THE BLUE GUIDES

Countries **Austria**
Belgium and Luxembourg
Channel Islands

1992

Denmark
Egypt
England
France
Germany
Greece
Hungary
Ireland
Northern Italy
Southern Italy
Malta and Gozo
Morocco
Portugal
Scotland
Sicily
Spain
Turkey: Bursa to Antakya
Wales
Yugoslavia

Cities Athens and Environs
Boston and Cambridge
Florence
Istanbul
Jerusalem
London
Moscow and Leningrad
New York
Oxford and Cambridge
Paris and Versailles
Rome and Environs
Venice

Themes **Churches and Chapels of Northern
England**
Churches and Chapels of Southern England
Gardens of England
Literary Britain and Ireland
Museums and Galleries of London
Victorian Architecture in Britain

Castle Campbell

BLUE GUIDE

SCOTLAND

JOHN TOMES

*Atlas, maps and plans
drawn by John Flower*

A. & C. Black
London

W. W. Norton
New York

Tenth edition 1992

Published by A & C Black (Publishers) Limited
35 Bedford Row, London WC1R 4JH

© A & C Black (Publishers) Limited 1992

Published in the United States of America by
W W Norton & Company, Inc
500 Fifth Avenue, New York, NY 10110

Published simultaneously in Canada by
Penguin Books Canada Limited,
2801 John Street, Markham, Ontario L3R 1B4

ISBN 0–7136–3426–X

A CIP catalogue record for this book
is available from the British Library.

ISBN 0–393–30841–3 USA

John Tomes was educated at Oxford, where he gained his degree in
Modern Languages, and, after careers in the Royal Air Force and the
aero engine industry, he was invited to update the Blue Guides to
Greece and Sicily. Subsequently, he became the author of *Blue Guide
Scotland, Wales, Belgium and Luxembourg* and *Holland*, a group
which he has now seen through several editions. A number of his short
stories have been published and broadcast, and his other travel books
include the *Shell Book of Exploring Britain* (A & C Black), of which he is
co-author with the late Garry Hogg.

Printed in Great Britain by
Butler & Tanner Ltd, Frome and London

PREFACE

This, the Tenth Edition of 'Blue Guide Scotland', reflects the steady consolidation and growth in Scotland's tourist industry; a growth not only in the infrastructure of essential practical facilities but also in the recognition that, increasingly, visitors are becoming eager for background. For many, simply to gape at a ruin or a stately home, however dramatic or however sumptuous, is no longer enough; the modern family asks questions—but wants the answers in a form it can readily absorb. To this trend the Scottish tourist industry is demonstrably alert and, while recent years have certainly seen the continuing opening of new sites, what is perhaps more significant is the emphasis today being placed on the informative and imaginative presentation of established sites; more and more, sites of all kinds now include associated visitor or heritage centres—these more often than not offering admirable interpretive video films—while the steady proliferation of site shops, most of them of good quality, both supports the sites and meets what is clearly a strengthening and more discerning demand for local literature and local souvenirs.

Acknowledgement is due first to all those who in one way or another have contributed to the compilation and high reputation of this book over the many years since its first appearance in 1927, special and most recent appreciation going to the late Stuart Rossiter, long associated with the Blue Guides as both editor and author. Particular thanks also go to the Scottish Tourist Board, whose headquarters in Edinburgh, office in London, and information centres of all levels throughout Scotland have been generous with advice and published material. Much help, too, has been given by many local authority offices and information centres; by those responsible for museums and art galleries; by the owners, administrators and curators of both official and private sites, many of whom went out of their way to explain detail and draw attention to special features; and by several organisations, these including the National Trust for Scotland, Historic Scotland, the Highlands and Islands Development Board (now H and I Enterprise), the Nature Conservancy Council (now Scottish Natural Heritage), the Royal Society for the Protection of Birds, the North of Scotland Hydro Electric Board, and the Forestry Commission.

Thanks also go to those users of 'Blue Guide Scotland' who have taken the trouble to send constructive criticism, corrections and also suggestions regarding new material and sites. All such have been carefully considered, most have been acted upon, and users of this Tenth Edition are assured that criticisms and suggestions, and especially those arising from personal discovery, will be most welcome. Particular thanks are due to Mr J. Morland Craig, whose comprehensive comments are reflected throughout this edition; and, as always, the author thanks his wife who so successfully combines the roles of navigator, researcher, typist and perceptive critic.

Background sources. From the many reference and other books constantly used, the author would in particular like to record the following: 'Mary, Queen of Scots' by Antonia Fraser (Weidenfeld and Nicolson). 'Portrait of the Border Country' by Nigel Tranter (Robert Hale). 'Ancient Stones of Scotland' by W. D. Simpson (Robert Hale). 'The Highland Clearances' by John Prebble (Secker and Warburg). 'The Burrell Collection' by John Julius Norwich, Richard Marks, Rosemary Scott, Barry Gasson, James K. Thomson and Philip Vainker (Collins, in association with Glasgow Museums and Art Galleries). 'A Concise Guide to

Historic Shetland' by G. A. Points (Shetland Tourist Organisation). 'Guide to Prehistoric Scotland' by Richard Feachem (Batsford). The 'Encyclopaedia Britannica'.

Illustrations. The drawings in this edition of 'Blue Guide Scotland' are by Marcus Lutyens. Those on pages 240 and 265 are based on photographs by Joanne Tomes. The engravings are reproduced from an edition of Walter Scott's 'Tales of a Grandfather', published in Edinburgh by A & C Black in 1860.

NOTES ON USING THIS GUIDE

This guide is in two parts. The first gives background and practical information. The second comprises ten geographic sections, each with an Introduction followed by a number of Routes. For the overall scheme of the Routes, see Atlas 16.

History and Antiquities. Throughout any tour of Scotland prehistory and history always accompany the traveller, usually in the visible form of monuments, ruined or still intact. To avoid repetition the first part of this guide includes an outline *History of Scotland* and also an essay describing the background to Scotland's *Antiquities and Later Buildings*. Also to avoid repetition the first part provides *Biographical Notes*. It would of course be impracticable to cover all the men and women who crowd Scotland's long history, and these notes aim only to identify selected personalities who make a particular, frequent or perhaps confusing appearance and who are not covered in the History or Routes texts.

Routes. In the second part, an *Introduction* at the beginning of each geographical section outlines the main features—historical, scenic and other—and a plan sketches that section's *Routes*, these designed, of course, to cover all places of tourist interest. Since some Routes inevitably merge with or run close to others, it is as well to be aware of neighbouring Routes, thus ensuring that places within easy reach but perhaps described under another Route are not missed.

Opening Times of Sites. Few sites, official or private, are willing to commit themselves for even a year ahead. Rather than offer information which may well be misleading, this guide therefore provides a telephone contact for virtually all sites with formal opening arrangements, these numbers usually being that of the site itself but in some cases that of the nearest Tourist Information. Historic Scotland (Ancient Monuments, AM) publish a Standard Opening Time, this being Easter–September: Monday–Saturday, 09.30 to 19.00. Sunday, 14.00 to 19.00. October–Easter: Monday–Saturday, 09.30 to 16.00. Sunday, 14.00 to 16.00. Nevertheless there are constant variations, and intending visitors are advised to check with 031-244-3101, this being the department's Visitor Facilities number for the whole of Scotland. See also Practical Information, Organisations. For *National Trust for Scotland* (NTS) properties, local telephone numbers are given, but information for all properties will be provided by 031-226-5922. See also Practical Information, Organisations.

Tourist Information offices will also of course provide information on Opening Times.—No firm guidance can be given regarding Sundays and public holidays, but increasingly the trend is towards opening.

Tourist Information offices are operated by various levels of the tourist industry; from the Scottish Tourist Board down through Regions, Island Areas, Districts, Cities and Towns. Also, approaching towns and usually beside a layby, there are often local information notice boards, useful if only for their town plans. In this guide, the entry *Inf.* after the name of a town advises that there are manned Tourist Information facilities. Addresses are given only in the cases of larger towns. Elsewhere, offices, often temporary caravans, tend to move around and also to be closed from roughly end September to Easter. Offices are usually clearly signed from towns' road entrances.

Maps. The Atlas provided with this guide shows principal places mentioned in the text and indicates main physical features. The maps, designed for broad reference and planning, have deliberately not been overcrowded and are not intended to take the place of motorists' maps. Of such there is a wide choice from which four may be mentioned. The *Scottish Tourist Board* publish (as companion to their '1001 things to see in Scotland') a Touring Map clearly overprinted with the names of most places listed in the publication. The map is to a scale of 5m to an inch and covers the whole of Scotland on reverse faces. *Ordnance Survey* Routemaster maps 1 to 4, on single faces, cover Scotland as follows: Orkney, Shetland and the Western Isles; Northern Scotland; Western and Central Scotland; and Central Scotland and Northumberland. These maps are physical and to a scale of 4m to an inch. However, for detailed exploration, most visitors will choose the relevant single face Ordnance Survey Landranger sheets (1:50,000. 1m to 1¼ inches). Also, and good for general use, is *Michelin* Sheet 401 (6.30m to an inch), a modestly physical map covering all Scotland on reverse faces.

Distances. The preamble to each Route (other than those devoted to individual towns) gives both its total distance and a breakdown of distances between principal places. In both the preambles and the texts italicised distances are those between points along the Route, i.e. each italicised distance represents the distance from the previous one. Other distances (e.g. along diversions) are in Roman print. For a number of obvious reasons distances can only be approximate.

Hotels. In response to requests, especially from overseas visitors wishing to plan and book their tour well ahead, the names of a few hotels are, as a convenience, given at the start of each Route. Although these are believed to be good—as a generalisation they are in the middle to higher category—it must be emphasised that these hotels have not necessarily been inspected by the author. It is equally important to emphasise that they are no more than a small selection from the choice available and that the omission of a name certainly does not imply any doubt or criticism. In the larger towns the aim has been to name hotels which are central and, whenever possible, with car parking.—See also Practical Information, Accommodation.

Telephone Numbers. Britain's telephone system is being modernised to digital switching, this resulting (other than in large cities) in four-figure area codes followed by six-figure numbers. This process seems likely to extend over some years, during which numbers not conforming to the above pattern will change. For some time after change—generally until the publication of a new directory—a recorded announcement will give the new number. If nevertheless in difficulty, callers may dial Directory Enquiries on 192.

Asterisks draw attention to places of special attraction or interest.

Abbreviations. In addition to generally accepted and self-explanatory abbreviations, the following occur:
AM   = Ancient Monument (Historic Scotland)
FC   = Forestry Commission
NTS = National Trust for Scotland
RSPB = Royal Society for the Protection of Birds
SNH = Scottish Natural Heritage
STB = Scottish Tourist Board

CONTENTS

MAPS AND PLANS

A NOTE ON BLUE GUIDES

The Blue Guide series began in 1918 when Muirhead Guide-Books Limited published 'Blue Guide London and its Environs'. Finlay and James Muirhead already had extensive experience of guidebook publishing: before the First World War they had been the editors of the English editions of the German Baedekers, and by 1915 they had acquired the copyright of most of the famous 'Red' Handbooks from John Murray.

An agreement made with the French publishing house Hachette et Cie in 1917 led to the translation of Muirhead's London Guide, which became the first 'Guide Bleu'—Hachette had previously published the blue-covered 'Guides Joannes'. Subsequently, Hachette's 'Guide Bleu Paris et ses Envrions' was adapted and published in London by Muirhead. The collaboration between the two publishing houses continued until 1933.

In 1933 Ernest Benn Limited took over the Blue Guides, appointing Russell Muirhead, Finlay Muirhead's son, editor in 1934. The Muirheads' connection with the Blue Guides ended in 1963 when Stuart Rossiter, who had been working on the Guides since 1954, became house editor, revising and compiling several of the books himself.

The Blue Guides are now published by A & C Black, who acquired Ernest Benn in 1984, so continuing the tradition of guidebook publishing which began in 1826 with 'Black's Economical Tourist of Scotland'. The Blue Guide series continues to grow: there are now more than 40 titles in print with revised editions appearing regularly and many new Blue Guides in preparation.

'Blue Guides' is a registered trademark.

BACKGROUND INFORMATION

Introduction to Scotland

Although constitutionally part of Great Britain ever since the union of the parliaments in 1707, Scotland in the minds of most people still ranks as a country in its own right, particularly since it has its own legal, educational, and ecclesiastical systems. Additionally the banks issue their own notes and the postage stamps carry the Scottish lion, two among the many indications of Scotland's individual identity that will strike visitors once they have crossed what is, significantly, still known as the border.

The name Scotland derives from that of the Irish people (Scoti) who came across during the 6C, but it was not generally used until the formation of a single kingdom during the 11C; to the Romans the northern lands had been known as Caledonia. The broad division of the country into Highlands and Lowlands has no formal significance. But for much of Scotland's history, the two, separated by culture, language and geography, had little in common, and it has really only been in recent times that the differences, however artificially still maintained, have in fact begun to fade.

As a holiday choice Scotland can hold its own against most competition. It boasts scenic variety which ranges from the pastoral lands of the Borders with their woods and rippling rivers, through the open down and moorland expanses stretching across much of the south and far north, to the lonely grandeur of the true Highlands, whose mountains towards the north west pile up to a wild and fretted coast. Beyond are the largely unspoilt island groups of the Hebrides in the west and Orkney and Shetland to the north. Within this scenery crowds the visible legacy of Scotland's long and romantic history: a wealth of prehistoric remains, beautiful though ruined medieval abbeys, castles (some ruined, some still inhabited), great houses with superbly decorated and furnished interiors and surrounded by fine parks.

In the sphere of holiday sport Scotland offers, to name only some of the possibilities, golf and fishing (both at a cost far below that in England); water sport, pony trekking, walking and climbing, gliding, wildlife study and skiing.

With so much scenic grandeur and variety, sport and stirring history, all to be found in a country which is easily accessible, has good internal communications and good accommodation, and which is populated by an attractive and friendly people, it is scarcely surprising that Scotland's holiday popularity is growing so rapidly.

Scotland's weather, sometimes maligned, is not that much more uncertain than that of England, due allowances being made for the country's northerly geography and the effect of mountains which meet the weather systems moving in from the Atlantic. Nevertheless, superb though the weather can often be, the term 'Scots mist' was not born of nothing and the visitor must be prepared for days that can be as wet as others can be hot and dry. The north west coast, in the direct path of the Gulf Stream, can be surprisingly mild, and along it there are several sub-tropical gardens.

The main tourist season is from about Easter to the end of September, and outside this period many though by no means all facilities and some sites are closed. In July and August the more popular districts can be overcrowded, but even at this time there are still remote and lonely corners to be found by those willing to explore the smaller roads. Undoubtedly the best times for touring are May, June and September. While October can also be a good touring month, there can be a chill in the air and the evenings start to shorten.

Aspects of Scotland

Bagpipes, kilts, Highland dancing—these are just some of the things instinctively associated with Scotland and which the visitor will expect to see and hear. Any visitor staying only a day or two is likely at least to meet a kilt. For the whole scene, though, the best course is to arrange to attend a Gathering (see below), of which there are a large number, especially in summer, their dates being listed in the STB's annual publication 'Events in Scotland'. Many hotels and local tourist centres also organise Highland Evenings and suchlike, where, if no cabers are tossed, at least there is a good chance of eating haggis.

Bagpipes, though perhaps most associated with Scotland, are not peculiar to that country. The instrument is one of great antiquity and can be traced in early forms to ancient Persia, Egypt, and Greece, where it was certainly known by AD 100. It was introduced to Britain by the Romans (a bronze figure excavated at Richborough is playing bagpipes), becoming popular in Ireland and Scotland and in the latter developing into something of a status symbol (clan chiefs all had their hereditary pipers by the 16C) as well as a military instrument that inspired the warlike Highlanders, so much so in fact that together with Highland dress the pipes were banned after Culloden.

The instrument itself comprises an airtight bag and pipes of three kinds, a blow-pipe, a chaunter for melody, and drones producing the continuous note which is the bagpipes' main characteristic. The bag may be inflated either by blowing or by small bellows worked by the arm.

Ceilidh is Gaelic for 'visit'. Remote communities were forced to rely for entertainment on their own resources, and it was the custom for groups to meet in one another's homes, each person in turn contributing music, a song, a poem, or whatever else he had to offer. The ceilidh today tends to be more commercial and to be held in halls or hotels, although the occasion is still informal and the entertainment traditional. Visitors should consult their hotel, the local press, or Tourist Information.

Clans. In Gaelic 'clann' means 'children' or 'family'. The start of the clan system may perhaps be traced to the 6C when, after establishing themselves at Dunadd, the Scots began to spread out, dividing the lands between their leaders. A similar process would have been going on elsewhere, and from now on for many centuries the powerful who acquired land acquired also the people living there. Such landowners, though, and especially in the Lowlands, were by no means necessarily Scots and indeed several clans and names have Norman roots, not least that of the great Bruce.

A principal characteristic of the system that developed was the absolute and (an important feature) the willing subservience to the chief. Below the chief there was a recognised hierarchy, descending through the lesser chieftains and the gentlemen (both these being kinsmen of the chief) down to simple clansmen, who did most of the manual work and were the main strength when it came to fighting. Fighting was of course frequent, not only because of clan rivalry, largely over land and cattle, but because loyalty to chiefs ran counter to loyalty to kings, who all the time sought to impose their authority, no easy task with many of the clans living on islands or in remote valleys. Often this was achieved by the king (notably James IV) receiving allegiance in return for formally confirming the chiefs' position by charter (parchment documents known as 'sheepskin grants'). This in turn led to further fighting among the clans, with one chief claiming land by tradition and another by virtue of his royal grant. The Statutes of Iona (1609), signed under duress by nine chiefs 'of the Isles', did much to discourage such fighting, but it was not until 1688 that the last clan battle was fought (at Keppoch).

Culloden killed what was left of the Highland way of life and with it the clan system, but around the turn of the century came the birth of the Highland and clan cult (largely a matter of costume, games, piping, and an urge to 'belong') that on an international scale still flourishes today.

James Pringle Archive Computer, Edinburgh (Rte 18F). Inverness (Rte 51). *Museum of Scottish Tartans*, Comrie (Rte 25B). *Clan Centres:* See under individual names in the index.

The Scottish **Flag**, a white St. Andrew's cross on a blue background, is first recorded as the national emblem at the end of the 13C and derives from St. Andrew being the country's patron saint. St. Andrew was crucified in c 69 and buried at Patras in Greece; he is said to have asked for a cross of diagonal beams (saltire) because he considered himself unworthy to die on an upright cross as Christ had done. According to legend St. Regulus, hearing in 370 that the saint's bones were to be removed to Constantinople, took some relics, fled by sea, and was wrecked in Scotland at the spot which is now St. Andrews. More probably the relics came to Scotland in the 8C, and it was at this time (736) that Angus, son of the king of the Picts, adopted St. Andrew as his patron saint.

Another legend is that of the white St. Andrew's cross seen against the blue sky when in the 10C the Picts defeated the Northumbrians at what is now Athelstaneford (Rte 1).—Scotland's other emblem, the **Thistle**, is said to date from an incident at the battle of Largs (1263). One of Hakon's men, barefooted and advancing in the dark to surprise the Scots, trod on a thistle, letting out such a cry that the Scots were alerted and the day was saved. The battle of Luncarty, fought against the Danes in 990, is credited with the same incident.

Highland Dances, though now all in relatively modern form, have ancient origins. The Romans reported that the Caledonians danced wildly around their swords, stuck upwards in the ground, and certain characteristics—sudden high leaps, clockwise movement, chains—allow Celtic origins to be claimed. It has been suggested that the patterns of some dances reflect both ancient sun worship ritual and, more recently, the shape of the Celtic High Cross, and that the circle of the reel symbolises the circle of life.

In 1561 Mary, Queen of Scots, arrived, with her French custom of having musicians and dance-masters to organise court entertainment, and from this date on began a continuous process by which the old dances were tamed and formalised, while others were introduced. Change accelerated with the enthusiasm for everything Highland which followed the repeal in 1782 of the Act of Proscription, new development being to a great extent military as the pipers and dance-masters of the 20 or so Highland regiments became increasingly competitive and inventive.

Highland Dress. Although the word 'tartan' does not appear until 1471, the Romans referred to the Caledonians' 'chequered garments'. There are similar references in later centuries, and in 1578, writing about the ancient customs and dress of the Highlanders, a bishop records that everyone in Scotland wore mantles of the same kind though the nobles favoured many colours.

These mantles would have been plaids, which served both as a single garment and as a blanket. Dressing in a plaid (described as 16 yards of tartan) seems to have been a rather complicated business, involving spreading it on the ground, folding it into pleats, then lying on it, crossing it over the body, and finally belting it. By the 16C, the clan territories were well defined and varied tartan plaid designs developed, to some extent probably as a means of identification.

The kilt is one of the earliest known forms of dress; it appears for instance in the Bronze Age frescoes of Knossos in Crete and was also the dress of the ancient Egyptians. In Scotland, however, the kilt seems to date only from the early 18C when, presumably for reasons of convenience and comfort, the plaid was divided into two halves.

After Culloden Highland dress was forbidden by the Act of Proscription, but with the repeal of the act in 1782 and the explosion of the Highland cult came the development of more or less official tartans, a trend confirmed in 1822 when George IV appeared wearing the Royal Stuart. Today's tartans are defined by sets (which may be registered at the Court of the Lord Lyon), the principal ones being those distinguishing clans, these in turn in many cases sub-dividing into hunting and dress tartans. But it is no longer only the clans who boast tartans. There are sets individual to chiefs and their immediate families, regimental sets, district sets, a clerical set, and even a general set for those with no specific claim.—*Scottish Tartans Society*, Museum of Scottish Tartans, Comrie. Rte 25B.

Highland Games (Gatherings) probably originated as fairs organised in very early times by kings and chiefs. There seems also, at least on occasion, to have been a military purpose, Malcolm Canmore being credited with the first Braemar Gathering, when he summoned the clans to contests which would enable him to select the best men to be his warriors. Ceres, in Fife, held a Gathering after Bannockburn to honour the village's returning bowmen, and today claims that their games have since been held annually without a break, other than during the two world wars. Like everything else Highland, Gatherings became of widespread popularity after the repeal of the Act of Proscription, and Queen Victoria's patronage of Braemar ensured that Gatherings became the important feature in the Scottish calendar that they remain today.

Among the features of Gatherings are competitions in Highland dancing; tossing the caber (the largest Braemar caber is 19ft 3 inches long and weighs 120lbs); putting the stone (weighing up to 22lbs); throwing the hammer (weighing up to 22lbs); wrestling; and all manner of piping events.—For dates of Gatherings, see STB annual booklet, 'Events in Scotland'.

Deer Forests. Deer are as much valuable stock as are cattle and sheep, but, being wild, have not until recently been herded on farms and normally have to be culled only in their natural habitat. Deer forests (mostly open mountain and moor) should therefore be regarded as deer farms and are not, as often thought, merely sport shooting lands.

Whisky (Celtic visque-beatha = water of life). Although the earliest historical reference to something like whisky ('aquavitae') appears only in 1494, there can be little doubt that long before this the Highland crofters distilled spirits from barley and the art may even have been brought to Scotland by the Dark Ages Irish missionaries. A century and a half after that first official mention, the government awoke to the revenue possibilities, passing the first Excise Act in 1644. This, with variations, lasted until the Union of the Parliaments in 1707, after which confusion and illicit distilling flourished until the situation was brought under control by the British parliament's Distilleries Act of 1823. There are two kinds of Scotch whisky—Malt from malted barley solely; Grain made from malted barley together with unmalted barley and other cereals. As to what gives Scotch whisky its special character, the answer probably lies in a combination of factors—the secrets of the distilling process allied to the natural elements of Scotland's climate, peat and, above all, soft water.

Distilleries with visitor facilities will be found in many parts of Scotland, though notably in the North East where special Distilleries Circuits are outlined along Rtes 38 and 39. For more information, contact the Scotch Whisky Association, 20 Atholl Crescent, Edinburgh, EH3 8HF. Tel: 031-229-4383; or 17 Half Moon Street, London W1Y 7RB. Tel: 071-629-4384.

History of Scotland

Prehistoric Period (BC).
From midden excavations, tombs and settlements, it is known that Scotland was inhabited in Middle and New Stone Age times, say 5000 and more years ago, these people probably originating from coastwise maritime movements which over millennia brought early man northward along Europe's western shores. Stone circle ritual sites, fortified hill camps and finally earth-houses and brochs continued the story through the Bronze and Iron Ages down to about the time of the birth of Christ, by when the inhabitants must have been many tribes of diverse origins.

The Romans (82–208).
The Romans made their first appearance in 82 under Agricola, penetrating into the North East and defeating the tribes at the battle of Mons Graupius (84), the site of which may have been Raedykes near Stonehaven or Bennachie to the west of Inverurie. The Romans mention one Calgacus, a tribal chief, the first Scot to appear by name in history. Withdrawal soon followed. A second invasion lasted from 142–185, the area up to the Firth of Forth being occupied and the Antonine Wall built from Forth to Clyde. There followed another withdrawal, after which, apart from a punitive expedition by Septimius Severus in 208, Scotland did not again see the Romans.

Christianity, the Four Kingdoms and the Birth of Scotland (208–1034).
(Kenneth I, Macalpine, 843–860. Constantine I, 863–879. Donald I, 892–900. Constantine II, III and Donald II, 900–943. Malcolm I, 943–954. Kenneth II, 954–994. Malcolm II, 1005–1034)

In 397 the Christian Church was founded at Whithorn by St. Ninian, and in the following two centuries other missionaries, of whom the best known are St. Columba and St. Mungo (or Kentigern), were spreading the Faith.

Gradually the tribes, original inhabitants and new arrivals, formed into four kingdoms. These were the Scots, Celtic Christians (amongst them, Columba) who crossed from Ireland in the early 6C and settled in Argyll to found the Kingdom of Dalriada; the Picts in the North, of uncertain origin but probably mixed Celtic and aboriginal (Pictland); the Britons, the people of the South West (Strathclyde); and the Angles, who in the late 6C colonised the eastern Lowlands (Lothian, a part of Bernicia and much of the time subject to or a part of the neighbouring English Kingdom of Northumbria). The Norsemen appeared around the end of the 8C, soon occupying the Hebrides, Orkney and Shetland, and establishing settlements around the mainland coasts.

Under Kenneth Macalpine the Scots and Picts merged, forming the Kingdom of Alba, later Scotia. He and his successors were constantly engaged with both the Norsemen and Northumbria, and it was not until 1018 that Malcolm II finally defeated the latter at Carham, near Coldstream, and thus joined Lothian to his kingdom. In 1034 Malcolm II was succeeded by his grandson, Duncan I. Duncan had already inherited the remaining independent Kingdom of Strathclyde and thus the single Kingdom of Scotland was born. The Norsemen, though, still held the islands and parts of the mainland.

Development of English Influence (1034–1286).

(Duncan I, 1034–1040. Macbeth, 1040–1057. Malcolm III, Canmore, 1057–1093. Donald Bane, 1093–1094. Duncan II, 1094. Donald Bane and Edmund, 1094–1097. Edgar, 1097–1107. Alexander I, 1107–1124. David I, 1124–1153. Malcolm IV, 1153–1165. William I, the Lion, 1165–1214. Alexander II, 1214–1249. Alexander III, 1249–1286)

Duncan I was murdered by Macbeth, himself killed in 1057 and succeeded by Malcolm III (Canmore). Malcolm III's reign was important less because of himself than because of his queen, the English princess, Margaret, to whom, for a man of those times, he seems to have given remarkably free rein. A determined and pious woman, later canonised, she was staunchly English. She started the anglicisation of the Church, till then essentially Celtic, she introduced an English-speaking court and English-speaking clergy, and she brought up her six sons in the English tradition. Three of these, all as pious and as English in outlook as their mother, subsequently reigned and continued her work, which could be said to have changed Celtic Scotland into a feudal kingdom like Norman England. In this task their strongest influence was the Church, and David I, the last son to reign, was particularly active in founding abbeys and granting land to Norman nobles. At this time, too, towns or burghs, as opposed to villages, began to grow; those founded by kings or later granted charters enjoyed the title of Royal Burgh.

Nevertheless relations with England remained uneasy, with the Scots determined to annex Northumbria and the English kings, relying on the wording of a 10C alliance against the Danes, claiming feudal authority over Scotland. William I, the Lion, defeated and captured at Alnwick in 1174, was forced to do homage, but 15 years later the English Richard I (Coeur de Lion), in return for a Scottish contribution to his crusade, annulled this. Then in 1236 Alexander II renounced claim to Northumbria. The long reign of his son, Alexander III, sometimes called the 'Golden Age', was stable and prosperous. It also saw the expulsion of the Norsemen from the Hebrides as the result of Alexander's victory at Largs in 1263. (They had already withdrawn from the mainland 70 years earlier and remained therefore in occupation only of Orkney and Shetland.)

Alexander III's death in 1286 marks a watershed. He was the last of the old line of kings; Border warfare was about to erupt and would continue on and off for three centuries; and from now on English influence would gradually yield to that of France.

Wars of Succession and Independence (1286–1371).
(Margaret, Maid of Norway, 1286–1290. Interregnum, 1290–1292. John Balliol, 1292–1296. Interregnum, 1296–1306. Robert I, The Bruce, 1306–1329. David II, 1329–1371)

Alexander III's heir was his infant granddaughter, Margaret (The Maid) of Norway, but there were rival claimants, John Balliol and Robert Bruce. Scotland's choice thus lay between an infant girl, not even in the country, or civil war between Balliol and Bruce. The Grand Council (barons and clergy) opted for Margaret and her succession was guaranteed by Edward I of England, who, set upon the union of the two countries, arranged for her betrothal to his son. But four years later (1290), on her way to Scotland, Margaret died. Edward I then declared himself feudal overlord and chose John Balliol as his vassal king. Foolishly, but probably egged on by Scottish opinion, Balliol soon revolted, whereupon Edward started to earn his reputation as 'Hammer of the Scots'. He claimed total sovereignty, easily defeated the Scots at Dunbar, and went on to destroy the Great Seal and remove to London the Stone of Destiny, the sacred stone, brought from Ireland to Dalriada and thence to Scone, upon which Scottish kings had been crowned since the 6C. The following year (1297) saw the uprising by Sir William Wallace.

Born about 1270, **William Wallace** lived for some years at Dunipace near Stirling. Being declared an outlaw, for killing an Englishman who had insulted him, he gathered many adherents and frequently attacked the English, perhaps his best known early exploit being the burning of the barracks (barns) of Ayr. Later, when confronted by an English army at Irvine, many of his supporters deserted him, whereupon Wallace gathered a new army in the North. He won outright victory at Stirling Bridge, expelled the English and ruled Scotland as 'guardian'. Edward I retaliated in force, defeating Wallace at Falkirk (1298). Wallace escaped, but was betrayed in 1305 and put to death as a traitor.

In 1306 the rival Scots factions met in Greyfriars Church, Dumfries, to concert plans for resistance to the English. But a quarrel broke out and Bruce slew Comyn ('the Red'), the representative of the Balliols, and then had himself crowned Robert I.

Robert Bruce was born at either Lochmaben or Turnberry in 1274. Of Norman ancestry and owning lands in England, he probably spent his youth at the court of Edward I. As Earl of Carrick he supported Wallace, but later deserted him at Irvine. After the incident at Dumfries, Bruce declared himself unequivocally for Scotland and was crowned at Scone. Defeated at Methven and Dalry, proclaimed an outlaw, excommunicated, and with his wife and daughter in English hands, Bruce's cause seemed hopeless. He spent 1306–07 as a fugitive (some of the time on the island of Rathlin off Ireland, probable scene of the legendary encounter with the persistent spider). But in 1307 Edward I died, being succeeded by his incompetent son, Edward II. There followed seven years of struggle (during which Bruce defeated all rivals, especially the Comyns in the North East), culminating in the defeat of Edward II at Bannockburn in 1314. Only in 1323, though, was Bruce's title as King of Scotland recognised by the Pope. In 1327 the Treaty of York with Edward III declared Scotland's independence. Bruce died, probably of leprosy, at Cardross in 1329. He was buried at Dunfermline, but his heart, after being taken on a crusade by Sir James Douglas, is believed to lie at Melrose Abbey.

Bruce was succeeded by his infant and weak son, David II, whose reign was marked by revolts of the Balliols and other nobles disinherited by Bruce, wars with Edward III and the birth of Scottish French alliances against the English. Captured in battle, David II was held in London from 1346–57, and it was in order to raise his ransom that the constitutional change was made under which representatives of the royal burghs were invited to join the barons and clergy on the Grand Council. David II was succeeded by his nephew, Robert II, the first of the Stewarts.

The Early Stewarts (1371–1542).
(Robert II, 1371–1390. Robert III, 1390–1406. James I, 1406–1437. James II, 1437–1460. James III, 1460–1488. James IV, 1488–1513. James V, 1513–1542).

From the accession of Robert II to the abdication of Mary, Queen of Scots, in 1567, Scotland's story is a complicated one of wars with England, and the internal intrigue, rebellion, and anarchy resulting from the constant endeavours of kings to impose their authority on people who recognised only that of their chiefs and on chiefs who recognised none. Though at times threatened, the monarchy nonetheless prevailed, notable landmarks being the wholesale execution of the powerful Albany family by James I in 1425, the defeat of the equally powerful Douglases by James II, the introduction by James IV of land grants ('sheepskin grants') in return for formal allegiance, and the assumption for the crown by the same king of the title Lord of the Isles. Also on the positive side, Orkney and Shetland were given to James III in 1469, as a pledge for the dowry of his wife, Margaret of Denmark. The pledge has never been redeemed, and the islands were in any case formally annexed by Scotland in 1472.

James IV, set on helping the French, unnecessarily went to war with England and suffered disastrous defeat at Flodden in 1513. He was followed by James V, who made two French marriages, the second being to Mary of Guise. During his reign the Reformation, encouraged by pressure by Henry VIII in England, began to make progress in Scotland, but James refused to follow Henry's lead and dissolve the Scottish monasteries. Henry then invaded Scotland, and James, little supported by his nobles, who resented the French influence and who also, more realistically than their King, had their eyes on the wealth of the Church, was defeated in 1542 at Solway Moss. He died soon after, leaving as his heir his six-days-old daughter, Mary.

Mary, Queen of Scots (1542–1567; died 1587).
The reign opened with an uneasy balance between the regent, Arran, who was inclined towards the Reformation, and the court and the Church. However the savage ravaging of southern Scotland in 1544–45 (the 'English' or 'rough wooing') by the Earl of Hertford, consequent upon the Scots' refusal to ratify a treaty of marriage between the infant Mary and Henry VIII's son, pushed Scotland towards France. Hertford (now Lord Protector Somerset) invaded a third time, winning the battle of Pinkie (1547), whereupon the Scots sent Mary, aged 5, to France. She stayed there 13 years, marrying the French boy heir in 1558. The following year her husband became King.

But in Scotland it was the beginning of the end for Catholic power and the French alliance. The Protestant leaders (Lords of the Congregation as they styled themselves) increasingly resented the French influence. Mary of Guise, now regent and backed by French troops, reacted by denouncing the Protestants as heretics. In reply the Protestants, fired by John Knox's sermon in Perth, started to destroy the religious houses and in 1559 deposed the regent queen, seeking the protection of Elizabeth of England for so long as 'the marriage shall continue between the Queen of Scots and the French King'. The next year they formally abolished Roman Catholicism and forbade the celebration of Mass. In that year, too, Mary's husband died.

Such was the situation to which Mary, not yet 20, a devout Catholic and a widow, returned in 1561. Although barely seven years were to elapse between her return and her flight to England, these were so charged with intrigue and violence and have left such a mark on Scotland that this period, with its romantic and tragic heroine, demands more detailed description than either its length or its historical significance warrants.

Mary's principal home was Holyrood and it was here, only a month after her return, that she had the first of her interviews with the reformer, John Knox, and started her unsuccessful struggle for toleration for Roman Catholicism. This apart, the early years were not unhappy and Mary saw something of Scotland. In 1562 she made a royal progress through the North East, combining this with suppressing a revolt by the Earl of Huntly (see Introduction to VI North East), and in 1563 there was another progress, this time through the South West. In 1565 she married Henry, Lord Darnley, with whom she was infatuated. Elizabeth of England's attitude was equivocal—she was always very conscious that Mary was her heiress presumptive—and she halfheartedly supported a rebellion by the Earl of Moray, Mary's half-brother. This failed, and Moray fled. Darnley, a youth as weak as he was ambitious, then set his heart on the Crown Matrimonial, a device which would have given him personal royal status. But when Mary, encouraged by her Italian secretary, Rizzio, refused this, Darnley went over to Mary's enemies, personally taking part in the brutal murder of Rizzio before Mary's eyes at Holyrood in March 1566. Moray and other banished lords then returned to Scotland. However Darnley promptly betrayed his fellow conspirators and fled with Mary to Dunbar, whence, escorted by the Earl of Bothwell and a small army, they returned three days later to Holyrood. Rizzio's murderers fled to England, but Darnley was allowed to protest that he was an innocent dupe. Three months later Mary gave birth to her son, James.

Not only was Bothwell now in the ascendant, but it was also becoming increasingly obvious that the marriage with the impossible Darnley, who had made enemies of everyone, could not last. Although in January 1567 Mary visited him in Glasgow when he was seriously ill (possibly poisoned), and although she then accompanied her to Edinburgh, their brief stay there at the house called Kirk o'Field was their last time together. In early February, when Mary was at Holyrood, Kirk o'Field was mysteriously blown up and Darnley's body, showing evidence of strangulation, found in the garden.

Whether or not Mary had any hand in this murder plot, hatched at Craigmillar Castle, is unproven, but Bothwell was undoubtedly a ringleader, although he successfully overrode all accusations and even achieved formal acquittal by the Privy Council. He virtually abducted Mary to Dunbar, speedily arranged a divorce from his wife, and then married Mary in Edinburgh in May 1567. For Mary, the marriage was the beginning of the end. There was immediate rebellion and, under suspicion for Darnley's murder and discredited by the marriage, she had to flee with Bothwell first to Borthwick, then to Dunbar. In June she surrendered at what was a farce of a battle at Carberry Hill, Bothwell galloping away never to be seen by her again. Five days later, imprisoned in the island castle of Lochleven, she abdicated in favour of her infant son, Moray being appointed regent.

The following year Mary escaped with the aid of the Douglas family.

She rode west through Niddry and Hamilton, but suffered final defeat in May 1568, at Langside, whence she fled to England. Not yet 26 years old, she was to face nearly 20 years imprisonment before being executed in 1587.

The Union of the Crowns (1603) to the Union of the Parliaments (1707).

(James VI/I, 1567–1625. Charles I, 1625–1649. Charles II, 1649–1651. Commonwealth, 1651–1660. Charles II, restored, 1660–1685. James VII/II, 1685–1688. William III of Orange and Mary, 1688–1694. William III to 1702. Anne, 1702–1714)

In 1603, on the death of Elizabeth, James VI of Scotland became also James I of England. But this union of the crowns did not mean the union of the two countries and for a century and a half longer Scotland's story continues as a complicated and violent one, its main features being bitter quarrels about the Church, the English and later Scottish civil wars, and Scottish support of Charles II and the Stuart pretenders. (Mary had changed the spelling from Stewart to Stuart.) In simplest terms the church quarrels sprang from two sharply opposed views. One was the extreme Protestant Presbyterian belief, personified by the Covenanters, which stood for pure Reformation simplicity, the Church's separation from the civil power, the equality of all ministers and little formal worship. The other party believed in more formal liturgy and a hierarchy with bishops (episcopacy), possibly holding authority from the crown. Again in simplest terms, the former were Lowlanders and tended to be supporters of parliament; the latter Highlanders, who, since the Stuarts were by preference episcopalian, tended to be royalist and Jacobite.

The Covenants. James VI/I succeeded in grafting episcopacy on to the Presbyterian Church, but Charles I went too far, particularly in attempting to introduce a new prayer book, the result being the National Covenant, signed with great enthusiasm at Greyfriars, Edinburgh (1638). This stood firm on the principles of the Reformation and led to the abolition of the bishops appointed by James VI/I. Charles I's attempts to impose his will failed, and, under the Solemn League and Covenant (1643; confirmed 1646), Scotland, led by the Earl of Argyll, sided with parliament during the crucial period before and at the start of the English civil war, parliament, for its part, undertaking to introduce Presbyterianism in England.

This turned out to be only a brief alliance, and Cromwell's inability to fulfil parliament's side of the bargain, followed by his execution of Charles I, led to deep divisions within Scotland. Scotland now defied Cromwell's Commonwealth, proclaiming Charles II as King (but only after he had signed both Covenants), and there were abortive invasions of England: in 1650 when Cromwell defeated the Scots at Dunbar, and in 1651 when another venture in support of Charles II ended in defeat at Worcester.

A prominent figure during the above period was James Graham, **Marquess of Montrose**, who achieved romantic fame as a betrayed and tragic hero. Montrose found himself having to play a double role. At heart a Covenanter, he was active in suppressing the initial opposition in the North East, but later, in 1640, largely because he could not accept the personal ambition of the dominant Earl of Argyll, he supported Charles I rather than the Solemn League and Covenant. When the Civil War broke out in England, Montrose won several minor battles in the North. But with Charles's defeat at Naseby, Montrose's Highlanders deserted him and he was himself defeated by the Covenanter general, Leslie, at Philiphaugh. Montrose escaped abroad, returning in 1650 when Scotland accepted Charles II. But the latter soon disavowed him, finding it more expedient to become King on Argyll's

Covenanter

terms, and Montrose, after failing to rouse the clans, was routed near Bonar Bridge, afterwards being surrendered by MacLeod of Assynt and hanged in Edinburgh in 1650. His enemy, Argyll, suffered the same fate ten years later.

For nearly nine years (1651–1660) Scotland was under Commonwealth military occupation. With the Restoration (1660), the Scottish parliament surprisingly annulled all Church legislation since 1633 and appointed bishops. Bitterness deepened until the extreme Covenanters rebelled, first in 1666 when they were defeated at Rullion Green in the Pentland Hills, then again in 1679. Initially successful, they held the Highlander Royalist Claverhouse at Drumclog, but, lacking support from the majority of Scotsmen, were themselves soon defeated at Bothwell Bridge. There followed years of suppression of the Covenanters, so savage that the period became known as 'the killing time', ended only by the English revolution against James VII/II (1688). His successor, William of Orange, agreed to the abolition of bishops. What was left of Scottish episcopalianism became Jacobite (i.e. supporting the Stuarts), but effectively died with its leader Claverhouse (now Viscount Dundee) on the field of Killiecrankie a year later. But the Highlanders continued unwilling to take the oath to William of Orange and Mary, so the last day of 1691 was set as the final date for submission. All the chiefs eventually swore, except Macdonald of Glencoe who delayed. The result was the notorious Massacre of Glencoe.

1707 brought the Treaty of Union, under which the parliaments of England and Scotland were united into that of the United Kingdom, Scotland receiving guarantees on the Presbyterian Established Church and on the maintenance of Scottish law and courts.

After Union.

(George I, 1714–1727. George II, 1727–1760. George III, 1760–1820. George IV, 1820–1830. William IV, 1830–37. Victoria, 1837–1901. Edward VII, 1901–1910. George V, 1910–1936. Edward VIII, 1936. George VI, 1936–1952. Elizabeth I/II, 1952–)

Despite the Treaty of Union, the Highlands were far from subdued and Jacobite sentiment clung on, erupting in the rebellions of 1715 and 1745. The '15, led by the Earl of Mar on behalf of the Old Pretender, failed to get either Lowland or the promised French support and ended in defeat at Sheriffmuir. To bring the Highlands under control General Wade was then given the task of building a network of military roads, but, despite this, there was another and more serious rising in 1745, this one led by Prince Charles Edward (the Young Pretender or Bonnie Prince Charlie). General Scottish support was patchy and after initial success at Prestonpans and an advance as far south as Derby the Prince had to withdraw until finally defeated by Cumberland at Culloden. After adventurous wanderings he escaped to France, while in Scotland Cumberland set about earning his nickname of 'butcher'.

The **Pretenders** were the end of the Stuart line. The son of James VII/II was James Francis Edward, James III to the Jacobites and the Old Pretender to the Hanoverians. A worthy but uninspiring man, he made three attempts to win his crown. In 1708 he came by sea and was defeated in the Firth of Forth by Admiral Byng; the '15 ended at Sheriffmuir; and a final attempt in 1719 collapsed when the supporting Spanish fleet was lost in a storm and the Highland rising broke in Glen Shiel. He died in 1766. His son, Prince Charles Edward (born 1720), is a better known figure, and, as the Bonnie Prince Charlie of the '45 helped during his adventurous wanderings by Flora Macdonald, briefly even a romantic one. After the '45 he had long years of pathetic exile. He died in 1788, leaving no legitimate male issue, and with the death in 1807 of his celibate brother the Stuart male line ended. These last three Stuarts lie in the crypt of St. Peter's in Rome, unaware that their marble monument was in part paid for by the Hanoverian George III.

Culloden signalled far more than the end of Jacobite hopes. It signalled too the end of a centuries-long Highland way of life. The Lowland Scots and the English were determined to tame the Highlanders, and the Act of Proscription (1747; repealed 1782) formally banned Highland dress, etc., but the Act was scarcely necessary for complete change was inevitable. For centuries the clansman crofter had paid his rent to his chief in warrior service; now, with fighting a thing of the past, and with the chiefs increasingly attracted by the glitter and comforts of London, the latter required rent in cash. But this their tenants did not have, so instead the chiefs turned to Lowland and English sheep farmers only too anxious to buy or lease Highland land, provided always that the crofters were first removed. In the evictions that followed (between

IACOBO · III
IACOBI · II · MAGNÆ · BRIT · REGIS · FILIO
KAROLO · EDVARDO
ET · HENRICO · DECANO · PATRVM · CARDINA · LVM
IACOBI · III · FIL · IIS
REGIAE STIRPIS STVARDIÆ POSTREMIS
ANNO MDCCCXIX

BEATI MORTVI
QVI IN DOMINO MORIVNTVR

The Stuart Monument at St. Peter's, Rome. Here lie the last of the Stuarts—the Old and the Young Pretenders and the latter's prelate brother—their memorial in part paid for by the Hanoverian George III

about 1780 and 1860, now known as the Highland Clearances), the Highland people were dispossessed and dispersed. Some disappeared into city slums, others died trying to scratch a living from the miserable coastal sand plots allotted to them, thousands emigrated to Canada and Australia. By 1860 the Highlands had been virtually emptied.

In the South, though, during much the same period, Edinburgh took on new life, flourishing as a centre of the arts. Then in 1822 George IV made a State Visit, the first by the sovereign since the Stuarts. Instigated and organised by Sir Walter Scott, Holyrood was brought back to life and the trapping of the occasion included Highland dress, bagpipes, weapons and banners, even the King wearing the Royal Stuart tartan. This occasion, followed thirty years later by the royal purchase of Balmoral, marked the birth of the Highland cult which is today so much a part of what the tourist expects of Scotland.

The Victorian era saw medical landmarks, such as Simpson's use of chloroform in Edinburgh in 1847 and Lister's introduction of antiseptic surgery in Glasgow in 1865, and also great industrial expansion, this bringing far-reaching social change, with at one extreme mass poverty and slums, and at the other a personal and civic prosperity that encouraged noteworthy architectural movements (Scottish Baronial and Neo-Classical) and the founding of some of Scotland's most famous art collections. The era has left such an interesting and varied legacy that 'Victorian Scotland' has become an official theme of Scottish Tourist Board promotion.

Within the first part of the present century belong the gallantry of the Scottish divisions during two world wars, and the inauguration in 1947 of the Edinburgh Festival, quickly to earn international artistic renown. More recent years have seen the exploitation of North Sea oil, the debate on devolution and, in 1975, the local government reorganisation. The year 1983 was the year of the first Glasgow Mayfest, now an annual feature, and for 1990 Glasgow enjoyed acclaim as Cultural Capital of Europe.

Biographical Notes

Adam. Renowned family of Scottish-born architects, consisting of William and his four sons, John, Robert, James and William. Robert (1728–92) is the best known. The Adam style was basically Roman and Italian rather than native and extended beyond architecture to everything that went with the interior decoration of a gracious building. Adam achievements will be met throughout Lowland Scotland.

Adamnan, Saint (c 624–704). 9th Abbot of Iona. Important as author of the 'Life of St. Columba'.

Albany, Dukes of. 1. Robert Stewart (c 1345–1420). Natural son of Robert II. Became Regent of Scotland and retained this position even after the accession of his brother as Robert III. In 1398 his nephew, David, Duke of Rothesay and heir to the throne, became Regent. Uncle and nephew soon quarrelled and in 1402 the latter died in prison at Falkland. Although parliament recorded that Rothesay died from natural causes, Albany is generally held to have been responsible. Albany became Regent again and was succeeded by his son, Murdoch. 2. Murdoch Stewart ruled feebly on behalf of James I, captive in England. James, on his return to Scotland, resolved to curb the power of the great nobles and started by executing (1425) Murdoch, his son and his father-in-law. 3. John Stewart (c 1481–1536). Regent of Scotland (1515–23). He was active in furthering alliances with the French and negotiated the marriage between James V and Mary of Guise.

Angus. See Douglas (Red).

Argyll, Earls and Dukes of. 1. Archibald Campbell, 5th Earl (1530–73). Although an adherent of John Knox and a Lord of the Congregation, he later sided with Mary, Queen of Scots, but was nevertheless probably concerned in the murders of both Rizzio and Darnley. Commanded Mary's troops after her escape from Lochleven. 2. Archibald Campbell, 8th Earl (1607–61). A Covenanter, he became the most powerful man in Scotland. He sided with parliament in the Civil War and opposed Montrose on both personal and political grounds, their bitter rivalry leading to the latter's final defeat and death. Later Argyll supported Charles II, whom he crowned at Scone. At the Restoration, however, his earlier collaboration with Cromwell was proven and he was executed. 3.

Archibald Campbell, 9th Earl (1629–85). Staunchly Protestant he fell foul of James VII/II, supported Monmouth's rebellion, was defeated and executed.

Balliol. Important Norman-Scottish family, of whom the best-known are: 1. John (d 1269). Regent during minority of Alexander III, but was accused of treason and lost his lands. Went to England, fought for Henry III and established several scholarships at Oxford. 2. Devorguilla (d 1290). Daughter of Alan, Earl of Galloway, and wife of the above John Balliol. She founded Balliol College, Oxford, Sweetheart Abbey and several other religious houses. 3. John (1249–1315). Son of John and Devorguilla. Chosen by Edward I to be King of Scotland, in preference to the rival claimant, Robert Bruce.

Barrie, Sir James (1860–1937). Scottish novelist and dramatist. Among many works are: 'A Window in Thrums' (Kirriemuir), 'Quality Street', 'Peter Pan' and 'Mary Rose'.

Beaton. 1. James (d 1539). Archbishop of Glasgow and St. Andrews. Regent during minority of James V and chiefly responsible for the alliance with France. Burned many heretics, including Patrick Hamilton. 2. David (c 1494–1546). Nephew of James. Cardinal and Archbishop of St. Andrews. Strongly supported the Scottish-French alliance, and was a notorious persecutor of Reformers, his best-known victim being George Wishart. Murdered, in revenge, in St. Andrews Castle. 3. James (1517–1603). The last Roman Catholic archbishop of Glasgow. Nephew of Cardinal Beaton. From 1560 he lived in Paris, acting as ambassador for Scotland.

Bell, Henry (1767–1830). Scottish engineer who placed the first steamboat on the Clyde ('Comet'. 25 tons. 3 H.P. engine). He gave much

Cardinal Beaton. A notorious and enthusiastic persecutor of Reformers, he burnt George Wishart but was soon afterwards himself murdered in St. Andrews Castle

assistance to the American engineer, Fulton.

Bothwell, James Hepburn, Earl of (1536–78). Powerful and turbulent noble during the reign of Mary, whom he married in 1567 after taking the lead in the murder of her husband, Darnley. At Carberry Hill Bothwell offered to fight any of Mary's enemies single-handed, but Mary forbade this. After Carberry Hill Bothwell became leader of a band of pirates. In 1570 Mary was granted a divorce. Bothwell went to Scandinavia where he was held in solitary confinement in the Danish castle of Dragsholm, eventually dying insane.

Brahan, Seer of (Coinneach Odhar). Early 17C Scottish seer. After sleeping on a fairy hillock he awoke to find his head resting on a small stone with a hole in it. He put the stone to his right eye, which from then on was blind to everything except the truth and the future. He gained considerable fame, but was cruelly murdered by the Countess of Seaforth (at Fortrose) for telling her about her husband's infidelity.

Buchanan, George (1506–82). Best-known Scottish 16C humanist. Anticlerical, he satirised the religious houses and was forced by Cardinal Beaton to flee to France. Returning to Scotland, he became openly a Reformer. He was tutor both to Mary and James VI.

Burns, Robert (1759–96). Generally accepted as Scotland's greatest poet. His early years were spent in some poverty, he, his brother and his father together failing to make a success of farming at Lochlea, near Tarbolton. His first volume was published in 1786, and was so successful that he cancelled the passage he had booked to take up a job in Jamaica. At about this time he was in love with Mary Campbell of Dunoon. She inspired poems such as 'The Highland Lassie' and 'Highland Mary' and, after her early death, 'To Mary in Heaven'. After a period in Edinburgh, where he was lionised but continued to have little financial success, he again tried farming, this time at Ellisland. In 1791 he accepted a post as excise officer in Dumfries, where he remained until his death. He married Jean Armour, by whom, both before and after marriage, he had several children. Among his many works were 'Tam o'Shanter', 'The Twa Brigs', 'Auld Lang Syne' and 'Hallowe'en'.

Chantrey, Sir Francis (1781–1841). English sculptor; well-known for his portrait-busts, notably one of Sir Walter Scott. Principal works include Washington (State House, Boston); George III (Guildhall, London); George IV (Brighton).

Claverhouse. See Graham of Claverhouse.

Cochrane, Robert (d 1482). Low-born favourite of James III, important also as an architect (Auchindoun Castle; Parliament Hall, Stirling). He became too powerful and was murdered by hanging (at Lauder) by jealous nobles led by Archibald Douglas, henceforth known as 'Bell-the-Cat'. (Some modern authorities suggest Cochrane may never have existed.)

Columba, Saint (c 521–597). A member of the Irish royal house, he founded a number of churches and monasteries in Ireland before in 563 settling in Iona with 12 companions. From here, by his preaching and holy life, he converted much of northern Scotland. As chief churchman of Dalriada, he gave formal benediction to his kinsman Aidan, thus officiating at what was probably the first Christian 'coronation'.

Crichton, William (d 1482). On the murder of James I, he seized the infant James II, took over the revenues, became Lord Chancellor and for long enjoyed absolute power. To secure his position (and that of the king) he arranged the judicial murder of William and David Douglas at the Black Dinner in Edinburgh Castle, and he was also present in 1452 when James II treacherously stabbed William Douglas to death at Stirling.

Oliver Cromwell. Parliamentarian, soldier, man of God, regicide

Cromwell, Oliver (1599–1658). Of yeoman stock, he became a member of parliament (England) in 1628. During the Civil War he rose to become parliament's leader and as such bore much of the responsibility for the execution of Charles I. After the execution he ruled as Lord Protector of England (Commonwealth period) until his death.

Cumberland, Duke of (1721–65). Son of George II. Best-known for his defeat of the Young Pretender at Culloden, after which his savage repression earned him the title of 'Butcher'.

Douglas. Ancient Scottish family which divides into the Black and Red branches. Of the *Black Douglases* the best known are: 1. Sir James, the Good (1286–1330). A staunch supporter of Bruce, he gained the name of 'black' from his savage excesses in raids along the border. (One of his exploits was so barbaric that it became known as the 'Douglas Larder'.) He took Bruce's heart on a crusade, but fell fighting the Moors in Spain. 2. Archibald, the Grim (1328–c1400). Natural son of 'good' Sir James. Became Lord of Galloway, and built Threave Castle, whence he ruled his lands as absolute master. Black Douglas power overshadowed that of the crown during the weak rule of Robert III, and Douglas's daugher, Marjorie, married Robert III's son and heir, the Duke of Rothesay. 3. William and David (d 1440) were sons of the 5th Earl. When little more than boys they were treacherously executed in Edinburgh Castle (the Black Dinner). This murder, arranged by Chancellor Crichton, broke the Douglas power. 4. William (c 1425–52), 8th Earl, temporarily recovered Black Douglas power, but, although under safe-conduct, was murdered by James II at Stirling Castle. 5. James (1426–88) rebelled to avenge his brother, but was defeated (losing Threave) and the lordship of Douglas passed to the Red Douglas, 4th Earl of Angus. Of the *Red Douglases* (Earls of Angus) the best-known are: 1. Archibald (c 1450–c 1514), 5th Earl, who earned the title of 'Bell-the-Cat' for taking the lead in hanging several low-born favourites of James III. 2. Bishop Gavin (c 1474–1522). Third son of the 5th Earl. Churchman, diplomat and poet. Abbot of Arbroath, Bishop of Dunkeld and of St. Machar, Aberdeen. 3. Archibald (c 1489–1557), 6th Earl, who married Margaret, sister of Henry VIII and widow of James IV. He became very powerful and was hated by his stepson (James V), whom for a while he held and controlled. In 1528 Margaret got a divorce, James freed himself and Douglas fled. James then avenged himself by burning Douglas's sister (Janet, Lady Glamis) at the stake, as a witch for conspiring against him. By Margaret this Douglas became grandfather to Darnley, husband of Mary, Queen of Scots.

Dundee, Viscount. See Graham of Claverhouse.

Duns Scotus, John (c 1265–1308). A Franciscan, born at Duns, he became a leading divine and the greatest medieval philosopher. Known as 'Dr Subtilis'. He lived in Oxford, Paris and Cologne.

Fingal. In origin probably a 3C Irish warrior called Finn MacCumhael. Finn attracted much legend to himself and became a mythological figure dominating Gaelic folklore. When not busy with the chase, he and his band of warrior heroes (the original Fenians) defended Ireland against foreign invaders. Traditionally father of Ossian.

Graham of Claverhouse, John (c 1649–89). Viscount Dundee ('Bonnie Dundee' of ballad). Scottish soldier, royalist, and notorious persecutor of the later Covenanters. After the revolution against James VII/II, he placed himself at the head of the Stuart cause in Scotland, but was killed at Killiecrankie.

Hamilton, Patrick (1504–28). Titular Abbot of Ferne, he studied in Paris, was attracted by the teaching of Erasmus and became a convinced Protestant. A member of the university of St. Andrews, he had to flee the persecution of James Beaton. After visiting Luther and studying in Germany, he returned to Scotland, but Beaton had him burned for heresy. He is regarded as the Scottish proto-martyr of the Reformation.

Hertford, Edward Seymour, Earl of (1506–52). Also Duke of Somerset and brother of Jane Seymour, third wife of Henry VIII. In 1544 and 1545 Henry appointed him Lieutenant General of the North, with instructions to punish the Scots for their repudiation of the marriage treaty between the infant Mary and Henry's son, Edward. Hertford carried out his instructions with great savagery. After the death of Henry VIII, Hertford (Somerset) became Lord Protector of England, but was toppled by his rival, Warwick, and executed.

Hogg, James (1770–1835). Scottish poet, known, from his calling, as the 'Ettrick shepherd'. Protégé of Sir Walter Scott.

Jones, John Paul (1747–92). Son of John Paul, a gardener near Kirkbean, he went to sea, at first on slavers and then getting his own ships. In 1773 he changed his name to Jones, after killing the leader of a mutinous crew, an act he always deeply regretted. He received a commission in the new American navy and was the first to raise the Union flag on a warship (the

'Alfred'). Thereafter he spent several years in European waters harassing the English, but usually acting with chivalry. In 1788 he entered Catherine the Great's Russian navy as an admiral, but soon retired disillusioned. He died in France. A century later his body was brought back to the USA and laid in the naval chapel at Annapolis.

Keith. Ancient NE Scottish family whose leaders bore the hereditary title of Marischal of Scotland. 1. Robert (d 1346) had the title confirmed and made hereditary by Bruce. He commanded the Scottish cavalry at Bannockburn. 2. William (d c 1407) built the great Keith stronghold at Dunnottar. 3. Another William (d 1581) was a guardian of Mary, Queen of Scots, and later became an adherent of the Reformation. He retired to Dunnottar and became known as William of the Tower. His daughter married the regent, Moray. 4. George (c 1553–1623), 5th Earl Marischal, was a highly cultured man. He arranged the marriage between James VI and Anne of Denmark. In 1593 he founded and endowed Aberdeen's Marischal College. 5. William (c 1617–61), 7th Earl Marischal, was a leading Covenanter. It was to his safe-keeping at Dunnottar that the Scottish regalia were entrusted. 6. George (c 1693–1778), 10th Earl, was a Jacobite, took part in the '15, fled to the continent and lost the family estates and titles. 7. James (1696–1758) is best known as Marshal Keith. Like his brother he fled abroad after the '15, but returned to take part in the even more abortive (Glen Shiel) rising of 1719. He thereafter served in the Spanish, Russian and Prussian armies, being given the rank of Field Marshal by Frederick II of Prussia. He had a distinguished career in Frederick's army during the Seven Years War before he was killed in battle.

Kelvin, William Thomson (1824–1907). Distinguished physicist. For 53 years he held the chair of natural philosophy at the University of Glasgow, during which period it became a source of inspiration for advanced research.

Kirkcaldy of Grange, Sir William (c 1520–73). Determined opponent of Cardinal Beaton whom, with the help of others, he murdered. He was a leader of the Lords of the Congregation; was accessory to the murder of Rizzio, but not to that of Darnley; he received Mary's surrender at Carberry Hill and was mainly responsible for her defeat at Langside. Later he sided with her (although she was by now imprisoned in England) and held Edinburgh Castle in her cause; here he was forced to surrender and hanged.

Knox, John (c 1505–72). Scottish reformer. In 1547, when in St. Andrews, he was taken prisoner by the French, spending 19 months in the galleys. Returning to Scotland he preached (1559) in Perth and St. Andrews the fiery sermons which led to the destruction of the monasteries. As minister of St. Giles in Edinburgh (1561) he held four Dialogues with Mary. Absent in England during the latter part of Mary's reign, he returned to Scotland in 1567 to preach at the coronation of James VI. In character Knox was dogmatic, yet had a sense of humour and tenderness belied by sermons which sparked an orgy of destruction well beyond anything he intended.

Lauder, Sir Harry (1870–1950). Mill boy and miner who became a famed writer and interpreter of Scottish songs.

Leighton, Robert (1611–84). Bishop of Dunblane and Archbishop of Glasgow. A scholarly and meditative man, he is best-known for his efforts to reconcile the Episcopalian and Presbyterian points of view, and for his representations against the persecution of the Covenanters.

Leslie, David (1601–82). Scottish Covenanter and general. After being a colonel of cavalry in the army of Gustavus Adolphus, he fought for parliament during the English Civil War and defeated Montrose at Philiphaugh. He led Scotland's army (in support of Charles II, 1650), but was defeated by Cromwell at Dunbar. The following year he accompanied Charles II to defeat at Worcester, thereafter being imprisoned in the Tower of London until the Restoration when he was made Lord Newark.

Macdonald, Flora (1722–90). After assisting the Young Pretender (see Rtes 62 and 66), Flora was arrested and imprisoned in the Tower of London. Freed under the 1747 Act of Indemnity, she married (1750), later (1773) emigrating to America. Her husband served the British government during the War of Independence and was taken prisoner. Flora returned to Scotland in 1779.

Macpherson, James (1736–96). Scottish poet and 'translator' of the Ossianic poems. He certainly collected a quantity of Gaelic material, but his so-called translations have been much questioned and are probably his own compositions based on Gaelic fragments.

Melville, Andrew (1545–1622). Scottish scholar, theologian and reformer. He studied at St. Andrews (classics), Paris (oriental languages) and Poitiers (civil law). In Scotland his academic appointments were Principal of Glasgow University (1574), raising the university from ruin to prosperity; and Principal of St. Mary's College, St. Andrews, in 1580. He became Rector ten years later. Melville at all times defended the Church against government encroachment, and spent four years in the Tower. His last years were passed in France as a professor at the University of Sedan.

Monk, George (1608–69). Parliamentary general, first against the rebels in Ireland and then in 1650 in Scotland at Dunbar. From 1653 until Cromwell's death in 1658 he governed Scotland. He then became commander-in-chief of the parliamentary forces and marched to London where, after devious manoeuvres, he engineered the Restoration and became Duke of Albemarle.

Monmouth, Duke of (1649–85). Natural son of Charles II by Lucy Walters. Married Anne Scott, Countess of Buccleuch. A Protestant, he claimed that Charles II had been married to Lucy and raised a revolt against James II. The revolt was easily crushed and Monmouth was executed.

Moray, Regent (c 1531–70). James Stuart, illegitimate son of James V, and half brother to Mary, Queen of Scots. He sided with the Lords of the Congregation and opposed Mary's marriage to Darnley, thereupon being declared an outlaw and fleeing to England. Pardoned, he returned to Scotland and became Regent on Mary's abdication. In 1570 he was shot while riding through Linlithgow.

Morton, Regent (?1525–1581). James Douglas, 4th Earl. Led the soldiery which secured Holyrood when Rizzio was murdered. Fought against Mary, Queen of Scots, at Langside. Elected Regent (for James VI) in 1572, but had many enemies and was executed in 1581 for connivance in the murder of Darnley.

Ossian. Shadowy 3C Gaelic bard, possibly son of Fingal. See Macpherson, James.

Park, Mungo (1771–?1806). Scottish surgeon and explorer, in the latter capacity especially active in West Africa and along the Niger river. In 1806, on a Niger expedition in which his aim was to trace the river down to the coast, he was drowned when hostile natives attacked his canoe while stranded on a rock.

Queensberry, 'Old Q' (1724–1810). 4th Duke. Notorious as a gambler, as also for other extravagances.

Ramsay, 1. Allan (1686–1758). Scottish poet, who tried to reawaken interest in the older national literature. Perhaps his best-known work is 'The Gentle Shepherd'. In 1736 he unsuccessfully opened a theatre in Carrubber's Close, Edinburgh. 2. Allan (1713–84). Well-known portrait-painter son of the poet.

Rennie, John (1761–1821). Scottish engineer whose specialities were marsh drainage (in Scotland: Solway); harbours and docks (Wick, Holyhead); and bridges (in London: Waterloo, Southwark and London).

Rob Roy (1671–1734). Robert MacGregor, known as Rob Roy (Red Robert) from the colour of his hair. Although represented by tradition and Sir Walter Scott as a romantic and genial outlaw akin to Robin Hood, Rob Roy was simply a cattle-lifter and free-booter. He was present at Sheriffmuir, as a Jacobite, but abstained from active help to either side. He submitted to General Wade in 1722, was imprisoned in London and pardoned in 1727.

Rothesay, Duke of (d 1402). Eldest son of Robert III. See Albany.

Scot, Michael (c 1117–1232). 'The Wizard'. Although appearing in Scottish history mainly as an astrologer, alchemist and dealer in the occult, Scot was a scholar, mathematician and linguist. He was a scholar at the court of the Holy Roman Emperor, Frederick II, for whom he translated Aristotle and Arabic commentaries. The legends grew after his death and will be met in many places in Scotland. The opening of his tomb (Melrose Abbey) is a striking episode in Sir Walter Scott's 'Lay of the last Minstrel'.

Scott, Sir Walter (1771–1832). Scott's fame rests not only on his achievements as a prolific poet and novelist, telling the stories of Scotland's romantic past, but also on the way in which he publicised Scotland and restored something of the spirit that had been lost after the Act of Union and Culloden. It was he who instigated the successful search for the Regalia (1817), and it was he who organised the State Visit (1822) by George IV (see History). In 1825 Scott found that in the financial confusion following the collapse of his publisher he was personally responsible for £130,000 and his toil and determination to pay the debt are a famous chapter of literary history. (For Scott generally, see STB booklet, *Land of Scott*.)

Sharp, James (1618–79). Archbishop of St. Andrews. He played a devious role in Scottish Church negotiations with England, but when in 1661 Episcopacy was restored he came into the open and accepted the see of St. Andrews. When in 1666 the Covenanters rose, Sharp acted with cruelty towards the prisoners of Rullion Green. He was murdered by Covenanters at Magus Muir, near St. Andrews.

Smith, Adam (1773–90). Economist and philosopher, born at Kirkcaldy. While Professor of Moral Philosophy at Glasgow (1752–63) he published (1759) his 'Theory of Moral Sentiments'. Later, his concern turned more to political economy, in which subject he is best known for his 'Inquiry into the Nature and Causes of the Wealth of Nations' (1776).

Stevenson. 1. Robert (1772–1850). Scottish engineer, well-known for his lighthouses, the most important being Bell Rock. 2. Robert Louis (1850–94). Grandson of the engineer, Robert, and son of another engineer, he tried to follow the family profession but had to give up due to ill health, and instead became a famed and prolific literary figure. ('Treasure Island', 'Dr Jekyll and Mr Hyde', 'Master of Ballantrae', etc.)

Telford, Thomas (1757–1834). Scottish civil engineer, especially known for his canals (Caledonian), roads and many still surviving bridges.

Thomas the Rhymer (c 1220–97). Thomas Learmont of Erceldoune (Earlston). Scottish seer and poet associated with numerous fragments of prophetic verse, from which he has gained the name of True Thomas. Traditionally he had a romance with the fairy queen, spending three years with her in the Eildon Hills.

Wade, George (1673–1748). Distinguished English officer sent (as a major-general) to Scotland in 1724 to begin a system of metalled roads and stone bridges, of which he built 40. He tactfully disarmed the clans and is remembered by the couplet:

Had you seen these roads before they were made,
You would lift up your hands and bless General Wade.

Warbeck, Perkin (d 1499). Son of a boatman, he was put forward by the English Yorkist faction, the Scots and others as one of the princes murdered in the Tower and thus as rightful claimant to the English throne, rather than Henry VII. He made three futile invasions of England, one from Scotland being supported by James IV. After the third he was caught and executed.

Wishart, George (c 1513–46). Scottish reformer. Accused of heresy in 1538, he fled to England and then to Germany. Returning to Scotland in 1543, he began to preach, but was seized and handed over to Cardinal Beaton who had him burned at St. Andrews.

Wolf of Badenoch (d 1394). A natural son of Robert II, the Wolf was Alexander Stewart, Earl of Buchan. Also known as Alisdair Mor mae an Righ (Big Alexander, son of the King). Turbulent and vicious, he brooked no opposition and from his castles of Ruthven and Lochindorb terrorised and devastated the countryside, notably in 1390 after a quarrel with the Bishop of Elgin resulting in his excommunication.

Scotland's Antiquities and Later Buildings

Ranging from burial cairns and standing stones to castles, abbeys and mansions, the ruins and other evidence of Scotland's past cover a period of 4000 and more years. These notes try to relate these antiquities to their place within this period.

It is impossible to be precise about the dates of cultures which overlapped one another both geographically and in time by perhaps many hundreds of years. This is particularly so of prehistory. In this guide, whenever the description Stone Age is used it means New Stone Age (Neolithic), the time when man began to change from wandering food gatherer to crop-raising farmer, thus having to settle and build. As a very rough guide, in Scotland this New Stone Age stretched from 3000 BC or earlier to 2000 BC. It was followed by the Bronze Age, lasting to about the date of the birth of Christ and merging with the Iron Age, starting in Scotland around 200 BC and representing the period when prehistory shades into history.

Hill-forts, brochs, and also later defensive points, especially in the Highlands and Hebrides, all frequently appear on maps as 'Dun', with or without a name.

Chambered Cairns *(Stone and Early Bronze Age)*. Generally, chambered cairns are the oldest structures to be found in Scotland. Of varying shapes, both interior and exterior, the cairns are piles of stones covering well constructed corbelled burial chambers, these often having a number of side cells. Entrance is nearly always by way of a long, low and narrow passage. The four main cairn types are Circular, Stalled, Horned and Heel. Circular cairns are found all over Scotland, the supreme example being the huge *Maes Howe* in Orkney. Although on the mainland there is nothing to compare in size, the *Clava Cairns* (near Inverness) are of considerable interest, both as cairns and because they are encircled by standing stones. Stalled cairns, so called because of their interior partitions, are found largely in Orkney, the best being *Midhowe* on the island of Rousay. Horned cairns, with their strange crescents, are rare and unique to Scotland; a good example is the *Grey Cairns of Camster*, south of Wick. Heel cairns are special to Shetland.

Most cairn tombs seem to have been used over many generations, possibly for a community but more likely just for the ruling families who would have had the necessary organising skill and call on labour. The cairn builders may be pictured as people with some social structure, able to make pottery and having both domestic animals and a developing agriculture.

Stone and Bronze Age Settlements. Scotland's most easily recognisable Stone Age settlement is that at *Skara Brae* in Orkney. Other Stone Age structures are *Knap of Howar* on Papa Westray (Orkney) and *Stanydale* on Shetland's Mainland. The outstanding Bronze Age settlement is *Jarlshof* in Shetland.

Stone Circle Ritual Sites *(Late Stone and Bronze Age)*. Ritual sites are of three main types. These are a single ring or concentric circles (*Ring of Brodgar*, Orkney); a ring enclosing a burial cairn (*Clava*); or parallel lines of stones (*Hill o' Many Stanes*, near Wick). A fourth group, confined to the district around Aberdeen, includes a recumbent stone between uprights. The builders were mainly Bronze Age people, who must not only have had skill and the ability to command a large labour force, but also some compelling motivation to erect sites as massive as these. What rituals these monuments saw will probably never be known, but the honouring of the dead certainly played a major part. The sites are often laid out with precision, both in themselves and in relation to conspicuous landmarks, a feature which has prompted some archaeologists to suggest an astronomical significance. Many lone standing stones date from this same period, as do also the mysterious but presumably ritual cup, ring and other markings found on so many stones and natural rocks.

Hut Circles *(Bronze and Iron Age)*. Found all over Scotland, often within hill-forts, a typical hut circle is a ring of earth and stone about 3ft thick and rarely more than 2ft high enclosing an area of 20 to 30ft in diameter. An entrance can sometimes be traced, and occasionally the interior is in part paved. When occupied, the huts' walls would of course have been higher and a frame would have supported a roof of perhaps wattle or skin. Such primitive huts were probably in use until well into historic times; the age of any particular site can normally only be determined from the relics found there.

Hill-Forts *(Late Bronze and Iron Age)*. Hill-forts is a loose description for a variety of enclosures, such as earth ramparts, dry-stone walling or a combination of both. In large part these were defended villages, evidence of a growing knowledge of metals and competence with tools as well as of how the tribes in the increasingly populated Lowlands were beginning to organise themselves to combine domestic life with defence both against their neighbours and later against the Romans. Hill-forts are, in fact, the earliest evidence of miliary architecture. While some go back to the Bronze Age, relics excavated place most within the Iron Age. Forts vary greatly. Some, on mountain tops and without water supply, would have been occupied only in emergency. Others, such as the complex on *Traprain Law* near Dunbar, would have been permanently occupied villages, while that at *Dunadd* in Argyll

BROCH

0 feet — 10

0 metres — 3

Section

Stairs in Wall

was the capital of the kingdom of Dalriada. It was to hill villages such as these that the early Christian missionaries would have made their way.

A defensive and strengthening feature of the walls was the use of timbers. These were however liable to catch fire, the intense heat then partially melting some types of stone. This, with the impression of burnt timbers, can still be seen today, such forts being called vitrified. About 50 of these are recorded.

The Brochs *(Iron Age).* The defensive round towers known as brochs are unique to Scotland. Although the name is Norse, the brochs were built many centuries before the arrival of the Norsemen and for a long period must have overlapped with the hill-forts. Typically, a broch is a hollow round tower, some 40ft high, enclosing an interior of about 40ft diameter at ground level but tapering towards the top. The ingenious double walls are the unique feature. Standing on a solid base, the outer and inner walls are bonded at roughly 5ft vertical intervals by continuous stone lintels forming a series of galleries. Also within the wall is at least one stairway to the top of the broch. This construction, entirely dry-stone, ensures the combination of lightness and strength essential for such a tower, and it seems unlikely that the galleries had any purpose other than structural. The only entrance is narrow and low, with a stone door secured by a drawbar and beside it one or more guard cells. Features in the courtyard often include a hearth and a cistern or well.

The size of the brochs suggests that they were intended for the households of chiefs, though in times of danger doubtless many others would have crowded in. Eventually, around perhaps 200, there seems to have been less demand for the security the brochs provided and they became centres of farming and other settlements. There are some 500 broch sites in Scotland, most now no more than mounds and stones. Some, though, still stand, the finest being *Mousa* in Shetland. On the mainland the best preserved are a pair in *Glen Beg*, near Kyle of Lochalsh.

Wheel-Houses *(Iron Age)*. These are round dry-stone dwellings, with curious radial partitions off a common central area. Found in the north they are often built within or alongside brochs (*Gurness*, in Orkney, and *Jarlshof*, Shetland). Wheel-houses are thought to have remained in use until about the time of the first Christian missionaries.

Earth-Houses (Souterrains) *(Iron Age, or earlier)*. Neither the purpose nor the age of these strange underground structures has been satisfactorily decided. A typical earth-house is reached by steps down to a long, narrow passage which gradually descends in a curve to an underground chamber, usually with well-built walls and roof and measuring perhaps 12ft by 6ft and over 6ft in height. As to date, some in southern Scotland incorporate Roman stonework; on the other hand those at *Jarlshof* are within a complex of Bronze Age buildings. Earth-houses may have been used as refuges, stores, or even as winter dwellings. Among good and accessible examples are *Culsh*, near Tarland (Deeside); three near Dundee (*Tealing, Ardestie* and *Carlungie*), all now unroofed; one by *Loch Eriboll* in the far north; and two (*Grain* and *Rennibister*) near Kirkwall, Orkney.

Crannogs *(Iron Age and later)*. Crannogs are man-made islets on which stood usually single defended dwellings. They were built up in shallow water, simply by sinking a wooden base (normally circular) and then piling stones on to it. Access was either by boat, or by sunken causeway. A large number of small, round islets in lochs are crannogs, an easily seen example being *Cherry Island* in Loch Ness at Fort Augustus.

Roman Period *(80–200)*. Scotland's Roman remains are all military, the best being the *Antonine Wall*, several stretches of which can be well seen along the line linking the Forth to the Clyde. This was turf or earth on a stone foundation, with a ditch, a military road and forts at intervals. Other Roman sites are all fortified camps, these being either permanent bases (*Cramond*, Edinburgh; *Ardoch*, between Stirling and Crieff), or marching camps (*Lyne*, near Peebles).

Early Christian *(5–12C)*. The first evidence of Christian presence is in the form of grave-slabs, the earliest being in the South West, where St. Ninian preached Christianity about the year 400. Notable collections are at *Whithorn* and *Kirkmadrine*, at the former being the Latinus (or Barrovadus) Stone of 450, probably the oldest Christian memorial in Scotland. St. Columba's mission in the 6C was of wider and more lasting effect than that of St. Ninian. His Celtic Church was monastic in organisation, its early small buildings being circular and thus known as beehive cells, remains of which can still be seen in the more inaccessible Hebrides (*Garvellach Islands*). Later years saw the construction of Celtic churches and monasteries, but with the 7C the Roman Church began to displace the Celtic influence, this process accelerating as between about 850 and 1050 Scotland coalesced into a single kingdom. It is from the end of this period that the Round Towers, of which there are three in Scotland, can be dated. These are on *Egilsay* (Orkney) and at *Abernethy* and *Brechin*, this last being the oldest (probably 10C). These round towers, serving as belfries, landmarks and refuges, are typical of the Culdee order in Ireland and can be considered as eastward late Celtic (Culdee) intrusions.

The main reminders of Scotland's Early Christian period are the

An example of Ogham writing

variety of sculptured stones and crosses, these broadly being of Celtic origin in the west and of Northumbrian in the east. The latter, often bearing the knotwork patterns common on the continent, are generally the older, the supreme example being *Ruthwell Cross* (first half 8C). Of mixed Northumbrian and Pictish origin are slabs carved with a cross in relief, knotwork pattern, foliage, human and animal figures and Pictish symbols of unknown but presumably Christian meaning. Crosses or slabs are also common in the west, but the more typical monument here is the free-standing cross, or High Cross, its arms frequently linked to form a ring. Both in form and in their often rich ornamentation these crosses are essentially Irish. They served many purposes (to commemorate the dead, to mark boundaries or preaching sites) and they continued to be erected throughout the western Highlands down to the Reformation. Of the really early crosses two intact examples are *St. Martin's* (10C) on Iona, and *Kildalton* (8C) on Islay. To this general period also belong stones bearing Ogham inscriptions, the oldest written form of Celtic Gaelic. The writing takes the form of strokes or notches along a base-line. The oldest examples are in Argyll (*Dunadd*), and there are later, Pictish Ogham stones in the North East (e.g. *Brandsbutt Stone*, Inverurie).

Holy wells, still found near many Early Christian sites, recall the baptismal and also often healing activities of the early missionaries.

Norse Remains *(9–14C)*. If one discounts a monument such as St. Magnus Cathedral in Kirkwall (built by a Norse earl, but Norman in style), true Norse remains are few and largely confined to Orkney and Shetland. At *Brough of Birsay* there survives something of Earl Thorfinn's Christ Church and Hall, and here also, as at *Jarlshof* and a few other places, there are the outlines of long-houses, the buildings most commonly associated with the Norsemen. Although over the long period of Norse occupation there must have been change, a typical long-house may be imagined as perhaps 100ft long and 20ft broad, built of earth within dry-stone facing and having a turf and wood roof. There would have been two or more rooms, each with its hearth. Perhaps the most interesting Norse remains are their carefully executed graffiti, notably within the chambered cairn of *Maes Howe*.

In the 11 and 12C Malcolm III (Canmore), his queen, Margaret, and the three of their sons who became kings, changed Celtic Scotland into a feudal kingdom of the Anglo-Norman pattern. The change was felt as much in architecture as in other fields, and the period of the 12 and 13C marks the start of large architecture in the form of monastic houses, their associated church buildings, and increasingly formidable castles. This period, which includes first Romanesque, or, as often called in Britain, Norman architecture, and then, by gradual transition, Gothic, continued through to the outbreak of the wars of succession and independence in the 14C. These wars ended two centuries of freedom of movement between Scotland and England, thus opening the way for developments in local style, to some extent influenced by the continent; the 15C can claim to be the second and the more individual of Scotland's great building periods.

Monastic Houses. The monasteries suffered severely from the Reformation and in consequence their remains (that is of the domestic buildings as distinct from their churches) are few and fragmentary. Though there were variations to meet the requirements of each order, the monasteries were of a more or less standard pattern: the whole was enclosed by an outer wall, often with an imposing gatehouse, within which the nucleus was the cloister, an arrangement of buildings around a central court, usually on the south and thus more protected side of the church. Around the court stood the abbot's lodging, the guest house (hospitium) and various domestic buildings while the infirmary usually stood to the east of the church. The eastern range buildings were normally of two storeys, the lower rooms serving various administrative purposes and including the chapter-house which, as the general meeting place, was often the most handsomely built. Above was the monks' dormitory (dorter) with a sanitary provision (reredorter), and, at the end abutting the church, a night stair by which the monks descended to night worship. The south side of the cloister contained the dining hall (refectory or frater), a kitchen and a warming house, this last a common living room with a fireplace. The cloister walk in most cases ended at a door at each end of the south wall of the church.

Some good portions of outer wall can be seen at *Sweetheart Abbey* and the best gatehouse is at *Crossraguel*. The best surviving domestic buildings are at *Dryburgh*.

Cathedrals and Churches. Among the characteristics of Norman architecture are great length of church plan; rounded arches; broad and shallow buttresses; arcading and massive round columns. Bell towers, later absorbed into their churches (as at *Dunblane*), became square and apses angled rather than round. There is also a distinct if crude decorative richness, in which geometric designs such as zigzags are popular. Examples of this period abound in Scotland, though nearly always combined with later styles. The nave of the abbey church at *Dunfermline* is outstanding, with round columns and arches, blind arcading and zigzag decoration, while at *Kirkwall Cathedral* the contrast between Norman and later work can be well seen. Of many smaller churches, probably the most visited is Edinburgh's *St. Margaret's Chapel*, while *Dalmeny* and *Leuchars* rank among Scotland's best Norman work.

Although there was a Transitional (mixed styles) period, the Gothic (or Pointed) style was taking over by the latter part of the 12C. Generally the first phase is known as Early English, others following being Decorated (so called because of the increasing use of rich stone carving) and Perpendicular; in Scotland, though, the later stages of Gothic were characterised more by borrowings from French Flamboyant and earlier Romanesque or Norman styles. The basis of Gothic architecture is structural, arising from the wish to build churches completely vaulted in stone, the main feature for this purpose being the general use of the pointed arch. Other features are ribbed vaults; large areas for stained glass; the use for decorative purposes of what had previously been essentially structural, e.g. buttresses and arcades; and an increasing lavishness in carving. Generally there was an urge towards soaring height in preference to the squat solidity of the Norman style. Most of the great abbeys are good examples of the transitional period and after, the long nave at *Jedburgh* being one of the best, while *Glasgow Cathedral*, mainly Early English but with other periods, is outstanding among Gothic buildings.

When from the 15C on Scotland's builders found themselves freed from Anglo-Norman influence, they both looked back to the past and also innovated to met the needs of their age. From the past they resurrected round-arch doorways and apse, the latter now three-sided as in *Crossraguel Abbey*. Sometimes the need was to fortify church buildings, this explaining the castellation of *Torphichen Preceptory* and the turreted gatehouse at *Crossraguel*. But the most important innovation of this period, arising from the declining interest in monasteries, was the founding instead of collegiate churches (originally chantries), where a 'college' or group of clergy was bound by deed to sing masses and pray for the souls of the wealthy founder and such relatives and friends as he might require. Such churches might be either new or simply older parish churches converted to collegiate status. Later, collegiate churches often became parish churches, as at *Corstorphine*. Many collegiate churches are still in use today, the best known being *Roslin Chapel*, with its unsurpassed richness of carved stone.

Following are explanations of some principal church architecture terms.

Nave	Main body of the church from the W door to the choir.
Aisles	Almost any division of a church, but usually the areas parallel to and separated by pillars (piers) from the nave, transepts or choir.
Transepts	The transverse (N and S) parts of a cruciform church.
Crossing	Where the transepts cross the nave-choir; usually supports the tower.
Choir (Chancel)	E part of the church reserved for the clergy, choir etc. Often railed off. Strictly the chancel is that part beyond the choir and nearest the altar, the word coming from the altar screens ('cancelli').
Apse	Small extension, usually of the choir and often containing the altar and sedilia (stone seats).
Chapels	Dedicated to saints and others, chapels may be anywhere around the church interior. A Lady Chapel is dedicated to the Virgin and is normally E of the altar.
Sacristy	Repository for vestments, vessels, etc.
Sacrament House (Aumbrey)	Wall recess in which the Sacrament, holy vessels etc, are placed. Often richly carved. Most found in the NE.
Triforium	Gallery (usually arcaded) above the arches of the nave, transept and chancel.
Clerestory	(Clear storey). Part of the upper wall, with windows, above the aisle roofs.

Castles. The feudal castle came to Scotland in the 11 and 12C, with the new Norman ruling class, although during these early centuries few bore much resemblance to the massive structures that were to follow. The castle started as a ditch surrounding an earth mound on which stood a timber tower. Annexed to this mound, and protected by a palisaded rampart and ditch, there was often an enclosure with further timber buildings. The mound was called a 'motte' or 'mote', this being the same as 'moat', the word meaning equally a ditch or what had been heaped out of it. The annexed enclosure was the 'bailey'. Numerous remains of these motte-and-bailey castles survive, though only of course in the form of their earthworks. Good examples are *Peel of Lumphanan, Hawick* and *The Bass* near Inverurie.

Stone castles appeared as early as the mid 12C, though there are now few remains as old as this. Exceptions are *Castle Sween,* with Scotland's only Norman keep and generally accepted as the oldest 'real' castle, and *Kisimul Castle* on Barra, whose tower probably dates from 1120. It was not until the 13 and 14C that stone castles became general, at first being essentially stone versions of the motte-and-bailey pattern, the stone towers (also called keeps or donjons) often rising on the same mottes as had supported the earlier timber towers. *Duffus Castle* well illustrates this.

Throughout this time defensive tactics were based on these massive keeps, regarded as the last line of defence and therefore usually in the remotest or safest corner of the enclosure. But a departure from the strict motte-and-bailey plan came towards the middle of the 14C as the belief grew that defence should be forward on the enclosure rather than within or to the rear. At *Tantallon* and *St. Andrews,* for instance, the chief tower or keep is placed forward of the courtyard and the castle's main entrance is carried through the base of the tower. Another and more significant design change is apparent at *Doune,* where a two-storey building of the kind known as the 'hall', hitherto always an independent building within the enclosure, is now placed alongside the main tower. Indeed with the 15C the hall, together with its kitchen and other domestic rooms, increasingly determined the plan of new castles and of alterations to older ones, the result being that enclosure walls became buildings and, with warfare becoming more mobile, towers decreased in importance. In Scotland, structures where the emphasis was on the hall became commonly known as 'palaces', regardless of whether the owner was a king, a church dignitary, an earl or a mere laird. Later though, the description 'palace' was reserved for larger places, more modest ones being described as 'mansions' or 'houses' or reverting to the old style of 'castle'. On the grand scale *Linlithgow* superbly illustrates the gradual development from a tower of 1302 to a 16C palace, while of smaller, part-fortified houses there are many.

With the shift from defence to residence came also structural artistic taste, Renaissance styling being a favourite source of inspiration. When, for instance, to complete the quadrangle, the north side of *Crichton Castle* was erected in 1585, it was given an elaborate, embossed, Italianate inner stonework decoration. Another example is *Caerlaverock* where a formidably defensive exterior contrasts with the Renaissance elegance of the courtyard. This development of taste was apparent also in the new castles built in the late 16 and 17C, especially in Scotland's North East. Increasingly, defensive features were treated as ornamentation and turreted projections became popular, so that castles such as *Crathes* and *Craigievar,* often with fine internal plasterwork, became as much works of art as defensive strongholds. This style, known as Scottish Baronial, was to be revived during the 19C at Balmoral and many other places.

A type of castle special to Scotland and spanning the 14 to the 17C is the Tower-House, typically a tower to which was normally attached an enclosure (barmkin) for service buildings. In the Borders district these are called 'Pele' towers, the word coming from the Latin 'palus' meaning a stake or palisade. For the most part tower-houses, the majority being built later than the 14C, were the defended homes of the lesser nobility. An early development was the addition of one or two towers built on to the corners of the original (L-plan or Z-plan). Initially this was a defensive requirement to meet the tactical changes of the early 16C when the increasing power of artillery was shifting defence from the parapet to ground level: square or round towers on opposite corners, provided with ground level gunloops, enabled all four sides of the main tower to be covered. Later, as the demand for private accommodation grew, these wings, particularly if square and of several storeys, were used for this purpose. However, original tower-houses onto which extensive additions have been grafted must rank, according to their development, as full castles, palaces or mansions. The more pleasing tower-houses are those which have retained their tower character, often embellished with the many turrets which were to lead to the Scottish Baronial style already referred to. Examples of all kinds of tower-houses are many. The oldest is probably *Threave Castle*; *Borthwick Castle* has typical massive wings; *Craigmillar* and *Crichton*, both starting as tower-houses, received so many additions that they became complex castles. Of tower-houses still retaining their original character, *Smailholm*, free of any additions, best represents the essentially military Borders pele tower, while *Claypotts* is turreted.

The word 'castle' has become somewhat overworked in Scotland today and will be found describing almost anything from a massive feudal stronghold to a modest country mansion.

Dovecots (Doocots). Dovecots are an attractive and interesting minor form of older architecture. It was only in the 18C that turnips and swedes were introduced, thus making it possible to feed livestock throughout the winter; before this only breeding stock could be kept, the remainder being slaughtered and salted. Pigeons then provided fresh winter meat. The most distinctive types of dovecot are round-domed (beehive) structures with a circular hole in the roof for the birds (*Northfield* at Old Preston and *Phantassie* at East Linton); square plan, with a slated, sloping roof with entry holes part way down (a pair may be seen at *Tantallon Castle*); incorporated in towers (*Hailes Castle*).

17 and 18C Military Works. Something survives of the military works erected by the English in the 17 and 18C, first by Cromwell and later by the Hanoverian governments. Of what Cromwell built most was destroyed at the Restoration, but his great fort at *Lerwick* (Shetland) still stands, though reconstructed in 1781. Rather more can still be seen of the Hanoverian works, notably the intact *Fort George* near Inverness and, near Kingussie, the shell of *Ruthven Barracks*, standing on an ancient motte.

Building after the Union of the Parliaments. Presbyterianism had triumphed at the revolution of 1688, and Culloden in 1746 was the last battle to be fought on Scottish soil. The former meant simple yet dignified churches to match a simple form of worship, the latter the end of major military building. Activity turned to the erection of fine civic buildings and, in the country, great mansions. In both spheres the Adam family were pre-eminent, their work embracing achievements as diverse as *Culzean Castle*, Glasgow's *Trades' House*, the splendid mansions of *Hopetoun, Haddo* and *Mellerstain*, and the north side of Edinburgh's *Charlotte Square*. The Georgian elegance of Edinburgh's New Town grew between 1767 and the early 19C, to be followed by the Victorian era, with, roughly in succession, the grandiose revival of the Scottish Baronial, Neo-Classical solidity, probably still best seen in Glasgow despite much demolition and the steady intrusion of modern tower blocks, and Art Nouveau, of which the principal exponent was C.R. Mackintosh of Glasgow.

The Church in Scotland

The Celtic Columban Christianity brought to Scotland in the 6C was soon displaced by the Roman forms favoured by the powerful kings of Northumbria, and from the early 8C until the Reformation Scotland was Roman Catholic. (However, the *Culdees*, Servants of God, spanned the earlier part of this period. Coming from Ireland in about the 8C, this order—apparently living to no formal rule and whose particular interests were, it is said, the care of the poor and the study of liturgical music—followed a fringe half-monkish, half-secular path. By the 12C the Culdees had become absorbed under Roman canonical rule). The 16 and 17C saw first the strife between the Roman Catholics and the reforming Protestants, and then the struggles within the Protestant faith between the covenanting Presbyterians and the Episcopalians. This struggle ended with the revolution of 1688, the triumph of Presbyterianism and the formal establishment of the Church of Scotland.

Church of Scotland. The Presbyterian and national united established *Church of Scotland* is the Church to which the overwhelming majority of Scottish Presbyterians belong today. This Church has emerged only after a long and confusing history of secessions and unions which began soon after the establishment of the Church of Scotland and continues to the present day. Throughout this period of some 250 years all the seceding groups remained strictly Presbyterian, their differences with the Established Church being not on points of faith but rather on aspects of the relationship between Church and State, and between congregations and elders or the assembly. The main events are summarised below.

1689. James VII/II deposed in favour of William and Mary. Presbyterianism established, with the *Church of Scotland* administered by an assembly. Abolition of patronage. (The right of the crown, local landowner or other patron to nominate or 'present' the minister).

1706. Secession of the *Cameronians* (originally followers of the fanatical Covenanter, Richard Cameron). An extremist group, they rejected any supremacy of the State in ecclesiastical matters.

1712. The Act of Toleration allowed Episcopalian dissenters to use the English liturgy, and the same parliament restored patronage, an act which led to much subsequent trouble.

1733–45. The *Secession Church* founded by Ebenezer Erskine; largely in opposition to an assembly decision that, when patrons failed to present a minister, then the minister would be chosen, not by the local congregation, but by the elders.

1743. The Cameronians assumed the name *Reformed Presbyterian Church*.

1747. The Secession Church split into the *Burghers* and the *Anti-burghers*. This split arose out of a religious clause in the oath required of burgesses in Edinburgh,

Glasgow and Perth. ('I confess and allow with my heart the true religion presently professed within this realm and authorized by the laws thereof'.) The anti-burghers condemned the swearing of such an oath as sinful.

1761. The *Relief Church* seceded. Adherents objected to patronage and any other lay interference and stood for 'the relief of Christians oppressed in their Church privileges'.

1799 and 1806. The Burghers and the Anti-burghers each split into the *Old Light* and *New Light* groups. The split was basically one between the views of conservative and other elements on the issue of the jurisdiction of the civil authority in ecclesiastical affairs.

1822. The two New Lights merged to form the *United Secession Church*.

1841. The two Old Lights merged to call themselves the *Original Seceders*.

1843. The Disruption. 451 ministers (of a total of 1203), headed by Dr Thomas Chalmers, resigned their livings, largely on the issue of patronage, and formed the *Free Church*.

1847. The United Secession Church joined with the Relief Church to become the *United Presbyterian Church*.

1874. The Patronage Act, conferring on congregations the right of electing parish ministers, removed a long-standing grievance.

1876. The Free Church absorbed the Reformed Presbyterian Church (formerly Cameronians).

1893. After a protest by the Rev. Donald Macfarlane of Raasay at the 'despotic power' exercised by many Free Church office bearers, some Free Church congregations, mainly in the Highlands, seceded and formed the deeply fundamental *Free Presbyterian Church*.

1900. The Free Church and the United Presbyterian Church united to become the *United Free Church*. But a few Free Church congregations, chiefly in the Highlands, remain outside this union and retain the name of Free Church; colloquially these are called the *'Wee Frees'*.

1929. The United Free Church joined the Church of Scotland, the two becoming the (united established) *Church of Scotland* under a General Assembly, presided over by a Moderator.

1956. The Original Seceders (Old Lights) joined the united established Church of Scotland.

1989. A decision to suspend an elder of the Free Presbyterian Church who had attended two Catholic requiems for old friends led to the secession of many adherents of the Free Presbyterian Church and the formation of the *Associated Presbyterian Churches*.

Episcopal Church in Scotland. After 1688 Episcopalian incumbents who took the oath of allegiance were allowed to retain their benefices, and an Act of 1712 protected the Episcopal Communion. Although suspect at the time of the '15 and the '45, an independent Episcopal Church survived. The Church has seven bishops, direct successors of those consecrated at the Restoration, and all the sees (except Edinburgh, founded by Charles I) are pre-Reformation. The sees are Aberdeen and Orkney; Argyll and the Isles; Brechin; Edinburgh; Glasgow and Galloway; Moray, Ross and Caithness; St. Andrews, Dunkeld and Dunblane. The bishops constitute the synod and elect their own Primus.

Roman Catholics. At the Reformation a considerable part of the population, especially in the Highlands and Hebrides, remained faithful to the 'old religion' which, strengthened by the immigration of Irish and others, still flourishes today. A new RC hierarchy was established in 1878 and now includes two archbishops (St. Andrews and Edinburgh; Glasgow) and six bishops (Aberdeen; Argyll and the Isles; Dunkeld; Galloway; Motherwell; Paisley).—Modern Scotland's first saint, John Ogilvie, a priest hanged in Glasgow in 1615, was canonised in 1976.

PRACTICAL INFORMATION

Organisations

Local Government. Under the 1975 local government reorganisation the counties of Scotland disappeared as such. Instead the country is now administered as nine Regions and three Island Areas (see Atlas 16). Sub-divisions comprise 51 Districts, many of these bearing the names of the former counties. The nine Regions are: Highland, Grampian, Tayside, Fife, Lothian, Borders, Central, Strathclyde and Dumfries-Galloway. The three Island Areas are Western Isles, Orkney and Shetland.

The **Scottish Tourist Board** (STB) has its headquarters in Edinburgh at 23 Ravelston Terrace, EH4 3EU. Tel: 031-332-2433. The next level comprises some 36 Tourist Areas, below these being the town and other centres' Tourist Information Offices, many of the smaller of which are open only during the summer. STB also has a London office and information centre at 19 Cockspur Street, SW1Y 5BL (just off Trafalgar Square). Tel: 071-930-8661.—A wide range of attractive and informative publications (many free) is provided by all levels.

The **National Trust for Scotland** (NTS), with its headquarters in Edinburgh (5 Charlotte Square, EH2 4DU. Tel: 031-226-5922), was formed in 1931 with the purpose of promoting the preservation of places of historic interest or natural beauty. Currently the Trust has in its care over 100 properties covering some 100,000 acres. The Trust is not a government department, but a charity supported by the subscriptions of its members, the entrance fees charged at the larger sites and the voluntary contributions received at others. Membership (quickly arranged at most sites) is well worth considering as much for the merit of the cause as for the practical reason that it affords free entry to all NTS sites as also to those in the care of the National Trust in England, Wales and Northern Ireland.—The Trust offers many general and local publications (some free), a summary of properties being in the annual 'Guide to Properties', which provides current opening times.

Ancient Monuments (AM) officially in the care of the nation are the responsibility of **Historic Scotland**, 20 Brandon Street, Edinburgh, EH3 5RA. Tel: 031-244-3101. This is the official Visitor Facilities number which will provide up-to-date information on opening times for all sites in Scotland. For principal sites there is an entrance fee, but a season ticket (obtainable at most sites and through some Tourist Information centres) giving access to all sites and valid for one year could be a considerable saving.

Forestry Commission (FC), 231 Corstorphine Road, Edinburgh, EH12 7AT. Tel: 031-334-0303. In Scotland the Commission owns some two million acres, about half of which are plantation. The Commission aims to produce as much home-grown timber as possible, both through its own forestry enterprises and through encouragement and financial incentives to private landowners. At the same time it has to meet other important objectives, regarding amenity and landscape design, wild-life conservation and the provision of facilities for public access and recreation.

For the tourist the Commission provides several superb forest parks, as well as information centres, picnic areas, forest cabins and holiday houses, outstandingly attractive caravan and campsites, and way-marked forest trails. All forest roads are open to walkers, but cars are not permitted other than along designated Forest Drives.— Publications, notably the admirable forest park guides, are obtainable from local booksellers, FC information centres and local district offices, and often from Tourist Information.

Scottish Natural Heritage (SNH) is the outcome of the merger in 1992 of the Nature Conservancy Council for Scotland and the Countryside Commission for Scotland. The broad terms of reference for SNH are nature and landscape conservation and the public enjoyment of the countryside, this including the establishment and management of nature reserves. It is the intention that regional offices should play an increasingly important role. For further information: 12 Hope Terrace, Edinburgh, EH9 2AS. Tel: 031–447–4784. Or Battleby, Redgorton, Perth, PH1 3EW. Tel: 0738–27921.

Highlands and Islands Enterprise, Bridge House, 20 Bridge Street, Inverness IV1 1QR. Tel: 0463-234171. Successor (since 1 April 1991) to the Highlands and Islands Development Board, this new agency has two main functions—to help the people of the Highlands and Islands to improve their social and economic conditions; to enable the Highlands and Islands to play a more effective part in the economic and social development of Scotland. Financed by the government, the agency has a wide range of powers, these including land acquisition; factory construction; the provision of equipment and services; the establishment of businesses; the granting of financial assistance and advisory services etc.

Scotland's Gardens Scheme, 31 Castle Terrace, Edinburgh EH1 2EL. Tel: 031-229-1870. The scheme promotes the occasional opening, in aid of charity, of about 300 gardens. A programme can be obtained from the above address, and local Tourist Information offices will advise on gardens open in their areas.

Getting around Scotland

Visitors planning to make extensive use of public transport—rail, sea, air or road—should ask about the selection of discount tickets on offer (most Tourist Information offices should have up-to-date information on these).

'Getting around the Highlands and Islands', published twice yearly in association with Highlands and Islands Enterprise, details (with current timetables, booking addresses and telephones), all forms of transport in the Highlands and Islands.

Road. Main road motoring in Scotland is generally little different from elsewhere in Britain. What is different is that many roads in mountain and moorland districts and on the islands are single track and often winding, with the additional hazards of humpbacked and thus blind bridges and loose sheep and cattle. Surfaces are nearly always good and gradients long rather than steep, and there are frequent passing places, normally well marked and clearly visible from a distance. Motorists are asked to remember, though, that these are passing and not parking places, and also that, if travelling slowly, it is courteous to draw in and allow others to overtake. It is also worth remembering that in the remoter districts, and on the islands, petrol stations can be far apart and unlikely to be open late or on Sundays.

The opening of bypasses and the realignment of roads seems to be a continual process; motorists aiming for particular sites should therefore be alert to exits and may well also find that access to sites between towns is from the old road.

Automobile Association, Fanum House, 18–22 Melville Street, Edinburgh, EH3 7PD. Tel: 031-225-3301. *Royal Automobile Club*, RAC House, 200 Finnieston Street, Glasgow, G3 8NZ. Tel: 041–248–4444.

Public Transport. For those with the time it is possible to see much of Scotland by using the network of scheduled bus services, the obvious generalisation being that the more inhabited the district the better the service. Nevertheless dependence on public transport must limit the choice of sites that can be visited, as also the length of time spent there, and in some remoter areas where buses may run only once a day, or even only once or twice a week, the practicability of breaking a journey at sites along the way is small.—*Coach Tours*, lasting anything from a few hours to several days and covering all the more popular areas, start from many of the larger Scottish towns during the season; also from London and other English towns.

Rail. Scotland's mainland is quite well covered by rail, the principal routes coming in from the south to Edinburgh and Glasgow and serving the populated areas around and between these cities. Main lines continue to Perth and Dundee, with a direct mountain route from Perth to Inverness (at Drumochter reaching the highest level of any railway in Britain, 1484ft), and an eastabout route linking Dundee, Aberdeen and Inverness.

Smaller lines run down the south-west coast to Stranraer; from Glasgow to Oban, and via Fort William to Mallaig; from Inverness north to Wick and Thurso; from Inverness west to Kyle of Lochalsh. Services on the smaller lines, especially in the north, can be infrequent, and restricted on Sunday.

Some of the rail routes are very scenic, notably Glasgow to Mallaig (with, on certain days, a steam service from Fort William) and Inverness to Kyle of Lochalsh. See Rtes 48 and 54.

Information (including services, discounts, luxury land cruises etc) from Passenger Sales Office, Scotrail House, 58 Port Dundas Road, Glasgow, G4 0HG. Telephone information from either 041-204-2844 or 031-556-2451. Also from InterCity Land Cruise Office, 104 Birmingham Road, Lichfield, WS14 9BW. Tel: 0543–254076.

Air. A network of services covers the mainland centres of Edinburgh, Glasgow, Aberdeen, Inverness, Wick and Campbeltown, and there are also services to and within the Hebrides and the Orkney and Shetland groups. The principal operators are British Airways and Loganair, the emphasis of the latter being on the islands for which the company operates virtually all the inter-island services. *British Airways*. Tel: 0345–222111. *Loganair*, Glasgow Airport, Paisley, Renfrewshire. Tel: 041-889-3181.

Sea. For ferries, see the relevant Routes.

Accommodation. Food and Drink

Scotland offers **Accommodation** of all kinds, ranging from luxury hotels (some in mansions or castles) to simple bed-and-breakfast premises, these latter increasingly also providing an evening meal. Most hotels serve dinner in the evening; a few still provide the rather earlier high tea, a usually excellent meal with fish or meat course and very likely a selection of local breads and cakes. It should be remembered that in summer, and particularly in popular districts, there is considerable pressure on accommodation and that booking, if only a few hours ahead, is virtually essential; also that accommodation may be sparse in some remote areas and that some hotels are directly associated with fishing or other sporting facilities. Some country hotels close during the winter.

For the traveller without sophisticated demands bed-and-breakfast establishments, whether in town or country, can be recommended. They are clean, comfortable and surprisingly cheap, the food is usually generous, and they offer the opportunity to meet local people.

STB publish annually four books (charge) covering all aspects of accommodation and filled with comprehensive information on prices and facilities. The books are: 'Where to Stay: Hotels and Guest Houses'. 'Where to Stay: Bed and Breakfast'. 'Self-catering Accommodation'. 'Camping and Caravan Parks'. Additionally all area Tourist Boards provide comprehensive booklets, a welcome feature of these being that most premises are illustrated.

All Tourist Information centres will help over finding local accommodation, and at many a telephone or telex advance booking service (Book-a-bed-ahead) is operated, well worth using for the cost of a small fee and the telephone charge.

See also Notes on using this Guide, Hotels.

Food and Drink. While in most hotels and restaurants the food served is of standard, international type, Scotland does have its own specialities which have evolved locally or from long French or Scandinavian association. Among many specialities are Scotch Broth and Cock-a-leekie, soups that are a meal in themselves; trout and salmon from local rivers and lochs; sea fish cured and smoked in the Norse tradition (Arbroath Smokies, Finnan Haddies); from the moors, vension and game. Haggis, a minced mixture of animal organs with suet and oatmeal, looks and tastes better than it sounds. From the bakers come Selkirk bannocks and a whole delicious range of oatcakes, scones and baps, while for the sweet-toothed there are Edinburgh rock and butterscotch. Scotland's cheeses, notably Islay and Orkney, are becoming increasingly better known; and Scotch beef, Dundee cake and Dundee marmalade are as world famed as is also of course Scotland's whisky.

A book, 'A Taste of Scotland', lists hotels and restaurants (identified visually by a special sign) participating in a Taste of Scotland scheme.

Sundry Information

Banking and Currency. Scotland has its own banks, and branches of

English banks are rare. However, English banks have arrangements under which their cashpoint cards can be used at associated Scottish banks.—Main banks are open Mon., Tues., Wed., 09.30 to 12.30. 13.30 to 15.30. Thurs., as above but also 16.30 to 18.00. Fri., 09.30 to 15.30. Some city banks do not close over lunchtime, and are also open on Saturdays.— Scotland uses British currency, but locally issued bank notes circulate as well. Scottish notes are not always willingly accepted in England but can always be exchanged without loss at banks.

Credit cards. The major credit cards are widely accepted, but may well be refused in remote districts or modest establishments.

Events. Coming events of all kinds are listed in the annual STB publication 'Events in Scotland'.

Licensing Hours are currently standard throughout Scotland, pubs being open Mon.–Sat., 11.00 to 14.30. 17.00 to about 23.00. Increasingly, also, licences are being granted for Sun. opening. Hotel bars conform to the same hours and are open on Sun., 12.30 to 14.30. 18.30 to 23.00. Residents in licensed hotels may order drinks at any time. Persons under the age of 18 may not drink in licensed premises.

Postal Services. Scottish stamps attractively carry a lion but the postage rates are the same as in England. Main Post Office hours are normally Mon.—Fri., 09.00 to 17.30. Sat., 09.00 to 12.30.

Public Holidays. The Bank Holidays, which are also general holidays in England, do not apply as such in Scotland. In Scotland, in principle, these bank holidays are for banks only, though they increasingly also apply to some professional and commercial offices. Christmas Day and a period of two or three days over New Year are treated as general holidays. Additionally most towns and districts have local public, trades' and other holidays which vary from place to place and year to year but are usually in Spring or Autumn.

Shopping. Normal shopping hours are 09.00 to 17.30 or 18.00, though, in the case of smaller establishments, with a break over lunchtime. Many shops enjoy a weekly early closing (13.00) day, this varying from place to place. However, early closing is rare, at any rate in summer, in the case of shops of tourist interest in popular areas.

Sports Holidays

Scotland abounds in opportunities for holiday sport. For all activities STB will, on request, provide specialist information, accommodation lists and suchlike.

Climbing and Hill Walking. The climbing and walking attractions of Scotland are obvious, the possibilities ranging from skilled rock climbing on the Cuillins of Skye down to simple upland walking along well defined paths. Yet too many people still get lost, in most cases through inexperience, lack of correct clothing and equipment and an unwillingness to believe how suddenly the weather can close in. The rule is always to ask local advice, and also, in the case of anything perhaps venturesome, to ensure that the police or somebody else responsible know what is planned. Hill walkers should also seek local advice before venturing far during the shooting seasons.—STB's 'Scotland: Hillwalking' describes in detail over 60 of the more arduous walks and scrambles, while 'Scotland: Walks and Trails' lists over 200 waymarked easy walks. FC also provides guides to its forest walks, as does also NTS for ranger/naturalist walks (annual programme guide).

Curling, although traditionally Scotland's national winter game, is today mostly played on indoor rinks, notably at Edinburgh, Perth (museum), Stranraer and Aviemore. The game, which may very roughly be described as bowls played on ice, has been popular in Scotland for approaching 500 years, the oldest dated curling stone bearing the date 1511, though yet older stones have been found in rivers and lochs.

Dry Skiing. The largest artificial slope in Britain (almost $\frac{1}{4}$m and with a chairlift) is at Hillend on the Pentland Hills just south of Edinburgh. There are also slopes at a number of other places.

Fishing. Scotland is famed for its salmon and trout fishing, but what is less well known is how cheaply fishing may be enjoyed. Salmon fishing, admittedly, is usually, though not necessarily, expensive, but trout fishing permits are reasonably priced and sometimes free. Coarse fishing can also be inexpensively enjoyed, particularly in southern Scotland, permits being obtainable from local owners or leasing clubs, or sometimes simply through Tourist Information.

Gliding. For information apply Scottish Gliding Union, Portmoak Airfield, Scotlandwell, Kinross. Tel: 059284-543.

Golf is Scotland's national game and courses will be found almost everywhere, the great majority of them accepting visitors without introduction. The cost is small compared to most other countries, England included, and Sunday play is now the rule rather than the exception.

Pony Trekking and Riding holidays may take the form of ordinary riding instruction, pony trekking or, for more experienced riders, trail riding. Trekking is becoming increasingly popular as a means of exploring tracts of wild country, not otherwise easily accessible, and most centres providing trekking offer accommodation which may range from hotel to simpler farmhouse standard. STB will, on request, provide lists of establishments.

Water Sport. Canoeing of all kinds is popular and can be well combined with bird and even seal watching and other nature study. Among fast rivers the Spey and Tay are well known, the Grandtully rapid on the latter being used for slalom competitions.

Winter Sports. Skiing facilities are most developed at five places: the Cairngorms (Rte 50), Cairnwell (Rte 28), Glen Coe (Rte 44), Nevis Range (Rte 50), and the Lecht (Rte 38). At or near all these will be found accommodation, après ski, instruction, equipment hire, access roads to lifts and tows.

Language

The language of Scotland is English, spoken with the distinctive Scots accent, itself having local variants clear enough to the expert ear. But the virtually universal use of English dates from comparatively recent times, and over its history Scotland has used at least three other languages. These were the original Pictish in the North East; Gaelic, brought across by the Irish who in the 6C settled in what is now Argyll and carried far and wide by Christian missionaries; and Norn, the language of the Norsemen. As the Irish, or, as they became, Gaelic-speaking Scots, spread across Scotland, the three languages mixed, with Gaelic predominating and becoming the main language of all Scotland other than Orkney, Shetland and some parts of the Lowlands. Pictish disappeared early but Norn held on until about 1800 when it finally died, last being used on the Shetland island of Foula. Gaelic remained in common use throughout the Highlands until after the Clearances in the 19C. It is still spoken by many people, mainly in the Hebrides and remoter districts, although the number of these who have no English is negligible.

So far as the visitor to Scotland is concerned Pictish, Norn and Gaelic survive mainly as the whole or part of place names and, although intermixed, it is still possible to identify origins. Places, for instance, beginning with *Pit* or *Pet* may be Pictish, the word meaning a plot of land or a homestead, while from Norn come such words as *by* (village), *lybster* (farmstead), *vick* or *wick* (bay), *thing* or *ding* (council), and *brough* (same word as broch, a fortified place).

Where English was Scotland's language, it developed local dialect forms, generally known today as Lowland Scots.

The glossaries below may both interest and help the visitor.

Gaelic (with some Norn and Pictish)

Aber, mouth or confluence of a river.
Aird, ard, height, promontory.
Allt, ault, stream.
An, of the.
Aros, dwelling.
Auch, ach, field.
Auchter, see *Uachdar.*
Ay, island.

Ba, bo, cow.
Bal, baile, town, homestead.
Ban, white, fair.
Barr, promontory, top.
Beag, beg, little.
Bealach, balloch, mountain pass.
Bean, woman.
Ben, beann, beinn, mountain.
Bhlair, blar, plain.
Bhuidhe, bui, vuie, yellow.
Bister, busta, bost, dwelling.
Bo, ba, cow, cattle.
Brae, braigh, bread, upper part.
Breac, vrackie, speckled, variegated.

Cailleach, nun, old woman.
Cam, cambus, crooked.
Caolas, a strait, a firth.
Car, a bend or winding.
Carn, cairn, heap of stones.
Ceann, ken, kin, head, end.
Cil, kil, church.
Clach, cloich, stone.
Clachan, place of stones, helmet.
Cladach, shore, beach.

Cnoc, hill, knoll.
Coillie, killie, wood.
Coire, corrie, hollow.
Creag, craig, rock, cliff.
Cruach, rick, stack.
Cul, coul, back, recess.

Dal, dail, field.
Dalr, valley.
Damph, damh, ox, stag.
Darach, an oak.
Dearg, red.
Dour, water.
Droichead, drochit, bridge.
Druim, drum, ridge, back.
Dubh, dhu, black, dark.
Dun, hill fort.
Dysart, desert (i.e. hermitage).

Eaglais, church.
Eas, esh, waterfall, ravine.
Eilean, island.
Ey, island.

Fada, long.
Fail, rock, cliff.
Fear, fir, fhir, man.
Fetter, fothir (for), field or wood.
Fionn, fyne, white, shining.
Fraoch, heather.

Gabhar, gower, goat.
Garbh, garve, rough, rugged.
Gart, an enclosed place.

Gearr, gair, short.
Geo, gia, gio, chasm, rift.
Gil, ravine.
Gille, lad; pl. *gillean.*
Glass, grey.
Gleo, gloe, mist.
Gobha, gowan, blacksmith.
Gorm, blue or green.

Holm, uninhabited island.
Hope, small bay.
How, haugr, burial mound.

Inch, innis, island.
Inver, inbhir, mouth of a river.

Ken, kin, head, promontory.
Kil, church, burying-place.
Knock, knoll.
Kyle, a strait, a firth.

Lag, laggan, hollow.
Larach, site of an old ruin.
Larig, pass, mountain track.
Leac, flagstone.
Leana, a plain.
Learg, pass, hill-slope.
Liath, grey.
Linn, linne, pool.
Lis, lios, fortress, now a garden.
Loch, lake; *lochan,* lakelet.

Machar, plain by the sea.
Maol, meal, mam, bald headland
Mhor, great, large.
Moine, bog.
Mon, monadh, moorland.
Mor, more, great, extensive.
Moy, a plain.
Muc, muic, sow.
Muli, mull, promontory.
Na, nam, nan, of the.

Ob, oba, oban, bay.
Ochter, high-lying.

Pit, pet, homestead, hollow.
Poll, pool.

Quoich, cuach, cup.

Rath, fort.
Reidh, smooth.
Riach, riabhach, brindled.
Ross, peninsula, forest.
Ru, rhu, row, rubha, point.

Sgeir, skerry, sea, rock.
Sgor, scuir, sgurr, sharp rock.
Slochd, sloc, hollow, a grave.
Spideal, spittal, hospice.
Stob, point.
Strath, broad valley.
Strone, sron, nose, promontory.
Struan, sruth, stream.

Tarbert, tarbet, isthmus.
Tigh, tay, house.
Tir, land.
Tobar, well.
Tom, hillock, bush.
Torr, round hill, heap.
Tulloch, tilly, tully, knoll.

Uachdar, high-lying, upper.
Uamh, cave, 'weem'.
Uig, nook, sheltered bay.
Uisge, esk, water.

Voe, narrow bay.

Wick, vik, bay or creek.

Lowland Scots

Aiblins, perhaps.
Arles, earnest-money.
Ashet, meat-dish.

Bailie, alderman.
Bairn, child.
Bannock, flat cake, generally of oatmeal.
Bap, breakfast roll.
Bawbee, halfpenny.
Beadle, church officer, verger.
Ben, see *But and Ben.*
Bien, well-to-do, prosperous.
Biggin, a building; *big,* to build.
Bing, slag-heap.
Birk, birch-tree.
Blate, shy, timid.
Blether, to talk nonsense.
Bothy, farm-hands' barrack.
Brae, rising ground, hill.
Bramble, blackberry.
Branks, scold's bridle (comp. 'jougs').
Braw, fine, handsome.
Breeks, trousers.
Brig, bridge.
Bubblyjock, turkey.
Burn, stream.
But and Ben, two-roomed cottage.
Byre, cowhouse.

Ca', to be set in motion; also to call; *ca'canny,* be cautious.
Caller, fresh, cool (of air).
Canny, cautious, gentle.
Clarty, dirty.
Close, common entry to a tenement-house.
Clout, to patch, a cloth.
Clype, a tell-tale.
Corbie, a crow.
Coup, to upset; a rubbish-heap or dump.
Crack, to converse.
Creel, basket, usually large.
Croft, small-holding, often with a common grazing, peat-bog, fishery, etc.
Cuddy, donkey.
Cutty, short; *cutty-stool,* stool of repentance.

Daft, mentally deranged, silly.
Daunder, to stroll.
Ding, to smash, to worst.
Doo, dove.
Douce, sober, quiet, prudent.
Dreigh, tedious, dull.
Drumly, muddy (of water).

Factor, bailiff, land-steward, agent.
Farl, segment of oatcake.

LANGUAGE **55**

Fash, to trouble, to vex.
Feu, to let (house or land).
Fey, under mystic influence.
Flesher, butcher.
Flype, to turn a stocking inside out.
Forbye, besides.
Fou, intoxicated.
Fushionless, insipid, weak-kneed.

Gab, the mouth, incessant talk.
Gey, very, 'pretty'.
Gigot, leg of mutton.
Girdle, round iron baking-plate.
Glaur, mud.
Gleg, ready, sharp.
Gowan, daisy.
Gowk, cuckoo, foolish person.
Greet, to weep.
Grieve, farm-overseer.
Grozet, Gooseberry.

Haar, drizzling rain; hoar-frost; mist.
Handsel, gift for luck.
Hantle, a small amount.
Harl, to roughcast a wall.
Haugh, alluvial plain.
Haver, to talk nonsense.
Heugh, a low hill.
Hog, unshorn lamb.
Hogmanay, New Year's Eve.
Howe, a hollow or sheltered place.
Howff, meeting place, resort.
Howk, to dig.
Howm, a dell.
Huntygowk, fool's errand (April 1st).
Hurl, to wheel (a barrow).

Ilk, the same; 'of that ilk' indicates that a landowner's surname and the name of his property are the same.
Ilka, each, every.

Jink, to dodge.
Jougs, scold's bridle (comp. 'Branks').
Jouk, to duck (e.g. to avoid a blow).

Kail, cabbage.
Keek, to peep.
Keelie, street-arab.
Kelpie, water-sprite; river-horse.
Kenspeckle, conspicious.
Kitchin, relish, or seasoning.
Knowe, a knoll, head.
Kye, cows.

Laigh, low, south.
Laird, landed proprietor.
Land, a tenement-house.
Lave, the rest, remainder.
Law, conical hill.
Leal, loyal.
Lift, the sky.
Limmer, rogue.
Links, sand-dunes.
Lith, section (of an orange).
Loan, loaning, lane.
Lug, ear.
Lum, chimney.

Mair, more; *maist*, most, almost.
Manse, clergyman's official residence.
March, boundary.

Mavis, song-thrush.
Meikle, great, much.
Minister, clergyman.
Muckle, large.

Neeps, turnips.
Nieve, fist.

Outwith, outside.

Partan, crab.
Pawky, shrewd, sly, arch.
Philabeg, kilt.
Pickle, small quantity.
Pig, earthenware pot.
Plenishing, furniture.
Ploy, enterprise, something to do.
Poke, a bag.
Policies, private grounds.
Provost, mayor.
Puddock, frog.

Quaich, drinking-up.

Reek, smoke.
Rig, a ridge.
Roup, auction-sale.

Sark, shirt.
Saugh, willow.
Scunner, dislike.
Sheriff, county court judge.
Sheiling, hut.
Shinty, hockey.
Siccar, sure, certain.
Siller, money, silver.
Skail, dispersal of a meeting.
Skelp, to whip.
Smeddum, mettle, sense.
Sneck, snib, latch, hasp.
Sonsie, jolly, good-looking.
Sort, to arrange, to put right.
Soutar, shoemaker.
Speir, to ask.
Spunk, a match (for lighting).
Steek, to shut.
Stey, steep.
Stour, dust.
Stravaig, to wander aimlessly.
Sumph, dunderhead.
Sweer, averse.
Swither, to vacillate, to hesitate.
Syne ago, since.

Tassie, small cup.
Tawse, leather strap used for corporal punishment.
Teinds, tithes.
Tent, heed; *tak' tent*, take care.
Thole, to bear; to put with, bear with.
Thrang, crowded, busy.
Thrawn, stubborn, misshapen.
Threap, to assert.
Tine, to lose; *tint*, lost.
Tocher, dowry, marriage-portion.
Tod, a fox.
Toom, empty.
Tow, a rope.
Twine, to part.

Unco', strange, monstrous; very.
Usquebaugh, whisky.

Vennel, an alley.

Wale, to choose.
Wame, belly.
Wean, child.
Whaup, curlew.

Wight, Wicht, strong, powerful.
Wynd, an alley.
Wyle, blame.

Yett, gate.

I SOUTH EAST

South East Scotland divides itself into two parts. The district loosely known as The Borders (roughly the modern Borders Region) lies south of the line of the Lammermuir, Moorfoot and Pentland hill ranges and east of Annandale and the upper valley of the Tweed. The other and much smaller part, Lothian, is sandwiched between the hills to its south and, to the north, Edinburgh and the Firth of Forth. During the Dark Ages (say 600–1000) most of this South East, colonised by Angles from the Continent, grew to become the 'Kingdom' of Lothian, which was though for much of the time subject to Northumbria to the south. In 1018 Malcolm II decisively defeated Northumbria at Carham, just south of the Tweed near Coldstream, but despite this there were still some 650 years to follow during which the South East, and especially The Borders, would be under frequent English threat and occupation.

The Borders

The Borders is thus a land fought over with little respite from Roman times until the mid 17C. Of the Romans there remains little beyond earthworks and occasional foundations, but of the savage centuries that followed the evidence is everywhere in ruined towers, castles and abbeys (these last also of course suffering the neglect following the Reformation) as well as in the stories that still live on in the pageantry of local festivals. The towns today are prosperous, but it should not be forgotten that scarcely one did not several times change hands, on most such occasions being razed then rebuilt by the surviving citizens. With the more peaceful times starting in the mid 17C came the stable growth of the towns, the construction of great mansions, and of course, in the 19C, the era of Sir Walter Scott, man of letters and publicist for Scotland, who, from his years spent at Ashiestiel and Abbotsford, and from his writings so intimately concerned with that area, has left such a mark that a whole district centred on *Abbotsford* is known as the *Scott Country*. This indeed is the heart of The Borders and, a little extended, includes all four of the great abbeys (*Kelso, Jedburgh, Dryburgh* and *Melrose*) as well as towers and castles such as *Smailholm, Greenknowe* and *Hume* and the Adam mansion of *Mellerstain* (Rtes 3, 4 and 5, while Rte 6 extends as a westward arm up the Tweed to historic *Traquair House* and *Peebles*).

The Borders is also Scotland's horse country, with roots going back to the marauding freebooters (or reivers or moss-troopers) of medieval times. Today the tradition continues with breeding and sales and the growing popularity of holiday trail riding and pony trekking, while more picturesque links with this past are provided by the Common Ridings which are a central feature of several towns' summer festivals. (In the past, as a guard against encroachment, towns carried out periodic rides around their bounds. Today's Common Ridings, with sometimes 300 or more riders, are a re-enactment of this precaution, the rides also often being accompanied by pageantry recalling some brave skirmish with the English.)

Scenically The Borders offer in the east rolling wooded and pastoral country, threaded by famous fishing rivers such as Tweed and Teviot. West of a line through Galashiels, Selkirk and Hawick lie the moors, often lonely upland, with rounded mountains, some over 2000 feet. Throughout this area, even in summer, the many small roads can be surprisingly uncrowded.

Many visitors will associate The Borders with weaving, tweed and knitwear, the practical and profitable result of the fortunate union of lush sheep pasture, soft river water and the fact that the early monks of the great abbeys continued the clothworking traditions of their native Flanders, Hainault and Artois. Soon rich in sheep, the abbeys mass-produced wool both for export and local use, at the same time introducing the local people to more sophisticated spinning and weaving skills and thus starting a cottage industry which only in the 19C became centralised.—Contrary to widely held belief, the word 'tweed' has no proper link with the river of that name. The Borders weavers called their product 'tweel', a local variant of course of 'twill', and it was a London merchant who jumped to the conclusion—in this case happy enough—that what was really meant was 'tweed'. And then it was Sir Walter Scott, ever the publicist, who by sporting chequered trousers in London sparked an enthusiasm that would spread around the world. In the Borders today *Galashiels*, *Hawick* and *Walkerburn* (Scottish Museum of Woollen Textiles) are the main, though by no means only centres. Some firms can be visited, and shops selling their work will be found throughout most of The Borders.

Lothian

Lothian is a shallow strip some 50m long and 10m deep between the

Firth of Forth and the succession of hill ranges to the south. Partly, though not only because of the relationship to Edinburgh, the district includes more sites likely to attract the visitor than its size might suggest. The closeness to Edinburgh also means that the visitor has the choice between being based in Edinburgh, thence making excursions into Lothian, or alternatively choosing one or more of Lothian's attractive small towns as bases from which both to tour around and to visit the city.

History in Lothian visibly spans some 4500 years. *Cairnpapple Hill* is Stone, Bronze and Iron Age, and the Roman period is represented by their fort at *Cramond* near Edinburgh and the remains of the *Antonine Wall* at Falkirk (Central Region). Medieval times live on in the humble 15C *Soutra Aisle*, the triangular plan of *Dirleton* village and, above all, in castles (*Hailes, Tantallon* and *Dirleton* in the east, *Craigmillar* and *Crichton* to the south of Edinburgh, and to the west the great palace of *Linlithgow*); while, travelling on in time, *Hopetoun House* reigns as the supreme example of 18C palatial elegance. But it is the brief but stirring seven years of Mary, Queen of Scots, that tend to dominate Lothian's past. She was born at *Linlithgow*; the plot to murder Darnley was hatched at *Craigmillar*; three times she took refuge in *Dunbar*'s castle; from *Borthwick* she had to escape disguised as a man; *Carberry Hill* was the scene of her defeat and of the last time she saw Bothwell; and the following year, after her escape from Loch Leven, she experienced a brief but last encouragement at *Niddry*.

Lothian is not outstanding scenically, and in fact the west, with slagheaps, urban spread, motorways and the petro-chemical works around Grangemouth in adjoining Central Region, is not inviting, although here are some of the more interesting sites, such as Cairnpapple Hill, Linlithgow and Hopetoun House. But the *Pentlands* offer good upland, and the wooded slopes of the *Lammermuirs* with Stenton, Nunraw Abbey and Gifford, are quiet, lost country. There is also a particular charm to the Forth coast east of Edinburgh with its links and dunes. Much of this shore is controlled by public authorities who have made it a model of conservation planning with coastal parks, picnic areas, camping sites, and seabird sanctuaries at *Aberlady* and on the islands.

1 Berwick-upon-Tweed to Edinburgh via Dunbar and Haddington

A1 to Burnmouth. A1107 to Cockburnspath. A1 to Edinburgh.— Agricultural and pastoral with coastal views. Alternatives touch the Lammermuir Hills, part open upland and part wooded, with quiet roads and valleys.

SOME HOTELS. **Berwick-upon-Tweed**. *King's Arms*, 43 Hide Hill, TD15 1EJ. Tel: 0289-307454. **Dunbar**. *Bayswell*, Bayswell Park, EH42 1AE. Tel: 0368-62225. **Gifford**. *Tweeddale Arms*, High Street, EH41 4QU. Tel: 062-081-240. **East Linton**. *Harvesters*, Station Road, EH40 3DP. Tel: 0620-860395. **Haddington**. *George*, 91 High Street, EH41 3ET. Tel: 062082-3372.

Total distance 50m.—*6m* **Burnmouth**.—*2m* **Eyemouth**.—*3m* **Coldingham**.—*9m* **Cockburnspath**.—*7m* **Dunbar**.—*10m* **Haddington**.—*13m* **Edinburgh**.

Berwick-upon-Tweed (see also 'Blue Guide England'), for all its tentative feel of Scotland, is wholly in England, for the border, which from well to the west of Coldstream has run with the Tweed, loops sharply northward as soon as the river comes in sight of the town. That there is nevertheless an anticipation of Scotland here is hardly surprising, for not only is Scotland a mere 3m away but also, over centuries, Berwick belonged first to one country, then to the other, until it was finally ceded to England in 1482. Even then Berwick was not allowed to forget the Scots as it saw itself both fortified and administered as a bastion against them, and the virtually complete Tudor *Ramparts*, begun in 1558 but not completed until 1747, still stand as the town's most distinguished feature. They are best appreciated as the town is approached from the south across one of the impressive Tweed bridges. Of the castle in which in 1291 Edward I concluded the assembly begun at Norham (see below) and pronounced in favour of John Balliol's claim to the Scottish crown only fragments survive, just west of the station.

Before setting out northward along A1, two alternative and quieter entries to Scotland are worth considering.

BERWICK TO COLDSTREAM (A698, south west 13m). This road remains in England, but short diversions north reach places of interest in or closely associated with Scotland, such as *Union Suspension Bridge*, approached by a minor road off A698 about 2m west of Berwick. This Tweed bridge, linking England and Scotland and built by Samuel Brown in 1820, was the first of its type in Britain designed for road traffic. It was in the church at *Norham*, north off A698 some 7m from Berwick, that Edward I opened the assembly called to weigh the contesting claims to the Scottish throne of Bruce and Balliol, later, at Berwick Castle, ruling in favour of the latter. *Norham Castle* (English Heritage. Tel: 028-982-329), a huge Norman keep of c 1160 and long a stronghold of the prince-bishop of Durham, was the place in which Scott set the opening scenes of 'Marmion'. At *Ladykirk*, in Scotland just north of Norham, the church was built by James IV in 1500 in gratitude for an escape from drowning; his bust (19C) is on the interior west wall of the nave, near it being a small blocked window used by the priest whose room was behind (steps). Of the tower at the west end only the lower part is original, the upper levels having been added in 1743 from a design by William Adam. For **Coldstream**, 6m south west of Norham by A698, see Rte 3.

BERWICK TO DUNS (A6105, north west 14m). Before entering Scotland the road runs below *Halidon Hill* on which in 1333 a Scottish army marching to raise the English siege of Berwick was defeated with great slaughter. At *Foulden*, across the border, there is, beside the road, a most attractive two-storeyed tithe barn with an outside stair, while at *Chirnside*, 3m farther, the tower of the parish church incorporates a Norman doorway. But the Norman chancel arch at *Edrom*, another 3m west, is perhaps more noteworthy, for here it has been rebuilt on its own in the churchyard. *Manderston* (Tel: 0361-83450), off A6105 2m east of Duns and ranking among the best of Britain's Edwardian country mansions, boasts a silver staircase, believed to be unique. Also of interest are the spacious domestic quarters and the splendid stables and dairy. **Duns** is a modest market town which first stood on the south west slope of nearby Duns Law, until wholly destroyed by the English in 1545. It was rebuilt on its present site 43 years later. The town claims (as do also Down in Northern Ireland and Dunstane in Northumberland) to be the birthplace in c 1266 of John Duns Scotus, the medieval philosopher, and a statue to him stands in the public park. A very different native was Jim Clark, the motor racing champion killed in 1968, a collection of whose

trophies is displayed in the *Jim Clark Memorial Room* at 44 Newtown
Street (Tel: 0361-82600). On the summit of Duns Law the *Covenanters'
Stone* commemorates that Leslie's army camped here in 1639. *Fogo
Church*, 3m south west of Duns, has an unusual outside staircase of 1671
leading up to the laird's loft.

Along the A1 the border is crossed *3m* north of Berwick-upon-Tweed at
Lamberton Bar where once, as at better known Gretna, the toll-keeper
performed marriages for runaway couples. The now ruined church in
the hamlet is mentioned in the marriage contract of 1502 between
James IV and Margaret, daughter of Henry VII of England.—*3m*
Burnmouth, where this Route temporarily leaves A1, forking right for
Eyemouth and Coldingham. However some motorists may prefer the
Lammermuir alternative suggested immediately below.

LAMMERMUIR ALTERNATIVE. A1 is followed past *Ayton Castle* (Tel:
08907-81212), a conspicuous red sandstone Scottish Baronial edifice of
1846 (James Gillespie Graham), as far as Grantshouse, 10m from
Burnmouth. Here A6112 leads south towards Duns, in about 3m reaching a sign for *Edin's Hall Broch*, for those interested in Iron Age antiquities a worthwhile objective at the end of a long mile's walk. On a
commanding crest above a wooded valley, this substantial broch-like
structure, occupied in Roman times and one of few of its kind in
southern Scotland, stands within a complex of earthworks which may
represent both hill-fort and settlement. The broch remains comprise a
thick base wall 4 to 5ft high, parts of side chambers and a few steps of the
stairway between the walls. After returning to the car, a pleasant circuit
can be made by continuing south 2m to Preston, there bearing north
west along B6355 before in another 3m turning north along a minor road
for **Abbey St. Bathans**, a lost little place on a lovely stretch of the
Whiteadder Water. Here the village church incorporates parts of the
walls of the 13C church of a nuns' priory dedicated to St. Bathan, possibly a cousin of St. Columba and his successor at Iona, while the effigy
of an early prioress, found during 19C building work, now lies in a niche
in the east wall. And here, too, there is a Trout Farm, doubling as an
interpretive centre of the life of this valley from prehistoric to modern
times. Roads north from here rejoin A1 in 7m at Cockburnspath. Alternatively B6355 traverses the heart of the Lammermuir Hills on its way
to Gifford and Haddington.

2m (from Burnmouth) **Eyemouth** is an incidental small town combining
the activities of minor seaside resort, with angling festivals and competitions, and the business of commercial fishing. The harbour stretching up the river is both picturesque and lively, and the *Eyemouth
Museum* in the Auld Kirk in Market Place was opened in 1981 as a
centenary memorial to what has become known as the Great East Coast
Fishing Disaster when 189 local men lost their lives. A tapestry stitched
by local people portrays the tragedy, while at the same time the
museum provides an insight into many aspects of local life (Tel: 08907-
50678).—*3m* **Coldingham** lies just inland from Coldingham Bay which,
with St. Abb's and West Loch, forms a popular summer holiday corner.
In the village are the remains of a 13C *Priory* founded in c 1098 by King
Edgar as successor to a nunnery founded in the 7C on St. Abb's Head by
Ebba (a Northumbrian princess saved from a shipwreck here) and
burned by the Norsemen in c 870. The priory was much damaged by
Hertford in 1545 and its domestic buildings were largely demolished by
Cromwell in 1648. The *John Wood Collection* (Tel: 08907-71259), in

Fishers Bray, is an unusual exhibition of photographs, printed from original glass plates and recording Borders life in the early 1900s. *St. Abb's Head*, a sheer headland with cliffs 300ft high, is a nature reserve (visitor centre) known for its nesting and migrating seabirds. *Fast Castle*, 4m north west of Coldingham, although little more than battered fragments, stands stark and dramatic on its lonely crag above the sea at the foot of high grassy cliffs. The approach road, off A1107, ends at the clifftop, along which a short walk brings the ruin into sight at the end of the path far below. Of uncertain origin, Fast was by the end of the 14C a stronghold of the Homes and later held by the Logans. Margaret of England, aged only 14 and on her way to marry James IV, stayed here, but left her retinue of 1500 people to overnight under what must have been somewhat overcrowded conditions at Coldingham.

9m (from Coldingham) **Cockburnspath**, where the church has a distinctive 16C round beacon-tower, was the birthplace of John Broadwood (1732–1812), the pioneer piano craftsman. About 1m north, and delightfully sited in the grounds of Dunglass House, will be found the partially restored *Dunglass Collegiate Church*, a typical mid 15C example of its kind, with much rich detail both inside and out. The arched tomb niches suggest that the founder, Sir Alex Hume, intended the church to serve as his family burial place. A1 continues north between coast and railway, passing a nuclear power station, just beyond which, and opposite a prominent cement works, a sign directs to *Doon Hill* (road and motorable track), site of a c 6C Dark Ages settlement. There is little or nothing original to be seen, but the site is excellently described and the foundations have been outlined of, for example, two halls and a burial ground. For the part played by Doon Hill in the Battle of Dunbar of 1650, see immediately below.

6m **Broxburn**, the fork where A1 bears west to bypass Dunbar, is the place near which anyone interested in battles should stop, for it was here, in 1650, that Cromwell decisively defeated the Scottish supporters of Charles II under Leslie. Leslie had the advantage for he was massed around Doon Hill (582ft), 1m south west of this road fork, while Cromwell's army, enfeebled by hunger and disease, was strung across the low ground towards Dunbar. However, urged on by fanatical Covenanting clergy, Leslie came down, pushing forward his right wing to occupy the low ground at what is now Broxburn, whereupon Cromwell, quick to seize his opportunity, sent in his cavalry which drove the Scots back in total disorder. About 3000 Scots lost their lives and 10,000 were made prisoner.

1m **Dunbar** (6000 inhab. *Inf.*), historic fortress port and royal burgh, has in modern times developed as a holiday town.

History. In 1295 Dunbar saw the defeat of the Scots by England's Edward I, when suppressing the revolt unwisely launched by his protégé, John Balliol. Nineteen years later, Edward II, fleeing from his defeat at Bannockburn, ignominiously escaped by sea from here. In 1339 'Black Agnes', Countess of Dunbar, successfully defended the fortress for six weeks against the English until it was relieved by supplies brought in by sea. Over two centuries later, in 1566, Mary, Queen of Scots, and Darnley found refuge here during the dangerous days following the murder of Rizzio. Within a month, though, Mary made Bothwell governor of the castle, and the following year twice visited it with him, the first occasion being after he had carried her off from Edinburgh, the second after their interrupted honeymoon and flight from Borthwick. After Mary's defeat at Carberry Hill, the castle was razed by the regent, Moray. Oliver Cromwell was here in 1650, totally defeating the supporters of Charles II (see above) and later further destroying the castle by using its stones to improve the harbour.

After being razed by Moray and used as a source of building material by Cromwell it is hardly surprising that of the historic and once formidable *Castle* all that now remains are fragments picturesquely clinging to the small headland which forms one abrupt arm of the entrance to the harbour. The contrastingly busy upper town stretches the length of the broad High Street, midway along the east side of which is the steepled 17C *Town House*, claiming to be the oldest civic building in Scotland in continuous use. The *John Muir House* (Tel: 0368-63353), also in High Street, was the birthplace of John Muir (1838–1914), naturalist, writer and founder of America's National Parks, while, at the north end of High Street, *Lauderdale House*, now owned by the local authority, was built by Robert Adam. John Muir is also remembered by *John Muir Country Park*, north west of the town and offering woodland and shore (Tel: 0620-842637).

From Dunbar there is a choice of three approaches to Edinburgh. This Route follows the main A1, but, immediately below, first suggests a meandering southerly alternative through Gifford, only 3m longer and running below the northern slopes of the Lammermuir Hills. The coastal road through North Berwick is described as Rte 2.

DUNBAR TO EDINBURGH VIA GIFFORD. Approaching **Stenton**, the curious small conical structure beside the north side of the road marks the site of an ancient pilgrims' well. The village, once notorious for the burning of witches, is now a quiet little unspoilt place, protected as a conservation area and with some cottages still showing traces of their original external stairs. On the green stands the *Wool Stone*, or tron, used for weighing wool at the wool fair, while behind there is a dovecot with crow-step gabling, once the tower of a now ruined church.—In 3m B6370 reaches Garvald, above which stands *Nunraw Abbey*, built by Cistercian monks in 1948, their first Scottish foundation since the Reformation. What in fact happened was that the monks bought the property in 1946, building this large new abbey and leaving the old Tower-House (15C with additions) to serve as a guest house (Tel: 062083-228). In origin Nunraw (Nuns' Row) was a grange belonging to the convent at Haddington, founded in c 1158, the nuns accepting the bizarre obligation to maintain a four-gun fortification for use in case of invasion. During the 16C the property became first the preserve and then, after three Hepburn prioresses, the residence of the Hepburn family. In 1548 the Scottish parliament met here and took the decision to send their five-year-old queen, Mary, to France to marry the heir to the French throne. Today the most important interior feature is the painted ceiling of 1610, bearing the initials of the then owner and his wife, Patrick and Helen Hepburn, and the arms of medieval monarchs. In the grounds there is a 16C dovecot with 450 nests.

Gifford, 4m farther, is a neat 17–18C village, specially laid out to meet the needs of the many people who had settled around Yester House at that time. A plaque on the church wall commemorates the birth in Gifford in 1723 of the Rev. John Witherspoon, one of the signatories of the American Declaration of Independence and first president of what is now Princeton university. At **Pencaitland**, 6m west of Gifford, the church preserves a 13C north choir aisle, while *Winton House* here (only by prior arrangement and for those with a particular interest. Tel: 0875-340222) dates from 1620 and is known for its plasterwork ceilings and carved stone chimneys, the former in honour of a visit by Charles I. At the pleasant village of *Ormiston* (2m west) a 15C cross adds to the charm of the tree-lined street. The main A1 can be rejoined in 2m at *Tranent*, some 7m short of central Edinburgh.

Along the main Route, *5m* (from Dunbar) **East Linton**, with a part 13C church and a 14C bridge, is best known for *Preston Mill and Phantassie Doocot* (NTS. Tel: 0620-860426). On a quiet river bank where there may have been a mill from the 11 or 12C, Preston as seen today dates from the 16C and is one of the oldest water-mills still working in Scotland and was even in commercial use until as late as 1957. Although the machinery has been regularly renewed, the system remains unchanged and the technical ingenuity of the past can be appreciated in something like its original setting. *Phantassie Doocot*, a beehive type once with 544 nests, is a short walk away. John Rennie (1761–1821), the engineer and architect, was born at the mansion, an event commemorated by a memorial on A1 East Linton bypass.

Hailes Castle (AM. Tel: 031-244-3101), south of A1 and 1½m south west of East Linton, is the place to which Bothwell, the then owner, brought Mary, Queen of Scots, on their way to Dunbar. Architecturally the castle is notable for the substantial amount of its 13C masonry, to this period belonging much of the lower structure east from and including the central tower, while that extending west and south is of the following century. But for many people the most lingering memory will be of the two grim pit prisons, one in each tower, with narrow air and lavatory shafts angling away through the massive walls.

Traprain Law (734ft), the distinctive whale-back hill to the south, may have been occupied during the Stone Age and certainly was an Iron Age fortified site, the city of the Votadini, spreading over some 40 acres. The Votadini are thought to have been in some form of alliance with the Romans, but much of the defensive surrounds may date from later, Dark Ages, times and it seems that the site continued in use until perhaps as late as the 11C. A treasure of 4C Christian and pagan silver, excavated here in 1919, is now in the Edinburgh Royal Museum of Scotland (Queen Street).

Within a 2m-wide belt paralleling A1 on the north between East Linton and Haddington there are various places worth either looking at or visiting. As a start, in a field just west of East Linton and just north of A1, a lone standing stone is thought to have been a Bronze Age route marker. Beyond, B1347 leads north to *Athelstaneford*, a place associated with the origin of Scotland's flag. Tradition tells that the Scots, fighting a battle here in the 10C against the Northumbrians under Athelstane, saw a white St. Andrew's Cross against the blue sky and, thus encouraged to victory, made a banner which became the Scottish flag. A flag now flies beside the church where a pictorial plaque tells the story. At nearby East Fortune airfield the *Museum of Flight* (Tel: 062-088-308 or 031-225-7534), an outstation of Edinburgh's Royal Museum of Scotland, shows aircraft such as a 1930 De Haviland Puss Moth, a Comet airliner, a Vulcan bomber, a Spitfire and a Lightning, while other exhibits include a Blue Streak rocket and several varieties of aero engine dating from 1909 onwards. The airfield itself has its niche in history as the starting point of the airship R34 when it made the first double crossing of the Atlantic in 1919, and the museum shows contemporary material. To the north west of Athelstaneford rises the hill-fort of *Chesters*, posing something of a riddle because, although obviously a defensive complex with multiple banks and ditches, it nevertheless stands in a tactically ridiculous situation below a high ridge. The *Hopetoun Monument*, 1m north of Haddington and as conspicuous today as its erectors always intended it to be, commemorates the 4th Earl who fought with distinction in the Napoleonic wars. *Stevenson House* (Tel: 062082-3376), off A1 2m from Haddington, although largely dating from restoration of about 1560, has its roots in the 13C at which time the estate belonged to Haddington's Cistercian nunnery.

5m (from East Linton) **Haddington** (8000 inhab.), noted today for its dignified 17–19C streets, in fact dates from at least the 12C when it was made a royal burgh by David I. At that time what are now Market, Court and High streets marked the town's triangular plan around an open centre which was not built on until some 400 years later. Alexander II was born here in 1198 and John Knox in 1505. The town was several times burned by the English, and was held by them against the Scots and French in 1548–49.

A tour of Haddington's buildings of architectural and historic interest can best follow the route suggested and explained in a booklet called 'Walk around Haddington', obtainable in local shops, and also shown on a plan on the wall of the *Town House* (William Adam, 1748 but enlarged 1830). The *Court House* (William Burn, 1833) stands on the site of the royal palace, and the *Knox Memorial Institute* (1879), with a statue of the reformer, is the successor to the school at which Knox was educated. The *Church of St. Mary* (Tel: 062082-5111), near the river and perhaps the town's most important building, dates from around the 14C, though there has been much restoration, notably and recently (1982) of the choir and transepts which had been in ruins since the siege of 1548–49. Near the east end of the choir is the tomb of Jane Welsh (1801–66), wife of Thomas Carlyle and a native of Haddington. From the church Pleached Alley leads to *St. Mary's Pleasance*, the garden of Haddington House now restored as a 17C garden (rose, herb, cottage and sunken gardens). There are two museums. The *Haddington Museum* (Tel: 062082-2531), in the 19C public library in Newton Port, shows local historical material, while the *Jane Welsh Carlyle Museum* (Tel: 062082-3738), in Lodge Street, was the home of Jane Welsh, wife of Thomas Carlyle who courted her here; furnished as it was in the days of Jane's parents (1830s), the house also shows portraits of people associated with the Carlyles. The names Abbey Bridge and Nungate Bridge, both 16C in origin, recall a Cistercian nunnery founded by the Countess of Northumberland in c 1159, while, as another link with the past, the Customs stone, set in the grass behind the George Hotel, was once the seat of the official levying local petty dues.

Maitland of Lethington, 'Secretary Lethington' to Mary, Queen of Scots

Lennoxlove House (Tel: 062082-3720), 1m south of Haddington on B6369, is now the home of the Duke and Duchess of Hamilton. Originally called Lethington, this was the seat of the Maitlands, one of whom (William Maitland, 'Secretary Lethington') was secretary to Mary, Queen of Scots. Acquired by the Richmond and Lennox family in the 17C, the house was renamed Lennoxlove after the celebrated beauty known as 'La Belle Stuart'; daughter of a physician, she became mistress of Charles II, but in 1667 eloped with Charles Stuart, Duke of Richmond and Lennox. The house now shows the Hamilton Palace collections of portraits, furniture and porcelain.

6m. The mining and industrial town of **Tranent**, an outlier of the Edinburgh conurbation, has two niches in history—as the place from which the Highlanders advanced to their victory of Prestonpans (see Rte 2), and as one of the two stations of the first railway in Scotland; built in 1722, the railway's purpose was to carry coal the 2m north to ships berthed at Cockenzie and its course is now a popular walk.—*3m* **Musselburgh** earned the title of the 'Honest Toun' as long ago as 1332 when Bruce's nephew, the Earl of Moray, died here and the citizens disclaimed any reward for honouring his body. Golf has been played since 1672 on the Links Course and the town also boasts the oldest racecourse in Scotland. Although for the most part a busy, modern place, Musselburgh still has attractive corners. For instance, *Pinkie House* (Tel: 031-665-2059), off A1 at the east end of the town, is known for its plaster ceilings and painted gallery of c 1620, while the old *Esk Bridge* and nearby *Tolbooth* (the latter built partly with the stones of a once famous pilgrim chapel, Our Lady of Loretto) are both of the 16C.

Inveresk, immediately south of Musselburgh, once the Roman station at the north end of Dere Street and today a contrastingly quiet suburb, has several pleasing Georgian houses. Here *Inveresk Lodge Garden* (NTS. Tel: 031-226-5922) specialises in plants for the small garden. Rather over 1m farther south is the site of the battle of Carberry Hill at which in 1567 Mary, Queen of Scots, and Bothwell were defeated by the rebel lords.—*4m* central **Edinburgh**, see Rte 18.

2   Dunbar to Edinburgh via North Berwick

A198 to Musselburgh. A1 to Edinburgh.—Pastoral and coastal, with cliffs and islands around North Berwick; links and dunes along the Firth of Forth.

SOME HOTELS. **North Berwick**. *Marine*, Cromwell Road, EH39 4LZ. Tel: 0620-2406. *Nether Abbey*, 20 Dirleton Avenue, EH39 4BQ. Tel: 0620-2802. **Gullane**. *Greywalls*, Duncur Road, Muirfield, EH31 2EG. Tel: 0620-842144. **Aberlady**. *Kilspindie House*, Main Street, EH32 0RE. Tel: 08757-682. *Green Craig House*, EH32 0PY. Tel: 08757-301.

Total distance 32m.—*12m*. **North Berwick**.—*7m* **Aberlady**.—*9m* **Musselburgh**.—*4m* **Edinburgh**.

Dunbar, see Rte 1, is left by A1, a turn north on to A198 being made after 2m.—*5m* (from Dunbar) *Tyninghame*, a place which, together with Whitekirk (see below), is associated with St. Baldred, an 8C holy man remembered by two rocks on the shore bearing his name, St. Baldred's Cradle here near Tyninghame and St. Baldred's Boat farther north below Tantallon Castle. The first of these, we are told, was originally between Bass Rock and the shore and thus a danger to shipping; however in response to Baldred's prayers God shifted the rock a couple of miles southward.—At (2m) **Whitekirk** there is a large 15C church beside which is a two-storeyed 16C tithe barn, long ago used by the monks of Holyrood Abbey for the storage of their grain. At that time, and during preceding centuries, Whitekirk boasted a miraculous crucifix and a holy well, possessions which attracted several thousand pilgrims a year during the 15C, amongst them being the later Pope Pius II who is reputed to have walked here barefoot from Dunbar, thus contracting the rheumatism which plagued the rest of his life.

3m *Tantallon Castle (AM. Tel: 031-244-3101) is a massive red sandstone ruin, occupying a breathtaking position, long impregnable, on a towering cliff promontory. On three sides defence is assured by sheer drops to a rock-strewn sea, on the fourth by a double moat. A notorious lair of the Douglases, the main ruin now comprises a central tower, flanking towers and linking ramparts, the walls being 14ft thick and the well plunging 100ft deep into the rock. Dating from c 1375, Tantallon was never taken until 1651 when Cromwell's general, Monk, destroyed it, though only after 12 days of bombardment.

Bass Rock, prominent about 1½m out to sea, is a precipitous basalt island 350ft high and a mile in circumference. There was a castle here from early times and traces still remain of fortifications and a chapel, the latter tenuously associated with St. Baldred, who may indeed have lived here. The rock was used as a prison for Covenanters after 1671, one of these being 'Prophet' Peden, (see Rte 11, Cumnock and Sorn), and, soon after, for Jacobite prisoners who in 1691 dramatically seized the fort and successfully held it until 1694 when they were granted an amnesty. Today Bass Rock is the home of huge colonies of noisy seabirds, including several thousand gannets. Boat trips round the rock from North Berwick.

2m **North Berwick** (5000 inhab. *Inf.*), a royal burgh of Robert III, was developed during the 19 and early 20C as a holiday and golf resort, and the confident Victorian and Edwardian architecture of that period seems to set the tone in this still popular place. The most interesting area of the town is around the rocky spit with the small harbour and bays on either side. On the spit stands the ruin of the notorious *Auld Kirk*, with 12C foundations and a 16C porch; notorious because it was here in 1591 that a gathering of witches and wizards negotiated with the Devil to bring about the death of James VI. North Berwick's other antiquity is the so-called *Abbey*, in fact a fragment of a 12C nunnery. The ruin is in the grounds of the house called Abbey Home, owned by Edinburgh corporation, but its relics in the *Borough Museum* in School Road are perhaps more interesting (Tel: 0620-2197).

Behind the town rises *Berwick Law* (613ft; path). At the top there are a view indicator; a watchtower from Napoleonic times, when the Law was one of a chain of beacons ready to warn of the approach of French invaders; concrete buildings used for a similar purpose against the Germans in 1914–18; and a curious arch made of a whale's jawbones. The origin of this arch seems to be unknown, but one was erected in about 1709 and there have been a number of replacements.—Seawards, in addition to Bass Rock, there are four islands, all alive with seabirds. From east to west these are *Craigleith*, *Lamb*, *Fidra* (a childhood home of R.L. Stevenson and said to have inspired his 'Treasure Island') and *Eyebroughty*.

2m *Dirleton, with its castle, two triangular greens and the way in which its buildings are grouped in the traditional style of a medieval feudal township, is often, and with good reason, described as the prettiest village in Scotland. The ruined *Castle* (AM. Tel: 031-244-3101) was started in about 1225, but later centuries saw many additions to this ancient keep, notably a 15C hall and a 17C Renaissance mansion. In 1298 the castle held out for Wallace against England's Edward I, and it was finally demolished by Cromwell in 1650. Within the walls there are a garden and a 17C bowling green, while a 17C dovecot, built with 1100 nests, stands at the east corner.—*2m* **Gullane** is a name almost synonymous with golf, here being five courses including the championship course of Muirfield. *Heritage of Golf* (by appointment. Tel: 08757-277), on West Links Road, is an exhibition telling the story of golf after the game's arrival in Scotland from Holland in the 15C. Gullane Bay, with extensive sands and many parking and picnic places, is the focus of a major sand dunes control scheme.

Approaching (*3m*) **Aberlady** are Luffness Castle and Myreton Motor Museum. *Luffness Castle* (by appointment. Tel: 08757-218), with its foundations on the site of a Norse camp, centres on a 13C keep. *Myreton Motor Museum* (Tel: 08757-288) shows vintage cars, cycles and commercial vehicles. Aberlady once enjoyed maritime status as the port of Haddington, but the bay in which so many ships once anchored is now a silted nature reserve, the haunt of some 200 recorded species of birds, including all five types of tern. *Gosford House* (Tel: 08757-201), on Gosford Bay between Aberlady and Longniddry, was built in 1800 by Robert Adam but only his central block survives, the wings having been replaced in 1890. The grounds are known for their ornamental waters and wildfowl.

4m **Seton Collegiate Church** (AM. Tel: 031-244-3101) dates from the 15–16C but followed a church of 1242. The oldest portion of the present church are the foundations (in the transept) of a south aisle added to the original church of c 1410 but demolished a century later. The choir is of c 1460; the 4th Lord Seton added the sacristy and in 1492 established the church as collegiate (ruins of the domestic buildings can be seen); the 5th Lord Seton, killed at Flodden, probably lies in the choir to which he had added glazed windows and paving; his widow built the transept

Prince Charles charging at the head of the clans at Prestonpans. 'The sun broke out, and the mist rose from the ground like the curtain of a theatre' (Scott)

and spire, in so doing demolishing the south aisle wall of c 1410. External features are the truncated stone spire and the stands for statues on the buttresses. Worth noting inside the church are, in the south transept, a Renaissance monument with a delightful inscription; the crossing's vault with a hole for hoisting the bells; and, in the choir, sedilia set at a curiously awkward height, and what are probably the effigies of the 5th Lord and his wife.

Seton Castle (1790; no adm.), nearby, stands on the site of Seton Palace, home of the Lord Seton who was such a staunch supporter of Mary, Queen of Scots. It was to Seton Palace that Mary and Darnley fled after Rizzio's murder, and the following year Mary was here again, this time with Bothwell after Darnley's murder.

Approaching (*2m*) **Preston**, a cairn beside A198 at a road fork commemorates the Battle of Prestonpans of 1745 when the Young Pretender's Highlanders, approaching from Tranent across a morass, in a ten-minute dawn charge routed the government forces under General Cope, losing only 30 men and killing 400 of the enemy. The village is known for its magnificent 17C *Market Cross*, complete with unicorn, lockfast chamber and crier's platform, as also for its compact and elegant group of 15–17C buildings. These include the part-ruined 15C tower, with a 16C addition perched on top and an attached lectern dovecot; turreted 16C Northfield House; 17C Hamilton House; and, beside A198, a 16C beehive dovecot.—**Prestonpans**, immediately north of Preston, is a straggling industrial community which traces its name back 700 years to the time when monks from Newbattle Abbey, near Dalkeith, extracted salt here by using local coal to heat sea water in metal pans. *Scottish Mining Museum: Prestongrange Site* (Tel: 031-663-7519. See also Lady Victoria Colliery, Rte 5) makes use of a former colliery site (now closed after some eight centuries of activity) just west of Prestonpans on the coast road. The main exhibit, in its 5-storey shed, is a huge beam engine, Cornish-built in 1874 and in operation until 1954. The mine's former power house now serves as an exhibition hall, while other attractions here include steam locomotives and a colliery winding engine.—*3m* **Musselburgh**, see Rte 1.—*4m* central **Edinburgh**, see Rte 18.

3   Coldstream to Edinburgh via Kelso and Lauder

A698 to Kelso. A6089 and A697 to Lauder. A68 to Edinburgh.—Tweed valley to Kelso, followed by gently rising pastoral country to Lauder. Beyond Lauder, upland moor across the west flank of the Lammermuir Hills (1130ft) with views northward over Edinburgh and the Firth of Forth.

SOME HOTELS. **Kelso**. *Cross Keys*, The Square, TD5 7HL. Tel: 0573-23303. *Ednam House*, Bridge Street, TD5 7HT. Tel: 0573-24168. **Lauder**. *Lauderdale*, 1 Edinburgh Road, TD2 6TW. Tel: 05782-231. **Dalkeith**. *County*, High Street. Tel: 031-663-3945.

Total distance 50m.—*6m* **Kelso**.—*9m* **Gordon**.—*9m* **Lauder**.—*18m* **Dalkeith**.—*8m* **Edinburgh**.

Coldstream (2000 inhab.), a small Border town above a wooded curve of the Tweed, today with a bridge built by Smeaton in 1766, was earlier known for a ford which all too frequently provided military passage during the long years of Border warfare. Edward I crossed here in 1296, as did also Bruce several times when fighting Edward II. In 1513 James IV forded the river on his way to defeat and death at Flodden, 3m south east, where today there is a monument to the brave of both nations. Montrose, too, crossed here in 1640, and, 20 years later, General Monk, on his way southward to play his devious part in the business of the Restoration. Monk was accompanied by a regiment, soon to become famous as the Coldstream Guards, which he had personally raised in Coldstream in 1659, and the site of the original headquarters of this regiment, in Market Square, now houses the *Coldstream Museum* (Tel: 0890-2486). At the east entrance to the town an obelisk honours Charles Marjoribanks, the first Member of Parliament for Berwickshire after the Reform Bill of 1832.

Wark, south of the Tweed just west of Coldstream, still shows fragments of a castle defended in 1344 against David II by the beautiful Countess of Salisbury. The battle of *Carham*, in which in 1018 Malcolm II defeated the Northumbrians and annexed the kingdom of Lothian, was fought immediately east of Wark.

A mile to the west of Coldstream, A697 forks north, a short way along this road being the entrance to *The Hirsel*, seat of the Douglas-Home family. The grounds are open daily, dawn to dusk, and include an Estate Exhibition Centre in an old farm by the loch (Tel: 0890-2834).

6m **Kelso** (5000 inhab. *Inf.*), a compact market town at the confluence of the rivers Teviot and Tweed, has as its two main features its famed ruined abbey and its spacious, elegant Georgian square.

History. Known in the 12C as 'Calkou' (Chalk Hill), Kelso was never a fortified place, optimistically relying for its defence on its status as an abbey town, and, earlier, on the neighbouring great castle of Roxburgh. Nevertheless it was repeatedly sacked by the English, notably in 1522, 1544 and 1545, and also became an accepted assembly place for Scottish armies on their way south. James III was crowned here in 1460. In 1715 the Old Pretender was proclaimed James VIII in the main square, and in 1745 his son, retreating north, stayed here for two days.

Two minor curiosities merit a glance. One is a horseshoe set in the road in Roxburgh Street marking the spot where the Young Pretender's horse shed a shoe; the other, two lamps on Rennie's bridge of 1803, these being from London's Waterloo Bridge, modelled by Rennie on this Kelso bridge but demolished in 1935. *Kelso Museum* (Tel: 0573-25470) is in Turret House, Abbey Court, a 17C building which once served as a skinners' workshop; the theme is local history, with some emphasis on skinning and tanning.

As seen today, **Kelso Abbey* (Tel: 031-244-3101) probably represents no more than the west end of what was one of the greatest of the Borders abbeys.

History. The original foundation was by Alexander I at Selkirk in 1113, but the monks (from Picardy) moved to Kelso when David I founded his abbey in 1128. For several centuries the abbey enjoyed great wealth and influence, its abbots at one time claiming precedence over even St. Andrews, but the end came in 1545, when Hertford, finding the place garrisoned, slaughtered the 100 defenders, including 12 monks, and razed the buildings. From 1649 to 1771, when the roof collapsed, the transept was used as parish church.

Architecturally the abbey as seen today—that is, what is left of the great church—is mixed Norman and Gothic Early English, surviving being the west façade, transepts and tower and two bays of the nave. By far the most striking aspect is the façade of the north-west transept, unaltered for 800 years. Here, mounting one above the other over the fine doorway, are an ornamental arcade and a gable with diamond patterning; two levels of Norman windows; a round window; and at the top two turrets with, between them, another gable. The tower was supported by four great arches, of which two remain.

The massive earthwork with fragments of masonry just outside Kelso beside the Selkirk road (A699) is all that remains of *Roxburgh Castle*, below which once clustered the town of the same name, an important walled royal burgh which became so large that, as early as the 12C, some of its inhabitants had to be dispersed to the medieval equivalent of a satellite town near the site of the present village of Roxburgh 2m to the south. In 1460 the town and castle, both long in English hands, were being besieged by James II, when he was killed by the bursting of a cannon he was inspecting. A yew tree in the grounds of Floors Park (see below) marks the spot. When the Scots finally took Roxburgh, they wholly destroyed both castle and town.

At *Ferneyhill*, 1½m north of Kelso by B6461, an obelisk remembers James Thomson (1700–48), born at nearby Ednam and author of the words of 'Rule Britannia'.

B6352 wanders south east to *Town Yetholm* and *Kirk Yetholm*, twin villages divided by the Bowmont Water, the latter once noted as the home of the Scottish gypsies. Kirk Yetholm is also at one end of the Pennine Way, a 250m path running south into Derbyshire. The round can be continued on B6401 to *Morebattle*, 2m beyond which a minor road leads south past 14C *Cessford Tower*.

Kelso is left by A6089 which soon passes **Floors Castle** (Tel: 0573-23333), seat of the Duke of Roxburghe. Built by William Adam between about 1721–25, the mansion was added to and given much of its present aspect by W.H. Playfair during the 1840s. It was in the park that James II was killed (see above), a yew tree now marking the spot.—A tour of the interior includes the oak-panelled Entrance Hall with ceiling and fireplace attributed to William Adam; the Ante Room showing an early 16C Brussels tapestry (Pentecost and Descent of the Holy Ghost); the Sitting Room, in which a painting of 1809 by William Wilson well shows Adam's Floors before the changes made by Playfair; the Drawing Room, displaying late 17C *Brussels tapestries (Triumphs of the Gods); the Needle Room, a tower-room said to be a replica of a room at Versailles and decorated in Louis XVI style; the elegant Ballroom, a Playfair addition of 1841 now showing 17C Gobelins tapestry. Most rooms house exquisite French and English furniture (Chippendale, Kent and others) and Chinese and European porcelain, while the many paintings include works by such as Raeburn, Kneller, Hogarth, Gainsborough, Hoppner and Reynolds.

Although A6089 for the present remains the axis of this Route, smaller roads can conveniently be chosen first to the west to visit Smailholm Tower followed by the mansion of Mellerstain, then to the east for Hume Castle.

Smailholm Tower (AM. Tel: 031-244-3101) is 7m west of Kelso off B6404. Perched on an isolated green hillock with rocky outcrops beside a small loch, and with unspoilt all-round vistas, this must surely be the most satisfying of all the Borders towers, of which it is a typical and exceptionally well preserved 16C example. The interior construction can be readily enough understood, and a neat domestic touch is provided by a small privy with seat, window and niche for a lantern. Nearby Sandyknowe Farm, the home of Sir Walter Scott's paternal grandfather, was often visited by the poet, and Smailholm houses an exhibition on the theme of his 'Minstrelsy of the Scottish Border'.

Mellerstain House (Tel: 057381-225), 7m north west of Kelso off A6089, was begun by William Adam in 1725 (he built both wings) and completed in 1778 by his son, Robert—an architectural partnership which resulted in what is arguably the most attractive 18C mansion in all Scotland. The elegantly proportioned front is approached through a park rich in superb and varied trees, while the rear overlooks contrastingly formal Italian terraced gardens below which the grounds slope to a lake. The interior, with exquisite Robert Adam ceilings and decoration, is a treasure-house of antique furniture, with work by Chippendale, Sheraton and Hepplewhite. There are two libraries, one accepted as among the finest of Adam's creations, and the notable collection of paintings includes works by Gainsborough, Allan Ramsay, Constable, Veronese, Bassano, Van Goyen and Nic. Maes.

Due north east across A6089, and prominent on a hilltop, stands the dramatic if somewhat bogus outline of **Hume Castle**. Reaching back to the 13C and once the seat of the earls of Home, the castle fell to Cromwell in 1651, after which it was neglected until 1794 when the Earl of Marchmont not only patched up the ruin but for good measure added sham medieval battlements.

9m (from Kelso) **Gordon** recalls through its name a long if distant association with the Gordon family, who moved to north-east Scotland in the 14C when Bruce presented the fortress of the Comyn at Huntly to his supporter, Sir Adam Gordon. *Greenknowe Tower* (AM. Tel: 031-244-3101), on A6105 just west of Gordon, is a well preserved and warmly attractive fortified house of 1581, possibly unique for still having its iron gate.

9m **Lauder** is a quiet little royal burgh, known today for its *Church* (William Bruce, 1673), curious for having an octagonal spire and a ground plan in the shape of a Greek cross with the congregation occupying all four aisles. The 17C *Town Hall* was once the tolbooth, the cellar gaol of which remained in use as such until 1840. The town's annual Common Riding (July, August) is one of the older such, although it was discontinued from 1841 to 1911.

But for many visitors Lauder tends to be overshadowed by **Thirlestane Castle** (Tel: 05782-430), which has long been the home of the Maitland family, whose earlier tower is represented by a ruin some 2m east, and just south of the Kelso road (A697). It was during the time of this earlier castle, in 1482, that Archibald Douglas earned his title of 'Bell-the-Cat' by taking the lead in seizing and hanging from a bridge a group of humbly-born favourites of James III of whom he and the other nobles were jealous. Among those hanged was Cochrane, the king's architect. The present castle, representing stages of building between 1590 and the mid 19C, is notable for its 16 and 17C state rooms with some of Scotland's finest plasterwork ceilings, while children should enjoy the family nurseries with their collection of over 7000 early toys. In the grounds will be found the *Border Country Life Museum*, admirably illustrating, through both displays and demonstrations, the development of country life in these Borders lands from prehistoric to modern times.

A68 now ascends Lauderdale, beyond (*4m*) *Oxton* breasting the open western slopes of the Lammermuir Hills to reach (*4m*) *Soutra Hill (1130ft), a noted viewpoint sweeping Edinburgh and the Firth of Forth. Just north, up B6368, there hides a modest and roofless little stone building, in part possibly of the 15C or earlier, said to be *Soutra Aisle*, a hospice for the poor founded in 1164 by Malcolm IV.

The road now drops sharply, in some *4m* reaching minor roads which lead west for 2m to *Crichton Castle (AM. Tel: 031-244-3101). Crowning a hillock on the steep flank of a quiet valley, Crichton is important as an example of how a once plain 14C tower-house grew into an elegant mansion with elaborate 16C Italianate decoration; earlier rooflines, walls and other details can be well seen, enabling much of the sequence of structural change to be appreciated. Originally owned by Sir William Crichton, chancellor to James II, the castle passed to the Bothwells, and it was the 5th Earl, who had visited Italy, who was responsible for the decorative work (c 1585) of which the most striking feature is a high wall with diamond bosses. Equally, if very differently striking, is the contrast provided by the castle's grim oubliette. The building alongside the castle is also worthy of attention, for this was a defended stable, with an unusual trefoil gunport and a double-horseshoe door.—Nearby *Crichton Collegiate Church*, in continuous use since built in 1449, is known for its barrel-vaulting.

6m **Dalkeith**, which owes its origins to the 12C or earlier castle now represented by *Dalkeith Palace* (no adm.), is a place of some historical interest in the context of the 17C. Dalkeith has been a seat of the Scotts of Buccleuch since the 2nd Earl purchased the castle from the Douglases of Morton in 1651. His surviving heiress daughter, Anne, had Cromwell's General Monk for a guardian at the time when, here at Dalkeith, he was plotting the Restoration. At the age of 12 Anne was married to Charles II's natural son James (he himself was only 14), later made Duke of Monmouth and Buccleuch and executed in 1685 after the failure of his Protestant rebellion against James VII/II. Later, in c 1700, Anne commissioned James Smith to build the present palace around the old castle. Although the palace does not admit visitors, *Dalkeith Park* (Tel: 031-663-5684) is open and offers woodland walks beside the river Esk, as well as nature trails, a Robert Adam bridge and, for the children, an adventure play area. In the town the *Church of St. Nicholas*, made collegiate in 1406, contains the tombs of Duchess Anne as also of the 1st Earl of Morton and his deaf and dumb wife Joanna, daughter of James I.

In a little under *4m*, and now in the outskirts of Edinburgh, A68 passes (right) a group of houses known as *Little France*, recalling that here was the home of some of Mary, Queen of Scots' French attendants. Here also, beside the road, is the stump of a tree planted by Mary in 1561.

Above stands *°Craigmillar Castle* (AM. Tel: 031-244-3101), one of Mary's favourite residences and the place where, with or without her connivance, the murder bond was signed that Darnley, 'sic ane young fool and proud tirrane', should be 'put off by one way or uther'. The castle still impresses as a formidable pile, despite the modern development which has crept towards it. The heart is the L-shaped tower-house of about 1374, with, on the first floor, a great hall served by four stairways, the way in which one of these changes direction at a landing being one of the castle's several defensive features. The year 1427 saw the addition of the strong wall with round corner towers, the gunports in the north east tower being among Scotland's earliest examples of this kind of defence. Destruction in 1544 by Hertford was followed by the building of the three-storeyed east side courtyard buildings, this probably resulting in the Craigmillar Mary would have known. Interesting features are the kitchen with drain and service hatch, and a dungeon in which in 1813 a skeleton was found. The outer wall with its defended dovecot dates from about this same period, but the west courtyard buildings belong to the mid 17C when the emphasis was no longer on defence.

4m central **Edinburgh**, see Rte 18.

4   Carter Bar to Edinburgh via Jedburgh and Melrose

A68.—Much of this Route runs with the general line of the Roman Dere Street which, after leaving the Cheviots near Woden Law, crossed the Tweed near Melrose and the large camp of Trimontium (today Newstead) then ascended Lauderdale to reach the Firth of Forth at Inveresk. After descending from Carter Bar this Route crosses the pastoral and wooded valleys of the Teviot and Tweed before gradually rising with Lauderdale (see Rte 3).

SOME HOTELS. **Jedburgh**. *Glenbank*, Castlegate, TD8 6BD. Tel: 0835-62258. *Glenfriars*, The Friars, TD8 6BN. Tel: 0835-62000. **Melrose**. *Burts*, Market Square, TD6 9PN. Tel: 089682-2285. *George and Abbotsford*, High Street, TD6 9PD. Tel: 089682-2308.

Total distance 60m.—*10m* **Jedburgh**.—*12m* **Melrose**.—*4m* **Earlston**.—*6m* **Lauder**.—*28m* **Edinburgh**.

Carter Bar (1371ft), at the lofty south-west end of the Cheviot range, is one of the best known and scenically most exciting gateways into Scotland. The Reidswire Stone here reminds of the Raid of Reidswire of 1575, the last true Borders skirmish between the Scots and the English, but somehow—and especially on a clear day when their earthworks can be picked out—the Roman presence seems stronger. Their great camp of *Ad Fines* spreads across lonely border moorland 6m to the east, and from it Dere Street started northward past unmistakable *Woden Law* (1388ft), with Iron Age and Roman earthworks, the latter perhaps constructed as part of their training by the garrisons at *Pennymuir* between Kale Water and Oxnam Water at the hill's north-west foot. And it is easy to get closer, for 2m north below Carter Bar a minor road ambles east for 5m to a point where it crosses Dere Street. Northward, from this point, there is no more than a track, but southward a little road, actually named Dere Street, aims straight at Woden Law, beside the road being clear traces of those Pennymuir camps mentioned above.

Approaching Jedburgh, the road passes, first, 16C *Ferniehirst Castle* (Tel: 0835-62201) where a 17C stable houses an information centre on the history and families of the Borders, and then, on the left, the *Capon Tree*, reputedly 1000 years old and perhaps once the local hanging tree.

10m (from Carter Bar) **Jedburgh** (4000 inhab. *Inf.*), once known as Jedhart, is a royal burgh of c 1300, most visited today for its abbey and Mary, Queen of Scots' House. Also of interest are the Castle Jail Museum and medieval Canongate Bridge.

Jedburgh's history is essentially that of its abbey and castle, for both of which see below.—Jedburgh Festival (Callants Festival) lasts over a period of two weeks, usually in June–July.—'Jedhart Justice' was to hang a man first and try him afterwards. The expression seems to have grown out of a single incident involving a gang of thieves during the reign of James IV.—A 'Jedhart Staff', a well-known Borders weapon, was an 8ft-long shaft with a head shaped as a hook or an axe.

•Jedburgh Abbey (AM. Tel: 031-244-3101) survives as a mainly 12–15C red sandstone ruin, standing above the Jed Water down to which once spread the domestic buildings, reduced now to foundations.

This has long been a Christian site. A 9C chapel gave place to the priory founded in c 1138 by David I for monks from Beauvais, this being raised to abbey status in 1147. In 1285 Alexander III was married here to Yolande, daughter of the Count of Dreux. Later the abbey suffered the usual Borders cycle of sacking, rebuilding and neglect, the worst destruction being by Hertford in 1544–45. After the Reformation part of the nave served as parish church until 1875.

The abbey is entered through the admirable Interpretation Centre, which, with much else, includes an instructive model of the complex as it was in about 1510, so positioned that the visitor can both study the model and at the same time relate to the adjacent ruins. Here too are artefacts discovered during excavations in 1984, especially noteworthy being the Jedburgh Comb.

The tour of the ruins follows an excellently explained series of numbered Viewpoints, starting immediately below the Interpretation Centre with (1) the Cellars which should be pictured as a large vaulted area. Steps bring the visitor to (2) at the south-east corner of the Cloister with, below, the site of the Refectory. Viewpoint (3), along the cloister east walk, is at the Chapter House, the late 15C remains seen today being the third, last and smallest (due to the steady drop in the number of monks) of a series reaching back to the 12C. Beyond, the Church is entered through the Norman (12C) East Processional Doorway to reach (4) at the crossing below the tower. Here, the choir to the east is of architectural interest for the unusual way in which the Norman piers rise to a triforium in a semicircular arch embracing two smaller arches. From the crossing, the 12C Transitional nave of nine bays stretches away westward, features to note being the unbroken range of windows and the three levels. First there is a lofty main arcade; next a triforium (where round arches enclose pointed ones); and at the top the clerestory has pointed arch windows.

Viewpoint (5) is at the west end of the nave, the part which, rebuilt in 1671, served as parish church until 1875. Here the visitor should walk out of the west door to view the magnificent *West Front and also to visit the adjacent masonry display.

The nave is left by the West Processional Doorway (replica Norman of 1876), the tour continuing along the cloister west walk to reach (6) the south-west corner above the site of the Kitchen, beyond continuing through domestic ruins and just above the Great Drain with its feeders. Viewpoint (7) embraces the western domestic range.

The *Castle Jail Museum* (Tel: 0835-63254), in Castlegate up the hill from the abbey and town centre, is on the site first occupied by Jedburgh's castle and later by the prison built here in 1825. This latter was designed to meet the requirements of the penal reform thinking of the early 19C, and the rooms have been imaginatively reconstructed to illustrate this prison period.

The *Castle*, roughly contemporary with the abbey, was one of five fortresses surrendered by the Scots to England under a treaty of 1174 as surety for the ransom of William the Lion after his defeat and capture at Alnwick. Later the castle became a favoured royal residence, and it was here, at Alexander III's wedding feast in 1285, that the appearance of a spectre was interpreted as a warning of early death; and correctly, because in the following year Alexander was thrown from his horse and killed. Later the castle became such a magnet for English attacks that the Scots demolished it in 1409.

When Mary, Queen of Scots, came to Jedburgh in 1566 for the assizes, she lived in what is now known as *Mary, Queen of Scots', House* (Tel: 0835-63331). Built less than 20 years earlier, and thus a modern house, Mary chose it, or so it is said, because it was the only house in Jedburgh with indoor sanitation, and it was from here that she rode in one day to Hermitage Castle and back—a good 40 miles in all—to visit the wounded Bothwell, on her return falling dangerously ill and nearly dying. At that time the house was surely crowded and lively, but today little emphasis is given to Mary's stay here and the house now serves as a somewhat austere and sparse Visitor Centre. Of note are the ground level kitchen with its original cobble flooring and showing a death mask and other memorabilia; and, on the second floor, a rare portrait (1565) of Bothwell and also Mary's watch, found 250 years after she had lost it in what is now known as the Queen's Mire, close to Hermitage. The tiny room in which Mary lay sick is between the first and second floors, while the even more cramped space in which her ladies, the four Marys, slept is immediately above.

Canongate Bridge (15C), one of the few medieval three-arch bridges still in use in Scotland, survives as something which readily conjures back the past. Mary almost certainly rode across these arches; the Young Pretender certainly did. Well received in Jedburgh, the latter lodged in a house in Castlegate.

A68 crosses the Teviot, in *4m* from Jedburgh reaching the intersection with B6400. At *Ancrum*, a secluded village immediately to the west, there is a 13C cross on the village green. Just east of the crossroads will be found the *Woodland Centre* (Tel: 08353-306), a pleasant and original interpretation centre, the main theme of which is timber and the care and use of woodland. The *Waterloo Monument*, to the north on Penielheugh Hill (741ft), was erected by the Marquis of Lothian and his tenants shortly after the victory.

Ascending north, A68 in just over *2m* reaches the spot known as *Lilliard's Edge*, on Ancrum Moor, where in 1545 an English force, returning laden with booty from a raid, was attacked and defeated with great slaughter. The name perpetuates the memory of the legendary Maid Lilliard who fought here, her courage told in the spirited lines:

Fair Maid Lilliard lies under this stane
Little was her stature, but great was her fame:
Upon the English loons she laid many thumps,
And when her legs were cuttit off, she fought upon her stumps.

All the way since Jedburgh the Romans' Dere Street has been angling in on the east, and at Forest Lodge, less than 1m north of Lilliard's Edge, it merges with A68 which now enters what is sometimes known as the 'Scott Country'. Centred on Sir Walter Scott's home at Abbotsford, the district (quartered roughly by Selkirk and Galashiels and Dryburgh and Melrose) has many associations with both Scott's life and his works.—*2m* (from Lilliard's Edge) **St. Boswells** derives its name from one Boisel, a prior of Old Melrose, a monastery founded in the 7C within a loop of the Tweed 2m north of here, below what is now known as Scott's View (see below). *Mertoun Gardens* (Tel: 0835-23236), 2m north east of St. Boswells by B6404, offer walks, river views and a circular 16C dovecot.

*Dryburgh Abbey (AM. Tel: 031-244-3101) is reached by car by following B6404 east from St. Boswells to cross the Tweed, and then returning along the other bank. An alternative is to walk, using a lane off A68 just south of Newtown St. Boswells and then a footbridge. Within a lovely pocket of the river and amid handsome trees, Dryburgh is of outstanding interest because of the exceptional completeness of the 12 and 13C monastic buildings. Here, better than at any other Scottish abbey, it is possible to get reasonably close to the day-to-day life of the monks. The abbey church shelters the tombs of Sir Walter Scott and of Earl Haig, the Allied commander during the 1914–18 war.

History. On a site once occupied by the 6C sanctuary of St. Modan, holy man son of an Irish chieftain, the abbey was founded in 1150 for Premonstratensians, probably by Hugh de Morville, Constable of Scotland. In 1322, 1385 and finally in 1544 it was destroyed by the English, after the last occasion never to be rebuilt. In about 1700 the abbey lands belonged to the great-grandfather of Sir Walter Scott, but they soon passed from the family who retained only the quaint right to 'stretch their bones' there.

The *Church* is badly ruined, but the remains still include parts of the nave, transepts and choir. Especially to be noted are the moulded west door of the nave, with, strangely, a semicircular Norman arch despite the date being as late as the 15C; and the processional doorway (which, though Transitional, also has a semicircular arch) leading from the nave into the cloister. The tombs of Scott and Earl Haig, as also of members of their families, are by the north transept. From the south transept a night stair, used for attending night worship, descends from the remains of the dormitory which once stretched as an upper floor along the length of the east side of the cloister.

The *Monastic Buildings* are for the most part on the east and south sides of the cloister. Nearest the church is the vaulted Vestry (or sacristy or library), later converted into a chapel dedicated to St. Modan. Next comes the Parlour, or slype, the only place where the monks were permitted to receive visitors. The Chapter House, virtually intact and entered through a fine doorway with another semicircular arch, was the main place of formal assembly. The room is surrounded by a stone bench, the abbot occupying the east end with its arcade, and the large openings on either side of the door enabled the lay-brothers to listen to the discussions and readings inside. A day stair beside the chapter house gave access to the dormitory. The next room is the Warming Room, with a large fireplace and remains of elegant vaulting columns, best considered as the medieval monastic equivalent of an academic common room. Beyond, a passage leads into the Novices' Room, above which would have been their dormitory. The Refectory, the west gable of which has a large rose window, stretches the length of the south side of the cloister, the kitchens being just beyond. Just south of the cloister are the remains of a gatehouse.

From the hill north of the abbey a huge statue (1814) of William Wallace surveys the scene.—B6356, beside the abbey, in 1m passes *Bemersyde*, seat of the Haigs since 1162 (no adm. Relics of Earl Haig are in Huntly House Museum, Edinburgh). The mansion's 16C tower-house can be seen from the road. Beyond is *Scott's View*, overlooking Old Melrose where once stood the monastery in which Boisel was a prior (see above), the Tweed and the Eildon Hills. Here, at this spot so loved by Scott, the cortege taking his body to Dryburgh paused a while.

Melrose is approached by A6091 out of Newtown St. Boswells, a road which curves across the north-east slopes of the **Eildon Hills**—for challenging walking and a touch of prehistory and the Romans. For romantic legend, too, for Arthur and his knights lie below this turf in enchanted sleep, and it was here also that Thomas the Rhymer (see Earlston below) was given his power of prophecy by the Fairy Queen—

an event marked, anything but romantically, by the *Rhymer's Stone* on the north verge of A6091 about a mile short of Melrose. The hills lift as three volcanic summits, the central one of which is the highest (1385ft, with an orientation table). The north summit shows traces of a prehistoric or Iron Age settlement and was probably also used as a signal station by the Roman garrison of Trimontium near today's Newstead (see below).

4m (from St. Boswells) **Melrose** (2000 inhab. *Inf.*) is a compact small town, known perhaps more for its abbey than for itself. Yet with its Cross of 1642 and several attractive old houses, some with carved stones pillaged long ago from the abbey, the town as such merits at least a glance. *Priorwood Garden*, near the abbey and with a visitor centre and picnic area, specialises in flowers suitable for drying (NTS. Tel: 089682-2555). *Melrose Motor Museum* (Tel: 089682-2624), also near the abbey, is primarily concerned with the period between 1914 and the late 1930s.

*Melrose Abbey (AM. Tel: 031-244-3101) is of architectural and artistic interest for its examples of elaborately carved stonework, and of possibly more popular and romantic curiosity as the burial place of Bruce's heart and of that legendary all-rounder, Michael Scot, the Wizard.

History. The abbey was founded in 1136 by David I for Cistercian monks from Rievaulx in Yorkshire and also as successor to the 7C monastery of Old Melrose. Alexander II was buried here in 1249, probably in the choir. Lying in the path of the English invasions, the abbey was repeatedly destroyed, notably in 1322 and 1385. Bruce restored Melrose in 1326, following the first English destruction, and bequeathed his heart to the abbey, but, apart from the short north wall of the sacristy, the present remains are a mixture of the rebuilding after 1385 together with work of the mid 15C. After Hertford's passage in 1545 there was no real restoration, and for a long time the ruins were pillaged as a source of building material.

What stands today represents the east part of the nave of the church, into which projects the unusual monks' choir; the transepts, with remains of the tower; the main choir; and much of the south nave aisle. As indicated above, perhaps the abbey's finest feature is its elaborate stonework, in particular the bosses and capitals of the columns with intricate and delicate foliage in which the leaves of curly kale stand out as typical of the skill and fancy of the Scottish stone carvers of the time (note especially the capitals at the east end of the Monks' Choir).

The South Nave Aisle was flanked by a row of chapels, of which eight remain, each one the burial place of an important family. By comparison, the North Nave Aisle, because it abuts on the cloister, is narrow, undistinguished and without chapels. A stone screen separates the central aisle from the Monks' Choir, the elegant pointed arches of which are hidden on the north side by piers and arches erected in 1618 as part of conversion to a Presbyterian church, a role which it played until 1810. The Tower still preserves its two west piers, the capitals of the clustered shaft on the south-west pier bearing particularly fine examples of curly kale carving. The South Transept provides the best window in the abbey, with five lights, 24ft high and 16ft wide, and a wealth of lovely tracery. A tablet in this transept mentions one John Morow as master mason (mid 15C). Off the North Transept opens the Sacristy, with its 12C north wall representing the oldest part of the whole abbey. Under the lower threshold step (worn inscription) is buried Joan, wife of Alexander II and sister of Henry III of England.

The Choir still shows its fretted stone roof, and the windows retain their early Gothic design of c 1387, though with later mid 15C tracery, perhaps the work of Morow. Below the east window was the traditional resting place of the heart of Robert Bruce, buried here when brought back from Spain whither Sir James Douglas had carried it on his way (cut short because of his death in battle) to the Holy Land. An embalmed heart found in a casket here in 1920 and reburied in the chapter house (plaque) could well have been Bruce's. Also in the choir are Douglas tombs, and possibly that of Alexander II, while what may be the tomb of Michael Scot, the Wizard, is the flat one in the chapel off the south side of the choir.

North of the church are the Cloisters, the south walk of which has some good shallow arcading, while the earlier arcade on the east is also attractive. Excavation in 1921 exposed the whole ground plan and identified also the foundations of the chapter house (on the east) and other parts of the monastic buildings.—The *Abbey Museum* (across Cloisters Road) is housed in what was the Commendator's House, built in 1590 on the site of the abbot's palace but since much altered. Relics include material from Roman Trimontium, and in the museum area further foundations have been exposed, as also the course of the great drain.

Abbotsford House (Tel: 0896-2043), Sir Walter Scott's flamboyant creation and home for the last 20 years of his life, is 2½m west of Melrose.

Scott bought the farm here in 1811, renaming it Abbotsford, because the monks of Melrose formerly crossed the river here. Five years later he added an armoury, dining room, study, conservatory and some bedrooms. In 1822 he demolished the old farmhouse, replacing it with the main block of today's Abbotsford. (The west wing and the entrance lodge were added after Scott's death.) When financial disaster overtook Scott, the house was presented back to him by his creditors, since when it has remained in the family.

Abbotsford, together with its park, is essentially Scott's personal achievement, a place which, however it may strike the modern visitor, was as much in sympathy with 19C taste as it reflected its builder's unfettered romantic imagination. A mock baronial complex of turrets and gables, Abbotsford is part original and part copied from elsewhere. The garden screen wall, for instance, reflects the cloister at Melrose, the porch that at Linlithgow Palace, and the library ceiling has designs from Roslin Chapel.

Today Abbotsford is a museum not only of Scott but also of the many and curious historical relics he so enthusiastically collected. The Study, surprisingly small and dark and with a restricted view, is little altered. The Library and the Drawing Room both offer views along the river. The former contains a bust of Scott (Francis Chantrey, 1820), a portrait of him by Raeburn, and oddities such as Napoleon's cloak-clasp, Rob Roy's purse, Burns's drinking glass and a lock of The Young Pretender's hair. The Armoury is a museum of Scottish and other weapons of various periods, these including Scott's own blunderbuss, Claverhouse's pistol and Rob Roy's sword; here also are an interesting contemporary portrait of James IV, and a bizarre painting of the head of Mary, Queen of Scots, made by Amyas Cawood the day following her execution. The Dining Room, with family portraits, is the room in which Scott died, his bed near the window within sight of the Tweed.—Outside, in the South Court, five medallions in the south wall are from the old Edinburgh Cross, pulled down in 1756; and, above the porch, there is a more macabre souvenir, the door of the upper floor of the Edinburgh tolbooth through which condemned prisoners emerged for execution.

Returning to Melrose, A68 can be reached by way of *Newstead*, close to the site of Rome's Trimontium, so called of course from the triple peaks of the Eildon Hills. Nothing visible remains, but an inscribed stone beside the road east of the village outlines the history of the camp.

4m **Earlston** was the home of Thomas Learmont (c 1220–97), known as Thomas the Rhymer, or True Thomas, because of his famous verse prophecies, a gift which he claimed to have received from the Fairy Queen (see Eildon Hills above). It is a measure of his fame that a stone on the church wall still records 'Auld Rhymer's race lies in this place', and that a small ruin, which may have been his tower home, continues to be known as Rhymer's Tower.

For (*6m*) **Lauder**, and for Lauder to (*28m*) **Edinburgh**, see Rte 3.

5 Canonbie (Carlisle) to Edinburgh via Hawick, Selkirk and Galashiels

A7 (alternative B6357 and B6399 to Hawick).—As far as Selkirk, much lonely open moor with heights approaching 2000ft. Included also along this stretch are diversions such as Eskdale and the Ettrick and Yarrow valleys, all providing a scenic mix of valley and upland moor broken by afforestation. Between Selkirk and Edinburgh the road ascends the Gala Water and touches the comparatively modest Moorfoot Hills.

SOME HOTELS. **Carlisle** (both hotels north on A7). *Cumbria Park*, 32 Scotland Road, CA3 9DG. Tel: 0228-22887. *Crest*, Kingstown, CA4 0HR. Tel: 0228-31201. **Canonbie**. *Riverside Inn*. DG19 0UX. Tel: 03873-71295. **Langholm**. *Eskdale*, Market Place, DG13 0JH. Tel: 03873-80357. **Eskdalemuir**. *Hart Manor*, DG13 0QQ. Tel: 03873-73217. **Hawick**. *Kirklands*, West Stewart Place, TD9 8BH. Tel: 0450-72263. **Selkirk**. *Philipburn*, TD7 5LS. Tel: 0750-20745. **Ettrickbridge**. *Ettrickshaws*,

TD7 5HW. Tel: 0750-52229. **Galashiels**. *Kingsknowes*, Selkirk Road, TD1 3HY. Tel: 0896-58375.

Total distance 78m.—*7m* **Langholm**.—*22m* **Hawick**.—*11m* **Selkirk**.— *6m* **Galashiels**.—*20m* **Borthwick Castle**.—*12m* **Edinburgh**.

The border is 12m north of **Carlisle** (see 'Blue Guide England'), A7 initially following the line of a Roman road and crossing the Esk at Longtown, just west of which is *Solway Moss*, scene of the defeat of James V in 1542. The border is more or less marked by *Scotsdyke*, the remains of an earth and stone wall defining the border (as agreed in 1552) where it crosses between the Esk and Sark rivers (see also Rte 7, Sark Bridge).

Canonbie is 2m north of the border. From here there is a choice of roads to Hawick, similar scenically and in distance: either A7 through Langholm, whence Eskdale and the moors across to Ettrick can be reached, or B6357 and B6399 up Liddesdale, passing Hermitage Castle and providing approaches to Border Forest Park.

Canonbie to Hawick via Langholm

2m Gilnockie Tower, also known as Holehouse and dating from the 16C, was one of the lairs of Johnnie Armstrong of Gilnockie, a dashing Borders bandit who, despite a reputation for never molesting a Scotsman, was nevertheless eventually taken by James V and hanged near Teviothead (see below) together with some 36 companions.—*5m* **Langholm** (2500 inhab. *Inf.*) is a long, enclosed small town at the confluence of the Esk, Ewes and Wauchope waters and of the roads which run with their valleys. Historically it is known for the battle of 1455 in which James II finally crushed the Douglases. The obelisk on a hill to the east is a memorial to Sir John Malcolm, an 18C Indian administrator.

ESKDALE (B709), ascending north west out of Langholm—at first pastoral, then forest, then sweeping upland moor—provides an ever-changing scenic cut across to the Ettrick Valley, some 28m away. In about 3m the road bends sharply west, across the river here being *Burnfoot*, the home of that Sir John Malcolm whose monument stands above Langholm. *Bentpath* comes next, with, 1m north opposite Westerkirk school, a memorial (1928) to Thomas Telford, born in 1757 near here. Beyond, B709 crosses the river before plunging into Castle O'er Forest to meet (in 2m) the White Esk, beside which are two groups of standing stones, first the battered stone circle known as the *Girdle Stanes*, then, just beyond, the *Loupin' Stanes*, a more scattered and shapeless group which does however include a small circle. From *Eskdalemuir*, some 13m now from Langholm, a track up the left bank of the river in 1m reaches *Raeburnfoot*, an important Roman fort on the road to Trimontium, while, in startling contrast beside B709 beyond Eskdalemuir, suddenly appears a *Tibetan Monastery*, founded by refugees in 1967 and now complete with pagoda, prayer wheels and perhaps even a glimpse of a monk. Beyond *Eskdale Observatory*, an important meteorological station, the watershed is crossed at 1095ft, the road then dropping beside the afforested valley of Tima Water to reach Ettrick (see below).

From Langholm A7 ascends the Ewes Water and the Mosspaul Burn to (*10m*) *Mosspaul Hotel* before starting to descend to (*4m*) *Teviothead* with, in its churchyard, a memorial stone to the bandit Johnnie Armstrong, hanged by James V at Caernlanrig, ½m to the south west; the stone, set in the wall of the part of the cemetery across the road from the church, bears an inscription which leaves little doubt where local loyalties lay. Now dropping with the upper Teviot, A7 in *8m* reaches **Hawick**.

Canonbie to Hawick via Hermitage

B6357 ascends Liddesdale, to the east of which spreads the huge *Border Forest Park*, virtually the whole of which however is in England. *10m Newcastleton*, just north of which there is a road fork from which B6357 to the right reaches the heart of the park by way of Saughtree from where a minor road curves away south east for the lovely expanse of man-made Kielder Water. This Route, though, takes the left fork (B6399) for (*6m* from Newcastleton) *Hermitage Castle (AM. Tel: 031-244-3101) which, beside Hermitage Water and in bleak, lonely open plain, impresses as a grim place of defiant impregnability.

History. The original 13C castle belonged to the Soulis family, of unsavoury reputation and one of whom, William (the 'Wizard'), is said to have forfeited his lands in 1320 for conspiring against Bruce. The Douglases took Hermitage in 1341, and the following year the castle was the scene of the cruel fate of Sir Alexander Ramsay, whom Douglas starved to death, although the unfortunate but determined man survived for 17 days on corn trickling through from the granary above (the pit prison can still be seen). In 1492 the Douglases exchanged Hermitage for Bothwell Castle near Glasgow, and in 1566 it was fleetingly visited by Mary, Queen of Scots, who, in residence for the assizes at Jedburgh, rode the 40 miles round journey to Hermitage and back in one day in order to visit Bothwell who had been wounded in a foray against the English. This ride is still remembered by the map entry 'Queen's Mire' 3m north west of the castle.

Much restored on the outside, today's ruin is mainly of the late 14C and comprises a keep and corner towers, joined by great arches at the east and west ends, the whole having a corbelled parapet. The south-west tower was extended during the 15C. In the much ruined interior survive remains of the original Soulis 13C tower.

Continuing north, B6399 skirts a hill known, because of its stone circle, as *Nine Stane Rig*, where, it is said, the cruel Lord Soulis was boiled alive, though the more prosaic truth is that he died as a prisoner in Dumbarton Castle. Beyond, and now in lonely countryside, a patch of woodland is crossed (Wauchope Forest, a Scottish outrider of Border Forest Park) immediately beyond which (*5m* from Hermitage), at a spot called Robert's Linn Bridge, the road meets the mysterious *Catrail*, a wide ditch and embankment which runs from Peel Fell on the border north west to Borthwick Water and thence towards Galashiels but the purpose of which must remain a matter for individual guesswork.—*8m* **Hawick**.

Hawick (pron. Hoik. 16,000 inhab. *Inf.*) is important as a main Scottish textile centre. Entering the town A7 becomes Buccleuch Street which kinks north east to become High Street. By this kink, Howegate, leading south, soon reaches the only survival of medieval Hawick, the *Mote*, a high mound which was once the base of a Norman defensive work and later became the meeting-place of the Manor Court; and of 16C Hawick there is (merged with other building in High Street) just a tower which managed to survive the destruction of the town by the English in 1570. The English were here a few years earlier, too, in 1514, when the local youths (callants) defeated a marauding force at Hornshole, 2m east, and captured their banner. This skirmish is recalled both by a monument in High Street and also annually as part of the Common Riding pageantry (June).

It was in the predecessor of *St. Mary's Church* (1764; restored) that in 1342 Douglas seized Sir Alexander Ramsay, carrying him off to

Hermitage and death by starvation in the pit. In the west outskirts of the town are the grounds of *Wilton Lodge*, now a public park along the banks of the Teviot. The estate originally belonged to the Langlands, friends of Wallace, who is said to have visited here in 1297 and to have tethered his horse to a tree near the house (memorial stone). The house is now *Wilton Lodge Museum* (Tel: 0450-73457), exhibiting material relating to the knitwear industry, Borders history and archaeology and natural history, while the Scott Gallery shows 19 and 20C Scottish paintings. *Trow Mill* (Tel: 0450-72555), 2m east on A698, offers visitors the opportunity both to watch tweed being made and to buy it. Opened in the 1750s as a meal-grinding mill powered by water, Trow converted to textiles production in c 1880 but continued to use water power until 1965.

11m **Selkirk** (5500 inhab. *Inf.*) sprawls over a hillside high above the Ettrick river.

History. Selkirk was declared a royal burgh by David I in 1113, and it was here in the late 13C that Wallace was proclaimed Guardian of Scotland. After Flodden the town was burned by the victorious English. In 1645 Montrose slept here (in West Port) the night before his disastrous defeat by Leslie at nearby Philiphaugh.

The town centre is the dignified, triangular Market Place, where a statue of Sir Walter Scott, county sheriff for 27 years, stands in front of his spired Court Room. Here too is *Halliwell's House Museum and Gallery* (Tel: 0750-20096), housed in a neat row of restored 18C dwellings and devoted to local history. The Gallery mounts changing exhibitions. At the other end of High Street there is a particularly fine statue, with African figures, of the explorer Mungo Park (1771–1806), born at nearby Foulshiels (see below), while a more martial memorial, with a virile standard-bearing man-at-arms, commemorates Flodden, whence of the 80 townsmen who fought only one returned. But he came back with honour and a banner, and the parading of the banner is a highlight of Selkirk's Common Riding (June), with its many riders one of the Borders' most colourful, and celebrated for five centuries without a break.

ETTRICK AND YARROW DIVERSIONS. From Selkirk tours can be made up the quietly lovely pastoral and moorland Ettrick and Yarrow valleys. Although each is described separately below, a circuit of c 30m is possible, at least in part, by using B709 between Tushielaw on the Ettrick and Gordon Arms Hotel (Mountbenger) on the Yarrow. This upland area was once the great Ettrick Forest, rich with game and secure refuge for Wallace, and perhaps also for Bruce, as well as for the Borders freebooters and indeed for any man on the run. In 1528 James V, with a retinue of, it is said, 12,000, hunted here (thieves, it appears, as much as game), but it seems also to have been he who later so increased the number of sheep that eventually the forest became the peaceful moor and downland hills that it is today. Both Ettrick and Yarrow were long the subject of ballads—which, in these valleys, tend to get confused with reality—and they also inspired poets such as Scott, Wordsworth and Hogg.

Ettrick Valley (B7009. 17m to Ettrick). *Oakwood Tower* (16C), above the road on the left 4½m from Selkirk, is said to be successor to a 13C home of Michael Scot, the Wizard. On the hillside 1½m west of Ettrickbridge stands *Kirkhope Tower*, a lair of the freebooter, Wat of Harden, and perhaps the tower to which he brought his bride, Mary of Dryhope, the 'Flower of Yarrow' of ballad. *Tushielaw*, 7m farther west, was the home of another freebooter, Adam Scott, hunted down and hanged by James V during his foray of 1528. From here B709 climbs north west high across wild moorland to drop down to the Yarrow at Gordon Arms Hotel, while the valley road (now B709) continues south west to reach (in 2m) *Ettrick*, perhaps best known as the home of James Hogg (1770–1835), the poet called the 'Ettrick Shepherd' and protégé of Sir Walter Scott. A monument marks his birthplace and his grave is in the churchyard. From Ettrick B709 bears south to climb across the moors to Eskdale, while a smaller road accompanies the river towards its source.

Yarrow Valley (A708. 17m to Tibbie Shiel's Inn on St. Mary's Loch). Below Selkirk the road crosses the Ettrick and bears west, here traversing the site of the battle of Philiphaugh (1645) at which Leslie decisively defeated Montrose. *Bowhill* (Tel: 0750-20732), just beyond and across the river, has long been the home of the Scotts of Buccleuch. The present house, started by the 3rd Duke of Buccleuch in c 1795, contains an outstanding collection of French furniture, as well as pictures by, amongst others, Leonardo da Vinci, Gainsborough, Reynolds, Claude, Canaletto, Guardi and Raeburn. There are also relics of the Duke of Monmouth and Sir Walter Scott. In the grounds there are nature trails and, for the children, an adventure woodland play area. Nearby *Newark Castle* (for entry apply Bowhill), now a ruined 15C oblong tower-house, stands on the site of an earlier royal hunting lodge. It was in the courtyard here in 1645 that Leslie shot in cold blood 100 of Montrose's supporters who had been made prisoner at Philiphaugh.

Newark Castle can also be seen across the river from A708 at *Foulshiels*, where beside the road are the remains of the cottage in which the explorer Mungo Park was born in 1771. From here the road gently ascends beside Yarrow Water, leaving woodland for bare country and reaching first *Yarrow*, with a church of 1640 and a bridge (Deuchar) of 1653, and then *Gordon Arms Hotel*, from where B709 provides a remote moorland link across to Tushielaw in the Ettrick valley. James Hogg must have known this crossroads well, for he farmed unsuccessfully for nearly ten years (1821–30) at Mountbenger, immediately north. In just over another 2m the east end of St. Mary's Loch is reached at Dryhope, where *Dryhope Tower*, visible north of the road, dates from c 1600 and, at that time four storeys high, was the home of Mary, the 'Flower of Yarrow' (see also Ettrick Valley, Kirkhope, above). *Tibbie Shiel's Inn*, on the spit separating St. Mary's Loch from Loch of the Lowes, perpetuates the name of the lady who was the innkeeper here for many years after 1823 (born in 1783, she lived until 1878). Her inn was a favourite meeting-place of such men of letters as Scott, Carlyle, Stevenson and James Hogg, the last of whom now sits as a statue beside the road here.

For the motorist not wishing to retrace to Selkirk there are now two choices, both scenically outstanding. One is to continue along A708 to cross the watershed at 1100ft, beyond dropping steeply towards Moffat (see Rte 7), on the initial descent passing *Grey Mare's Tail Waterfall* hurling itself 200ft down a bare mountain cleft. This dark and remote country is under the care of the National Trust for Scotland who maintain a path to the foot of the waterfall.—The other choice is the minor road, surely one of the loneliest in southern Scotland, which breaks away westward from St. Mary's Loch to hug Megget Reservoir and climb to nearly 1500ft before—and with breathtaking views—winding abruptly down to dark *Talla Reservoir* and the hamlet of *Tweedsmuir* (see Rte 7).

Leaving Selkirk A7 curves down to the confluence of the Ettrick and

Tweed, here crossing the latter, though B6360 along the right bank should be taken if Abbotsford (see Rte 4), 2m from the bridge, is the objective.

6m (from Selkirk) **Galashiels** (12,000 inhab. *Inf.*), a long, rather grey town, was founded as a kind of staging camp for pilgrims to Melrose; hence the name, meaning Huts on the Gala Water. That Galashiels also played its part in the constant struggle against the English is recalled by its arms, a fox reaching for plums, the origin being a successful skirmish with a body of English surprised when gathering wild plums. The annual Braw Lads Gathering in June, though dating only from 1930, lacks little in spirit.

Today Galashiels is known for its textile manufacture and as the home of the internationally important Scottish College of Textiles, and visitors interested in this field may visit the *Peter Anderson Woollen Mill* (Tel: 0896-2091). Here not only can the manufacturing process of tweeds, tartans and suchlike be followed, but the mill also serves as a museum of the local past, both industrial and social. The oldest house in Galashiels is the *Old Gala House* (Tel: 0750-20096), in Scott Crescent; dating from 1583 and long the home of the lairds of Gala, the house now serves as a local interpretation centre as also focus for exhibitions.

A7 now accompanies the Gala Water, reaching (*7m*) *Stow*, where, beside A7 to the south of the village, there is a battered packhorse bridge of 1655, before climbing along the east flank of the modest and rather dull Moorfoot Hills.—*13m* *Borthwick Castle*, to the east of A7 at North Middleton, although not open to the public can be well seen from the outside. And the short diversion is worthwhile on two counts—architecturally because, built in c 1430, this castle with its twin towers and two wings is the strongest and most massive of all Scotland's tower-houses; historically because it was to Borthwick that Bothwell brought Mary for a brief and dramatic visit after their wedding. When almost at once the place was surrounded by their enemies, Bothwell slipped away to Dunbar and Mary, disguised as a page, followed two days later. The village of *Temple*, 3m west, is so named because this was the Scottish seat of the Knights Templar, suppressed in 1312; there survives a roofless 13–14C church.—*3m* **Newtongrange**, with *Lady Victoria Colliery* (Tel: 031-663-7519), a Victorian colliery taken over by the Scottish Mining Museum Trust when it closed in 1981 and now showing much of interest including a visitor centre in which a day in the life of a Victorian pit village is recreated. See also Prestongrange, Rte 2.—*3m* (just beyond Eskbank) *Edinburgh Butterfly Farm* (Tel: 031-663-4932) shows exotic free-flying butterflies from worldwide habitats.—*6m* central **Edinburgh**, see Rte 18.

6   Galashiels to Edinburgh via Peebles

A72 to Peebles. A703 to Edinburgh.—As far as Peebles along the largely wooded valley of the Tweed, A72 following the north bank while a smaller and quieter road follows the other. From Peebles northward, below generally bare rounded hills, with the Pentlands to the west and the Moorfoot Hills to the east.

SOME HOTELS. **Walkerburn**. *Tweed Valley*, Galashiels Road, EH43 6AA. Tel: 089687-636. **Peebles**. *Park*, Innerleithen Road, EH45 8BA. Tel: 0721-20451. *Hydro*, Innerleithen Road, EH45 8LX. Tel: 0721-20602. **Roslin**. *Roslin Glen*, 2 Penicuik Road, EH25 9LH. Tel: 031-440-2029.

Total distance 41m.—*11m* **Innerleithen (Traquair)**.—*6m* **Peebles**.—*13m* **Penicuik**.—*3m* **Roslin**.—*8m* **Edinburgh**.

A72 curves westward out of Galashiels, on the right at the curve, *2m* from the town centre, being *Torwoodlee House* (by appointment. Tel: 0896-2151), a small Georgian mansion of 1783 with Victorian modifications on an estate which has been the home of the Pringle family for approaching 500 years. *Torwoodlee Broch and Fort*, just north of the house, is one of southern Scotland's rare examples of this kind of structure and one also about which, unusually, a little seems to be known, or at any rate deduced. The native fort seems to have been built first, only however to be destroyed by the Romans during their first penetration in c 82. With the Roman withdrawal soon afterwards, Picts may have moved in from the north to build the broch, in which they seem to have stored Roman pottery and glass, perhaps abandoned at Trimontium. However, the Romans were back by 140 and seem soon to have destroyed the broch, perhaps also killing the woman whose skeleton was found here.—In another *2m* A72 reaches the Tweed and bears west, opposite across the river being *Ashiestiel*, the house tenanted by Sir Walter Scott for several years before moving to Abbotsford.—*5m* **Walkerburn**, where the *Scottish Museum of Wool Textiles* (Tel: 089687-281), associated with a large shop, has imaginative displays illustrating the rearing of sheep, how a weaver once lived and worked, dying and spinning, the origins of knitting and other themes.—*2m* **Innerleithen**, with a mineral spring (St. Ronan's Well) and also *Robert Smail's Printing Works* (NTS. Tel: 0896-830206) set up in 1866 and closed by Robert Smail's grandson in 1985. This latter was unenthusiastic about modernisation or change and today's visitor can step back a century or so to appreciate such features as 'guard books' (with examples of every job printed) reaching back 100 years, letterpress, two water-wheels in use until 1930, the Victorian office and much else.

Traquair House (Tel: 0896-830323), beyond the river 1m south of Innerleithen, claims to be the oldest continuously inhabited home in Scotland, and certainly the impression today is of a mature home rather than of a formal mansion. It was the residence of William the Lion, who held court here in 1209, and it is further claimed that 27 Scottish and English monarchs (including Mary, Queen of Scots, Darnley, and their baby, the future James VI/I) have visited here. The 1st Earl is said to have betrayed Montrose's plans to Leslie before the battle at Philiphaugh and then denied Montrose entry after his defeat, the latter having ridden from Philiphaugh in a direct line across Minch Moor (1856ft). The 5th Earl, however, received the Young Pretender, and when the latter departed through the avenue's Bear Gates swore that they should not open again until a Stuart regained the throne; so, they remain closed. The house is largely of the 17C, but with a very ancient tower, and many relics are on view in its historic rooms and passages, which include a priest's room and escape stairway. Other attractions are an 18C brewhouse, still producing ale, several craft workshops, a maze and woodland walks.

Peebles may now be approached either by A72 north of the river, or by the pleasanter, quieter and wooded B7062 along the south bank, the latter passing *Kailzie Gardens* (Tel: 0721-20007), with a walled garden of 1812. The main road runs immediately south of *Glentress Forest*, with an information room and several trails.

6m (from Innerleithen) **Peebles** (6000 inhab. *Inf.*) is a country town set among gentle wooded hills on a broad stretch of the Tweed.

History. Legend insists that St. Mungo visited Peebles in the 6C. Be this as it may, it is known that its castle, now vanished, was a favourite hunting lodge of the early Scottish kings, and particularly of Alexander III, and that David II granted royal burgh status in 1367. More than once sacked by the English, Peebles was later occupied by Cromwell in 1649 and, briefly, by the Young Pretender in 1745. The home of the Queensberry family, it was the birthplace of 'Old Q' (1725–1810), the notorious gambling 4th Duke, as also of the publishers, William and Robert Chambers, born here in 1800 and 1802.

The Beltane Festival (June) is probably of Celtic origin. Revived in 1899, it now lasts a week, the highlights being the Common Riding and the crowning of the Beltane Queen.

Only fragments of the old town wall remain, near the former railway station. In High Street the *Tweeddale Museum* (Tel: 0721-20123), with material of local interest, is housed in the Chambers Institute, once the town house of the Queensberry family, while, also in High Street, No. 31 is *The Cornice* (Tel: 0721-20212) with a reconstruction of a turn-of-the-century plasterer's casting workshop; here, too, there is a 'hands-on' area offering visitors the chance to test their own skills. The *Tweed Bridge*, though widened at least twice, is basically of the 15C, but Peebles's oldest site is the ruin of *Cross Kirk* on the west edge of the town. Built by Alexander III in the 13C, the church was associated with a Trinitarian friary, the foundations of which can still be seen.

Neidpath Castle (Tel: 0721-20333), 1m west of Peebles on A72, stands dramatically amid woods on a green hillock immediately above the north bank of the Tweed. Built through the 13–15Cs, and with later additions, this was the stronghold first of the Frasers and then of the Hays. The castle held out for Charles II, but the old tower, which had only recently been raised a storey, was soon battered by Cromwell's cannon and the castle surrendered after a long siege. Later, in 1686, Neidpath was bought by the 1st Duke of Queensberry, whose worthless successor, 'Old Q', was denounced in a sonnet by Wordsworth as a 'degenerate Douglas' because he cut down the timber. For today's visitor perhaps Neidpath's main interest lies in the way in which it developed from grim fortress complete with pit prison into a (for the times) comfortable 17C residence.

At *Lyne*, 3m west of Neidpath, there are the remains of a Roman camp, contained within a loop of A72 immediately east of the river bridge. Belonging to the first foray into Scotland, the camp was built in c 84 but survived only until 117. In the tiny church of Lyne (c 1645) there are a contemporary pulpit and two good canopied pews.

From Peebles this Route continues north by A703 up the valley of the Eddleston Water. The road can either be taken direct out of Peebles, or, if Lyne has been visited, joined at Eddleston, the minor cross-country road to which affords a good view across the valley to the earthworks of the large Iron Age fort of *Milkieston Rings*.—*13m* (from Peebles) **Penicuik**, below the Pentland Hills, marks the south limit of the Edinburgh conurbation. Here the *Edinburgh Crystal Works* (Tel: 0986-75128. No children under 10), arrange conducted tours for visitors interested in the glassmaker's craft and, in particular, the production of high-grade crystal.

3m **'Roslin (or Rosslyn) Chapel** (Tel: 031-440-2159), to the east of A703, houses within its comparatively small space the most lavish, most intricate and in its themes most intriguing stone carving in Scotland, if not in Britain.

History. Founded in 1446 by William Sinclair, 3rd Earl of Orkney, the chapel was made collegiate in 1521. It was the burial place of the Sinclairs, reputedly interred in full armour until 1650 when the widow of that year broke the ancestral custom, 'thinking it beggarly to be buried in that manner'. The chapel was damaged by the Edinburgh mob in 1688, partly repaired during the 18C, and thoroughly restored in 1862 by the Earl of Rosslyn for Episcopalian use.

Architecturally the chapel represents the choir of a church of which the nave was never built and the transepts only begun. The central aisle, of five bays, is separated from the side aisles by clustered columns, all with extravagantly carved capitals. It is barrel-vaulted with transverse ribs, and the roof of each bay is worked with a different flower. The side aisles are crossed by transoms covered on both sides with elaborate bas-reliefs. On one are the Seven Deadly Sins and the Seven Cardinal Virtues; on another is a Dance of Death; on a third the opinion 'Forte est vinum, fortior est rex, fortiores sunt mulieres, super omnia vincit veritas'.

The *Prentice Pillar, entwined by particularly complex flowers and foliage, is at the east end of the south aisle. The not very original story is that the pillar was carved by an apprentice in the absence of his master, and that the latter, on his return, killed the apprentice in a fit of jealousy. The story is rounded off by the suggestion that the three heads at the end of the nave are those of the apprentice, his master and his sorrowing mother.

At the east end of the north aisle a slab in the pavement showing a knight in armour with a dog at his feet is said to represent the founder of Roslin Castle, but is probably of later date. This story tells that Sir William Sinclair wagered his lands against the lands of Pentland that two of his hounds would pull down, before it reached a certain burn, a deer that had often escaped the royal huntsmen. The deer was killed exactly at the burn and Robert Bruce at once awarded the estate to Sinclair. In gratitude Sir William built the church of St. Katherine in the Hopes, now drowned beneath Glencorse reservoir in the Pentlands.

Behind the altar, a Lady Chapel shows carved pendants descending from the central ribs. At the south-east angle of the choir steps descend to a chamber projecting beyond the east end of the chapel. The altar and piscinae show that this was a chapel, while the fireplace and other secular conveniences suggest use also as a vestry or perhaps priest's room.

Roslin Castle (ask at chapel), below the chapel to the south and perched on the edge and against the face of a cliff overhanging the North Esk, was perhaps built by an earlier Sir William Sinclair than the founder of Roslin Chapel; perhaps, even, it was that Sir William who earned his lands from Bruce by means of the wager described above. More certain is that the keep was enlarged by the founder of the chapel. Destroyed by Hertford in 1544, the castle was gradually restored and converted to a 16–17C fortified house, and it is this rebuilding that is most in evidence today. Of the original little remains, bar some sections of 14C wall, and rooms, dungeons and passages part wedged into the cliff. One intriguing feature is an escape slide from the lower part of the castle to below the water level in the moat. Today the castle is in part arranged as holiday accommodation.

3m Burdiehouse is thought to derive its name from 'Bordeaux House', a settlement of the French attendants of Mary, Queen of Scots.—*5m* central **Edinburgh**, see Rte 18.

7   Gretna to Edinburgh via Lockerbie and Moffat

A74 to Lockerbie. A709 to Lochmaben. B7020 to Beattock (Moffat). A701 to Broughton. B7016 to Biggar. A702 to Edinburgh.—As far as Lockerbie a rather dull and busy main road, followed, after

Lochmaben, by a smaller parallel road a mile or two to the west of the main road. Beyond Moffat, a climb to the watershed at 1330ft, followed by moorland down the valley of the upper waters of the Tweed. North of Biggar A702 runs below the bare Pentland Hills.—*Note:* A74 is a dual-carriageway trunk road and as such bypasses the places along it mentioned below. Care must therefore be taken to choose the relevant exits.

SOME HOTELS. **Gretna**. *Gretna Chase*, CA6 5JB. Tel: 0461-37517. *Solway Lodge*, Annan Road, CA6 5DN. Tel: 0461-38266. **Lockerbie**. *Lockerbie House*, Boreland Road, DG11 2RG. Tel: 05762-2610. *Dryfesdale House*, DG11 2SF. Tel: 05762-2427. **Moffat**. *Moffat House*, High Street, DG10 9HL. Tel: 0683-20039. *Beechwood Country House*, DG10 9RS. Tel: 0683-20210. **Tweedsmuir**. *Crook Inn*, ML12 6QN. Tel: 08997-272. **West Linton**. *Medwyn House*, Medwyn Road, EH46 7HB. Tel: 0968-60542.

Total distance 89m.—*15m* **Lockerbie**.—*4m* **Lochmaben**.—*14m* **Moffat**.—*28m* **Biggar**.—*12m* **West Linton**.—*16m* **Edinburgh**.

The bridge over the river Sark marks the border as agreed in 1552. Prior to this the tract between the Sark and Esk rivers, roughly 8m by 4m, was simply known as the Debatable Land, the lair of Borders freebooters. Gretna on the border, and Gretna Green a short way farther, are names instantly associated with elopements and romantic secret marriages.

For a long period English people seeking secret marriages had to resort to London's Fleet Prison where imprisoned clerics, having nothing to lose from breaking a law which was in any case ill defined, were happy to oblige for a fee. A law of 1573, however, required banns, a licence and marriage in a church, so from then on couples had to go to Scotland where marriages by declaration before two witnesses were legal. At Gretna and Gretna Green the ceremony was performed by the blacksmith, the ferryman, the tollgate keeper or almost anyone else convenient. After 1856 immediate marriage by declaration became illegal and one of the parties had to have a residential qualification, and in 1940 marriage by declaration ended altogether.

At **Gretna**, immediately beside the road, the *Old Toll House* (Tel: 0461-37439), the first house in Scotland, shows its Wedding Room, appropriately musty and Victorian and earlier with massive visitors' books and period pictures. A short way farther on, at **Gretna Green**, is the *Old Blacksmith's Shop* (Tel: 0461-38224), an altogether more ambitious place with the original anvil, a coach museum, a restaurant and tweed shops.

3m **Kirkpatrick Fleming**, where signs direct to *Bruce's Cave* (Tel: 04618-285), in which Bruce is said to have been hidden for about three months by Irving of Bonshaw, then owner of the adjacent house from which there was a passage to a small tower above the cave. At that time the only access was by swinging down by rope over the cliff, but today's visitor has a path. Whether it was here, or on Rathlin in Ireland, or at a choice of other places, that Bruce took new heart from watching the persistence of a spider must be a matter of personal judgement, but, Bruce apart, this cave half-way down the cliff face is interesting for having been hollowed out by prehistoric men whose tools have been found by the river below.—*2m* Beside the south-bound carriageway of A74 stands the *Merkland Cross*, a 9ft-high cross of 1494 believed to have been set up to commemorate the death of a Maxwell in battle.

4m **Ecclefechan** was the birthplace in 1795 of Thomas Carlyle, the essayist and historian. The *'Arched House'* (NTS. Tel: 05763-666), in which he was born (built by his father and uncle, both master masons), is now a museum with letters and relics. His tomb is in the churchyard. *Hoddom Castle*, 2m south west, a mainly 15C Maxwell stronghold, stands below Repentance Hill (with a watchtower), a name said to commemorate the remorse of a Lord Herries for having pulled down a church in order to build the castle. An alternative story is that he repented for having thrown his prisoners overboard during a storm while returning from a sea raid on the English coast.

B725 running east out of Ecclefechan soon reaches two Roman or earlier sites. *Burnswark* (920ft)—a hilltop confusion of earthworks representing a native fort and Roman camps—is reached by taking a minor road north off B725 almost immediately after crossing the railway just outside Ecclefechan. This minor road deteriorates into a track at the base of the hill more or less at the point at which the Romans' road angled north west. It is thought that the Romans may have besieged the native fort, afterwards using the hill and its surrounds as a battle-practice zone complete with camps. Some eight centuries later, in 937, a greater battle may have been fought here, Burnswark being one of several places claiming to be the site of the battle of Brunanburh at which the English king Athelstane routed an army of Scots, Norsemen and Irish, *Blatobulgium*, the other Roman site, is reached by continuing along B725 to Middlebie, a minor road south out of which crosses the site, a station occupied with breaks from 80 to 180.

6m **Lockerbie**, a small market town important since the 17C for its lamb fairs, and in modern context tragically associated with the destruction by terrorists in December 1988 of an American airliner, is historically notorious as the focus of bloody feuding between the Maxwells, who held the lower end of Annandale, and the Johnstones who controlled the central reaches. So savage indeed was the fighting and the feeling that the Johnstones adopted the custom of slashing the faces of defeated Maxwells, a practice which became known as the 'Lockerbie Lick'. Much of this feuding took place beside the Dryfe Water which angles down from the north east to join with the Kinnel Water and flow through a sandy, marshy tract to the north of A709 between Lockerbie and Lochmaben. Here the Johnstones decisively defeated the Maxwells (the latter losing 700 men including their chief) in revenge for the burning by the Maxwells of the Johnstones' Lochwood Castle (see below). And here, too, it is said, a lady of the Johnstones, while pretending to surrender, brained a Lord Maxwell with her castle key.

Approaching (*4m*) **Lochmaben**, A709 skirts the north shore of Castle Loch with, in a nature reserve on a promontory on the south shore, *Lochmaben Castle*, the early 14C successor of a castle of the Celtic-Norman De Brus (Bruce) family in which Robert Bruce may have been born (but see also Turnberry, Rte 15). Later, Lochmaben became a favourite residence of James IV and was also visited in 1565 by Mary, Queen of Scots, and her husband Darnley. Today, though, there survive only shattered creeper-clad remains surrounded by earthwork evidence of past grandeur. Castle Loch is only the largest of a group bordering this quiet, small town in which, in the main street, a statue of Bruce recalls the De Brus family association.

The **Forest of Ae**, some 7m north west of Lochmaben, forms a large irregular triangle measuring roughly 7m from north to south and the same from east to west. The map shows a scatter of intriguing names, such as Souter's Grave, Bruce's Well, King's Well, Glenae Tower and, at the south-east corner of the forest, Wallace's House, said to be the ruin of a tower held by Wallace in 1297. *Ae Village* is half-way along the forest's south fringe, just over 1m north of here being a FC parking and picnic area from which start forest walks.

B7020 followed north in *6m* reaches the minor crossroads of *Springwells*, 1m east of which on A74 the name Johnstonebridge recalls those who once held power here.—*3m Lochwood Castle*, just west of a crossroads and dating from the 15–16C, was long the principal centre of the Johnstones, whose earlier wooden 12C castle is represented by the motte just to the north. But 16C life at Lochwood was not peaceful. Occupied by the English between 1547–50, the castle was again attacked and burnt in 1585, this time by the neighbour Maxwells, an act bloodily avenged by the Johnstones beside the Dryfe (see above). Abandoned by the Johnstones in the early 18C, the castle fell into ruin, the scanty and flattened remains seen today being but the core of what was once an extensive complex.—*4m* **Beattock**, where Rte 10 continues north west on A74 while this Route takes A701 due north.

1m **Moffat** (2000 inhab. *Inf.*), lying well clear of A74 with its heavy traffic, is a quiet small town, probably best known for its main street, notable for being the broadest in Scotland, for the trees which break the street's centre line, and for the Colvin Fountain (1875) which with its pleasing figure of a ram emphasises the long-standing importance here of sheep farming. *Moffat Museum* (Tel: 0683-20868), in the south of the town opposite St. Andrew's church and in a building in turn cottages, workshop and bakery, tells the local story, this including the period during the 18 and 19C when Moffat's mineral well gave it the status of spa (today's Town Hall was built in 1827 as Baths Hall and Pump Room). Among Moffat's distinguished residents was James Macpherson, who worked as a tutor at Moffat House (now a hotel, but in Macpherson's time a residence of the Earl of Hopetoun) and in 1759 published his controversial translation of the Ossianic fragments, while a distinguished son was Lord Dowding (born 1882), Commander-in-Chief during the Battle of Britain and honoured by a memorial in Station Park. From Moffat A708 penetrates NE up the dark glen of Moffat Water to reach (10m) *Grey Mare's Tail* waterfall (see Rte 5, Yarrow Valley).

Beyond Moffat A701 climbs north to reach (*6m*) a sharp loop in the road which here skirts the precipitous rim of the **Devil's Beef Tub**, so named because it was in this vast, gloomy hollow which forms the head of Annandale that the Johnstones hid the cattle they had lifted in raids on their neighbours, notably the Maxwells. In 1746, it is said, a follower of the Young Pretender here escaped his guards by diving into the Beef Tub's mists, but the roadside stone near here recalls one who was less fortunate, John Hunter, who in 1685 was shot as a Covenanter and whose body now lies in the churchyard at Tweedsmuir. About 1m farther on there is another memorial, this one at the spot where in 1831, and in a blizzard, the mail coach lost the road and overturned, killing both the driver and his companion.

A short way beyond, the road breasts the watershed with, to the east, *Tweed's Well* (1500ft), the source of the Tweed, then, accompanied now by the quickly maturing stream, begins to fall to (*10m*) the hamlet of *Tweedsmuir*. Here there is a Border Collie and Shepherd Centre (Tel: 08997-267), housed in what is said to have been the smallest school in Scotland (1900–37) and today offering a photographic exhibition as also sheepdog handling demonstrations. *Talla Reservoir*, 1m south east, is a long artificial loch filling a sombre narrow cleft of a valley overhung by steep bare mountains gashed by rocky corries. The small road skirting the north shore of the reservoir scrambles steeply through remote and wild country to drop down to St. Mary's Loch (see Rte 5, Yarrow Valley).—*6m* (from Tweedsmuir) *Rachan Mill*.

B712, leading east, almost at once crosses the Tweed at a spot called Merlindale, one of the many legendary sites of Merlin's grave but one strengthened in its claim by Thomas the Rhymer who foretold that 'when Tweed and Powsail meet at Merlin's grave, England and Scotland shall one monarch have'. And, it seems, on the day of the coronation of James VI/I, the Tweed did here overflow into the little Powsail stream. *Tinnis Castle*, just beyond and reached by a short path, is the ruin of an early 16C stronghold of the Tweedies. Two miles east again is *Dawyck Botanic Garden* (Tel: 07216-254) with rare trees and shrubs and woodland walks. A chapel in the grounds was designed by William Burn.

The Tweed now curves away eastwards while this Route continues north for just over *1m* to reach **Broughton** in which is the *John Buchan Centre* (Tel: 0899-21050). Housed in what was the United Free Church, the centre is devoted to this distinguished Scottish statesman (1875–1940) who as John Buchan thrilled a generation and more with his gripping fiction, and then, as the 1st Lord Tweedsmuir, went on to become Governor General of Canada.

At Broughton this Route bears west along B7016 for (*5m*) **Biggar** (2000 inhab. *Inf.*), where, thanks in large part to the vigour of the Biggar Museum Trust (Tel: 0899-21050), the attractions awaiting the visitor well exceed what might be expected of a town so relatively small. First there is the *Gladstone Court Museum*, in which the visitor can wander around the shops, a bank, a schoolroom, a telephone exchange, a library and much else of the 19C. Nearby, in Burn Braes, *Greenhill Covenanters' House*, once a sadly neglected 17C farmhouse, decaying some 10m away from Biggar, was rescued, re-erected and restored here to serve as a museum of local life during the 17C, some emphasis being placed on Covenanting times. Also nearby is the *Moat Park Heritage Centre*, occupying a now redundant church and, largely by means of models, telling the story of the upper Clyde and Tweed valleys from the geology of volcanic and glacial days up to recent times. Other displays feature agriculture, Church, school and natural history. Lastly there is the *Gasworks Museum* (Tel: 031-225 7534, Dept. of Technology), site of the Biggar Gas Light Company which served the town from 1839 to 1973. Now classified as an Ancient Monument and operated as an outstation of Edinburgh's Royal Museum of Scotland, the buildings (essentially major reconstruction of 1914) serve as a museum of the coal-gas industry. Finally, Biggar was from 1899 until after the end of the Second World War associated with Albion Motors which grew to become a major manufacturer of commercial vehicles. The company's archives are held by the Museum Trust and a motor museum is planned.

Beside the *Church of St. Mary*, the last pre-Reformation foundation in Scotland (by Lord Fleming, 1546), are the graves of Gledstanes or Gladstones, ancestors of William Gladstone, the statesman, whose grandfather left Biggar for Leith in c 1756. Only one small tower remains of *Boghall Castle* ($\frac{1}{2}$m south), one time seat of the Flemings. On A72, 1$\frac{1}{2}$m south west of Biggar, there is a particularly good motte.

Generally following the course of a Roman road, A702 in *12m* arrives at **West Linton** below the south-east slopes of the Pentland Hills. Although today something of a lost little place, West Linton was once the rough and lively gathering place for drovers accompanying their herds across the Pentlands' pass of Cauld Stane Slap (1500ft), a period celebrated today by the annual Whipman festivities in June. But West Linton was also once famed for the skill of its masons, two interesting examples of whose work survive, both associated with the Gifford family. *Lady Gifford's Well*, with the lady's figure on top, was carved in 1666, while, roughly opposite, a curious bas-relief (1660 and 1678) on a house shows figures representing 'the six progenitors of James Gifford, his awne portract and eldest sone'.

A702 continues north east immediately below the **Pentland Hills**. Running for some 16m south west from Edinburgh, these hills are four to five miles wide and, with their streams and reservoirs, many signed paths and wide views, offer some exhilarating upland walking. The highest point is Scaldlaw (1898ft), and the higher ground generally is easily reached either by car to Castlelaw, by various paths on foot, or by means of the chairlift at Hillend.

The more gradual and less interesting west slopes can be seen from A70, the direct road between Edinburgh and Lanark. Along this road, at Currie (5m from central Edinburgh), *Rosebank Open Farm* (Tel: 031-449-4401) should with its many animals attract the children, while, 2m farther south at Balerno, *Malleny Garden* (NTS. Tel: 031-226-5922) is best known for its shrub roses and the National Bonsai Collection. The house (no adm.) dates from c 1635.

6m (from West Linton) *Silverburn*, just beyond which a path climbs between Scaldlaw and Carnethy Hill to reach Loganlea Reservoir, thence dropping to Balerno and Malleny House, some 6m from Silverburn.—*2m* The name *Rullion Green*, a farm off the left of the road, recalls the battle here of 1666 at which General Tam Dalyell (See Rte 9, The Binns) decisively defeated the Covenanters who were marching on Edinburgh. Less than a mile beyond, a small road ascends to *Glencorse Reservoir*, the water of which covers the ancient church of St. Katherine in the Hopes, perhaps built by Sir William Sinclair in gratitude for his successful wager with Bruce (see Rte 6, Roslin Chapel). Beyond, again, another small road is the approach to *Castlelaw*, an Iron Age hill-fort of three concentric ramparts, within which there is an earth-house.—*4m* (from Rullion Green) *Hillend*, a Country Park (Tel: 031-445-3383) with one of the longest dry-ski slopes in Britain and a chairlift (open to non-skiers) to a point offering views over Edinburgh.—*4m* central **Edinburgh**, see Rte 18.

8   Edinburgh to Glasgow via Bathgate

There are four main approaches to Glasgow from Edinburgh, these being, from north to south:

1. Via Linlithgow and Falkirk. See Rtes 9 and 22.

2. Via Bathgate. Described below as this Rte 8. (A8. A89).

3. Motorway M8. Of no interest.

4. Via Mid Calder (A71). The few places of interest are included below as diversions from this Rte 8.

SOME HOTELS. **Edinburgh**. See Rte 18. **Uphall**. *Houston House*, EH52 6JS. Tel: 0506-853831. **Livingston**. *Hilton*, Almondvale, EH54 6QB. Tel: 0506-31222. **Airdrie**. *Tudor*, 39 Alexander Street. Tel: 0236-64144. **Glasgow**. See Rte 19.

Total distance 40m.—*10m* **Broxburn**.—*8m* **Bathgate**.—*22m* **Glasgow**.

Edinburgh is left by A8 through *Corstorphine* (see Rte 18), 1m beyond which, at Gogar, a road drops 1m south for *Suntrap* (NTS. Tel: 031-339-7283), a gardening advice centre catering primarily for owners of small gardens. The main road passes south of Edinburgh (Turnhouse) Airport and Ingliston, the latter the site of the Royal Highland Show and also home to the *Scottish Agricultural Museum* (Tel: 031-225-7534) covering many aspects of rural life including farming, crafts and both home and social life. A short way beyond, a road leading south soon reaches Ratho on the Union Canal (see also Rte 9, Linlithgow) where the *Canal Centre* (Tel: 031-333-1320) offers a visitor centre and boat trips.

A8 crosses the motorway to become A89 and reach (*10m* from central Edinburgh) *Broxburn*, a short way north west of which is *Niddry Castle*

(Tel: 0506-890174), the 15C–16C tower-house home of the Setons, and later the Hopes, which after centuries of neglect until it was no more than a forlorn and blackened keep, has now been impressively restored. It was to this castle of her supporter Lord Seton, that Mary, Queen of Scots, rode after her adventurous escape from Loch Leven, the story being that next morning she came out to receive the acclaim of the local people with her long auburn hair flowing undressed in the breeze, so eager was she to show herself.—*2m Uphall.*

From Uphall a road drops south to **Livingston-Mid Calder**; it was at Calder House that the first Protestant Communion was administered by John Knox in 1556 (see picture in John Knox House, Edinburgh) and here also Chopin visited in 1848. *Almondell Country Park* (Tel: 0506-882254), 1m east off A71, is a wooded and riverside country park with a visitor centre. Off A705, to the west of Livingston, *Almond Valley Heritage Centre* (Tel: 0506-414957) is a restored 18C farm steading and mill with a countryside museum, attractions for children, a riverside nature trail and a feature on the Scottish shale-oil industry. (James 'Paraffin' Young, born at West Calder and the son of a Glasgow joiner, in 1851 established at Bathgate the world's first commercial oil works, using oil shale and starting an industry which sold oil lamps worldwide.)

6m **Bathgate**, a mainly industrial town, was the birthplace of James Simpson, a pioneer of anaesthesia, who first used chloroform in 1847. The *Bennie Museum* (Tel: 0506-634944), in Mansefield Street, features both James Simpson and James 'Paraffin' Young. From Bathgate there is a choice between continuing direct to Airdrie and Glasgow (A89, of no interest) or making a northerly loop (adding some 3m) across the Bathgate Hills, rewarding for their views and with two worthwhile sites, namely prehistoric Cairnpapple Hill and medieval Torphichen Preceptory. This northerly loop is described immediately below.

NORTHERLY LOOP. *°Cairnpapple Hill* (AM. Tel: 031-244-3101), 2m north of Bathgate, is reached by B792 and a minor road leading off north east at Ballencrief Toll just clear of Bathgate. Here, on this isolated open hill with superb all-round views, primitive man worshipped his god or gods and buried his dead over the immense span of perhaps 2500 years, from around 2500 BC to the 1C AD. Five archaeological phases have been identified. Ritual of some probably never-to-be-known form, but perhaps associated with cremation and observed within a henge with boulders, ditch and bank, seems to have been the primary purpose of the Neolithic people of the first two phases, say 2500 to 1650 BC. Then in the third phase (Bronze Age, c 1600 BC) a large cairn was erected and the emphasis shifted from ritual to burial, this continuing down through the Bronze and into the Iron Age centuries. This great cairn was built within and on top of the earlier complex, the original henge stones being either removed or perhaps incorporated. A fourth phase (c 1300 BC) saw urn cremations built into the by now enlarged cairn, while a fifth (possibly early Iron Age) saw four elongated graves cut into the stone mass.

Today, while much of the original can still be seen, the site (archaeologically perhaps the most important in Scotland) has been imaginatively reconstructed, the whole being made clearer to the visitor by means of a model and a taped commentary.

Torphichen Preceptory (AM. Tel: 031-244-3101), 1m north west of Cairnpapple, was founded in 1153 by the Knights of St. John of Jerusalem as the preceptory (or community) that was to be their Scottish centre. With all the air of an elegant small castle, what remains today is partly ruin dating from the 13–15C and partly the 18C parish church built over the original Norman nave. This site is not only an outstanding and attractive example of the way in which during the 15C defensive features had to be incorporated even in church architecture, but it also provides an interesting exhibition illustrating the history of the founding Order. Torphichen village was the birthplace of Henry Bell (1760), pioneer of the steamboat.—From Torphichen A89 may be rejoined in 10m at Caldercruix by way of B8047 and B825.

10m (from Bathgate by A89) *Caldercruix.*—*2m* **Airdrie**, marking the start of Glasgow's eastward industrial spread, within which is (*5m*) **Coatbridge**, with, in West Canal Street, the *Summerlee Heritage Trust* (Tel: 0236-31261), a museum of industrial and social history with working machinery in reconstructed contemporary buildings. The complex includes ironworks (1835), an electric tramway, steam machinery and a restored stretch of canal.—*5m* central **Glasgow**, see Rte 19.

9   Edinburgh to Stirling via South Queensferry, Linlithgow and Falkirk

A90 and B924 to South Queensferry. A904 and A803 to Linlithgow. A706 to Bo'ness. A904 to Grangemouth. B904 and A803 to Polmont and Falkirk. A9 to Stirling.—Flat and agricultural mixed with a central core of urban driving between Linlithgow and Larbert to the north of Falkirk. Some views along and across the Firth of Forth.

SOME HOTELS. **Edinburgh**. See Rte 18. **South Queensferry**. *Forth Bridges Moat House*, EH30 9SF. Tel: 031-331-1199. **Linlithgow**. *Star and Garter*, High Street, EH49 7AB. Tel: 0506-845485. **Grangemouth**. *Grange Manor*, Glensburgh Road, FK3 8XJ. Tel: 0324-474836. **Polmont**. *Inchyra Grange*, Grange Road, FK2 0YB. Tel: 0324-711911. **Falkirk**. *Stakis Park*, Camelon Road, Arnothill, FK1 5RY. Tel: 0324-28331.

Total distance 38m.—*8m* **South Queensferry**.—*10m* **Linlithgow**.—*5m* **Grangemouth**.—*5m* **Falkirk**.—*10m* **Stirling**.

Edinburgh (see Rte 18) is left by Queensferry Road (A90) which in rather over *4m* reaches a roundabout (*Barnton*), feeding in A902 from the south. Here the smaller road north in 1m reaches the quiet and most attractive village of ***Cramond**, standing beside the Firth of Forth at the mouth of the little river Almond; a place for Roman and medieval remains, restored 18C houses, and pleasant walks up the Almond and in both directions along the Forth, to the west through Dalmeny Park to the Forth Bridges, to the east to Lauriston Castle. The *Roman Fort*, of which the foundations are laid out, is by the church of 1656. Built in c 142 to guard the harbour, this fort may well have been used by Septimius Severus as a base for his punitive expedition of 208 against north-east Scotland. A good display plan and some admirable illustrations bring this place to life, and objects excavated here are on display in Edinburgh's Huntly House Museum. Just east of the fort stands a 15C tower, thought once to have belonged to the bishops of Dunkeld.

A short way beyond the Barnton roundabout A90 crosses the Almond by Cramond Bridge, just downstream of which is *Cramond Old Bridge* (1619), which, standing on the site of an older bridge, has a curious link with James V who was attacked here by footpads. The local miller, Jack Howieson, rescued his king and brought him water, the king in gratitude granting land to the family on the quaint condition that they always had a basin and ewer ready whenever a sovereign should pass. Such were in fact offered to George IV in 1822, to Queen Victoria in 1842, to George V in 1927, and in 1952 to the present Queen.

In a little under *2m* beyond Cramond Bridge B924 forks right, just beyond the fork and to the west being *Dalmeny Church, dating from the 12C and one of the most satisfying examples in Scotland of a small Norman church. Of special note are the south door with its arch of double mouldings and interlaced arcade of five arches; the stone-vaulted choir and apse, both in their original state and showing two sculpted circular arches; and the round-headed windows with their typical chevron mouldings. The west tower, which collapsed in the 15C, has been rebuilt, and on the north side of the nave an addition has been made for the Rosebery Aisle built in 1671 by Sir Archibald Primrose. The Primrose (Rosebery) family have for over three centuries been the owners of **Dalmeny House** (Tel: 031-331-1888) standing in its park beside the Firth of Forth. Built in 1815 by William Wilkins, the house is not only the first but also one of the grandest examples of Scottish neo-Gothic, a style and splendour represented inside by a fine hammer-beam hall. The paintings, furniture, tapestries, porcelain and much else are in keeping, especially notable being the Rosebery Collection, reflecting the many interests—historical, literary, artistic, racing and political—of the earls of Rosebery; the collection of 18C portraits by Reynolds, Gainsborough and Lawrence; the Mentmore Collection of 18C furniture, porcelain and other works of art; and a Napoleon room, with some interesting relics, including the furniture the Emperor used when in power and the simpler pieces he had to accept on St. Helena.

2m **South Queensferry** somehow manages to retain a character of its own despite the dominating presence of the two great bridges far above. The town owes its name to Queen Margaret, wife of Malcolm Canmore, who frequently passed through here when journeying between Edinburgh and her palace and abbey across the Forth at Dunfermline. This was in about 1070, so there was a ferry here for at least 900 years, until the opening of the rail bridge in 1890 sounded the first

The famed Forth Bridge of 1890 contrasting with the modern (1964) Road Bridge behind

warning and that of the road bridge in 1964 finally closed the long chapter. Today, inevitably, it is the two lofty bridges which first force themselves on the visitor's attention, though something of the town's past can be learnt from a visit to the small *South Queensferry Museum* in the Burgh Chambers (Tel: 031-331-1590).

The *Rail Bridge*, the achievement of Sir John Fowler between 1883–90, was one of the great engineering feats of its day. The length of the bridge proper is just over one mile; the railway track is 157ft above the water; there are two spans of 1710ft each and two of 690ft; and the painted surface represents 135 acres. Below the bridge, in mid Firth, the island of Inchgarvie has a 15C fort which held out against Cromwell in 1650 and was rebuilt in 1779 when the American privateer John Paul Jones was in the offing.—In 1964 the Queen opened the *Road Bridge* (toll, but free for pedestrians and cyclists). The bridge proper is almost 2000 yards long, the central span 3300ft and the side spans 1340ft each. The towers are 512ft high.

3m ***Hopetoun House** (Tel: 031-331-2451), superbly situated in parkland beside the Firth of Forth, can be reached from Queensferry by way of the small shoreside road, or from A904 by a turn north 2m west of that road's departure from A90. If the two Forth bridges represent the constructive genius of the 19 and 20C, then this, one of the most splendid of Scotland's mansions, surely represents that of the 18C; more particularly that of William Adam and his son John, who between 1721 and 1754 rebuilt and enlarged the original structure of about 1700 which had been put up by William Bruce for the 1st Earl of Hopetoun, ancestor of the present Marquis of Linlithgow. And it was John Adam who was largely responsible for the interior decoration of the main state apartments (especially noteworthy being the yellow drawing room and the ballroom) which today house a distinguished collection of paintings by, amongst others, Rubens, Raeburn and Canaletto as well as portraits by Gainsborough and Scottish artists. Additionally the house offers a museum of costumes and other bygones; a roof platform with Forth views; and in the stables an exhibition devoted to 'Horse and Man in Lowland Scotland'.

In the park will be found a flock of rare four-horned black St. Kilda sheep, and also two deer herds; red deer in the North Park, reached by a woodland nature trail, and fallow deer in the South Park in which there is also a picturesque ruined 17C tower.

From Hopetoun it is convenient to visit the secluded church of *Abercorn*, ½m west of the house and reached by an unclassified road. Founded in the 5C, and later (681–85) the seat of a short-lived Northumbrian bishopric, the church as seen today dates in part from the 12C (a blocked Norman doorway), but suffered from overrestoration which amounted almost to reconstruction in 1579 and 1893. To be seen here are a splendid 8C Anglian cross-shaft with interlaced pattern, an ancient hog-backed tombstone, and the burial place of the colourful Thomas (Tam) Dalyell of the Binns, though those who prefer legend to fact will argue that his body was in reality carried off by the Devil.

3m The **House of the Binns** (NTS. Tel: 050-683-4255), just north of A904, derives its rather curious name from the old Scots word 'bynnis', meaning twin hills, a reference to two such hills which slope up to the east. This old Scots name well reflects the antiquity of this estate, documentary evidence of whose existence reaches back to 1335, although it was not until 1612 that house and lands were bought by Thomas Dalyell, a cadet of an ancient family, the senior line of which later achieved the earldom of Carnwath. This Thomas Dalyell accompanied James VI/I to London, made his fortune and returned to build this house, then as now a fine example of a comfortable 17C home developed from a 15C nucleus. A western range was added later in the 17C, and the main fronts were remodelled in the 19C, at which time also (1826) the tower on the hill was erected (paid for with money won in a wager), but, despite these changes, the house remains essentially the creation of the man whose initials still so ubiquitously intertwine with those of his wife, Janet Bruce. Fine carpets, antique furniture and valuable china are all on display here, but far and away the most notable feature is the elaborate *plasterwork, much of it dating from 1630 in anticipation of a visit by Charles I. The park offers a woodland walk to a viewpoint above the Firth of Forth.

The most colourful member of the Dalyell family was 'General Tam' (1599–1685), son of Thomas. A staunch Royalist, he was captured at Worcester, escaped from the Tower of London, and then served the Tsar in Russia until recalled by Charles II at the Restoration. In 1666 he soundly defeated the Covenanters at Rullion Green on the Pentland Hills, and in 1681 he raised the Scots Greys. Though legend insists that his body was carried off by the Devil, his tomb, with or without contents, is in Abercorn church.

Blackness Castle (AM. Tel: 031-244-3101), occupying a Forth promontory 1m north of the House of the Binns, could scarcely provide a greater contrast in situation, appearance or purpose. Built in the 15C, this was once one of the most important fortresses in Scotland and one of the four which under the Articles of Union (1707) was to be left fortified. In Covenanting times Blackness served as a prison, and during the 1870s as a powder magazine.

4m (from the Binns) **Linlithgow** (9000 inhab. *Inf.*), chartered by David I and probably from at least that time a royal residence, is today best known for the well-preserved ruins of Scotland's most splendid fortified palace, as also for one of the country's most interesting churches.

History. The history of the town and palace are interwoven. After David I's charter Linlithgow became a place of some importance. England's Edward I camped here in 1298 before the battle at Falkirk against Wallace, wintered here in 1301, and in 1302 built a tower, later to become incorporated into the palace planned and partly built by James I over 100 years later. The capture of this tower in 1313 by a handful of Scots concealed in a load of hay is one of the many romantic feats that abound in Scottish history. Here in 1513 Queen Margaret waited in vain for her husband, James IV, to return from Flodden. James V was born in the palace the year before this, and his daughter, Mary, Queen of Scots, in 1542. Edinburgh University moved temporarily to Linlithgow in 1545–46 when the plague was raging in the capital. Charles I was the last monarch to sleep in the palace, in 1633 at a time when he was considering making Linlithgow the Scottish capital, and from 1651–59 the town was garrisoned by Cromwell. The Young Pretender visited the palace during the '45, and the following year, when occupied by government troops, it was burned, probably accidentally. In 1914 George V held a court here.

**Linlithgow Palace (AM. Tel: 031-244-3101) is approached through a Gateway erected by James V in c 1535. On the 19C parapet are the badges of four orders of knighthood to which James belonged: the Garter of England (three lions), St. Andrew of Scotland (one lion), the Golden Fleece of Spain (castle and lions), and St. Michael of France (fleur de lys).

Of any residence David I may have had here there is now no trace, the oldest visibly surviving part of the palace being the tower at the southwest angle built by Edward I in 1302. For over a century this was probably all there was, until in 1425 James I laid out the plans from which would grow the great palace beside the loch. The west side of the quadrangle dates partly from this time, but the south and east sides, architecturally the richest, are mid 16C (James V), while the north, which collapsed in 1607, is a reconstruction of 1618–30.

The Quadrangle is the heart of the palace, with round towers at the angles and an octagonal tower of 1620 on the north side. Above the modern entrance (south side) can be seen part of an Annunciation, while to the east is the palace's earlier massive entrance across the moat, which should of course be pictured with a drawbridge. Above this entry there are three canopied niches, once housing statues. In the centre stands an ornate fountain, a wedding present from James V to Mary of Guise, said on that glittering occasion to have run with wine.

Around the quadrangle everything is on the grand scale, the chief apartments being on the first floor. Here, along the east, stretches the Great Hall, 94ft long with tall windows, a huge fireplace and ornamental mantelpiece, and a curious kind of side-passage within the inner wall. Elsewhere halls and rooms, notably their fireplaces, are in proportion and, though roofless, intact enough to enable something of the life of their times to be imagined. In the south wing are the Chapel, which has five lancets, and another hall. The Royal Apartments, along the west side, include the King's Hall, the Presence Chamber with a curious horizontal window, and the Bedchamber. Two recesses in the north wall represent the royal oratories. The room in which Mary of Guise gave birth to Mary, Queen of Scots, was probably in the north wing, later rebuilt; and at the top of the north-west tower a little octagonal turret known as Queen Margaret's Bower may have been the place where Margaret, doubtless all too well aware of the ghostly warning conveyed to her husband in St. Michael's church (see below), so anxiously awaited the news from Flodden.

The *Church of St. Michael*, adjacent to the palace, is the largest pre-Reformation parish church in Scotland and a good example of the Scottish Decorated style.

Consecrated in 1242, the church was largely rebuilt in 1424 after a fire. The nave is the oldest part, the choir (c 1497) and tower being of later date and the apse not completed until 1531. Until 1821 the lofty, pinnacled tower carried an open stonework crown, added by James IV, this being replaced in 1964 (by helicopter) by a modern work (Geoffrey Clarke). Beneath the tower there is a notable doorway, and there is another entrance on the south side under an elegant porch with a priest's chamber and an unusual oriel above it. The image of St. Michael at the south-west angle is the only image to have survived the Reformation.

Inside the church the broad, handsome nave comprises five bays, with pointed arches resting on clustered pillars. The triforium and clerestory, each with a main arch enclosing two smaller lights, deserve attention, as does also the church's varied and graceful window tracery, especially that of the Flamboyant window in the south transept. It was in this transept, known as St. Catherine's Aisle, that, just before Flodden, an apparition warned James IV against war with England. At the end of the church is a three-sided apse of tall windows and tracery that is surprisingly severe.

Within Linlithgow town there are a few 17C houses, notably *West Port House* (c 1600) at the west end of High Street, while, near the town hall, the *Cross Well* with its quaint figures is an 1807 reproduction of an earlier fountain said to have been here during the reign of James V.—The Union Canal, opened in 1822 and originally running from Edinburgh to join the Forth–Clyde Canal (see below), crosses the southern part of the town. Here, today, the *Canal Museum* (Tel: 0506-842575), housed in stables of 1822, shows records and relics and provides an audio-visual display, while for those in search of a closer nostalgia there are cruises on the 'Victoria', a replica of a 19C boat.

From Linlithgow A803 provides the direct approach to (7m) Falkirk, but this Route takes a northerly loop through Kinneil, not to be missed by anyone with an interest in James Watt's engineering research, and the petro-chemical town of Grangemouth.

3m **Bo'ness** is a contraction of Borrowstounness. *Kinneil House* (AM. Tel: 031-244-3101), on the west of the town and just south of A904, is the tall shell of a 16–17C fortified seat of the dukes of Hamilton. The building shows outstanding contemporary wall and ceiling paintings, but, apart from these, is perhaps less interesting than its grounds, now a public park containing a small Roman fort and the remains of the outhouse in which in 1765 James Watt developed his steam engine (by arrangement with the then occupier of the house, the owner of the Carron Ironworks, who was financing Watt's research). Alongside, an iron cylinder, cast to Watt's design for a local mine pump, was set up in 1946 as a memorial. The *Bo'ness Museum* (Tel: 0324-24911), nearby in converted 17C stables, is devoted mainly to local industrial history, but also tells about the Roman fort, while, for rail enthusiasts, the *Bo'ness and Kinneil Railway* (Tel: 0506-822298) operates steam over $3\frac{1}{2}$ miles, using locomotives and rolling stock representing various former Scottish railway companies.

2m **Grangemouth** (24,500 inhab.), a large industrial complex with extensive docks and oil-refining and chemical works, would never claim to be a tourist's town. Yet with its massed oil tanks and often pervasive petro-chemical atmosphere it has an individual character and sense of purpose that can hardly be ignored. Founded in 1777 at the east end of the Forth–Clyde Canal (see below), Grangemouth grew during the 19C but remained relatively unimportant until the 1940s when its expansion really began. Today Scotland's principal petrochemical centre, Grangemouth's oil tanks are fed by North Sea oil pipeline. The *Grangemouth Museum* (Tel: 0324-483291 or 24911), in the Victoria Library, Bo'ness Road, is mainly concerned with the story of the canals of central Scotland, but also displays material on the 'Charlotte Dundas' (see immediately below) and on modern Grangemouth.

The **Forth–Clyde Canal**, now long commercially disused, was built by John Smeaton in 1768–90 and in large part still runs for some 38m roughly below the line of the Romans' Antonine Wall (see below). The canal started at Grangemouth, crossed Falkirk (from where the opening of the Union Canal in 1822 provided a link into Edinburgh), and ended on the Clyde at Bowling where its basin is now a marina. The tug 'Charlotte Dundas', engined by William Symington and the world's first practical steamboat, appeared on the canal in 1802. For canal cruises Tel: 0324-612-415.

From Grangemouth there is a choice of approaches to Falkirk, but this Route takes B904 which crosses the M9 motorway to join A803 at Polmont. A short way to the west, and immediately south of A803 between the road and a high-rise housing estate (Callendar Park), a good length of Antonine Wall ditch will be found.

5m (from Grangemouth) **Falkirk** (37,500 inhab. *Inf.*) is an industrial town, known historically for two battles. In the first, fought on the south side of Callendar Wood in 1298, Edward I, advancing from his encampment at Linlithgow, defeated Wallace. In the second (January 1746), at Bantaskyne, just 1m west of the first, the retreating Young Pretender inflicted a severe repulse on the pursuing government forces. *Falkirk Museum* (Tel: 0324-24911), at 15 Orchard Street, covers the archaeology and history of the district, with some emphasis on local pottery and foundry products.

The Romans' ANTONINE WALL, four good sections of which are in or close to Falkirk, was built between the Firth of Forth at Bridgeness, 1m east of Bo'ness, and Old Kilpatrick on the Clyde, a length of 37 miles. Its date is c 140, its building resulting from a decision by the Emperor Antoninus Pius to abandon Hadrian's Wall across northern England, built only ten years earlier, and adopt a more forward policy towards Scotland. The work was entrusted to the II, VI and XX Legions under the orders of Quintus Lollius Urbicus, governor of Britain. Unlike Hadrian's Wall, which is of stone, the Antonine was a turf rampart on a stone base, with a ditch to the north and a military road along the south side. Spoil from the ditch was tipped to form an outer obstacle, and there were forts about every two miles. The wall was abandoned by the end of the 2C, possibly as early as 163. Inscriptions, sculptures, distance slabs (erected by the legionaries to mark the completion of their length) and other finds can be seen in the Edinburgh Royal Museum of Scotland (Queen Street) and in the Hunterian Museum in Glasgow. Sections of the wall survive at several points along its length.

The two sites in Falkirk are the ditch at *Callendar Park* mentioned above, and another particularly well preserved length of ditch known as *Watling Lodge*. This latter, in the west suburbs of Falkirk, is reached by turning south off A803 through Camelon to cross the Forth–Clyde Canal for Tamfourhill Road (B816).

Rough Castle, by far the most extensive and best preserved fortified site, is on the hills 1½m from Bonnybridge (4m west of Falkirk) from where there are signs. The road reaches the wall, the line of which it follows to a car park, 300 yards east of which is the complex of earthworks of about one acre which makes up the fort. The fort's rampart abuts that of the wall itself, and the military road runs through the fort. Although little else is now recognisable, the barracks are known to have been to the north of the road, while to the south lay, in succession, the commander's house, the granary and the headquarters buildings. Earthworks well seen just east of the fort are the remains of an annexe with baths.—*Seabegs Wood*, beside B816 2½m west of Rough Castle, shows a stretch of rampart, ditch, mound and military road.—For some other good and accessible Antonine Wall sites, see Rte 20, *Duntocher*; Rte 21, *Bearsden*; Rte 22, *Castlecary*.

Leaving Falkirk A9 passes to the west of *Stenhousemuir*, a name recalling the great days of droving when cattle fairs were held on the 'muir' monthly between spring and autumn. Immense herds of livestock crowded here from far and near, including cattle from the Western Isles, sheep from Ross and Sutherland, even ponies from Shetland, and after sale found their way farther south by the great drove roads.

8m **Bannockburn**, a name as resounding in Scotland's history as it is inglorious in England's. The actual site of the battle (1314) in which Robert Bruce so spectacularly defeated Edward II is disputed, but most maps seem agreed on an area, about 1m north of today's town, between the railway and A905. For the *Bannockburn Memorial and Information Centre*, 1m west, see Rte 23.—*2m* **Stirling**, see Rte 23.

II SOUTH WEST

Lying to the side of the popular through-roads, and too often thought to have little to offer scenically, the South West is a district relatively little visited. Yet much of Scotland's story has its roots here and the visitor willing to make the detour will be the richer for it. Those heading for Highland Scotland may then use the interesting and scenic island of *Arran* as a stepping-stone across the Clyde estuary to Kintyre. Alternatively the island of *Bute*, with its unique round castle at Rothesay, or the car ferry from *Gourock* to *Dunoon*, can both serve as gateways to the North by way of the Cowal peninsula.

Scenically much of the inland South West may be unexciting moorland, but *Galloway Forest Park*, the nearest approach in southern Scotland to Highland grandeur, is a superb 200 square miles with 10 summits of over 2000ft, while along the *Solway* coast there is a rolling, wooded and pastoral countryside, which with its neat small towns, many of them 17–18C in character, offers pleasant and undemanding touring; and the Firth itself, a shallow estuary of sandy flats, bays and beaches, for much of its length untouched by a main road, has many lost and unspoilt corners. The *West Coast* is bolder and more incidental, with views across to the Clyde islands. But though superficially more scenic than Solway, this coast loses through being hugged by a busy main road linking a string of sometimes undistinguished resorts.

Historically the early South West took shape as the Kingdom of Strathclyde to the north and independent Galloway to the south, while the coasts were subject to Norse raiding and settlement. In 1034 Duncan of Strathclyde succeeded Malcolm II as king of the rest of Scotland and Strathclyde was thus absorbed as the single Kingdom of Scotland was born.

Aspects of the South West

Today's traveller will hear many references to Galloway, the name still used for the ancient territory which once embraced virtually the whole of the southern part of the South West. He will also soon become aware that the South West was the cradle of Christianity in Scotland; the cradle too, through the early struggles of Wallace and Bruce, of Scotland's fight for independence; the land through which Mary, Queen of Scots, made a royal progress in 1563 and a desperate flight five years later; and the scene, during the following century, of the strife into which Christianity slid and under which the Covenanters so bitterly suffered. Finally, in the mid 18C, the South West was the home of Scotland's national poet, Robert Burns. Each of these aspects is discussed individually below.

Galloway. Until the end of the 12C Galloway comprised the whole of the South West roughly west of Nithsdale and south of the river Doon (Loch Doon to Ayr). The district immediately south of the Doon, then, as now, known as *Carrick*, broke away at the end of the 12C, leaving, as Galloway, what would later become the counties of Wigtown and Kirkcudbright. The name derives from 'Gallwyddel' ('stranger Gaels'), a term anciently applied to the Celts of this region. These were an independent people, who fraternised with the Norse raiders when they began to settle towards the end of the 9C, and who refused formal allegiance to any Scots Crown until the reign of Malcolm Canmore (c 1060). Even then Galloway maintained a partial independence under its own lords until the death of the last of these in 1234, and thereafter the tradition still lived on in the power and lawlessness of the great families. In the 14C the chief such families were the Balliols and Comyns, bitter enemies of the Bruces, earls of Carrick. In c 1370 the lordship of Galloway was obtained by the Douglas family who exercised a haughty dominion until 1455 when, by reducing *Threave Castle*, James II crushed their power. Galloway then passed fully to the Crown, though, as elsewhere in Scotland, there were hereditary sheriffs until 1747.

Christianity. Christianity was brought to Scotland in c 400 when St. Ninian built his church at *Whithorn*, and its story in the South West can be followed in stone from soon after that until modern times. Although traces have been found of what may have been St. Ninian's church, these can no longer be seen. What can be seen are Early Christian memorial stones, surviving as evidence of how Christianity established itself and spread. Examples are the *Latinus Stone* (450) at Whithorn; the *Kirkmadrine Stones* (5–12C) on the Rhinns of Galloway, and the cross at *Ruthwell*, near Dumfries. Possibly the earliest church building still surviving, though only as foundations, is the 10 or 11C *Chapel Finian*, but of the work of the immediately following centuries there are many examples, starting with humble chapels and flowering into the great medieval abbeys. Of the first category, mention may be made of the 12–13C *Chapel of St. Ninian* at Isle of Whithorn and the fragment of 12C *St. Kentigern's* at Lanark, where Wallace may have been married. Of the great abbey churches, though, there is more to be seen and the South West is rich in these. The best are *Sweetheart*, with its touching story of Devorguilla Balliol and her husband's heart; *Dundrennan*, where Mary, Queen of Scots, last slept in Scotland; *Whithorn Priory*, built on the site of St. Ninian's church; *Glenluce, Crossraguel*, and *Paisley* with its early Stuart tombs. There followed the Reformation and the building of Greenock's *West Kirk*, the first post-Reformation church to be built in Scotland, now known also for its Burne-Jones and Rossetti stained glass.

Wars of Independence. Wallace and Bruce both started their patriotic struggles in Scotland's South West and, though no physical remains are to be seen, the visitor is constantly reminded that these heroes were active here. A monument at *Elderslie*, near Paisley, commemorates Wallace's birth there, and it was at *Lanark* that he took up arms after the death of his wife at the hands of the English. A fragment survives of the church where he may have been married, and *Cartland Crags*, where he hid, can be visited. In 1297 *Ayr* was the scene of one of his most famed exploits, the burning with all the occupants of the English barracks known as the Barns of Ayr. The same year, though, at *Irvine*, Wallace was deserted by his supporters and thus forced to flee to northern Scotland.

Bruce was born in c 1274 at either *Lochmaben* or *Turnberry*, both strongholds of his powerful Norman-Celtic family. In 1306 he killed Comyn at Greyfriars, *Dumfries*, and thus rekindled the war of independence. Two places can be seen where he may then have hidden: *Bruce's Cave*, near Gretna, and the fort on *Tynron Hill*, near Moniaive. He next appears in the wild country that is now *Galloway Forest Park*, where two memorial boulders mark the sites of his successful skirmishes. A plaque at *Girvan* records the granting of a charter, but after 1307 Bruce was mostly elsewhere in Scotland. He returned towards the end of his life when he made a pilgrimage to *Whithorn* and then, sick with leprosy, founded a hospital for lepers at Prestwick, beside *Bruce's Well* where he had been refreshed; the well and the hospital chapel can be seen.

Mary, Queen of Scots. Mary was twice in the South West. The royal progress of 1563 started at *Seagate Castle*, Irvine, then made a sweep south and east to finish at *Drumlanrig* in Nithsdale. Many of the places at which she stayed can be seen, amongst them *Dunure* and *Ardstinchar* castles, the abbeys of *Glenluce* and *Whithorn*, and *Kenmure Castle*. She is reported to have had 18 horses and six baggage mules and to have been escorted by barons and local lairds. Five years later, after the defeat at Langside, this pomp had been replaced, to use her own words, by having 'to sleep upon the ground and drink sour milk'. Her exact path is uncertain, but she seems to have ridden south across *The Glenkens*, continuing past *Kenmure* down the west bank of the Ken to cross the Dee near *Tongland*. From here she made for *Terregles*, near Dumfries, on the way stopping at *Corra*. The decision taken to leave Scotland, she then retraced the route to *Dundrennan* and embarked to cross Solway.

Covenanters. The Covenants were obstinately supported in the South West, this support being recalled today mainly in the form of numerous memorials either to victories or more often to martyrs. Notable early victories were the taking in 1640 of *Caerlaverock* and *Threave* castles. Another, later, was the defeat of Claverhouse in 1679 at *Drumclog*, though this was soon followed by defeat at *Bothwell Bridge*, near Hamilton. *Sanquhar* twice became famous, in 1680 and 1685 when the first and second Declarations of Sanquhar were affixed to the town cross. The leader on the first occasion, Richard Cameron, was killed at *Airds Moss* and that of the second, James Renwick, had the dubious distinction of being the last Covenanter to be executed (1688). His monument is at *Moniaive*. The worst period for the Covenanters was 1684–88 (the 'killing time') and the majority of the South West's memorials, most of them carrying stirring words, are to the victims of these years. Three may be mentioned as particularly poignant: the bleak and lonely site of the *Wigtown Martyrs'* stake on the estuary flats where two women were left to drown; the little stone tomb in *Galloway Forest Park*, with engraved upon it the names both of the six Covenanter martyrs and of the men who killed them; and at *Douglas* the stone carved in protest by a Covenanter tailor who had had his ears cut off with his own shears.

Robert Burns. The poet spent his life in the South West, he and his work being most associated with two areas; that around *Ayr*, and *Dumfries*. At most places there is a monument or a museum. Burns was born at *Alloway* in 1759, and the scene of his famous poem 'Tam o' Shanter' is laid between Ayr and Alloway Brig o'Doon. *Ayr Auld Brig* has been made famous by the poem 'The Twa Brigs'. In 1777 his family moved to Lochlea Farm near Tarbolton. At *Tarbolton* he founded the Bachelors' Club and at nearby *Mauchline*, the scene of 'The Holy Fair', he was married. The first edition of his poems was published at *Kilmarnock*. In 1788 Burns tried farming at *Ellisland* in lower Nithsdale, but three years later he accepted a post as an excise officer at *Dumfries* where he died in 1796.—A Burns Heritage Trail (leaflet) traces the poet's life in some detail.

Castles. Of the South West's many castles, six (other than Lochmaben and Turnberry as possible birthplaces of Bruce) merit particular mention. These are *Caerlaverock*, for its triangular shape and elegant Renaissance interior; *Threave*, for its grim aspect; *Craignethan*, for defensive features; *Bothwell*, as perhaps the finest 13C castle in Scotland; *Culzean*, as an 18C masterpiece of Robert Adam; and *Rothesay* (Bute), for its unique round shape.

10   Gretna to Glasgow via Beattock (Moffat) and Lanark

A74 to Douglas. A70 and A73 to Lanark. A72 to Hamilton. Choice of roads into Glasgow.—As far as Douglas, a busy arterial road across varying moorland, with high passes westward through the Lowther Hills; A74 closely follows the line of the Roman Watling Street. Around Lanark, woods and orchards, in places gashed by river ravines.—*Note*: A74 is a dual-carriageway trunk road and motorway and as such bypasses the places along it mentioned below. Care must therefore be taken to choose the relevant exits.

SOME HOTELS. **Beattock**. *Auchen Castle*, DG10 9SH. Tel: 06833-407. *Beattock House*, DG10 9QB. Tel: 06833-403. **Hamilton**. *Avonbridge*, Carlisle Road. Tel: 0698-420525. **East Kilbride**. *Bruce*, 35 Cornwall Street, G74 1AF. Tel: 03552-29771. *Stuart*, 2 Cornwall Way, G74 1JR. Tel: 03552-21161. **Bothwell**. *Silvertrees*, 27 Silverwells Crescent, G71 8DP. Tel: 0698-852311.

Total distance 100m.—*32m* **Beattock** (for Moffat).—*29m* **Douglas**.— *11m* **Lanark**.—*18m* **Hamilton**.—*10m* **Glasgow**.

For **Gretna** to (*32m*) **Beattock** (**Moffat**), see Rte 7. Beyond Beattock A74 ascends for some 7m before reaching the watershed at 1029ft and starting its descent into the upper valley of the Clyde.—*13m* (from Beattock) *Elvanfoot*, whence two roads angle south west across the Lowther Hills to reach Nithsdale (Rte 11). One of these (A702), a Roman route, ascends the Powtrail Water to cross the long, bare and winding Dalveen Pass (1105ft), but first, 2m south of Elvanfoot, throws off a minor road to Daer Reservoir. The other road (B7040, becoming B797) climbs up to **Leadhills** (1350ft) and **Wanlockhead** (1380ft), curiously, despite being in the Lowlands, the bleakly sited highest villages in all Scotland, once prosperous through mining lead, gold and silver. Local gold went into the crowns of James V and his queen and, in our century, provided a ring for George V's Queen Mary and a brooch for Elizabeth, the Queen Mother. Leadhills was the birthplace of William Symington (1763–1831), pioneer of marine steam engines, and of Allan Ramsay (1686–1758), the poet, the latter's name perpetuated in that of the *Allan Ramsay Library* (Tel: 065974-326), a lead miners' library founded in 1741 and showing some rare books and mining documents. At Wanlockhead the *Museum of the Scottish Lead Mining Industry* (Tel: 065974-387) offers both indoor and outdoor sections, the former covering some 250 years of lead mining, including examples of local minerals, while an outdoors trail visits a water-tunnel, beam engines, a smelt mill and much else.

2m Crawford, where there is a fragment of Tower Lindsay, once seat of the Lindsays, earls of Crawford. Here Wallace fought a skirmish with the English, and here too James V pacified foreign ambassadors, disgruntled by a poor day's hunting, by presenting them with gold 'bonnet' pieces. The gold came from Leadhills and the pieces bear a portrait of the king wearing a Scottish bonnet.

14m **Douglas** was long a Douglas centre, and it was here in 1307 that the misnamed 'Good' Sir James destroyed his own English-occupied castle, using such barbarity that to this day the exploit is known as the 'Douglas Larder'; knowing that the English would soon return in strength, he made a great pile of all the grain and other foodstuffs, poured on all the wine and ale, killed all his prisoners, throwing their corpses onto the mix, filled the well with slaughtered horses and, finally, fired the castle. The later castle, a rebuilding of the 18C, in 1938–48 suffered a less bloody if by some standards perhaps less dignified demolition as the result of undermining by a coal seam.

What has survived is the ancient part-ruined *St. Bride's Church*, founded in the 12C and still sheltering the Douglas mausoleum, less

Douglas Castle, scene in 1307 of the notorious 'Douglas larder'

sombre than many such and interesting for the canopied tombs and effigies below which lie some historically colourful if, even by the custom of their day, often brutal characters (see also under Biographies). Among the tombs is that of 'Good' Sir James (1286–1330) of 'Douglas Larder' infamy; the man, too, who earned the title of 'Black' from his English victims, but that of 'Good' from the Scots because in 1330 he undertook to carry Bruce's heart to the Holy Land, in so doing losing his life in Spain in battle against the Moors (since then a heart has always been part of the Douglas arms). Here too lies a later James (died 1443) beside his wife Beatrice Sinclair, daughter of the Earl of Orkney, their tomb attracting attention not so much for its rather undistinguished occupants as for the appealing frieze of their ten children. On the floor, under glass, rest caskets with the hearts of 'Good' Sir James and of Archibald 'Bell-the-Cat', another who thought nothing of hanging those lesser men who incurred his displeasure (died 1514: see Rte 3, Thirlestane Castle). The clock (1565) on the tower, said to have been a gift from Mary, Queen of Scots, is reputedly the oldest still-working public clock in Scotland; it chimes three minutes before the hour, thus keeping faith with the Douglas motto of 'Never Behind'.

Beside the road leading to St. Bride's, what must surely be a unique monument—a stone with carved scissors and a human ear—provides a reminder, as sharp as it is poignant, of the hazards of 17C life. In 1684 James Gavin, a Covenanter tailor who lived here, had his ears cut off with his own shears before being transported to the West Indies. On his return, years later, he erected this stone in protest against the outrage he had suffered.

Lesmahagow, 5m north and just west of M74, takes its name from St. Machutus, a 6C Culdee missionary. A priory, dedicated to the saint, was founded in 1144 and its foundations can still be seen beside the south side of today's church of 1803. Although largely destroyed at the Reformation, the nave of the priory church served as parish church until the present one was built.

A70, followed north east, skirts the north west flank of *Tinto* (2320ft), an isolated hill mass famous for its views and easily climbed by a path up the east side from near Thankerton. To have to carry a stone to Tinto's summit was long a recognised penance, and today some people still take up a stone to add to the ever-growing cairn.

11m (from Douglas) **Lanark** (9000 inhab. *Inf.*). Standing above the Clyde and today a busy market town, Lanark is historically associated with the start of Wallace's rebellion as also, in more recent times, with the social experiments (at New Lanark) of Robert Owen.

History. By the 10C Lanark was already sufficiently important for Kenneth II to have held a parliament here in 978. The town was made a royal burgh by David I in 1140, and later Wallace is thought to have lived in Castlegate. He is said to have killed an English soldier during a brawl, then fled to Cartland Crags, whence, on learning that his wife had been murdered, he returned with a band of supporters, overthrowing the English garrison, killing its commander and thus committing himself to rebellion. Three centuries later Lanark was a Covenanter centre (the Declaration of Lanark of 1682 was a confirmation of that of Sanquhar), this period now recalled by a monument in the churchyard.

Lanark's traditional festival is the Lanimers (Land march), lasting throughout the first week in June and in origin going back to the granting of the status of royal burgh in 1140. The highlight is the Lanimer Day procession which includes the riding of the marches or bounds.

Architecturally about all that remains of ancient Lanark are some Early English pointed arches of what was once the 12C *Church of St. Kentigern*, the church in which Wallace may have been married. This church's ancient bell (recast in 1659, 1740 and 1836) also survives, although it now hangs and still tolls in the tower in front of the *Church of St. Nicholas* (1774). Here too, above the door to this tower, Wallace is remembered by a statue (1822), the work of Robert Frost, a Lanark man who claimed to have taken the likeness from an authentic old print.

*New Lanark, beside the Clyde, was founded in 1784 as an industrial village by David Dale, a merchant, and Richard Arkwright, pioneer in cotton spinning, and soon developed into a large complex involving some 2000 people. Later (1800–25), the village became the scene of the early social experiments of Robert Owen, Dale's son-in-law and mill manager over this period. Convinced that better living conditions meant better output, he, amongst other things, opened a free school, provided a club and operated a co-operative store. Today the principal buildings have been accurately restored and converted for use as modern housing and shops, including craft shops, and a monorail and descriptive leaflet enable visitors to make a self-guided tour (New Lanark Conservation, Mill Three Visitor Centre. Tel: 0555-61345).—The former dyeworks now house a Scottish Wildlife Trust *Falls of Clyde Centre* (Tel: 0555-65262), telling the story of the nearby *Falls of Clyde Nature Reserve*, a wooded gorge with waterfalls.

Blackhill (NTS), 3m west of Lanark between A72 and A74, is a hill-fort offering views over the Clyde valley.—*Castledykes*, 3m east of Lanark and just east of A70, was a Roman fort; and at *Carnwath*, on A70 4m farther east, there is a motte and also, abutting the west end of the parish church, an attractive and intriguing survival in the form of the transept of a collegiate church of 1424.

6m *Craignethan Castle (AM. Tel: 031-244-3101) will be found 2m west of Crossford on A72, and for anyone even slightly curious about medieval defensive ingenuity few castles can be as rewarding as this, or, because of the intactness of the ruins and the careful restoration, as easy to understand. Its defensive aspect apart, this site is particularly attractive with its spacious open court and its surrounds of parkland and wooded river defile.

Built in the 15–16C, Craignethan was a stronghold of the Hamiltons, staunch supporters of Mary, Queen of Scots. Inevitably, as with so many others, the castle suffered after Mary's flight to England, but about a century later, in 1665, a new mansion was built in the court by the Hay family.

But despite dismantling and change of ownership Craignethan has preserved its main and most fascinating defensive feature, its caponier, possibly the earliest example in Britain of such a structure. The castle was built at the time when the ever-increasing power of artillery was shifting the target of siege attack away from the soldiery manning the ramparts and down to the vulnerable base of the walls, and the caponier—a large, vaulted chamber set solidly across the floor of a broad, dry moat—was the defensive reply to these new tactics. This chamber was, and still is reached by a stair in the castle wall (this suggesting that the caponier was integral with Craignethan's original design), and from inside it can at once be seen how effectively gunports on both sides commanded the moat and thus the length of the base of the keep—the defenders' task of course made simpler by the fact that on the remaining three sides the keep stood above steep cliffs.

12m **Hamilton** (52,000 inhab. *Inf.*) owes its industrial growth to the discovery and mining of coal, but, with the closing of the pits, has now much diversified.

History. There was a settlement here in prehistoric times, and later this area became known as Cadzow, a name which stuck until 1445 when a charter from James II to the first Lord Hamilton officially changed the name to that of the family. This early township (Netherton) clustered around Mote Hill, still a name on modern Hamilton's northern edge. In 1568 Mary, Queen of Scots, came here to confer with her supporter the 4th Marquis of Hamilton before the battle at Langside. Cromwell set up his headquarters here for a short while in 1651, and in 1679, after their defeat at Bothwell Bridge, many of the fleeing Covenanters sought refuge in the woods of Hamilton Palace where they were protected by Anne, the then duchess, who pressed the victorious Monmouth not to disturb the game in her coverts.

The Hamilton family dominated the town from as early as the 14–15C, their palace standing in the area later known as the Low Parks and now absorbed by Strathclyde Country Park. The palace was pulled down in the 1920s because of the subsidence resulting from coal workings; however, slabs of its basement flooring now pave the choir of Paisley Abbey.

In the town, beside the *Old Church* built by William Adam in 1732, stands the Netherton Cross, probably pre-Norman in date and for long the Cross of the township around Mote Hill. The macabre 'Heads Memorial', on the churchyard east wall, commemorates four local Covenanters beheaded in 1666; the text gives a grim insight to the viciousness of the times. *Hamilton District Museum* (Tel: 0698-283981), at 129 Muir Street in the north part of the town, occupies an interesting building that was originally a coaching inn (1696) but was enlarged in 1790 to provide an assembly hall. The museum records the social and industrial development of Hamilton and includes a reconstructed Victorian kitchen, a section devoted to transport, and material on Sir Harry Lauder who is buried in the town's Bent cemetery. The nearby *Cameronians (Scottish Rifles) Regimental Museum* (Tel: 0698-428688), telling the story of this Covenanter regiment (see also Rte 11, Sanquhar), is housed in the Duke of Hamilton's former stables in Mote Hill.

Strathclyde Country Park (Tel: 0698-66155) occupies both sides of the M74 motorway between the Hamilton and Bothwell interchanges (A723 and A725). The park has absorbed the former unsightly coal-working subsidence area known as Hamilton Low Parks, itself once the gracious park—that same park in which Duchess Anne sheltered the Covenanters—of imposing Hamilton Palace. A major feature is the 200-acre loch (formed by diverting the Clyde) which is a national watersports centre. Other amenities include a nature reserve (entry by permit), a caravan and camping site, many sports facilities and even some Roman remains. Within the park bounds stands the strange *Hamilton Mausoleum*, a square edifice with a cupola built in 1840 by David Bryce for the 10th Duke who died in 1852. The interior is a solemn octagonal chapel, notorious for producing an echo so resounding that the chapel could not be used as such. The huge original bronze doors, now kept inside, bear mouldings illustrating Bible stories and are facsimiles of panels on Ghiberti's doors at the Baptistry in Florence.

The name *Chatelherault Country Park* (Tel: 0698-426213), 1m south east of the town by A72, recalls that the dukes of Hamilton also bear the title of Duke of Chatelherault. Formerly the High Parks of the Hamilton estate, today's country park offers much of interest, including the ruins of Cadzow Castle, a royal residence until the time of Bruce when it passed to the Hamiltons and was eventually destroyed by Moray after Langside; ancient oaks said to have been planted by David I to replace yet earlier trees once part of the Caledonian forest; Iron Age earthworks; a herd of white cattle, descendants of the wild white cattle of Britain to which Scott refers in his ballad of 'Cadyow Castle'; and, in the restored William Adam Lodge, a visitor centre.

EAST OF HAMILTON. *Carfin*, 2m north of Motherwell east of the motorway and river, once with a population largely of Irish and Polish origin, is visited for its Grotto, dedicated in 1922 to Our Lady of Lourdes and still much visited by pilgrims. The original shrine is modelled on that at Lourdes and there are a number of other shrines within the grounds.

WEST OF HAMILTON. *East Kilbride*, 5m west, was Scotland's first satellite town, built in the 1950s and 1960s and with some interesting architecture of that period, such as St. Mark's Episcopal Church, of triangular elevation (Noad and Wallace, 1956), and the seven-sided Church of Scotland (Robert Rogerson, 1964). The new town sprawls generally to the south of the site of the original village, in which, in 1653, the first Scottish meeting of the Society of Friends was held. A memorial in the town commemorates the brothers John and William Hunter, the 18C anatomists, both born in this parish.—*Calderglen Country Park* (Tel: 03552-36644), off A726 to the south of East Kilbride, stretches for some 3m along the wooded cut of Calder Water and offers nature trails, waterfalls, picnic areas, a children's zoo, and a visitor centre telling the story of the local environment.—It was near *Eaglesham*, 4m south west of East Kilbride, a 'model' village laid out in 1769 by the Earl of Eglinton, that the Nazi leader, Rudolf Hess, made his sensational parachute landing in 1941.—For the *Livingstone National Memorial*, 3m north west of Hamilton by A724, see below.

Leaving Hamilton northwards A74 passes the racecourse and then dips to *Bothwell Bridge* (spanning the Clyde), where a monument recalls the battle here in 1679 in which the royal troops under Monmouth and Claverhouse, marching down from the north, routed the Covenanters on the south who lost 500 killed and 1000 as prisoners. This bloody affray can be more easily pictured if today's bridge is ignored in favour of one which was barely 12ft wide, with a steep hump at the centre where it was barred with a gate.

2m (from Hamilton) **Bothwell**, where the *Church of St. Bride* was founded in 1398 by Archibald, 3rd Earl of Douglas ('The Grim', whose daughter Marjory was married to the unfortunate Duke of Rothesay; see Rte 33, Falkland). The original choir with stone-slab roof and generous buttresses is well seen from outside, while inside the church the sedilia are noteworthy, as are also some capitals from an earlier (Norman) church, the grave-slab of Walter de Moravia, builder of Bothwell Castle, and the Burne-Jones east window. A door beside an elaborate monument to the 3rd Duke of Hamilton (died 1694) leads into the 14C sacristy.

David Livingstone (1813–73), the explorer, was born at Blantyre, immediately west of Bothwell, and today the mill tenement in which he was born, in a 'one-room' dwelling, and the adjoining houses have been restored as a ***Livingstone National Memorial** (Tel: 0698-823140). Here, in these almost unbelievably cramped and dingy surroundings, he spent his youth—going to school, working long hours in the mill, and studying until he achieved the qualifications which enabled him to escape to London to become a doctor and missionary. This Memorial is not only an instructive museum of Livingstone's career as mill 'piecer', missionary, explorer and fighter against the slave trade, but the section devoted to his birth and early years also gives a fascinating if sobering insight into the life of the poor during the Industrial Revolution in the early 19C. Livingstone's last journey, when his body was carried by his devoted African bearers 1500 miles from the interior to the coast (and eventual burial in Westminster Abbey) is movingly captured in sculpted wood by Pilkington Jackson. Other features here are a pavilion devoted to modern Africa, and a museum illustrating the history of local agriculture, cotton spinning and mining.

**Bothwell Castle (AM. Tel: 031-244-3101) is 1m north west of Bothwell church. A sprawling red ruin amid woods high above the steep-sided Clyde, this is held by many to be the finest 13C castle in all Scotland.

During its first 200 years Bothwell's story was rarely free of blood and drama. It all started in c 1270 with Walter de Moravia (later the name became Moray and then Murray) who in that year probably began to build his castle here. Soon afterwards, in 1289–90, the castle was held for Edward I, but eventually carried by the Scots after a siege lasting 14 months. But only 11 years later, in 1301, Edward I was back again and Bothwell remained in English hands until Bannockburn when the governor, Fitzgilbert, had no choice but to surrender both the castle and the many important English who had taken refuge here to Robert Bruce's brother Edward. Although then dismantled, Bothwell was occupied again by the English from 1331–36, during which period it was rebuilt by the master-mason John de Kilburn—only to be destroyed a year later when taken by the Scots, led by Sir Andrew Moray, to whom the castle by right belonged and who under the 'scorched earth' policy of the day was obliged to dismantle his own property. In 1361 Bothwell passed by marriage to the 'black' Douglases, who rebuilt it, only to lose it in 1445 after the Douglas defeat by James II. Patrick Hepburn, created Earl of Bothwell, became the new owner, but four years later he exchanged the castle for Hermitage, the property of Archibald, Earl of Angus, the 'red' Douglas.

Towards the end of the 17C a mansion (demolished 1926) was built beside the castle, the latter suffering yet further destruction in the process.

After some 700 years of war, destruction, rebuilding and neglect these ruins are inevitably very complicated and visitors in serious search of structural detail are advised to buy the site booklet which helps out with plans and photographs. Below, however, is an outline of the main features.

Along the north curtain wall, crudely built and with buttresses at either end, a gap indicates the position of the main entrance. The great 13C *Keep*, the oldest part of Bothwell, stands half-wrecked at the castle's south west corner, a notable feature here being the way in which the moat which separates the keep from its own court has in part been hacked out of the rock. Designed not only for defence but also as a residence, the keep's interior was of several levels—cellar, the lord's hall, the garrison's hall, the lord's private room, and a defensive top. From this keep a massive curtain wall, running south east to the prison tower and postern, was extended in the early 15C as far as the south east tower. At the south east corner of the court are the remains of the *Chapel*, with aumbrey and piscina, while at the court's east end, on the first floor, was the *Great Hall*, rebuilt in c 1500. Two interesting features here are the absence of a fireplace, this indicating that there would have been a central hearth, and the arrangement for a drawbridge on the square tower; the rectangular recess into which the small door is set would have housed the drawbridge when raised, and above can be seen the channels into which slotted the bar and hoop by which the bridge was lifted.

8m central **Glasgow**, see Rte 19. This approach to the city passes *Calderpark Zoo*.

11   Gretna to Glasgow via Ruthwell, Dumfries and Kilmarnock

A75 to Annan. B724 and B725 to Dumfries. A76 to Kilmarnock. A77 to Glasgow.—As far as Dumfries, agricultural countryside with views across Solway Firth. Nithsdale, gently ascended after Dumfries, is cultivated and lightly wooded with moor and downland rising behind. After Nithsdale, generally open and cultivated countryside.—Many Robert Burns associations.

SOME HOTELS. **Annan**. *Queensberry Arms*, High Street. Tel: 04612-2024. *Corner House*, 78 High Street, DG12 6DL. Tel: 04612-2754. **Dumfries**. *Cairndale*, English Street, DG1 2DF. Tel: 0387-54111. *Station*, 49 Lovers Walk, DG1 1LT. Tel: 0387-54316. **Thornhill**.

Buccleuch and Queensberry, 112 Drumlanrig Street, DG3 5LU. Tel: 0848-30215. **Sanquhar**. *Mennockfoot Lodge*, DG4 6HS. Tel: 0659-50382. **Cumnock**. *Royal*, 1 Glaisnock Street, KA18 1BP. Tel: 0290-20822. **Kilmarnock**. *Howard Park*, 136 Glasgow Road, KA3 1UT. Tel: 0563-31211. **Strathaven**. *Strathaven*, Hamilton Road, ML10 6SZ. Tel: 0357-21778.

Total distance 104m.—*8m* **Annan**.—*6m* **Ruthwell**.—*13m* **Dumfries**.—*26m* **Sanquhar**.—*16m* **Cumnock**.—*7m* **Mauchline**.—*8m* **Kilmarnock**.—*20m* **Glasgow**.

Gretna, see Rte 7.—*8m* **Annan**. A75 here provides the direct road to Dumfries but this Route leaves A75 for B724 to reach (*6m*) **Ruthwell** (pron. Rivvel), a village famous for the *******Ruthwell Cross* which stands in its church. Shaped and carved in the early 8C and one of Europe's most important Early Christian monuments, the cross was in 1642 judged idolatrous and smashed, the pieces being consigned to below the church floor, until in 1823 the cross was re-assembled in its present form. The shaft (18ft) is original, but the cross-arm is restoration although a detached piece of the original can be seen. Excellent descriptive boards explain the detail of the elaborate carving.

The *Henry Duncan Cottage Museum* (Tel: 038-787-640), in Ruthwell village, is on the site of the first Savings Bank, founded here in 1810 as one of his pastoral initiatives by Henry Duncan who was minister at Ruthwell in 1799–1843, and did much to restore Ruthwell Cross. Although philanthropic and not operated for profit, the bank was run on firm principles and imposed what must have been an almost unbearable discipline on its usually impoverished members who, for example, could be fined if they defaulted on the regular deposits to which they had hopefully committed themselves. So successful was Duncan's venture that within 15 years similar societies had sprung up all over Britain.—*Comlongon Castle* (Tel: 038787-283), just north of Ruthwell off B724, is now a hotel attached to a 15C keep.

Continuing west along B725, this Route in 1m passes *Brow Well*, an ancient mineral well once visited by Burns on medical advice.

4m ***Caerlaverock Castle** (AM. Tel: 031-244-3101). With its unusual triangular plan, its Renaissance carving and its moat still full of water, Caerlaverock ranks among Scotland's best both for structural interest and visual satisfaction.

This stronghold of the Maxwells, later earls of Nithsdale, dates from c 1290 when it succeeded an earlier castle which lay to the south. It was taken by Edward I in 1301, but by 1312 was back in the hands of Sir Eustace Maxwell, a supporter of Bruce. Later, once more with an English garrison, it was assaulted and taken by Sir Roger Kirkpatrick who seems to have destroyed much of the building. Repaired by Lord Maxwell in 1593, and elegantly extended and modified in 1634 by the 1st Earl of Nithsdale, Caerlaverock eventually capitulated to the Covenanters in 1640 after a siege lasting 13 weeks.

The castle's symmetry, and particularly that of the massive gateway at the triangle's apex with its formidable drum towers, is immediately striking, as is also the contrast between the wholly defensive 14–15C exterior and the 1st Earl's elegant Renaissance interior of 1634. Here, around a triangular courtyard, are what must have been exquisite rooms, incidental in shape, with large windows on two sides, and most with generous fireplaces. This, at the time known as 'Lord Nithsdale's dainty fabrick'—and the adjective is not ill-chosen—was enjoyed by its owner, a supporter of Charles I, for a mere six years before his achievement was largely destroyed by Covenanter rebels. However, the Maxwell crest and motto still obstinately survive above the gateway.

Caerlaverock National Nature Reserve embraces 13,594 acres of salt-marsh, tidal mud and sand extending along six miles of coastline along the Nith estuary and Solway Firth. The reserve is noted for its winter wildfowl, especially many thousands of geese, these including the entire Spitsbergen barnacle goose population. The unreclaimed salt-marsh, the largest such in Britain, is the most northerly breeding site of the natterjack toad, remarkable for having legs so short that it runs rather than hops.

9m **Dumfries** (32,000 inhab. *Inf.*), with a historic and violent past typical of a Borders town, is today a lively centre, of interest to visitors mainly because of the associations with Robert Burns, for the picturesque Nith waterfront with its 15C bridge, and for ruined Lincluden Abbey in the north suburbs.

History. Probably originating as a settlement on the Roman road up Nithsdale, Dumfries became a village protected by the early castle (now vanished, but its site recalled by Castle Street). The town was made a royal burgh in the 12C, possibly by William the Lion, and of subsequent charters the best known is Robert III's of 1395. In 1301 Edward I seized the castle, but perhaps the town's most historic date is 1306 when Bruce and Roger Kirkpatrick here murdered Balliol's man Comyn and thus started the long war of independence. Later, Dumfries was burned or sacked by the English in 1448, 1536 and 1570. In 1745 the Young Pretender passed through here on his northward retreat from Derby, treating the town with some severity because of the hostility shown to him on his southward march. During the 1939–45 war Dumfries was the headquarters of the Norwegian forces in Britain (tablet in St. Michael's Church).—The town motto, A'Loreburn!, derives from the Saxon. Meaning 'To the muddy burn', it was a rallying cry for the weakest part of the defences, recalled today by the name of a street to the north east of Greyfriars.

Robert Burns lived in Dumfries from December 1791 until his death in 1796, working as an excise officer and here writing over 100 of his poems. His first home was a three-room flat in the Wee Vennel (now Bank Street), but in May 1793 he moved to a better house in Mill Vennel (now Burns Street) where he died.

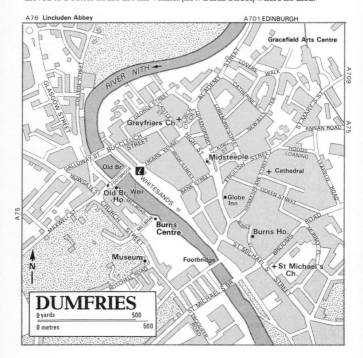

DUMFRIES

The best of Dumfries can be seen by walking the length of High Str\
from Greyfriars Church southward to St. Michael's Church, a distan\
of about half a mile, and then returning northward along the waterfrol\
(Whitesands).

Greyfriars Church, with a statue of Burns in front, is a prominent red
building of 1867 within the angle of Academy and Castle streets. The
church occupies the site of the ancient castle but should not be confused with the 13C Franciscan Greyfriars Friary, founded either by
Alan of Galloway or his daughter Devorguilla Balliol. This stood on the
west side of today's Castle Street and it was here (plaque) that Bruce
and Kirkpatrick murdered ('the Red') Comyn. Tempers rose while
Bruce was conferring with Comyn, who had come here as the representative of John Balliol, the rival claimant to the crown. Bruce stabbed
Comyn, then ran out of the friary, crying 'I doubt I have slain the
Comyn', whereupon Bruce's supporter, Roger Kirkpatrick, replying 'I'll
mak siccar', went in and finished Comyn off.—*Gracefield Arts Centre*
(Tel: 0387-62084), to the north east at 28 Edinburgh Road, shows a collection of Scottish paintings and mounts regular exhibitions of contemporary art.

Midsteeple (1707), the former tolbooth, marks the town centre. On it
there is a plan in relief showing how Dumfries was in Burns's time, and
also a distance table which includes the distance to Huntingdon in
England, once the end of the road for the Scots cattle drovers. Farther
south, Bank Street, dropping west off High Street, was formerly the Wee
Vennel in which Burns found his first home (plaque). Burns gave this
street yet another name, Stinking Vennel, because an open culvert here
carried blood and offal from the meat market down to the river. It was in
the building opposite English Street (then the Commercial Hotel, later
the County Hotel and now a shop) that the Young Pretender held a
council. Just beyond, off the other side of the road, Burns's favourite
tavern (or howff), the *Globe Inn*, with the poet's chair and other relics,
still welcomes those in search of atmosphere and a drink. *Burns House*,
in Burns Street a short distance beyond, was the poet's second and last
home in Dumfries, and the home also of his wife, Jean Armour, until her
death in 1834. Admirably refurbished, the house now serves as a Burns
museum (Tel: 0387-55297). The *Archive Centre* (Tel: 0387-69254), opposite Burns House, is at the service of family and other researchers.

St. Michael's Church, a few yards farther south across a main road,
was built in 1750. A tablet on a pillar near the entrance marks the Burns
family pew, and in the churchyard stands the *Burns Mausoleum*, an
elaborate Grecian edifice to which his body was moved in 1815 and
within which also rest his wife and several of his children. The monument contains a sculptured group by Peter Turnerelli depicting the
Muse of Poetry finding Burns at the plough. But Burns is not the sole
focus of interest in this melancholy churchyard which contains many
weird tombs, one being the mass grave of the hundreds who died in the
cholera outbreak of 1832. And here, too, near the mausoleum, a grey
granite pyramid marks the tomb of three Covenanters, executed (two in
1667, one in 1685) on Whitesands beside the river (see also below).

The waterfront (Whitesands), perhaps the most attractive part of
Dumfries, extends between two main road bridges, in between being
two footbridges and the weir (or caul), this latter built during the 18C to
provide power for grain mills. By the east side of the road, roughly
opposite the weir, a cairn commemorates one James Kirko, a Covenanter shot in 1685, one of the three remembered on the memorial in St.
Michael's churchyard. The part-15C six-arched *Old Footbridge*, immediately above the weir, is last in a succession of bridges here the first of

which was a wooden structure put up by Devorguilla Balliol in the 13C. This was followed by a stone bridge of 1431, a part of the west arch of which is said to have survived the destruction by floods in 1620. After the flood damage, the bridge was rebuilt, close to the original design and using much of the original stone.

Across the river there are three museums, the first, built into the west end of the Old Footbridge, being the *Old Bridge House* (Tel: 0387-56904), dating from 1660 and today housing a museum of local life with period rooms. Mill Road, leading south beside the river, soon reaches the *Robert Burns Centre* (Tel: 0387-64808) which, housed in the town's 18C water mill, uses video and displays to tell the story of Burns's association with Dumfries. In Church Street, 200 yards south, the *Dumfries Museum* (Tel: 0387-53374), centred on an 18C windmill tower, has Solway, Dumfries and Galloway as its main theme, among the subjects being prehistory, early Christianity, natural history, and life in Victorian times. And here, too, there is a camera obscura of 1836, recalling that this tower once served as an observatory and today offering the visitor a panoramic view.

This Route leaves Dumfries northward by A76 which in *1m* reaches **Lincluden Abbey** (AM. Tel: 031-244-3101). Founded in the 12C for Benedictine nuns, the house was made collegiate (the site is sometimes called Lincluden College) by Archibald the Grim in 1389. Of this early structure little if anything remains, what survives today being mainly the choir and part of the south transept of the small but exquisite 15C church. Of particular note are the carvings from the life of Christ on the stone screen at the entry to the choir; the effigy and decorated canopied tomb (c 1430) of Margaret, daughter of Robert III and Countess of Douglas; and, beside the tomb, the carved doorway bearing the Douglas heart (see also Rte 10, Douglas). Of the domestic buildings little survives other than garden terraces to the east. A motte stands beside the site.

5m **Ellisland Farm** (by advance notice. Tel: 0387-74426), on the east side of A76, is where Burns, as always unsuccessfully, experimented with new farming methods in 1788. As a poet, though, he was more successful since it was during his time here that he wrote 'Tam o' Shanter', 'Auld Lang Syne' and 'Mary in Heaven'. There are various Burns exhibits and, in the granary, agricultural material. *Craigenputtock*, some 10m west of Ellisland through Dunscore, is the bleak moorland farm which was Thomas Carlyle's home from 1828–31; it was the property of his wife's mother and it was here that he wrote most of 'Sartor Resartus'.

7m **Thornhill**, where the Buccleuch and Queensberry Hotel stands on the site of a cobbler's shop to which Burns brought his shoes for repair. *Keir*, 2m south west, was the birthplace of Kirkpatrick Macmillan who in 1840 here built the first real bicycle; he rode his machine all the way to Glasgow and was fined for 'furious driving' and knocking down a girl. *Tynron Doon*, a hill fort 2m west of Thornhill, is said to have been the refuge to which Bruce fled after the murder of Comyn at Dumfries.—The village of **Moniaive**, 7m south west of Thornhill, was the birthplace of James Renwick, son of a weaver (1662–88; see also Sanquhar below), hanged in Edinburgh and the last of the Covenanter martyrs; his monument stands above the village. *Maxwelton House* (Tel: 08482-385), on B729 2m east of Moniaive, was the birthplace (1682) and home of Annie Laurie, subject of the haunting ballad. The original song was written by William Douglas of Fingland in c 1700; the more modern version by Lady John Scott in 1835. The early 17C house incorporates part of a 14–15C castle, originally a stronghold of the earls of Glencairn, while modern attractions include woodland walks and a museum of agriculture and early domestic life.

2m (from Thornhill) **Carronbridge**, where A702 forks north east to cross Dalveen Pass, a long and bare ascent to 1105ft following the line of a Roman road traversing the Lowther Hills. About 1m along A702 a minor road bears south east across the railway for *Morton Castle*, a small ruin of c 1480 beside a loch. A castle here was occupied during the 14C by Randolph, 1st Earl of Moray, as regent for David II; it later passed to the Douglases, a branch of whom became earls of Morton. At *Durisdeer*, off A702 4m after leaving Carronbridge, the small 17C church contains a particularly fine black-and-white marble monument (by Van Nost) to the 2nd Duke of Queensberry (died 1711) and his duchess (died 1709).

*Drumlanrig Castle is set in glorious parkland just north west of Carronbridge (Tel: 0848-31682). This home of the Duke of Buccleuch and Queensberry, occupying the site of a 15C Douglas stronghold and close to that of a Roman fort, is a huge palace of local pink sandstone, forming a central courtyard with corner towers, built (probably by James Mylne) between 1679–90 for the 1st Duke of Queensberry. Among the superb paintings are works by Rembrandt ('Old Woman Reading'), Holbein, Murillo, Ruysdael and Rowlandson, while family portraits are by Kneller, Reynolds and Ramsay. The collection of out-standingly fine French furniture includes a cabinet given by Louis XIV to Charles II, who in turn presented it to his natural son the Duke of Monmouth and Buccleuch, and there are also some interesting relics of the Young Pretender, displayed in the bedroom in which he spent a night while on his retreat from Derby. Other attractions include craft workshops, a tearoom in the old Kitchen, an adventure playground, ranger-guided walks, and a cycle collection.

5m beyond Carronbridge A76 reaches *Enterkinfoot* where the Enter-kin Burn, descending from the north east, flows into the Nith. It was up this burn, along its short, narrow and steep-sided cut into the flank of the Lowther Hills, that Covenanters holding the heights forced a party of English Dragoons to hand over prisoners they were escorting, an incident described by Daniel Defoe in his 'Memoirs of the Church of Scotland'.—*4m Mennock* is at the foot of the pass of the same name (B797) which ascends to 1409ft to reach Wanlockhead and Leadhills, for both of which see Rte 10.

2m **Sanquhar**, the southern entry to which is marked by ruined *San-quhar Castle*, built in the 15C and in 1630 bought by Sir William Doug-las of Drumlanrig whose grandson, the 1st Duke of Queensberry, lived here while the present Drumlanrig Castle was under construction, and until his death in 1695. The 2nd Duke—the one honoured by that marble monument at Durisdeer—abandoned Sanquhar when he moved into Drumlanrig.

Sanquhar is famous in the story of the Covenanters, for it was here in 1680 that Richard Cameron, a schoolteacher born in Falkland, with a band of armed supporters affixed to the town cross the first 'Declaration of Sanquhar', renouncing allegiance to Charles II. Soon afterwards, and with a price on his head, he was killed in a skirmish on Aird's Moss north east of Cumnock, but the survivors of his band were later amnestied by William III and became the nucleus of the regiment, the Cameronians. The year 1685 saw the second Declaration, affixed by James Renwick (see Moniaive above), a young man who, fired by his theological studies in Holland, returned to his native Scotland to become a field preacher. Sadly, Sanquhar's historic cross has not sur-vived, though its site is now marked by a monument. But something else, equally historic if very different, has survived, namely Britain's oldest *Post Office* which was providing service as long ago as 1783, a year before the introduction of the mail coach service. Another survival is the *Tolbooth* (William Adam, 1735) which houses the local museum (Tel: 0659-50186).

16m **Cumnock** (10,000 inhab. *Inf.*) was for most of his life the home of James Keir Hardie (1856–1915), the early Socialist leader. Already at work in the coal mines at the age of ten, he later (1888) helped in the founding of the Scottish Labour Party and was elected to parliament in 1892. His bust, the work of Benno Schotz, stands outside the town hall, and here too is a monument to Alexander 'Prophet' Peden (c 1626–86), a leading Covenanter divine who, after burial at nearby Auchinleck, suffered the indignity of being exhumed by the English soldiery and re-interred in unconsecrated ground here at Cumnock.

CUMNOCK TO MUIRKIRK (A70, north east, 9m). Bello Mill, at *Lugar*, was the birth-place of William Murdoch (1754–1839), pioneer of coal-gas lighting. Beyond Lugar, A70 skirts *Aird's Moss*, a dreary moor which was the scene of the skirmish in which Richard Cameron (see Sanquhar above) lost his life, and then reaches *Muirkirk* where a cairn marks the site of John McAdam's tar works.

2m **Auchinleck**, associated with James Boswell (1740–95), lawyer and man of letters, best known as the close friend and biographer of Dr Johnson. Boswell's father, the Edinburgh lawyer Alexander Boswell, on being raised to the bench took the title of Lord Auchinleck, a place in which his family had long had roots. Father and son are both buried in the mausoleum built by the former in 1754, now serving as a memorial museum to both Boswell and William Murdoch (by appointment. Tel: 0290-21185).

5m **Mauchline** is a village which, with Dumfries and Alloway, will surely be an obligatory stop for all Burns enthusiasts. Here in 1788 the poet was married to Jean Armour, daughter of a local mason, in Gavin Hamilton's house near the 15C Mauchline Tower, and the cottage at which he afterwards lived is now the *Burns House Museum* which includes Jean Armour's upper floor room, furnished in the style of her time (Tel: 0290-50045). *Poosie Nansie's Tavern*, inspiration and setting for part of 'The Jolly Beggars', is still a public house, and in the church-yard, scene of 'The Holy Fair', are buried four of the poet's children and several of his friends.

Nor are Burns associations confined to the village. *Mossgiel*, just north west, was the site of the farm (since rebuilt) at which between 1784–88 the poet and his brother Gilbert lived and farmed, as always unsuccessfully, while *Lochlea*, farther north west, was the Burns family home before this, another disastrous farm and the place where Burns's father died. Yet more will be found along or close to B743 linking Mauchline with Ayr. At *Failford* a monument marks the place where, it is popularly accepted, Burns bade farewell to Mary Campbell, his 'Highland Mary', his betrothed for the few months she had yet to live and, after her death, the subject of the poignant 'To Mary in Heaven'. Then comes Tarbolton, associated with the youthful Lochlea period and particularly with the *Bachelors' Club*, a 17C house in which Burns and some friends founded their literary and debating society; in which, too, Burns was initiated as a freemason (NTS. Tel: 0292-541940). To the west of Tarbolton, 2m south of B743 and 4m east of Ayr, there is *Leglen Wood* (on some maps *Laighland*) in which Wallace is believed to have hidden before burning the Barns of Ayr. Burns, to whom, understandably, Wallace was a hero, often visited here 'with as much devout enthusiasm as ever pilgrim did the shrine of Loretto' and a cairn of 1929 now commemorates his visits. The *Barnweil Monument* of c 1860, 2m north of Tarbolton, marks the height from which Wallace is thought to have watched Ayr burning.

Sorn, 3m east of Mauchline, is a straggling village with, at its west end, a most attractive bridge and a 17C church with jougs hanging on the wall. Alexander Peden (see Cumnock above) ended his days as a fugitive in a cave near here.

8m **Kilmarnock** (52,000 inhab. *Inf.*), today a largely industrial town, was in its quieter 18C days well known to Burns, for here in 1786 was published the first edition of his poems, an event which brought the poet fame and £20 and a century later (1879) led to the erection of the *Burns Monument* in Kay Park in the north east part of the town.

Kilmarnock's museum is the *Dick Institute*, in Elmbank Avenue off London Road (Tel: 0563-26401). Here are a good geological collection, local archaeological material, a natural history section, a display of Scottish weapons, and an art gallery with changing exhibitions. *Dean Castle*, in Dean Road off Glasgow Road (Tel: 0563-26401), in turn 14C stronghold and 15C palace, was the seat of the Boyds, lords Kilmarnock, the last of whom lost his head after Culloden. Arms and armour, tapestry and musical instruments are among the collections here, while the grounds have been designated a Country Park (Tel: 0563-22702).—Kilmarnock is also known as a home of John Walker Whisky (tours of blending and bottling plant, in Hill Street. Tel: 0563-23401).

ENVIRONS OF KILMARNOCK. To the north, *Kilmaurs* (3m by A735) has a delightful, almost miniature tolbooth, still with jougs hanging from its wall. *Rowallan Castle*, north east of Kilmaurs off B751, is an outstanding example of a 16–17C mansion.— For *Dundonald Castle*, 5m west, see Rte 16.—Wallace is thought to have spent much of his youth at his uncle's farm at *Riccarton*, 1m south.

KILMARNOCK TO STRATHAVEN (A71, east, 18m). *Cessnock Castle*, just south of Galston, was visited by Mary, Queen of Scots, soon after her defeat at Langside. Sir Alexander Fleming (1881–1955), discoverer of penicillin, was born at *Darvel*. *Louden Hill*, 11m from Kilmarnock, a prominent rocky knoll immediately north of the road, is the spot where in 1306 Bruce, with only 600 men, defeated the Earl of Pembroke's six thousand. To the north of *Drumclog*, 2m farther east, an obelisk commemorates 1 June 1679 when Claverhouse (Dundee), leading Lifeguards and Dragoons, was routed by a mere 200 Covenanters. **Strathaven** (pron. Strayven) offers the visitor ruined 15C *Avondale Castle*; the *John Hastie Museum* of local history (Tel: 0357-21257); and the *Town Mill and Granary*, abandoned as such when the dukes of Hamilton moved out of the castle in the early 18C and now restored and put to good use as a club, theatre and arts centre.

20m central **Glasgow** (see Rte 19), the approach to the city passing close to Pollock Park with *Pollock House Art Gallery* and the *Burrell Collection*.

The Battle of Drumclog (1679). Claverhouse's Dragoons are defeated by a modest force of Covenanters

12   Dumfries to Newton Stewart via Kirkcudbright

A710 to Dalbeattie. A745 to Castle Douglas. A75 and A711 to Kirkcudbright. A755 and A75 to Newton Stewart.—Mainly rolling pastoral country, rounding first Criffel (1868ft) and, later, Cairnharrow (1496ft). Views along the Solway coast, with many small roads down to a shore with shallow, sandy bays.

SOME HOTELS. **New Abbey**. *Abbey Arms*, 1 The Square. Tel: 038785-215. *Criffel Inn*, 2 The Square. Tel: 038785-244. **Castle Douglas**. *King's Arms*, St. Andrew's Street, DG7 1EL. Tel: 0556-2626. *Imperial*, King Street, DG7 1AA. Tel: 0556-2086. **Kirkcudbright**. *Selkirk Arms*, Old High Street, DG6 4JG. Tel: 0557-30402. **Gatehouse of Fleet**. *Cally Palace*, DG7 2DL. Tel: 05574-341. *Murray Arms*, High Street, DG7 2HY. Tel: 05574-207.

Total distance 67m.—*6m* **New Abbey**.—*5m* **Kirkbean**.—*15m* **Dalbeattie**.—*6m* **Castle Douglas**.—*10m* **Kirkcudbright**.—*10m* **Gatehouse of Fleet**.—*15m* **Newton Stewart**.

From **Dumfries** (see Rte 11) there is a choice of roads to Dalbeattie; the direct A711, or (this Route) the more scenic and more interesting A710. Those who choose the A711 will nevertheless pass two historic sites, both close to Kirkgunzeon, 9m from Dumfries. One of these is *Corra Castle*, on A711 immediately south of Kirkgunzeon; once a Maxwell stronghold but today a mere fragment half lost among farm buildings, Corra was one of a number of places which afforded shelter and rest to Mary, Queen of Scots, during her flight from Scotland. The other site is *Drumcoltran Tower*, just over 1m north of Corra; also once belonging to the Maxwells, Drumcoltran survives as a typical example of a sternly simple mid 16C tower-house.

Along A710, *6m* **New Abbey** is a modest village, visited for its ruined abbey, its costume museum and its corn mill.

*Sweetheart Abbey (AM. Tel: 031-244-3101), an unfortunate modernisation of this place's Latin name of Dulce Cor, is so called because of the touching devotion of its founder, Devorguilla Balliol, to the memory of her husband. After his death she not only founded this abbey (in 1273; for Cistercians from Dundrennan) but also carried his heart around with her wherever she went until her own death at the age of 90 in 1290, when she and the heart were buried in front of the high altar. Fragments of her tomb have been incorporated in a reconstruction in the south transept, while a memorial slab (1966; from Balliol College, Oxford, which she founded) marks the original site.

Architecturally the red sandstone ruins are essentially those of the abbey church (largely Early English) and include all the main arches, part of the clerestory of the nave (oddly combined with an inside passage to form a triforium), much of the transepts and choir, and a tall central tower. The fine wheel above the three lights of the great west window is of particular note. Only the aisle of the south transept still carries its roof, groined and with shields at the intersections. Of the domestic buildings little remains bar the west door of the cloister, such wholesale destruction perhaps explained by the fact that the last abbot, Gilbert Brown of Carsluith who died in 1612, was such a doughty opponent of the Reformation. Finally, and perhaps the most impressive feature of this site, there is the great boulder precinct wall which encloses some 30 acres.—In the village an amusing note is provided by a small stone, once part of the abbey but now set into a house, depicting a boat carrying three ladies who, the story goes, ferried stone for the abbey across the Nith. The tower on the hill to the west commemorates the victory of Waterloo (footpath from village).

New Abbey Corn Mill (AM. Tel: 031-244-3101), a still working watermill, though in its present form dating from the 18C, is probably on the site of the original abbey mill.

Shambellie House Museum of Costume (Tel: 031-225-7534) is housed in an unpretentious mid 19C manor designed by David Bryce. An outstation of Edinburgh's Royal Museum of Scotland, Shambellie displays material from that museum's Charles Stewart Collection of European Fashionable Dress, donated by the collector in 1977; the emphasis is on women's dress and accessories of the late 18 to early 20C.

A710 rounds the conspicuous mass of Criffel (1868ft) to reach in *5m* **Kirkbean** where the church contains a memorial font presented by the US Navy, a reminder that *Arbigland*, 1m south east, was the birthplace in 1747 of John Paul Jones whose father was an estate worker here. The woods, and formal and water gardens, are open to visitors (Tel: 038788-283).—*9m* **Rockcliffe**, a village by the shore 1m south west of White Loch on A710, is associated with a number of nearby NTS properties, notably several acres of coastline beside Rough Firth, and also *Mote of Mark*, a large earthwork fort overlooking *Rough Island*, also NTS and a bird sanctuary (because of ground-nesting birds, please do not try to visit in May and June).—*Hestan Island*, off Auchencairn Bay to the south of Rough Island, once a home of Edward Bruce, was the 'Isle Rathan' of Crockett's 'The Raiders' (see Rte 13, Raiders' Road Forest Drive).

6m **Dalbeattie** (4000 inhab. *Inf.*) is a small town built largely of a local grey granite which until a century ago was widely exported, while *Mote of Urr*, just over 2m north beside B794, is a notable example of mixed Saxon and early Norman fortification, in which an almost circular mound, surrounded by a deep trench, rests on a massive platform. *North Glen Gallery* (Tel: 055660-200), at Palnackie 3m south by A711, offers the opportunity to see crafts such as glass blowing, sculpture assembly and steel working, while *Orchardton Tower*, 1m farther south, is a rare and most attractive circular tower-house built in the mid 15C by John Cairns.

A745 now leads westward, in 1m passing the entrance to Buittle Place, close to which stood Buittle Castle, still marked on some maps, where John Balliol was born in 1249 and where his mother, Devorguilla, in 1282 signed the charter founding Balliol College, Oxford.

6m (from Dalbeattie) **Castle Douglas** (3400 inhab. *Inf.*), standing above the west end of Carlingwark Loch, is a town which has known three names. Originally, or at any rate as far back as can be traced, this was Causewayend, from an ancient causeway which led to one of the wooded islets in the loch. Next it took the name of its loch, retaining this until 1789 when its purchase by a merchant called Douglas resulted in the present name. Long before this, though, this place was subject to the Douglases of nearby Threave, and the name Gallows Plot, still sometimes used for the south end of the loch, is a reminder of what their rule was like. The ruined Douglas castle (Threave), together with Threave gardens and wildfowl refuge, are the three attractions here for today's tourist.

Threave Castle (AM. Tel: 031-244-3101) is a tower stronghold, stern and daunting enough as such and even more so for its island situation. Built between 1369–90 by Archibald the Grim, 3rd Earl of Douglas, who died here in 1400, it was the last Douglas castle to surrender to James II in 1455 during the struggle between the Crown and that family, and then only after James had brought against it the cannon Mons Meg (see also

Rte 18, Edinburgh Castle). Repaired after Flodden, Threave was seized
in 1640 by Covenanters who finally wrecked the interior. The tower,
some 70ft high and now but a shell, once sheltered five storeys, each a
single room—store, kitchen, great hall and two domestic levels—while
from the kitchen a stair spiralled within a corner turret. The curtain wall
represents addition during the 15C, and the 'gallows knob' still projecting over the doorway survives as a grim reminder of owners who
boasted that it 'never wanted its tassel'.

Threave Gardens (NTS. Tel: 0556-2575), of over 60 acres, include park,
and peat, rock, formal and water gardens, and in April and May there is a
superb display of naturalised daffodils. There is also a visitor centre,
with a shop, while the Victorian house (no adm.) is the NTS School of
Practical Gardening.—*Threave Wildfowl Refuge* (NTS. November–
March. Tel: 0556-2575), on the Dee, attracts many species of geese and
duck.

This Route leaves Castle Douglas by A75 and in just under 4m forks left
along A711 to reach (*8m* from Castle Douglas) *Tongland Power Station*
(Tel: 0557-30114), a unit of the Galloway Hydro Electric Scheme (see Rte
13, New Galloway).

2m **Kirkcudbright** (pron. Kir-coo-bree. 3500 inhab. *Inf.*) owes its name
to the Kirk of Cuthbert, an ancient church here which for a while sheltered that saint's bones. A small royal burgh (of 1455) and stewartry capital on the Dee, Kirkcudbright's open waterfront, long quay and wide,
dignified 18C streets have rightly earned it the distinction of being the
most attractive of the Solway towns and a place popular with artists.

The term 'stewartry' is a survival from the time when the overlordship of the
Balliols, followed by that of the Douglases, was annulled in the mid 15C and their
lands were placed under a royal steward. From 1526 onwards the office of steward
became the hereditary right of the Catholic Maxwells, one of whom is said to have
offered Kirkcudbright harbour to Philip II of Spain for use by the Armada of 1588.

Of ancient Kirkcudbright only two traces survive. One is the name
Castledykes, a road leading towards the river and recalling that the 13C
castle once stood beside the water some 200 yards north of the west end
of Castledykes. The other is a fragment in 19C *Greyfriars Church* of the
13C Franciscan friary church, thought to have survived into the 16C and
to have been host to Mary, Queen of Scots, in 1563. Greyfriars preserves a
16C aisle of its predecessor, in this being the tomb and effigy (1597) of Sir
Thomas Mclellan who, in 1582 and using stones from the old friary, built
himself the elegant castellated and turreted mansion which today,
under the name *Mclellan's Castle* and long a ruin, still overlooks the
harbour (AM. Tel: 031-244-3101).

Also of interest in Kirkcudbright are the *Market Cross* of 1610, standing beside the 16–17C *Tolbooth* in which John Paul Jones was once
imprisoned, having been charged with the manslaughter of his ship's
carpenter who had died after a flogging; the *Stewartry Museum* (Tel:
0557-30797), in St. Mary Street, with a collection of Galloway historical,
domestic and crafts material as also a section devoted to John Paul Jones;
Broughton House (Tel: 0557-31217), in High Street, an 18C mansion
which was the home of the landscape artist E.A. Hornel who on his death
bequeathed Broughton House and its contents to the town (Antiquarian
reference library. Furniture, ornaments, Victoriana. Special exhibitions); and *Harbour Cottage Gallery* (Tel: 0557-30528), a riverside cottage
showing paintings and crafts.

A visit to Kirkcudbright would scarcely be complete were it not to
include ***Dundrennan Abbey** (AM. Tel: 031-244-3101), just under 6m
south east and quickly reached by A711. Certainly no one who, be it

historically or geographically, has followed the tragic story of Mary, Queen of Scots, would wish to miss this place where it all ended, at least so far as Scotland was concerned.

Founded in 1142 for Cistercians by either David I or Fergus, Lord of Galloway, Dundrennan achieved its poignant footnote in history on 15 May 1568 when Mary came here, in all probability to sleep her last night in Scotland though possibly only to rest, having already slept at Lord Herries's mansion at Terregles near Dumfries. In sharp contrast to Niddry (Rte 8) less than two weeks before, when she could scarce wait to show herself, she arrived here in secret and with her hair shorn for disguise. She wrote a letter to Queen Elizabeth asking for sanctuary, then descended the burn to the little bay now called Port Mary, whence she crossed to England.

In 1606 the abbey came into the possession of the Earl of Annandale, but although the church served as parish church until the late 17C, Dundrennan was generally neglected and used as a quarry. Dundrennan village is partly built of the abbey's stones.

Essentially the ruins are those of the abbey church, together with some remains, notably of the chapter house, around the cloister. What remains of the nave is entered by a west door, the central one of an original three. Note in a recess in the now blocked north door a particularly fine effigy of an abbot, of particular interest for the dagger near his heart and a disembowelled figure at his feet, symbols perhaps indicating that he died violently; the graveslab here is that of a 15C cellarer. From the west door seven nave bays stretch away to the point at which a screen (pulpitium) divided the lay area (west) from the monks' choir (east), this latter filling the nave's eighth bay and much of the crossing. Both transepts survive, in the northern being an effigy thought to be that of Alan, Lord of Galloway (died 1234), father of Devorguilla Balliol. To the east, in the presbytery, features of interest are the double piscina and the triple arcade once covering sedilia. The chapter house (rebuilt 13C), off the east cloister walk, is entered by a particularly fine doorway with elegant windows on either side. Graveslabs here are mostly those of abbots.

Kirkcudbright is left by A755 for (*10m*) **Gatehouse of Fleet** (*Inf.*), a small place at the head of the estuary of the Water of Fleet. *Fleet Forest*, with a visitor centre and forest walks, lies to the south, while 1m to the west beside A75 will be found *Cardoness Castle* (AM. Tel: 031-244-3101), a ruined 15C tower-house of four storeys above a vaulted basement, particularly interesting on account of its original stairway, stone benches and elaborate fireplaces. Cardoness—and hence its name—belonged originally to the De Cardines, but by 1450 ownership had passed to the McCullochs of Galloway. In the churchyard at *Anwoth*, just north of Cardoness, there is an 8C Christian cross.

A75 skirts Cairnharrow (1496ft) and runs above wooded and rocky Ravenshall Point before crossing Kirkdale Burn (*5m* from Gatehouse of Fleet). On the shore, a short way east of the burn's mouth, is *Dirk Hatteraick's Cave* (see Scott's 'Guy Mannering'), the largest of several here, while the woods to the north east hide the remains of *Barholm Castle*, a 16–17C McCulloch stronghold. And it is worth driving half a mile up the glen to find the two chambered cairns together known as *Cairn Holy*. At the first a stone cist can be clearly seen, as can also standing stones in front of which funerary rites would have been celebrated. The more modest cairn just to the north is interesting for its double chamber.—*2m* *Carsluith Castle*, a roofless 16C tower-house built to the L-plan, was the home of Abbot Brown who at Sweetheart Abbey so staunchly opposed the Reformation.—*3m* **Creetown** enjoys the odd distinction of having supplied the granite for the building of Liverpool's docks. A turning opposite the clocktower leads to the *Gem Rock Museum*, displaying a large collection of gems, rocks and minerals of worldwide provenance.

Cutting, shaping and polishing can all be viewed, and there is also a shop (Tel: 067182-357).—*2m Palnure*, just north of which the FC *Kirroughtree Forest* offers a forest garden, a visitor centre and several trails.—*3m* **Newton Stewart**, see Rte 13.

13 Dumfries to Stranraer and Rhinns of Galloway via New Galloway and Newton Stewart

A75 to Crocketford. A712 to Newton Stewart. A75 to Stranraer.— Pastoral and downland countryside as far as New Galloway, between which and Newton Stewart A712 skirts the south edge of Galloway Forest Park with the finest 'Highland' scenery in southern Scotland.

SOME HOTELS. **New Galloway**. *Ken Bridge*, DG7 3PR. Tel: 06442-211. *Leamington*, High Street, DG7 3RN. Tel: 06442-327. **St. John's Town of Dalry**. *Lochinvar*, Main Street, DG7 3UP. Tel: 06443-210. **Newton Stewart**. *Creebridge House*, Minnigaff, DG8 6NP. Tel: 0671-2121. *Bruce*, 88 Queen Street, DG8 6JL. Tel: 0671-2294. **Stranraer**. *North West Castle*, Portrodie, DG9 8EH. Tel: 0776-4413. **Portpatrick**. *Fernill*, Heugh Road, DG9 8TD. Tel: 077-681-220.

Total distance 64m.—*9m* Crocketford.—*15m* New Galloway.—*17m* Newton Stewart.—*14m* Glenluce Abbey.—*9m* Stranraer.

Dumfries, see Rte 11.—*6m Deanside* is little more than a name on the map, but it is from here that a minor road leads north through Shawhead to reach in 3m *Glenkiln Reservoir* beyond the west end of which occasional sculpture pieces by such as Henry Moore, Epstein and Rodin stand somewhat strangely on the moorland slopes and ridges.—*3m* **Crocketford** where this Route forks north west along A712.—*13m Balmaclellan* for (2m south) *Blowplain Open Farm* (Tel: 06442-206) providing an insight into the activities of a local hill farm.

2m **New Galloway**, a place which, though no more than a village (established in 1633 by Viscount Kenmure), nevertheless enjoys the distinction of being a royal burgh. It also stands at the heart of the Galloway Hydro-Electric Scheme and on a crossroads offering the motorist a choice of diversions.

Galloway Hydro-Electric Scheme. Using the waters of the Dee and Ken, this was the first of Scotland's large-scale power schemes (1929–36). There are five generating stations. Kendoon, Carsfad and Earlstoun, in the hills between Dalry and Carsphairn, are supplied by reservoirs created by damming the Ken; Glenlee is fed from Clatteringshaws Loch, 6m west of New Galloway, whence the water is piped through a tunnel; Tongland (see Rte 12), above the Dee estuary, utilises its own headpond and storage water from Loch Ken, raised by a dam at Glenlochar (2m north of Castle Douglas) to form a reservoir. Loch Doon, at the north end of the system, serves as an extra storage reservoir. Fish-passes for salmon have been built at Tongland, Earlstoun and Carsfad, and there is a regulated level pass at Loch Doon.

SOUTHWARD DIVERSION. Two pleasant roads run south from New Galloway, both, and particularly A713, running close to Loch Ken, one of southern Scotland's leading water sports centres and popular also for nature reserves, walks, pony trekking and bird watching. A713 (to Castle Douglas) skirts the length of the loch's east shore, along this 10m stretch being most of the attractions mentioned above.—The other road, A762, soon passes *Kenmure Castle* (15–17C), long the seat of the Gordons of Lochinvar. The family was host to Mary, Queen of Scots, in 1563 during her western tour, and, after Langside, it was Lochinvar who gave her the clothing in which she disguised herself. The 6th Viscount Kenmure was executed for his part in the '45. Beyond, this road (to Kirkcudbright) skirts part of Loch Ken's west shore below the fir-clad slopes of Cairn Edward Forest, and at Bennan, 4m south of New Galloway, it passes the east entrance of *Raiders' Road Forest Drive* (see below).

NORTHWARD DIVERSION (To Dalmellington. A762 and A713. 20m. B7000 and B729 offer a lonelier and hillier alternative to the east of Lochs Earlstoun, Carsfad and Kendoon). This diversion crosses the empty mixed pastoral and moorland district known as *The Glenkens*, with the heights of the Rhinns of Kells (c 2600ft), marking the south east flank of Galloway Forest Park, away to the west. It is generally accepted that it was across this lonely country that Mary, Queen of Scots, fled after Langside. *St. John's Town of Dalry*, just north of New Galloway and long a stage along the pilgrim way to Whithorn, is so named because here was once a church (St. John's) of the Knights Templar. Three miles east of Dalry a gated road off A702 leads to *Lochinvar*, with an islet and fragments of a castle, the home of Young Lochinvar of ballad fame.— From Dalry A713 continues north through Carsphairn to reach (17m from Dalry) a little road which angles away south west to reach *Loch Doon*, once a small loch but now a long and narrow reservoir. Here, beside the loch near the road's end, stands a ruined 14C castle, interesting less for itself than for the fact that it once occupied the islet which can still be seen when the water is low. In danger of drowning when the loch was converted to a reservoir, the castle was taken down and then re-erected on this new site. At *Dalmellington*, 1m north of the Loch Doon road junction, four 18C weavers' cottages, now Cathcartson Visitor Centre (Tel: 0292-550633) use video and an exhibition to recall their past.

Between New Galloway and Newton Stewart, and especially along the stretch west of Clatteringshaws Loch, this Route traverses its most scenic miles; miles, moreover, which were known to Mary, Queen of Scots, who in 1563 travelled this road on her way from Alexander Stewart's house at Garlies near Newton Stewart to the Lochinvar castle of Kenmure.—*5m* (from New Galloway) **Clatteringshaws Loch**, site of the *Galloway Deer Museum* (FC. Tel: 06442-285) with attractively displayed and instructive material covering not only deer (information on the nearby Red Deer Range) but also feral goats, trout (live exhibit) and the history, botany and mineralogy of this wild district. *Bruce's Stone* adjacent, marks the site of the Battle of Rapploch Moss (1307), a successful skirmish by Bruce against the English. The west entrance to *Raiders' Road Forest Drive* (FC. Tel: 0671-2420) is a short distance beyond the Deer Museum. The drive takes its name from S.R. Crockett's novel 'The Raiders' (1894) set in the period immediately following the '15 and describing a raid by the Faas and Marshalls who, following the line of today's drive, lifted cattle from the Maxwells' Solway lands and drove the herds back along the Black Water of Dee and into the hills around Loch Dee, 3m west of Clatteringshaws Loch. Crockett knew this land well, for Little Duchrae, just north of Kirkcudbright, was his birthplace. The drive (10m) is mainly through woodland planted in the last 30 or so years, but at the east end the Sitka spruce and Douglas fir were planted some 55 years ago. Many species of birds may be seen, including buzzards; there are several picnic sites, and, at the south east end of the drive at Stroan Loch, a viaduct of 1863 recalls the railway which until 1965 ran this way to Stranraer.

Continuing west along A712, just beyond the dam marking the end of Clatteringshaws Loch, the road skirts (north) first the *Red Deer Range* and then the *Wild Goat Enclosure* in which the animals, the goats feral rather than wild, can normally be seen close to the road. Opposite the enclosure there is a parking area for a path to *Murray's Cottage*, birthplace of Alexander Murray (1775–1813) who, reared here as a shepherd boy, and despite death at the age of 38, nevertheless became Professor of Oriental Languages at Edinburgh University. A short way beyond, Murray's memorial rises above the road, just below being the FC *Talnotry* estate with camping and a choice of forest trails (Tel: 0671-2420).

12m (from Clatteringshaws Loch) **Newton Stewart** (2000 inhab. *Inf.*) is less important for itself than as a base for visiting Galloway Forest Park to the north and the interesting Machars district (Rte 14) to the south. The town is relatively modern, having been built in the late 17C by William Stewart, a son of the then Earl of Galloway, as the result of a charter granted in 1677 by Charles II. A long main street runs above the west bank of the river Cree, which is crossed by a bridge with, at its west end, a memorial to the 9th Earl of Galloway. The town *Museum* (Tel: 0671-2646), in the former St. John's church in York Road, covers the past of a wide area, including the Machars and the west part of the Stewartry of Kirkcudbright. Period costumes, lace and a fine collection of photographs are among the features.—*Minnigaff*, just north east of Newton Stewart, has a 19C church by William Burn, as also does *Penninghame*, 2m north west, while the map entry *Garlies Castle* recalls that this home of Alexander Stewart was one of the places visited by Mary, Queen of Scots, during her royal tour in 1563.

*GALLOWAY FOREST PARK (FC. Tel: 0671-2420), rising immediately north of Newton Stewart, embraces some 150,000 acres of varied forest, moor, bog, loch, burn and mountains of which ten are higher than 2000ft. *Merrick*, at the centre of the park and its highest point, rises to 2766ft, and the wild, high wastes of moor hold the headwaters of at least six rivers: Stinchar, Girvan, Doon, Dee, Fleet and Cree. The reserve shelters much wildlife, such as red and roe deer and feral goats, while among the many birds are species, including the golden eagle, normally associated only with the Highlands. Only the walker can enjoy the remote best of the park, and the Forestry Commission has opened up many miles of trails far removed from any road.

The motorist can enjoy two areas. The southern area traversed by A712 and including Clatteringshaws Loch has already been described above, but the heart of the park (*Loch Trool*, 10m from Newton Stewart) is equally easily reached by a choice of roads leading north either side of the Cree river. Of these, A714 along the west bank is faster, but the minor road from Minnigaff along the east bank passes *Wood of Cree Nature Reserve* (RSPB. Tel: 0671-2861), a surviving area of native oak and birch protecting woodland birds. The roads meet at Bargrennan where a right fork leads first to *Glentrool Village* (for forest workers) and then up the glen to Loch Trool. This loch, with its steep wooded banks and backdrop of mountains, is superbly spread below the road which climbs its north flank and commands views across a wild and remote country which successively provided refuge for Bruce and, centuries later, Covenanters. Both are commemorated. On a bluff high above the loch and beside the road, the *Bruce Stone* recalls a skirmish of 1306 when Bruce defeated the English by rolling boulders down on to them, while, below, a path from the camp and caravan site near the foot of the loch leads to the sad little *Memorial Tomb* of six Covenanters murdered here while at prayer; a stone records their names and those of their killers.—Visitors aiming for Girvan or Ayr may continue north either by A714 or by the minor road out of Glentrool Village; both roads are scenic, especially the latter as it runs with the Water of Minnoch.

From Newton Stewart A75 runs west to reach (*14m*) **Glenluce Abbey** (AM. Tel: 031-244-3101). Founded in 1192 by Roland, Earl of Galloway, as a daughter-house of Dundrennan, Glenluce will surely appeal as much to the romantic as to the connoisseur of abbatial architecture. In these surroundings the former will readily enough accept that this was the home during the 13C of Michael Scot the Wizard; that it was to these walls that he lured the plague, and then imprisoned it in a vault; that, moreover, his books on alchemy and the occult lie buried here. Others, though, will enthuse over the intact vaulted Chapter House of 1470, entered by an ornamental round-arched doorway and having within an elegant central pillar and some Decorated windows. Also worth noting are the possibly unique interlocking red-clay water pipes. The abbey's cloister walls still stand, but of its church little remains save the foundations and a gable of the south transept.—*Glenluce Motor Museum* (Tel: 05813-534) shows vintage and classic vehicles—*Castle of Park* (AM. Tel: 031-244-3101), just west of Glenluce, is a castellated tower-house of the Hays, built by Thomas Hay in 1590 making good use of stones from the by now neglected abbey to which, as illegitimate son of the last abbot, he claimed some shadowy right. To the south west stretch *Luce Sands*, with dunes which long threatened the fertile land behind but are now checked by planting.

6m ***Castle Kennedy Gardens** (Tel: 0776-2024) are those of *Lochinch Castle* (1867; no adm), the stately home of the Earl of Stair. Long neglected, the gardens were restored in about 1847 to their original 17C form. The notable pinetum was the first such in Scotland, while one of the main attractions here today is the broad avenue of monkey puzzle trees, now about 100 years old and 70ft high. Within the grounds, on an isthmus between the White and Black Lochs (with a crannog), stand the ivy-clad ruins of *Castle Kennedy*. Built during the reign of James VI, the castle was the seat of the earls of Cassillis before passing to the Stair family during the 17C, only to be destroyed by fire in 1716. Park features such as Mount Marlborough and Dettingen Avenue recall the campaigns of the 2nd Earl of Stair (died 1747) who became a Field Marshal; he was also ambassador to France and, inspired by Versailles, it was he who first laid out the grounds round the old castle, unashamedly using soldiers of the Royal Scots Greys and Inniskilling Fusiliers, officially supposed to be hunting down Covenanters.

3m **Stranraer** (10,000 inhab. *Inf.*) is important as a market centre, as a holiday resort and base from which to tour the Rhinns, and, together with Cairnryan on the east side of Loch Ryan, as a port for car ferry and passenger sailings to Larne in Northern Ireland. The crossing takes just over two hours and specially priced day excursions are popular. Stranraer's only historic survival is a fragment of the *Old Castle of St. John*; over the years it served many purposes and in 1632 it was occupied for a while by Claverhouse during his persecution of the Covenanters (exhibitions. Tel: 0776-5088). *North West Castle*, opposite the pier and now a hotel, was the residence of Sir John Ross (1777–1856), the Arctic explorer. At 55 George Street, the old Town Hall, the *Stranraer Museum* (Tel: 0776-5088) covers local history with both permanent and temporary exhibitions.

Rhinns of Galloway

Rhinns of Galloway is the name given to the hammer-shaped double peninsula that marks the south west corner of Scotland. The Rhinns are sometimes incorrectly called the Mull of Galloway, this in fact being only the south extremity.

NORTH ARM. *The Wig*, a scoop of a bay along the west shore of Loch Ryan, was used during the 1939–45 war as a repair base for flying boats. The explorer, Sir John Ross, was born at Balscalloch, some 3m north west. On the north shore stands *Corsewall Lighthouse*, built by Robert Stevenson; the view can embrace Ireland and the island of Ailsa Craig (Rte 15).

SOUTH ARM. **Portpatrick**, 5m south west of Stranraer, is a thriving if small holiday resort and the only town of significance on the Rhinns. During the 17–19C, however, it was of wider importance since between 1661 and 1849 the little harbour with its narrow entrance handled all regular sailings to Northern Ireland. Then came steam and with it the transfer of the service to Stranraer; and Portpatrick's new harbour works, constructed only six years previously, were abruptly abandoned. The ruins of early 15C *Dunskey Castle* stand on a promontory (dangerous cliff area) immediately to the south.

B7042 angles across to Sandhead on the east coast, rather over 1m south west of which, in the ancient churchyard of a little church, will be found the *Kirkmadrine Stones*, generally accepted as being among the earliest Christian memorials in Britain (5–12C). Some of the stones bear Latin inscriptions and the 'Chi-Rho' symbol, formed by combining the first two letters of Christ's name as written in Greek, and it is interesting that the stones suggest the successful presence of Christianity in this remote corner only a few years after the arrival of St. Ninian at Whithorn in c 400.—*Ardwell House Gardens* (Tel: 077686-227), 2m farther south, offer daffodils and rhododendrons, while *Logan Botanic Garden* (Tel: 077686-231), another 2m south, shows sub-tropical plants flowering in a district which enjoys the mildest climate in Scotland. Cabbage palms and tree ferns are among the southern hemisphere species to be seen here. One mile south, on the north shore of Logan Bay, will be found a tidal *Sea Fish Pond* (Tel: 077686-300). Built in 1800 as a larder for Logan House, but closed 1939–55 due to war and damage by a mine, the pond now contains fish (mainly cod) sufficiently tame to be fed by hand.

Mull of Galloway (paved road) is a bold headland with cliffs 200ft high and a lighthouse. Double Dykes, two earthworks across the west end of the Mull, was traditionally the site of the last defence of the Picts against Scots pressing down from the north.

14 Newton Stewart to Wigtown, Whithorn and Glenluce

A714 to Wigtown. A746 to Whithorn. A750 to Isle of Whithorn. A747 to Glenluce.—Farmland and modest coastal scenery.

SOME HOTELS. **Whithorn** *Castlewigg*, DG8 8DL. Tel: 09885-213. **Isle of Whithorn**. *Steam Packet*, Harbour Row, DG8 8LL. Tel: 09885-334. *Queen's Arms*, 22 Main Street, DG8 8LF. Tel: 09885-369. **Port William**. *Corsemalzie House* (Mochrum), DG8 9RL. Tel: 098886-254. *Monrieth Arms*, DG8 9SE. Tel: 09887-232.

Total distance 44m.—*7m* **Wigtown**.—*10m* **Whithorn**.—*4m* **Isle of Whithorn**.—*23m* **Glenluce Abbey**.

Newton Stewart, see Rte 13.—*7m* **Wigtown**, a little royal burgh (1457) with a dignified, spacious square, is known for the Wigtown martyrs; Margaret Lachlan, aged 62, and Margaret Wilson, a girl of 18, two Covenanters who in 1685 were tied to a stake in the estuary and left to drown in the rising tide. Together with other Covenanter martyrs they now rest in the churchyard. The *Martyrs' Monument*, on high ground above the town, was erected in 1858, but the *Martyrs' Stake*, standing lone by the traditional site on the bleak estuary flats, is a great deal more moving. The small town, sprawled over a hill, boasts two Burgh Crosses (1738, 1816), a *Town Museum* (Tel: 0776-5088) and, lower down the hill, the church incorporates a ruined Gordon chantry. To the north of the river mouth, once with a harbour, a grassy mound marks the site of the old castle, but of a Dominican priory founded here by Devorguilla Balliol there survives no trace. *Torhouse Stone Circle*, 3m west beside B733, comprises 19 stones forming a circle 60ft in diameter with three individual stones in the centre.

5m A746 runs through *Kilsture Forest* with trails starting from the Forest Office.—*1m Sorbie*, from where B7052 leads east for 2m to reach *Galloway House Gardens* (Tel: 09886-225), with ancient beech and other trees, spring flowers, a walled garden and a heronry. The house (no adm.), now owned by Help the Aged, was built by Lord Garlies in 1740. *Cruggleton Church*, between B7063 and the sea a mile or so south of Galloway House, is one of the few examples of Norman architecture in this part of Scotland. By the shore an arch is about all that remains of what was once a Comyn coastal defence fortress.

4m (from Sorbie by A746) **Whithorn**. Although a royal burgh since the time of Bruce, this little place enjoys a more ancient and, some would say, more important past as the place where in 397 St. Ninian, a local man who had made a pilgrimage to Rome and studied there, introduced Christianity to Scotland, building a small stone church which he covered with white plaster. This stone and plaster, contrasting with the dark wattle of the peasant huts, earned the building the Anglo-Saxon name 'huit aern' (becoming Whithorn) meaning a white house (also called in Latin the 'Candida Casa').

According to Bede, writing centuries later, St. Ninian dedicated his church to his master in Rome, St. Martin of Tours, who is also reputed to have sent masons to help shape the walls after the Roman fashion. (Excavations of c 1895 and 1948–63 revealed the walls of an ancient building, with a coat of light-coloured plaster over the masonry; for preservation, these remains are now covered.) Christianity throve here, Whithorn becoming an important monastery, missionary centre and shrine. The bishopric—first Celtic, and then in the 8–9C Northumbrian—was revived in c 1125, and in c 1160 a Premonstratensian priory was founded here to serve the shrine. For many generations Whithorn was visited by pilgrims of all ranks and many nationalities, some of the better-known pilgrims being Bruce (1329) and James III, IV, and V, James IV being particularly devoted and coming here almost annually. After 1560 the nave of the church served as a cathedral for the now Protestant bishop, and from 1689 to 1822 it was the parish church.

Priory and Museum (AM. Tel: 031-244-3101). Today's site is approached through what is known as The Pend, a 17C arch flanked by 15C pillars with sculpted coats-of-arms and surmounted by a panel with the Scottish arms as borne before the Union. Of the Priory all that remains above ground is the 13C nave of the church, with some 17–18C alterations. On the south side of the church are two doorways, that at the west end, with fine mouldings, dating from the 12C; the other is 13C, with a rich outer archway of c 1500. Inside the church, on the north side, there are two canopied tombs of c 1300 and a 17C arched recess. The choir and east chapels have disappeared, but the crypts (c 1200) beneath the latter have survived, in them being late medieval tombs overlying an early Christian cemetery.—The *Museum is of its kind outstanding, with graphic and admirably clear explanations of local history and an important collection of Early Christian crosses and stones. The *Latinus (or Barrovadus) Stone of 450, the earliest Christian memorial in Scotland, records the burial of one Latinus and his daughter (very probably members of St. Ninian's flock) and the fact that the stone was set up by Latinus's grandson, Barrovadus. The St. Peter Stone (7C) is also of particular interest as bearing lettering of a type normally found only in Gaul.

What has become popularly known as the *Whithorn Dig* (Tel: 09885-508), an excavation by the Whithorn Trust just across the lane beside the Priory and Museum, is a major long-term project (about 1988–98). The period likely to be revealed spans from Dark Ages early Christian to medieval times, and excavation has already produced evidence of the early (8–9C) monastery, Norse settlement and burial grounds of various periods. Unlike at many excavations, visitors are welcome and there are frequent guided tours, while nearby, beside the Pend in the main street, the Trust has opened a visitor centre.

Rispain Camp (1m south west of Whithorn, off A746) is a rectangular Iron Age fortified enclosure, probably the home of a farming community.

4m **Isle of Whithorn** is not in fact an island, but a little port within a rather desolate coast of low rocks. It is a popular centre for tope and shark fishing, while ruined *St. Ninian's Chapel*, dating from c 1300 and on the foundations of an even older building, was probably used by pilgrims to Whithorn arriving from overseas.

Isle of Whithorn is left by A750, this Route soon forking left along A747. One mile beyond the fork a minor road drops seaward for *St. Ninian's Cave* (1½m walk each way), said to have been used by the saint as an oratory and certainly a place of pilgrimage until at least the 11C. Small votive crosses on the wall and on the rocks outside date from about the 8C. For much of the next 20m the road runs along a coast of low rock, with several small sites of interest either beside the road or within 4m of the shore.

8m (from Isle of Whithorn) *Barsalloch Fort*, on the inland side of A747 by Barsalloch Point, is an Iron Age fort sprawled over a bluff some 60ft high and surrounded by a wide and deep ditch.—*2m* **Port William**, whence A714 in 3m reaches *Drumtrodden Stones*, two groups of exceptionally clear Bronze Age cup-and-ring markings on natural rock. Four hundred yards south there is an alignment of standing stones.—*Mote of Druchtag*, just north of Mochrum less than 2m NW of Drumtrodden, is a typical motte of about the 12C.—*5m* (from Port William) *Chapel Finian*, beside A747, although now little more than foundations, a wall and traces of a well, was once a 10–11C chapel dedicated to St. Findbarr. An evocative, modest ruin, standing beside an inlet in the rocks, the chapel may be pictured as serving pilgrims landing here on their way perhaps to Glenluce, perhaps to Whithorn.—*Old Place of Mochrum* (4m inland off B7005. No adm. but seen from the road) is a 15–16C castle with two towers.—*8m* **Glenluce Abbey**, see Rte 13.

15   Stranraer to Ayr

A77, with alternatives after Turnberry.—A coastal road offering access to a rocky and often seaweedy shore; some sandy bays. Views across the water to Ailsa Craig and Arran. The road runs through the former territory of the Kennedys, successors to the earls of Carrick (a title held by Bruce) and later earls of Cassillis. Of this once powerful family—the ruins of whose castles and watchtowers will be found crumbling along the coast and up many glens—doggerel asserts:

'Twixt Wigtown and the town of Ayr,
Portpatrick and the Cruives of Cree,
No man may think for to bide there,
Unless he court St. Kennedie.

SOME HOTELS. **Girvan**. *Westcliffe*, 15 Louisa Drive, KA26 9AH. Tel: 0465-2128. *King's Arms*, Dalrymple Street. Tel: 0465-3322. **Turnberry**. *Turnberry*, KA26 9LT. Tel: 0655-31000. **Alloway**. *Belleisle House*, KA7 4DU. Tel: 0292-42331. **Ayr**. *Caledonian*, Dalblair Road, KA7 1UG. Tel: 0292-269331. *Station*, Burns Statue Square, KA7 3AT. Tel: 0292-263268.

Total distance 45m.—*15m* **Ballantrae**.—*10m* **Girvan**.—*5m* **Turnberry**.—*15m* **Ayr**.

Leaving **Stranraer** (see Rte 13), A77 runs northward skirting the east shore of Loch Ryan, once used as an anchorage by the Romans who knew it as Rerigonius Sinus. In just under 2m the hamlet of *Innermessan* is reached, with a motte by the shore, while just beyond, to the east of the road, ruined *Craigcaffie Castle* provides an example of 13C architectural ingenuity, for this late 16C keep rests on 13C foundations, laid, it is said, on bags of wool because the ground was so boggy.—*5m* (from Stranraer) **Cairnryan** is the port for a car ferry service to Larne in Northern Ireland. During the 1939–45 war the harbour facilities here were of some importance, latterly controlled by the Americans, and components of the 'Mulberry Harbour' used in the 1944 Normandy invasion were made here.

Briefly leaving the shore the road now ascends wooded Glen App, in just over 3m crossing the Water of App at *Altimeg*, reputed site of the violent death of Appin, a king of Dalriada who in 741 unsuccessfully invaded Galloway.—*10m* **Ballantrae**, on the coast, is not, as might be thought, the scene of R.L. Stevenson's 'The Master of Ballantrae' (this was Borgue, south west of Kirkcudbright). Stevenson did, though, visit here in 1876 and recorded that people threw stones at him because of the eccentricity of his dress. Above the village stands the shell of *Ardstinchar Castle*, host to Mary, Queen of Scots, during her royal progress of 1563 and coastal (Ard) guardian of the Stinchar valley, today ascended by B7044 (becoming A765), roads which pass fragments of Kennedy strongholds.—*5m* **Carleton Castle** (above the village of Lendalfoot), now a ruin but once one of a line of proud Kennedy watchtowers along the coast, has achieved a more lasting fame in ballad, in which the castle was the seat of a baron who rid himself of seven wives by pitching them over the cliff, but was finally himself similarly disposed of by his eighth, a redoubtable lady called May Cullean. Beyond, another reminder of this coast's former lords, the road reaches first Kennedy's Pass and then 16 and 18C Ardmillan Castle, despite its name a Kennedy possession until the 17C when it passed to the Crawfords.

5m **Girvan** (8000 inhab. *Inf.*) is a sizeable resort, typical of this coast, with a spacious waterfront and good sands. A touch of history can be found in the public gardens on Knockcushan Hill above the harbour where a stone records that Bruce presented a charter and held his court on this hill, the name of which means the Hill of Justice. *Penkill Castle* (by appointment. Tel: 046587-261), 3m north east at Old Dailly, traces its origin to c 1420 and was until recent years the seat of the Boyds, one of whom, Spencer Boyd, in 1857 castellated his by then largely 16–17C mansion. But it is for its Pre-Raphaelite association that Penkill is best known for in the 19C this was the home of William Bell Scott (1811–90) who here welcomed Rossetti and several of his contemporaries and even built a gallery to house their works.

Ailsa Craig, also sometimes known as 'Paddy's Milestone' for being half-way between Belfast and Glasgow, is a solid 1114ft-high mountain island 10m offshore from Girvan. In Gaelic the name may mean Fairy Rock—singularly inappropriate for such a lump of granite—and Burns surely showed a finer perception when, in 'Duncan Gray', he wrote that 'Meg was deaf as Ailsa Craig'. In medieval times the rock belonged to Crossraguel Abbey, and it is no surprise to learn that it may have been used as a place to which the abbot exiled his less tractable monks. Later, during the Reformation, Ailsa Craig became a refuge for Catholics, some of whom at one time openly declared that they were holding it on behalf of Philip II of Spain. Once famed as provider of the best granite curling stones, today the island is part bird sanctuary (gannets, puffins, guillemots and other seabirds). In summer there are boat excursions from Girvan, time being allowed for a walk around the rock (c 2m) at low tide or for a climb to the top, on the way passing a medieval tower.

B741, ascending Girvan Water, offers two scenic northern approaches to *Galloway Forest Park* (Rte 13). The first road is from Crosshill, the second from Straiton, the two merging in the heart of Carrick Forest to follow the lovely course of the Water of Minnoch.—*Blairquhan Castle* (Tel: 06557-239), just west of Straiton, is an early 19C replacement (by William Burn) of a 14C original. Features are a walled garden, a pinetum and a picture gallery.

5m **Turnberry** is an internationally-recognised golf centre with two courses overlooked by a huge hotel. *Turnberry Castle*, fragments of which adjoin the lighthouse, which probably stands on the medieval courtyard, claims (as does Lochmaben, see Rte 7) to be the birthplace of Bruce. But, whether he was born here or not, Turnberry was long the

A lighthouse marks the site of Turnberry Castle, closely associated with Bruce

centre of intrigue to put him on the throne, a role which was probably the cause of the castle's destruction in 1307, the year in which, lured it is said by a mystic fire, Bruce came across from Arran.

At Turnberry a choice must be made between the coastal or inland roads to Ayr, the former passing Robert Adam's elegant Culzean Castle, the latter the equally elegant but ruined abbey of Crossraguel. There are several linking roads enabling a criss-cross course to be planned.

Coastal Road to Ayr

4m ***Culzean Country Park and Castle** (pron. Cullane. NTS and others. Tel: 06556-269 (park) or 274 (castle)). The showplace along this part of the coast, the Culzean complex comprises the fine mixed woodland park, a visitor centre, and the great Robert Adam castle sprawled above the sea. The estate, the seat of the Kennedys since the 14C, was given to the National Trust for Scotland in 1945.

Visitors are rightly encouraged to go first to the *Visitor Centre*, a most successful and pleasing conversion of the 1777 Robert Adam Home Farm. The centre is the base for the park's ranger service, the starting point for guided walks and the venue for talks and films. Facilities include an auditorium, exhibition, shop and restaurant. The *Country Park*, of 560 acres and the first (1970) in Scotland to be declared such, includes a beautiful and mellow walled garden established since 1783, an adventure playground, a deer park and some 17m of woodland walks through rare trees and shrubs.

Culzean Castle, one of Robert Adam's outstanding achievements, was built between 1772–92 for the 10th Earl around an ancient Kennedy tower. Particular features are the handsome Oval Staircase, the Round Drawing Room, and the plaster ceilings now restored to Adam's original colouring. A flat in the castle was presented to General (later President) Eisenhower for his use during his lifetime and an Eisenhower Presentation now illustrates the General's link with Culzean.

. Beyond Culzean A719 soon passes a road (B7023) to Maybole on the inland route to Ayr and then reaches (*5m*) *Dunure Castle*, the stark cliffside ruin of a 13C castle in which in 1563 Mary, Queen of Scots, spent one of the first nights of her royal progress. Here, too, only seven years later in 1570, the then Earl of Cassillis is said to have roasted in soap the lay-abbot of Crossraguel in an attempt to persuade him to surrender the rich abbey lands. Whether or not this treatment succeeded does not seem to be recorded, but the abbey's days were in any case numbered and by 1592 it had succumbed to the Dissolution.—*6m* **Ayr**, see below.

Inland Road to Ayr

From Turnberry A77 angles north east to reach in *3m* **Kirkoswald**, a village where Burns went to school. Here *Souter Johnnie's Cottage* (NTS. Tel: 06556-603 or 274) was the home of John Davidson, the original of the Souter (cobbler) Johnnie of Burns's 'Tam o' Shanter', Tam being Douglas Graham of nearby Shanter Farm. The cottage shows Burns material, contemporary furniture and the tools of a village cobbler, while in the restored ale-house are life-size stone figures (by James Thom) of Souter, Tam, the innkeeper and his wife. Both Davidson and Graham are buried in the village churchyard.

2m ***Crossraguel Abbey** (AM. Tel: 031-244-3101) was founded in 1244 by Duncan, Earl of Carrick, for Cluniac monks from Paisley, these remaining in occupation until 1592, probably later than at any other abbey in Scotland. The abbots enjoyed the convenient privilege of mint-ing their own coins. More intact and extensive than many of their kind, these ruins, and especially the gatehouse, dovecot and abbot's house, allow a clearer picture than is usual of abbey life. The ruins (13–16C) are entered near the east end of the *Church*, the choir of which, largely rebuilt in the 15C, ends as a triple apse and contains a piscina and sedilia, these latter, rather unusually, of four seats. From the south west corner of the choir there is access to the cloister, along the east walk of which are (north to south) the sacristy, the chapter house, the treasury and the inner parlour. The vaulted *Sacristy*, 15C in date, occupies the position of the early south transept, foundations of which can be seen, while in the handsome 15C *Chapter House* the principal feature is the groined vaulting sweeping from a slender central pillar. Back in the church, a central door in the wall separating the choir from the nave gives access to the latter, largely of the 13C (south) and 14C (north). The *Gatehouse*, the abbey's most conspicuous survival, stands south west of the nave's west front. Dating from the mid 16C and with contemporary curtain walls, it was perhaps built by that same lay-abbot, Allan Stewart, who was roasted in soap at Dunure. The exterior recalls the increasing militarisation of Scottish life at this time, but, inside, the three storeys are provided with comforts such as window seats, garderobes and fireplaces. The *Dovecot*, at the south west corner of the South Court, was of course essential to the community's economy, as was the adjacent bakehouse, traces of which survive.

A walk across the large South Court passes, to the south, remains of pensioners' dwellings and reaches the extensive area used by the abbot, this being essentially the *Abbot's House*, with courts on either side. The *Tower House* beyond, dating from about 1530 and serving as residence for the later abbots and governors, comprises a vaulted ground floor (probably a store) and three upper levels, of which the first was the hall.

2m **Maybole** (5000 inhab.), sprawled over a hill, has long been the centre for the district of Carrick. The *Town Hall*, in High Street and on the site of what was once the south gate, represents a variety of previous buildings and uses ranging from tolbooth to theatre, while farther north, on the other side of High Street, the *Castle* (in origin probably 16C) marked the north entrance to the town; it now serves as Cassillis estate offices. To the east, below High Street, are the ruins of the 15C *Collegiate Church* (college founded 1373), the sacristy of which was early enlarged as a Kennedy burial place, while, adjacent, the old graveyard is on the site of a 12C church founded by Duncan, Earl of Carrick.

B7024 is now followed north for (5m) **Alloway**, the village in which Burns was born in 1759 and lived his first seven years and, more even than either Dumfries or Mauchline, today a focus of Burns pilgrimage. Approaching the village the road crosses the river, on the right being the startling *Burns Monument* (Tel: 0292-41321), a Grecian temple of 1823. Just below, and in pleasing contrast, the river is spanned by *Brig o' Doon*, a single arch, possibly of the 13C, which features in 'Tam o' Shanter' as the means by which Tam escaped from the witches who dared not cross running water. Just beyond the monument (left, beside the main road, opposite a modern church) is the *Auld Kirk* which was a ruin even before Burns's time. The poet's father is buried here, and it was through the east window that Tam o' Shanter watched a witches' orgy. The *Land o' Burns Centre* (Tel: 0292-43700), roughly opposite, is a visitor centre with an exhibition and video presentation. In about another ½m comes *Burns Cottage and Museum* (Tel: 0292-41215). Originally a clay hut, this thatched cottage was rebuilt by Burns's father with his own hands and served as the family's home between 1757 and 1766 (Burns was born here in January 1759) when they moved to Mount Oliphant, a farm about a mile to the south east. Adjoining the cottage is the Burns museum.

The *Maclaurin Gallery*, at Rozelle House just north of Alloway and just east of the Ayr road, offers a change from Burns. Both the gallery proper, in the servants' quarters and stables, and the main house are used for exhibitions of fine art, sculpture, crafts and local history (Tel: 0292-45447).

2m **Ayr** (50,000 inhab. *Inf.*) is a large, busy town which with its extensive sands and many amenities ranks as the principal resort along this coast,

Alloway, Burns Monument. Incongruous today, but in 1820 imperatively Classical

while for visitors with interests more literary than recreational there are a number of Burns associations.

History. A settlement as far back as the 8C, Ayr received its first charter in c 1202 from William the Lion. Less than a century later Wallace was active here, one of his earliest, best known and bloodiest exploits (1297) being the burning, with 500 English soldiers, of the 'Barns of Ayr', a collection of temporary wooden barracks erected by Edward I. A year later, to prevent its occupation by the English, the castle near the river mouth was demolished by Bruce. In 1315 the parliament which settled the succession of the Scottish crown in the event of Bruce's death met in the (old) church of St. John, a church which later was absorbed into the great fort covering 12 acres built by Cromwell in 1652. In medieval times Ayr harbour saw Perkin Warbeck sail in 1497 to his final defeat, and James IV berthed and anchored his fleet here in 1513.

Alloway Street, extended by High Street, forms Ayr's curving main axis, most places of interest lying close either side over a distance of roughly half a mile between the station in the south and the New Bridge in the north.

Burns extolled Ayr as unsurpassed 'for honest men and bonnie lasses' and thus earned himself the statue (George Lawson, 1891) in front of the railway station. The *Tam o' Shanter Museum*, on the right of the road by the start of High Street, is generally accepted as the starting point of the wild ride so vividly described. Today a museum, in Burns's time this was a brewhouse to which Douglas Graham of Shanter, the real life Tam, supplied malted grain (Tel: 0292-284196). Beyond, Burns yields place to Wallace, commemorated by the *Wallace Tower* built in 1828 on the site of an ancient tower in which, tradition holds, Wallace was imprisoned and from which he made a daring escape. A statue of the hero, by the local sculptor James Thom, looks out from a niche.

Farther on, and again on the right, an alley (Kirk Port) off High Street leads through an arch (with mort-safes, once placed over new graves to prevent body-snatching) to *Auld Kirk*, also known as the New Church of St. John because both the church and its gateway were built in 1654–56 using money given by Cromwell in compensation for the old Church of St. John which he had absorbed into his great fort (see below). Here Burns was baptised. Restored in 1952 as a war memorial, the church preserves the panelling of the original pulpit and is particularly interesting for its three lofts—merchants', traders' and sailors'. The churchyard, beside the river and a haven away from the traffic of High Street, allows a pleasant and detached view of the *Auld Brig*, dating from c 1491 and for 300 years Ayr's only bridge—and an indifferent one, too, according to Burns, who in his dialogue, 'Twa Brigs', writes scornfully of a 'poor narrow footpath of a street where twa wheelbarrows tremble when they meet'.

Opposite the south end of Auld Brig once stood the Fish Cross, symbol of the town's main market centre; today the site is remembered by a cobbled cross and a plaque. Beyond, where High Street meets a T-junction, are the spired *Town Buildings*, built by Thomas Hamilton in 1820–28, and, to the right, the *New Bridge*, first built in 1788 and the other participant in Burns's dialogue. The new bridge's abutments, adorned with allegorical figures, roused the ire of the Auld Brig which prophesied that this newcomer would not last, a prediction which came true when a newer bridge was built in 1877. *Loudoun Hall* (Tel: 0292-284196), nearby in Boat Vennel, is the oldest house in Ayr. Dating from the turn of the 15–16C and beautifully restored, the house, once the home of a wealthy merchant, is a fine example of the better type of domestic architecture of the period.

Fort Street, running south from Loudoun Hall, is a reminder that it

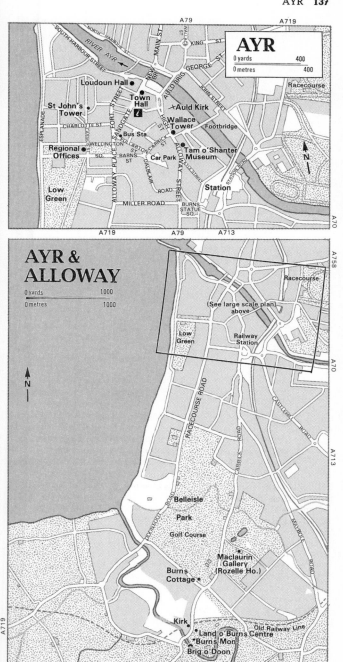

was in this corner of Ayr that Cromwell built his huge fort, using, it is said, stones from the medieval castle and incorporating the 12C Church of St. John as an armoury. Citadel Place, another reminder of the fort, leads west out of Fort Street to *St. John's Tower*, the restored tower of the militarised church. From here Eglinton Terrace and Cassillis Street drop south to Wellington Square in which are the *Regional Buildings* (Robert Wallace, 1820–22 but later extended) and a monument to John McAdam, the road builder, who was born in Ayr in 1756.

16   Ayr to Paisley and Glasgow Round the Coast

A78 and A770 to Greenock and Port Glasgow. A761 via Paisley or A8 via Renfrew to Glasgow.—As far as Ardrossan, generally flat with golf courses and resorts, the last few miles industrialised. After Ardrossan, improving, with coastal scenery, good Clyde views and moorland inland. East from Gourock increasingly built-up and industrial. There is a large area of empty upland (Clyde-Muirshiel Regional Park) within the north loop of this Route.

SOME HOTELS. **Prestwick**. *Carlton*, 187 Ayr Road, KA9 1TP. Tel: 0292-76811. *Parkstone*, Esplanade, KA9 1QN. Tel: 0292-77286. **Troon**. *Marine Highland*, 8 Crosbie Road, KA10 6HE. Tel: 0292-314444. *Piersland*, Craigend Road, KA10 6HD. Tel: 0292-314747. **Irvine**. *Hospitality Inn*, 46 Annick Road, KA11 4LD. Tel: 0294-74272. **Kilwinning**. *Montgreenan Mansion*. Tel: 0294-57733. **Ardrossan**. *Blair Lodge*, South Crescent. Tel: 0294-68436. **Largs**. *Elderslie*, John Street, KA30 8DR. Tel: 0475-686460. **Skelmorlie**. *Manor Park*, PA17 5HE. Tel: 0475-520832. **Gourock**. *Stakis Gantock*, Cloch Road, PA15 1AR. Tel: 0475-34671. **Greenock**. *Tontine*, 6 Ardgowan Square, PA16 8NG. Tel. 0475-23316. **Paisley**. *Stakis Watermill*, Lonend, PA1 1SR. Tel. 041-889-3201.

Total distance 66 or 62m.—*9m* **Irvine**.—*18m* **Largs**.—*6m* **Wemyss Bay**.—*7m* **Gourock**.—*2m* **Greenock**.—*2m* **Port Glasgow**.—*22m* **Glasgow** via **Paisley**, or *18m* **Glasgow** via **Renfrew**.

THE CLYDE AND CLYDE CRUISING. The *Clyde* rises in the hills of Tweeddale, some 80m above Glasgow. Below the moors the river's course to the city is known as Clydesdale, a district of orchards and market gardens interspersed with industry. Along this course the Clyde is used for hydro-electric purposes near Lanark, and near Hamilton it has been diverted and canalised as part of the planning of Strathclyde Country Park (Rte 10). At Glasgow the river is broadish and fairly shallow, and it is interesting that up to about the close of the 18C it was still fordable here. Below Glasgow all changes as the river suddenly reaches maturity—wide, navigable, and, as far as Greenock on the south and Dumbarton on the north, its banks in large part lined by industry. Further west the river becomes the Firth of Clyde, at Gourock curving south to open as a broad and scenic estuary stretching across to hilly Kintyre and embracing the islands of Arran, Bute and Cumbrae. To the north, sea lochs pierce deep into Cowal (Rte 47) and Argyll. The combination of islands, sea lochs and many cheerful summer resorts makes these waters popular for day cruising.

Cruising may be by either one or a combination of the scheduled routes, or in summer by taking a cruise as such. The principal scheduled routes are those to the islands (see Rte 17), day round-trips, often including an island coach tour, being popular; and those from Gourock across the Clyde to Dunoon and Hunter's Quay on Cowal, to Kilcreggan on the

Rosneath peninsula, and to Helensburgh on the east side of Gare Loch. The services to Kilcreggan and Helensburgh do not carry cars. Gourock, Wemyss Bay, Largs and Ardrossan all have connecting train services with Glasgow.

Visitors in search of a unique cruise and experience will choose the Paddle Steamer 'Waverley' (built in 1946 as a replacement for the 1899 'Waverley' sunk at Dunkirk in 1940), the last paddle steamer designed for use on the Clyde. During summer there is a variety of Clyde cruises from Glasgow, as also sailings much farther afield. The same company also offers cruises on the MV 'Balmoral'. Information from Waverley Excursions Ltd, Anderston Quay, Glasgow G3 8HA. Tel: 041-221-8152.

The principal Clyde operator is Caledonian MacBrayne Ltd, Ferry Terminal, Gourock PA19 1QP. Tel: 0475-33755. This firm publishes a useful twice-yearly leaflet 'Cruises and Crossings on the Firth of Clyde'. Other operators include Western Ferries Ltd, 16 Woodside Crescent, Glasgow G3 7UT. Tel: 041-332-9766 (for Gourock-Dunoon, Hunter's Quay); and Clyde Marine Ltd, Princess Pier, Greenock PA16 8AW. Tel: 0475-21281 (for cruises, and services between Gourock, Helensburgh and Kilcreggan).

The northern suburbs of **Ayr** (see Rte 15) merge with the southern suburbs of Prestwick, and it was to this, then very different corner that Bruce came towards the end of his days; to the spot now called *Bruce's Well*, today within a bungalow estate at the southern approach to Prestwick (sign west off Ayr Road). Tradition tells that Bruce, in sombre mood and fearing that he had leprosy—which he probably had for he is thought to have died of it—sank down here exhausted, at the same time striking his spear into the ground. Water miraculously welled up, which Bruce drank, at once feeling restored. Be this as it may, Bruce did endow a leper hospital here and the ruin beside the well may be that of its Chapel of St. Ninian.

1m (from Ayr) **Prestwick** (13,500 inhab. *Inf.*), although noticeably overshadowed by Ayr, remains a resort in its own right, particularly for golf, for which, together with its international airport, it is probably best known. The town's origins go back to at least the 12C, at which time it was held by Walter Fitzalan of Dundonald (see below), Lord High Steward. But of Prestwick's remoter past there is but one remain, its c 15C *Cross*, and even this was rebuilt in 1779 and moved to its present central position opposite the post office in 1963.

Prestwick Airport was started up in 1935 by the Duke of Hamilton and Group Captain D.F. McIntyre, the first men to fly over Everest (1933). At first just the grass field of Scottish Aviation Ltd, Prestwick's fog-free record led to rapid development during the war when it became the headquarters of RAF Ferry Command and of the USAF Transport Command. After the war the same fog-free characteristic ensured growth to international civil airport status.

At *Monkton*, just north of the airport, there is a monument to James Macrae (died 1744), a poor local boy who went to India and became Governor of Madras. He returned a wealthy man and is said to have begun this monument himself. His tomb is in Monkton churchyard, with a 12C church, though there is a local belief that his bones were disinterred and placed within the monument. At *Symington*, a short way north east on A77, the small church preserves three 12C Norman windows.

3m **Troon** (11,000 inhab. *Inf.*) is a summer and golf resort, refreshingly smaller and quieter than the Ayr-Prestwick complex. There are good beaches, as also several golf courses in the neighbourhood. The place derives its name from the Troone (nose), the rocky arm of land which hooks seaward. *Lady Island*, 3m offshore, is a bird sanctuary.— *Dundonald Castle* (AM. Tel: 031-244-3101), 3m north east of Troon, a rough but striking ruin on a hill above its village, is a place which demands to be visited by anyone with a feel for Scotland's history, for this was the cradle of the Stuart line. This came about because the castle was held by the Fitzalans, Lord High Stewards, one of whom married the daughter of Bruce, their son becoming Robert II, the first of the Stewarts or Stuarts. Both Robert II and his son Robert III lived and died here (1390 and 1406), but after their time the castle fell into neglect. The early structure (13C) seems to have been a keep-gatehouse with two towers. This, however, was largely destroyed during the wars of independence, afterwards being rebuilt as a large tower-house by Robert II. The great hall was on the third floor, its upper part, however, being removed in 1644 by the 1st Earl of Dundonald to provide material for his castellated mansion of *Auchans*, a mile to the south and also now a ruin.

5m **Irvine**—although in an industrial setting and, together with Kilwinning (see below), since 1966 a New Town—is in fact an ancient royal burgh (first charter c 1240) which has played its part in Scotland's history, for it was here in 1297 that Wallace was deserted by his supporters (who signed the Treaty of Irvine with the English), thus being forced to flee to the Highlands to gather fresh allies. Today a sprawling and confusing place, Irvine is effectively in two parts; the town proper (Old Burgh) and Harbourside. In the Old Burgh there are two places of visitor interest, Seagate Castle and Glasgow Vennel. *Seagate Castle*, overlooking the site of the early harbour, though of older origin, in its present form is the drab shell of a mansion built by the 3rd Earl of Eglinton between 1546–85, during which period Mary, Queen of Scots, is thought to have been received here. *Glasgow Vennel* (Tel: 0294-75059) is the street in which Burns lived (at No 4) and worked (No 10) as a flax-dresser between 1781–84. Both places have now been restored to their 18C character and there is a small museum. Others associated with the town (both natives) were John Galt (1779–1839), the novelist and traveller who gave his name to the town of Galt in Canada, and J.B. Dunlop (1840–1921), born at Dreghorn 2m east), the vet who in 1888 invented the pneumatic tyre.—The main features in Harbourside are the *Magnum Leisure Centre*; *Sea World* (Tel: 0294-311414), specialising in marine creatures of the Ayrshire coast; and the *Scottish Maritime Museum* (Tel: 0294-78283), a scattered long-term project aiming to expand from its opening base of some modest ships, several small boats, a shipyard worker's home, a shop and suchlike.

2m Eglinton Country Park (visitor centre, Tel: 0294-51776), roughly half-way between Irvine and Kilwinning, was the scene of the extravagant 'Eglinton Tournament' of 1839, a romantic if dotty attempt to revive the forms and ceremonies of ancient chivalry. Prince Louis Napoleon (Napoleon III) was one of the knights, as was also, and more appropriately for this district, the Earl of Cassillis; Lady Seymour, a granddaughter of Sheridan, was Queen of Love and Beauty, and the tournament provided Disraeli with material for his novel 'Endymion'. The ruins here, the last in a series, are those of a mansion completed by the 12th Earl in 1802.—*2m* **Kilwinning**, with Irvine now a New Town, claims to be the earliest home in Scotland of freemasonry, possibly introduced by foreign workers who came to build the *Abbey*. This, founded about 1150 by Richard de Morville on the site of a church built by the 6C Irish St. Wynin (hence the town's name), was largely destroyed in 1561 and the ruins left today are scanty. Nevertheless they provide the town with an attractive central feature alongside the parish church with its detached tower of 1815. Among the remains are the south transept wall with gable and three lancets, the doorway into the east cloister walk, the chapter house entrance and part of the west front.—*Dalgarven Mill* (Tel: 0294-52448), 2m north of Kilwinning on A737, is a working water-powered flour mill, now home to a museum of Ayrshire country life and costumes.—*3m* **Saltcoats**, now a harbour and resort on the depressing fringe of an industrialised district, owes its name to the saltworks established here by James V. The *North Ayrshire Museum* (Tel: 0294-64174), in the 18C former parish church, well illustrates the industrial and maritime development of this region and includes some early 19C interiors.—**Ardrossan**, another resort and port (sailings to Arran), although physically joined to Saltcoats, achieves some individuality through having been laid out to a formal plan in 1806. *Ardrossan Castle*, a small 12C ruin above the town, was taken by Wallace from the English and finally destroyed by Cromwell. *Horse Island*, just offshore, is a bird sanctuary.

The coastal road now clears the industrial belt to reach (*4m*) **West Kilbride** where late 15C *Law Castle* was a tower-house of the Boyds. The ruined castle by the shore at *Portencross*, 2m west, is a 15C keep, successor to earlier strongholds used by the early Stuarts, notably Robert II, before crossing to Rothesay on Bute. A nearby cannon is said to have belonged to an Armada galleon sunk by a local witch. *Blackshaw* (Tel: 0563-34257), 2m east of West Kilbride by B781, is an open farm park.—Continuing north, A78 passes *Hunterston Nuclear Power Station* (by appointment. Tel: 0294-823668) and British Steel Corporation's huge deep-water iron ore terminal (1979) on the way to (*4m*) **Fairlie**, a pleasant modest resort looking across to Cumbrae and known also for its castle, a small, creeper-clad 16C keep standing above the town in a pretty glen with a waterfall.—*Kelburn Country Centre* (Tel: 0475-568685), just north of Fairlie, offers gardens, walks, adventure trails, pony riding, and a group of 18C farm buildings set around a green and today housing information, café, shop and suchlike. The castle, seat of the earls of Glasgow, is not normally open to visitors. High above Kelburn, a short distance up A760, there is a viewpoint well rewarding a brief diversion.

3m **Largs** (10,000 inhab. *Inf.*), below green hills and with views across to Cumbrae, is as popular for itself and its holiday amenities as for being the port for the Cumbrae ferries. A burial chamber and traces of a hillfort, both in Douglas Park, are evidence of Neolithic and Iron Age settlement, while a motte (see below) survives from medieval fortification. But it is the *Pencil* tower (1910), on the shore at the south edge of the town, that records Largs's honoured place in Scottish history, for it was here, at the Battle of Largs in 1263, that Alexander III fought and routed Hakon of Norway. The battle—part naval and part land as a storm drove Hakon's galleys ashore—was won by the Scots after two days of fighting, the victory meaning that the Hebrides and the Isle of Man, held by the Norsemen for some 400 years, were ceded to Scotland.

Near the town centre, the *Skelmorlie Aisle* (AM. Tel: 031-244-3101), a few yards east of the pier, was originally the north transept of the parish church, but was converted in 1636 into a mausoleum by Sir Robert Montgomerie of Skelmorlie and now ranks as one of Scotland's most elegant examples of Renaissance work. The adjacent *Largs Museum* (Tel: 0475-687081) is that of the Largs and District Historical Society. Largs also offers two curiosities, the closer of which, the *Three Sisters* (off Waterside Street, a few minutes walk south east from Skelmorlie Aisle), three stone columns on top of the medieval motte, were erected for astronomical measurement purposes by General Sir Thomas Brisbane (1773–1860), a native of Largs, governor of New South Wales and a distinguished astronomer. The other curiosity is the *Prophet's Grave* in Brisbane Glen (home of Sir Thomas) on the north east of the town; this commemorates one William Smith, the local minister, who died of the plague in the 17C while continuing to care for his flock who had fled into the glen.—The minor road north out of Largs up Noddsdale Water climbs over moor to reach *Cornalees Bridge*, see below.

CLYDE-MUIRSHIEL REGIONAL PARK. A760, leading east to reach Lochwinnoch in 14m, skirts the southern boundary of Clyde-Muirshiel Regional Park (Tel: 041-887-2806), which embraces much of the empty, roadless upland moor enclosed by this road; by B786 and B788 between Lochwinnoch and Greenock; and by the minor road leading south from Greenock past Loch Thom and down Noddsdale Water to Largs (but a pocket reaches beyond A78 to the Clyde estuary). Hill of Stake (1711ft) rises at the heart of the park, which has four visitor centres—Cornalees Bridge at the north west, and, at the south east and close to Lochwinnoch, Castle Semple Country Park, Lochwinnoch Nature Reserve, and Muirshiel Country Park.

Before descending into **Kilbirnie** the ruin of *Kilbirnie Place* may be glimpsed a few fields away to the south; this seat of the Crawfords was built in the 14C and burnt down in the 18C. In the town, *Kilbirnie Church* (nave and tower, 1470–90. North aisle, 1597) is known for its Laird's Loft of 1642, adorned in 1703 by the 1st Viscount Garnock with 18 heraldic shields of the Lindsay lineage.

Approaching **Lochwinnoch**, the 16C tower of *Barr Castle* is seen on the right. The town has a local *Museum* (Tel: 0505-842615), in Old School Buildings in Main Street, and is close to three Clyde-Muirshiel Regional Park centres. *Castle Semple Country Park* (Tel: 0505-842882), with the loch of the same name as its main feature, was created mainly for sailing, canoeing, rowing and coarse fishing. *Lochwinnoch Nature Reserve* (RSPB. Tel: 0505-842663) offers an observation tower, hides, exhibition and gift shop. *Muirshiel Country Park* (Tel: 0505-842803), off B786 4m north of Lochwinnoch, was opened in 1970 as a contribution to European Conservation Year. Here, in an area of upland rolling moor and mixed woodland, the amenities include a visitor centre, ranger services and several trails of varying length.—Beyond the north east end of Loch Semple, on a hill, can be seen *The Temple*, a folly said to have been built to enable a crippled Lady Semphill to watch the hunt. *Castle Semple Collegiate Church* (AM. Tel: 031-244-3101), 2m north east of Lochwinnoch, represents a foundation of 1504. The remains include a square tower and a three-sided apse, each side with three Gothic windows.

Leaving Largs A78 keeps to the coast, passing two former Montgomerie strongholds; *Knock Castle* (late 16C), just visible among trees, and, conspicuous on a rise, *Skelmorlie Castle* of 1502.—*6m* (from Largs) **Wemyss Bay** (pron. Weems) is the port for the ferry to the island of Bute.—*2m* **Inverkip** where there is a nuclear power station. From here a small road climbs to open upland on which is *Cornalees Bridge* (Tel: 0475-521458), one of the centres of Clyde-Muirshiel Regional Park. Here the interesting 2m-long Cornalees Trail follows first the Greenock Cut, an aqueduct designed and built in 1827 by Robert Thom (after whom the nearby loch is named) to provide Greenock with drinking water and power for its mills; the trail then continues down the wooded glen of Kip Water, to return by the Kelly Aqueduct which once carried water along the hillside from Kelly Reservoir near Skelmorlie.—At Inverkip A78 is left for A770 which soon rounds *Lunderston Bay*, a shore picnic area at the point where Clyde-Muirshiel Regional Park meets the coast, beyond (*3m* from Inverkip) reaching *Cloch Lighthouse* (1797) marking the great bend from the Firth of Clyde into the Clyde proper.

2m **Gourock** (11,000 inhab. *Inf.*). Although on the fringe of the urban and industrial strip stretching east through Greenock and Port Glasgow, Gourock remains essentially a resort. Standing, too, on the bend where the Clyde changes direction, the town enjoys wide views across the estuary and is busy with ferries. There are frequent daily car ferries (20 minutes) to Dunoon on the Cowal peninsula (Caledonian Mac-Brayne from Railway Pier to Dunoon Pier; Western Ferries from McInray's Point to Hunter's Quay), and passenger ferries (Clyde Marine) also run north to Kilcreggan on the Rosneath peninsula and to Helensburgh on the east side of Gare Loch. On Gourock Pier are the offices (booking) of Caledonian MacBrayne Ltd, the main west coast operators of ferries, both within the Clyde and, from West Highland ports, to the Hebrides.

Gourock also has one curious local antiquity, namely the *Kempock Stone* (or Granny Kempock's Stone), to be found above the library within the curve of A770. Probably prehistoric, the stone was used by fishermen in rites to ensure good weather, and also by couples about to marry who encircled it for good luck. In 1662, one Mary Lamont was burned as a witch after confessing she had intended to throw the stone into the sea and thus cause shipwrecks.

A770 now plunges into a virtually uninterrupted urban and industrial strip, sandwiched between the Clyde and the steep hills behind and extending from Gourock through Greenock to the east edge of Port Glasgow. Yet it could be a mistake to hurry through, for both places have something to offer.

2m **Greenock** (69,500 inhab. *Inf.*), long connected with shipbuilding, was the birthplace in c 1645 of Captain Kidd, the privateer and pirate, and also of James Watt (1736–1819), engineer and inventor of the condensing steam engine.

Today's visitor should aim first for the east end of the long, elegant Esplanade which runs westward out of the main town. Here stands the *Old West Kirk* of 1591, interesting on three counts. It was the first church built after the Reformation and the first Presbyterian church confirmed by parliament; in 1920, to make room for commercial development, it was removed from its original site and rebuilt here; and it has stained-glass windows by Burne-Jones, Morris and Rossetti. Moving into the main town, Broughton Street and Grey Place are followed by Dalrymple Street which meets a roundabout with local government buildings to the north and south. James Watt's birthplace was in William Street, just beyond municipal buildings immediately south east of the roundabout. High Street runs west from the roundabout, on the right being shopping precincts, beyond which West Burn Street was the street in which John Galt (see Irvine, above) died; he is buried in the old graveyard in Inverkip Street, the westward extension of High Street. Off George Square, about 100 yards north of the junction of High Street and Inverkip Street (by Kilblain Street) run Nelson Street (south west) and Union Street (north west). In the former stands the (new) *West Kirk* (David Cousin, 1841–53), and this same street ascends to the cemetery in which is the tomb of Mary Campbell, Burns's 'Highland Mary', removed from the original graveyard of the Old West Kirk. In Union Street, soon on the left, is the building (Edward Blore, 1835), commissioned by Watt's son as a memorial to his father. Here, now, is the *McLean Museum and Art Gallery* (Tel: 0475-23741) showing, in the art gallery, works by, amongst others, James Guthrie (1859–1930), a native of Greenock; and, in the museum, local and natural history exhibits, model ships and material associated with James Watt.

In 1940–45 Greenock was the chief Free French naval base in Britain, and a great granite *Cross of Lorraine* and anchor, the French memorial to their men who died in the Battle of the Atlantic, stands on Lyle Hill above the town.

  2m **Port Glasgow**, built in the 17C as the furthest deep water port up the river and the place where, in 1812, Henry Bell's steamer, the 'Comet', was constructed by John Wood; of about 25 tons and with a 3 horsepower engine, the boat achieved a speed of 7mph. *Newark Castle* (AM. Tel: 031-244-3101), beside the Clyde at the east end of the town, is an almost intact turreted mansion of the Maxwells, for the most part of the 16–17C but with a 15C tower. This elegant building, with its dovecot, once solitary and gracious beside the river, today contrasts almost startlingly with the ugly industry which has now engulfed it.

  From Port Glasgow to Glasgow there is a choice between the inland road (A761) through Paisley or the faster Clydeside road (A8, M8) through Renfrew.

Inland Road to Glasgow

A761 climbs steeply out of Port Glasgow, offering wide and interesting views before reaching open upland.—*10m* **Kilbarchan**, just south of the main road, was once well known for its tartan weaving, and the 18C *Weaver's Cottage* (NTS. Tel: 05057-5588) is typical of those in which home weaving was practised until as recently as 1940. Weaving is demonstrated and the cottage and garden contain looms, contemporary furniture and an eclectic collection of interesting and curious period articles. On the town steeple there is a figure of Habbie Simpson, a famous 17C local piper.—At *Elderslie*, just west of Paisley and the traditional birthplace of Wallace in c 1272, a memorial, with dramatic pictorial plaques, put up by the Clan Wallace Society, stands beside A737 at the west entrance to the town.

  5m **Paisley** (85,000 inhab. *Inf.*) is a large, busy town which, although essentially industrial, is nevertheless a place of some spaciousness and character and with sufficient buildings of architectural merit to warrant an official waymarked town trail. It is best known for its abbey and for the shawls with their distinctive pattern woven here during the 19C. Born here were Alexander Wilson (1763–1813), poet and American ornithologist, and Robert Tannahill (1774–1810), the weaver poet.

  Virtually all that remains of *Paisley Abbey* is its church, the nave of which has long served as parish church. The main architectural phases are Transitional (12C) in the three bays at the east end of the south aisle of the nave; Gothic First Pointed (13C), the west end of the church; Gothic Decorated (15C), nave interior and transepts; and post-Reformation restoration.

The priory of Pasletum was founded by Walter Fitzalan (ancestor through Bruce's daughter of the Stuart kings, see Dundonald Castle) who in about 1163 here installed 13 Cluniac monks from Wenlock, in Shropshire, his native home. The relics of St. Mirren or Merinus (c 7C), whose cell had stood here, were transferred to the church and his shrine soon became a place of pilgrimage. The priory rapidly grew to be a wealthy house and was promoted to abbey in 1219. It was destroyed by the English in 1307 and, although favoured by the Stuart kings, was not rebuilt until after 1450, to which date much of the present structure belongs. Further destruction came with the Reformation, at which time the tower collapsed, destroying the choir in its fall. The church, with the exception of the nave and one chapel, then fell into decay and the lower part of the west front and the south wall of the nave are all that survive of the early church. The nave roof was replaced in 1780. The main restoration, begun in 1897 by Rowand Anderson and McGregor Chalmers, was completed by Sir Robert Lorimer between 1922–28.

The West Front has a deeply recessed Early English doorway flanked by two blind arches and surmounted by three traceried windows. The

Nave is remarkable for a richly developed triforium of broad round arches, and on the left of the west door there is a memorial to John Hamilton, the last abbot, executed in 1571 for alleged complicity in the murder of Darnley. The place of the south transept is occupied by *St. Mirren's Chapel (1499), with a fascinating series of panels (one missing), probably of the 12C, depicting episodes of doubtful authenticity from the life of the saint. The Choir, surprisingly paved with slabs from the basement of Hamilton Palace and with stalls designed by Lorimer, is historically the most interesting part of the abbey, for here are the Stuart Tombs. A recumbent female effigy may be that of either Euphemia Ross, wife of Robert II, or, more popularly, of Marjory Bruce, Bruce's daughter and Robert II's mother. She was killed in 1316 at the age of 23 while hunting at Knock, just north of Paisley. Here also are buried six High Stewards, the first, Walter Fitzalan, being the founder of the abbey and the sixth the husband of Marjory; two wives of Robert II; and Robert III.

Place of Paisley, adjoining the church on the south, was in origin a part of the abbey's domestic buildings dating from c 1475. After the Dissolution the buildings were converted to a mansion (or palace, which word has corrupted to Place) of first the Hamiltons and then the earls of Dundonald, and it was either here, or perhaps in the church, that Jean Cochrane, granddaughter of the 1st Earl, was married to Claverhouse in 1684. In 1764 the Abercorn family bought the mansion, but it was later so neglected that the old kitchen became used as a tavern. However in 1903 the Place returned to Church ownership, since when there has been constant improvement culminating in the 1950s in the conversion of the upper levels to Abbey Manse.

From Place of Paisley, Bridge Street (Cotton Street) crosses the river, after which a right turn along Orchard Street leads into New Street in which, by the junction with Shuttle Street, stands the *Laigh Kirk* of 1738, successor to the abbey nave as parish church and of particular interest to Americans because the Rev. John Witherspoon, the only cleric to sign the Declaration of Independence, was minister here for 12 years before emigrating in 1768. Farther along New Street, the *Bull Inn*, built in 1901, is known for its Art Nouveau interior. New Street meets High Street, with, to the west, the *Thomas Coats Memorial Church* (Hippolyte Blanc, 1894), the cruciform church of the Baptist community and perhaps the most conspicuous building in Paisley.

The *Paisley Museum and Art Gallery* (Tel: 041-889-3151) is in High Street at the opposite end to the abbey. Founded in 1870, but now admirably modernised and with an art gallery, the museum covers local history, archaeology (with excellent explanations of prehistoric dwellings, etc) and natural sciences. Perhaps the most important section is the display of *Paisley Shawls and Plaids, of which the museum has some 700, as well as much other material (design books, looms etc) relating to this former industry.

At the end of the 18C British and French soldiers returning from India brought back Kashmir shawls. These—warm, light and with beautiful designs—were soon copied at several places in both countries, one of these being Paisley, where shawl weaving was started in 1805. The 'pine motif' (virtually synonymous with the term 'Paisley pattern', though in fact there were many other designs) was Kashmiri in origin, there known as 'Baandaam' and deriving from the shape of the native almond in its early green state. It was copied and developed at most weaving centres, but nowhere more efficiently than at Paisley, which soon became as famous for its mass production (after c 1840 boosted by increased use of the Jacquard mechanised loom) as it was notorious for its imitation of others' designs. By the second half of the century Paisley had achieved a virtual monopoly in Britain. Printed shawls date from about the 1840s; reversed shawls, with the pattern on both sides, began to appear in about 1865. The 1870s saw the sudden end of the popularity of the Paisley shawl and plaid, largely because this decade also saw the passing of the crinoline for which the large plaids had been about the only possible over-cover. Fortunately the new demand for cotton thread was ready to provide alternative employment.

The *Coats Observatory and Weather Station* (Tel: 041-889-2013), an outstation of Paisley Museum, is in Oakshaw Street, north of and roughly parallel to High Street.

7m central **Glasgow**, see Rte 19.

Clydeside Road to Glasgow

This road connects to M8, the quickest way into Glasgow. Also to *Erskine Bridge* (toll) which, built in 1971, superseded a ferry and now provides a main Clyde crossing, particularly useful for traffic heading north and wishing to avoid Glasgow.—The *Blantyre Obelisk*, north of B815 and 2m west of Erskine Bridge, commemorates the 11th Lord Blantyre who lost his life in Brussels in 1830 during the fighting for Belgian independence.

Clear of Port Glasgow A8 passes first *Parklea Farm*, between road and river, a NTS property leased to Inverclyde District Council as a recreational area, and then (*3m*), on the right, *Finlaystone House* (Tel: 047-554-285), with a 14C core but 18 and 19C additions. Long a seat of the Cunningham earls of Glencairn, the estate is now the home of the chief of Clan MacMillan and a clan centre. The house shows a collection of dolls, and the grounds provide gardens, woodland walks and play areas.

9m **Renfrew**, today an industrial town, has also long been a royal burgh which gives the title of baron to the Prince of Wales. Somerled, Lord of the Isles, was defeated and slain here by Malcolm IV in 1164, and it was here too that the 9th Earl of Argyll, who was supporting Monmouth's rebellion, was taken (and later executed) in 1685.—*6m* central **Glasgow**, see Rte 19.

17   The Clyde Islands (Arran, Bute, Cumbrae)

The islands of Arran, Bute and Cumbrae, all lying in the Firth of Clyde, are scenically pleasant, though, with the exception of Arran, not outstanding. Popular family resorts, all are on the whole quiet and with something of an old-fashioned flavour. In summer, accommodation should be reserved in advance.

Car ferries serve all three islands. Timetables are, however, subject to annual and seasonal changes. For latest information, apply to Caledonian MacBrayne Ltd, Gourock, PA19 1QP. Tel: 0475-33755. Telex: 779318.

Island of Arran

Tourist Information. The Pier, Brodick. Tel: 0770-2401 or 2140.

Access. 1. Car ferry from Ardrossan to Brodick, with train connections from Glasgow. Several times daily, but restricted timetable on Sun. and in winter. Advance booking for vehicles essential in summer; passenger embarkation (reservation) tickets also required for some sailings at peak periods. Crossing 55 minutes. 2. Car ferry from Claonaig (Kintyre) to Lochranza. Several times daily, approx mid May to end Sept. No winter service. Small ship; services liable to cancellation in poor weather. Crossing 30 minutes.

Local companies operate coach tours around the island and to

Brodick Castle, times related to specific ferries. Self-drive cars are available.

SOME HOTELS. **Brodick**. *Auchrannie*, KA27 8BZ. Tel: 0770-2234. *Invercloy*, KA27 8AJ. Tel: 0770-2225. **Lochranza**. **(Catacol)**. *Catacol Bay*, KA27 8HN. Tel: 077083-231. **Blackwaterfoot**. *Kinloch*, KA27 8ET. Tel: 077086-444. **Kilmory (Lagg)**. *Lagg*, KA27 8PQ. Tel: 077087-255. **Lamlash**. *Glenisle*, Shore Road, KA27 8LS. Tel: 07706-559 or 258.

History. The many standing stones and burial cairns show that Arran was well populated in prehistoric times. Later the island became a part of the kingdom of Dalriada, but was soon taken by the Norsemen who held it until Somerled, Lord of the Isles, wrested it from them in the mid 12C. Bruce, fired by the example set by the spider while on the Irish island of Rathlin, landed here in 1306 on his way to Turnberry to start in earnest the war of independence. In 1503 Arran was awarded by royal charter to the Hamilton family. The island has been a holiday resort since the early 18C and at one period it was fashionable to come here to drink the allegedly health-giving wild goats' milk.

Arran is about 20m long by 10m wide, much of the island being uncultivated moor and mountain, the latter rising in the north to a serrated range, with Goatfell (2866ft) the highest peak. The island belongs almost wholly to the Hamilton family and the National Trust for Scotland, whose combined successful policy has been the exclusion of offensive development. Among the many recreational possibilities are swimming, boating, fishing, golf, climbing and pony-trekking, while for those in search of the past there are medieval castles and a profusion of prehistoric and Iron Age sites.

The description below makes an anti-clockwise circuit of 55m starting from Brodick.

Brodick, the island's capital and with many hotels, straggles around the bay of the same name. The *Isle of Arran Heritage Museum* (Tel: 0770-2636) occupies buildings which were once an 18C croft. Local history, archaeology and geology are among the fields covered, and there is also a picnic area.—2m **Brodick Castle** (NTS. Tel: 0770-2202) is the ancient seat of the dukes of Hamilton. Built on the site of a Viking fort, the castle dates in part from the 13C (north wing) and was extended in 1652 and 1844. It was held by Edward I, and later by Cromwell's troops, who however were massacred by the islanders. The drawing room has a rich plaster ceiling with coats of arms, and the series of rooms contain silver, porcelain and paintings—Watteau, Turner and Rowlandson are among the artists—from the collections of the dukes of Hamilton, William Beckford and the Earl of Rochford. There are two gardens. The formal walled garden dates from 1710; the woodland garden of some 60 acres was started in 1923 by the late Duchess of Montrose and is now accepted as one of the finest rhododendron gardens in Britain. Both gardens now form *Brodick Country Park* (Tel: 0770-2462).

Goatfell (2866ft), rising to the north above Brodick Castle, forms part of a NTS property which includes Glen Rosa to the south and Cir Mhor (2618ft) to the north, an area which provides some superb scenic walking. The walk, of around 11m, from Brodick, up Glen Rosa, across the saddle (1500ft), then down wild Glen Sannox to Sannox Bay is well worth considering. The ascent of Goatfell is best made by a path which starts from Brodick Country Park and climbs to the summit by way of the mountain's eastern shoulder.

5m Sannox Bay, from where Glen Sannox cuts across the north flank of Goatfell towards Cir Mhor.—*7m* **Lochranza**, a village below mountain and high moor and strung along the narrow sea loch of the same name, is reputed to be the place where Bruce landed in 1306 or 1307 on his return from Rathlin. It is said, too, that there was a nunnery here which gave shelter to Bruce's sister, but of this, if indeed it ever existed, there is now no trace. What does survive, though, is *Lochranza Castle*, a ruin with two square towers, built during the 13–14C and enlarged in the 16C. The car ferry to Claonaig on Kintyre sails from Lochranza.

The road south hugs the shore, affording a continuous view across Kilbrannan Sound to Kintyre and passing in *6m* the hamlet of *Pirnmill*, a name recalling the 'pirns', or wooden bobbins, once used at the mill here.—*7m Auchagallon Stone Circle*, a somewhat battered site on the east of the road close to a road junction, comprises a circle of 15 stones around a burial cairn of possibly rather later date. The moor (***Machrie Moor**) within the triangle formed by the main coastal road, the small road leading east from Auchagallon, and B880 heading NE from Blackwaterfoot, is (on the south side of the Machrie Water) exceptionally and visibly rich in prehistoric remains, these including burial chambers and at least six stone circles, some marked by uprights 12–18ft in height. For detailed study some walking is necessary—the normal approach being a path just south of the Machrie Water near Tormore—but much can also be seen from the roads, especially from the slightly higher ground crossed by the small one from Auchagallon.

4m **Blackwaterfoot**, from where B880, a road known as The String and built in 1817, skirts the south east flank of Machrie Moor. *Shiskine*, 1m up this road, claims to be the burial place of St. Molaise, also known as St. Luserian, who, despite deliberately contracting 30 diseases in expiation of his sins, is nevertheless popularly believed to have lived to the age of 120. A rough stone on a wall of the church is said to have once covered the saint's remains. *King's Cave*, reached by a 2m walk along the shore from the golf course at Blackwaterfoot and the largest of a group, was, tradition asserts, used by Fingal and his followers, as also later by Bruce who, needless to say, here watched that spider while his companions drew the rough hunting scenes on the walls. A sign about 1m south of Blackwaterfoot directs to *Kilpatrick Dun* (short walk), an unusual site at which a small Iron Age fort has been surrounded by a turf and stone cashel (enclosing an area of about two acres) which would seem to be of Celtic Christian origin; while at Corriecravie, rather over *3m* from Blackwaterfoot, a second sign suggests another short walk, this time to the Iron Age fort of *Tor Chaistel*.

3m **Kilmory** village, in which, 500 yards down a path, will be found *Torrylin Cairn*. Now no more than a mound, this Stone or Bronze Age tomb once had several compartments in which were found the remains of four adults and two children. And, for those prepared to face a seven-or-so-mile moorland trudge, there is *Cairn Ban* (sign east of Kilmory. 3½m), a large and well preserved chambered cairn lying at 900ft way out on the moors.—At (*6m*) *Kildonan* the ruined medieval keep by the sea is that of a castle first granted in 1406 by Robert III to his bastard son, John.

The road now curves north with the coast, in *5m* reaching **Kings-cross**, a name recalling that it was from Kingscross Point that, lured by a mystic fire, Bruce set sail for Turnberry in 1307. Only 44 years earlier Lamlash Bay, of which Kingscross Point marks the southern arm, had witnessed a very different scene as King Hakon here tried to rally his shattered fleet after its defeat at Largs. *Holy Island*, which with its quite impressive 1000ft peak protects the seaward side of the bay, owes its name to St. Molaise (see Shiskine above) who used a cave on the west shore as his meditative cell. Runic inscriptions here were, it is tempting to suppose, left by Hakon's defeated followers.—*3m* **Lamlash** is, after Brodick, Arran's largest village. From here there is a scenic footpath to Brodick (4½m), passing the Iron Age fort of *Dun Fionn*.—*4m* (by road) **Brodick**.

Island of Bute

Tourist Information. Rothesay. Tel: 0700-502151.

Access. 1. Car ferry from Wemyss Bay to Rothesay, with train connections from Glasgow. Several times daily, but restricted timetable on Sun. and in winter. Crossing 30 minutes. 2. Car ferry from Colintraive (Cowal) to Rhubodach. Frequent daily service. Crossing 5 minutes.

SOME HOTELS. **Rothesay**. *Ardmory House*, Ardmory Road, Ardbeg. Tel: 0700-502346. *Craigmore*, Crichton Road. Tel: 0700-503533.

Bute is 15m long by 3m broad, with gentle scenery, mostly farming land with patches of moor. Its northern part is tucked into the Cowal peninsula, from which it is separated by the narrow and beautiful straits known as the *Kyles of Bute*, while the southern island runs out to Garroch Head on the way to which there are remains of interest. The island's history is essentially that of Rothesay Castle, but that man was here millenia before its construction is clear from the island's several prehistoric sites, a few visible from the road, others to be discovered by using a special historical map obtainable from Tourist Information.

The sizeable and popular resort of **Rothesay** is the island's capital, a royal burgh which gives the title of Duke to the Prince of Wales. The first holder of the title—the premier Scottish title of the Heir to the Throne—was the ill-fated David, son of Robert III (see Rte 33C, Falkland Palace). *Bute Museum* (Tel: 0700-502248), in Stuart Street beside the castle, has exhibits illustrating local and natural history and archaeology. The museum also provides information on the island's prehistoric sites, as well as on the several nature trails arranged by the Bute Natural History Society. Local history, with emphasis on the holiday resort aspect, is also the theme of an exhibition in the *Winter Garden* (Tel: 0700-502487) in Argyll Street. *St. Mary's Chapel*, on A845 just south of the town, is a ruin beside the High Kirk of 1796. Built in the 16C as the chancel of the parish church, the small ruin houses two canopied tombs (13–14C), probably of the Stewarts of Menteith, and also a recumbent effigy. It is said that here also are buried five 14C bishops of Sodor and Man.

*Rothesay Castle (AM. Tel: 031-244-3101) is a historic and attractive ruin, of particular interest for being round in shape.

History. The castle dates from at least the early 13C, first appearing in history in 1230 when it was stormed by the Norsemen. Only a few years later, in 1263, the Norsemen were here again, but this time only briefly because they were soon routed at Largs. During the Stuart period, Rothesay was a royal residence, much used by Robert II and Robert III. Later, James IV and V both based themselves here during their operations against the Lords of the Isles, and it was these two kings who added the Great Tower. Much battered during the Civil War, the castle was burned by Argyll in 1685, thereafter remaining a neglected ruin until repaired during the 19C by the 2nd and 3rd Marquises of Bute.

Today's still impressive remains include the 12 or 13C Circular Wall (unique in Scotland), with four round towers, and the Great Tower of James IV and V, the forework through which the castle is entered. Within the Great Tower, on the first floor, is the Great Hall which has been restored. Inside the round open courtyard are the well and the roofless Chapel (appropriately dedicated to St. Michael, patron of warriors) in which the piscina and sacrament house can still be seen. Behind the chapel is the Bloody Stair, on which, the story goes, the daughter of a High Steward stabbed herself in order to escape from an unwelcome bridegroom.

NORTH OF ROTHESAY. **Port Bannatyne**, 2m north of Rothesay, is a resort on Kames Bay, at the head of which stands *Kames Castle*, dating in part from the 14C. The writer John Sterling (1806–44), known less for himself than as the subject of a biography by Carlyle, was born here. From Port Bannatyne A886 runs north with the shore of the eastern arm of the Kyles of Bute, with views across to Cowal, and in 5m reaches *Rhubo- dach* (for the ferry to Colintraive), while two roads branch west for the sands of Ettrick Bay; to the south of the northern of these roads a stone circle can be seen in a field about ½m after the fork.

SOUTH OF ROTHESAY. The coastal road (A844) leads past (at Kerrycroy) the gates of *Mount Stuart* (1877), seat of the Marquis of Bute, to reach *Kingarth*, 5m from Rothesay. Beyond, the small road down the centre of the peninsula (signed to St. Blane's Chapel) passes within about ½m a cart track into the wood on the left. A few yards down this, in a clearing on the right, there are three massive standing stones. The small road continues to its end, whence a path climbs (10 minutes walk) to *St. Blane's Chapel*, in origin perhaps of c 1100 and named for a 6C native saint who studied in Ireland and preached in Scotland (perhaps estab- lishing a monastery here on Bute), being best known in connection with Dunblane.

Island of Cumbrae

Tourist Information. Stuart Street, Millport. Tel: 0475-530753.

Access. Car ferry from Largs to Cumbrae Slip, with train connections from Glasgow and bus from Cumbrae Slip to Millport. Frequent. Crossing 10 minutes.
   In summer, island-circuit coach tours.

HOTEL. **Millport**. *Millerston*, West Bay Road, KA28 0HA. Tel: 0475- 530480.

Cumbrae, or more properly Great Cumbrae, although only ten minutes offshore, has a character surprisingly different from that of the busy mainland. One road (about 12m) circles the island, and in summer much of its traffic is made up of families riding hired bicycles.

Millport, the only town, curves round its bay for 1½ miles, and with its pleasantly incidental sandy beach, broken by rocks and a scatter of islets, rightly claims to be a family resort. The episcopal church (Wil- liam Butterfield, 1849) was in 1876 consecrated as Cathedral of Argyll and the Isles and claims to be the smallest cathedral in Britain, if not in Europe. The *Museum of the Cumbraes* (Tel: 0475-530741), in Garrison House, is devoted to the history of the local way of life, a feature being Cumbrae in Victorian and Edwardian times. The *University Marine Biological Station* (universities of Glasgow and London), or *Robertson Museum*, just north of Millport, is concerned with the study of marine life in Clyde waters and admits visitors to its interesting aquaria (Tel: 0475-530581).

Little Cumbrae, immediately to the south, was maintained as a deer forest by Robert II and Robert III. On an islet off the east shore are the remains of a tower erected in 1527 to control deer poaching and destroyed by Cromwell in 1653.

18 Edinburgh

Tourist Information. *Edinburgh Tourist Centre*, Waverley Market, Princes Street (east end). Tel: 031-557-1700.—*Scottish Travel Centre*, South St. Andrew Street. Tel: 031-557-5522. For information about Scotland generally.—'*What's on in Edinburgh*', published monthly, provides comprehensive, factual and up-to-date practical information, including opening times of sites, entertainment and suchlike.

Public Transport buses are operated by Lothian Regional Transport, Waverley Bridge. Tel: 031-226-5087. A choice of *City Tours* leave from Waverley Bridge; also full and half-day excursions to several places in this part of Scotland.—The *Coach Station*, for scheduled services beyond the city, is off St. Andrew Square. For services and tours, Tel: 031-556-8464.

Walking Tours (guided) are perhaps the best way to appreciate the city's detail. A wide choice is available ranging from medieval through Georgian to witchcraft, ghosts and murder.

Scottish Entertainment is offered by several hotels and restaurants, as advertised in 'What's on in Edinburgh'.

British Rail. Waverley Station, below east end of Princes Street. Tel: 031-556-2451.

Airport. 6m west. Tel: 031-333-1000.

Opening Times of Sites. Telephone numbers are given for most sites. Latest information is also available from the Edinburgh Tourist Centre or from the current edition of 'What's on in Edinburgh'.

Edinburgh Festival. *Festival Offices*: 21 Market Street, EH1 1BW. Tel: 031-226-4001. Started in 1947, the Edinburgh International Festival of Music and Drama has now long been accepted as one of the world's leading festivals of its kind. It extends over a period of three weeks (usually the last three weeks in August) and although the emphasis is on music and drama, many other aspects of the arts are included, one of the most popular events being the spectacular military searchlight tattoo staged on the Castle Esplanade with the floodlit castle as a dramatic backcloth.

What has come to be known as *The Fringe* (Offices: 180 High Street, EH1 1QS. Tel: 031-226-5257) is now firmly established as companion to the Festival proper. It may be described as 'that vast range of entertainment available during the Festival period just beyond the official Festival programme... adventurous, irreverent, and invariably intriguing'.

Edinburgh becomes very full indeed during the Festival, and advance booking both for events and accommodation is strongly advised. Information, programmes, bookings and accommodation reservation all through the official Festival offices.

SOME HOTELS. The following, all in the more expensive category, are in the city centre and have parking. *Caledonian*, Princes Street, EH1 2AB. Tel: 031-225-2433. *George*, 19–21 George Street, EH2 2PB. Tel: 031-225-1251. *King James*, Leith Street, EH1 3SW. Tel: 031-556-0111. *Sheraton*, 1 Festival Square, EH3 9SR. Tel: 031-229-9131.

Some other central hotels. *Roxburghe*, 38 Charlotte Square, EH2 4HG. Tel: 031-225-3921. *Carlton*, North Bridge Street, EH1 1SD. Tel: 031-556-7277. *Mount Royal*, 53 Princes Street, EH2 2DQ. Tel: 031-225-7161. *Old Waverley*, 43 Princes Street, EH2 2BY. Tel: 031-556-4648.

Some outer city or suburban hotels, all to the west near the approaches to the airport and the Forth Bridge: *Hilton National* Bell Mills, 69 Belford Road, EH4 3DG. Tel: 031-332-2545. *Post House*, Corstorphine Road, EH12 6UA. Tel: 031-334-0390. *Crest*, Queensferry Road, EH4 3HL. Tel: 031-332-2442. *Barnton Thistle*, 562 Queensferry Road, EH4 6AS. Tel: 031-339-1144.

EDINBURGH
Central

0 yards 500
0 metres 500

Routes to and from Edinburgh. Several of the Routes in this guide run into or out of Edinburgh. To Edinburgh from *Berwick-upon-Tweed*, *Dunbar* and *Haddington*, see Rte 1; from *North Berwick*, see Rte 2; from *Coldstream*, *Kelso* and *Lauder*, see Rte 3; from *Jedburgh* and *Melrose*, see Rte 4; from *Canonbie*, *Hawick*, *Selkirk* and *Galashiels*, see Rte 5; from *Peebles*, see Rte 6; from *Gretna*, *Lockerbie* and *Moffat*, see Rte 7.

From Edinburgh to *Bathgate* and *Glasgow*, see Rte 8; to *Linlithgow*, *Falkirk* and *Stirling*, see Rte 9; to *Aberfoyle* and *The Trossachs*, see Rte 21; to *Dunfermline*, *Culross*, *Alloa* and *Stirling*, see Rte 31; to *Perth*, see Rte 32; into *Fife*, see Rtes 33A and 33C.

Justly held to be one of Europe's most distinguished and most dramatic capitals, Edinburgh is a city of style and dignity, a place well aware that Scotland has just about everything to offer and that this, its capital—and for many visitors their introduction—must not disappoint. It is a responsibility the city accepts with confidence and discharges with instinctive flair; a confidence and flair both born of that same vision which shook off the trauma of lost status, of becoming second to London, and in the 18–19C exploded into an era of brilliance in the arts and of elegant expansion. Now, in the 1990s and in this same tradition, Edinburgh is studying bold suggestions projecting well into the 21C and designed to continue to present the city as a positive and contemporary visitor experience; a more vivid appreciation of the rich social and architectural centuries of the Royal Mile, various proposals for an opera house, the creation in Leith of an international arts focus, and even the return of Nor' Loch are among the several themes under consideration.

Yet, for all its sense of style, this is no stuffy city. Festival and Fringe can live together, as can gourmet restaurants with the extrovert cheerfulness of Victorian pubs, the sedate, established shops of Princes Street with the brasher denizens of modern precincts.

History. Recent discoveries prove Bronze and Iron Age occupation of Castle Rock. Later the Romans were here, building their fort at Cramond, but after their departure from Britain the Angles of Northumbria subjugated Lothian and in the 6C their king, Edwin, rebuilt an earlier fortress whose name of Dun Eadain, the Fortress on the Slope, readily if inaccurately applied to Edwin's Burgh. For many centuries Edinburgh's story was that of this fortress or castle, the town as such really only starting to develop during the 11C when markets began to spring up in the area where High Street now runs. On accession in 1124 David I moved his capital from Dunfermline to Edinburgh, founding his abbey at Holyrood four years later, and the progress in the town's growth is marked by the granting of a charter by Bruce in 1329.

The reigns of James II to IV (1437–1513) marked an outstanding period in Edinburgh's history. It saw the construction (1436) of the first effective town wall, Wellhouse Tower at the north foot of Castle Rock being about the only surviving trace; the start in c 1500 of the construction of Holyrood Palace; much patronage of the arts and education, including the granting of a charter (1506) to the Royal College of Surgeons and the setting up in 1508 of Scotland's first printing press; and finally, with the disaster of Flodden in 1513, the hasty building of the Flodden Wall, a part of which can still be seen south of Grassmarket.

But Flodden ushered in what was to prove a century or more of darkness and disaster. In 1544, and again in 1547, the years of the 'rough wooing' (see History of Scotland), England's Henry VIII, baulked in his plan of marriage between his son and Mary, the infant Queen of Scots, devastated the city. Then in 1561 Mary returned from France, and Edinburgh and the surrounding district became the stage on which was played much of the tragedy and turbulence of her seven years in Scotland—years which presaged that day in 1603 when Mary's son, James VI, becoming James I of England, moved with his court to London, leaving Edinburgh as a deserted capital of secondary importance. Not that this new status brought any compensating tranquility, for the city was now to experience much of the bitter religious and associated struggle that, born in Mary's short reign, reached its climax during the 17C. Among the events of these years were the signing of the National Covenant at Greyfriars in 1638; Cromwell's occupation of the city in 1650 and the execution here of Montrose in the same year; the continued burning of witches on the castle esplanade; and the martyrdom in Grassmarket of over 100 Covenanters.

The 18C got off to a bad start. Although with the Restoration Charles II had rebuilt Holyrood Palace, Edinburgh was soon to become even less of a capital when the Act of Union was passed in 1707, and in 1745 there followed that moment of divided loyalty, when the Young Pretender held court at Holyrood while the castle remained in Government hands. Then, and suddenly, there was that explosion of brilliance referred to above. In the broad field of the arts Allan Ramsay, Adam Smith, Hume, Goldsmith, Sir Walter Scott and R.L. Stevenson are only some of the galaxy of names associated with the 18 and 19C. At the same time, with the bridging of Cowgate, Edinburgh shook itself free of its tenemented rock as buildings began to spread southwards beyond the Flodden Wall and, more significantly (starting in 1767), northwards to become over the ensuing 70 or so years the most distinguished and most extensive area of Georgian architecture in Britain.

Of many important 18 and 19C landmarks, the years 1818 and 1822 are perhaps the most deserving of mention, both closely associated with Sir Walter Scott. In 1818 a search made in the castle at his instigation rediscovered the Scottish regalia, forgotten since 1707; and in 1822 he organised a highly successful visit by George IV, the first royal visit for over a century and one which not only brought Holyrood back to life but, so far as Scotland as a whole was concerned, could be said to have signalled the end of the aftermath of Culloden. The Industrial Revolution brought little visible harm to what had long been an essentially professional rather than industrial city (the railway is well hidden) and, though inevitably there are sores, 20C development is on the whole being kept clear of the best areas of old and Georgian Edinburgh.

Central Edinburgh divides itself into three distinct yet adjacent areas and is thus easy for the visitor. The older city sprawls across a conspicuous, sloping volcanic rock along which stretches historic **Old Edinburgh**, or the **Royal Mile**, linking the Castle, high on its precipitous crag at the west, with Holyrood Palace and Abbey at the slope's foot in the east. On either side of this spine there are roughly parallel valleys, gouged out during the Ice Age. The valley to the north, until 1816 filled by a loch (Nor'Loch), is now the long panoramic sweep of Princes Street, renowned for its dramatic setting and as Edinburgh's main shopping street. From Princes Street there extends northward, up and over the ridge which carries George Street, the spacious and dignified mainly 18C **New Town**. To the rock's south there is a sheer drop to the area of **Grassmarket and Greyfriars**, both of historical interest, while beyond spreads a district of only limited attraction for the visitor, where Georgian and Victorian streets and squares are gradually giving way to modern development.

However short the time available most visitors will not fail to see the Castle, the Royal Mile and Holyrood, as well as Princes Street and George Street, with perhaps something of their Georgian neighbours. The Grassmarket and Greyfriars district, though of less immediately obvious interest, retains, despite some development, much of the feel of 17 and 18C and early Victorian Edinburgh and will certainly attract any student of the Covenanter years. Which of Edinburgh's many museums and art galleries are chosen will be a matter of time and taste, but three may be mentioned here. The National Gallery of Scotland is among the most distinguished of Europe's smaller galleries. The Royal Museum of Scotland (Queen Street) shows prehistoric and historic material from all over Scotland and a browse around can be a rewarding accompaniment to sites already visited, or to be visited, throughout the country. The City Museum at Huntly House, on the other hand, is concerned exclusively with Edinburgh and offers invaluable background to anyone wishing to get below the surface of this city's story.

Although Edinburgh divides into the three main areas referred to above (Old Edinburgh, Grassmarket and Greyfriars, and New Town), for descriptive convenience these are covered below as five sections:

A. Edinburgh Castle. B. Royal Mile and Holyrood. C. South Edinburgh (Grassmarket, Greyfriars and beyond). D. Princes Street. E. North Edinburgh (New Town). A sixth section (F.) describes other places of interest within the city or its environs, while a seventh (G.) covers the National Gallery of Scotland. A whole day should be allowed for the Castle, Royal Mile and Holyrood, all conveniently combinable as one walk. South and North Edinburgh can each comfortably be covered in a half day, although this does not of course allow for time spent in the several museums and galleries.

A.   **Edinburgh Castle

Famed for the views from its lofty bastions, Edinburgh Castle (AM. Tel: 031-244-3101) is perhaps less significant as a castle than for what its walls embrace—a rich and varied offering which includes ancient (11C) St. Margaret's Chapel; the deeply impressive Scottish National War Memorial; the old palace, with the Crown Room in which are proudly displayed the regalia of Scotland, and with Queen Mary's Apartments, these including the room in which the future James VI/I was born; the handsome 15C Old Parliament (or Banqueting) Hall, scene of at least two treacherous murders; an ancient and historic cannon; and three military museums.

Many improvements are being carried out in a programme (until about 1997) which includes in its opening phase a new vehicle tunnel, leaving the original road within the castle clear for pedestrians, and also new visitor reception facilities by the main gate. Later phases provide a restaurant, a video presentation, access to David's Tower, several special displays, and access to the French Prison. The above work may cause occasional inconvenience, as also some changes to the sequence and detail of the description below.

History. With recent evidence of Bronze and Iron Age occupation, so natural a defensive position was clearly a fortress from earliest times, and indeed in monkish legends this site is mentioned as Castrum Puellarum, Castle of the Maids, presumably a safe retreat for the daughters of Pictish kings. In the 6C the Northumbrian king Edwin rebuilt the older fortress as a strong northern bastion of his lands, and 500 years later, in the 11C, Malcolm Canmore seems to have lived both here and in Dunfermline, his saintly wife, Queen Margaret, building in c 1076 the simple little chapel which bears her name. She died in the castle in 1093, while it was being besieged by Donald Bane, and her body was secretly let down the cliff and taken to her priory at Dunfermline. In 1174, after his defeat and capture at Alnwick, the castle was surrendered by William the Lion to England's Henry II, and from 1296 to 1313 it was again in English hands (Edward I) until retaken by the Earl of Moray after a daring climb up the cliff; then, in accordance with Bruce's scorched earth policy, the castle was largely dismantled. David II rebuilt and did much to strengthen the defences, part of his great keep, in which he died in 1371, still surviving, though as a ruin.

It was in the castle that Mary, Queen of Scots, gave birth in 1566 to the future James VI/I, and two years later, when she was captive in England, her former enemy, Kirkcaldy of Grange, held the castle in her cause for an epic five years; he was finally defeated by cannon brought from England and, later, hanged. Cromwell seized the castle in 1650, and in 1745 it declined to open its gates to the Young Pretender, then installed in some state in Holyrood Palace after his victory at Prestonpans. During the Napoleonic wars French prisoners were confined here.

The castle is approached across the spacious sloping **Castle Esplanade**, the dramatic stage for the Festival's Military Tattoo. Around the Esplanade are a number of military memorials recalling past glories and disasters, and also two other memorials, not military and of more general interest. The first is against the wall, immediately on the right on entering the Esplanade. Here the *Witches' Well* marks the spot where more than 300 witches were burned between 1479 and as late as 1722, a sharp reminder both of past attitudes and of past spectacles staged here. Nor were the victims all wretched old crones, for one of their number (1540) was the beautiful Janet, Lady Glamis, found guilty of mixing potions but in reality one of the many casualties of James V's implacable hatred of the Douglas family. The well bears a curious if somewhat equivocal design with a wicked head (bad witches), a serene head (witches who may have been benevolent), and a serpent representing both evil and wisdom. The other memorial of general, or at any rate Canadian interest, is at the opposite end of the Esplanade where a plaque commemorates the spot where, at a ceremony in 1625, the Earl of Stirling received formal possession of the lands of Nova Scotia; in other words a gift from the Crown of huge tracts of land in what is now Canada (see also Rte 23, Stirling, Argyll's Lodging; and Rte 25C, Menstrie Castle).

The entrance to the castle proper is across the moat and through an outer gateway (1888), flanked by statues of Bruce and Wallace, the path then bearing right for the *Portcullis Gate*, just before which (above, left) there is a memorial stone to Kirkcaldy of Grange. The Portcullis Gate stands below the *Constable's Tower*, later called *Argyll's Tower* because the 8th Earl of Argyll was held in the gateway dungeon before his execution in 1661. The old prison here, built by David II in 1369, was destroyed by English cannon in 1573 during the closing hours of Kirkcaldy's stand and, though rebuilt in the following year, required reconstruction in 1890. The path curves upward past the *Argyll Battery*, named after the victor of Sheriffmuir (1715) and overlooking Princes Street, to reach a slope down to an 18C courtyard across the end of which runs a short battlements walk (the Western Defences). Off this courtyard are a section of the Scottish United Services Museum and also the museum of the *Royal Scots Dragoon Guards*.

Another regimental museum, that of the *Royal Scots*, is close to the top of the slope referred to above. Here, before ascending through Foog's Gate, the visitor may bear right for the entrance to the **Vaults** which, lying directly below Old Parliament Hall, served variously as store, gun room, barracks, bakery and prison. Today, all this is admirably explained, the principal feature being *Mons Meg*, a great bombard made at Mons in Belgium in 1449 and presented to James II by the Duke of Burgundy. Later, in 1497, the cannon was used by James IV against the English Norham Castle, and, a century and a half later, it was still formidable enough to warrant inclusion—as the 'great iron murderer, Muckle Meg'—in the inventory of castle guns captured by Cromwell. However, the cannon's operational life came to an undignified end in 1682 when it burst while firing a salute in honour of the Duke of York. In 1754 it was removed to the Tower of London, but in 1829, at Sir Walter Scott's request, restored to Edinburgh.

Many distinguished prisoners were held in these vaults and later, during the Napoleonic wars, they housed French prisoners who, it seems, were so well treated that they penned a note of thanks to the governor.

Returning to the main tour, beyond Foog's Gate the *King's Bastion* is reached, the highest platform of the castle and a spot affording a famous view.

St. Margaret's Chapel was probably built by Margaret in 1076, though some hold that it may have been founded rather later in her honour by her son, David I. Although the chapel early acquired

Mons Meg, perhaps forged in Belgium in the 15C. Described in a Cromwellian inventory as the 'great iron murderer, Muckle Meg'

sanctity—that the dying Bruce made provision for restoration work is evidence enough—it was not always treated with reverence and as recently as 1845 it was used for storing the gunpowder with which ceremonial salutes were fired. However, later years brought more enlightened attitudes, starting with a restoration by Sir David Wilson in 1853 when the five small windows were given stained glass, this being replaced in 1921 by figures of St. Margaret, St. Andrew, St. Columba, St. Ninian and Wallace, all by Douglas Strachan. Further restoration in 1929 was sealed by the rededication of the chapel in 1934. However approached, this little place will surely not disappoint. As a link with a remote past, and even allowing for restoration and the modern windows, the simple interior cannot be very different to the chapel that Margaret knew and in which she probably spent her last hours; architecturally this is the oldest building in Edinburgh, an example of humble Norman, complete with zigzag moulding around the chancel arch; and if a sense of piety is sought, then it is surely more present here than in many a more pretentious edifice.

In the south part of this general area will be found the *Forewall Battery*, the *Well* and the *Half Moon Battery*, this last erected over, and as replacement for, the ruins of *David's Tower*, the name given to the keep built by David II in 1367, battered down by the English cannon during Kirkcaldy of Grange's famous defence, and effectively hidden by the Half Moon Battery until discovered by chance in 1912. On the wall above the battery perches the ironwork cage within which, at the close of the tattoo and picked out by spotlight, stands the lone piper.

Around Crown Square—the heart of the castle complex—are the Scottish National War Memorial, the Crown Room, Queen Mary's Apartments, the Old Parliament or Banqueting Hall, and the United Services Museum.

The **Scottish National War Memorial**, an inspired achievement by Sir Robert Lorimer (1927), covers a site on which once stood a church, then barracks, a part of the walls of which has been incorporated into the present building. The memorial comprises a long Gallery of Honour with bays at either end, and, centrally opposite the entrance, the octagonal *Shrine*, within which, strikingly on an outcrop of natural rock, stands the marble Stone of Remembrance, bearing a wrought-steel casket containing records. The stained glass windows, depicting war as a mysterious element in the destiny of man, are by Douglas Strachan, while below, and perhaps more readily understood, are reliefs by Morris and Alice Meredith Williams portraying types of all who served, men and women, as also animals and birds. The *Gallery of Honour* is divided into recesses devoted to the Scottish regiments. The West Bay commemorates the Women's War Services and the Air Force; the East Bay the Navy, Cavalry, Yeomanry, Artillery and Engineers.

The east side of Crown Square represents the medieval royal palace, dating from the 15C but with additions of 1566 and 1615. Here now is the **Crown Room** in which are shown the Regalia, or, more romantically, the 'Honours of Scotland'—the crown, the sceptre and the sword, generally accepted as the oldest regalia in Europe. After their gallant and romantic rescue from Dunnottar Castle, followed by some years beneath the pulpit of Kinneff church (see Rte 35), the regalia were returned to Edinburgh at the Restoration, but on the union of the parliaments were ignominiously deposited in a chest and virtually forgotten. But not by Sir Walter Scott who in 1818 instigated a search resulting in their discovery here in this then sealed Crown Room.

The Crown, made of Scottish gold and said to incorporate the circlet with which Bruce was crowned at Scone in 1306, is decorated with 94 pearls, ten diamonds and 33 other stones. Refashioned in 1540, when James V added the mound and cross at the top, the crown was last used for the coronation of Charles II at Scone in 1651, nine years before his restoration to the English throne. The Sceptre (1494; refashioned 1536), a gift to James IV from Pope Alexander VI, shows a Madonna, St. James and St. Andrew. The Sword, a sumptuous Italian masterpiece, was presented to James IV in 1501 by Pope Julius II. The other objects, displayed separately and bequeathed to George IV by Cardinal York, the last of the Stuarts, include the Collar and George of the Order of the Garter presented by Elizabeth to James VI/I, the latter's badge of the Order of the Thistle, and a ring given by him to the future Charles I.—The exit from the Crown Room (back into Crown Square) is through sections of the Scottish United Services Museum.

In **Queen Mary's Apartments**, in the south east corner of Crown Square, is the modest little room in which, on 19 June 1566, Mary, Queen of Scots, gave birth to the son who, only a year later, would succeed her as James VI of Scotland and who in 1603 would triumphantly move to London as James I of England. A bizarre scene may be pictured as—with Mary in long and painful labour—the Countess of Atholl resorted to witchcraft in an attempt to transfer the pangs to a seemingly willing Lady Reres lying on a bed nearby.

The **Old Parliament Hall** (or Banqueting Hall), occupying the south side of Crown Square, is of early 15C origin but was extensively rebuilt by James IV. Here, in the predecessor of this handsome hall with its lofty open-timber roof, another bizarre scene, though one with a darker outcome, was played—the so-called Black Dinner of 1440. Chancellor Crichton—self-appointed guardian of James II, then only eight years old, and determined to smash the powerful Douglases—treacherously invited the boy Earl of Douglas and his younger brother to a banquet to meet James. And here they were seized and executed, having first been cruelly warned of their fate by the bringing on of a black bull's head, in the Scotland of the time the customary sign of violent death.

Used as the meeting-place of the Scottish parliament until 1639, and still in good condition in 1648 when Cromwell was entertained here by the Marquis of Argyll, the hall later declined, at one time being converted into storeys and used as a military hospital, and it was not until

1892 that it was restored, by the effort and purse of William Nelson, the publisher. It now houses a fine display of armour and weapons. Below the hall are the Vaults (see above).

The **Scottish United Services Museum** (Tel: 031-225-7534) was opened in 1931 as the Scottish Naval and Military Museum, receiving its present title when, after wartime closure, it reopened with an Air Force section. The longest established institution of its kind in Britain, the museum, with its comprehensive reference library, plays an important research and archival role. Additionally a unique collection of some 10,000 contemporary prints provides a valuable pictorial reference to changes in military uniforms from the early 18C to the end of the 19C, while some modern subjects are covered by an equally large collection of photographs.

B.   Royal Mile and Holyrood

From those medieval centuries when traders and others gradually began to settle along the track between the castle and David I's abbey of Holyrood, right up until the explosive expansion of the 18 and 19C, this long slope, now popularly known as the Royal Mile, was the busy spine of Edinburgh life; the place where or close to which most of the inhabitants both lived and worked. Today it is paved and clean, relatively quiet, almost staid, but the Royal Mile of the past should be pictured as a narrow way, not too clean and certainly smelly, crowded with stalls and booths, behind which rose the ever taller tenement buildings (lands) inevitable with a fast-growing population and lack of space within the town wall. Off this bustling main thoroughfare a maze of dark wynds and closes or courts (the first a throughway wide enough for a horse, the last two generally blind alleys) led to business or residential courts, many of which, some admirably restored, can still be explored today. A visit to the City Museum in Huntly House will prove a great help towards understanding Edinburgh as it once was.

The distance between the castle and Holyrood is just about the one mile of this stretch's name; a mile surely unique for its crowding sequence of surprising and curious corners, for its kaleidoscope of associations with a long past, and for the throng of characters—royal, aristocratic, intellectual, criminal and humble—who in one way or another have left their mark. It is a mile that must be pottered on foot.

The Royal Mile leaves the Castle Esplanade as Castle Hill, the house at the top of Castle Wynd steps, which drop down to Grassmarket, being known as *Cannonball House* (1630) because of the ball still embedded in its west gable. Traditionally this was fired from the castle in 1745 and intended for Holyrood, then occupied by the Young Pretender. Just below is the **Scottish Whisky Heritage Centre** (Tel: 031-220-0441), aiming to introduce the visitor to the centuries-long part played by whisky in the story of Scotland. The Centre includes displays, a video presentation, a model distillery, a shop, and an electric car ride, with commentary, through three centuries of history. **Outlook Tower** (Tel: 031-226-3709), across the road, has been a popular Edinburgh attraction for close on 150 years; since the 1850s when an upper level was added to a 17C tower and, equipped with a viewing platform and a camera obscura, Short's Popular Observatory began to pull in visitors. This camera obscura—reflecting a living, moving picture of Edinburgh on a white table while a guide provides a commentary—remains the principal and most popular feature here, but, ever since the close of the 19C when the tower gained its present name, there has been a progressive programme of other features, such as, today, laser holography and space photography.—Below, with a fine tower and spire, is the now redundant *Church of Tolbooth St. John* or, more popularly, the Highland Church, built in 1842–44 by Gillespie Graham and A.W.N. Pugin (heritage project, early 1990s).

Mylne's Court, just below Outlook Tower, recalls Robert Mylne, Master Mason to Charles II and the man responsible, with William Bruce, for Holyrood Palace as it now is. Dating from 1690, this court has been restored by the University of Edinburgh as student accommodation.

Castle Hill now becomes Lawnmarket, the western section of High Street and once, as its name suggests, the centre for linen merchants. Here, on the left, is **Gladstone's Land** (NTS. Tel: 031-226-5856), dating from 1620 and a typical example of a lofty (six storeys) tenement, with an arcaded front, outside stair and stepped gables. Both externally and internally—with reconstructed booths showing 17C goods, and, inside, painted ceilings and the main rooms refurbished in the style of the period—this house provides a glimpse, as accurate as is reasonable to expect after a lapse of some 300 years, of an Edinburgh that would have been familiar to a comfortable merchant, such as was Thomas Gledstanes. And *James Court*, alongside, provides a similar glimpse, both visually and historically, for here, before becoming one of the first to succumb to the attractions of the New Town, lived the historian David Hume (1711–66) and here, too, in the same flat, lived James Boswell who in 1773 entertained Dr Johnson here.

Hume earlier lived opposite in *Riddle's Close*, where he wrote a part of his 'History of England', while the inner court here, known as *Macmorran's Close*, was the home of the ill-starred Bailie Macmorran, a wealthy merchant who was shot in 1595 while attempting to quell a school riot. Three years later his son entertained James VI and his queen, Anne of Denmark, in this fine late 16C house, today an adult education centre.

So far all place names have been those of respectable citizens. At *Brodie's Close*, however, the pattern changes since here lived the notorious Deacon Brodie, by day an esteemed town councillor, but by night a thief. Finally caught trying to rob the Excise Office in Chessel's Court (see below), he was hanged in 1788, the mechanism of the 'drop' being of his own design and apparently more successful than the steel collar he wore which was supposed to save his neck.

Opposite, a short close descends to **Lady Stair's House** (Tel: 031-225-2424. Ext. 6593), much restored but retaining some features of the house of 1622 which was the home of the beautiful Lady Stair (died 1731), whose story as Lady Primrose (during her first marriage) forms the basis of Scott's story 'My Aunt Margaret's Mirror'. Today the house serves as a museum of all manner of material on Scotland's three great literary figures, Burns, Scott and Stevenson. Below the house, and built over the site of the palace of Mary of Guise, is the *Assembly Hall* of the General Assembly of the Church of Scotland.

Lawnmarket ends at a busy crossroads (Bank Street and George IV Bridge), at the south east corner of which brass strips on the road mark the site of the scaffold, scene of public hangings until 1864. From here the Royal Mile continues as High Street, with, immediately on the right, Parliament Square, not immediately recognised as a square since most of its centre is filled by St. Giles Cathedral.

The heart of Edinburgh until the expansion of the 18C—and still the heart so far as the visitor to Old Edinburgh is concerned—**Parliament Square** still provides several links with the city's past, starting, on the west near a statue of the 5th Duke of Buccleuch, with the '*Heart of Midlothian*', a cobblestone heart and outline marking the site of the entrance to the Old Tolbooth, built in 1466, extended by the New Tolbooth some time after 1561 and demolished in 1817. Here stood a building which over its centuries met many needs—in turn chapter house for St. Giles, meeting-place of parliament, the law courts, the town council and, in the 1560s, of the General Assembly of the Reformed Kirk—until degraded to the role of prison, the place, too, on which many an aristocratic head was displayed; those of the regent Morton in 1581, of Montrose in 1650, and of the 8th Earl of Argyll in 1661. This site later achieved fame as the scene of the opening of Scott's novel 'The Heart of Midlothian', the author having acquired the tolbooth keys and the great wooden door, all now to be seen at Abbotsford.

The south side of Parliament Square was once the cathedral cemetery, in which, it is thought, John Knox was buried in 1572. Here an equestrian Charles II poses as a martial Roman, a statue (of 1685, by an unknown Dutch sculptor) enjoying the esoteric distinction of being the only leaden one in Scotland.

Parliament House (Tel: 031-225-2595) fronts the south side of Parliament Square. Erected in 1632–40, but given its present Italianate façade in 1808–14, this was the meeting-place of the Scottish parliament from 1639, the year in which it abandoned the castle, until it abolished itself under the Act of Union of 1707, the building then becoming, and remaining to this day, the legal heart of Scotland, the home of the Court of Session and the High Court. For the tourist the main interest will lie in the *Parliament Hall*, now used as a concourse—and a lively one, too,

Old Tolbooth of Edinburgh, built in 1466 and demolished in 1817. Here during the 16 and 17C the citizens gathered to stare at severed aristocratic and humbler heads

when crowded with gowned and wigged advocates, solicitors and clients—a majestic Gothic place with an open timber roof, a great window depicting the inauguration of the Court of Session in 1532 by James V, and several legal portraits by, amongst others, Kneller and Raeburn. Access to the splendid *Signet Library* (Robert Reid, 1815) is by written application only.

This circuit of Parliament Square ends on the east side, where the *Mercat Cross* marks the true city centre, the traditional place, today as over a long past, of Royal Proclamations by the Lord Lyon, King of Arms, one such, in 1745, being that of the Young Pretender as James VIII. The tradition, though, is older than this cross which, though incorporating parts of its 14–16C predecessor, is essentially 19C, a gift to the city by the statesman W.E. Gladstone, who also composed the Latin inscription.

*St. Giles Cathedral** (Tel: 031-225-4363) is a courtesy title for what is more properly the High Kirk of Edinburgh; a courtesy earned because this church was in fact twice a cathedral, albeit over only brief periods. The first was under Charles I who established a bishopric of Edinburgh in 1633; the second under Charles II and James VII/II, this however ending in 1689 when episcopacy was disestablished in Scotland. For today's visitor the cathedral's principal features are, outside, the famous Crown of St Giles atop the square tower, and, inside, the memorials to famous Scots, some the victims of hanging, execution or murder.

History. It is known that there has been a church on this site since at least 854 and that this was replaced by a Norman structure in c 1120, the church at this time being subordinate to the bishopric of St. Andrews which in 1243 authorised the dedication to St. Giles (see below). This Norman church was destroyed by Richard II of England in 1385 (although today's massive central piers may, if only in part, be survivals), the successor Gothic church then growing over the course of the 15C during which three significant dates were 1454 when Sir William Preston gifted the church a bone from the arm of St. Giles; 1467 when, by achieving collegiate status, the church gained independence from St. Andrews; and 1495 which saw the construction of the tower completed.

At the Reformation, when amongst other damage the church lost its 44 altars

ST GILES CATHEDRAL (HIGH KIRK)

0 yards 20
0 metres 20

North Door

Albany Aisle

St Eloi's Chapel

N.E. Chapel

West Door

NAVE

CHOIR

Preston Aisle

S.E. Door

Royal Pew

(Moray Aisle)

Organ

Chapel of the Thistle

1. Marquis of Argyll.
2. Jenny Geddes.
3. Marquis of Montrose.

Regent Moray's Tomb

Chepman's Aisle

PARLIAMENT SQUARE

(one at each pillar, and one in each side chapel) and its statue of St. Giles was thrown into Nor'Loch, John Knox became minister (1559–72), and it was in this capacity that he had his debates with Mary, Queen of Scots. The two subsequent bishopric periods have already been mentioned, and it was during the first of these, in 1637, that there occurred the incident when Jenny Geddes, incensed at hearing the episcopal service being read, hurled her stool at the preacher, thus launching the first blow of the movement that would be formalised the following year by the signing of the National Covenant at Greyfriars. During the 18 and 19C St. Giles was divided into four separate churches, and also at times in part used for secular purposes, only becoming one again with successful restoration work carried out between 1872–83, largely at the expense of William Chambers, the publisher. The Chapel of the Order of the Thistle, Scotland's highest order of chivalry, was added in 1911.

St. Giles, who died in c 710, seems to have been a Provençal by birth and to have lived his hermit life on land given to him by the local king Wamba. One day Wamba shot at a hind, which Giles was sheltering, missing the hind but crippling Giles with an arrow. St. Giles, by then the patron of cripples and beggars, became hugely popular in medieval times—perhaps simply because there were so many cripples and beggars—and throughout Europe many churches were dedicated to him. Here in the cathedral the story of St. Giles and the hind is portrayed in four places: outside, on the west door, below the archway; and, inside, in a window in the north nave, in a south clerestory window in the central chancel, and in the Chapel of the Thistle.

The description below of the cathedral's interior follows a clockwise course starting from the west door below the Burns Memorial Window of 1985 and first travelling the length of the north aisle. First comes the *Albany Aisle*, said to have been built in c 1410 by the Duke of Albany as a prudent expiation of his murder by starvation of the Duke of Rothesay (see also Rte 33C, Falkland Palace). Rededicated in 1951 as a war memorial, the aisle now houses military memorials and, in a recess the original purpose of which is unknown, the Roll of Honour of the 1939–45 war. *St. Eloi's Chapel*, next to the east, recalls a French saint (c 588–c 660), who, himself a skilled metalworker, became patron of the Guild of Hammermen whose chapel this once was and whose hammer is outlined on the floor. Today the main feature here from the past is the handsome memorial to the Covenanter 8th Earl of Argyll who lost his head in 1661, while modern times are represented by the Queen's Standard of No. 603 (City of Edinburgh) Squadron, Royal Auxiliary Air Force, a squadron which, operating in Gladiator biplanes from the grass field at Turnhouse (now Edinburgh airport) defended both the city and the fleet at Rosyth during the early months of the last war. The *North-East Chapel*, beyond the north door, originally a memorial to William Chambers who financed the church's 19C restoration, now serves as a Chapel of Youth, while, as noted earlier, the central piers near here may be survivals from the earlier Norman church.

The church is now crossed to the south east corner and the *Chapel of the Thistle*, entered through an ante-chapel listing the names of members since the founding of this Most Ancient and Most Noble Order of the Thistle in 1687 by James VII/II. This, Scotland's premier Order, consists of the sovereign and 16 knights and long used Holyrood Abbey as its chapel. The 12th Earl of Leven bequeathed funds for the restoration of Holyrood, but when this proved impracticable the bequest was directed to the construction of this new chapel, designed by Sir Robert Lorimer and opened in 1911. An admirable self-guide board details architectural and other information, the principal features being the lofty groined roof, the elaborate canopies of the carved oak stalls, the heraldic windows, and the floor of Ailsa Craig granite with a memorial slab to George VI; and, for connoisseurs of the quaint, there is that angel playing bagpipes, to be found by the upper right side of the entrance arch.

Back in the church proper, the *Preston Aisle* was founded in 1454 to honour Sir William Preston who died in that year having presented the church with an arm-bone of St. Giles. Two hundred years later (1643) this aisle was the scene of the signing of the Solemn League and Covenant, under which Scotland sided with the Puritan Cromwell—an occurrence which would hardly have pleased the obviously devoutly Catholic Sir William Preston. The main feature here today is the carved Royal Pew, with stalls for the Queen and the Duke of Edinburgh and, below, those occupied on ceremonial occasions by Lord Lyon, King of Arms, and his heralds and pursuivants. *Chepman's Aisle*, off the south west corner of the Preston Aisle, was a gift from Walter Chepman (died 1532) who in 1508 set up the first printing press in Scotland. Although remembered by a plaque here, Chepman is overshadowed by the great Marquis of Montrose, hanged in 1650, whose dismembered remains were collected and buried here in 1661 and whose monument is on the east wall. Here too is an original (Queensferry) parchment of the National Covenant signed at Greyfriars (see below) in 1638.

The original *Moray Aisle* (in which Lord James Stewart, later Regent Moray and leader of the Reformers against Mary of Guise, was buried after his murder in Linlithgow in 1570) was in the south transept, but the name Moray Aisle is now rather loosely given to the whole area west of the south transept. The Regent Moray Memorial (1864) is in the south east corner of this area, in what was once the Holy Blood Aisle, here too being a window (Noel Paton) depicting both the murder and John Knox preaching at the funeral. Roughly opposite, on the floor on the north side of this new Moray Aisle, a tablet marks the traditional spot from which Jenny Geddes launched her stool.

Across High Street from St. Giles Cathedral stand the *City Chambers* (1753–61; entrance archways 1902), originally built to serve as a Royal Exchange but taken over by the city council in 1811. In the quadrangle there is a lively statue of Alexander the Great and his horse, Bucephalus, and the city's war memorial Stone of Remembrance is beneath the central arch. In *Anchor Close*, alongside, once stood the Anchor Tavern, a favourite pub of Burns, and also the printing works of William Smellie who in 1768 published the first edition of the 'Encyclopaedia Britannica' and in 1787 the first Edinburgh edition of Burns's poems.

High Street next reaches its second busy intersection, here with the streets known as North Bridge and South Bridge. Here *Tron Church* (1637–47) recalls through its name the tron or public weighbeam which stood nearby, merchants risking being nailed by their ears to the beam if they gave short measure. No longer in use, the church may be converted to house a visitor centre. Below the intersection, off the north side of High Street, the narrow Carrubber's Close was the site of Edinburgh's first theatre, opened in 1736 'at vast expense' by Allan Ramsay; but Edinburgh was not yet ready for this kind of thing and the place was soon closed by the magistrates. The close leads to *Old St. Paul's Episcopal Church* (1883), standing on the site of a wool store which served as church for those who quit St. Giles in 1689 when the Episcopal Church was disestablished. In the present church a chapel commemorates the contentious Samuel Seabury, who worshipped here while a student and went on to become in 1783 the first bishop of the American Church. By contrast, a sculpted relief over the entrance to nearby *Paisley Close* recalls the cheerful courage of a mere lad who, trapped below a collapsed tenement in 1861, encouraged his rescuers by shouting 'Heave awa', I'm no deid yet'. Blackfriars Street, opposite, was formerly Blackfriars Close, during the 16–18C one of Edinburgh's most aristocratic quarters.

Edinburgh, Canongate Tolbooth. Long the civic centre of independent Canongate.

John Knox House (Tel: 031-556-6961) next juts into High Street. Dating in appearance from c 1560, the house incorporates in its lower part work of c 1473 and of the early 17C above. Whether in fact John Knox ever lived here can be debated, but it does seem that he may well have occupied the second floor from 1561, when the house was raised a storey, until his death in 1572. In any event the house shows material on Knox, including a film, as also some interesting pictures of old Edinburgh, and with its wood panelling and hand-painted ceiling is one of the most attractive old houses in Edinburgh.

Opposite is the attractive and unusual **Museum of Childhood** (Tel: 031-225-2424), the world's first museum devoted to the history and theme of childhood. With displays illustrating such aspects as upbringing, clothing, health and education, this is in many respects a museum of more interest to parents than to children. But toys, dolls, books and suchlike are here too, so, however serious the museum's intent, the children tend to swamp the adults in what has been described as the 'noisiest museum in the world'.

Below John Knox House is the site of *Netherbow*, a spot at which to pause for here once stood the lower gate of the city, removed in 1764 but still recalled by a pictorial sign on the Church of Scotland Art Centre and by brass strips on the ground. Imagination can conjure much from the past here, but perhaps no scene as dramatic or dashing as that of the early hours of 17 September 1745. Edinburgh, in a turmoil of terror and ambivalent loyalty with the Young Pretender encamped at Duddingston and faced with a demand for surrender by 2 a.m., sent a delegation to the rebel camp to plead for time. Spurned by the Young Pretender, the delegation returned, its coach passing through Netherbow sometime after midnight. Soon afterwards a force of Highlanders under Lochiel assembled below the gate but, on being refused entry and with dawn not far away, decided to retire. Then, to their amazement, the gate opened—simply to allow out the city deputation's coachman who happened to stable his horses outside the walls— whereupon Lochiel stormed through to take the city.

The Royal Mile now becomes *Canongate*, running through a district which, being outside the Netherbow, enjoyed the status of independent town until absorbed in 1856. The name derives from the canons or clerics of Holyrood Abbey, while 'gait' is a walk or road, and Canongate was for long the smart residential quarter of the aristocracy, anxious to be close to Holyrood Palace. Recent years have seen much successful restoration aimed at reconciling the best of the old with modern requirements. *Chessel's Court*, for instance, on the south and once the Excise Office, the robbing of which was Deacon Brodie's last crime, has now been reconstructed as flats, while *Playhouse Close*, on the same side, recalls an early theatre which, opening 11 years after Allan Ramsay's unsuccessful venture in Carrubber's Close, flourished from 1747–69.

Built in 1625 by the Dowager Countess of Home, and receiving its name from her daughter the Countess of Moray to whom it passed in 1645, **Moray House** (south), now a college of education, was visited by both Charles I and Cromwell. From its balcony in 1650, while here at his son's wedding party and 11 years before his own execution, Argyll watched Montrose pass in a cart on his way to his death; and in 1707, when Commissioners were discussing the Treaty of Union in a summerhouse in the garden, they were assailed by an angry mob and forced to flee to a cellar in High Street. Part of Moray House is an archway across St. John's Pend where the Knights of St. John once had their quarters.

The *City Museum** (Tel: 031-225-2424. Ext. 6689), devoted to the story of Edinburgh, occupies Huntly House, dating from 1517, bought and restored by Edinburgh Corporation in 1926, and opened as a museum in 1932. The wide range of exhibits—from decorative art to a clay pipe workshop, from an original copy of the National Covenant to material on Earl Haig—is admirably displayed through an attractive, rambling series of rooms.

Canongate Tolbooth, opposite, dates from 1591 but is successor to a much older tolbooth. With its projecting clock, hall used as council room and law court, and prison below, this tolbooth long served as the civic centre of independent Canongate. Today it is an appropriate home for *The People's Story* (Tel: 031-225-2424. Ext. 6638), a museum devoted to the working, domestic and political lives of the ordinary people of Edinburgh from the late 18C to the present day.

A switch can now be made from the past to the present, from sightseeing to stylish shopping, for *Acheson House* (1633), next door to Huntly House, is the home of the **Scottish Craft Centre** (Tel: 031-556-8136), founded several years ago as a charity charged with encouraging the highest standard of Scottish craft work and today offering the widest range of quality products in the country.

Canongate Church, opposite, was built in 1688 by James Smith to serve the parishioners ejected from Holyrood's Chapel Royal by James VII/II, but in 1745 was treated with scant respect by the Young Pretender who found it to be a convenient place in which to hold the several officers he had taken at Prestonpans. The remains of Rizzio are said to lie under a stone in the south east corner of the church, while in the churchyard are the graves of Adam Smith (south west corner) and, north of the church, the poet Robert Fergusson (1750–74), best known for his 'Auld Reekie' but here perhaps of more interest for the fact that his headstone was paid for by his admirer, Robert Burns.

At the foot of Canongate, with Holyrood just beyond, there are four places deserving attention. First, a cobbled circle on the road marks the position of the *Girth Cross*, the western limit of the Sanctuary of Holyrood which, until the abolition in 1880 of imprisonment for debt, offered a refuge to debtors, derisively known as 'abbey lairds'. *White Horse Close*, north off Canongate and possibly so-named after Mary, Queen of Scots' white palfrey, was once a busy coaching station with a long courtyard at the end of which stood the White Horse Inn, in 1745 much frequented by the Young Pretender's officers. Dating from the 17C, the Close, now private homes, has been sensitively restored and, architecturally at least, still conveys the essence of its early character. *Nos 11–15 Canongate* make up a typical 17C tenement building, or land, now restored as flats and a shop. Lastly, round the corner, on the edge of Holyrood grounds, will be seen the curious, small turreted lodge, obscurely called *Queen Mary's Bathroom*. The tradition that Rizzio's murderers escaped by way of this lodge may well be true; another, that Mary habitually bathed here in white wine, seems less likely.

**Holyrood comprises the Palace of Holyrood House, with its State and Historical Apartments, and, behind, the much older and ruined Holyrood Abbey. Thus for the visitor there is a tangible and visible identification spanning from modern state splendour, back through the brief but turbulent and bloody days of Mary, Queen of Scots, down to the ruins of medieval piety and superstition.

Holyrood means Holy Cross, and its use here may stem from that fragment of the True Cross said to have been treasured by Queen Margaret, mother of David I, founder of the abbey. A more stirring tradition is that David, out hunting and in danger of being gored by a stag, was saved by the miraculous intervention of a Cross.

Palace visits are by conducted tours, these being frequent and lasting about 40 minutes. The Abbey ruins are visited on leaving the Palace after the tour. The Palace is normally completely closed for some two weeks in late May and again for the same time in late June and early July when it is occupied by the Lord High Commissioner and the Queen respectively. Intending visitors should refer to Tourist Information or telephone 031-556-7371.

The **Palace of Holyrood House**, or simply Holyrood Palace, has, with varying fortunes, been a royal residence since the reign of James IV, his predecessors having frequently used Holyrood Abbey's guest house for the same purpose. However, except for the north west tower—and even this was altered—the building seen today essentially represents major rebuilding and extension of 1671–80. Today the palace is the Queen's official residence when visiting Edinburgh.

History. Starting in c 1500, and using the abbey's guest house as a nucleus, James IV and James V completed what may be called the first palace, which, however, was burnt by the Earl of Hertford in 1544 and again badly damaged three years later, only the north west tower significantly surviving. Mary, Queen of Scots, spent only six years here at Holyrood—in that north west tower—but they were eventful ones. Hither the young widowed queen came from France in 1561, and here took place her famous disputation with John Knox, her marriage (in the abbey) to Darnley, the butchery before her eyes of Rizzio, and her hasty marriage to Bothwell (in the predecessor of today's Gallery).

But change came in 1603 with the departure for London of James VI/I, since which date, although occupied by royalty from time to time, Holyrood has never been a royal residence in any permanent sense. Cromwell occupied the palace in 1650, even ordering some repairs after a fire, but it was during the reign of Charles II, between 1671–80, that the major work (design by Sir William Bruce, executed by Robert Mylne) took place which converted what was essentially just the north west tower and some ruins into the great palace as seen today.

Despite this major work, the use made of the palace from now on was only intermittent. James VII/II, as Duke of York, resided here on and off between 1679–82; and in 1745, from 17 September to 31 October, the Young Pretender held his court here, beneath the guns of the hostile castle, though he often passed the night with his troops at nearby Duddingston. The Comte d'Artois, afterwards Charles X of France, occupied a suite of rooms for some years after 1795, and again, as an exiled monarch, in 1830–32. George IV held a levée here in 1822, Queen

Holyrood Gate and wing of Palace containing Queen Mary's Apartments

Victoria came from time to time on her way to and from Balmoral, and her son, Edward VII, lived here for some months in 1859 when studying in Edinburgh.

The spacious *Outer Court* is enclosed by wrought-iron gates which, together with a statue, form a national memorial to Edward VII. The fountain in the centre, a Victorian replica of that at Linlithgow Palace, provides a link back to James V and Mary of Guise, as also do their badges on the tower, or wing, projecting to the left, the only significant survival of that king's 16C palace.

The visitor starts his tour of the interior by the Grand Stair, which shows the first of the fine 17C ceilings prominently displaying the Honours of Scotland, from here diverting to the Household Dining Room with its Adam-style green and white decoration.

The *State Apartments*, or Charles II Great Apartments (something of a courtesy name, referring to the rooms' date rather than Charles II, who in fact never came here), are visited next, starting with the Throne Room (Charles II's Guard Hall), converted to throne room use at the time of George IV's visit of 1822. Still used for investitures and dinners, this room shows four works by Lely and one by Wilkie. Beyond come the Evening Drawing Room and the Morning Drawing Room, the latter with particularly fine decoration, both these rooms formerly designated as audience chambers. The tour now turns left (north) to pass through the Ante Chamber, Bedchamber and Closet, all three presented today as they would have been in 1680 when the future James VII/II held court here as Duke of York and Albany, with his wife Mary of Modena and their child, the future Queen Anne. Most of the furniture shown here is original, including the restored State Bed, and what is not original is for the most part contemporary. Finally there are three smaller state rooms, formerly the king's domestic rooms (Wardrobe, Dressing Room and a room allotted to the Page of the Back Stairs) which today display various relics associated with the palace and its historical users, of particular note being a 15C service book, one of the very few medieval liturgical books surviving in Scotland.

The *Picture Gallery*, extending the length of the northern range of the rebuilt palace, has long been and still is a kind of royal promenade, used for a variety of court events, including, in 1567, though in an earlier form, the marriage between Mary and Bothwell (according to Protestant rite and a sombre occasion compared to the pageantry and festivity of the marriage to Darnley two years earlier), and, in 1745, a ball given by the Young Pretender, a description of which will be found in Scott's 'Waverley'. But what will most attract the attention of today's visitor will surely be the astonishing collection of portraits of 89 Scottish kings, the prolific and highly imaginative outcome of a government commission executed in 1684–86 by Jacob de Wet the Younger.

The tour now moves to the *Historical Apartments* (in what little is left of the 16C palace of James V), dividing into Darnley's and thence, by way of a private stair in the wall, Mary's above. Darnley's rooms (antechamber, bedroom and dressing room) show Mortlake tapestry, portraits and antique furniture, including a set of contemporary Turkeywork chairs, but are without the historical association of Mary's, comprising Outer Chamber or Audience Room, Inner Chamber or Bedroom and, in turrets opening off the latter, small North and South Cabinets or closets. The Outer Chamber was undoubtedly the scene of John Knox's famous interview with Mary when she arrived in Scotland in 1561, but whether the supper from which Rizzio was dragged took place in the North or the South Cabinet is disputed. Either way, it was in one of these two small rooms that on 9 March 1566 Mary was supping with, amongst others, her favourite and secretary David Rizzio when a party led by Darnley and Ruthven burst in. Seizing Rizzio they dragged him through the bedroom to the outer chamber where he was left dead with 56 dagger wounds. A plaque on the floor marks the spot where his body lay, but the alleged indelible stain of blood, if indeed it exists, is concealed by floor covering.

Holyrood Abbey. Of the once great abbey, with its guest house large and important enough to serve as a court residence, only the church survives, and of that only the ruined nave, the remainder having in part been demolished at the Reformation and again (south-west corner) to make way for Sir William Bruce's enlargement of the palace in 1671–80. The collapse of the roof in 1768 completed the process of ruin.

History. The abbey was founded in 1128 by David I, his church however being replaced in the 13C by a grander edifice. During the 15C the abbey became a regular court residence of James I, II and III—all of whom doubtless found this valley site preferable to their bleak quarters up in the castle—James II being born and crowned here, while he, James III and James IV were all married in the church. Like the palace, the abbey was burnt in 1544 by Hertford, and suffered again in 1547, but less than 20 years later, in 1565, the church was in good enough condition for the wedding of Mary and Darnley, followed a century later (1633) by the coronation of Charles I, in preparation for which the king ordered extensive refurbishment. Under Charles II the church became a Chapel Royal, and under James VII/II the chapel of the Order of the Thistle.

A Norman arch, visible behind the royal vault (south east corner), is about the sole vestige of David I's church, today's ruins being essentially those of the 13C replacement. Worth noting are the West Front (remodelled for Charles I's coronation), the small but richly arcaded north west tower, and the blind arcading either side of the nave. David II, James II and his queen, James V and Darnley (as King Henry) were all buried near the high altar; this, however, was desecrated in the religious rioting of 1688, and now, by order of Queen Victoria, they lie together in the royal vault. Rizzio, also, may lie somewhere in the ruins, though tradition also places his grave in Canongate Church.

For **Holyrood Park**, or Queen's Park, adjoining the palace, see F. Other Districts of Edinburgh.

Buses return up Canongate and High Street. An alternative is to return to Canongate Church, there taking Old Tolbooth Wynd, beyond which a footpath climbs up to Regent Road (with the Burns Monument and Calton Hill), the eastward extension of Princes Street.

C. South Edinburgh (Grassmarket, Greyfriars and beyond)

A pleasant way to start this walk is by the path leading off Princes Street opposite the foot of Castle Street. This crosses the gardens to King's Stables Road, once a tilting ground but now with a large car park.

To the south west of King's Stables Road, within the angle with Lothian Road, are *Usher Hall* (1814), a fine hall for meetings, concerts etc., and the *Royal Lyceum Theatre*, an extensively renovated opulent Victorian theatre (1883).

Grassmarket is soon reached, a drab rectangle, to anyone so attuned still oppressive with echoes from a dark past, bloody, violent, even ghoulish. For long this was the main place of execution, the many victims including over 100 Covenanters who here were martyred, or, in the cynical words of the Earl of Rothes, 'glorified God in the Grassmarket'. Today a cobblestone cross within a railed enclosure at the east end both marks the site of the gallows and remembers those who died. Here too, in 1736, Captain Porteous was lynched. Commander of the guard when the thief Wilson (see Rte 33A, Pittenweem) was hanged, he panicked when the mob—judging the robbing of an Excise officer to be no great crime—got ugly, ordering his men to fire and causing several deaths. Tried and found guilty of murder, Porteous was however reprieved, only to be dragged from the tolbooth and hanged here in Grassmarket from a dyer's pole. And the evil Burke and Hare had their den near here (in Tanner's Close, now gone but once the last close off the north of West Port beside Lady Lawson Street), in 1827–28 enticing at least 18 men and women here so that they could suffocate them and sell their bodies to doctors. Even the disaster of Flodden is recalled here, for in Vennel, reached by steps off the south west of Grassmarket, there survives a section of the *Flodden Wall*, hastily built in 1513 but still serving as the west wall of George Heriot's School (see below). But on Grassmarket's north side a lighter note is struck, for here stands the old *White Hart Inn*, once the convivial haunt of Burns and other writers.

Three streets lead out of the east end of Grassmarket, in West Bow (becoming Victoria Street), the northernmost, being the *Traverse Theatre*, a leading experimental theatre in an 18C building. **Magdalen Chapel** (Scottish Reformation Society, Tel: 031-220-1450), of unusual interest as a charitable and guild chapel, will be found a short way up Cowgate, the central of the three streets and the one in which in 1508 Scotland's first printing press operated.

The chapel was founded in 1547 by Janet Rynd (buried here; widow of Michael Maquhen, a prominent citizen whose wishes she was carrying out) as a chapel and hospice for seven bedesmen (pensioners). Although well cared for, the pensioners did not have an easy life, amongst other obligations having to attend three lengthy services daily, including repeating the Lord's Prayer five times and the Creed 50 times before breakfast, and before supper praying for the souls of the founders and their relations. The chapel was placed under the patronage of the Hammermen, the guild of all metalworkers (except gold), and so remained until 1857, though the last bedesman had left in 1665. During the 17 and 18C, probably because of the closeness to the Grassmarket gallows, the chapel was used as a mortuary.

The Hammermen's insignia, with the crests of the founders, may be seen on a panel over the principal door. The main features of the interior are the boards recording charitable gifts for the benefit of the poorer members of the craft; below the dais a wrought-iron railing with the craft insignia; and the stained glass in the central window, the only important pre-Reformation stained glass in Scotland still in its original building.

St. Cecilia's Hall, farther along Cowgate beyond South Bridge, was built in 1762 by Robert Mylne (using the Teatro Farnese in Parma as a model) for the Musical Society of Edinburgh who used the hall until 1802. Later serving as a Baptist chapel and a Freemasons' Hall, St. Cecilia's has since 1960 belonged to Edinburgh University Faculty of Music, and is used, mainly during the Festival, for small musical and other recitals. The hall houses the *University Collection of Historic Musical Instruments* (Tel: 031-667-1011, Ext. 4415).

Candlemaker Row, the southernmost of the three streets leading out of the east end of Grassmarket, reaches Greyfriars Place at the junction with George IV Bridge, a spot at which dog lovers will surely pause, for here sits the appealing small statue of *Greyfriars Bobby*, a Skye terrier which for 14 years after 1848 kept watch over his master's grave in Greyfriars churchyard opposite. At one time, in danger of being destroyed as a stray, the dog was given a special licence collar (now in Huntly House City Museum) by the then city provost.

Greyfriars Kirk and Kirkyard, as the name suggests on the site of a 15C Franciscan friary, offers both history and one of Scotland's most extraordinary collections of weird and pretentious tombs. This is, of course, a place sacred in Scottish religious history, because it was here that the National Covenant was signed in 1638, some of the names being written in blood. The many consequent martyrs are commemorated by a stirringly worded memorial against the north wall of the kirkyard, while in the south is the enclosure where 1200 Covenanters taken prisoner at Bothwell Bridge in 1679 were held for five months, rigorously guarded, without shelter and poorly fed. Among those buried here are the Regent Morton (1581), George Buchanan (1582), the artist George Jamesone (1644), Captain Porteous (1736), Allan Ramsay (1758), Duncan Ban MacIntyre (the 'Burns of the Highlands', 1812), and, of course, John Gray (1848), owner of Greyfriars Bobby, whose simple grave, with a red granite stone erected by American admirers of Bobby, may be seen to the left of the path leading from the kirkyard entrance to the Martyrs' Memorial.—*Greyfriars Kirk*, dedicated on Christmas Day 1620, was the first to be opened in Edinburgh after the Reformation.

Just south west of Greyfriars, but reached by Forrest Road and Lauriston Place, is *George Heriot's School, one of the most handsome and original buildings in Edinburgh (visitors may walk around the exterior and the quadrangle). Endowed by George Heriot (died 1624), jeweller and banker to James VI/I, the building, sometimes ascribed to Inigo Jones, grew between 1628–93, the large quadrangle being particularly pleasing with over 200 windows, said all to be different in decoration. The Vennel, with remains of the Flodden Wall, marks the school's west boundary. The Scottish Baronial *Royal Infirmary* (David Bryce, 1879) is to the south of the school on the other side of Lauriston Place.

To the east of Greyfriars the two places of principal interest are the Royal Museum of Scotland (Chambers Street) and the complex, old and new, of Edinburgh University. A clockwise round, starting along Chambers Street, is suggested.

The *Royal Museum of Scotland (Chambers Street)*, until 1985 called the *Royal Scottish Museum* (Tel: 031-225-7534), on the south side of Chambers Street, is almost as worth visiting for its soaring, airy design (Fowke and Matheson, 1861–66) as for the astonishing variety of its exhibits. The museum was established in 1854, but the foundation stone of the present building, appropriately reminiscent of his Crystal Palace in London, was laid in 1861 by Prince Albert. As its name indicates, this is a Scottish as opposed to city museum, the home of national collections of seemingly limitless scope in both time and subject. The time scale spans from fossils formed in remote ages up to the most modern technology, the principal fields embraced being the decorative arts (the national fine arts collections are in the National Gallery in Princes Street), archaeology, ethnology, natural history in its widest sense, and technology. Additionally there is a programme of specialised temporary exhibitions, while for those in search of more than just a browse around there are lectures, films and gallery talks.

The older buildings (Old College) of **Edinburgh University** occupy the south west angle of Chambers Street and South Bridge, while the new buildings are just to the south and south west, generally along Lothian Street and around Bristo Square.

The youngest of Scotland's historic universities, Edinburgh in large measure owes its origin to the generosity of two brothers, William and Clement Little, and one James Lawson, an associate of John Knox. It was in 1580 that Clement Little presented his collection of 300 books to provide a library, and in 1582 the university was founded as the Town College. In the following year James VI granted a charter, the name then being changed to College of King James. In more recent times Edinburgh was one of the first universities to admit women (1884).

The *Old College* stands partly on ground once belonging to the collegiate Kirk o' Field, where stood the house in which Darnley met his violent and mysterious death. In classical style, the Old College was designed by Robert Adam in 1789 (the portico is judged to be one of his most distinguished achievements) and completed by W.H. Playfair in 1834, the delay being because of the Napoleonic wars. The dome (by Rowand Anderson), surmounted by a figure of Youth (by J. Hutchison), was added in 1884. The *Talbot Rice Art Centre* (Tel: 031-667-1011) houses, in a fine gallery designed by Playfair, the Torrie Collection of 16 and 17C European painting and sculpture, while an adjacent gallery is used for temporary exhibitions. To the south west are the *New University Buildings*, an imposing group designed by Rowand Anderson in 1884, with, facing Teviot Place, the Medical Faculty (1897). The large Student Centre flanks the north east side of the large open Bristo Square, off the diagonal corner being the McEwan Hall of 1897. The above complex, effectively forming a campus, on the south merges with George Square, dating from about 1770 when the gentry began to move out of the Old Town (Sir Walter Scott lived his first 25 years here) but today with much of its former dignity exchanged for functional modern university buildings.

The Meadows, just south of George Square, were a fashionable 18C promenade, while James IV is said to have played golf on *Bruntsfield Links*, farther south across Melville Drive. At one time both Meadows and Links formed part of the Burgh Muir, a frequent rallying place for Scottish armies.

Archers' Hall (no adm.), at the north east of The Meadows, built in 1776 and later extended, is the headquarters of the Royal Company of Archers. Constituted by the Privy Council in 1676 and chartered in 1704, the Company was formally appointed as King's Bodyguard in Scotland on the occasion of George IV's visit in 1822. Enjoying high rights of precedence, the Company consists of some 500 noblemen and gentlemen, commanded by a Captain General, who is invariably a distinguished Scottish peer. When the monarch holds court in Edinburgh they are on duty as escort, guards and gentlemen-in-waiting.

In Leven Street, just west of The Meadows, the *King's Theatre* was opened in 1906 and today, grandly refurbished, still shows its Baroque frontage and Rococo interior.

The return to Princes Street can be made along George IV Bridge (from Greyfriars at the west end of Chambers Street), passing on the left the *Central Library* (Tel: 031-225-5584), with comprehensive reference collections on Scottish and local history (including an admirable Edinburgh Room), music and the fine arts. Opposite is the **National Library of Scotland** (Tel: 031-226-4531), occupying a building (by R. Fairlie, 1956) the main façade of which carries statues by Hew Lorimer typifying seven branches of learning. This is one of the largest libraries in Britain, developed from the Advocates' Library founded in 1682, formally opened as a law library seven years later, and since 1710 enjoying the right to claim a copy of every book published in Britain. In 1922 the library was offered to the nation (the Faculty of Advocates reserving for themselves the specifically legal works), and in 1925 it assumed its present name. Books apart, the library owns an extensive collection of illuminated manuscripts, specimens of early printing, and historical documents, amongst these being the last letter of Mary, Queen of Scots, written on the eve of her execution; the order resulting in the massacre of Glencoe; and letters and papers of Hume, Boswell, Burns, Stevenson, Scott and Carlyle. Frequent special exhibitions are also mounted.

D. Princes Street

Completed in 1805 as part of the New Town concept of 1767 (see E. below), and named after Prince George, later George IV, Princes Street is Edinburgh's main thoroughfare. With its eastern extension, Waterloo Place, it is just about a mile in length, its north side an architectural and functional hotchpotch of shops, banks, clubs, hotels and suchlike; its south side, by contrast—and it is this that gives the street its exciting character—a panoramic sweep of gardens backed by the steep-sided long slope of the Royal Mile rising to the battlemented mass of the historic castle sprawled over its precipitous rock. Add the street's airy width, its unbroken straightness, its several monuments both beside the street and in the gardens, and that astonishing eastern wall provided by Calton Hill and its curiosities, and it is easy to see how Princes Street has earned its fame.

Waverley Market (with Tourist Information), at the street's east end, can be regarded as the modern heart of Edinburgh. The description below therefore starts here, afterwards first looking eastward to Waterloo Place and Calton Hill before travelling westward the length of Princes Street.

Waverley Market, a precinct of the 1980s filling much of the slope within the east angle of Princes Street and Waverley Bridge, is more imaginative than many such and at any rate successfully hides what was once the desolate roofscape of Waverley Station (likely to undergo major change during the 1990s). Here, in the market, *Tourist Information* occupies spacious modern premises. Waverley Bridge descends past *Waverley Station* and over the railway to reach a crossroads at the foot of the slope. From here Cockburn Street winds up to the Royal Mile, while Market Street runs east–west below the slope. To the west, at No. 21, are the *Festival Offices*; to the east, and opposite one another, the City Art Centre and the Fruitmarket Gallery.

The **City Art Centre** (Tel: 031-225-2424. Ext. 6650), housing the city's permanent fine arts collection and the focus, too, of a diverse programme of temporary exhibitions, occupies an interesting warehouse of 1899, used in turn for storing newsprint and then fruit and vegetables but now skilfully converted to reconcile architectural integrity with the sophisticated needs of a modern art centre. The city's permanent collection (sometimes withdrawn to allow space for temporary exhibitions) comprises some 3000 works—paintings, drawings, prints, sculpture—mainly by Scottish artists active between the 17C and the present day, and, quite apart from artistic enjoyment, the visitor can, through the many topographical views and portraits, conjure up much of old Edinburgh and its distinguished citizens. The *Fruitmarket Gallery* (Tel: 031-225-2383), opposite at No. 29 Market Street in a 1920s warehouse, mounts temporary exhibitions of modern, and particularly contemporary, Scottish and international fine art, the emphasis tending to be on one artist or one theme.

EASTWARD from Waverley Market Princes Street ends at a major intersection with North Bridge (south) and Leith Street (north), on the south east corner being the *General Post Office* (1861) with the *Philatelic Bureau* (Tel: 031-550-8370) with stamp displays and a service for collectors. Opposite, behind a statue (by Steell) of the Duke of Wellington, extends the long, symmetrical façade of *General Register House* (Scottish Record Office), built between 1774–1827 largely to the design of Robert Adam though completed by Robert Reid. Here are housed Scotland's legal and historical public records, some dating from the 13C, and here too, in the entrance hall or in the gallery below Adam's dome, are mounted special exhibitions (Tel: 031-556-6585.—See also West Register House under E. North Edinburgh). Behind General Register House, within the general angle of Leith Street and York Place and in sorry contrast to Adam's fine taste, sprawls the externally drab and ponderous *St. James Centre*, with a hotel, shops, offices, multi-storey parking etc.

Princes Street is extended east by **Waterloo Place**, off the south east corner of which is *Calton Old Burial Ground*, with the Lincoln Monument (1893), dedicated also to the Scottish-American soldiers who fell in the American Civil War; the tomb of David Hume designed by Robert Adam; and an obelisk honouring five early political reformers, found guilty of sedition (1793–94) and sentenced to transportation by a government nervous of contagion from the spreading and bloody revolution in France.

Calton Hill can be ascended either by steps at the corner of Waterloo Place and Regent Road, or by a road a little farther on. It is an ascent well worth making if only for the views, even though that over the main city is now somewhat blocked by the mass of St. James Centre. This can to some extent be overcome by climbing the *Nelson Monument* (Tel: 031-556-2716), erected between 1807–15 to honour the admiral. However, even without doing this, grand views can still be enjoyed across to Leith and its harbour, across and along the Forth, and, best of all, over Holyrood and Arthur's Seat. The attempt to honour the Scottish dead of the Napoleonic wars, and their 'glorious naval and military achievements', was less than successful, for the grandiose and ambitious *National Monument*, intended to be a reproduction of the Parthenon— perhaps because this was a temple to Athena, Goddess of War—though begun in 1822 was before long abandoned when funds, and memories too perhaps, ran dry. However the relatively obscure philosopher Dugald Stewart (1753–1828), professor of moral philosophy at the university, was for some reason deemed worthy of a place on this hill where he is remembered by a reproduction of the monument of Lysicrates in Athens. Cannon up here include a Portuguese one of 1624, captured at Mandalay in 1886, while the buildings represent the *Observatory* (see F. Royal Observatory).

Opposite the steps up Calton Hill, the south side of Regent Road is lined by the long block of *St. Andrew's House* (1937–39), while across the road and just beyond stand the *Crown Office Buildings* (Thomas Hamilton, 1825–29), an adaptation of the Temple of Theseus in Athens and long the home of the Royal High School, the pupils of which included such as Robert Adam, Alexander Graham Bell, George Borrow, James Boswell and Sir Walter Scott. A short distance beyond stands the classical *Burns Monument* (Hamilton, 1830), close to which a path leads down to Old Tolbooth Wynd and then Canongate near the foot of the Royal Mile.

WESTWARD from Waverley Market Princes Street runs beside the **East Gardens**, with, beside the road, the **Scott Monument**, a lofty Gothic spire forming a canopy over a statue of Scott with his dog (by Steell) and with niches in which are historical figures and characters from Scott's novels. Erected in 1840–44 the monument is the design of George Kemp who, however, did not live to see his work completed. (Ascent. Tel: 031-225-2424. Ext. 6596). Just beyond stands the confident figure of Adam Black (1784–1874), Provost of Edinburgh, Member of Parliament and founder in 1807 of the publishing house of A. and C. Black which in the 19C acquired the copyright of Scott's novels and is today the publisher of the 'Blue Guides'. Beyond, the East Gardens end at the two dignified classical edifices, both by W.H. Playfair, of the Royal Scottish Academy (beside Princes Street) and the National Gallery of Scotland, the latter beside the street called The Mound which, built on the dumped debris of the New Town excavations, now curves up to meet the Royal Mile at the foot of Lawnmarket.

The **Royal Scottish Academy** (Tel: 031-225-6671), in a building of 1823–36, was founded in 1826. Normally there are two main exhibitions; one, showing the work of the elected members and contemporary artists, running from late April to early August, the other a special Festival Exhibition.

For the **"National Gallery of Scotland**, see section G.

The **West Gardens** spread southward across the railway to the foot of the castle cliff, at the gardens' north east corner, immediately below the angle of Princes Street and The Mound, being the *Floral Clock*, dating from 1903 and believed to be the oldest of its kind in the world. The *Ross Open Air Theatre* is a central feature of the gardens, near here being the ornate Ross fountain and a contrastingly simple and effective boulder to the Norwegian Brigade 'raised and trained in Scotland'. The *Scottish American War Memorial* (by R. Tait McKenzie of Philadelphia), symbolising 'The Call, 1914' and erected by Americans of Scottish blood and sympathies, is in the gardens below the level of Princes Street, while the *Royal Scots Greys Memorial* (Frank Mears, 1952) is beside the street. Others remembered here, by statues, are the poet Allan Ramsay (1686–1758); Sir James Simpson (1811–70), who in 1847 introduced the use of chloroform as an anaesthetic; and Dr Thomas Guthrie (1803–73), apostle of the Ragged Schools (1844) for the education of the poor. Finally, beyond the railway and at the foot of the castle rock, *Wellhouse Tower* survives as the last vestige of the town wall of 1436.

The West Gardens end with two churches, the one beside Princes Street being the 19C *St. John's*, worth entering for William Burn's neo-Gothic nave of 1817. *St. Cuthbert's*, just to the south, is an ancient foundation, perhaps of the 7C, although today's church, except for its tower of 1789, is a rebuilding (1894) by Hippolyte Blanc. In the yard are the graves of the writer Thomas de Quincey (1785–1859) who died in Edinburgh, of George Kemp (1795–1844), architect of the Scott monument, and of the painter Alexander Nasmyth (1758–1840). But the mathematically-inclined visitor should head for the church's vestibule where there is a monument to John Napier of Merchiston (1560–1617), inventor of logarithms and of various rules and formulae in spherical trigonometry.

Rose Street, running parallel to and just north of this western section of Princes Street, is known for its pubs, some showing Victorian or Edwardian interiors as opulent as they can be inviting.

E.   North Edinburgh (New Town)

In 1767 the decision was reached that Edinburgh—hitherto essentially a confined tenemented maze clinging to its rock ridge between Holyrood and the castle—must breathe. Thinking in enviably bold and radical terms, in which space rather than the lack of it was the key, the authorities sponsored a competition, the winner of which was James Craig, aged only 23. His grand and formal scheme was based on George Street, named after George III, to run along the natural ridge; Queen Street, parallel to the north, named after George's consort; and Princes Street, for the Prince of Wales, along the valley to the south.

Work soon started and was continued by successive planners and architects until well into the 19C. The north and west extension is largely the achievement of Robert Reid (1802); the east that of Archibald Elliot in 1815 and William Playfair in 1819; J.G. Graham planned the north west in 1822, while to Henry Raeburn (up to 1823) must go the credit for much of what lies beyond the Water of Leith. The outcome is a confident and extensive grid of solid wide streets, of spacious crescents and squares, of restrained symmetrical classical buildings, and of elegant urban views, all impeccably combining as a monument to Georgian vision and achievement and as much a part of the character of today's Edinburgh as are the older historical and architectural associations of the Royal Mile.

The New Town is of course an officially designated conservation area, subject to strict planning control. Well aware of the value of this heritage, the City of Edinburgh and the Historic Buildings Council in 1970 embarked on a conservation programme, many interesting aspects of which are explained at the *New Town Conservation Centre*, 13A Dundas Street, which is the northward extension of Hanover Street (Tel: 031-557-5222). Here are an exhibition of conservation work in progress and a library, while for the enthusiast there is a programme of conducted walks.

The fortunate visitor will have the time to explore. Others, inevitably, will have to be content with the essentials which, at their barest, may be pruned to Charlotte Square and a taste of George Street. For the most part, though, the New Town, or Georgian Edinburgh, is professional and residential, with correspondingly relatively light traffic, and the visitor with a car will be able to enjoy a good overall impression simply by driving around.

The description below starts in the east at St. Andrew Square; follows George Street west to Charlotte Square and, beyond, the districts of West End and Dean; then returns east along Queen Street to the National Portrait Gallery and Royal Museum of Scotland.

St. Andrew Square, architecturally something of a mixture, lacks both the essential character and the dignity of other New Town squares. However, there can be no complaint about the stylish premises of the *Royal Bank of Scotland* on the square's east flank, the bank occupying the mansion built in 1772–74 by William Chambers for Sir Lawrence Dundas who, as owner of the land, insisted on a family town residence here in preference to the church originally planned. Other notable buildings here are No. 26 (by Chambers) and No. 38 (by Bryce, 1851–52), while in the square's centre soars the lofty fluted column of the *Melville Monument*, supporting a statue (Robert Forrest, 1828) of Henry Dundas, 1st Viscount Melville (1742–1811).

The Royal Museum of Scotland and the National Portrait Gallery, both described below, are in Queen Street one block north of St. Andrew Square.

George Street now swathes westward along its ridge from which, at the several intersections, there are glimpses north towards the Forth and south to the spine of the Royal Mile. *St. Andrew's Church* (1782–85, by Andrew Fraser; steeple of 1789 by Andrew Sibbald), on the north just after leaving St. Andrew Square, is of interest not only as the first to have been built in the New Town but also because this was the scene in 1843 of the Disruption when 451 ministers, seceding from the Established Church, marched out to found the dissenting Free Church of Scotland.

Opposite, the Corinthian bank building is by David Rhind (1847), while farther along on this south side the *Assembly Rooms* were designed in 1784–87 by J. Henderson and later added to by William Burn. The bank at No. 25 is by David Bryce (1847), and No. 22 has, since 1909, been the seat of the *Royal Society of Edinburgh*, Scotland's leading scientific society, incorporated in 1783 and numbering Scott and Kelvin among its presidents. Scott lived in this district, too; at No. 107 George Street soon after his marriage in 1797, then successively at Nos. 10 and 39 Castle Street, the latter being his home from 1802–26 and the place at which he wrote many of the Waverley Novels.

**Charlotte Square, the epitome of the New Town, was designed in 1791 by Robert Adam who, however, died soon afterwards. Nevertheless the superb north side, a masterpiece of restrained symmetry and accepted as one of Europe's most distinguished frontages, is entirely his; his 'again', one might write, because thanks to the imagination and drive of the 4th Marquis of Bute during the 1920s and '30s, the depredations of the Victorians—lowered windows, dormers added, doors altered—were largely erased and this north side restored as nearly as possible to its original state. After the death in 1956 of the 5th Marquis of Bute, the three houses (Nos. 5–7) passed to the *National Trust for Scotland*, No. 5 now being the headquarters of the Trust, while No. 6 (Bute House) is the official residence of the Secretary of State for Scotland. No. 7 is now the *Georgian House* (NTS. Tel: 031-225-2160), the lower floors of which have been furnished as a typical wealthy New Town home generally of the period 1790–1810; the home, in fact, of the first owner, John Lamont of Lamont, 18th chief of Clan Lamont. The furnishings apart, the house shows several notable paintings, among the artists being (in alphabetical order) Ferdinand Bol, Jan van Goyen, Melchior de Hondecoeter, George Morland and Alexander Nasmyth, as also, for portraits, Dobson, Hoppner, Kneller, Ramsay and Raeburn.—The upper floors of the house are the official residence of the Moderator of the General Assembly of the Church of Scotland.

Two other places in Charlotte Square, both on the west side, may be of interest. The *Scottish Arts Council Centre*, at No. 19, provides detailed information on arts events of all kinds throughout Scotland (Tel: 031-226-6051); and nearby *West Register House*, since 1962 occupying the former church of St. George (Reid, 1810–14), offers a permanent exhibition of documents relating to Scotland's history (Tel: 031-556-6585. See also General Register House under D. Princes Street).

WEST OF CHARLOTTE SQUARE. Visitors with time may now choose a worthwhile and varied meander (in large part also motorable) in the general area to the west and north west of Charlotte Square. Others may descend the short distance south into Princes Street, or perhaps make their way east along Queen Street for the portrait gallery and Royal Museum of Scotland.

Behind West Register House, Randolph Place runs into busy Queensferry Street, across which is Melville Street, a broad and dignified creation of 1820–26 with a monument to the 2nd Viscount Melville (1802–61) and, at the street's end, the triple-spired *Episcopal Cathedral of St. Mary* (1874–1917), designed by George Gilbert Scott and one of the largest Gothic churches built in Britain since the Reformation. The path along the cathedral's north side passes *Easter Coates House*, a gracious small house of about 1615, now St. Mary's Music School.

Queensferry Street, followed north west, soon reaches **Dean Bridge**, built by Telford in 1832 and much acclaimed, not least by coach travellers who hitherto had had to negotiate the steep and sometimes treacherous valley. Today the Water of Leith, over 100ft below and flowing through a wooded cleft, is scarcely noticed. Yet it should be, for this modest river was once of huge economic importance, turning some 70 mills over its brief course between the Pentlands and the Forth, no fewer than 11 of these being in the neighbourhood of **Dean Village**, just west below the bridge and reached (from the south side) by the street called Bell's Brae. A milling centre for at least four centuries—indeed an active life of twice that length is sometimes claimed—this almost secret jumble of houses and converted mills all cramped within the narrow valley provides a startling contrast to the spacious Georgian elegance above. There is a riverside path here too, bearing back below the bridge to reach *St. Bernard's Well*, a small Doric temple of 1789, popular with 18 and 19C strollers who paused here beside the figure of Hygieia, Goddess of Health, to sip the waters.

From the south side of Dean Bridge the superb sequence of Randolph Crescent, Great Stuart Street and Ainslie Place lead to St. Colme Street, representing the westward extension of Queen Street (see immediately below).

From the north east corner of Charlotte Square, North Charlotte Street quickly reaches the west end of Queen Street, a broad largely residential thoroughfare running along the north face of the New Town ridge and flanked on the north by gardens, across which, at No. 17 Heriot Row, Robert Louis Stevenson lived from 1859–79.

At Queen Street's east end are the **Royal Museum of Scotland (Queen Street)** and the **National Portrait Gallery**, occupying respectively the east and west wings of a red sandstone building (by Rowand Anderson) dedicated by the munificence of J.R. Finlay, a proprietor of 'The Scotsman', to 'the illustration of Scottish history'. And this indeed is just what this museum and gallery do, for here can be seen, in physical or portrait form, much of what to the touring visitor can be no more than a printed historical reference or the mention of a name. What the imagination may have pictured is here brought to reality.

The Museum and Gallery are either side of a central balconied well, below the balcony being a colourful if imaginative frieze of Scottish historical figures, starting with prehistoric man and finishing with Carlyle. And around the first floor balcony are equally colourful and probably equally imaginative battle and other scenes, these including Stirling Bridge (1297), Bannockburn (1314), Largs (1263), and, by way of contrast, the Good Deeds of David I and the Landing of Queen Margaret at Queensferry (1086). If neither the frieze nor the battle and other scenes lay great claim to either artistic merit or historical authenticity, at least it can surely be said of both that they stimulate the imagination.

The ***Royal Museum of Scotland (Queen Street)** (Tel: 031-225-7534), until 1985 the *National Museum of Antiquities*, provides a rich and immensely varied background to any tour of Scotland, the material illustrating many aspects of Scottish life from earliest to quite modern times. The museum is arranged on three levels, the Ground Floor being the Historic Gallery (with also Dark Ages sculpture); the 1st Floor, the Prehistoric and Viking Gallery; and the 2nd Floor, the Roman Gallery. The following paragraphs claim only to offer a (roughly chronological) glimpse of the wealth of material exhibited.

1st Floor. Prehistoric and Viking. Cases display palaeolithic to Bronze Age artefacts—articles which, even if in their earliest forms they perhaps strike the layman as no more than stone chips and slivers, nevertheless remind that primitive man had a lifestyle here millenia ago. But gradually the artefacts become recognisable—as ornaments or tools or weapons—later even exciting aesthetic admiration as, for instance, gold jewellery, jet necklaces or sophisticated Pictish silver chains of double rings. And in the same category, if of a later period, there is the *St. Ninian's Isle Treasure, a silver hoard of c 800, the sight of which may tempt the viewer to that fragment of Shetland ruin in which, after perhaps being hidden from Viking raiders, it was discovered in 1958 (Rte 68). Additionally, everyday objects enhance the human aspects (from remote Stone Age to Viking) of sites such as Skara Brae (Rte 67), of which there is an instructive model, and Jarlshof (Rte 68), while pottery, largely from burials, adds meaning to the cairns, cists and suchlike the traveller will meet over so much of Scotland. And examples of cup-and-ring stones are shown too, as unexplained here as they are on their moorland sites.

2nd Floor. Roman. Roman sites in Scotland tend to be little more than earthworks or stone foundations and are thus hard to people. But the many finds displayed here—admirably arranged by themes such as army, cooking, transport, religion, burial, hypocausts—go a long way to suggest what life may have been like along the exposed length of the Antonine Wall (Rte 9); or at, for instance, more comfortable Cramond (Rte 9) beside the Forth; or at Trimontium (Newstead, Rte 4), once a considerable camp but now little more than a notice board; or within the wide defences of Ardoch (Rte 25B).

But the highlight in this Roman section is the *Traprain Treasure (Rte 1), a hoard of Christian and pagan silver, largely Roman work of the 4C, found on Traprain Law in 1919 and thought perhaps to represent the loot brought back from an early 5C raid southwards, possibly even into Gaul.

Ground Floor. Historic Gallery. Here the scope of the exhibits greatly broadens, spanning from the Dark Ages through medieval antiquities and on into the 18C. From the Dark Ages there are grave contents, including finds from Whithorn (Rte 14), as also, finely set in a special room, originals and casts of 6–11C sculptured stones, some bearing strange symbols peculiar to Scotland. Weapons of many kinds and periods are shown here too, as are also instruments of law and order, including the Maiden, which removed the heads of the Regent Morton in 1581, and of the 8th and 9th earls of Argyll in 1661 and 1685. Near the entrance the visitor stands below the Rossend Castle ceiling (see Rte 33, Burntisland). Also shown are domestic exhibits of many, and often strange kinds; bagpipes and other musical instruments; and personal relics of, for example, Mary, Queen of Scots and the Young Pretender (his *Canteen, a unique set of Jacobite silver).

The ***National Portrait Gallery** (Tel: 031-556-8921) records Scottish history, from the 15C onwards and in its broadest sense, by means of portraits of men and women who in one way or another have contributed to the whole. As might be expected, royalty is strongly represented, starting with that tragic sequence of James I to Mary, Queen of Scots, every one of whom—except for James V who is said to have died of heartbreak after his defeat at Solway Moss—met a violent end. Mary is contrastingly shown—in white mourning for her husband Francis II of France and in a *portrait of 1578 by P. Oudry. Her mother, Mary of Guise, is here too (painted, it is thought, by Corneille de Lyon), as are also her son James VI/I and his son Charles I, the latter painted with his queen (after Van Dyck) and on the scaffold by an unknown artist. And the royal sequence continues, notably with *Charles II as a boy by William Dobson, James VII/II by Lely, George II by John Shackleton and *George IV by Thomas Lawrence.

From Scotland's deeply scarred 17C many famous faces look down, led perhaps by James Graham, Marquis of Montrose (after Honthorst), and his enemies the Covenanter general David Leslie (by Lely), the man responsible for the massacres of prisoners at Philiphaugh and Dunaverty, and the 8th Earl of Argyll (by David Scougal). The devious General Monk (by Lely) represents the Commonwealth and the Restoration; Claverhouse (or Bonnie Dundee) the final throw, at Killiecrankie, on behalf of James VII/II.

The Pretenders, Old and Young, hang here too—as do the latter's courageous guide 'over the sea to Skye', Flora Macdonald (painted by Richard Wilson); Henry, Cardinal York, the last of the Stuarts; and even Charlotte, Duchess of Albany, the Young Pretender's natural daughter, who may or may not have been mother of that self-styled Count Roehenstart who lies in Dunkeld cathedral.

When it comes to portraits of the 18C onwards, the artist increasingly begins to claim as much attention as the sitter. And rightly so, for several of these artists are in themselves a part of Scotland's history. Allan

EDINBURGH Environs

0 miles 1
0 kilometres 2

PORT

NEWHAVEN

DOCKS

Firth Of Forth

COMMERCIAL

L E I T H

ROAD

James Pringle
Woollen Mill

St Mary's

LEITH WALK

SEAFIELD

ROAD

RESTALRIG

LONDON

Meadowbank
Sports Centre

ROAD

PORTOBELLO

ROAD

Central Area
(See large scale plan)

Waverley
Station

Palace of
Holyroodhouse

St Margaret's Loch

stle

Holyrood Park

Dunsappie Loch

DUDDINGSTON

MILTON ROAD

Arthur's
Seat

Duddingston
Loch

PORTOBELLO

A1

tsfield
nks

DALKEITH

Braid Burn

NIDDRIE

NETHER
LIBERTON

Blackford
Hill
Observatory

Craigmillar Castle

OLD DALKEITH ROAD

N

Braid Hills

GILMERTON

NORTHFIELD

ROAD

FERNIEHILL

A68

LIBERTON

GILMERTON

IRMILEHEAD

KAIMES

SLIN

A701

A7 DALKEITH

Ramsay portrays David Hume; George Willison, James Boswell; William Aikman, Allan Ramsay the poet; Henry Raeburn, *Sir Walter Scott; Andrew Geddes, Scott and the artist David Wilkie; Alexander Nasmyth, Robert Burns (twice); and William Nicholson, James Hogg the 'Ettrick Shepherd'. And, moving into the present century, a strong Scottish Socialist flavour is provided by J.J. Dobson's James Keir Hardie; A. McEvoy's Ramsay Macdonald (also appearing as a bust by Epstein); and John Lavery's Clydesider James Maxton.

The Gallery's main collection is supported by engravings, water-colours, drawings and other material, the *Print Room* also containing a reference archive of many thousands of engravings and photographs of portraits. There is also the largest existing collection of work by the pioneer photographers D.O. Hill and Robert Adamson.

The eastward extension of Queen Street is York Place, in which No. 32 was the home and studio of Sir Henry Raeburn, while at No. 36 the Royal Pharmaceutical Society shows a *Late Victorian Pharmacy* with a collection of historic pharmaceutical material (Tel: 031-556-4386). *St. Paul's and St. George's* (1816–18), at the north east corner, was built by Archibald Elliot, the man responsible for much of this east part of the New Town. Picardy Place, beyond, recalling in its name a settlement of French weavers, was the birthplace (No. 11) of Arthur Conan Doyle (1859–1930), creator of Sherlock Holmes. In Union Street, just north of Picardy Place off Leith Walk, will be found the *Printmakers Workshop*, representing an Association devoted to promoting all aspects of the art of printmaking. There is a continuous programme of exhibitions, and visitors are welcome to view and, if they wish, buy members' original prints (Tel: 031-557-2479).

F.   Other Districts of Edinburgh

This section covers, in alphabetical order, places of interest not already included under the previous five sections.
   There are also a number of outlying places which can conveniently be visited from Edinburgh, but which are described along other Routes. The principal such places are: On Rte 1—Musselburgh. Inveresk. Carberry Hill. On Rte 3—Dalkeith. Butterfly Farm. Craigmillar Castle. On Rte 6—Edinburgh Crystal (Penicuik). Roslin Chapel. On Rte 7—Pentland Hills. On Rte 8—Suntrap. Ingliston. Canal Centre. On Rte 9—Cramond. Dalmeny. South Queensferry and the Forth Bridges.

The **Caiy Stone** (NTS) is an ancient standing stone, 9ft in height and, on its east face, bearing traces of cup markings. The stone will be found on the north side of Oxgangs Road, about 4m south of Waverley Market and best reached by A702, the road by which Rte 7 enters Edinburgh.

Once the hunting reserve of kings, and perhaps the place where the miraculous Cross saved David I from being gored by a stag, **Holyrood Park**, sometimes called Queen's or King's Park, stretches away southward from Holyrood Palace. At Holyrood Lodge, opposite the south entrance to the palace, there is a *Visitor Centre* (Scottish Wildlife Trust. Tel: 031-556-7561) with an exhibition covering the history, geology and wildlife of the park.—Some 4m in circumference, the park is one of hilly and craggy moorland, the most prominent feature of which, with of course a superb view, is *Arthur's Seat* (822ft). The climb to the top, best started from Dunsapie Loch (parking), is less formidable than it may appear. The origin of this hill's name is shadowy; it claims no connection with Britain's legendary king, and no knights slumber here, but the name may relate to a 6C Prince Arthur of Strathclyde. Among other suggestions are a simple corruption of 'Archer', or 'Ard Thor', Gaelic for the Height of Thor.

Queen's Drive makes the clockwise (one way) circuit of the park, soon after leaving Holyrood Palace reaching St. Margaret's Loch, near which are *St. Margaret's Well* and, higher up the hill, the small ruin of *St. Anthony's Chapel*. Both places are tenuously associated with afflictions of the eyes, the well reputedly brought here during the reign of James IV from Restalrig (see entry below), where a spring was credited with alleviating eye disease. The chapel is thought to date from the 15C, and its dedication may indicate some kind of connection with a hospital for sufferers from 'St. Anthony's Fire' (erysipelas) known to have been founded by James I at Leith in c 1430. Beyond the loch (Restalrig is ½m north east from the exit here) Queen's Drive curves east, then south, to reach *Dunsapie Loch* (see above), beyond slicing between the Lion's Haunch (north) and Samson's Ribs (south) to arrive at the foot of *Salisbury Crags*. Here a road hairpins back to reach *Duddingston* village, beside its bird-sanctuary loch and known for its church with a Norman south door and chancel arch and, near the gate, a horse-mounting block, the village jougs and a small watch-tower for the guard against body-snatchers. It was here at Duddingston that the Young Pretender's army camped for six weeks in 1745.

Inchcolm Island. For detail, see Rte 33A. From Edinburgh there are cruises to the island (two hours, of which one ashore) by the 'Maid of the Forth' from Hawes Pier near the Forth railway bridge (Tel: 031-331-1454).

Lauriston Castle, off Cramond Road North (which is off Queensferry Road) some 4m north west of Waverley Market, was built in about 1590 by Sir Archibald Napier (father of John Napier of Merchiston, the mathematician and inventor of logarithms) and later occupied by John Law (1671–1728), the buccaneering financier who in 1716 established the first Bank of France. Napier's turreted and corbelled tower was later much extended, mainly by William Burn during the 19C, and stands today as a gracious Edwardian mansion showing period furniture, objets d'art and a notable collection of Derbyshire Blue John ware. The fine grounds extend down to the Forth. (Tel: 031-336-2060).

Leith, the port of Edinburgh, straddles the Water of Leith which flows into the sizeable harbour, comprising the large, open outer or western harbour, and, running away south east, an inner harbour complex of docks—an area which in recent years has become increasingly popular for its lively restaurants and pubs and which may see the development of an international arts and media centre, including an opera house. For the present, Leith's main tourist attraction, and particularly so for overseas visitors, is the James Pringle Woollen Mill with its Clan Tartan Centre.

History. As the port of the capital, Leith has experienced its touches of history—violent, ceremonial and even sporting, for its Links, on the east of the town, represent one of the world's most venerable golf courses. Vulnerable beside the water, Leith was frequently ravaged by the English, but the year 1561 brought a more welcome landing, when, returning after the years in France, Mary, Queen of Scots, came ceremonially ashore here, to be entertained by a local merchant, Andrew Lamb, whose house in Burgess Street still stands. In the following century, in 1641, Charles I was here, receiving the ominous news of the Irish insurrection while he was enjoying a game of golf; but, only a few years later, in 1650, Cromwell had

taken over and was building a great waterside fort. The Jacobite Highlanders
seized this fort in 1715, and in 1822 it was the turn of ceremonial again when
George IV landed here at the start of his State Visit.

The approach from the east end of Edinburgh's Princes Street is by
Leith Street and Leith Walk, the latter in rather over a mile reaching a
major intersection at the south apex of a triangle of roads—clockwise,
Great Junction, North Junction, Commercial, Bernard and Constitution streets—which define central Leith. Great Junction Street, followed north west, in about five blocks reaches Bangor Road (south) in
which is the *James Pringle Woollen Mill* (Tel: 031-553-5100. Courtesy
transport makes morning calls at leading hotels). Here, in addition to a
huge shop area, there is a Clan Tartan Centre in which an Archive
Computer, fed with a surname, will present the applicant with a printed
certificate detailing, if there is such, any clan connection, together with
information regarding the clan chief, its origins, heraldic emblems,
plant badge, tartans and other historic information, including even the
clan war cry. Postal applications may also be made to the Clan Tartan
Centre Ltd, 70–74 Bangor Road, Leith, Edinburgh EH6.
   Visitors wishing to make the round of Leith should continue north
along Great and then North Junction streets, at the end of the latter
bearing east along Commercial Street which runs beside (north) the site
of Cromwell's fort, recalled on the south by the names Cromwell Place
and Citadel Place. After crossing the Water of Leith, Commercial Street
becomes Bernard Street which turns south as Constitution Street.
Within the angle, in Burgess Street, is *Andrew Lamb's House* (NTS. Tel:
031-554-3131), the house in which Mary, Queen of Scots, was received
on her arrival from France in 1561. Typically combining residence and
warehouse, the house (now an old people's day centre) is four storeys
high and has a projecting staircase-tower. Historic *Leith Links* are to
the east for most of the length of Constitution Street which, at its south
end, becomes Leith Walk.—*Newhaven*, to the west of Leith, was founded by James IV in c 1500 as a naval dockyard. *Granton*, farther west,
was a creation of the Duke of Buccleuch, who in 1835 began the construction of the harbour, now mainly used by pleasure craft.

Mathematicians may choose to make a pilgrimage to **Merchiston**,
some 2m south of Waverley Market, the approach road (Bruntsfield
Place) skirting *Bruntsfield Links* (see C. above). Merchiston takes its
name from an estate which belonged since 1483 to the family of Napier,
their seat being *Merchiston Tower* (15C; now appropriately incorporated into Napier Technical College), in which in 1560 was born John
Napier (see also D., Princes Street, St. Cuthbert's Church).

The **National Gallery of Modern Art** (Tel: 031-556-8921) is housed in
the classical former John Watson's School (William Burn, 1823) on Belford Road, rather less than a mile west of Dean Bridge between the
Water of Leith and Queensferry Road. The surrounding extensive
grounds provide a good setting for some larger sculpture.
   Founded in 1960, the gallery has aimed to build up a representative
collection of the essential forms of 20C art with works by most of the
major European and American artists. Names include Matisse, Picasso,
Kirchner, Klee, Hepworth, Moore and Hockney; Braque, Léger and
Mondrian; Ernst, Miró, Giacometti and Magritte; and contemporaries
such as Lichtenstein, Lewitt, Kitaj and Chia. There is also a programme
of temporary exhibitions.

Portobello, on the coast 3m east of Princes Street, owes its exotic name not to topographical beauty, though this is a pleasant enough corner, but to one George Hamilton who built the first house here and named it after Portobello in Panama, at the capture of which he had fought in 1739. Later, and especially during Victorian times, Portobello became a popular resort. Sir Harry Lauder was born at 3 Bridge Street in 1870.

Restalrig Church (in an east suburb just north of Holyrood Park), although a 19 and 20C restoration, has ancient and confused roots associated with St. Triduana, a saint who, regrettably, never existed, the name in fact deriving from a three-day fast practised by the old Celtic Church. Founded probably in those Celtic times, the church was destroyed by a Reformist mob in 1560, but restored in 1837 and again in 1910. Adjoining is a small hexagonal chapel, with a groined roof supported by a central pillar, successor and in part survivor of the chapel of a college founded here in 1478 by James III. During restoration in 1908 the new floor paving was suddenly burst by a spring, this enabling the building to be identified as the successor of a hitherto more or less legendary *Chapel of St. Triduana*, famed for a spring once resorted to for diseases of the eye (see also Holyrood Park, St. Margaret's Well, above).

Founded in 1670 on the site of Waverley Station, the **Royal Botanic Garden** moved in 1823 to its present site in the district of Inverleith, a mile to the north of Princes Street. Among the oldest botanic gardens in Britain, the main features here are a magnificent collection of rhododendrons; woodland, heath and rock gardens; plant houses with landscaped exotic plants; and an exhibition hall. (Tel: 031-552-7171).

The **Royal Observatory** (Visitor Centre. Tel: 031-667-3321) was built on Calton Hill in the early 19C but moved in 1894 to its present site on Blackford Hill, rather over 2m south of Princes Street.

Edinburgh's **Zoo** (Tel. 031-334-9171) is 3m west of Waverley Market, the approach being along West Coates and Corstorphine Road. This road passes (north) *Donaldson's School*, a set-back, dignified building by W.H. Playfair, founded by James Donaldson (died 1830) for the education of poor children and now used for the education of the deaf, and soon afterwards crosses the Water of Leith at *Coltbridge*, scene of the 'Canter of Coltbridge', an incident during the '45 when a body of Dragoons, taking fright at the appearance of the Young Pretender's Highlanders, turned tail and are said not to have drawn bridle until they reached Prestonpans, 9m distant. The Zoo, perhaps best known for its penguins, was established by the Royal Zoological Society of Scotland in 1913 and now spreads over more than 70 acres on Corstorphine Hill.

G.   The **National Gallery of Scotland

The **National Gallery of Scotland** (Tel: 031-556-8921), in a building of 1845–58 with a lower floor new wing of 1978, shows distinguished collections spanning the 15C to the 19C and including Dutch, Flemish, French, German, Italian and British (especially Scottish) artists. The Gallery is in two parts, with Main and Upper Floors showing, generally in chronological order, the permanent collections of European and British paintings, while the Lower Floor (or New Wing) is the home of some principal Scottish works.

Also on the Lower Floor are the Library and the Print Room. The important collection of drawings and prints (shown on request) includes works by Old Masters (e.g. Tintoretto, Rubens, Rembrandt, Dürer), by English artists (Blake, Palmer), and, above all, by a range of Scottish artists. Selections from the collection are shown in the Prints and Drawings Gallery (Main Floor, Room VIII).

The Vaughan Bequest of 38 watercolours by *J.M.W. Turner* is exhibited annually in January and may at other times be seen by advance request.

The Gallery is outstanding for the clarity and detail with which the paintings, and other incidental exhibits, are described, a feature, all too rarely found elsewhere, which can add hugely to the visitor's enjoyment. The following paragraphs, though mentioning only a fraction of the works shown, will, it is hoped, indicate the Gallery's level and scope.

Beyond the entrance, with the bookshop and other facilities, the tour starts in **Room A1 (Early Northern)**, outstanding here being, by *Hugo van der Goes*, the Trinity Altarpiece or the Trinity College Panels (James III and IV. Margaret of Denmark, queen of James III. Holy Trinity. Sir Edward Bonkil). The Collegiate Church of the Holy Trinity, standing near what is now Waverley Station but demolished in 1848, was founded in 1462 by Mary of Gueldres, widow of James II. Sir Edward Bonkil was its first provost and may have commissioned the artist. The panels were almost certainly the wings of an altarpiece the centre of which was destroyed at the Reformation.

MAIN FLOOR. **Rooms I and II (Venetian. 16C)**. *Raphael*: Holy Family with a palm tree. Bridgewater Madonna. *Titian*: Diana and Actaeon. Diana and Calisto. Three Ages of Man. *Andrea del Sarto*: Portrait of Becuccio Bicchieraia. *Paolo Veronese*: St. Anthony Abbot as patron of a kneeling donor. *Tintoretto*: The deposition of Christ. *Filippino Lippi*: Nativity with two angels.—**Room III (European. 16C and 17C)**. *Hendrik Avercamp*: Winter landscape. *Jan de Bray*: Portrait of a gentleman. Portrait of a boy. *Lucas Cranach the Elder*: Venus and Cupid. *J.D. de Heem*: Still-life. *Meindert Hobbema*: Waterfall in a wood. *Hans Holbein the Younger*: Allegory of the Testament. *Quentin Massys*: Portrait of a man. *P.P. Rubens*: Reconciliation of Jacob and Esau.—**Room IV (French, Italian, Spanish. 17C)**. *Nicholas Poussin*: Mystic marriage of St. Catherine. *Claude Lorrain*: Landscape with Apollo and the Muses. *Guido Reni*: Moses with a crown. *El Greco*: St. Jerome. Saviour of the World. *Velasquez*: Old woman cooking eggs.—**Room V** is devoted to the Seven Sacraments by *Nicholas Poussin*.—**Rooms VI and VII (Dutch. 17C**. Room VII is also used for temporary exhibitions). *Aelbert Cuyp*: View of the Valkhof at Nijmegen. *Frans Hals*: Portrait of a gentleman. Portrait of a lady. Verdonck. *Philips Koninck*: Onset of a storm. *Rembrandt*: Self-portrait, aged 51. *Jacob van Ruisdael*: River banks.

Room VIII (Prints and Drawings) shows changing selections from the Gallery's important collection of prints and drawings.

Room IX (Flemish and Dutch. 17C). *A. van Dyck*: St. Sebastian. The Lomellini family. Portrait of an Italian nobleman. *Rembrandt*: Woman in bed. Young woman with flowers in her hair. *P.P. Rubens*: Feast of Herod. *Frans Snyders*: Mischievous monkeys. *Jan Vermeer*: Christ in the house of Martha and Mary.—**Room X (British. 18C)**. *Thomas Gainsborough*: Portrait of the Hon. Mrs Graham. Portrait of Mrs Hamilton Nisbet. *Gavin Hamilton*: Achilles lamenting the death of Patroclus. *Angelica Kauffmann*: Portrait of Michael Novosielski. *Joshua Reynolds*: The Ladies Waldegrave. *George Romney*: Portrait of Mrs Wilbraham Bootle. *Richard Wilson*: Landscape with a ruined castle.—**Room XI (British and American. 19C)**. *Frederick W. Church*: Niagara Falls. *John Constable*: Dedham Vale. *Edwin Landseer*: Rent day in the wilderness. *J.M.W. Turner*: Modern Rome, Campo Vaccino, 1839. Somer Hill. *David Wilkie*: General Sir David Baird discovering the body of Tippoo Sahib.—**Room XII** is largely devoted to works by *Henry Raeburn*.

UPPER FLOOR. Beside the stairs hangs the Albacini Collection of plaster portrait busts. Rooms A2 to A6 show European works of the 18 and 19C.—**Room A2**. *Jean Chardin*: Still-life. *J.-B. Greuze*: Girl with a dead canary. Boy with a lesson book. *Francesco Guardi*: St. Mark's, Venice. *Gavin Hamilton*: Andromache bewailing the death of Hector. *Allan Ramsay*: Portrait of Jean-Jacques Rousseau. Portrait of Lord Robert Manners. *Antoine Watteau*: Fêtes Vénetiennes. This room also houses charming tapestry chairs depicting children at play.—**Room A3**. *John Crome*: A sandy bank. The Beaters. *Thomas Gainsborough*: Rocky landscape. Landscape with Cornard village. *John Hoppner*: Portrait of Admiral Duncan. *John Martin*: Macbeth. *George Morland*: The comforts of industry. The miseries of idleness. *Henry Raeburn*: The Rev. Robert Walker, skating. *Joshau Reynolds*: Portrait of Alexander, later 10th Duke of Hamilton. *David Wilkie*: The Confessional.—**Room A4**. *J-B. C. Corot*: Ville d'Avray. Entrance to the wood. Portrait of the artist's mother. *Eugène Delacroix*: Arabs playing chess. Vase of flowers. *J.E. Millais*: Portrait of Sophie Gray.—**Room A5**. *Gustave Courbet*: Trees in snow. The Wave. *Vincent van Gogh*: Head of a peasant woman. *J.E. Millais*: Sweetest Eyes. *Claude Monet*: Seascape by moonlight. Boats in harbour. Church at Vétheuil. *Camille Pissaro*: The Marne at Chennevières. Kitchen garden. *Auguste Renoir*: Mother and child. *Alfred Sisley*: Molesey weir.—**Room A6**: *Paul Cézanne*: The big trees. *Edgar Degas*: Group of dancers. Portrait of Diego Martelli. Before the performance. Also three bronzes. *Paul Gauguin*: The vision after the sermon. Martinique landscape. Three Tahitians. *Vincent van Gogh*: Olive trees.

The LOWER FLOOR is devoted to Scottish artists, the Gallery's collection being too large for the space available and the works being changed at intervals. However, representative artists and works likely to be seen are listed below (in alphabetical order of artists). *William Aikman*: Self-portrait. *Andrew Geddes*: Summer. Portrait of the artist's mother. *James Guthrie*: Oban. Pastoral. *George Jamesone*: Portrait of Lady Mary Erskine. *Horatio McCulloch*: Inverlochy Castle. *William McTaggart*: Spring. The Storm. The coming of St. Columba. *Jacob More*: Falls of Clyde. *Alexander Nasmyth*: Edinburgh Castle. *Noel Paton*: Oberon and Titania. Luther at Erfurt. *Henry Raeburn*: Several portraits, including a self-portrait. *Allan Ramsay*: Several portraits, including the artist's wife. *David Wilkie*: Pitlessie Fair. Irish whiskey still. Self-portrait. Distraining for rent. The letter of introduction.

IV   GLASGOW

19   Glasgow

Tourist Information. *Greater Glasgow Tourist Board*, 35 St. Vincent Place (off George Square). Tel: 041-204-4400.—'*What's on in Glasgow*', published monthly.

Public Transport. Strathclyde Transport is an integrated system which includes underground, buses and local trains. *Travel Centre*, St. Enoch Square. Tel: 041-226-4826.—For city and regional tours, apply Tourist Information or the Travel Centre.

British Rail (Tel: 041-204-2844). There are two main stations, Central and Queen Street, linked by a special bus service. *Central Station* for services to England (west line) and Wales, and to Scottish destinations in the south and west. *Queen Street Station* for services to the West Highlands; to Loch Lomond; to North and East Scotland; and to Edinburgh and the east line to England.

Airports. *Abbotsinch*, 8m west (Tel: 041-887-1111). Coach service from Central and Queen Street stations and from Anderston Cross and Buchanan bus stations. See also Rte 16, *Prestwick* (Tel: 0292-79822).

River Cruises. From Broomielaw (Jamaica Street corner). Tel: Clyde Marine Cruises, 041-221-8702.—*Paddle Steamer 'Waverley'*, Waverley Terminal, Anderston Quay. Tel: 041-221-8152. See also Rte 16, the Clyde and Clyde Cruising.

Festival Mayfest, held over three weeks each May (Mayfest Ltd, 18 Albion Street, Glasgow G1. Tel: 041-552-8000). Founded in 1983 and organised by Glasgow city and Strathclyde Region.

Opening Times of Sites. Telephone numbers are given for most sites. Latest information is also available from the Greater Glasgow Tourist Board, or from Glasgow Museums and Art Galleries, Tel: 041-357-3929.

SOME HOTELS (all with parking). **Central Area**. *Hospitality Inn*, 36 Cambridge Street, G2 3HN. Tel: 041-332-3311. *Holiday Inn*, 500 Argyle Street, G3 8RR. Tel: 041-226-5577. *Albany*, Bothwell Street, G2 7EN. Tel: 041-248-2656. *Crest*, 377 Argyle Street, G2 8LL. Tel: 041-248-2355.—**West Area** (North of the Clyde; for Kelvingrove and Hunterian art galleries and museums). *Stakis Grosvenor*, Grosvenor Terrace, Great Western Road, G12 0TA. Tel: 041-339-8811. *Jurys Pond*, Great Western Road, G12 0XP. Tel: 041-334-8161.—**West** (for Exhibition Centre). *Moat House*, Congress Road, G3 8QT. Tel: 041-204-0733.—**South West Area** (for Pollok Park and Burrell Collection). *Tinto Firs*, 470 Kilmarnock Road, G43 2BB. Tel: 041-637-2353. *Swallow*, 517 Paisley Road West, G51 1RW. Tel: 041-427-3146.

Routes to and from Glasgow. Several of the Routes in this guide run into or out of Glasgow. To Glasgow from *Edinburgh*, see Rte 8; from *Lanark*, *Moffat* and *Gretna*, see Rte 10; from *Kilmarnock*, *Dumfries* and *Gretna*, see Rte 11; from *Paisley* and *Ayr*, see Rte 16.

From Glasgow to *Dumbarton* and *Tyndrum*, see Rte 20; to *Aberfoyle* and *The Trossachs*, see Rte 21; to *Stirling*, see Rte 22.

History. Although in the 5C St. Ninian is supposed to have blessed the ground on which the cathedral now stands, Glasgow probably started as a cluster of huts around the church built on the same site by St. Mungo (Kentigern) in the 6C. This site was known in Celtic as 'Glas Cau', the 'Green Place'. St. Mungo is Glasgow's patron, and the attractive city arms represent his miracles. (The tree is the frozen branch with which he rekindled the monastery fire; the bird is the decapitated redbreast he restored to life; the salmon, with a lost ring in its belly, was a miraculous capture to save the honour of a princess; and the bell was brought by the saint from Rome). The city motto—in full, 'Let Glasgow flourish by the preaching of the word'—recalls that it was to convert its inhabitants that St. Ninian came here to Strathclyde.

A charter granted by William the Lion in 1175 marks the official start of Glasgow's history, the cathedral then growing in importance between the 12–15C and with it the adjoining bishop's palace. Thus this district was long the heart of the town until it gradually shifted south to Glasgow Cross. Some key dates are 1300 when Wallace defeated the English at Bell o' the Brae, now the upper part of High Street; 1451 when the university was founded; 1568 when Mary, Queen of Scots, was defeated at Langside, near today's Queen's Park; 1611 when Glasgow was made a royal burgh; 1615 when a Catholic priest, John Ogilvie (canonised in 1976), was hanged in Glasgow; 1650–51 when Cromwell was here; and 1745–46 when the Young Pretender stayed here, without however receiving significant support. By this time Glasgow Cross had become the town centre, the present centre, George Square, still being only marshland.

Rapid growth came with Georgian times, and then the Industrial Revolution, during which period Glasgow took on the solidly prosperous Victorian face that, despite much bold modern development, is still likely to be a main impression for today's visitor. In 1990 the city's architectural and cultural achievements earned it the official accolade of Cultural Capital of Europe.

Modern Glasgow sometimes likes to call itself the Renaissance City. And deservedly. Although the city's roots reach back to early Christian and medieval days, in popular estimation Glasgow has long been synonymous with everything Victorian, as much for its handsome, if sooted, buildings as for its industry, commerce and notorious slums. But recent years have witnessed a dramatic transformation—the best of the Victorian buildings preserved, converted and increasingly sandblasted clean; the slums swept away; and imaginative modern developments (notably the airy central shopping precincts, a new concert hall, and the ambitious Cathedral Precinct project) now successfully mingling with the old. One reward—already mentioned and which speaks for itself—was the title in 1990 of Cultural Capital of Europe. With all this has come an impressive upsurge in visitors, increasingly aware of Glasgow's wealth of places of cultural distinction and historical and other interest. To mention but a few, the Cathedral is a superb example of Early English Gothic and its Lower Church a gem among interiors of that period; the city is the home of Scottish opera; the Art Gallery and Museum at Kelvingrove Park are world-famous, while the Hunterian Museum and Art Gallery within the imposing 19C University buildings increasingly enjoy a similar distinction; the Museum of Transport is outstanding among those of its kind; and finally, in Pollok Park, there is the Burrell Collection, as priceless in itself as it is superbly housed.

For the visitor Glasgow can conveniently be divided into two areas, (A). East and Central, and (B). West. A third section (C.) covers selected places in other districts, while a fourth (D.) introduces the Burrell Collection.

A.   East and Central Glasgow

The following tour, for the most part through the busiest part of the city, is only practicable on foot. If all the places mentioned were visited the distance could add up to perhaps 5m. However, a good mile of walking can be cut out, after leaving the cathedral, by taking a bus from Cathedral Square to Jocelyn Square. Also, so much of the round is within the concentrated central area in which perhaps most visitors are likely to be staying that it can conveniently be split into several parts to suit individual preferences. Not much less than a whole day should be allowed if the Cathedral, Provand's Lordship and People's Palace are given the time they deserve.

**GLASGOW
Central**

0 yards   700
0 metres   700

Dignified **George Square**, laid out in 1781 and named for George III, may be considered the heart of modern Glasgow. However George III has not achieved a statue here, the place on the pillar (80ft high) intended for him having been taken by Sir Walter Scott, wearing, as was his custom, his plaid on the 'wrong' shoulder (John Greenshields, 1837). Other statues in the square include equestrian figures of Queen Victoria and Prince Albert, both by the Italian Marochetti; Robert Burns (George Ewing, 1877), with, in his hand, the 'wee modest, crimson tipped flower'; James Watt (Chantrey, 1832); two prime ministers, Gladstone (Hamo Thornycroft, 1902) and Peel (Mossman, 1859); and, the first statue to be honoured with a place here, Sir John Moore (Flaxman, 1819), born in Glasgow and hero of Corunna during the Peninsular War. Also in the square is the *Cenotaph* (John Burnet), unveiled in 1924 by Earl Haig before an immense crowd (an interesting photograph in the People's Palace records the scene).

Of the buildings around the square the most important is the **City Chambers** (Tel: 041-221-9600). Built in 1883–88 by William Young, and extended to the east by John Watson in 1923, and occupying the whole of the east side of the square, this imposing mass with a 216ft-high tower and built in Italian Renaissance style, is as impressive inside as it is outside. From the loggia, built to the plan of a Roman Renaissance church, there rise two staircases, one to the Council Chamber, the other to reception rooms and the Banqueting Hall, with murals by Glasgow artists depicting the city's growth. Throughout there is a richness of mosaic, majolica and fine wood.—Other buildings around George Square are the *General Post Office* (1876) on the south; *Queen Street Station* on the north; and, on the west, the *Merchants' House* (Tel: 041-221-8272), built by John Burnet in 1874 and home of Glasgow Chamber of Commerce, the oldest in Britain.

George Street leads out of the north east corner of George Square, with, on the left, the length of the *University of Strathclyde* (the more modern buildings of which fill the area between George Street and, to the north, Cathedral Street), a technological university with roots going back to 1796 but not achieving its present title until 1964. A plaque here commemorates a former student, John Logie Baird, pioneer of television, while, in adjacent Richmond Street, the university's *Collins Gallery* (Tel: 041-552-4400. Ext. 2682) mounts varied exhibitions and acitivites. Beyond, High Street is reached, the district around the intersection once being known as Bell o' the Brae (recalling a bell in a turret at the top of the rise or brae) where in 1300 Wallace defeated Percy, the English governor holding the castle.

High Street leads north to reach the Cathedral, to the west and south of which is the area of the Cathedral Precinct project (1986–1990s) among the aims of which are the enhancement of the cathedral's setting and the creation at the same time of an elegant focus for visitors. The project, which embraces the 15C Provand's Lordship, includes a new road system with tunnel and parking; a visitor centre, partly on the site of the medieval Bishop's Palace and aimed primarily at providing an introduction to the cathedral; a new, pedestrian public square extending westward from the cathedral's west door; a processional way; and the use of the now redundant 19C Barony Church as a ceremonial hall of the university of Strathclyde.

Provand's Lordship (Tel: 041-552-8819), just opposite the cathedral, is Glasgow's oldest house, built in about 1471 probably for the priest in charge of the then nearby St. Nicholas Hospice, which had been founded for a priest and 12 old men. James II and IV may have stayed here, as very likely also Mary, Queen of Scots, in 1566, when she visited the very ill Darnley prior to taking him to Edinburgh and his murder at Kirk o' Field. The house in which Darnley lay ill may have been in the southern part of the cathedral precincts, and in the People's Palace there is a model showing the house and this area as it was at that time.

Glasgow Cathedral, or the Cathedral Church of St. Mungo, is, both historically and architecturally, one of Glasgow's most important buildings. Smaller than most cathedrals, the style is mainly 13C Early English, though several other periods are represented. Among striking features are the very modest projection of the transepts, and, because of the sloping ground, the construction of the east end in two storeys, so that the crypt is really the Lower Church. This Lower Church and the Blacader (or Fergus) Aisle are from the visitor's point of view the two most noteworthy parts of the interior.

History. The story goes that in the 6C St. Mungo (or Kentigern), coming from Culross, found a holy man, Fergus, on the point of death. He placed the body on a cart, yoked to it two untamed bulls, and bade them drag the cart to the place determined by God. The bulls halted at a cemetery, consecrated two centuries earlier by St. Ninian, and there the body of Fergus was buried at a spot now covered by the Aisle of Car Fergus or Blacader's Aisle. St. Mungo at the same time founded a church on the same spot. Other churches doubtless followed, until today's cathedral was founded by David I and Bishop Achaius in 1136. Soon destroyed by fire, the church was rebuilt by Bishop Jocelin in 1197. Of this, however, only a fragment remains (visible in the Lower Church). Crypt, choir and tower were completed by Bishop de Bondington (1233–58). Bishop Lauder (1408–25) added the stone spire and also finished the chapter house or crypt below the sacristy. Bishop Cameron (1425–47) completed the sacristy. The nave, begun early in the 14C, was not finished until 1480. Archbishop Blacader (1483–1508) constructed the stair from the nave to the crypt and founded the Blacader Aisle; he is also generally credited with the beautiful choir screen.

In 1560 James Beaton, the last Roman Catholic archbishop, carried off the treasure and the archives to France, whence they have never returned. At the Reformation the church was purged of 'monuments of idolatry', but the building was saved from destruction by the intervention (1578) of the city trade guilds. Later it was divided into three congregations (in the nave, in the choir and in the crypt). An unusual episode occurred in 1650 when Cromwell sat in the nave and heard himself denounced, in a two-hour-long sermon, as a 'sectary and blasphemer' by Zachary Boyd, rector of the university and minister of the church then occupying the crypt. Cromwell's revenge was to invite Boyd to dinner, after which he subjected him to prayers lasting three hours. When, in 1801, the crypt ceased to be used as a church, it was part filled with earth and used as a cemetery.

Entry is normally by the south west porch, outside which is a monument to Thomas Hutcheson, one of the founders of Hutchesons' Hall (see below). The *Nave* is stately and well proportioned, with a triforium of two arches to each bay and a clerestory. The clustered columns separating it from the aisles have plain capitals. On the walls are numerous monuments and regimental flags and on the easternmost column on the north side of the nave hangs a 17C Italian Nativity. The Victorian stained glass was of poor quality but good modern glass (1950–58) has replaced it in most of the windows; the great west window, with the Creation, is by Francis Spear (1958). The *Choir*, a beautiful example of Early English, now used as the High Church, is raised 3ft above the nave and is entered by a low elliptic-arched doorway in the fine *Rood Screen*, on the corbels of which appear the Seven Deadly Sins. It is separated from its aisles by clustered columns with flowered capitals, and has a peculiarly fine triforium. The choir pulpit was made c 1600 for use in the lower church. A window in the south aisle shows the arms of the fourteen incorporated trades. The east end has four slender lancet windows instead of the more usual three or five, and its arrangement is interesting. Here is a double aisle, the west half forming an ambulatory, while on the east are chapels, separated by elegant

GLASGOW CATHEDRAL

0 yards   30
0 metres   30

Sacristy
(Chapter
House below)

Abp.Law

N. CHOIR AISLE

CHOIR

(Lower Church
below)

S. CHOIR AISLE

SOUTH TRANSEPT
(Blacadar Aisle below)

N. AISLE

NAVE

S. AISLE

SOUTH WEST
PORCH

N

West
Door

TOWER
(site of)

TOWER
(site of)

Processional Way (Visitor Centre)

shafts supporting the vaulted roof. In the south east chapel is the tomb of Archbishop Law (died 1632). Adjoining the choir on the north east is the *Sacristy*, a square chamber with its original oak door (with, above the handle of the left door on entering, small bullet holes, evidence of a turbulent past) and a central shaft on which appear the arms of the founder, Bishop Cameron (died 1446), and those of James I.

From the south transept steps descend to the *Blacader Aisle*, a fine vaulted crypt founded by Archbishop Blacader (died 1508). The exquisitely carved ceiling bosses can be appreciated with the help of excellent modern lighting. As related under 'History', this aisle, or chapel, reputedly occupies the site of the cemetery blessed by St. Ninian, to which St. Mungo brought the body of Fergus. A carving over the north pier (visible just above and ahead on entering) shows a body on a cart, surrounded by the inscription 'This is ye ile of Car Fergus'. The *Lower Church*, with its rich vaulting, its proportion, the simple altar marking the traditional site of the tomb of St. Mungo and the row of four chapels, is an outstanding example of medieval Scottish architecture and the chief glory of the cathedral. The date is mid 13C, but a pillar with a capital differing from those of the others (ahead right, on entering by the south steps) is probably a vestige of Bishop Jocelin's church of 1197. In the Chapel of St. Andrew, one of the row of four, there is an effigy of Bishop Wischart, who gained fame and favour for his support of Bruce, whom he absolved of the murder of Comyn and later crowned.—At the north east angle of the Lower Church is the *Chapter House* (13–15C),

LOWER CHURCH

founded by Bishop de Bondington and connected by a turret staircase with the sacristy immediately above. Here are preserved a bell of 1594 (recast in 1790) and a gravestone commemorating in a quaint rhymed inscription nine martyred Covenanters.

Over the hill behind the cathedral sprawls the *Necropolis*, with many elaborate tombs and memorials, the most conspicuous monument being a Doric column erected in 1825 to the memory of the Reformers and crowned by a statue (by Robert Forrest) of John Knox.

Castle Street and High Street are now retraced, noting that the railway area on the east of the latter, roughly opposite College Street, was the site of Glasgow university from 1632 to 1870. **Glasgow Cross**, a short way beyond, followed the area around the cathedral as the town centre and so remained until the 19C. Today this is still a busy crossroads, marked by the *Cross* (a 1929 replica of the medieval original removed in 1629) and the isolated *Cross Steeple*, all that remains of the tolbooth of 1626, alongside which once stood the Tontine buildings, much used by the 'tobacco lords' in the 18C.

This tour continues west along Trongate (see next paragraph), but, first, the area to the south east and south of Glasgow Cross is described. Gallowgate runs east, once the road to the gallows but today known for the 'Barras', Glasgow's weekend flea-market, founded in the late 19C and covered since the 1920s. Saltmarket, the southward road and once what its name suggests, reaches Jocelyn Square and the river, the former once known as Jail Square and as recently as 1865 the scene of a public hanging watched by some 30,000 people. On the west stands the *High Court* (Stark, 1814), while, opposite, in Turnbull Street leading north off Greendyke Street, *St. Andrew's Church* (1750) is worth a visit for its dignified Corinthian-pillared front and elegant 18C interior. Glasgow Green, dating from 1662 and the oldest of Glasgow's parks, stretches away south east beside the river, here being a monument (1806) to Lord Nelson, of interest for being the first in Britain to be erected to the admiral, and also the **People's Palace** (Tel: 041-554-0223), so named because it originated (1898) as a cultural centre for the people of the eastern districts of Glasgow. Today it consists of a museum devoted to the story of Glasgow from its official foundation in 1175 through to modern times, and also winter gardens housing some splendid tropical plants and birds. The wide-ranging survey of Glasgow's history—the emphasis being on the 19 to 20C—embraces, among many others, themes such as trade and industry, politics, the press, housing and health, women's suffrage, entertainment and sport, admirable use being made of a rich collection of paintings, prints and photographs to bring home, often startlingly, the changes and developments of the last century and more.

The fourth street out of Glasgow Cross is Trongate which, in an area undergoing much development and with many shops, heads west, passing *Tron Steeple* (1637), all that is left of St. Mary's Church, burned down in 1793. There is a northward glimpse up Candleriggs to St. David's Church (see below) beyond the City Hall (1841), then another glimpse up Hutcheson Street to Hutchesons' Hall (see below). On the Royal Bank of Scotland, on the right at the corner of Glassford Street, there is a plaque recording that this was the site of Shawfield House where the Young Pretender stayed during his northward retreat.

A southward diversion may be made along Stockwell Street (birthplace of James McGill, founder of Montreal's McGill University) to reach the Clyde at Victoria Bridge (John Walker, 1851–54), successor to a medieval bridge at the south end of which once stood a leper hospital. Here is moored the *SV 'Carrick'* (no adm.), a three-master clipper of 1864, once named the 'City of Adelaide' and now a Royal Naval Volunteer Reserve headquarters. And here, too, starts the Clyde Walkway, leading nearly 2m westward to reach the *Scottish Exhibition Centre* (1985). In Bridegate, off Clyde Street running east from Victoria Bridge, the *Merchants Steeple* is all that survives of the Merchants' House of 1655 (attributed to William Burn).

Beyond its crossing with Glassford and Stockwell streets, Trongate becomes Argyle Street, in part pedestrian and one of Glasgow's busier shopping stretches. Argyle Street passes between two major late-1980s precincts. To the north is the stylish *Princes Square*, with a mosaic courtyard, glass-fronted lifts and wrought-iron balconies; to the south is St. Enoch Square (named after St. Mungo's mother, Enoch being a corruption of 'Thenew') with the Strathclyde Transport *Travel Centre*, in the curious little underground station of 1896, and the soaring glass structure which covers the *St. Enoch Shopping and Leisure Complex*. Immediately to the south of St. Enoch the Clyde is crossed by four bridges, these being, from east to west, a pedestrians' bridge of 1871; Glasgow Bridge (sometimes called Broomielaw or Jamaica), a massive structure opened in its present form in 1899 but successor to bridges of 1772 and 1836, the latter by Telford; the railway bridge serving Central Station; and George V Bridge opened in 1928.

Just west of Enoch Square is the *Central Station*, beyond again being Anderston Cross, site of one of the city's two main bus stations and by the start of the westward-running Clydeside Expressway.

From the crossing of Trongate and Stockwell and Glassford streets, this tour continues north along the latter, near the top of which is the domed *Trades House*, built by Robert Adam in 1794 but today with an interior much altered to meet the modern needs of the city's incorporated trades who administer large charitable funds. Glassford Street ends at Ingram Street, to the right along which there are three buildings of interest. The first is *Hutchesons' Hall* (NTS. Tel: 041-552-8391), an attractive and compact spired house built in 1805 to a design by David Hamilton but considerably enlarged and heightened by John Baird in 1876. Originally a charitable institution founded in 1641 in Trongate by two brothers—their statues stand here in niches—for poor old men and orphan boys, the building now not only serves as NTS regional offices, with a visitor centre and shop, but is also used as an elegant setting for concerts, small conferences and suchlike. The *Sheriff Court*, opposite, date from 1824 (Courthouse Fashion Centre, with shops, workshops and a Museum of Costume, early 1990s). *St. David's Church* (Thomas Rickman, 1824), beyond on the north side of Ingram Street, is, curiously, also known as 'Ramshorn', possibly from a monastery which once stood here until its walls reputedly collapsed when threatened by Reformers as did the walls of Jericho before Joshua's rams' horns. Until 1835 the pavement in front of the church was a part of its cemetery and the initials R.F. and A.F. carved into it are over the graves of the Foulis brothers, 18C printers and founders of Glasgow's first School of Art.

Followed west, Ingram Street ends at the *Royal Exchange*, in front of which stands a particularly lifelike Marochetti equestrian statue of the Duke of Wellington, with, around the plinth, some vivid action friezes. Today housing Stirling's Library, Glasgow's central lending library and known for its books on music and the pictorial arts, the Royal Exchange building has as its core a mansion of 1780 built as a suburban home by one of Glasgow's prosperous 'tobacco lords' (see Glasgow Cross above). To this were added in 1832 a great hall to the rear and, to the front, an imposing portico, both necessary for the needs and dignity of the Exchange which opened here in the same year.

Buchanan Street, part pedestrian and running behind the Royal Exchange, is now followed north through Nelson Mandela Place, surrounded by buildings worth noting. On the south side is the *Stock Exchange* (John Burnet, 1877), with a visitors' gallery (Tel: 041-221-7060); in the centre stands *St. George's Tron Church* (William Stark,

1807); and on the north the *Athenaeum* (John Burnet, 1888), once home of the Royal Scottish Academy of Music and Drama, carries statues (by George Mossman) of Reynolds, Wren, Purcell and Flaxman. At the top of Buchanan Street are the *Buchanan Centre* and the *Concert Hall* (Sir Leslie Martin), both of 1990.

Sauchiehall Street, Glasgow's perhaps best known and certainly most 'popular' street, stretches westward for almost 2m across the M8 motorway to Kelvingrove Park and the city Art Gallery and Museum (see next section). At its east end the street is a pedestrian shopping precinct. Here it crosses Hope Street, a short way north up which is the *Theatre Royal* (Tel: 041-331-1234), a gem of a theatre restored to all its Victorian splendour in 1975. The name Cowcaddens, just north of the theatre, preserves a rather different link with the past, this name recalling that what is now a busy street was once the common pasture. A little farther along Sauchiehall Street, connoisseurs of early 19C architecture will walk south down Blythswood Street to enjoy Blythswood Square; while admirers of Glasgow's perhaps most distinguished architect, C.R. Mackintosh (1868–1928; see also Charles Rennie Mackintosh Society below), will aim north up Scott Street to the corner of Renfrew Street to find his *Glasgow School of Art* (Tel: 041-332-9797), built in two stages, the first being the east façade to the main entrance (1897–99) and the second, the remainder of the building, 1907–09.

Accommodation of a very different kind can be savoured about 300 yards north west (145 Buccleuch Street) at the *Tenement House* (NTS. Tel: 041-333-0183), a capsule from the past enabling the modern visitor to walk straight into the flat of Miss Agnes Toward, a typist with a shipping firm. The tenement house was built in 1892—at a time when this was a genteel neighbourhood—and Miss Toward lived in this flat (parlour, bedroom, kitchen) from 1911 to 1965, little concerned, it would seem, with modern domestic progress though in 1959 she did exchange her gas lighting for electricity. In 1965 she was taken to hospital, and for ten years, until her death, the flat was unoccupied and time suspended. Today, the gas has been restored, the fire in the cast-iron grate has been rekindled, Miss Toward's heavily-draped table has been set for tea, and a partly finished dress lies across the ancient sewing machine to which her mother was doubtless devoted.

The *Third Eye Centre* (Tel: 041-332-7521), at 350 Sauchiehall Street, is a multipurpose art centre mounting exhibitions ranging from contemporary art to historical and social documentary. Farther west, at 518 Sauchiehall Street just before the motorway, the *Museum of the Royal Highland Fusiliers* (Tel: 041-332-0961) covers the histories of the Royal Scots Fusiliers and the Highland Light Infantry, amalgamated in 1959. Beyond, in Kent Road the other side of the motorway, is the *Mitchell Library* (Tel: 041-221-7030), built by W.B. White in 1911 but founded in 1874 out of a bequest by the tobacco merchant Stephen Mitchell. In this, the largest public reference library in Europe, the specialist collections include Robert Burns, Scottish poetry, Music, Celtic literature and Glasgow.

From St. George's Cross, half a mile north of the Mitchell Library, Great Western Road leads north west, soon passing on the right the graceful *Episcopal Cathedral of St. Mary* (George Gilbert Scott and J.O. Scott, 1871–93). Half a mile north again, at 870 Garscube Road, the *Charles Rennie Mackintosh Society* has its headquarters and a small exhibition in the former Queen's Cross Church, built by Mackintosh in 1897 (Tel: 041-946-6600).

B.   West Glasgow

The three places most likely to attract the visitor (the Art Gallery and Museum, the Museum of Transport, and the University with the Hunterian Museum and Hunterian Art Gallery) are either side of Kelvingrove Park, about 1½m west of George Square, while Victoria Park with its unique Fossil Grove is the same distance westward again. The round can conveniently be made by bus, or even by car, and at least a whole day should be allowed if the above are to be given the attention they deserve. A choice of buses run west from the city centre.

The ****Art Gallery and Museum** (Tel: 041-357-3929) occupy a palatial red sandstone building of 1901 by J.W. Simpson and Milner Allan.

The **Art Gallery*, with Britain's finest civic collection of British and European paintings, is spread over two wings on the first floor, the east wing housing British and the west wing Continental works. The balconies are in general devoted to applied art, with sculpture (Rodin, Epstein and several others), ceramics, silver, glass and jewellery, while the corridors show water-colours, drawings and prints. In almost all categories the collection is larger than the display space and the exhibits are therefore changed from time to time. Some representative artists and works are mentioned below.

The most publicised and popular painting is Salvador Dali's Christ of St. John of the Cross, normally awarded an individual balcony setting. Painted in 1951 at Port Lligat, Spain, the artist has stated that the picture was inspired by the 16C drawing of the Crucifixion by the Spanish Carmelite friar who became known as St. John of the Cross. The landscape is Port Lligat; the figure on the left derives from a drawing by Velazquez, and that by the boat from the detail of a peasant in a painting by Le Nain. Dali has also stated that his aim was to avoid the usual 'expressionistic and contortionist' portrayal and to achieve instead a Christ who 'would be beautiful as the God that he is'.

The Continental Wing comprises Italian, Flemish, Dutch and French galleries. Among the many outstanding Italian works are Giorgione's The Adultress brought before Christ, with Head of a Man, now separated but once the top right hand figure in the first picture; and Salvator Rosa's romantic landscapes. Flemish works include Nature adorned by the Graces (an interesting joint effort by Rubens and Jan Brueghel the Elder) as also paintings by such names as Jacob Jordaens (Fruit Seller), Van Dyck (portrait of Antoon Triest, Bishop of Utrecht), David Teniers the Younger (Visitation) and Bernard van Orley (Virgin and Child by a fountain).—The Dutch are represented by Rembrandt's A Man in Armour, and, contrastingly, also by a good choice of genre works, Benjamin Cuyp's The Quack Doctor being a notable example. Other Dutch artists include W. van de Velde the Younger ('Eendracht' and other ships of the line), Jacob van Ruisdael (Landscape with a ruined tower), Josef Israels (Frugal Meal) and Jan van Huysum (Flowers in a terracotta urn). There is also, by Herman Moll, an interesting map of the United Provinces, with margin drawings of Amsterdam, Middelburg, Utrecht, Groningen and the palace of Het Loo.—The rich collection of French works (notably Barbizon, Impressionist and Post-Impressionist) includes, to mention only a few, artists such as Courbet, Corot, Millet, Monet, Degas and Watteau.

The British Wing is divided into a Modern Gallery (III), and three others as below. Gallery I (16C to early 19C) shows several portraits by such as George Jamesone, Allan Ramsay, Joshua Reynolds, George Romney and Henry Raeburn. Also, by unknown artists, interesting portraits of Mary, Queen of Scots, and of Montrose.—Gallery II (late 18C to early 20C) includes works by several Pre-Raphaelites. Also works by David Wilkie (the Cottar's Saturday night), George Harvey (Battle of Drumclog), Horatio McCulloch (a dramatic Glen Coe), William McTaggart (a delightful Grandmother's Pet), W.Q. Orchardson (Farmer's daughter. Marriage of convenience) and J.M.W. Turner (Modern Italy).—Gallery IV (Glasgow School and Scottish Colourists), the several artists here including S.J. Peploe, William Strang, F.C.B. Cadell, William Kennedy, George Henry and E.A. Hornel.

The *Museum* occupies the entire ground floor either side of the vast central hall with its organ (recitals). To the west the central gallery shows a collection of Arms and Armour of international repute. Around the armour hall the gallery on the south is for Special Exhibitions, those on the west cover History and the Glasgow Style (Mackintosh. Art Nouveau), while that along the north is devoted to Archaeology with some particularly interesting models of Antonine Wall forts and reconstructions of Bronze Age cists, showing their contents as discovered.— In the east wing the theme of the central gallery is the Natural History of Scotland, around this being galleries devoted to Ethnography, Biology, Birds, World wildlife and Geology.

The **Museum of Transport** (Tel: 041-357-3929) is opposite the Museum and Art Gallery, in Kelvin Hall which also houses a sports and recreation complex. A free ground plan is provided. With some emphasis on Glasgow and the Clyde, the museum presents an array of aspects of the story of transport all the way from horse-drawn to relatively modern. Among the highlights are a Glasgow street of 1938 with period shops and vehicles; a reconstructed underground station; a railway station platform allied to a collection of Scottish locomotives; and the *Clyde Room of ship models.

The University may be reached by walking across **Kelvingrove Park** (1852, Joseph Paxton) lying either side of the river Kelvin. Within the park are a war memorial to the Scottish Rifles (P. Lindsay Clarke, 1924) and monuments to Carlisle, Lister and Kelvin. The university, spread pretentiously along its hill to the north, dominates the park from that side.

The main building (George Gilbert Scott) of **Glasgow University** (Visitor Centre. Tel: 041-330-5511) is a vast late 19C Gothic edifice with a frontage of over 500ft and a tower and spire reaching to 300ft.

The university was founded in 1451 mainly through the exertions of Bishop Turnbull who became the first principal. Classes met first in a crypt in the cathedral, then in a house, but after c 1460 in High Street, where, however, the accommodation was very humble until 1632 when the chief parts of the Old College were begun. Here Adam Smith expounded his doctrines and Watt perfected his scientific discoveries. In 1870 the university moved to its present site.

The main buildings form two quadrangles, separated by a cloister of granite pillars which support the great Bute Hall, used for graduation and other functions. Other buildings of interest are the smaller Randolph Hall, the Tower and the War Memorial Chapel of 1929. Reminders of the Old College are the Lion and Unicorn balustrade in a stone stair opposite the Principal's Lodging in Professors' Square, and Pearce Lodge, at the university entrance, which incorporates stonework of the High Street frontage.

At the north end of the cloister (in which there is a plaque to James McGill, 1744–1813, student here and founder of McGill University, Montreal, Canada), are stairs up to the Hunterian Museum.

The *Hunterian Museum* (Tel: 041-330-4221) originated in a bequest by Dr William Hunter (1718–83), Doctor of Medicine, Professor of Anatomy in London and Physician Extraordinary to Queen Charlotte. Opened in 1807, when the university was still in High Street, the museum is the oldest in Scotland. Now housed here in the main building of the university, the nucleus of the museum remains Hunter's collections, but it has since attracted many other and varied bequests. The archaeological, geological and numismatic exhibits are notable, as is also one on the history of the university and the achievements of its staff and students, while the Roman material includes many carved slabs from the Antonine Wall. Special application must be made to see the collections in the anatomical and zoological departments and in the University Library Special Collections Department.

The *Hunterian Art Gallery* (Tel: 041-330-5431) is entered from Hillhead Street immediately north of the university. Opened in 1980 and the recipient of several awards, this gallery now houses the university's art collections, of which William Hunter's bequest, with works by Chardin and Stubbs, forms the core. Among major holdings are works by James McNeill Whistler—paintings, drawings and prints, as also furniture and personal items—and a notable collection of works by Scottish artists of the 19 and 20C. Here too are the university's print collection, the largest in Scotland; a sculpture courtyard displaying large modern pieces; and—a major feature of the gallery—*Mackintosh House, a reconstruction of three floors of the interiors of the major rooms of the Glasgow home of the architect and designer C.R. Mackintosh (1868–1928), incorporating original furniture and other features.

University Avenue skirts the north side of the main university building, and buses from here run to Victoria Park, home of the *Tree Fossil Grove* (Tel: 041-959-2128). In 1887, when this area was taken over as a park, the cutting of a path across an old quarry revealed these erect stumps and other fragments of trees of the carboniferous period of some 300 million or more years ago. What is seen is not petrified wood, but casts formed by mud which set within the bark. That these were trees of a species not known today can be seen from their symmetrically forking roots; and these were in fact the trees which after millions of years became the Clydeside coal of today.

C.   Other Districts of Glasgow

This section covers, in alphabetical order, places of interest not already included under the previous two sections.

There are also a number of outlying places which can conveniently be visited from Glasgow, but which are described along Routes. The principal such places are: On Rte 10—Livingstone Memorial, Blantyre. Bothwell Castle. On Rte 16—Paisley. Renfrew. On Rtes 20 and 21—Duntocher and Bearsden (Antonine Wall).

Botanic Gardens (Tel: 041-334-2422). On the corner of Great Western Road and Queen Margaret Drive, to the north of the university and 2m north west of the city centre.

Founded in 1817 as the Royal Botanic Institute on a site in Sauchiehall Street (now Fitzroy Place), the gardens moved to their present site of 40 acres beside the river Kelvin in 1841 and were acquired by the city 50 years later. They early became famous because of the distinguished work of Sir William Hooker, then Professor of Botany at the university. The main range of *Glasshouses* contains a fine collection of orchids, begonias and tropical plants, while the striking *Kibble Palace*, with an exhibition on the Plant Kingdom, shows tree ferns and

BEARSDEN & MILNGAVIE A81

Dawsholm Park

KELVINDALE

MARYHILL

LAMBSHILL

BISHOPSBRIG

SPRINGBU

A82 DUMBARTON

GREAT WESTERN ROAD

Ruchill Park

Queen's Cross

Royal Botanic Gardens

PARTICK

Springburn Museum

DUMBARTON ROAD

University

Kelvingrove Park

KELVINSIDE

PORT DUNDAS

M8

ROVAN ROAD

GOVAN

IBROX

River Clyde

Central Area
(see large scale plan)

Cath +

Central Station

A8

Glasgow Rangers FC

ROAD

M8

A737 Crookston Cas M8

Bellahouston Park

M77

DRIVE

ST ANDREW'S

POLLOKSHIELDS

Glasgow Green

RUTHERGLEN

Haggs Castle

Pollok Country Park

Burrell Collection

Pollok House

POLLOKSHAWS

BARRHEAD RD

Camphill House

Queen's Park

GOVANHILL

Victoria Infirmary

LANGSIDE

Hampden Park

KING'S PARK

KILMARNOCK ROAD

CATHCART

NEWLANDS

MERRYLEE

THORNLIEBANK

GIFFNOCK

Linn Park

CROFTFOOT

A77 Rouken Glen & KILMARNOCK   CLARKSTON

GLASGOW Environs

| 0 miles | 1 |
| 0 kilometres | 2 |

A80 STIRLING

BALORNOCK

STEPPS

BARMULLOCH

MILLERSTON

PROVANMILL

Hogganfield Loch

GARNGAD

M8

M8

Provan Hall

M8 EDINBURGH

Alexandra Park

A8 EDINBURGH

COMBERS

CARNTYNE

A89 BAILLESTON

STREET

OWGATE

BARLANARK

SETON

SHETTLESTON ROAD

ON ROAD

TOLCROSS ROAD

Tollcross Park

SHETTLESTON

Calderpark Zoo A74/M74

PARKHEAD

BRAIDFAULD

Golf Course

ROCK ROAD

HAMILTON ROAD

LONDON ROAD

CAMBUSLANG ROAD

CARMYLE

River Clyde

ERGLEN

STREET

EASTFIELD

HIGH CROSSHILL

CAMBUSLANG

BURNSIDE

FLEMINGTON

A749 EAST KILBRIDE

HAMILTON A424

N

temperate plants. There are also a Herb Garden, with culinary and medicinal plants; a Chronological Border showing when common garden plants were introduced to cultivation in Britain; and a Systematic Garden with plants grouped in botanical families.

The **Clydebank Museum** (Tel: 041-941-1331. Ext. 402) tells the story of the Clydebank shipyards and of this town which grew beside them. Clydebank was also the home of Singer sewing machines and the museum shows a collection spanning from 1851 to 1980. The museum is in the Old Town Hall, Dumbarton Road, Clydebank, some 6m west of the city centre.

Crookston Castle (AM. Tel: 031-244-3101) is 4m south west of the city centre, reached by Paisley Road and Crookston Road, then, after crossing the White Cart Water, Brockburn Road. A 14C stronghold of the Stewarts of Darnley, the ruin preserves walls and a tower and is surrounded by the 12C earthworks of the earlier castle built here by Robert Croc, whose name if little else has survived. The Stewarts of Darnley were ancestors of Henry, Lord Darnley, who married Mary, Queen of Scots, and the couple spent some days at this castle after their marriage.

Greenbank Garden (NTS. Tel: 041-639-3281) is the garden of a Georgian house (no adm) of 1763. There are 2½ acres of garden and 13 acres of other grounds. Greenbank is 6m south of the city centre, off B767 which is off A77, the Kilmarnock road.

Haggs Castle (Tel: 041-427-2725) is about 3m south west of the city centre at the south west end of St. Andrews Drive off the north east edge of Pollok Country Park. In origin of 1585 but much converted, Haggs is now a museum and centre aimed primarily at activities for children. The theme here is the ways in which life has changed over the last 400 years, and an 18C cottage in the grounds now serves as an activities workshop, with facilities for spinning, weaving, candle making and suchlike.

Langside (battle). The site of the battle at which Mary, Queen of Scots, met final defeat is close to the Victoria Infirmary at the south east corner of Queens' Park, some 2½m south of the city centre. Here a plaque on the corner of Battlefield Road and Sinclair Drive reads 'Battlefield May 13, 1568', and at the top of Battlefield Road, in Battle Place, there is a memorial pillar. The suburb, then village, of Langside is immediately south west. Here, 11 days after her escape from Loch Leven and making for the shelter of loyal Dumbarton, Mary was defeated by Moray. Much of the battle was fought in what was then the narrow street of the village of Langside, Mary's defeat being largely caused by disputes among her supporters and the incompetence, or, it is sometimes suggested, defection of her commander Argyll. She is thought to have watched the battle, or at any rate awaited its outcome, from Court (or Queen's) Knowe in Linn Park (see below) over a mile to the south, though it is known that at one stage she rode forward in a vain attempt to encourage her men.

Linn Park is 4m south of the city centre and 1m south of Queen's Park. Covering over 200 acres beside the White Cart Water, the park includes at its north tip the ruin of *Cathcart Castle*, abandoned in 1750, nearby being *Court Knowe* (or Queen's Knowe), perhaps the spot from which Mary, Queen of Scots, watched the battle in Langside.

Pollok Country Park and Pollok House. *Pollok Country Park* is some

3m south of Glasgow Bridge and can be reached either by car or by bus to the park's Pollokshaws Road (A77) entrance from where there is a minibus service to the Burrell Collection (see D. below) and Pollok House. Gifted to the city, together with the house, in 1967 by Mrs Maxwell Macdonald, the park of 361 acres also provides nature trails and is home to the Pollok herd of Highland cattle.

Pollok House (Tel: 041-632-0274), long an ancestral home of the Maxwells, dates from c 1750 but was extended (Rowand Anderson, 1890–1908) by Sir John Stirling Maxwell. The house is visited both as an interesting home of this style and period, for its stylish plasterwork (possibly by Thomas Clayton, Robert Adam's plasterer), and as the home of the William Stirling Maxwell collection of paintings. These, together with sculptures, are scattered around the several rooms which show furnishings—including musical instruments, books, silver, china and glass—some long associated with the house, others more recent acquisitions. There are self-guide information boards in each room.

The *Paintings include one of the most representative Spanish collections in Britain, the examples starting with a late 16C work by Jeronimo Cosida (San Ildefonso receiving the Chasuble) and then ranging across much of the field, among the more famous names being two religious works by Murillo, two pictures of boys at play by Goya, and two portraits by El Greco.

But if the Spanish enjoy pride of place, the British and Dutch schools run close, while names such as Hackaert, Signorelli, Guardi, Dughet, Jordaens and De Crayer represent the Germans, Italians, French and Flemish. The British representation is particularly strong in portraits, many of the Maxwell family (by, for example, Etty and Nicholson), while William Blake contributes five works and Hogarth provides a portrait of James Thomson, author of the words of 'Rule Britannia', as also a fascinating historical glimpse into the Tower of London in 1745. From the Dutch, there are landscapes by Jan Both and Claes Berchem, a delightful portrait of a small girl by Johan van Loenen, and a guitarist and listener by Godfried Schalcken.—The Sculpture, of both bronze and marble, is largely British (William Reid Dick, Alfred Gilbert and F.J. Williamson being among the artists), but Canada is represented by R.T. Mackenzie and, outstandingly, Belgium by two typical and striking bronzes by Constantin Meunier.

Provan Hall (NTS, leased to Glasgow District Council. Tel: 041-771-1538) is north of the Clyde, in Auchinlea Park 4m east of the city centre. This well-restored 15C mansion, arguably the most perfect of its kind in Scotland, takes the form of two buildings either side of a courtyard. The original building, with a turret and stepped gable, was added to in the 17–18C, and an attractive wall garden adjoins.

Scotland Street School (Tel: 041-429-1202), at 225 Scotland Street (south of the Clyde, 1½m south east of the city centre) was designed by C.R. Mackintosh and opened in 1906. Today the school houses a museum of education.

602 (City of Glasgow) Squadron Museum (Tel: 0505-612-012 or 041-882-6201. Ext. 105), in Queen Elizabeth Avenue, Hillington, some 5m west of the city centre, is run by the Air Training Corps and tells the story of the local auxiliary squadron which achieved such a gallant and distinguished war record.

Springburn Museum (Tel: 041-557-1405), in Ayr Street, off the east side of A803 (Springburn Road) 1½m north of the city centre, illustrates the local story of a district which was once one of Europe's largest steam locomotive building centres.

Glasgow Zoo (Tel: 041-771-1185) is at Calderpark, 6m south east of the city centre.

D. **The Burrell Collection

The Burrell Collection (Tel: 041-649-7151) of decorative and fine art is brilliantly displayed in a specially designed building in Pollok Country Park (see C.), some 3m south of Glasgow Bridge, and can be reached either by car (ample parking) or by bus to the park's Pollokshaws Road (A77) entrance from where there is a minibus service every 20 minutes to Burrell and Pollok House. The walk through the park takes some 25 minutes.

Sir William Burrell (1861–1958) successfully combined the roles of wealthy Glasgow shipowner and compulsive and dedicated art collector, the former a prosperous inheritance, the latter an individual and self-taught passion of astonishing excellence, vision, range and scale. In 1916 he bought Hutton Castle near Berwick-upon-Tweed, a 15–16C keep and extension, the interior of which was during the following two decades sumptuously refurbished both as a home and as a setting for its owner's treasures. In 1944 Burrell and his wife donated the whole collection, by then totalling some 6000 items, to the city of Glasgow, a decision which, however, in no way reined his enthusiasm and by the date of his death in 1958 a further 2000 items had been added. Burrell in fact deliberately devoted his later years to strengthening areas he considered to be weak, notably the field of ancient civilisations, and to acquiring material which would add distinction to the museum he would in fact never see. For in making his gift, which was later accompanied by a large sum for a building, Burrell laid down stringent conditions, the essence of which was that the new museum was to be both close to Glasgow yet also in a rural setting; a seeming impossibility, resolved only in 1967 when Mrs Maxwell Macdonald presented the Pollok estate to the city.

The *Building*, designed by Barry Gasson and associates and opened in 1983, provides a fitting setting. Uncompromisingly yet unobtrusively modern in concept, it avoids all the drilled presentation of more conventional museums. Spacious yet always intimate, this is a place in which inviting vistas alternate with corners and surprises and sudden glimpses through medieval archways—the whole, moreover, set close against woodland, in spring a carpet of bluebells, which, for all that it is beyond a great glass wall, seems nonetheless as much a part of the Burrell experience as are the treasures on formal display.

A mezzanine is set aside for special study, special selections, and exhibitions, but, this apart, the entire collection is at ground level, arranged, as can be seen from the ground plan, as six principal sections. Physically, though, the divisions are not as precise as might appear, and essentially this is a place in which to drift from one world into another rather than follow a disciplined path. Everything on display is admirably identified and explained. Nevertheless the paragraphs below visit each section in turn, elaborating modestly where judged helpful and indicating a few representative themes or items.

BURRELL COLLECTION

Courtyard

Lecture Theatre

Temporary Exhibitions

The Hutton Castle Rooms

Ancient Civilisations

Oriental Art

Medieval & Post-Medieval European Art

Paintings, Drawings & Bronzes

Period Galleries

A service passage (shop, information, toilets) leads into the so-called Courtyard in which stands the massive Warwick Vase (not one of Sir William's acquisitions but a subsequent one by the Burrell trustees), once gracing Hadrian's villa at Tivoli and in more recent times a feature of the gardens of Warwick Castle.

Around the Courtyard are the three **Hutton Castle Rooms**, reconstructions of the drawing room, hall and dining room, the concept well explained by a notice in the Courtyard. It was Burrell's wish that the rooms into which he had worked some of his most valued acquisitions should be reproduced in the museum, and, as much for their size as for their sumptuous decoration and contents, they certainly provide a sobering picture of the castellar life still enjoyed by a magnate of good taste until only a few years ago. Panels, armorial decoration, heavy yet graceful and unfussy furniture, medieval sculpture, and, above all perhaps, priceless medieval tapestries and stained glass are the features here.

Ancient Civilisations here means Egypt, Mesopotamia (modern Iraq and Iran), Greece and Italy, and it was to the strengthening of this field that Burrell devoted much of his effort during his closing years. The *Egyptian* material forms the bulk of the collection—an exquisite small alabaster offering table and, by contrast, the heads of gods ('human' and animal), kings, queens and lesser men may be singled out—while the *Mesopotamian* collection, though relatively small, can in scope claim to be one of the most distinguished in Britain. Seals, always intriguing and always rewarding detailed study, represent workmanship of over 5000 years ago, while bronze work illustrates the 7C BC, amongst this a bull's head which has the added interest of being Burrell's final acquisition. From *Greece* and the eastern Mediterranean come the inevitable vases and jars of various periods, shapes and purposes, some attractive small statuary, and, from the later period (say the last 500 years BC) exquisite objects in gold such as a charming pair of bull's-head earrings. *Italy*, too, contributes pottery, notably a magnificent 4C BC Greek-style wine bowl (or krater) and, from the same period, an elaborate if perhaps inconvenient cup set into a sheep's head. The, later, Roman material includes stone sculpture and some superbly executed decorative mosaic.

The **Oriental Art** collection, the Burrell's largest and accounting for around a quarter of the whole, embraces the ceramic work of China and the Near East (this latter a wide belt of lands extending from Pakistan, Samarkand and Kabul in the east across to Istanbul, Cairo and Saudi Arabia in the west); the bronzes and jades, too, of China; the prints of Japan; and carpets from right across the Near East.

China's Pottery and Porcelain story spans from Neolithic to modern times, over the whole of which period of some 5000 years the country's skill and industry have rarely flagged and examples of most periods of which are shown here. Prominent, and certainly most publicised, is an almost life-size cross-legged Buddhist disciple (or lohan) of 1484, shaven, serene and smug. But from millenia before this there are painted and patterned Neolithic urns, and as the visitor tours the centuries recorded in this part of the museum he will find an impressive variety of subjects and colours and skills. A model storage tower, for instance, remarkable for its architectural detail and with purposeful figures on its external stair (from about the time of the birth of Christ); a sturdy, harnessed dog of about the same date; the inevitable horses and camels (largely Tang funerary, 618–907), as gorgeously decked out as are their human companions; fearsome tomb guardians of the 8C and others rather less intimidating of the Ming 14C era; and much handsome, sophisticated work in copper-red, blue and famille verte representing the later centuries.

The collection of *Near Eastern Ceramics* spans a shorter period, the 900 years between the 9 and 17C, but more than holds its own in deep richness of colour (notably turquoise for the twin practical reasons that it was not only readily to hand but also had a magic significance) and in daring yet distinctive design. Dishes and vessels of great variety predominate here in a dazzling display in which the design of each item repays detailed study, whether of the typically Islamic arabesques, of the gold leaf worked in with the dark cobalt of an elegant 12C Persian jug, or, by contrast, of two almost gaudy 17C Turkish jugs on which arabesques and blue-leafed flowers rest on tightly meshed blue, green and turquoise fish scales.

Aesthetically bronze can be a connoisseur taste and *Chinese Bronzes* are no exception, standing as they do in almost sombre contrast to the coloured exuberance of the ceramic. But if the ever-aging subtlety of the patina is perhaps lost on the layman, he can nevertheless enjoy the more obvious elegance and sometimes ingenuity of design as also the detail of the decoration. It may add interest to a study of the latter to look for specifics, such as dragons and also the masks (taotie) which, in a variety of forms, distinguish much ancient Chinese bronze (normally the masks, best identified by the eyes, are in twin mirrored parts). Eyes, for instance, stare out of the tripod legs which support an ingenious 11C BC food steamer, and also from the surface of what looks like a chamber-pot but is in fact a food vessel called a gui. For decoration perhaps the most important piece in the collection is a large cylindrical container (a lian, 1 or 2C BC), notable on a number of counts, such as the kneeling figures which support it, the masks holding the rings, and the decorative bands of birds in flight, birds walking and a delightful procession of stags and does. Finally, connoisseurs of weapons will note the crossbow mechanism, precisely dated to 147.

Chinese Jades. To the Chinese, jade (geologically the term is imprecise and jade may turn out to be any of several valuable, hard stones) has long been a favoured medium, and, as was the case with ceramics, the material in this collection spans from Neolithic to modern times. Given the choice of stones, the shades, though always sober, have a subtle range, while the articles made embrace weapons, ornaments, vessels, small figures and ritual and funerary objects, these last because jade was popularly supposed to prevent body decay.

The Burrell's *Japanese Prints* are all of the 18 and 19C and thus represent the art's most mature period. They are perhaps something of an acquired taste, but most visitors will surely find it hard not to smile with the apparently happily inebriated fisherman smoking his long, thin pipe (probably a self-portrait by the artist Hokusai). The *Near Eastern Carpets* shown here in the Burrell span the 16 to 19C and richly reflect the decorative imagination and skill, not to mention infinite patience (frequently the work was, and still is, executed by children), of a broad swathe of lands stretching from India through Persia to Turkey.

The very broad heading **Medieval and Post-Medieval European Art** embraces not only the strongest, and by Sir William most favoured, element in the whole collection but also the widest range of art-forms, extending from imposing sculptured doorways down to delicate silver and glassware and even needlework. Within this bracket of excellence, perhaps the tapestries and stained glass, each allotted its own gallery, can claim the most formal distinction.

Sculpture and Church Art. The large doorways, such as the heraldic portal of Hornsby Castle (early 16C) and the late 12C portal from Montron in France, fantastically carved with foliage and beasts, can hardly be missed. But the emphasis here—and there are over 300 pieces—is on stone and wooden statuary, largely from England, Spain, Germany and the Netherlands, some figures being individual, others once parts of retables (altar backings). Each piece has its own character, and each demands attention, whether, for example, for the naive charm of the painted wooden figures of St. John and the Virgin (13C, Spanish); or the poignancy of an early 16C German painted Lamentation; or the absorbed dedication expressed by Austrian 16C musician angels; or even the faintly comical, self-conscious group-photograph pose of the members of a late 15C English alabaster Adoration of the Magi.

In medieval times *Tapestries* were, to use the modern idiom, status symbols. Philip the Bold of Burgundy was, we are told, accounted immensely wealth with his 75. The Burrell Collection boasts over 150 (many displayed in the tapestry gallery and the Hutton Castle rooms), a world-famous assemblage ranging in date from a fragment of 1300 up to the 16C and with provenance from most of the major weaving centres, such as Germany, France, Burgundy and the Netherlands. If the heraldic designs hanging in the Hutton Castle rooms perhaps strike one as pretentious, there are plenty of others which can delight and even amuse. The sheer, idyllic innocence, for instance, of two young lovers hunting Fidelity (German, 15C); the purposeful and obviously well planned diligence of a group of peasants after rabbits (Franco-Burgundian, perhaps Tournai, 15C; sadly this tapestry shows only the start of the hunt—the setting of the nets—and journeys to San Francisco and Paris would have to be made to enjoy the actual hunt and the picnic that followed); or, in the Hutton Castle Drawing Room, a fashionably attired lady (Charity), improbably balanced astride an elephant and about to be anything but charitable as she prepares to cut down Envy, a craven little fellow allowed only a dog as a mount.

The Burrell's collection of more than 600 panels of *Stained Glass* is as world-famed as is its tapestry. The emphasis is on northern European work of the 15–16C and the glass is admirably displayed both in the Hutton Castle rooms and in a special gallery. For many people stained glass is perhaps instinctively associated with cathedrals and churches with their often stylised sacred themes. Here, though, the visitor also has the opportunity to enjoy lay themes, some of such panels revealing charming glimpses of contemporary everyday life.

The glass in the Hutton Castle rooms is both heraldic and religious, an interesting example (English) of the former, if only because the oldest, being a Dining Room pair of shields (first window on the left giving on the Courtyard) showing the royal arms and those of the Clares and dating back to the 13–14C. Less ancient (1537–47) are the roundels in the Hall framing several shields of arms, amongst these those of Henry VIII, Jane Seymour and their son the Prince of Wales. In the Hall, too, are three 15–16C German religious panels, one showing an Adoration of the Magi which can interestingly be compared with the alabaster rendering of the same date referred to above. Plenty more rich glass, some heraldic, some religious, graces the Drawing Room, much of this being English, as, for example, two 15C vertical strips showing St. Peter and an archbishop, each watched over by angels.

The subjects in the Stained Glass Gallery are of refreshing variety. Here a seated Solomon receives a kneeling Queen of Sheba (German, late 15C); St. Nicholas, protector of scholars, merchants and sailors, tries to halt a mass execution (Netherlands, early 16C); a prissy Princess Cecily, daughter of Edward IV, shows her displeasure (English, c 1485); a man toasts his toes before his fire (English, late 15C); and a Dutchman is seen busy at his task of making tiles (Netherlands, 17C).

Burrell's enthusiasm and taste ranged freely over much of the virtually infinite field of *Decorative Art*. His emphasis, though, tended to be on British examples of the 16–17C, a period in which Elizabethan and Restoration verve bracketed the brief years of simpler Commonwealth taste. Decorative Art exhibits, although largely in the Medieval and Post-Medieval area, will also be found in other parts of the museum, notably in the Hutton Castle rooms and in the three Period Galleries (see below). Among the forms represented are silver, ceramics, carved and decorated wood, glass and needlework, with also, to a more substantial physical scale, arms and armour and furniture.

Three **Period Galleries**—Elizabethan, 17–18C and Gothic Domestic—in part separate the Medieval and Post-Medieval European Art area of the museum from **Paintings, Drawings and Bronzes**, a field in which Burrell's tastes were conservative, or at any rate cautious. Here, although the collection's essential strength is 19C French, the total spread in fact is wide, reaching back to 15 and 16C masterpieces by Memling and the elder Cranach and at the other end of the scale touching the present century with the muted works of the Hague School (Anton Mauve and the Maris brothers). In between, the 17C Dutch find a distinguished place, exemplified by Rembrandt's Self Portrait of 1632 and Franz Hals's confident, patrician Gentleman of 1639.

The French paintings, including Impressionists, embrace a galaxy of names. Le Nain groups his rather surprisingly well dressed peasant children, even if one is without shoes. Géricault is here with his 'romantic' Prancing Grey Horse. Courbet's grotesque Dickensian Charity of a Beggar contrasts with Millet's gentle little shepherdess. Manet's blousy ladies quaff their beer; Boudin, Sisley and Cézanne provide sea and landscapes, Degas his usual horses and always charming young ballet dancers.

As to Sculpture, Burrell's taste in bronzes was as cautious as his attitude to paintings. No abstract compositions will be found here, but there is a place for such as Meunier, Rodin and a disciplined Epstein.

V EAST CENTRAL

East Central Scotland extends as a broad belt from Loch Lomond in the west clear across the country to the east coast. From south to north, from a narrow, thickly populated urban and industrial base between Glasgow and Edinburgh, it fans out into undulating farming land which in turn shades off into the wooded foothills, or braes, through which lovely valleys climb gradually into empty Highland moor, loch and mountain—the long Grampian range which defines the northern flank of this East Central belt. Yet, despite this Highland north, East Central Scotland, as a whole, is essentially Lowland in character.

In ancient times this was the land of the earliest Scotsmen, the Picts, people of unknown origin who had been established here, and in the Highlands behind, long before the Irish, Welsh and Angles began moving into the South West and South East (say, 5 and 6C). The Romans came during the 1 and 2Cs, establishing their great marching camps and defeating the tribes at Mons Graupius, the site of which may have been the high ground above Stonehaven, though Bennachie to the north west of Aberdeen is more favoured. But they did not stay long in the northern land, soon withdrawing behind their Antonine Wall between the Forth and the Clyde, and with their departure Pictland began to take shape, with its own kings, one of whom, Brude, in 685 at the battle of Nectansmere near Forfar, decisively defeated the Northumbrians and put a stop to their northward expansion. Christianity began to spread (the evidence is still to be seen in the many sculptured stones), and then in c 843 came the big change when Kenneth Macalpine united his western kingdom of Dalriada to that of Pictland, thus laying the first foundation on which the single kingdom of Scotland would grow. For some six centuries East Central Scotland remained the country's heartland—Perth was the capital and the kings were crowned at nearby Scone—and even after the transfer of the capital to Edinburgh in the mid 15C places such as Dunfermline, Stirling and Falkland remained favourite royal residences, while St. Andrews retained the spiritual primacy of Scotland down to the Reformation, when it became a centre of extreme religious persecution.

With such a background, and bordered by the Highlands, untamed until after Culloden, it is not surprising that this part of Scotland is rich in places of historical and other interest. But despite this richness—or perhaps because there is so much, so scattered—East Central Scotland has never really established itself as a touring region in its own right. Rather it is regarded by many as a belt (though an interesting one) to be crossed on the way to whichever of the 'gateways' to the Highlands has been chosen. Of these 'gateways', the main five are outlined below and suggestions are made regarding principal places of interest—historical, scenic, modern and other—along the way. **Stirling**, central and with its famous castle, is taken as the common starting point. Close to Stirling are the site of the *Battle of Bannockburn*, where Bruce won Scotland's independence from England (NTS Visitor Centre); *Doune Castle* which, more than any other, conveys what life in such a place may have been like; *Doune Motor Museum*; and *Scotland's (Blair Drummond) Safari Park*.

1. **Loch Lomond** (Rte 20). This is the road likely to be chosen by those heading for Glen Coe and the western Highlands and islands. At Tarbet, on the loch, an alternative road leads into the attractive Cowal and Kintyre peninsulas, and at Crianlarich, farther north, there is a choice between continuing north west, or instead bearing east for Loch Tay and the Central Highlands. Loch Lomond can be approached by way of Erskine Bridge across the Clyde, through Glasgow, or from Stirling along A811. The famous name 'Loch Lomond' apart, the attraction of this route is mainly scenic. However, if the approach is made from Erskine Bridge or Glasgow, two sites of interest are passed. At *Bearsden*, a north-western suburb of Glasgow, some good sections of the Roman Antonine Wall can be seen, and at *Dumbarton* the impressively sited castle is worth a visit.

2. **Pass of Leny and Strathyre** (Rte 24). This is a useful road which, near Killin on Loch Tay, offers a choice between west and east. *Blair Drummond Safari Park* and *Doune*, with its castle and motor museum, can be visited soon after leaving Stirling, and at *Callander* a short diversion leads to *The Trossachs* and *Loch Katrine*, renowned beauty spots, the territory of Rob Roy, the early 18C Robin Hood, and the setting of Scott's 'Rob Roy' and 'The Lady of the Lake'. *Lochearnhead* is a centre for sailing and water-skiing, and on *Ben Lawers*, high above Loch Tay, there is an outstanding National Trust for Scotland Visitor Centre in a mountain zone of exceptional geological and botanical interest.

3. **Sma' Glen** (Rte 25B). The glen—a pleasant, narrow valley climbing up to moorland—starts just east of Crieff which it links to Aberfeldy, where there is a choice between bearing west along Loch Tay or east for Pitlochry and the main A9. Along or close to the short stretch between Stirling and Crieff there are several places worth a visit. *Dunblane* has a superb Norman-Gothic cathedral, and just to the east is *Sheriffmuir*, the site of the battle of 1715 which ended the Old Pretender's hopes. Some other places are the great Roman camp at *Ardoch*; a 12C Norman tower at *Muthill*; and, at *Innerpeffray*, Scotland's oldest public library (1691).

4. **Pitlochry and Glen Garry** (Rte 27). This road (A9) is Scotland's main
south–north artery and carries heavy traffic. From Stirling it runs north
east to Perth, then heads north for Pitlochry, after which it climbs
through wooded Glen Garry on to desolate high moor before descending to meet the Fort William-Spey Valley road (Rte 50) at Newtonmore.
Stirling to Perth is described as Rte 25, and the town of Perth as Rte 26.
Nearby *Scone Palace*, although 19C, retains medieval parts and has
ancient associations, mainly with the crowning of Scotland's kings.
North of Perth, places worth noting are *Dunkeld*, with a ruined but
beautiful cathedral and a street of restored 17C houses; *Loch of the
Lowes*, a nature centre where ospreys may be seen; *Pitlochry*, in lovely
surroundings of loch and wood, with a fish-pass (observation chamber)
and, at *Killiecrankie*, a National Trust for Scotland Visitor Centre
which explains the battle here (1689) which, with that at Dunkeld three
weeks later, ended the hopes of James VII/II and assured the position of
William and Mary; and *Blair Castle*, the last castle in Britain to be
besieged.

5. **Glenshee and Cairnwell Pass** (Rte 28). This is the route for those
aiming for Royal Deeside and north-eastern Scotland. *Cairnwell Pass*
(2199ft) is the highest main road pass in Britain. *Scone Palace* (see
above) is passed just north of Perth, but after this the road's interest is
mainly scenic.

There remain two areas of East Central Scotland—Fife and the East
Coast—tours through both of which can conveniently be combined by
using the Tay bridge from Fife to Dundee. **Fife**, a self-contained touring
district in its own right and well worth a diversion of a day or two, is
described as Rte 33. Among its many places of interest are *Dunfermline*,
where Bruce and other Scottish kings lie buried in the abbey; *Falkland
Palace*, a historic Renaissance-style royal dwelling; the string of picturesque small fishing ports between Largo and Crail; and *St. Andrews*,
with its famous ruined cathedral and castle, Scotland's oldest university, and the world's premier golf club. The **East Coast** (including the
inland road through Forfar and Brechin), though of limited scenic worth
unless diversions are made north into the many lovely glens, compen-
sates by having along its roads an almost unbroken succession and
variety of places worth visiting. These are covered under Rtes 29 and 35.
The choice includes unique collections of Early Christian Pictish sculptured stones at *Meigle, Aberlemno* and *St. Vigean*; historic great castles
such as intact *Glamis*, ruined *Dunnottar* and *Edzell*, this last with a
famous early 17C walled pleasance; earth-houses, unusual for being
associated with huts, at *Ardestie* and *Carlungie*, near Dundee; and
ancient religious establishments such as the priory at *Restenneth*, the
great red sandstone abbey of *Arbroath* and the famous round tower at
Brechin.

20 Glasgow to Tyndrum

A82 (with A814 alternative).—Beyond Balloch the main road follows
the beautiful west shore of Loch Lomond into increasingly Highland
scenery. Despite new alignments and dual carriageway, this road can
be crowded in summer, especially beside Loch Lomond, and A814
from Dumbarton via Helensburgh and rejoining A82 at Tarbet offers a
highly scenic alternative only some 4m longer.

SOME HOTELS. **Dumbarton**. *Travel Lodge*, Milton, G82 2TY. Tel: 0389-65202. **Balloch**. *Balloch*, G83 8LQ. Tel: 0389-52579. **Drymen**. *Buchanan Highland*, Main Street, G63 0BQ. Tel: 0360-60588. **Luss**. *Colquhoun Arms*. Tel: 043686-282. **Tarbet**. *Tarbet*, G83 7DE. Tel: 03012-228. **Ardlui**. *Ardlui*, G83 7EB. Tel: 03014-243. **Crianlarich**. *Allt-Chaorain House*, FK20 8RU. Tel: 08383-283. **Tyndrum**. *Invervey*, FK20 8RY. Tel: 08384-219.

Total distance (A82) 61m.—*10m* **Dumbarton**.—*5m* **Balloch**.—*26m* **Tarbet**.—*16m* **Crianlarich**.—*4m* **Tyndrum**.

A82 leaves **Glasgow** (see Rte 19) as Great Western Road, passing the Botanic Gardens and in *8m* from the city centre reaching the road complex marking the north end of *Erskine Bridge* (see Rte 16). Here the elegantly functional bridge, the railway and the skeins of fast, purposeful traffic combine as a wholly modern ambience, yet the map entry 'Roman Fort' beside *Old Kilpatrick* just below reminds that it was here that the Antonine Wall met the river, while the strip of the *Forth Clyde Canal* (see Rte 9) closely paralleling the shore survives as a feat of traffic engineering as acclaimed in 1790 as was Erskine Bridge in 1971. But of the Roman presence at Old Kilpatrick there are now but scanty traces, the nearest significant Antonine remain being at *Duntocher*, 2m east, where there is a rampart base. A short way beyond Erskine Bridge *Auchentoshan Distillery* (Tel: 0389-79476) provides a dram at the end of a guided tour which covers brewing, distilling and warehousing. The Forth-Clyde Canal joins the Clyde at *(1m) Bowling* where the canal's basin, once busy with industrial barges, now serves as a recreational marina. A short mile to the west, by a castle ruin on the shore, the Bell Obelisk honours Henry Bell (1767–1830), engineer of the 'Comet' which, built across the water at Port Glasgow, was the first Clyde passenger steamer. And here, abruptly broadening, the Clyde matures from river to estuary.

1m **Dumbarton** (23,000 inhab.) is of interest for its historic and theatrically sited *Castle* (AM. Tel: 031-244-3101), visually best appreciated from a distance but also rewarding those who climb the 200ft to the top with far-reaching river and moorland views.

History. The name Dumbarton, a corruption of Dun Bretane, the Fort of the Britons, establishes the antiquity of this place which was probably the birthplace of St. Gildas (c 316–70) as also of St. Patrick (c 387–461), the latter being captured here by raiders in 405 and sold into captivity in Ireland. By the 13C the British dun had become a royal stronghold, the governor of which in 1305 was that Sir John Menteith who, if the verdict of tradition is accepted, treacherously captured Wallace and probably brought him here before the long journey to London and a cruel execution.

It was from here in 1548 that Mary, Queen of Scots, then a child of five, was sent to France, escorted by a French fleet all the way to Roscoff in Brittany. In 1571, despite their sovereign's final flight to England, Dumbarton was still held by Mary's adherents who, however, were overcome by a daring attack by 100 men who, at dead of night, scaled the least accessible face of the rock using ladders and ropes; and when, so the story goes, one of the band took vertigo and froze, he was lashed to the ladder which was then turned round so that his companions could climb past him. So total was the surprise achieved that none of the attackers was killed and only four of the garrison. But John Hamilton, Archbishop of St. Andrews, was less fortunate; taken in the attack, he was accused of complicity in the murder of Darnley and Regent Moray and four days later hanged at Stirling. In 1707, under the Treaty of Union, it was declared that Dumbarton should be maintained as one of the chief fortresses of Scotland.

The castle sprawls over much of a large, isolated basaltic rock which lifts abruptly from the shore of the Clyde and is cleft into two summits, the higher of which is known as Wallace's Seat. It is entered from the seaward side, the landward approach having been destroyed, near the entrance being a sundial presented by Mary, Queen of Scots. From the former Governor's House (1735–1832) a daunting flight of steps climbs within the cleft, passing the so-called Wallace's Guardhouse, on which a gable terminates in a crude head of Sir John Menteith, with his finger in his cheek, the conventional sign of betrayal. Beyond, the steps continue east past two gun batteries to reach the magazine; and west to the site of the White Tower, from which point there is a view (orientation table) which Dorothy Wordsworth judged to be 'sufficient recompense' for the climb.—In the town, in Castle Street, the *Denny Ship Model Tank* (Tel: 0389-63444) is the world's oldest surving experimental tank (1883).

Dumbarton to Tarbet via Helensburgh.

It was at (*4m*) *Cardross* that Bruce died in 1329, probably a victim of leprosy. *Kilmahew Chapel,*½m north on Darleith Road, beyond the golf course, was dedicated to St. Mayhew, a companion of St. Patrick, as long ago as 535; the present building, dating from 1467 and derelict since c 1840, was restored for parish use in 1955.

4m **Helensburgh** (13,000 inhab. *Inf.* Passenger ferry link to Kilcreggan and Gourock; also local cruises) is a residential and resort town of both dignity and character, named after the wife of Sir James Colquhoun of Luss who laid out the older part on a draughtboard pattern around the end of the 18C. Henry Bell (1767–1830), engineer of the 'Comet', the first Clyde passenger steamer (see also Rte 16, Port Glasgow), who lived and died here, is commemorated by an obelisk as also by the anvil and flywheel of the 'Comet', both of which are preserved in Hermitage Park. J.L. Baird (1888–1946), pioneer of television, was a native (bust) as was also the distinguished Glasgow architect, C.R. Mackintosh, whose memorial here is the *Hill House* (NTS. Tel: 0436-73900). Built in 1904 for the publisher W.W. Blackie, the house, which contains Mackintosh furniture and other material, is accepted as perhaps the most outstanding example of Mackintosh's domestic architecture.—In *Rhu*, a northern suburb of Helensburgh, Henry Bell is buried beside the church.

A814 now hugs the shore of Gare Loch which, sheltered and less than a mile wide, was an important Combined Operations base during the last war and today still serves both civil and naval maritime needs with shipbreaking yards at *Shandon* and a submarine base at (*6m*) *Faslane*. From this latter a minor road leading north east in under 2m enters *Glen Fruin*, peaceful and pretty enough today but a valley long bloodily and legally infamous in the feud between the MacGregors and the Colquhouns.

The battle fought here in 1603 was a typical example of the disputes that could arise out of 'sheepskin grants' (see Aspects of Scotland, Clans). The MacGregors held their lands by clan tradition, but the Campbells, flaunting an official grant, demanded rent from the MacGregors and, when this was refused, began to seize land. The impotent MacGregors could only live by cattle stealing, on one occasion raiding Colquhoun land at Luss on Loch Lomond. The Campbell chief encouraged the resultant bitterness and on 18 February 1603 the MacGregors and Colquhouns met here in Glen Fruin. Not only were many of the Colquhoun men killed, but a number of their onlookers (sons of the gentry of the district), who had been shut in a barn for safety, were massacred in cold blood by the victors. Sixty Colquhoun widows appeared before James VI at Stirling, each with the bloody shirt of her husband in her hand, and the king was so moved that he outlawed the MacGregors and proscribed their very name. Not until 1663 was the act of outlawry reversed by Charles II, as a reward for services rendered to Montrose, but it was renewed in 1693 by William III, and full legal rights were not finally restored until 1755, under George II.

1m **Garelochhead**, from where a road drops south to round the Rosneath peninsula as far as Coulport. A small road across the centre of the
peninsula completes the circuit, while Kilcreggan, on the south shore,
is linked by passenger ferry with Gourock and Helensburgh.—A814
now enters its most scenic stretch, climbing to the watershed between
Gare Loch and Loch Long, a spot offering wide views which include, to
the west, a glimpse of the entrance to Loch Goil. Loch Long is reached
at (*3m*) *Finnart*, an oil port where large tankers may be moored close to
the road. Between here and (*7m*) **Arrochar** (see Rte 45) the road runs
with the lovely east shore of Loch Long, above which to the west towers
the lofty and lonely skyline of Argyll Forest Park.—*1m* **Tarbet** where
A82 is rejoined.

Dumbarton to Tarbet via Loch Lomond

Between Dumbarton and Balloch at the south tip of Loch Lomond, A82
(bypassing towns) imperceptibly ascends the valley of the Leven, only
5m long and mainly given over to light industry. Once this was the land
of the Smolletts, and at (*2m*) **Renton** a monument, bearing a Latin epi-
taph by Dr Johnson, commemorates the novelist Tobias Smollett
(1721–71), born at the family home of Dalquharn (pron. Dalwhan),½m to
the south.—*2m* farther, **Alexandria** has neither Greek nor Egyptian
links but, less romantically perhaps, traces its name back to an Alexander Smollett.

1m **Balloch** (*Inf.*), virtually continuous with Alexandria, is a popular
resort and recreation focus straddling the outflow of the river Leven
from Loch Lomond. The attractive *Balloch Castle Country Park*, on the
east side of the outflow, offers woodland and lakeside walks, a nature
trail and a moated mound marking the site of ancient Balloch Castle,
while at the modern (19C) castle there is a local Interpretation Centre
(Tel: 0389-58216).

Loch Lomond, 24m long and varying in width between 5m in the
south and well under 1m in the north, is the largest stretch of inland
water in Britain as also one of the most varied and beautiful. To the
north the loch quickly narrows before piercing into the Highlands as a
narrow finger below ranges of high mountains, these including Ben
Lomond (east) and Ben Vorlich (west), both over 3000ft. In the south, by
contrast, the waters are broad and broken by many islands and islets
while the shores—those 'bonnie banks' of ballad (see below)—wash
modest pastoral and wooded scenery backed by green hills and more
distant mountains. *Inchmurrin*, named after the 7C St. Mirren who built
a chapel here, is the largest island, with, at its south west tip, the ruins of
Lennox Castle, built in 1390 when the earls of Lennox judged Balloch
not safe enough and later the retreat of the unfortunate Duchess of
Albany after the wholesale execution of her husband, sons and father.
Both this island and *Inchlonaig* opposite Luss were in the 18C used as
places of internment for 'persons disordered in their senses' as also for
'those of the fair sex, who were so unfortunate as to give pregnant proofs
of their frailty' and had therefore to 'avoid the reproach of the world'.
Inchcailloch (Island of the Old Women), off Balmaha, was the burial
place of the MacGregors who long took their oaths on those that slept
'beneath the grey stone of Inchcailloch'. This island, together with
adjacent *Clairinsh* and others, forms a national nature reserve (see
below).

Some History. The loch's ancient name was Leven, whence the surrounding lands
came to be known as Levenox or Lennox, and the leading clans were the MacGregors and the Colquhouns, who in 1603 met in bloody conflict in Glen Fruin (see

above). Magnus, King of Man, son-in-law of Hakon, is said to have dragged his galleys across the narrow isthmus from Arrochar on Loch Long to Tarbet in 1263 and to have harried the startled dwellers around the loch while Hakon was meeting defeat at Largs. Bruce is popularly supposed to have found refuge in Rob Roy's Cave at Inversnaid in 1306, the cave's name recalling that Robert MacGregor (Rob Roy) was the most colourful local figure in the early 18C. At about the same time, in 1715, the MacGregors, ever ardent Jacobites, seized every boat on the loch and assembled them at Inversnaid, where, however, they were speedily repossessed by a Hanoverian force that had dragged some armed boats up the Leven.—The popular ballad, 'The Bonnie Banks o' Loch Lomon', the lament of a Scottish soldier dying far from home, recalls the long-held belief that, on death, the spirit returned home underground ('the low road').

Loch Cruises. Operators include Maid of the Loch Ltd, Balloch Pier. Tel: 0389-52044, cruises (Easter–September) generally including one of 4½ hours calling at Luss, Rowardennan, Tarbet and Inversnaid; Loch Lomond Sailings, Riverside, Balloch. Tel: 0389-51481, main cruise (Easter–November) lasting one hour; and Sweeney's Boatyard, 26 Balloch Road. Tel: 0389-52376, providing daily services throughout the year. See also Balmaha and Tarbet, below.

The main A82, followed by this Route, travels the entire length of the west shore of Loch Lomond, but the small road along the east shore ends at Rowardennan. This latter, providing a rewarding diversion, is described immediately below.

BALLOCH TO ROWARDENNAN (18m). The road (A811) from Balloch to (8m) *Drymen* runs well inland of the loch shore and is of no great scenic or other interest. From Drymen (where, see below, intending visitors to the Loch Lomond Nature Reserve may wish to apply for information) B837 in 4m reaches the loch at **Balmaha**, a prettily situated village looking out to the group of wooded islands (Inchcailloch, Clairinsh, Torrinch, Creinch and Aber) which, together with a small area on the mainland on the south bank of the Endrick Water, make up the *Loch Lomond National Nature Reserve* (semi-natural deciduous woodland; aquatic invertebrates; botanical rareties; wintering wildfowl). Access to Inchcailloch, with a nature trail, is unrestricted to the casual visitor. Further information from the Warden, 22 Muirpark Way, Drymen. For island cruises and boats to Inchcailloch, apply MacFarlane and Sons, The Boatyard, Balmaha. Tel: 036087-214. Balmaha enjoys the additional attraction of being on the western fringe of Queen Elizabeth Forest Park (see Rte 21), two official forest walks of which start from the village car park.

Northward from Balmaha a narrow, minor road keeps close to the loch, passing Forestry Commission picnic sites and waymarked walks, to reach (6m from Balmaha) the road's end at **Rowardennan**. From here one path continues north along the shore, while another, starting from the pier picnic place and car park, climbs the steep, grassy slope to the summit of Ben Lomond (3192ft. 3½ miles, or maybe 3 hours, to the top).

Continuing north along the main Route, A82 in *6m* passes the estate of *Rhossdhu* (no adm.), long a seat of the Colquhouns whose 15C castle was replaced in 1773 by a house attributed to Robert Adam.—*2m* **Luss**, a pretty village enhanced by occupying one of the loveliest sites along this side of the loch, preserves in its church a 14–15C effigy of St. Kessog, a local evangelist of the 6C. A scenic road, affording views of the loch and its islands, ascends for 2m up Glen Luss.

Now close beside the water, A82 in *3m* reaches *Inverbeg*, from where a small road crosses westward by way of Glen Douglas to Loch Long.—*15m* **Tarbet**, a modest summer centre, stands at the east end of the 1½m-wide isthmus, today with a main road and a railway, across which Magnus, King of Man, hauled his galleys in 1263. For loch cruises, Tel: 03012-356 or 636. For Tarbet (Arrochar) to Lochgilphead and Kintyre, see Rte 45.—With the loch on one side, and the railway and woodland on the other, A82 in *3m* arrives at *Inveruglas Power Station*, operated by water from Loch Sloy, 2m north west below Ben Vorlich. Opposite the power station there is a pleasant parking and picnic area (orientation table).

Eilean Vow, reached in rather less than *3m*, is the next island, seat once of the Macfarlanes, the remains of whose castle still cling on, and the place also, or so it is said, where the far-seeing Bruce planted yew trees to ensure good bows for his descendants.—*2m* The village of *Ardlui* marks the head of Loch Lomond, here less than ½m wide, and the start of the glen of the river Falloch, wooded at first but the road soon entering a bleak mountain district, dotted with a few stunted survivors of the once great Caledonian Forest.—*8m* **Crianlarich**, popular with walkers and wildlife enthusiasts, stands at the junction of three fine Highland glens (Falloch, Fillan and Dochart) as also of the railway lines to Oban and Fort William. A85, bearing east through Glen Dochart, joins Rte 24 shortly before reaching Killin.

Now heading north west along Strath Fillan, and close beside the Oban railway, A82 parallels the Fillan Water, in which (roughly 3m from Crianlarich) is *St. Fillan's Pool*, a holy pool to which lunatics were brought to be cured by a method which could hardly have been simpler. After being plunged into the water the patient was bound and then left overnight in a corner of *Strathfillan Priory*, still surviving as a ruin on the far bank of the river; if, next morning, the knots were still tied, a cure was judged hopeless, but if he had managed to free himself then he was considered bright enough to be accepted as sane. St. Fillan, of Irish origin, retired to this strath and died here after years spent as a hermit at Pittenweem where his cave can still be seen (see Rte 33A). Centuries later, Bruce took his arm-reliquary to Bannockburn and, attributing his victory to the saint, founded this Augustinian priory in 1314.

A short distance farther, approaching Tyndrum, the railway takes a pronounced south west loop, the area within being known as *Dalry* (King's Field) and providing another, earlier and more dramatic association with Bruce. Fleeing after his defeat at Methven in 1306, Bruce was attacked here by John MacDougall of Lorne, a kinsman of the Red Comyn, at the head of a swarm of Highlanders. One of these seized Bruce's plaid and, though mortally wounded, held on so firmly that Bruce was compelled to abandon the garment together with its brooch fastening. This Brooch of Lorne is still treasured at Dunollie (Oban), but Bruce's sword, lost in the same encounter, is said to have finished up in nearby Lochan nan Arm, the Loch of the Sword.

4m (from Crianlarich) **Tyndrum**, a village in very Highland surroundings, enjoys the distinction of having two railway stations, one for the Oban and one for the Fort William line. Earlier very different travellers passed this way, for Tyndrum was an important stage along the drover route from the north before it split to reach the great cattle markets at Falkirk (Stenhousemuir) and Crieff. Here at Tyndrum the road forks, A82 continuing north (as Rte 44A) to reach Fort William via Glen Coe, while A85 heads west (as Rte 44B), aiming for Oban and Fort William by way of Connel.

21 Glasgow (Edinburgh) to Aberfoyle and The Trossachs

From **Glasgow**. A81 to Aberfoyle. A821 to The Trossachs.—After Strathblane the road runs below Campsie Fells, a tract of moor rising to 1800ft, and then into cultivated country. Beyond Aberfoyle the scenery quickly becomes more wooded and Highland.—From **Edinburgh**, the Trossachs district is reached in 61m via Stirling (by-passed) and Callander. See Rtes 9 and 24.

SOME HOTELS. **Strathblane**. *Country Club*, 41 Milngavie Road, G63 9AH. Tel: 0360-70491. *Kirkhouse Inn*, G63 9AA. Tel: 0360-70621. **Aberfoyle**. *Covenanters Inn*, FK8 3XB. Tel: 08772-347. **Kinlochard**. *Forest Hills*, FK8 3TL. Tel: 08777-277. **Brig o' Turk**. *Dundarroch and the Byre*, FK17 8HT. Tel: 08776-200.

Total distance 29m.—*10m* **Strathblane**.—*14m* **Aberfoyle**.—*5m* **The Trossachs**.

Glasgow (see Rte 19) is left by Maryhill Road for (*5m*) the northern suburb of **Bearsden**, near the southern entry to which Maryhill Road runs into the major intersection called Canniesburn Toll where this Route tends to the right along Milngavie Road which in½m is crossed by Roman Road (west) and Boclair Road (east), two roads tracing the course of the Roman military way accompanying the Antonine Wall. To the west, Roman Road soon passes (north) the remains of a bath-house, dating from about 140 and in modern times for over a century covered by houses until revealed as the result of demolition in 1973. Roman Road continuing west becomes in turn Thorn Road, Thorn Drive and Iain Road, steps off this last leading to a length of rampart base, partly still with its stones and ditch. To the east off Milngavie Road, Boclair Road in½m reaches *New Kilpatrick Cemetery* where there are two well-cleared lengths of rampart base, complete with stones and considered to be the best examples of rampart base along the whole wall.

A809 out of Bearsden leads via Drymen to (16m) *Balmaha* at the south east corner of Loch Lomond, see Rte 20. On the way (6m) *Queen's View* is reached (Auchineden Hill, 1171ft), so called because it was from here that Queen Victoria had her first glimpse of Loch Lomond. From the car park there is a signposted path to (1m) a curious chasm known as *The Whangie*.

2m **Milngavie** (pron. Milguy) marks the northern limit of the Glasgow conurbation. Here the *Lillie Art Gallery* (Tel: 041-956-2351. Ext. 226) shows a permanent collection of 20C Scottish paintings, sculptures and ceramics, as also a series of temporary exhibitions, while the *Heather-bank Museum and Library of Social Work* (Tel: 041-956-2687) is just what its name implies and includes a reference library of over 5000 volumes. Above the town are the adjoining Mugdock and Craigmaddie reservoirs, together feeding Glasgow, to the north of the former being *Mugdock Country Park* (Tel: 041-956-6100), with the remains of two castles. Just east of Milngavie, seen from A807 across a small loch, is mid 16C Bardownie Castle.

Leaving Milngavie A81 rounds Craigmaddie Reservoir and drops into the Blane valley to reach (*3m*) **Strathblane**, lying below the south west shoulder of Campsie Fells, a long, volcanic moorland hump lifting to over 1800ft.

CAMPSIE FELLS. A scenic circuit of some 17m can be made by driving east to Lennoxtown and then north across the centre of the Fells to return to A81 by way of Fintry and Killearn. *Craigend*, 2m east of Strath-blane, was the birthplace of Sir Thomas Mitchell (1792–1855), Surveyor

General of New South Wales and explorer of the Australian interior. The road across the Fells (B822; sometimes known as the Crow Road) tops 1064ft and affords fine views. And it is an ancient and historic road too, for, if the story is to be believed, it would have been over this Crow Road that St. Mungo and his bulls brought the body of Fergus (see Rte 19, Glasgow Cathedral). From *Fintry*, at the north end of the Crow Road, B818, running between Campsie Fells and the Endrick Water, completes the circuit, towards the end passing close to the village of *Balfron*, said to owe its name (Village of Sorrow) to the bizarre tradition that in some dark past all its children were devoured by wolves.

A81 continues north west along Strath Blane, in *3m* reaching Drumgoyne (by the junction with A875) where *Glengoyne Distillery* (Tel: 0360-50254) dates from 1833 or earlier. Just north, on A81, *Moss* was the birthplace of George Buchanan (1506–82), humanist, reformer, historian and tutor to Mary, Queen of Scots, and, more significantly, to her son James VI. He is commemorated by a large obelisk in the straggling village of *Killearn*, just north east on A875.—*3m* A small crossroads at which a short diversion east to *Gartness*, where the Endrick Water flows through a ravine with a salmon leap, can be recommended.—*6m* A81 crosses the Kelty Water, then in another *1m* the Forth, beyond which it skirts the east fringe of Queen Elizabeth Forest Park to reach (*1m*) a road junction just short of Aberfoyle. Here a short easterly diversion should be considered by anyone with a feel for ancient monastic houses, touched by history and beautifully set.

TO INCHMAHOME PRIORY. 3m. Ruined **Inchmahome Priory** (AM. Tel: 031-244-3101) stands on an island in Lake of Menteith. The name means Isle of St. Colmoc or Macholmoc. Also sometimes called the Isle of Rest, it is the largest of the islands in the lake. The priory was founded for Austin Canons in c 1238 by Walter Comyn, Earl of Menteith. In 1362 David II was married here to his second wife, Margaret, and in 1547, after their defeat at Pinkie, the Scots here hid Mary, Queen of Scots, then aged five. She stayed until July 1548 when she was stealthily moved to Dumbarton, whence she sailed for France. After the Reformation ownership passed to the Earl of Mar.

Of the original 13C church, in which David II was married, there still remain a part of the choir, the tower arch and two arches of the nave. The deeply recessed mouldings of the west entrance are particularly noteworthy. In the chancel is the tomb of Sir John Drummond (died 1390), and in the chapter house, partly rebuilt in the 17C, are those of Walter Stewart, Earl of Menteith, and his wife (died 1295 and 1286), presumably both placed here within about 50 years of the priory's founding. As to the spot known as Queen Mary's Bower, romantics will readily enough accept that this was the favoured playground of the little queen; others, that this was simply where the monks grew their vegetables.—The ruined castle on Inch Talla was long (1227–1694) a principal residence of the earls of Menteith.

The pleasant, overgrown and sometimes overcrowded village of **Aberfoyle** (*Inf.*), with macabre mort-safes flanking the entrance to the ruined church, rightly regards itself as the gateway to a district which—embracing The Trossachs as also lochs Ard, Chon, Venacher, Achray, Katrine and Arklet—has achieved fame partly because of its varied scenery, partly because it was the territory of the early 18C 'Robin Hood' Rob Roy MacGregor, and partly because it provides the romantic setting for Sir Walter Scott's 'Rob Roy' and 'The Lady of the Lake'. Those

familiar with Scott's works will readily recognise the many associations; others will enjoy the mountain, woodland, rock and loch scenery,
most of which is part of *Queen Elizabeth Forest Park*. Covering 67
square miles of one of the most scenic tracts in central Scotland, and
with many recreational facilities, trails and picnic areas, the forest—in
fact three, for it divides into Buchanan, Loch Ard and Achray—is the
essence of this district and the wise visitor will first make for the admirable Forestry Commission visitor centre *David Marshall Lodge*, 1m
north of Aberfoyle (Tel: 08772-258). Built by the Carnegie Trust, of
which David Marshall was chairman, the Lodge not only provides a
wide range of information but includes also a large picnic area, trails
and a viewpoint commanding much of the valley of the upper Forth.

ABERFOYLE TO INVERSNAID (LOCH LOMOND). Before continuing north
along A821, it is worth considering, on the grounds of both scenery and
interest, a longish diversion along B829 to Inversnaid on Loch Lomond.
No circuit is possible (other than the minor road from Kinlochard
through Duchray and the heart of Loch Ard Forest), and the distance to
Inversnaid and back is some 30 slow miles. There are Forestry Commission picnic sites and waymarked walks at Balleich, just outside Aberfoyle, at Renagour and Kinlochard on Loch Ard, and at each end of Loch
Chon.

B829 runs along the north shore of wooded *Loch Ard* with, on an islet
off the south shore, the foundations of a castle owned by Murdoch, 2nd
Duke of Albany, beheaded in 1425. *Loch Chon*, reached 2m after Kinlochard, though also wooded, is rockier and wilder than Loch Ard. *Stronachlachar*, 2m beyond Loch Chon, is the pier at the west end of Loch
Katrine (see below). Rob Roy was born at Glengyle, 2m north west of
here (no cars), and his wife, Helen, is popularly supposed to have been
born in Glen Arklet, now largely filled by *Loch Arklet*, doubled in size
since becoming a reservoir and now hugged by the unclassified extension of B829. Near the descent to the narrow northern finger of Loch
Lomond a farm, still known as 'The Garrison', incorporates as a sheep-
fold the remains of a fort, built in 1713 (and once commanded by Wolfe,
of Quebec fame) to overawe the unruly MacGregors. From *Inversnaid*,
on Loch Lomond opposite the power station of Inveruglas, a lochside
path wanders north (1m) to Rob Roy's Cave, rock crevices in which
Bruce is said to have hidden in 1306. This path continues to the head of
the loch and joins A82 (Rte 20) in Glen Falloch, while another path leads
south from Inversnaid to (7½m) Rowardennan, there meeting Loch
Lomond's east shore road from Balmaha (see also Rte 20).

Leaving Aberfoyle, and 1½m north of David Marshall Lodge, A821
arrives at the entrance to *Achray Forest Drive* (FC. Tel: 08772-383), a
glorious 7m-long forest and mountain drive touching four lochs. A
route map indicates parking and picnic areas, forest trails and a children's play area.

5m In a romantic setting of rocks and hummocks luxuriantly covered
with oak, birch, hazel, rowan and heather, **The Trossachs** ('the Bristly
Country') is, properly, simply the short gorge linking lochs Achray and
Katrine. The 'old pass', the one known to Sir Walter Scott, diverges as a
footpath to the north of the present road at the T junction, and in Scott's
time there was no exit 'excepting by a sort of ladder composed by the
branches and roots of trees'. Along the gorge, a road (no cars) diverges
south beside the Achray Water to arrive at the sluices of the Strathclyde
Water Department, on the far side of which rises *Bealach nam Bo* (the
'pass of the cattle'), through which the MacGregors drove their cattle
plundered from the Lowlands.

Loch Katrine, 9m long and 1m broad at its widest, derives its name, according to Scott, from the 'caterans' (freebooters) who once frequented its shores. Since as long ago as 1859 it has been one of the chief sources of water for Glasgow, a function which involved the raising of the water level by 17ft.

The west end of the Trossachs road reaches the loch at a huge car and coach park, from which however little can be seen of the water. So the best course is to enjoy a cruise to Stronachlachar on the steamer 'Sir Walter Scott' which, built in Dumbarton in 1900, dismantled, and then reassembled on the loch, survives as a much loved and much used piece of vintage nostalgia (Tel: 041-336-5333). An alternative is to follow the road on the north bank (no cars) for 1m to the *Silver Strand*, with a view described in 'The Lady of the Lake', the lady being the fair Ellen Douglas after whom the island here, Ellen's Isle, is named. Less romantically, this island was used as the cattle-pen and larder of the MacGregors who here hid their rustled herds.

A821, now heading east beside Loch Venacher towards Callander, has various Scott associations ('Rob Roy', 'The Lady of the Lake', and the ballad 'Glenfinlas, or Lord Ronald's Coronach'). This last was set in *Glen Finglas* which ascends north from Brig o' Turk at the west end of the loch. This glen was visited in 1853 by the painters Ruskin and Millais, the visit recalled by a celebrated portrait of the former. About 1m up the glen the public road ends at the reservoir dam (1965), but a path continues along the east side of the water.

22   Glasgow to Stirling via Kilsyth

A803 to Kirkintilloch. B8023 and B802 to Kilsyth. A803 and M80 to Stirling.—After breaking clear of Glasgow and Kirkintilloch, and as far as Banknock (Bonnybridge), the road runs below the Kilsyth Hills (up to 1870ft) on the north and, to the south, the partly bare and partly wooded ridge which carries the Antonine Wall.

SOME HOTELS. **Bonnybridge**. *Norwood House*, Larbert Road, FK14 1NX. Tel: 0324-812929. See also Rte 9, **Falkirk**.

Total distance 24m.—*8m* **Kirkintilloch**.—*3m* **Kilsyth**.—*4m* **Banknock**.—*9m* **Stirling**.

Glasgow (see Rte 19) is left by way of the cathedral, followed by Castle Street and Springburn Road.—*8m* **Kirkintilloch** in part stands on the site of a Roman fort, though nothing can now be seen. However *Barony Chambers Museum* (Tel: 041-775-1185), at the Cross, tells the more modern local story of weaving, mining, iron founding and other industrial activities. Beyond Kirkintilloch A803 provides the fast onward road, but B8023, followed by this Route, touches the Antonine Wall and the now quiet Forth-Clyde canal.—*2m* (from the junction of A803 and B8023), *Bar Hill*, with a fort, rampart and ditch, rises immediately to the south. The hill marks the south end of the best surviving continuous stretch of the wall, the north end being at Castlecary (see below).—Now running with the Forth-Clyde canal, B8023 in *1m* joins B802, immediately south east of the junction being the *Croy Hill* Antonine site with traces of a fort, a ditch and two beacon platforms.

It was around the loch to the east of **Kilsyth**, just north of Croy Hill, that in 1645 Montrose defeated the Covenanters, losing only ten of his own men but killing some 6000 of the enemy. *Colzium Country House and Park* (Tel: 0236-735077), 1m east on A803, is a 19C residence, now serving as a local museum with material about the battle, while more of Kilsyth's story is illustrated at the *Library Heritage Museum* (Tel: 0236-

823147).—*4m* **Banknock**, where A803 crosses A80 at the start of M80. *Castlecary*, just south of this point and beyond the canal, is another site of an Antonine Wall fort, but the site is crossed by the railway and little is now convincingly visible above ground. B816, followed east from here, reaches Bonnybridge and the Antonine sites of Seabegs Wood and Rough Castle, for both of which see Rte 9. **Cumbernauld**, 2m farther south by A80, although today a satellite spread, has its name in history through the signing in 1640 of the Bond of Cumbernauld by which Montrose, protesting against 'the particular and direct practising of a few', signalled his first move in his quarrel with the ambitious Argyll and the extremist Covenanters. *Palacerigg Country Park* (Tel: 0236-720047), 2m south east of the town and once hilltop farmland, now offers a visitor centre, rare breeds and a children's farmyard.

From Banknock M80 heads first east and then north, in *3m* passing *Dunipace*, reputedly a boyhood home of Wallace, and then (*3m*) reaching Junction 9 where the motorway should be left for (*1m*) the *Bannockburn Heritage Centre* and (*2m*) **Stirling**, for both of which see Rte 23.

23   Stirling and Environs

With a name prominent in the martial and political annals of Scotland, the royal burgh of Stirling (37,000 inhab.) stands proud and conspicuous on rising ground above the river Forth, with its famous castle higher still on a precipitous volcanic plug (250ft).

Tourist Information. Dumbarton Road. Tel: 0786-75019.

SOME HOTELS. *Park Lodge*, 32 Park Terrace, FK8 2JS. Tel: 0786-74862. *Granada Lodge*, Pirnhill Roundabout, FK7 8EU. Tel: 0786-813614.—At **Bridge of Allan**. *Royal*, 55 Henderson Street, FK9 4HG. Tel: 0786-832284.—At **Bannockburn Heritage Centre**, *King Robert*, FK7 OLJ. Tel: 0786-811666.

History. Stirling's history is substantially that of its castle. The early inhabitants may have been ancient Britons (Welsh) for the name appears to be a corruption from the Welsh for 'Place of Striving'. Another ancient name, probably poetical, was 'Snowdoun'. The Romans may have occupied the rock, and legend credits King Arthur with having later taken it from the Saxons, but it is definite that Alexander I died in the castle in 1124 and William the Lion in 1214. Stirling surrendered to the English in 1296 but was retaken the next year by Wallace after winning the Battle of Stirling Bridge and then became the last place in Scotland to hold out against Edward I. He laid furious siege to the castle in 1304, stripping lead from church roofs as far away as Perth and St. Andrews with which to feed his catapults bombarding from nearby Gowan Hill. When eventually the garrison capitulated, they numbered only 150 men. Ten years later the Scots under Edward Bruce besieged the castle and made a bargain with the governor, Sir Phillip Mowbray, whereby it would be yielded if not relieved by mid-summer 1314. Edward II marched to raise the siege, only to be routed at Bannockburn. The castle then surrendered and was dismantled in accordance with Bruce's normal policy. Under the Stuarts Stirling became a favoured royal residence. James III was born here in 1451. In 1488, after being defeated by rebel lords at Sauchieburn to the south, he was treacherously murdered and then buried at Cambuskenneth Abbey. After Flodden in 1513 James V was brought to Stirling for safety; later he spent much time here, making a practice of moving in disguise among his subjects, the better to understand them. His daughter, Mary, Queen of Scots, was crowned here at the age of nine months and stayed here until she left for France. Her son, James VI, also spent his childhood at Stirling, with George Buchanan as his tutor. In 1651 the castle was taken by General Monk, and in 1746 it was unsuccessfully besieged by the Young Pretender.—The office of the Keeper of Stirling Castle, hereditary in the Erskine family from 1370 (with one short break), was forfeited by the Earl of

Mar in 1715 after the battle of Sheriffmuir, but was restored to the Earl of Mar and Kellie in 1923.

Stirling Festival Fortnight of Music, Drama and the Arts, with exhibits and performances of international standard, is held annually in August.

Stirling Town.

The town centre may be taken as the *Old Burgh Building*, bearing a steeple and a figure of Wallace.

TOWARDS TOWN WALLS AND MUSEUM. From Old Burgh Building, Corn Exchange Road runs south west with, immediately on the right, the *Municipal Buildings* in which the town's history is told in stained glass. Just beyond there is a picturesque length of medieval town wall as Corn Exchange Road merges with Albert Place (a section of Dumbarton Road) with, on the left, another length of wall and, some 300 yards farther west, the **Smith Art Gallery and Museum** (Tel: 0786-71917), an arts focus offering a variety of exhibitions and events and also with permanent collections of fine art (the emphasis being on Scottish artists), archaeology and natural and local history. A short way beyond are King's Gardens with the mound known as the *King's Knot*, the pattern of a probably 17C knot garden, best appreciated from above from the castle.

NORTHERN STIRLING. OLD BRIDGE. In the north of the town, about $\frac{3}{4}$m from Old Burgh Building and reached by Barnton and continuation streets, the Forth is crossed by three bridges: the railway bridge in the south; the main A9 road bridge in the centre, carrying Rtes 25A and 25B to Perth; and then the *Old Bridge*. This last, built in c 1400, still a footbridge and used it is said by every Scottish sovereign between Robert III and Charles II, was long of key strategic importance as the most southerly crossing of the river. But the Stirling Bridge which gave its name to the battle won by Wallace in September 1297 would have been a wooden affair. Wallace was encamped around Abbey Craig, the rock now crowned with his monument. Refusing to accept terms, he waited until the bulk of the English army had foolishly crossed the bridge and then fell on them, killing most and driving the survivors into the river to drown.

TOWARDS THE CASTLE. Spittal Street climbs away north west from Old Burgh Building towards the castle, soon merging into St. John Street. Here No. 23 (restored), bearing a pair of scissors in relief, was a hospice founded 'for the support of the puir be Robert Spittal taillyour to King James the 4 anno 1530'. This Robert Spittal was clearly both a prosperous and charitable tailor and a man of varied talent for he also built the bridge over the Teith at Doune. Farther up, set back on the left, is the attractive **Cowane's Hospital** or **Guildhall** (Tel: 0786-62373), built between 1634–49 by John Cowane 'for the entertainment of decayed breithers', or, in other words, unsuccessful members of the Guild of Merchants. The outside of the building bears appropriately pious inscriptions, while inside (much altered in 1852) hang portraits of deans of the guild.

Just above is the **Church of the Holy Rude**, in which in 1544 Mary of Guise was appointed regent and in which also, in 1567, her grandson, then one year old, was crowned James VI, John Knox preaching the sermon. This is a fine Gothic edifice, built up a slope and thus with a choir noticeably higher than the nave. At the west end there is a plain, square, battlemented tower (90ft), still visibly bearing marks inflicted by Monk's siege guns in 1651. Inside, the nave of five bays with massive rounded piers was begun in c 1415, from which period survive an oak roof and vaulted arches, while the choir, in which the infant James VI

STIRLING

0 yards 400
0 metres 400

was crowned, dates from a century later (1520–23) and is notable for its high-pitched ceiling. In the vaulted north chapel there is a font which once served as a piscina in Cambuskenneth Abbey.

Alongside the church, and looking down Broad Street, sits the rather forlorn ruin known as **Mar's Wark**, all that survives of a palace started by the Earl of Mar in 1570–72 but never really completed. The fast eroding heraldry, sculpture and rhyming inscriptions, as also, above the entrance, the royal arms flanked by those of Mar and his countess, combine as a reminder of Renaissance taste and of the wealth to indulge it, while interest is added by reflecting that much of the stone was looted from Cambuskenneth. James VI and his queen lived here for a while, and the building remained a fine residence of the earls of Mar until 1715 when the misguided 6th Earl, leader of the '15, had to flee the country. Ironically the place was largely destroyed by Jacobite forces during the '45.

Opposite, and in some contrast, stands *Argyll's Lodging*, a handsome and complete example of a 17C town house, built in 1632 by Sir William Alexander of Menstrie (later Earl of Stirling). He soon died insolvent and his house passed (1655) to the Argyll family who enlarged it in 1674. In 1799 the Lodging served as a military hospital and in 1964 it became a youth hostel.

Beyond, the road reaches the **Castle Esplanade**, with a modern statue of Bruce in the act of sheathing his sword after Bannockburn and also a *Visitor Centre* (NTS. Tel: 0786-62517), providing an audio-visual introduction to the castle. From here a scenic walk rounds the castle, while another path, from the farther side of the Esplanade, descends in steps into the dip between the castle and the church of the Holy Rude. Once a tilting ground, with the lady onlookers arrayed along the western ridge, this is now part public garden and part cemetery, the latter a sombre and even eerie place with gaunt tombs inviting graffiti, a solid Covenanter memorial pyramid, and a desolate representation of the Wigtown Martyrs who languish in Victorian bathos under a glass dome.

The return to the lower town may be made down Broad, Bow and Baker streets, in the first of which the *Cross*, flanked by cannon, marks the spot where in 1571 Archbishop John Hamilton (see also Rte 20, Dumbarton) was tried and hanged on the same day; as a member of Mary's faction he was automatically judged guilty of complicity in the murder of Darnley. The adjacent Tolbooth of 1701 was the design of Sir William Bruce.

**Stirling Castle.

Stirling Castle (AM. Tel: 031-244-3101), with most of the principal buildings dating from the 15C and 16C, is a truly magnificent example of military and domestic architecture on a royal scale. The audio-visual presentation in the NTS Visitor Centre on the Esplanade provides an admirable introduction.

The outworks of the first moat date from the time of Queen Anne, and *Queen Anne's Garden* lies to the left. The drum-towers of the gatehouse were erected by James IV who also built the square *Princes' Tower* (left) in which James VI was educated by George Buchanan.

The **Lower Square** has on its left the Palace and, ahead, the Great Hall, both also forming sides of the Upper Square. To the right in the Lower Square, near the castle well, are some vaults that served as the palace kitchens, and farther on is the vaulted entrance (perhaps 14C) to the Nether Baillie.

Around **Upper Square** are grouped the Palace, the Great Hall, the Chapel Royal and the King's Old Buildings.

The *Palace* (c 1540) is notable for its curious pillars and emblematic figures, among these being types of Scottish soldiers of the 16C and grotesque representations of a king, a queen, a chamberlain, a cook, lust, Venus and others. The apartments surround the 'Lion's Den', traditionally the place where the royal beasts were caged (it is known that James III and IV both kept lions).—The *Great Hall* was built for James IV in about 1500.

The *Chapel Royal*, begun in 1501 by James IV as a collegiate church, was rebuilt in 1594 by James VI, who had been baptised in it. Today the line of the original chapel (in which Mary, Queen of Scots, was crowned at the age of nine months) can be traced by differently shaded stones outside, while James VI's chapel, with 17C frescoes, now serves as a Memorial Hall for the regiment, the Argyll and Sutherland Highlanders.

The *King's Old Buildings* (so called because the present buildings are probably on the site of an older palace) bear a tablet in memory of Sir William Oliphant, the heroic commander who in 1304 held out so long when besieged by Edward I. Here the *Museum of the Argyll and Sutherland Highlanders* (Tel: 0786-75165) includes a notable collection of medals.

A passage from the north west corner of Upper Square admits to the *Douglas Garden* in a room near which the 8th Earl of Douglas, a distrusted nobleman who had been invited to confer, was in 1452 stabbed by James II and then thrown out of the window (just above the end of the passage). A skeleton found in the garden in 1797 may have been his.

Beyond, at the north west corner of the ramparts, *Queen Victoria's Look-Out* has a balustrade bearing the initials of royal visitors, while a small round hole in the wall is said to have been made especially for the child Mary, Queen of Scots. The view embraces Campsie Fells to the south west; then, to the north west, Ben Lomond and Ben Vorlich above Loch Lomond, Ben Venue above The Trossachs and Loch Katrine, and Ben Ledi between Loch Venacher and the Pass of Leny. To the north east are the Ochil Hills while, closer, the twisting Links of Forth, the Wallace Monument and Cambuskenneth Abbey can be seen. Just below the castle is *Gowan Hill*, whence Edward I bombarded Stirling in 1304 and on which in 1746 the Young Pretender planted his batteries so as 'to oblige the citizens and spare the town', only to have them speedily silenced by the castle's guns. Near the hill's north angle is the Heading Hill, the place of execution.

Below the rampart, farther on, an ancient sally-port can be seen, very probably the exit used by James V when he went out in disguise to mix with the people.

Environs of Stirling.

Of the places mentioned below, Bridge of Allan, the Wallace Monument and Cambuskenneth Abbey are all north and east of Stirling and conveniently visited as a group. The Bannockburn Heritage Centre, however, is 2m south.

Bridge of Allan, 2m north, now a quiet and delightfully situated residential small town, was in Victorian times a popular and elegant spa, famed for its saline waters as also, since Burns wrote his 'Banks of Allan Water', for its river. To the south east of the town are the modern buildings of the *University of Stirling* (1967), blending surprisingly well into the parkland of the Airthrey estate, the castle of which (Robert Adam, with considerable 19C addition) is now a university department. The public are admitted to the grounds, in which a stone beside a road interestingly records 'Pathfoot village was built around this standing stone. Beside it was held an annual tryst (fair) in the 18C'. The university's MacRobert Arts Centre provides theatre, opera, ballet, films, concerts and exhibitions (Box Office. 0786-61081).

Immediately south of the university the ugly and over-conspicuous **Wallace Monument** (Tel: 0786-72140) perches high on the rock of Abbey Craig, around which Wallace camped in 1297, watching for the English to attempt the crossing of the Forth. Built in 1870 and bearing a statue of Wallace, the monument today houses an exhibition of armour, including Wallace's two-handed sword, while audio-visual displays tell the story of the district and its heroes.

The ruins of **Cambuskenneth Abbey** (AM. Tel: 031-244-3101) are enclosed within a crooked loop of the Forth, 1m south of the Wallace Monument (the only road approach) and the same distance east of Stirling (footbridge). The name, Field of Kenneth, reaches back to Kenneth Macalpine, traditionally supposed to have defeated the Picts here in the 9C, but three centuries would pass before this abbey was founded, in c 1140 by David I for Austin Canons. Because of its closeness to Stirling Castle the abbey was from time to time used for meetings of the Scottish parliament and other bodies, a notable occasion being Bruce's parliament of 1326. In 1570, by now a victim of the Reformation, the abbey was given to the Earl of Mar who reduced it to ruins in order to use the stone in the building of his palace in Stirling (Mar's Wark).

James III, murdered after Sauchieburn (see below), and his queen, Margaret of Denmark, were buried here, and two coffins, containing skeletons believed to be theirs, were found during excavations in 1864; on the instructions of Queen Victoria these were reburied beneath a memorial at the site of the high altar. The ruins include a 14C detached tower, the west doorway of the church, and another building thought to be part of the infirmary, later probably converted to dovecot.

The *Bannockburn Heritage Centre (NTS. Site always open. Visitor Centre, Tel: 0786-812664) is off M80/M9 at Junction 9, 2m south of central Stirling, from where the approach is by A872. The exact site of the battle, fought in June 1314, is disputed, but most visitors will readily enough accept that it was around here, and that the Borestone rotunda could well have been Bruce's command post.

Stirling Castle, held by the English, was being besieged by Bruce's brother, Edward. Impatient, Edward made a bargain with the English governor, Sir Philip Mowbray, that if by midsummer (1314) no English army had come within three miles of Stirling, then the castle would surrender. The English army, hastening to raise the siege, was led by Edward II in person and was greatly superior in numbers. But Robert Bruce, with a force almost entirely composed of pikemen, strengthened his carefully chosen position by strewing his front with caltrops (spiked iron balls) and planting sharp stakes in concealed pits, so as to break the attack of the English cavalry. Although thus defeated, the English stood their ground until the Scottish camp-followers, like a fresh army, suddenly appeared from over Gillies Hill (1m north west of today's memorial site). The subsequent English rout was complete and their losses immense. Stirling surrendered, Edward II fled to Dunbar, and the independence of Scotland was assured.

The memorial proper takes the form of a heroic, bronze equestrian statue of Bruce (Pilkington Jackson, 1964), while the rotunda alongside encloses the Borestone site, traditionally Bruce's command post. Fragments of the borestone, in which Bruce's standard is said to have been planted, can be seen in the visitor centre where an audio-visual presentation explains the events leading up to the battle and the battle itself. Facilities here include tourist information, food and a shop.

Bannockburn House, just east of Junction 9, served as the Young Pretender's headquarters in January 1746, and it was here that he first met Clementina Walkinshaw, later his mistress and mother of his natural daughter.—The name Sauchie appears frequently in the area a mile or so to the west of the motorway, a reminder of the battle of *Sauchieburn* in 1488. Here James III was defeated by the rebel lords, with his son more or less captive in their midst. As the king fled he was thrown from his horse and carried unconscious to a nearby mill, there being stabbed to death by a man disguised as a priest bringing the Last Sacrament. He was buried at Cambuskenneth Abbey, and tradition holds that his son, James IV, overcome with remorse, for the rest of his life wore an iron belt around his body.

For Stirling to **Edinburgh** via Falkirk and Linlithgow, see Rte 9; to **Edinburgh** via Culross and Dunfermline, see Rte 31; To **Glasgow**, see Rte 22; to **Pitlochry**, see Rte 24; to **Perth**, see Rte 25.

24   Stirling to Pitlochry via Killin and Aberfeldy

A84 to Lochearnhead. A85 and A827 to Killin, Aberfeldy (alternative through Glen Lyon) and Ballinluig. A9 to Pitlochry.—After Callander the scenery quickly becomes more grandly Highland, reaching its best along Loch Tay or the suggested alternative of Glen Lyon.

SOME HOTELS. **Doune**. *Woodside*, FK16 6AB. Tel: 0786-841237. **Callander**. *Roman Camp*, Main Street, FK17 8BG. Tel: 0877-30003. *Bridgend House*, Bridgend, FK17 8AH. Tel: 0877-30130. *Lubnaig*, Leny Feus, FK17 8AS. Tel: 0877-30376. **Lochearnhead**. *Mansewood Country House*, FK19 8NS. Tel: 05673-213. **Killin**. *Morenish Lodge*, FK21 8TX. Tel: 05672-258. **Kenmore**. *Kenmore*, PH15 2NU. Tel: 08873-205. **Aberfeldy**. *Guinach House*, Urlar Road, PH15 2ET. Tel: 0887-20251. *Crown*, Bank Street, PH15 2BB. Tel: 0887-20448.

Total distance 73 or 81m.—*8m* **Doune**.—*7m* **Callander**.—*16m* **Lochearnhead**.—*7m* **Killin**.—*22* or *30m* **Aberfeldy**.—*13m* **Pitlochry**.

Leaving **Stirling** (see Rte 23) by its north west corner, A84 at once crosses the motorway and in *5m* reaches **Scotland's (Blair Drummond) Safari Park** (Tel: 0786-841456). The wild animal reserves are toured either in the visitor's own car or by safari bus, and other attractions include a boat around Chimp Island, aquatic mammal shows, a hippo pool, pets' corner and an adventure playground.—The nearby church of *Kincardine-in-Menteith*, by the junction of A84 and A873, will be of interest to Drummonds for the several 17 to 18C family monuments, including a notable brass commemorating George Drummond who died in 1717.

3m **Doune**, once noted as a drover centre and for its sheep and cattle fairs, and during the 17C for the manufacture of pistols (crossed pistols still feature in the town's arms), is today visited for its castle, to the south, and its motor museum, to the north. The bridge here over the rapid river Teith was built in 1535 by Robert Spittal, formerly tailor to James IV (see also Stirling, Rte 23), reputedly to spite the ferryman who had refused him passage because he had no money on him.

*Doune Castle (AM. Tel: 031-244-3101). One of the largest, best-preserved and best-restored examples of late 14C military-domestic architecture in Scotland, and (to quote the authority, W.D. Simpson) 'the highest achievement of perfected castellar construction', Doune is outstanding, if not unique for the way in which it helps the visitor to assemble a picture of medieval life in such a place.

History. At the time of the castle's building the lands known as Albany comprised roughly modern Perthshire, Stirling and Fife. Strategically the two routes from Edinburgh to Inverlochy, and from Glasgow to Perth and Inverness, intersected at Doune and this, coupled with the feud between Albany and the Lord of the Isles over the claim to the earldom of Ross, probably prompted the building of this castle by Robert, Duke of Albany (died 1419) and his son, Murdoch. But when Murdoch was executed in 1425 Doune was forfeited to the Crown, later to be settled by James IV on his queen Margaret. Margaret's third husband was Lord Methven, a descendant of the dukes of Albany, and the office of constable of the castle became hereditary in his family, the earls of Moray, who today enjoy the title of Lord Doune. In 1745–46 the castle was held for the Young Pretender by

MacGregor of Glengyle and into it were herded the prisoners taken at Falkirk. By the end of the 18C Doune was a roofless ruin, so remaining until 1883 when the 14th Earl began a careful restoration.

Occupying a well-chosen triangular site, protected on two sides by the Teith and Ardoch and on the third by a deep moat, the castle encloses a large court with a square gatehouse tower, 95ft high, at the north east corner and another tower on the west side. The main block is of four storeys and an attic, while the round tower which flanks the portal rises to five storeys.

For the modern visitor the essence of the castle is the Gatehouse complex which, complete with its own water supply, formed a self-contained defensive residence. Here is still the entrance, from which a vaulted passage slopes up towards the court. Along this passage can be seen the slots for the portcullis, the great iron gate, and vaulted rooms on either side, the northernmost on the right-hand side being the prison. Standing in the court and facing north, the Retainers' Hall is to the left and the Lord's Hall to the right, both on the first floor, the former raised above vaulted cellars with service stairs. The magnificent Lord's Hall has been somewhat modernised, but some original features can still be noted; for instance, the fireplace in two compartments, and the passage through the thickness of the south wall leading to the steward's chamber, with a window opening on to the hall so that he could keep an eye on things.

A stair climbs to the Lord's Private Room in the corner round tower, complete with privy and, in the floor, a hatch through which water was drawn up direct from the well below. Another stair out of the Lord's Hall ascends to the hall above, this being the Solar or general living room of the lord and his household; it is provided with an oratory, complete with octagonal piscina and sacrament house. The Retainers' Hall is covered by an open timber roof which, though modern, follows the pattern of the original. The octagonal hearth is in the middle of the floor, and on the floor too can be seen the bases of the screens which defined the enclosure in which food brought up from the kitchens was cut up. These Kitchens, with an immense fireplace, are on the east of the court and linked to the Retainers' Hall by a service room, provided with a chute for rubbish.

Doune Motor Museum (Tel: 0786-841203) houses Lord Moray's collection of vintage and later thoroughbred cars, these including examples of, amongst many others, Hispano Suiza, Bentley, Jaguar, Lagonda, BMW and Aston Martin, as also the world's second oldest Rolls Royce. Nearly all the cars are maintained in running order and some even compete in Doune Hill Climb events held in April, June and September.

7m **Callander** (2000 inhab. *Inf.*), at the very foot of the Highlands and under 9m from the Trossachs (see Rte 21; reached by A821 along the shore of Loch Venacher), can at times be a somewhat over-popular resort. Nevertheless this beautifully sited place, with its several hotels, restaurants and other amenities, is an excellent touring base, while also, and especially for MacGregors, there is the *Rob Roy and Trossachs Centre* (Tel: 0786-75019), in the former St. Kessog's Church in Ancaster Square, with exhibits and a video telling about Rob Roy and this district which he made his own. In the east part of the town a small road leads north to a car park beyond which a path continues to the *Bracklinn Falls*; and, roughly opposite, a path off the south side of the main road reaches a strange, long, curving embankment, called Roman Walk and once thought to be the Roman camp known to have been established here. However the site of the camp, built by Agricola in the 1C, has now been officially located as having been near the farm of Bochastle, between the rivers 1m west of the town centre.

The **Pass of Leny**, 2m west of Callander, is a fitting gateway to the Highlands; a narrow glen into which are squeezed the road, the old railway and the river tumbling down as rapids and falls. Emerging, the road skirts the narrow length of Loch Lubnaig as the scenery becomes increasingly broken and wooded with bare moor and mountain looming above.—At (6m) **Strathyre**, in the heart of Strathyre Forest, a Forestry Commission *Information Centre* (Tel: 08772-383) and picnic area mark the starting points of trails on both sides of the river Balvag, those on the west being exacting and giving access to Beinn an Sithein (1800ft). It was at the farm of *Ardvoch*, just across the river, that the Gaelic poet and evangelist Dugald Buchanan (1716–88) was born.

The road continues through MacGregor country, with a *Clan Gregor Centre and Rob Roy Tryst* (Tel: 08774-216) at Kingshouse, and, 2m west of the main road, **Balquhidder**, where, beside the intermixed ruins of two ancient churches, are what are said to be the tombs of Rob Roy and close members of his family. It seems certain that he, his wife and his two sons lie somewhere here, so one might as well accept that the tombs are indeed those under the three unidentified stones within an iron railing, even though these stones would seem to date from long before Rob Roy's time. The central stone, claimed to be Rob Roy's, is a rough slab of slate, carved with a cross, with a sword on one side and a kilted figure with a dog or other animal at his feet on the other. A second stone, bearing the MacGregor arms (a pine torn up by the roots and crossed by a sword piercing a crown, an allusion to the claim to be of royal blood made by the chiefs of the clan) is supposed to commemorate Rob Roy's sons, Coll (died 1735) and Robert or Robin Oig (executed 1754). The last stone may be that of Rob Roy's widow Helen.

The adjacent ruins are those of two churches, the first dating back to the 13C or earlier, the other a church of 1631 which was built partly on top of the first. It was in the earlier church that in 1589 the Clan MacGregor gathered around the head of the king's forester and vowed to protect those who had cut it off (see Ardvorlich House under Lochearnhead below). Within the present 19C church can be seen the bell of the second church; a 17C chest, said to have belonged to Campbell of Glenorchy (died 1631); a Gaelic bible of c 1688; quaint long offerings ladles, dating from the 18C and still in use; and the St. Angus stone of the 8C together with an effigy of this shadowy local saint.

8m **Lochearnhead**, a popular centre for water sports and walking, marks the west extremity of *Loch Earn*, a lovely Highland loch overlooked by mountains rising to over 2000ft. Slicing seven miles eastwards to St. Fillans (see Rte 25B) the loch carries the main A85 along its north shore and a minor road beside the other. Along the latter *Ardvorlich House* (3m. No adm.) witnessed that grisly occasion of 1589 when the MacGregors, having murdered the king's forester in revenge for a real or supposed grievance, placed his severed head on a dish, with a crust between the teeth, and presented it to his sister. Nearby, beside the road, stands the tombstone of seven Macdonalds of Glen Coe, killed in a marauding attack on the house.

A85 (north) now steadily climbs wild and rocky Glen Ogle to reach the watershed in 4m at 948ft beside Lochan Larig Cheile, beyond which a steeper descent in rather over 1m makes the junction with A827, the road now followed. A85, heading west along Glen Dochart, in 10m meets A82 at Crianlarich on Rte 20.

2m **Killin** (600 inhab. *Inf.*) is approached beside the river Dochart, here tumbling as falls and rapids in its haste to swell Loch Tay, a short mile below the village. With a sharp bend A827 crosses the rapids by an old bridge at a point where the river is divided by two islets, the lower of which, *Inch Buie*, long served as the burial place of Clan MacNab, the most powerful family in this district until the MacNab emigration to Canada in 1833.

For all its small permanent population, Killin prospers as a year-round resort, in summer as popular with motorists and walkers as it can be busy with skiers in winter. Within the village *Killin Church*, dating from 1744 but on a very early Christian site, merits a visit for its seven-sided 9C font. The monument in front of the church is to the Rev. James Stewart, the first to translate the New Testament into Scottish Gaelic (1797). *Finlarig Castle*, ½m north, is reached by crossing the iron bridge over the Lochay opposite Queen's Court Hotel. A sombre and now dangerous ruin half-hidden on a tree-covered mound, this was once Clan Campbell's centre; the lair too of Black Duncan of Cowal, a notorious chief of that clan. The gruesome beheading pit, immediately adjacent and thought to be the only surviving example in Scotland, does not seem out of place in these gloomy surrounds.

Loch Tay (at a height of 335ft; 14m long and averaging ¾m in breadth; in places over 500ft deep) is grandly set below mountains and famous for its salmon as also archaeologically for its crannogs, some of which can be identified at low water, especially at the loch's east end near Kenmore. The loch's chief feeders are the Dochart and Lochay at the west end, while from its east issues the river Tay. Roads skirt both shores, that along the north being the main road and the shorter. The small south shore road keeps closer to the water and commands the finer views, especially across to Ben Lawers.

Between Killin and Aberfeldy, and keeping to the north of Loch Tay, there is a choice of two roads. The direct and fast road (22m) is A827 running beside and above the loch. The alternative (30m) is the more scenic and interesting, but slower, more northerly road through Glen Lyon, the wild setting for a brew of ancient settlement, early Christian legend, murderous clan feuding and, for good measure, modern hydroelectric engineering.

Killin to Aberfeldy beside Loch Tay.

Leaving Killin A827 crosses the Lochay and then bears east, in *4m* reaching the unclassified road which climbs to the *'Ben Lawers Visitor Centre* (just over 1m; see alternative road below) and then drops into Glen Lyon.—*8m* **Fearnan**, from where a road crosses (2m) into Glen Lyon. Now at loch level the road fringes the wood of *Drummond Hill*, with, just short of Kenmore, a Forestry Commission picnic site at the start of a network of walks.—*4m* **Kenmore** is a 'model' village at the outflow of the Tay, crossed here by a bridge of 1774. *Taymouth Castle* (no adm.), with its imposing turreted entrance in the village, is the early 19C successor of a mansion built in c 1573 by Colin Campbell of Glenorchy. In 1837 the Earl of Breadalbane reintroduced here from Sweden the capercailzie wood-grouse, which had become extinct in Scotland, and in 1940–46 the castle served as a hospital for Polish officers.

Climbing, and edging the south east flank of the Taymouth estate, with occasional views down to the baronial pile, the road in *2m* reaches *Croftmoraig*, with, near the south side of the road, a double stone circle and a cup-marked stone.—*4m* **Aberfeldy**, see below.

Killin to Aberfeldy via Glen Lyon.

The lochside road is followed for *4m*, at which point an unclassified road climbs up to (*1m*) the ***Ben Lawers Visitor Centre** (NTS. Tel: 05672-397). Ben Lawers (3984ft), declared a national nature reserve in 1975 and managed jointly by the National Trust for Scotland and Scottish Natural Heritage, combines fine scenery and views with much of outstanding natural history and geological interest. Geologically the mountain represents an overfold in which the oldest rocks, perhaps 600 million years old and then a deposit on the sea floor, are now those on the surface. Botanically the area is known for its alpine plants, while buzzard, kestrel, grouse, golden plover and curlew are among the birds that may be spotted from the nature trail (booklet). The Visitor Centre provides imaginative displays and an audio-visual presentation explaining the mountains's geology and natural history, advice on walks, ranger service, and leaflets and booklets as attractive as they are instructive.

The minor, unfenced road continues north across bare mountain to Lochan na Lairige, in scenery of dark grandeur, thence dropping to (*7m*) **Bridge of Balgie** in Glen Lyon. Here, although this Route turns east, it is well worth considering driving westward along the little road which, never straying far from the rock-strewn river, twists and switchbacks across open turf and moorland below broad-shouldered mountains to end at the foot of the great wall of Loch Lyon's dam. Here, and during the preceding mile or two, humps of turf or ribbles of stone, marked on the map as 'homesteads' or simply as tiny circles, represent what may once have been brochs or perhaps hut settlements.

St. Adamnan, 9th Abbot of Iona and best known for his 'Life of St. Columba', may well have spent his later years evangelising in this glen, living and building a meal-mill at what is now Milton Eonan (Mill of Adamnan) just south of the bridge of Balgie, while the church at nearby *Innerwick*, claiming to stand on the site of one founded by Adamnan, proudly guards the saint's handbell.

As the glen descends eastwards the scenery changes, the open moor giving way sometimes to defiles below hidden heights, sometimes to lengths and patches of woodland.—*6m* (from Bridge of Balgie) *Carnbane Castle*, now mere fragments high on a knoll above where the road kinks across a burn, recalls the bitter feud fought out in this glen between the Campbells of Glen Lyon, later to become notorious for the massacre in Glen Coe, and the MacGregors, the latter landless and thus little better than bandits. Here at Carnbane, and in easier days, the clan chief Gregor MacGregor had loved and married Marion Campbell. Now, in 1565 and on the run, he sought refuge here, only to be trapped by the Campbells and soon executed in the presence of his pregnant wife.

Just over *1m* farther the mansion called *Chesthill*, once the home of Campbell of Glen Lyon, appears on the left, opposite being perhaps the most charming combination of natural and man-made features to be found in the glen—a cascade dropping through the neat arch of a bridge which, Roman or not (for it is called *Roman Bridge*), is nevertheless perfection in this setting.—*2m MacGregor's Leap*, marked by a stand of larches, is the spot where Gregor MacGregor hurled himself across a river chasm in order to escape the Campbell hounds.

Almost immediately beyond, the tight and wooded glen opens abruptly before (*1m*) **Fortingall**, a place with a strange tale, for here, it has long been believed, was born Pontius Pilate, child of the union of a Roman envoy to the local chief (a Menzies forebear, it has been suggested) and of a woman of his tribe. And if the ancient yew still clinging to life in the churchyard is really, as claimed, 3000 years old, then it would have already known 1000 years by the date of Pilate's birth.

Older still, though, are the standing stones between the village and the river, tantalisingly mute evidence of even remoter people who once lived and held their rites in this valley.—*3m* **Coshieville** marks the junction with B846, originally one of Wade's military roads. Here *Comrie Castle*, a small ruined keep beyond the river, was an early stronghold of the Menzies, while *Garth Castle*, 1m north along B846 and across the Keltney Burn, was built by the Wolf of Badenoch. And a mile or so beyond Garth will be found *Glengoulandie Deer Park* (Tel: 08873-509), a scenic park showing red deer, highland cattle, rare breeds of sheep and much else of natural interest.

From Coshieville this Route continues east along B846 and in *2m*, near standing stones, passes below the hamlet of **Dull** in which an ancient one-armed cross, probably marking a limit of sanctuary, is all that survives of a distinguished monastic centre of learning. The place's origins are lost in a confusion of legend, but of several stories the most insistent goes back to St. Adamnan. On his deathbed higher up Glen Lyon he instructed that his body be carried down the glen to a point where a cord securing the body to the bier would snap. Here he was to be buried, a church was to be built and a teaching monastery was to be founded. All this duly happened at a place called Tulli. Be this as it may, this district is known as Appin of Dull (Appin meaning Abbey lands), and there can be no doubt that, from very early times, Dull was known as a seat of Culdee and, later, Catholic theology.

2m **Castle Menzies** (Tel: 0887-20982), now housing the Menzies clan museum, is a particularly fine example of a 16C Z-plan tower-house of the period marking the transition from fortification to residence. Weem Walk (1½m), starting from a FC car park close to the entrance to the castle, leads to a cave and well, both associated with St. Cuthbert (died 687).—*1m* **Aberfeldy** (see below).

Aberfeldy (1500 inhab. *Inf.*) stands on both sides of the Urlar Burn near where it meets the Tay, here crossed by **Wade's Bridge* of 1733–35, generally accepted as the most distinguished of the many he built, although the credit for the bridge's architectural elegance must of course go to its designer, William Adam. Optimistically Wade incorporated a plaque announcing that he laid the first stone on 23 April 1733 'and finished the work in the same year', whereas in fact he ran into problems—in his own words 'so much plague, vexation and disappointments that staggers my philosophy'—and it was not until 8 August 1735 that the bridge was formally opened. Beside the bridge a large cairn carrying a kilted figure (1887) commemorates Wade's raising of the Black Watch in 1739. The *Birks of Aberfeldy* (birk meaning silver birch), their immortality assured by Burns despite the suggestion that he really meant Abergeldie, line the Urlar Burn, about 1m up which are the *Falls of Moness*.

Twisting with the course of the Tay, A827 in *3m* reaches Grandtully Castle (pron. Grantly; no adm.), built in 1560 but since twice enlarged, ½m south west of which is 16C *St. Mary's Church*, with a contemporary wooden painted ceiling, lively with heraldry and all manner of symbolism.—*3m* The road crosses the Tay near standing stones and in another *3m* reaches *Logierait*, today no more than a village at the confluence of the Tay and Tummel but once the site of a court notorious for the despotic power wielded by the lords of Atholl. There was a prison here, too, from which Rob Roy escaped in 1717 and into which later the Young Pretender threw prisoners taken at Prestonpans.

A9 is met at *Ballinluig*, for which, as also for **Pitlochry** *4m* north, see Rte 27.

25   Stirling to Perth

There is a choice of three roads. A., via Auchterarder (33m), is the central and most direct. B., via Crieff (38m), the best scenically, also enables diversions to be made to the east end of Loch Earn or northward up the Sma' Glen. C., via Dollar (37m), represents a southerly loop. All three roads traverse generally pastoral country mixed with hills and woodland.

For **Stirling**, see Rte 23. For **Perth**, see Rte 26.

A.   Via Auchterarder

A9 (with bypasses) to Auchterarder. B8062 to Dunning. B934 to Forteviot. B9112 to Perth.

SOME HOTELS. **Dunblane**. *Cromlix House*, FK15 9JT. Tel: 0786-822125. *Stakis Hydro*, FK15 OHG. Tel: 0786-822551. **Auchterarder**. *Auchterarder House*, PH3 1DZ. Tel: 0764-63646. *Collearn House*, High Street, PH3 1DF. Tel: 0764-63553.

Total distance 33m.—*6m* **Dunblane**.—*5m* **Greenloaning**.—*9m* **Auchterarder**.—*13m* **Perth**.

Both M9 and A9, the latter passing the Wallace Monument and running through Bridge of Allan (see Rte 23), provide easy approaches to (*6m*) **Dunblane** (7000 inhab. *Inf.*), an ancient and incidental small town sprawled over hills and with some quaint narrow streets above the Allan Water, here crossed by a bridge in origin of 1409. The essence of the town, though, is its cathedral, standing within a gracious close of 17–19C houses.

*Dunblane Cathedral (AM. Tel: 031-244-3101) is a noble 13C Gothic edifice incorporating a part-12C Norman tower.

History. Dunblane was made a bishopric by David I who founded this cathedral in c 1150 on, it is believed, the site of a primitive church built in the 6C by St. Blane. But of David's work all that survives are the two lower storeys of the tower, and the existing church, including the tower's upper levels, must, apart from some alterations and additions of the 15C, be credited to Bishop Clement (1233–58). Neglected after the Reformation, the roof of the nave caved in during the late 16C, although the choir continued in use for 300 years as parish church. A thorough and admirable restoration of the nave was completed by Rowand Anderson in 1893, followed by that of the choir by Robert Lorimer in 1914.—Robert Leighton (1611–84) was bishop here from 1662 until his translation in 1670 to the archbishopric of Glasgow.

The West Front is the most noteworthy external feature, a good example of pure Early English comprising a deeply recessed portal surmounted by three tall lancets. Above, and seen only from the outside, is the so-called 'Ruskin Window', a pointed oval adorned with carved foliage, owing its name to the enthusiastic praise given to this West Front by John Ruskin.

Inside the cathedral the aisled Nave of eight bays has a fine clerestory with double arches towards the west and single towards the east. The stained glass and the roof are modern. At the west end are six carved stalls, known as the Bishop's Stalls because they were provided by Bishop Chisholm in 1486; and to the south is the entrance to 'Katie Ogie's Hole', a strange small vaulted chamber in the west wall, of unexplained name and unknown origin though more than likely to have been a hermit's cell. At the west end of the North Aisle is a stone of c 900 bearing a Celtic cross and allegorical carvings, while farther east lie effigies (1271) which may represent Malise, 5th Earl of Strathearn, and his countess. At the east end of the South Aisle, sometimes behind a curtain, will be found the effigy of Bishop Ochiltree who crowned James II in 1437.

In the Choir of six bays three slabs in the centre recall a mass murder of 1502, for they commemorate Margaret Drummond, mistress of James IV, and her two sisters, all poisoned at Drummond Castle by a group of nobles determined that the king should marry (as he did) Princess Margaret of England. An effigy on the north wall may be that of Bishop Clement, builder of the cathedral, or, some say, of Bishop Finlay Dermoch, responsible for the still surviving bridge over the Allan Water. The misericord stalls are attributed to Bishop Ochiltree and would thus be of the 15C, while the reredos and organ-case are by the Clow brothers working to Lorimer's design of 1914. The low-vaulted Lady Chapel, adjoining the choir on the N, serves as the war memorial (by Robert Lorimer; windows by Douglas Strachan).

In the close the 17C *Dean's House* (Tel: 0786-822217 or 824254) houses the small cathedral museum and library (enquire about Bishop Leighton's Library, in another 17C building opposite the Dean's House).

Sheriffmuir, 2½m east of Dunblane, was the setting of the battle of November 1715 which, although in itself indecisive, nevertheless marked the end of the '15 Jacobite rebellion. The moor is crossed by two unclassified roads, one running north east out of the south east outskirts of Dunblane, the other heading north out of Bridge of Allan, and the battle was fought within the angle of the junction of these roads. The forces of the Old Pretender, 12,000 strong, were led by the Earl of Mar; those of George I, 4000 strong, by the Duke of Argyll, whose object it was to prevent Mar from crossing the Forth to join his friends in the south. The right wing of each side was victorious, and the left of each routed, but it was Mar who judged it prudent to withdraw.

5m **Greenloaning**, where Rte 25B diverges north, soon passing Ardoch Roman Camp.—*7m* **Gleneagles**, a name often associated mainly with the famous golf hotel here, is in fact a southward-running wooded and moorland glen (whose name means 'churches' and, disappointingly perhaps, has nothing to do with eagles) through which A823 climbs across the Ochil Hills, from the watershed dropping down Glen Devon to meet Rte 25C at Yetts o' Muckhart.

2m **Auchterarder** (bypass) is a narrow, stretched kind of village which was spitefully burnt by the Earl of Mar after the fiasco on Sheriffmuir, and later, in 1834, figured in Scottish Church history as the scene of the first of the patronage disputes that culminated in 1843 in the Disruption and the founding of the Free Church of Scotland. The *Glenruthven Weaving Mill* (Tel: 0764-62079), in Abbey Road, boasts the only working steam textile engine in Scotland. Here, too, weaving is demonstrated while exhibits illustrate the history of steam and weaving and a shop sells local and other products. *Tullibardine Chapel*, 3m north west of Auchterarder by A823, was founded in 1446 and, being so complete and unaltered, is a notable survival of a rural collegiate chapel, the roof and heraldic detail being especially noteworthy. Formerly a mausoleum of the dukes of Atholl, the chapel is now that of the earls of Perth, and it may be noted that Tullibardine gives the courtesy title of marquis to the eldest sons of the dukes of Atholl, who were earls of Tullibardine before elevation to dukedom.

From Auchterarder A9 provides the fast approach to Perth, but this Route visits some places of minor interest along B8062, B934 and B9112 a mile or so to the south of the main road.

The church of Dunning with its fine 13C tower

5m **Dunning** where the church has a fine square tower of c 1210, not dissimilar to that at Muthill (Rte 25B). An outside stair beside the tower ascends past a blocked Norman archway, and at the top of the tower Norman arches with inset pillars are an unusual feature.—*3m Forteviot*, today a mere hamlet, bears no trace of its ancient importance as the capital of the Picts after the Roman departure; nor as the place in which Kenneth I, first king of the united Picts and Scots, died in 860; even less in support of the tradition that the mother of Malcolm Canmore was a daughter of a miller of Forteviot. At *Forgandenny*, 2m east by B935, the church shows some Norman fragments, has a belfry of c 1600 and an unusually elaborate font and bracket of 1744.—At Forteviot B934 crosses first the railway and then the river Earn, this Route then turning sharply east along B9112 to pass just south of the site of the battle of Dupplin of 1332. Here Edward Balliol and the 'disinherited barons' (i.e. the faction that had opposed Bruce and been disinherited by him) defeated the regent Mar, who was slain.—*5m* **Perth**, see Rte 26.

B.   Via Crieff

A9 to Greenloaning. A822 to Crieff. A85 to Perth.

SOME HOTELS. **Dunblane**. See Rte 25A. **Crieff**. *Crieff*, 45 East High Street, PH7 3HY. Tel: 0764-2632. *Hydro*, PH7 3LQ. Tel: 0764-2401. **Comrie**. *Royal*, Melville Square, PH6 2DN. Tel: 0764-70200. **St. Fillans**. *Four Seasons*, PH6 2NF. Tel: 076485-333. *Drummond Arms*, PH6 2NF. Tel: 076485-212. **Huntingtower**. *Huntingtower*, PH1 3JT. Tel: 0738-83771.

Total distance 38m.—*6m* **Dunblane.**—*5m* **Greenloaning.**—*10m*
Crieff.—*11m* **Methven.**—*6m* **Perth.**

For **Stirling** to (*11m*) **Greenloaning**, see Rte 25A.—*2m* **Braco** is a village
adjacent to **Ardoch Roman Camp**, today a complex of earthworks representing one of the largest Roman stations in Britain. Most active
during the 2C, it seems, however, probable that the station continued in
use as an outpost even after the completion of the Antonine Wall well to
the south. At the north end of Braco the road crosses the little river
Knaik, here, beside the modern bridge, being the overgrown arch of an
ancient predecessor, in origin surely Roman. The main Roman complex
is immediately east of the road just beyond the bridge. The central area
(420ft × 375ft) is on the customary Roman rectangular plan, with sides
roughly facing the cardinal points, but on the north and east, instead of
the usual rampart and ditch, there are five trenches with strong earthen
ramparts between them. The west and south sides are less well preserved. The camp buildings would have been of wood, and the stone foundations traceable in the middle of the area are those of a medieval
chapel and its churchyard walls.

Continuing north, A822 soon cuts across more, but only vaguely
visible Roman works to reach (*5m*) the small town of **Muthill**, known for
its ruined 15C Church. Here, embedded in the end of the nave, is a
square 12C tower of a tall type special to central Scotland and in which
the height and heavy stonework recall Saxon and even Celtic tradition.
Inside are effigies of Sir Muriel Drummond (died 1362) and of his wife.

1m **Drummond Castle Gardens** (Tel: 076481-257) form part of the
park extending to the west of the road. The main feature is the Italian-
style garden, laid out formally on a series of natural terraces and showing an extraordinary multiple sundial of 1630, the design of John
Mylne. The castle (no adm.) was founded in 1491 by John, Lord Drummond, and it was here, only a few years later in 1502, that Margaret
Drummond and her sisters were poisoned (see Rte 25A, Dunblane
Cathedral). Later the Drummonds became earls of Perth and staunch
Jacobites, their castle being badly damaged by bombardment by
Cromwell and later, in 1745, deliberately part demolished to prevent its
occupation by Hanoverian soldiery. Today only the square tower is
original, the remainder representing rebuilding in the old style. So
strong here was the contempt for the Hanoverians that, it is said, the
Pond of Drummond, to the north of the long drive, was dug in order to
flood ground 'desecrated' by being allotted to Hanoverian supporters.

2m **Crieff** (5500 inhab. *Inf.*) was, until superseded by Stenhousemuir
in 1770, long the site of one of Scotland's great 'trysts', or cattle markets,
thronged with drovers from the Highlands and buyers from the south.
Today, attractively situated above the river Earn, within easy reach of
Loch Earn, the Sma' Glen and similar scenic districts, and with many
hotels, the town is not only a popular touring centre but also a place
with several attractions of its own.

From James Square, the town centre, East High Street passes the
Town Hall, at the entrance to which can be seen the old stocks and also
the slender octagonal Cross (1688) of the 'Burgh of Regality of Drummond' which was for long the town's resounding name. Farther on, and
on the left, is the much older *Mercat Cross*, dating to the 10C, bearing
Celtic design and originally associated with an ancient church site. On
the south of the town there is a choice of museums and other attractions.
The *Highland Tryst Museum* (Tel: 0764-5202), in a restored weavers'
house, tells the story of Crieff and enables handloom tartan weaving to
be watched, while the Crieff Visitor Centre (Tel: 0764-4041) offers tours
around Scotland's oldest pottery (*Thistle Pottery*, which moved to

Crieff from Portobello in 1972); adjacent is *Perthshire Paperweights* where the manufacture of paperweights based on French 19C designs can be watched. Opposite, at *Stuart Strathearn Crystal* (Tel: 0764-4004), visitors can watch the creation of handmade crystal, see a video and buy from the shop.

In the grounds of 17–18C *Ochertyre House* (2m north west) a mausoleum stands on the site of a church where in 1491 many of the Murrays, with their wives and children, were burned by the Drummonds.—*The Knock* (911ft) is a wooded hill and public park immediately north of the town (view indicator).

Bibliophiles will surely drive 4m south east along B8062 to visit *Innerpeffray Library* (Tel: 0764-2819), Scotland's oldest library, founded in 1691 by David Drummond. Originally housed in the attic of the adjacent chapel, the collection was moved between 1750–58 to its present building, erected by Archbishop Hay Drummond who at the same time added his own library. The borrowers' ledger dates from 1747, and among the thousands of books, largely theological and classical, the oldest printing is of 1508 while historical interest is provided by the pocket bible Montrose carried at his last battle at Carbisdale.— Adjoining the library are the burial chapel of the Drummonds, founded in 1508 as a collegiate church on the site of an older chapel, and also a ruined tower-house of 1610. But long before this there was an important Roman ford and road junction here, both guarded by a fort at Strageath on the south bank.

CRIEFF TO LOCH EARN (A85 west. 12m). *Glenturret Distillery* (Tel: 0764-2424), beside the river Turret and reached in 1m, was established in 1775 and is thus one of Scotland's oldest. Today the visitor is offered a tour, a free dram, a video and a museum.—**Comrie**, a scenically situated summer resort half-way to Loch Earn, straddles the fault which, in geological terms, separates the Highlands from the Lowlands and is thus subject to occasional tremors which, however, rarely do more than perhaps rattle the crockery. In Drummond Street will be found the *Museum of Scottish Tartans* (Tel: 0764-70779), where the Scottish Tartans Society holds its collection of over 1300 tartans and much else of associated interest, including a reference library, prints, maps, documents and a system recording the details of every known tartan. Wool plucking, combing, dyeing and weaving—all as done before 1745—are demonstrated in an 18C weaving shed. The hill of *Dunmore* (837ft) rises 1m north of Comrie, the access path being linked with the scenic *Glen Lednock Circular Walk* (4m) which passes the Devil's Cauldron, a rock chasm through which falls force their way. The *Melville Monument*, crowning Dunmore, commemorates the statesman Henry Dundas, 1st Viscount Melville (1742–1811). He was also Baron Dunira, the name of an estate to the west of Comrie, and he retired to this district after impeachment (and acquittal) regarding his handling of Admiralty funds.

West of Comrie the mountains close in as the road follows the Earn to its outflow from Loch Earn at the village of *St. Fillans*. To the south east of the village, south of the river and beyond the golf course, there is a ruined chapel, dating from c 1500, since 1586 the burial place of the Stewarts of Ardvorlich (on the south shore of the loch near its west end; see Rte 24), and believed to mark the site of St. Fillan's 8C cell. Roads either side of Loch Earn in 7m reach *Lochearnhead* on Rte 24.

On the north east edge of Crieff A85 passes the Golf Course, on which there are three large standing stones bearing cup-and-ring markings, and in rather under *2m* reaches *Gilmerton*.

Here A822 heads north to enter in 4m the **Sma' Glen**, a stony moorland valley and historic Highland gateway through which the Young Pretender retreated and along which, soon afterwards, General Wade drove one of his military roads. The junction with B8063, 3½m north of Gilmerton, marks the site of a Roman signal station, while, c 1½m farther north, *Ossian's Stone*, between the road and the Almond stream, marks, to quote Wordsworth, the 'still place' where 'remote from men, sleeps Ossian in the narrow glen'.

3m **Fowlis Wester**, just north of A85, comes as a quaint hamlet with both ancient and very modern associations. The Cross, dating from the 8C, still carries a few links of the jougs, sufficient at any rate to conjure a picture of what it must have been like to be secured here by an iron collar. The *Church of St. Bean*, although built in the 13C (restored 1927), certainly occupies the site of a much older church, possibly founded by St. Bean who died in 720, and a Pictish stone, near the vestry and found embedded in the wall, is probably from St. Bean's time. Also near the vestry is an ancient headstone, a later copy of which surmounts the lych-gate, and in the churchyard there is a leper-squint. The modern association is provided by a piece of MacBean tartan, taken to the moon by the astronaut Alan Bean, and in the modern Ascension window the colouring of Earth was chosen from that of Earth as seen from the moon.—The very scanty ruins beside a minor road 2m south east of Fowlis Wester are those of *Inchaffray Abbey*, founded here in 1200 on the site of a Celtic church by Gilbert, Earl of Strathearn, and long famed for its silver reliquary of the arm of St. Fillan, taken by the abbot to Bannockburn and used to bless Bruce's army assembled before the battle.

At (*6m*) **Methven**, a name said to be a corruption of Vale of Bean, a fragment of a collegiate church of 1433 serves as a burial place for the Methven family. It was to the north of the village that Bruce was defeated in 1306 by the English under the Earl of Pembroke, and it was at Methven Castle (no adm.), to the east and well seen above the road, that Margaret Tudor, widow of James IV, died in 1541, 28 years after the loss of her husband at Flodden. *Tibbermore*, 2m south east, was the scene in 1644 of the first battle between Montrose and the Covenanters, when Montrose, leading a motley force of about 1100 ill-clad Irish and 1300 better clad but ill-armed Highlanders, defeated a mob of 6000 Covenanters, citizens of Perth and others hastily gathered together under Lord Elcho. Montrose then entered Perth.

4m **Huntingtower Castle** (AM. Tel: 031-244-3101), a compact and intimate tower-house, part well-preserved and part restored, was until 1600 known as Ruthven Castle, the home of the Ruthvens, earls of Gowrie, notorious even by the standards of the day for their involvement in conspiracy. The construction here is most unusual, the castle comprising two 15C towers, only 9½ft apart and united by a late 17C building. The space between the towers is romantically known as the Maiden's Leap, from the tradition that the daughter of the 1st Earl (who, with his father, had plotted the murder of Rizzio) sprang across to avoid detection in an illicit love affair. Wall and ceiling paintings of c 1540 decorate the hall on the first floor.

Huntingtower, or Ruthven as it then was, was the scene of the so-called 'Raid of Ruthven' of 1582. James VI, then an insecure adolescent of 14, accepted an invitation to this hunting lodge of the 1st Earl, but, on arriving, found himself in the hands of a band of jealous nobles whose demands included the dismissal of two royal favourites, the Earl of Arran and Esmé Stuart, the latter a French cousin, possibly James's first homosexual partner and soon created Earl of Lennox. When James attempted to leave, another conspirator, the Master of Glamis, planted his back against the door, at which outrage James burst into tears. James was held for some ten months and the 'raid' (not to be confused with the Gowrie Conspiracy, Rte 26) gave the control of Scotland to the Gowrie faction, at least until the earl was beheaded two years later.

2m **Perth**, see Rte 26.

C.   Via Dollar

A91 to Milnathort, where Rte 32 is joined to reach Perth by M90. As far as Milnathort the road runs below the often steep slopes of the Ochil Hills, cut by frequent small glens.

SOME HOTELS. See Rte 23 (**Stirling**) and Rte 32 (**Kinross**).

Total distance 37m.—*9m* **Tillicoultry**.—*2m* **Dollar**.—*4m* **Yetts o' Muckhart**.—*7m* **Milnathort**.—*15m* **Perth**.

5m **Menstrie Castle** (NTS. Nova Scotia Exhibition: by arrangement. Tel: 0738-31296), built in the 16C, was the birthplace and home of Sir William Alexander, 1st Earl of Stirling (c 1567–1640), a man who combined the roles of minor man of letters, courtier, and founder in 1621 of the colony of Nova Scotia, thanks to James VI/I's grant to him of huge tracts of land in what is now Canada. During the reign of Charles I Nova Scotia baronetcies were created, and today an exhibition shows their coats-of-arms.—*2m* **Alva** and *2m* **Tillicoultry** are both places born of the 19C textiles industry—recalled by a heritage display at *Clock Mill* in Tillicoultry (Tel: 0259-52176)—while the name Silver Glen, cutting in from the north between the two, recalls that silver mining was once important here. For *Gartmore Dam Country Park*, to the south on the way to Alloa, see Rte 31.—*2m* **Dollar** is known for Castle Campbell and for Dollar Academy, a distinguished school founded by John McNabb (died 1802), a poor local lad who became a wealthy sea-captain.

Castle Campbell (AM and NTS. Tel: 031-244-3101), perched on the steep slopes of the Ochils and guarded by deep clefts which meet 300 yards below, presides high and prominent above the town. The castle can be reached either by car to within ¼m or by a choice of taxing paths climbing through the woodland of Dollar Glen (NTS).

At one time called Castle Gloom—situated in the parish of Dolour (Dollar), beside the waters of the Burn of Sorrow, and with Gloom Hill just to the east—the castle came to the Campbells by marriage in the 15C, the present building being begun after 1481 by the Earl of Argyll who changed the name in 1489. John Knox preached here in 1556 and, though Montrose failed to take the castle in 1645, it was burned by Cromwell's troops nine years later. A vaulted pend of c 1600 admits to a court, where the 15C square north east tower, the castle's main feature, is joined to the 16C south wing by a 16 or 17C range with an open loggia. The great hall was on the first floor of the tower, with the entrance to a pit prison to the right of the fireplace, and the third floor is covered by a great ribbed barrel-vault, an early 17C addition.

4m **Yetts o' Muckhart**, from where two roads head north west and north to cross the Ochils and meet Rte 25A at Gleneagles and Dunning. To the south, at *Rumbling Bridge*, the river Devon, tumbling down a ravine, is spanned by three bridges—the present road bridge; a narrow arch of 1713 put up by a local mason; and a footbridge (steps and ramps lead down into the gorge). A mile or so east of Rumbling Bridge, approaching Crook o' Devon, will be found *Monarch Deer Farm* (Tel:

05774-310), with red deer, a shop and a picnic area by the river and its waterfall.—7m **Milnathort**, where Rte 32 is joined for (15m) **Perth**, see Rte 26.

26   Perth

A royal burgh of great antiquity and for a time capital of Scotland, and thus with a wealth of historical associations, Perth, with some 42,000 inhabitants, is today a mature and confident town spread along the west bank of the river Tay. The main town lies between the two large open park areas, about 1000 yards apart, known as North and South Inch.

>**Tourist Information**. The *Round House* (Tel: 0738-38353), Marshall Place; by the river at the north east corner of South Inch. Tourist Information is in itself interesting for occupying the former waterworks (1832), and here, today, the visitor can enjoy a tape-slide presentation on Perth and its county.

>SOME HOTELS. *Royal George*, Tay Street, PH1 5LD. Tel: 0738-24455. *Salutation*, 34 South Street, PH2 8PH. Tel: 0738-30066. *Stakis City Mills*, West Mill Street, PH1 5QP. Tel: 0738-28281. *Station*, Leonard Street, PH2 8HE. Tel: 0738-24141.

History. Whether or not Perth was once a Roman camp is disputed, though the city's rectangular street pattern suggests that it may well have been. Later, in 846, Kenneth Macalpine established at nearby Scone the first capital of the joint kingdom of the Scots and Picts (Alba, later Scotia), and from this doubtless sprang the first township, its name then the Celtic Abertha, the place at the mouth of the Tay. This township was swept away by a flood in 1210, and in that same year William the Lion founded a royal burgh where modern Perth now stands. As capital of Scotland until c 1452 Perth was a civil and religious centre of importance, home to the large monasteries of the Black Friars, the Grey Friars, the White Friars and the Carthusians—all of which, thanks to John Knox's iconoclastic sermons preached from St. John's church in 1559, have now vanished.

Fortified by Edward I, Perth nevertheless fell to Bruce in 1311; but after the battle of Dupplin in 1332 it was occupied by Edward Balliol until again taken and held by the English between 1335–39. It was from the garden of the Blackfriars' monastery that Robert III and his queen witnessed the extraordinary clan combat (see below) on North Inch, and it was in this same monastery that James I was assassinated in 1437. In 1559, as noted above, Knox here preached his momentous sermons, and in 1600 Perth was the scene of the Gowrie Conspiracy (see below). During the fighting in the 17 and 18C Perth again many times changed hands. Montrose marched in after his defeat of Lord Elcho's Covenanters at Tibbermore in 1644; Cromwell followed, after a day's siege, in 1651; Claverhouse seized Perth in 1689 and, finally, the Jacobites occupied the town in both 1715 and 1745, rallying on North Inch and on the former occasion proclaiming the Old Pretender as king.

The art critic John Ruskin (1819–1900) spent much of his boyhood at 10 Rose Terrace, on the south west edge of North Inch. John Buchan, 1st Lord Tweedsmuir, born in Perth, for a while lived in York Place at the town centre.

North Inch is a large, open riverside park offering a variety of sports activities including golf, putting, bowls and the many indoor facilities provided by *Bell's Sports Centre* (Tel: 0738-22301) on the west side of the park. But there was contest here of a more lethal kind in 1396 when North Inch served as the arena for a chivalric judicial fight between Clan Chattan and Clan Quhele (Kay), the point at issue being one of precedence—which clan should be entitled to the place of honour on a leader's right in battle. Thirty champions fought on each side, and as Clan Chattan was one man short they were joined by Hal o' the Wynd, a bandy-legged blacksmith who, though declaring himself an independent, not only contributed nobly to his side's victory but was also one of the few survivors. The affair is graphically described in Sir Walter Scott's 'The Fair Maid of Perth'.

Off the west of the park, and just north of Bell's Sports Centre, stands **Balhousie Castle** or, more grandly, the Tower-House of the Barony of Balhousie. First recorded in 1422, and probably built at about the same time, the castle was in more recent times rebuilt in Scottish Baronial style and now houses the *Museum of the Black Watch* (Tel: 0738-21281), a regiment which has had close connections with Perth ever since its raising at Aberfeldy in 1739. Farther north, on Inveralmond Industrial Estate, an insight is offered into two industries—glass and whiskey—at *Caithness Glass* (Tel: 0738-37373), with works tours, a paperweight museum and a shop, and at *John Dewar and Sons* (Tel: 0738-21231).

Beyond the south west corner of North Inch, at the junction of Atholl Street and North Methven Street, stands *St. Ninian's Cathedral*, Perth's handsome episcopal cathedral, begun in 1850 for the diocese of St. Andrews, Dunkeld and Dunblane and completed in 1900.

A plaque on the corner of Charlotte and Blackfriars streets, off the south of North Inch, reminds that this is a corner of Perth which has witnessed dramatic and violent occasions. For here stood *Blackfriars Monastery*, founded in 1231 by Alexander II and destroyed as the result of Knox's preaching in 1559. Here homage was paid to England's Edward I in 1291; from the monastery's garden in 1396 Robert III and his queen presided at that murderous clan combat; and here in 1437 James I was assassinated by Sir Robert Graham, in spite of the devotion of one of the queen's ladies, Catherine Douglas, who thrust her arm through the rings of the door to serve as the missing iron bolt. She survived, and later married one Richard Lovell of Ballumbie.

The **Fair Maid's House** (Tel: 0738-25976), in North Port (the site of Perth's castle) just south of Charlotte Street, was the old Glovers' Hall, chosen by Scott as the home of Catherine Glover, the heroine of his 'The Fair Maid of Perth'. The niche on the exterior corner once held a figure of St. Bartholomew, patron saint of the glovers, and inside there is a medieval wall, one of the oldest in Perth. The house now serves as a gallery, with changing exhibitions by Scottish artists (painting, sculpture, embroidery and other art forms), and also as a shop offering high quality Scottish craftwork and knitwear.

The city **Art Gallery and Museum** (Tel: 0738-32488), just east of the Fair Maid's House, is in George Street close to Perth Bridge, Smeaton's nine-arch work of 1723 (later widened). The building of 1935 incorporates the Classical façade of the old museum as also a statue of Provost Hay Marshall (1824). Among the varied permanent collections—fine and applied art, local history, archaeology, costume and suchlike—special mention may be made of the displays illustrating the whisky industry and local natural history.

From Perth Bridge, the wide tree-shaded Tay Street runs with the river, soon reaching the east end of High Street which, with Scott and South streets to the west and south, defines the compact heart of Perth. In High Street, near this corner with Tay Street, a plaque presented by 1st Polish Army reminds that Perth was the 'rallying place' for the Polish army in 1940–42. A short way farther along High Street, off the north side and opposite King Edward Street, the narrow *Guard Vennel* claims attention for having once housed the town guard and the mint, as also Wolfe (later General Wolfe, of Quebec fame) who lived here for a while as a young officer. Opposite, a shield on a house marks the site of the guildhall of 1722 (rebuilt 1907). Beyond, the intimate Victorian *Perth Theatre* (1900) stands on the north side of High Street near the junction with Kinnoull Street, while to the south, between High Street and South Street, is the contrastingly modern *St. John's Centre*.

Kinnoull Street is extended southward by Scott Street, which soon meets South Street, parallel to which on the south the name Charterhouse Lane recalls that near here stood the Charterhouse, an important Carthusian monastery founded in 1429 by James I and in which he and his queen, as also Margaret Tudor, widow of James IV, were all buried. Like all its fellows, the monastery was destroyed in 1559, and James I's tombstone was later removed to the church of St. John.

South Street, followed east, passes the *Post Office*, then reaching, set back in St. John Street, the **Church of St. John**, a church which has known much change and seen, too, something of history.

Founded in 1126 by David I, very possibly on the site of a Culdee church, and at the same time granted to Dunfermline Abbey, the church was first restored in 1328 by Robert Bruce, though work was soon halted by Bruce's death in the following year. There followed major restoration, amounting almost to rebuilding, during the 15 and 16C, the interior being divided in 1598 into two churches between which, in

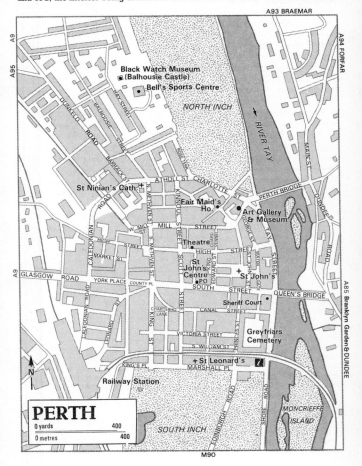

c 1773, a mid-church was inserted. The 19C brought further changes, some drastic, until finally, in 1926, yet more modification (by Robert Lorimer) enabled the church to house the County War Memorial. As to history, it was here, in David I's church in 1296, that the conquering Edward I kept the feast of the nativity of St. John the Baptist; and here, too, in 1335—though there seems no evidence for this tradition—Edward III slew his brother, the Earl of Cornwall. Then came 1559 and John Knox, preaching his inflammatory sermon urging the 'purging of the churches from idolatry' and sending an iconoclastic storm over Scotland, drastic and destructive far beyond the preacher's intentions if Knox's subsequent acid condemnation of the 'rascal multitude' was sincere. In 1644, after Tibbermore, Montrose confined 800 Covenanter prisoners here, and among the monarchs or would-be monarchs who worshipped here were Charles I in 1633, Charles II in 1650 and the Young Pretender in 1745.

As seen today the church is a cruciform edifice with a sturdy central tower carrying a 15C steeple. The north porch, with 15C vaulting, represents the lowest storey of a tower of David I's original church of c 1126, otherwise demolished in 1823; the choir dates from c 1440, the surprisingly low nave from about 50 years later, and the north transept stands as a rebuilding of 1828. The interior is said once to have boasted no fewer than 40 altars dedicated to as many saints, but these disappeared after Knox's sermon and today it is the choir, with its early roof and modern great east window (by Douglas Strachan), which is perhaps the most interesting area of the church. In part the choir is used to display the church's treasures, these including a call of early bells; the Hammermen's collecting box, once on their guild altar; the Nuremberg Cup (German, late 16 or early 17C); two steeple cups (London, early 17C); a baptismal basin (Edinburgh, 1593); pewter and various other items of interest.

The corner of South Street and St. John Street was once filled by the residence of the bishops of Dunkeld, built earlier than 1461 but demolished in 1861, and it is worth walking into Fountain Close, immediately east of St. John Street, where many snippets of information have been recorded on the whitewashed walls and at the end of which there is a pictorial impression of the bishops' house. Across the road, the *Salutation Hotel* (1695), with a distinctive frontage, is one of the oldest established hotels in Scotland, the place, too, chosen by the Young Pretender for his lodging in 1745, in Room 20 which is still in use.

South Street now meets Tay Street at Queen's Bridge, the building on the south-west corner of the crossroads, the *Sheriff Court* (R. Smirke, 1820), occupying the site of Gowrie House, scene of the still mysterious Gowrie Conspiracy of 1600. Today a bronze tablet in one of the blind windows gives the modern visitor a hint of the picturesque old mansion (1520) which in its day was one of the chief ornaments of the city.

There are at least two versions of the *Gowrie Conspiracy*, one portraying the 3rd Earl of Gowrie as the villain, the other ascribing the initiative to James VI. Under the first version Gowrie and his brother Alexander Ruthven, keen to repeat the success of the 'Raid of Ruthven' (see Rte 25B, Huntingtower Castle), lured the king to Gowrie House with a tale of foreign treasure, there leading him to an upper room where Ruthven, after some heated words, attempted to bind the king. James, however, succeeded in giving the alarm through an open window, whereupon his attendants forced their way to his rescue, both Gowrie and Ruthven being killed in the fracas. The alternative version suggests that the whole affair was stage-managed by James, still smarting from his experience at Huntingtower and determined to wipe out Gowrie and his family. Certainly James hunted down Gowrie's two younger brothers, forcing one to flee abroad and imprisoning the other (Patrick) until 1622. A curious footnote is that Patrick's daughter, Lady Mary Ruthven, became the wife of the painter, Van Dyck.

Either way, at this spot, approaching 400 years ago, James VI not only rid himself of the unpleasant Gowries but also proscribed the very name of Ruthven. By a strange quirk of history, though, Lady Mary Ruthven survives in several portraits by her husband.

Perth. The Waterworks of 1832 now house Tourist Information

A short way south, beside Tay Street, *Greyfriars Cemetery* spreads over the site of the Franciscan monastery founded by Lord Oliphant in 1468 and, with all the others, destroyed in 1559. Beyond, and below the railway and footbridge, Tay Street reaches *Tourist Information* in its distinctive converted 19C waterworks building, this standing on part of the site of a massive fort planted here by Cromwell in 1652.

The large, green open expanse of **South Inch**, though in part given over to boating, putting, minigolf and children's paddling and play areas, must surely be a more disciplined place now than it was in the days when used for uncontrolled archery, competitive hucksters, and the burning of witches. On the north side the church of *St. Leonard's in the Fields*, with its crown steeple, was built by J.J. Stevenson in 1884.

The railway bridge, with a footpath, crosses above the north end of the long *Friarton* or *Moncrieffe Island* in the Tay, on which James VI's golf course still flourishes. Beyond the bridge is **Branklyn Garden** (NTS. Tel: 0738-25535), begun by Mr and Mrs John Renton in 1922 on the site of an orchard. Within the garden's two acres are rhododendrons, herbaceous and peat garden plants, and, above all, alpines.—Beyond, *Kinnoull Hill* (729ft), rising abruptly above the Tay, is a noted local view point (indicator), with also a nature trail and woodland paths.—Below the hill, at Walnut Grove between A85 and the river, *Fairways Heavy Horse Centre* (Tel: 0738-25931), a working and breeding centre for Clydesdales, offers wagon rides, a video and the opportunity to see a blacksmith at work.

Elcho Castle (AM. Tel: 031-244-3101), on the right bank of the Tay 4m south east of Perth, was the home of that Lord Elcho who so unsuccessfully confronted Montrose at Tibbermore. Standing on or close to the site of a predecessor, said to have been one of Wallace's favourite retreats, the present castle is a well-preserved example of a 14–16C fortified mansion. The wrought-iron grills protecting the windows are especially noteworthy.

For **Scone Palace**, see Rte 28.—For Perth to **Stirling**, see Rte 25; to **Pitlochry**, see Rte 27; to **Braemar**, see Rte 28; to **Aberdeen**, see Rte 29; to **Dundee**, see Rtes 30 and 33D; to **Edinburgh**, see Rte 32.

27   Perth to Pitlochry and Newtonmore

A9 (old road between Pitlochry and Clan Donnachaidh museum).—Pastoral at first, becoming increasingly hilly and wooded after Dunkeld and, beyond Blair Atholl, ascending Glen Garry to break out on to high open moor bounded by bare mountains lifting to over 3000ft. The watershed is the Pass of Drumochter (1484ft), beyond which the road follows Glen Truim down to the gentler and more cultivated but still scenic valley of the Spey.

Note: This road was first laid out by General Wade in 1726–33, improved in 1830 by Telford, reconstructed in 1925–28, and, since then, has been under almost constant attention as Scotland's main north–south artery. Today a dual carriageway trunk road, the modern A9 bypasses virtually all the places mentioned along the Route below and, although signing is good, care must be taken not to get swept beyond the objective.

The railway follows much the same course as the road, at Drumochter reaching the highest level of any railway in Britain.

SOME HOTELS. **Dunkeld**. *Atholl Arms*, Tayside Terrace, PH8 0AH. Tel: 03502-219. *Stakis Dunkeld House*, PH8 0HX. Tel: 03502-771. **Pitlochry**. *Atholl Palace*, Atholl Road, PH16 5LY. Tel: 0796-2400. *Burnside*, West Moulin Road, PH16 5EA. Tel: 0796-2203. *Fishers*, 75 Atholl Road, PH16 5BN. Tel: 0796-2000. **Kinloch Rannoch**. *Loch Rannoch*, PH16 5PS. Tel: 08822-201. *Bunrannoch*, PH16 5PU. Tel: 08822-367. **Rannoch Station**. *Moor of Rannoch*, PH17 2QA. Tel: 08823-238. **Killiecrankie**. *Killiecrankie*, PH16 5LG. Tel: 0796-3220. **Blair Atholl**. *Atholl Arms*, PH18 5SG. Tel: 079681-205. **Dalwhinnie**. *Loch Ericht*, PH19 1AE. Tel: 05282-257.

Total distance 63m.—*13m* **Dunkeld**.—*12m* **Pitlochry**.—*7m* **Blair Atholl**.—*16m* **Pass of Drumochter**.—*15m* **Newtonmore**.

Perth (see Rte 26) is left by Dunkeld Road out of the city's north west corner, A9 soon being joined to cross, though scarcely noticeably, the small river Almond which flows into the Tay to the east of the road beyond the railway and close against the west bounds of Scone Palace park. Here at the confluence once stood the Roman station which later received the Celtic name of Abertha, forerunner of Kenneth Macalpine's capital.—*3m* **Luncarty**, to the east, was in 990 the site of a great battle in which Kenneth II crushed the Norsemen; a battle, too, which should interest anyone bearing the name of Hay since, or so the tale goes, the Scots were rallied at a critical moment by a peasant called Hay, armed with no more than a plough yoke. After the battle Hay was rewarded with land, and it is he who is the legendary ancestor of the Hays of Tweeddale; but, it must be said, several families of the name of Hay show a peasant with a yoke as part of their coats-of-arms. Another incident during the battle is said to have led to the adoption of the Thistle as the emblem of Scotland (see Aspects of Scotland, Thistle). Precisely where this battle was fought is disputed, but the hamlet of Battleby, ½m south west of Luncarty, is a tempting choice.—Beyond, at Bankfoot, is the *Highland Motor Heritage Centre* (Tel: 073687-696) showing vintage and classic cars, contemporary material and restoration workshops.

The road crosses the railway before curving west into the wooded *Pass of Birnam*, cutting between Birnam Hill (1324ft. west) and the Tay (east) and once known as the 'Mouth of the Highlands' out of which swarmed the Highlander bands of Montrose and the Young Pretender. The south slopes of the hill, with a hill-fort known as Duncan's Castle, are clothed by *Birnam Wood*, that same wood which, in Shakespeare's 'Macbeth', by moving to Dunsinane (see Rte 29), spelt the end for Macbeth. On Terrace Walk, which follows the right bank of the Tay for a mile below the village-resort of *Birnam*, some venerable trees are claimed to be survivors of the original forest. In the churchyard of *Little Dunkeld*, virtually joined with Birnam, lies Niel Gow (1727–1807), a fiddler of humble origins but great musical distinction, who, together with his four sons, did much both to preserve and add to traditional Scottish melodies and reels. Together the family edited the several volumes of airs preserved as the 'Gow Collection'.

This Route now breaks away from A9 to cross a sylvan reach of the Tay by Telford's bridge of 1809 and enter (*10m* from Luncarty) **Dunkeld** (1000 inhab. *Inf.*), a small and very ancient cathedral township in a tranquil riverside setting below wooded mountains. The setting apart, the main attractions for the visitor are the partially ruined cathedral and the early 18C Little Houses.—Dunkeld's Arts Festival is in June, and the Highland Games, among the oldest in Scotland, are held in late August.

History. First important as a residence of Pictish kings and soon afterwards a Celtic centre, Dunkeld is traditionally supposed to have been the site of a monastery founded in the 6C by St. Columba and St. Mungo, or perhaps a century later by St. Adamnan. Certainly, though, an abbey was established here by 729 by Celtic monks, who, driven out of Iona by the Norsemen, brought with them the relics of St. Columba for which they consecrated a shrine. Not long afterwards Kenneth Macalpine is said to have treated Dunkeld as joint capital with Scone, while a bishopric, founded here by either Alexander I or David I, flourished until the Reformation. This bishopric's perhaps most distinguished incumbent was Gavin Douglas (1474–1522), even if his life was devoted more to his literary pursuits (he is best known for a scholarly translation of the 'Aeneid') and to his political scheming than to the spiritual needs of his see.

In 1689, on 26 August, Dunkeld was the stage for the savage battle that was the aftermath of Killiecrankie. The town, including the cathedral, was held by 1200 Cameronians, the newly raised Lowland regiment of extremist Covenanters, against 500 Highlanders, victorious at Killiecrankie. Initially successful, the Highlanders penetrated the town, whereupon the Cameronian commander (Captain Munro, who had taken over from Colonel Cleland, already killed) resorted to fire and Dunkeld was virtually gutted. The Highlanders then withdrew, the cause of James VII/II was lost and the security of William and Mary assured.

Rising both elegant and ruined from tree-shaded lawns beside the Tay,

Dunkeld Cathedral (AM. Tel: 031-244-3101) dates in part from the 12C—the nave piers may well be contemporary with the original foundation of the see—but in general the remains are of the 14–15C. The nave and aisles have remained roofless since the savage Reformation desecration of 1560, but the choir, roughly repaired in 1600, was later thoroughly restored after 1815 and again in 1908.

Begun by Bishop Cardney in 1406 and consecrated by Bishop Lauder in 1464, the Nave is remarkable for the Flamboyant tracery of the aisle windows as also for the great west window which, curiously, is not truly centred in its gable. The massive tower at the end of the north aisle was started five years after the cathedral's consecration and took some 32 years to build, being completed in c 1501; it contains 15C murals and a hog-backed tomb. Buried in the nave are, near the west door, Colonel Cleland, the Covenanter commander (see above) and minor poet; Bishop Cardney, in the south aisle; and, at the west end, Charles Edward Stewart, self-styled Count Roehenstart (?1781–1854). A teasing question mark hangs over this grave. Source opinion varies, but Stewart appears to have been one of two well-born, exceptionally charming but eccentric brothers called Allan, both of whom claimed to be descendants of the Young Pretender, this one on the imaginative grounds that he was natural son of Charlotte (herself natural daughter of the Young Pretender and Clementina Walkinshaw) and the Swedish Count Roehenstart. The brothers' claim must have had some credibility—there was certainly rumour that Charlotte had some form of association with Roehenstart—for it seems to have been accepted in aristocratic circles, if only with amused tolerance. In 1854 Charles Stewart was killed in Dunkeld in a coach accident, and in resting here in the cathedral of Scotland's ancient capital he may be said to have achieved a form of recognition.

The aisleless Choir, now serving as parish church, was started by Bishop William Sinclair in 1318 but not completed until 1400. It has an attractive blind arcade (north) and good plain sedilia (south), while at the east end survive the remains of a statue of its founder who died in 1338. Nearby, a recumbent armoured effigy is believed to be that of Robert II's natural son, the arrogant and vicious Alexander Stewart, Earl of Buchan, more notoriously known as the 'Wolf of Badenoch'. Among memorials are those to the Black Watch and Colonel Cleland, both against the east wall; and to the Scottish Horse regiment (see museum in the town) and their founder, the 8th Duke of Atholl (died 1942), both on the north wall. Also to be seen in the choir are two sobering reminders of the cruel hazards of medieval life—the Lepers' Squint, now partially filled in (north wall, near the pulpit), and the Whipping Pillar, by the stair to the organ loft. The east window, with St. Columba as the central figure, was gifted by Sir Donald Currie, the benefactor responsible for much of the restoration of 1908.

Behind the cathedral the so-called 'parent larch' reputedly represents the first larch to be planted in Scotland, by the Duke of Atholl in 1737.

The *Little Houses*, which line Cathedral Street, delight both in themselves and as an inspiring example of imaginative conservation. Dating mainly from the rebuilding which followed the devastation caused by the battle of 1689, the houses, by 1950 in serious disrepair and in danger of demolition, then became the subject of an appeal by the National Trust for Scotland. So successful was this that the houses were restored, and, now let to tenants, provide a surely unique cathedral approach. One house, the *Ell House*, serves as the Trust shop (Tel: 03502-460).

In Dunkeld's delightful 18C square are *Tourist Information*, with a NTS photographic display and short audio-visual presentation, and also the *Museum of the Scottish Horse* (Tel: 03502-296), telling the story of this yeomanry regiment raised by the 8th Duke of Atholl, who died in 1942. *Stanley Hill*, behind the 'Little Houses', is a mound artificially land-scaped in 1730 as a fortification by the Duke of Atholl and his brother, Lord George Murray, the Jacobite general; the suggestion that the mound may include the original dun of Dunkeld can be left to the visitor's individual wishful thinking.

ENVIRONS OF DUNKELD. Perhaps the most popular local objective is the Scottish Wildlife Trust's *Loch of Lowes* nature reserve, beside the loch of the same name under 2m north east of Dunkeld by A923. The reserve shelters a variety of birds, plants and animals—the highlight being a hide from which ospreys may be watched if the visitor is lucky in his timing—and a centre explains the local natural history (Tel: 03502-337).

On the west side of the Tay there is the *Hermitage Woodland Walk* (NTS. 1m in length. Booklet) threading through the woods beside the Braan, the legacy of the interest in forestry, including the introduction of new species, shown by successive dukes of Atholl. Apart from offering much of natural beauty and interest, the walk passes a charming 18C bridge over a narrow gorge, a waterfall and two follies. The first folly is the Hermitage, or Ossian's Hall, built in 1758, converted to a romantic, mirrored waterfall room in 1783, largely destroyed by vandals in 1869 and now restored and refurbished. Beyond is Ossian's Cave, another 18C folly, neatly using a group of boulders and claiming to represent the kind of place in which such a bard would have lived.

This Route now continues north along A9 which crosses the Tay 2m out of Dunkeld and in under 3m reaches *Dowally*, beyond which a wide view opens out up the Tay, with the shapely Schiehallion (see below) and round-topped Farragon rising beyond the valley as the road approaches (3m) *Ballinluig* where Rte 24 comes in from the west. Here, at Ballinluig, the connoisseur of stone circles will enter the village and follow the old A9 northward for a few hundred yards, to the road's end where, on the east side, a modest circle survives. Beyond Ballinluig, if Pitlochry, Bridge of Garry and Loch Tummel, Killiecrankie and Blair Atholl are the objectives, care should be taken to choose the town road rather than the bypass. *Blair Athol Distillery* (Tel: 0796-2234), with a visitor centre, is by the south approach to Pitlochry.

4m **Pitlochry** (2500 inhab. *Inf.*), at the geographic centre of Scotland and at the heart too of a far-flung district of immensely varied natural beauty, is one of the most visited inland resorts in the country. With a touch of old-world elegance and with plenty of local attractions, these including a distinguished theatre and the famous fish-pass, and gen-erously provided too with hotels, Pitlochry is well sited as a base for day touring, whether perhaps to Aberfeldy and Loch Tay; or to Queen's View, followed by an exploration along Loch Tummel and the remote country around Loch Rannoch; or past the battlefield of Killiecrankie and then up to the high, wide mountain and moorland to the north with the pastoral Spey valley beyond and below.

Pitlochry Festival Theatre (Tel: 0796-2680), which started as a marquee in 1951, now occupies a purpose-built riverside (south bank) building opened by the Prince of Wales in 1981. The season of plays, concerts and other entertainment extends from May to October.—*Pitlochry Highland Games* are held annually on the second Saturday in September.

Immediately to the west of the town *Loch Faskally* curves away westward and northward, a lovely stretch of tree-surrounded water, 2½m long and created out of the Tummel river for hydro-electric purposes in

1950. Rowing and powered boats can be hired to enable the best of this loch to be enjoyed. At the south end of the loch, beside the large dam and power station, will be found the *Fish-Pass* or *Salmon Ladder* (Short walk from town centre. Motorists will find car parks on the north side of the river, whence they can walk across the dam. Alternatively the river can be crossed by Bridge Road at the south east of the town and signs then followed past the Festival Theatre. This latter approach is recommended to motorists planning to enjoy the drive along the south shore of Loch Tummel, described below). Yearly, between April and October, the salmon (electronically counted), spawned years earlier on the shingle beds of Scotland's northern streams and then finding their home in the Atlantic, make their way back to repeat the cycle. Provided with an observation room for the benefit of visitors, and with steps to the open top surface of the pools, the system is 900ft in length and comprises 34 pools connected by pipes.

Adjacent is the *Hydro-Electric Visitor Centre* (Tel: 0796-3152) where video films, a scale model, easily understood diagrams and photographs combine to illustrate not only the Tummel Valley hydro-electric scheme but also how salmon and man share Scotland's northern lochs and rivers.

The **Tummel Valley Hydro-Electric Scheme** covers a large area of wild and lonely countryside and makes use of many lochs and streams. Essentially the scheme operates as two sections, Rannoch and Tummel. *Rannoch* itself divides into two. In the far west the water flowing off the desolate Moor of Rannoch is collected in Loch Eigheach, with Gaur dam and power station (1953 and the first in the scheme to operate under remote control) at its east end. Well to the north, to the east of Dalwhinnie on A9 farther along this Route, are lochs An-t-Seilich and Cuaich, connected by tunnel and with a power station (1959) at the south end of the latter. From here water is discharged through an aqueduct across A9 and into Loch Ericht, which, dropping southward from Dalwhinnie, slices some 15 narrow miles through the mountains. Ericht also takes water from Loch Garry (5m to its east), the water arriving by tunnel at Loch Ericht power station (1962). From Loch Ericht, which represents the main Rannoch section storage reservoir, the water is tunnelled to Loch Rannoch power station (1930).

In the *Tummel* section there is a series of lochs, dams and power stations, some of these last (Errochty, Clunie and Pitlochry) constructed as part of the post-war Tummel-Garry scheme. Loch Rannoch and, high above to the north, Loch Errochty, are the main storage reservoirs. Travelling east and then south the lochs and power stations are Loch Dunalastair, channelling water by open aqueduct to the power station (1933) at the west end of Loch Tummel; Errochty power station, fed by tunnel from its loch; beyond the east end of Loch Tummel, Clunie dam, whence a tunnel carries water to Clunie power station at the north end of Loch Faskally; and, finally, at Loch Faskally's south end, Pitlochry dam and power station.

All the southern lochs lie along the roads from Pitlochry to Rannoch Station (see below).

From Pitlochry dam pedestrians may return to the town by crossing the dam; by the Port-na-Craig suspension footbridge a short way downstream; or, if more energetic, by skirting the wooded west shore of the loch, crossing to the east bank by a footbridge where the loch narrows by the boating station.

ENVIRONS OF PITLOCHRY. The *Black Spout*, a waterfall deep in woods 1½m south east of Pitlochry, is best reached by Knockfarrie Road (alongside the entrance to the Atholl Palace Hotel) and then through the woods.

Craigower (1300ft. NTS.), an 11-acre beacon hill rising immediately north of Pitlochry beyond the golf course and offering splendid views (indicator), can comfortably be climbed by following the signed Dunmore Trail. This varied circular walk of 3½m is named in honour of John, Earl of Dunmore (1939–80), member of the NTS Council, and of his father, Viscount Fincastle, killed in action in 1940.

From *Moulin*, just north of Pitlochry, a path ascends *Ben Vrackie* (2757ft) with a view indicator at the summit.—To the south east of Moulin, and reached by a short path, are the ruins of *Castle Dubh* (probably 13–14C), once a stronghold of Sir John Campbell of Lochow, a nephew of Bruce. Local tradition tells that when, in 1500, the garrison was stricken by plague, the castle was battered down by cannon to form a cairn over the dead.—*Edradour Distillery* (Tel: 0796-2095), a short way south off A924, dates from 1825 and enjoys the distinction of being the smallest in Scotland.

To the south (2m) of Pitlochry the 8C *Dunfallandy Stone* should not be missed by anyone with an appreciation of Pictish art. The stone is reached by crossing the river by Bridge Road to follow the little Logierait road southward close to the Tummel; this road runs below A9, passes the entrance to Dunfallandy House Hotel and immediately reaches another turn to the right across a cattle grid. The stone is atop a mound a short distance up this driveway. Originally near Killiecrankie, this stone, now well protected behind glass, bears on one side a decorated cross, together with figures of Jonah, beasts and angels; and, on the other, two figures apparently in earnest conversation (said to be Saints Paul and Anthony), a horseman and various symbols, all within a frame of two serpents.

PITLOCHRY TO RANNOCH STATION (B8019 and B846, west. 35m). One of a number of Scottish roads claiming the title of 'Road to the Isles', though this one stops abruptly at the railway well short of the western sea, this is a scenically highly rewarding drive into a remote and sometimes desolate countryside of loch, forest and mountain; in places, though, and especially of course in summer, trees can interfere with the views. There is no road escape at the far end, so the return, if to Pitlochry, must be by more or less the same route. However there are lonely Highland roads linking Tummel Bridge and Dunalastair to either Calvine or Dalnacardoch on A9 to the north; another, southwards, links Tummel Bridge with Rte 24 at Coshieville; and from Kinloch Rannoch a minor road rounds the northern slopes of Schiehallion to meet the Coshieville road. Various hydro-electric installations are passed—power stations, dams, pipes and reservoirs—and interest can be added by first calling at the Pitlochry hydro-electric visitor centre (see above, as also for an outline of the Loch Tummel Scheme). There are hotels at Kinloch Rannoch and Rannoch Station.

The south shore of Loch Tummel is reached from Pitlochry along the west shore of Loch Faskally, the approach being past the Festival Theatre and then negotiating the obstacle of A9 by following the signs to Foss, a village towards the west end of Loch Tummel. Narrow, and dipping and rising through woods, this pleasant and little-used small road first reaches, some 1½m beyond A9 and on the left atop a bank, an ancient (?6C) stone known as the *Priest's Stone* and bearing the outline of a cross. The *Clunie Memorial Arch*, immediately beyond, in the shape of a tunnel and marking the entrance to Clunie power station, honours five workers killed during the construction of the tunnel (2m long. 1946–50) through which the waters of Loch Tummel are brought from Clunie dam. Just beyond, again, a sign indicates *Lynn of Tummel View Point* (see below). The road continues along the loch's south side to join B846 which, taken southwards, travels through Strath Appin to pass Glengoulandie Deer Park and Garth Castle shortly before meeting Rte 24 at Coshieville; or, taken northwards, reaches Tummel Bridge where the modern bridge crosses the river beside its attractive stone predecessor of 1733. For west, north and east of Tummel Bridge see below.

The more important and more popular B8019 bears west across *Bridge of Garry* (about 3m north of Pitlochry. For Linn of Tummel, visited from here, see below) and in 4m arrives at the rocky spur known as ***Queen's**

View, a justly renowned beauty spot with a superb vista up the length of
Loch Tummel with the mass of Schiehallion as background. It is of
interest that this spot apparently won its name long before Queen Victoria came here in 1886, and it may well be that the name reaches back to
a visit by Mary, Queen of Scots, in 1564, the tradition being that she was
so taken with this district that she ordered her harpist to extol it in music.
Schiehallion (3547ft), which will dominate the southward view along
most of this diversion, is an isolated and graceful conical peak of quartzite which in 1774–76, and again in 1811, played a part in scientific history.
On the first occasion the mountain was used by Nevil Maskelyne, the
Astronomer Royal, in his experiments, through deviations of the plumb
line, into determining the attraction of the mass of mountains, and from
this the mathematician Charles Hutton deduced the mean density of
Earth. On the second occasion similar use was made of the mountain by
the Scottish mathematician John Playfair.

The Forestry Commission's *Visitor Centre* (Tel: 08822-335), with
admirable displays including a slide show, interprets the natural history,
forestry and other aspects of this district. Advice is also given on a choice
of forest walks which, starting from the nearby Allean picnic site and in
part rough and steep, visit an Iron Age fort and a reconstructed clachan
(homestead).

Close beside the water, and sometimes frustratingly deep in trees,
B8019 passes the Errochty power station and arrives at the loch's west
end to join B846 at *Tummel Bridge*, which bridge, flanked by its pleasing
stone predecessor of 1733, carries the latter road southward (see small
print above). Another road (at Trinafour becoming B847), wild and
remote as it travels northward, provides an opportunity, soon repeated
at Dunalastair, to join A9 in some 9m at Calvine or Dalnacardoch, the
former between Blair Atholl and the foot of Glen Garry and the latter
well up the glen. If Dalnacardoch is chosen, then on the way a fine
glimpse can be enjoyed of Loch Errochty and its dam.

The power station at Tummel Bridge is fed by aqueduct from the dam
at *Dunalastair*, rather over 3m farther on and at the east end of its reservoir. Beyond the other end of the reservoir the neat village of **Kinloch
Rannoch** stands, despite its name, at the foot rather than the head of Loch
Rannoch, a beautiful sheet of water some 10m long and 1m broad. In the
centre of the village an obelisk remembers Dugald Buchanan 'the Rannoch Schoolmaster, Evangelist, and Sacred Poet' (see also Rte 24, Strathyre). Roads fringe both sides of the loch, that on the north affording the
better distant views. The unclassified south shore road soon enters *Rannoch Forest* to cross (3m from Kinloch Rannoch) the Carie Burn, by which
the Forestry Commission's Carie Picnic Site is the start for a choice of
forest walks ranging from 1m to 5m in scope and climbing to high ground
overlooking the loch. *Dall*, 1½m farther along the south shore and now
part of a school, is a mansion built in 1855 as a 'clan-seat' of the
Robertsons, and, just beyond, the *Black Wood of Rannoch* shelters
ancient trees officially accepted as survivors of the Caledonian Forest.
At the west end of the loch the roads join, just west of the bridge over the
Gaur being a house called Rannoch Barracks, a reminder that it was built
to accommodate Hanoverian troops stationed here after the '45.

The river Gaur, barely 3m long and tumbling its way across desolate
country, links lochs Rannoch and the wilder and much smaller Eigheach, beyond the latter being the road's end at Rannoch Station on the
West Highland Railway (Glasgow to Fort William; see the introduction
to Rte 44A).

Along the main Route (continuing north out of Pitlochry but avoiding the trunk A9), *3m Bridge of Garry* is at the start of the lochs Tummel and Rannoch diversion described immediately above. Here there is a car park for the use of visitors to **Linn of Tummel** (waymarked walk of 2m; booklet from Killiecrankie), a popular NTS property of 47 acres of mixed woodland along the banks of the rivers Garry and Tummel and a place greatly admired by Queen Victoria whose visit here in 1844 is recorded by an obelisk. At the time of this visit the Tummel dropped as a sheer waterfall into the Garry, but much of this fall became a pool (Linn) in 1950 when the level of both rivers was raised by the creation of Loch Faskally. Today a wooden bridge crosses an early fish-pass, needed when the salmon were confronted by the then formidable Falls of Tummel, in their present more modest form still cascading a short way upstream.

Just north of Bridge of Garry, and now somewhat slashed by a ruthless trunk A9, starts the **°Pass of Killiecrankie**, the wooded gorge through which the river Garry forces its way to join the Tummel and the site of the latter part of the battle of 27 July 1689 when the English troops of King William were defeated by insurgent Jacobite Highlanders under Claverhouse (Bonnie Dundee of ballad).

Battle of Killiecrankie. The English, commanded by General Mackay, had emerged at the upper end of the pass and had formed up facing north on the plateau above the Haugh of Urrard when the Highlanders received the signal to charge. 'It was past seven o'clock. Dundee gave the word. The Highlanders dropped their plaids. The few who were so luxurious as to wear rude socks of untanned hide spurned them away. It was long remembered in Lochaber that Lochiel took off what possibly was the only pair of shoes in his clan, and charged barefoot at the head of his men. In two minutes the battle was lost and won... and the mingled torrent of red coats and tartans went raving down the valley to the gorge of Killiecrankie' (Macaulay). But for the Highlanders victory was soured by the death of their leader, Dundee. Fatally wounded, he is said to have been carried to Urrard House, in the woods near the old A9 north of the NTS Visitor Centre, and a stone in the grounds, visible from this road, marks the spot where he fell. Although the Highlanders won this battle, they were unable to survive this loss and were decisively defeated three weeks later at Dunkeld.—This Pass of Killiecrankie long continued to have a baneful effect, and in 1746 German troops employed in subduing the Young Pretender's supporters refused to enter the pass, insisting that they had reached the last outpost of civilisation.

An excellent *Visitor Centre* (NTS. Tel: 0796-3233) not only explains the battle and its historical background but also illustrates the local topography and natural history. At a corner of the car park, at the opposite end from the Centre, a small and rather unconvincing section of Wade's original road construction is indicated. From the Centre a path drops down the wooded hillside to the river far below, where the narrowest part of the gorge is known as the Soldier's Leap, a spot where a fleeing English soldier made a spectacular jump to escape the Highland pack hot on his heels. From here paths descend the gorge to Bridge of Garry and Linn of Tummel, for both of which see above.

Northward from the Visitor Centre the old A9 passes, to the right, the site of the battle proper, with the Claverhouse Stone marking the spot where the Jacobite commander fell, before reaching (*4m* from Bridge of Garry) **Blair Atholl**, the last place of any size before the ascent of Glen Garry. Here, although Blair Castle is likely to be the main objective, two more modest places propose themselves. One is the *Atholl Country Collection* (Tel: 079681-232), housed in the Old School (adjacent to a Craft Centre) and telling the story of village and glen life of the past. Among the features are a smithy, a crofter's byre and living room, and material on flax, on road, rail and postal services, and on the school, the church, the vet and the gamekeeper. At the other end of the village is the *Corn Mill* (Tel: 079681-321), a water-powered mill dating back to

1613, still working and offering for sale oatmeal, flour and home baking.

*Blair Castle (Tel: 079681-207). In wooded parkland at the end of a long avenue of limes, the castle is a straggling but elegant white Scottish Baronial mansion of various dates, as worth visiting for its historical associations as for its art and other contents.

The *Line of Atholl*. The last Celtic Earl of Atholl had died before 1211, the earldom then passing through the female line to David of Strathbogie (see also Rte 40, Huntly Castle) who however opposed Bruce and thus had his line forfeited. Later, in 1457, the earldom was conferred on Sir John Stewart of Balvenie (see Rte 39, Balvenie Castle), half-brother of James II and ancestor of the present family, and it was he who in 1475, when sent by James III to quell the uprising by the Lord of the Isles, received the uncompromising injunction, which later became the family motto, 'Furth Fortune and Fill the Fetters'. The direct succession ended in 1595, and until 1625 the earldom was held by the male heirs of the 1st Earl's brother, but in 1629 the title passed to John Murray, Master of Tullibardine. In 1703 the dukedom was created by Queen Anne.

Some **History**. Edward III visited here in 1336, and Mary, Queen of Scots, in 1564, on which occasion it is recorded that a hunt in Atholl Forest killed 360 red deer and five wolves. Garrisoned in 1644 by Montrose, held by Cromwell between 1652–60, and occupied by Claverhouse immediately before Killiecrankie, the castle was partly dismantled in 1690 to prevent its further occupation by the Highlander rebels. In 1746, just before Culloden and held by Cumberland, Blair was unsuccessfully besieged by the Jacobite Lord George Murray, brother of the Duke of Atholl, the castle thus achieving the distinction of being the last castle in Britain to come under siege. Queen Victoria visited here in 1844, afterwards granting the dukes the unique privilege of being allowed to retain a private army (the Atholl Highlanders).

The oldest part of the castle, Cumming's (or Comyn's) Tower on the north east, was built in c 1269 by John Comyn of Badenoch, and various alterations and additions have been made over the seven centuries that followed. By the mid 16C the castle had been extended southward, and the range of the great hall, between the two towers, had been built; there was major change in the 18C when the 2nd Duke remodelled Blair into a Georgian mansion, removing castellation and turrets to make way for low-pitched roofs and chimneys; and finally, in the later 19C, the 7th Duke recastellated, at the same time adding the present entrance and ballroom.

The numerous rooms on view present a remarkable picture of Scottish aristocratic life from the 16C to the present day. The collection of arms is one of the best in Scotland and includes the armour worn by Lord Glenlyon at the strange Eglinton Tournament (see Rte 16). Family portraits range over 300 years and include works by Lely, Ramsay, Zoffany, Landseer and Raeburn. Also on show are many Jacobite relics; a superb collection of china, especially Sèvres, Meissen and Dresden; Brussels tapestries made for Charles I, sold by Cromwell and later bought by the 1st Duke; and Georgian and Victorian toys. Additionally there is a Natural History Museum covering birds and animals native to the Highlands, and especially to Atholl.

Beinn a' Ghlo (3671ft; Mountain of the Mist) is a mountain group north east of Blair Atholl with three principal summits: *Carn nan Gabhar* (3671ft), *Carn Liath* (3193ft), and *Airgiod Bheinn* (3505ft). Carn Liath, 5m in a straight line from Blair Atholl, is the most easily reached, by way of the road from Blair Atholl up Glen Fender to Kirkton. The climb of c 2000ft is over rising moor to final steep slopes.

The old A9 in *3m* reaches the car park for the **Falls of Bruar**, the upper falls being found along a path which ascends through woods to a point where the Bruar cascades as rapids through a steep and narrow rocky cut. But there were not always woods here, and when Burns visited in 1787 he was so disappointed to find the stream tumbling through treeless moorland that he wrote 'The Humble Petition of Bruar Water', a plea which so touched the 4th Duke of Atholl that he planted this place with firs. The adjacent *Clan Donnachaidh Museum* (Tel: 079683-264)—the name is the Gaelic for the clan group, Donnachy—is the place for Robertsons, Duncans, Reids, MacRoberts, Duncansons, Colliers, MacIvers, Inches, Maclagans, MacConachies, Roys, MacInroys, Donachies, Starks, MacRobies, Roberts, Dunnachies, MacDonachies, Tonnochys and Skenes. Exhibits ancient and modern, including material on the '15 and '45, cover the story of these intricately related families.

The museum is beside the main A9, opposite being Glen Errochty along which B847 traverses open and empty country before dropping down into the Rannoch and Tummel valleys. A9, now rejoined by this Route, gradually ascends Glen Garry, achieving a mere 800ft in some 13m and passing (6m) *Dalnacardoch Lodge*, once well known as a coaching inn and standing on the site of the hut which was Wade's headquarters when he was building this stretch of the road in 1729. From here another small road makes its lonely way south through the hills towards the Rannoch and Tummel valleys, at a viewpoint on the way affording a striking glimpse of Loch Errochty. It was between Dalnacardoch and (5m) *Dalnaspidal Lodge* (1422ft) that Wade's troops working south from Inverness met those who had built up from Dunkeld, an occasion commemorated by a stone which over the years has suffered several moves as the road has been realigned and improved and which at present is seen only from the southbound carriageway. As the name suggests, Dalnaspidal was the site of a field hospital. Next, in *2m* and in increasingly desolate surroundings, the road arrives at the watershed **Pass of Drumochter** (1484ft) where the railway alongside breasts the highest railway summit in Britain. To the left the two prominent hog-backed hills are known as the *Sow of Atholl* (south) and the *Boar of Badenoch* (north).

6m **Dalwhinnie** (1180ft) is a bleak and frequently windswept village at the head of Glen Truim (north) as also of *Loch Ericht* which, today playing its part in the hydro-electric scheme, angles a narrow and lonely 15m southwards before discharging along the short river Ericht into Loch Rannoch. Here, below Ben Alder above the west shore towards the south end of the loch, Cluny's Cave, or Prince Charlie's Cave, is where the Young Pretender and Cluny Macpherson hid after Culloden (no road access). *Dalwhinnie Distillery* (Tel: 05282-264) offers tours, a visitor centre and a shop.

This wild and forbidding country around Dalwhinnie was long a favourite gathering place of the Highlanders, who here often successfully held their own against a far larger force of disciplined troops. Here Cromwell's Ironsides were checked by the men of Atholl, and here also in 1745 General Cope declined to encounter, in this their native stronghold, the Young Pretender's Highlanders descending from the Pass of Corrieyarrick. Cope retired to Inverness, leaving open the road to Edinburgh and the Lowlands, and thus assuring his own defeat at Prestonpans.

Descending Glen Truim into more fertile country, with opening views of mountains ahead, A9 enters the Spey valley close to the confluence of Truim and Spey, a spot to be noted by Camerons and Mackintoshes, for here in 1386 these two clans met in battle.—*9m* (from Dalwhinnie) **Newtonmore** (see Rte 50), bypassed by A9, lies just to the north beyond the Spey.

28   Perth to Braemar

A93.—Beyond Blairgowrie, and more steeply after Spittal of Glenshee, the road climbs into the mountains to the watershed of Cairnwell Pass (2199ft), the highest main road pass in Britain. Thence a scenic descent beside Clunie Water with views of the Grampian ranges ahead.

SOME HOTELS. **Blairgowrie**. *Altamount House*, Coupar Angus Road, PH10 6JN. Tel: 0250-3512. **Bridge of Cally**. *Bridge of Cally*, PH10 7JJ. Tel: 025086-231. **Kirkmichael**. *Log Cabin*, PH10 7NB. Tel: 025081-288. **Spittal of Glenshee**. *Dalmunzie, PH10 7QG. Tel: 025085-224.*

Total distance 51m.—10m **Bridge of Isla**.—*4m* **Blairgowrie**.—*6m* **Bridge of Cally**.—*15m* **Spittal of Glenshee**.—*7m* **Cairnwell Pass**.—*9m* **Braemar**.

Perth, see Rte 26, is left by way of Perth Bridge and Main Street, followed by a left fork on to Isla Road.

2m **Scone Palace** (pron. Scoon. Tel: 0738-52300). The present castellated mansion (1803–08), seat of the Earl of Mansfield, is the successor of a 16C house which itself succeeded the abbey and palace destroyed in 1559 by the Reformation mob after John Knox's sermon in Perth. However, the early gateway still stands and a part of the 16C house survives incorporated into today's building. But Scone's story starts many centuries earlier than any of these dates, and, though relatively modern in itself, today's palace offers the visitor not only ancient historical associations but also, in the more recent context, exquisite furniture, china, ivories and needlework, and an exhibition on estate management.

History. For most people Scone is first and foremost associated with the *Stone of Scone*, traditionally and obscurely linked with both Jacob's Pillow at Tara in Ireland and with Columba's Pillow on Iona. Said to have served as the throne on which Columba crowned Aidan at Dunadd in 574, and later to have been moved to Dunstaffnage, the stone, by now the sacred symbol of sovereignty, is supposed to have been brought to Scone in the 9C by Kenneth Macalpine, Scone thus becoming, perhaps in partnership with Dunkeld, the seat of government in those Pictish-Celtic times. Edward I removed the stone to London's Westminster Abbey in 1297, but, despite this, all the Scottish kings, including Bruce, were crowned here until James I. Later James IV upheld the tradition in 1488, and in 1651 Charles II did the same. Scottish romantics claim that the stone carried off by Edward I was a planted replica and that the real stone was hidden in a cave, where it still awaits discovery.
  The Moot Hill, still in front of the palace, was a solemn meeting-place even before Kenneth Macalpine's time. Later, in c 1120, a priory was founded here by Alexander I, this being raised to abbey status in 1164, and it was here that the parliament was held which decided that the Stewart line should succeed that of Bruce. Robert II, the first of these Stewarts, was buried here in 1390. Many centuries later, in 1716, the Old Pretender kept regal state here, and the Young Pretender slept here in 1745.

The ancient *Moot Hill* carries the family chapel, rebuilt at the same time as the palace but incorporating an aisle of a parish church of 1624, built by Viscount Stormont whose marble and alabaster tomb and effigy are here. The tour of the *Palace* embraces the main rooms, including the elegant Long Gallery. Among the things to be seen are a notable collection of 17 and 18C ivories; superb French furniture, including a writing table made for Marie Antoinette; embroidered bed hangings worked by Mary, Queen of Scots; and, on the Drawing Room walls, Lyons silk of 1804. The *Woodland Garden and Pinetum* (with, for the children, an adventure playground) include one of the finest collections of rare conifers in Britain, some of the trees being over 130 years old and 140ft high. David Douglas (1798–1834), the botanist after whom the Douglas Fir was named, was born on the estate and worked here as an under-gardener.

8m **Bridge of Isla** spans the Isla a little above its junction with the Tay, across the bridge being Meikleour House, the grounds of which are marked by a famous *Beech Hedge*. Planted in 1746 and now some 100ft high, the hedge borders the road for 580 yards.—*4m* **Blairgowrie** (7000 inhab. *Inf.*), known for its surrounding acres of raspberries, can be a useful stop before the mountains. The town centre, a small sloping area just above the river bridge, is known as Wellmeadow, a name recalling that this once was marsh much used for the supply of fresh water from an ancient well, traditionally associated with St. Ninian said to have camped here; today a modern well marks the spot. *Ardblair Castle* (by appointment. Tel: 0250-2960 or 0250-3155), 1m west by A923, although on 12C foundations, dates mainly from the 16C. The home of the Oliphants, who were staunch Jacobites, the castle houses Jacobite relics and also material on Lady Carolina Nairne (1766–1845, née Oliphant). Christened Carolina, in obstinate if belated honour of the Young Pretender, she achieved modest fame by writing a number of popular songs, amongst these being 'Charlie is my Darling' and 'Caller Herrin'. This road (A923) continues west to Dunkeld, soon passing a series of small lochs, in one of which (Loch Clunie) there is an island with the ruins of a castle built c 1500 by Bishop Brown of Dunkeld.

6m **Bridge of Cally** marks the junction with A924 running with Stra-thardle, a road providing a good connection across to (6m) Kirkmichael and (a further 11m) Pitlochry. A93 now starts to climb beside the Black Water, soon entering Glenshee and in *15m* reaching **Spittal of Glenshee** (1125ft), a village at the junction of Glen Beg and Glen Lochy whose streams here unite to form the Shee or Black Water. From its name perhaps once a travellers' hospice, Spittal of Glenshee is today popular in summer as a centre for walking and in winter as a base for skiing at Cairnwell. Diarmid's Tomb, $\frac{1}{2}$m east on the left bank of the Shee, is a tumulus.—Climbing more purposefully now the road makes for (*7m*) **Cairnwell Pass** (2199ft). Below Cairnwell (west. 3059ft) and Meall Odhar (east. 3019ft), the latter a spur of the mighty Glas Maol (3504ft), this bare and lofty ridge, the highest main road pass in Britain, is, with its chairlift, ski-tows, hang-gliding and ever expanding facili-ties, as popular in winter as it is in summer (Tel: 03383-320).

From Cairnwell the Clunie Water accompanies the northward descent of *9m* and 1100ft to **Braemar** (see Rte 37), sheltered beside the Dee below the Grampians rising beyond.

29   Perth to Aberdeen via Forfar and Stonehaven

A94 to Glamis. Choice to Brechin of A94 and B9134 via Forfar and Aberlemno, or A928, B957 and A94 via Kirriemuir and Finavon. B966 and A94 to Stonehaven. A92 to Aberdeen.—For the most part farmland, but with several outstandingly scenic glens meandering deep into the wooded foothills and mountains.

SOME HOTELS. **Meigle**. *Kings of Kinloch*, Coupar Angus Road, PH12 8QX. Tel: 08284-273. **Forfar**. *Royal*, Castle Street, DD8 3AE. Tel: 0307-62691. **Brechin**. *Northern*, Clerk Street, DD9 6AE. Tel: 03562-2156. **Kirriemuir**. *Thrums*, Bank Street, DD8 4BE. Tel: 0575-72758. **Edzell**. *Glenesk*, High Street, DD9 7TF. Tel: 03564-319. **Fettercairn**. *Ramsay*

Arms, AB3 1XX. Tel: 05614-334. **Stonehaven**. *County*, Arduthie Road, AB3 2EH. Tel: 0569-64386. *Heugh*, Westfield Road, AB3 2EE. Tel: 0569-62379.

Total distance 83m via Forfar. Via Kirriemuir is 3m longer.—*13m* **Coupar Angus**.—*12m* **Glamis**.—*5m* **Forfar**.—*11m* **Brechin**.—*5m* **Edzell**.—*5m* **Fettercairn**.—*17m* **Stonehaven**.—*15m* **Aberdeen**.

Perth, see Rte 26, is left by Perth Bridge and Main Street, followed by a right fork along Strathmore Street. After (*6m*) **Balbeggie** the Sidlaw Hills rise to the east, at their southern end, just north of B953 and about 4m out of Balbeggie, being *Dunsinane Hill*, bearing the remains of an ancient fort generally identified as the Dunsinane of Shakespeare's 'Macbeth'.

In the play the apparition foretold that Macbeth would never be vanquished until 'great Birnam Wood to high Dunsinane Hill shall come'. Later, while Macbeth held out in this fort of Dunsinane, his enemies met at Birnam (Rte 27) where their leader, Malcolm, ordered 'Let every soldier hew him down a bough and bear't before him'. Thus Birnam came to Dunsinane and Macbeth met his end. Although Shakespeare places the death of Macbeth at Dunsinane, it seems more probable that this occurred farther north at Lumphanan (see Rte 37).

7m **Coupar Angus** is so called to distinguish it from Cupar on the Fife peninsula. The tolbooth dates from 1762, and, beside the Dundee road (A923), there survives a fragment which is all that remains of a once wealthy abbey, founded in 1164 for Cistercians by Malcolm IV and destroyed in 1559. At Pitcur, 2m farther along this road, there is a square keep, once a seat of the Hallyburtons. Here an ancient holly tree is said to ᵐark where Claverhouse (Dundee) and Hallyburton breakfasted on 27 July 1689; in the evening both met their deaths at Killiecrankie.—*5m* **Meigle** is famed for its *Museum (AM. Tel: 031-244-3101) housing a notable collection of some 30 Early Christian inscribed stones of the 7–10C, all found at or near the old churchyard. The carvings are of great variety, curiosity and interest and it is rewarding to use the official leaflet which details each stone. *Belmont Castle*,½m south, was for many years the home of Sir H. Campbell-Bannerman (1836–1908), the prime minister; he is buried in Meigle churchyard.

From Meigle a pleasant diversion can be made northward to Alyth (4m) and thence up Glen Isla. *Alyth*, with the burn of the same name rippling along the main street, offers an arcade of a 13C church, a small Folk Museum (Tel: 0738-32488), and, on top of Barry Hill just north east, an Iron Age fort. *Glen Isla* winds up into hilly country to reach Glen Shee (Rte 28) in some 15m.

5m **Eassie**, where there is an elaborately carved Early Christian stone in the churchyard.—*2m* **Glamis** (pron. Glahms) is a neat village, most famed of course for its castle but also providing two more modest but nonetheless rewarding attractions. One of these, in the Manse garden, is the so-called *Malcolm Stone*, traditionally held to be the graveslab of Malcolm II, said to have died or been murdered in or near the castle in 1034. In fact this stone, nearly 9ft in height, is probably rather earlier in date, but may nevertheless have marked the burial place of some chieftain or leading churchman. Features of the stone are, on one side, serpent, fish and mirror symbols; and, on the other, a particularly fine cross with a variety of symbols in the quarters. The village's other attraction is the *Angus Folk Museum* (NTS. Tel: 030784-288), housed in an attractive terrace of restored early 19C cottages and illustrating local domestic and agricultural life in the 19C and earlier.

***Glamis Castle** (Tel: 030784-242), the imposing and historic family home of the earls of Strathmore and Kinghorne, has been a royal residence since 1372. It was the childhood home of the Queen Mother and the birthplace of Princess Margaret.

History. There has been a building here from very early times, and, as noted above, Malcolm II may have died or been murdered in or near the castle in 1034. In 1372 the estate was given by Robert II to Sir John Lyon, created Thane of Glamis, who four years later married Joanna, the king's daughter. Their grandson was in 1445 appointed Lord Glamis. In 1606 the 9th Lord Glamis was created Earl of Kinghorne, the 3rd Earl in 1677 becoming Earl of Strathmore and Kinghorne.

The castle, a five-storey L-shaped tower block, was originally a royal hunting lodge, but was extensively remodelled during the 17C. Today it comprises sumptuous rooms with a rich range of pictures, furniture, porcelain and tapestries.

The *Dining Room*, rebuilt in the 1850s with decoration of that period, is hung with family portraits. The *Crypt*, originally the Lower Hall, shows armour and weapons. The *Great Hall*, with its plasterwork ceiling of 1621, is the finest room in the castle. Portraits here include one of the 3rd Earl and his sons against the background of the castle (1683) and also one of Claverhouse ('Bonnie Dundee') by Kneller. A jester's motley is also displayed, the family enjoying the curious distinction of being the last in Scotland to offer such employment. The *Chapel* of 1688 shows painted panels of c 1686 by Jacob de Wet, and the *Billiard Room* Mortlake tapestries. The *King Malcolm Room*, so named because by tradition he died here, is today distinguished by blue-linen wall hangings of 1683, embroidered by Helen (died 1708) wife of the 3rd Earl, and by a collection of family china.

The *Royal Apartments* were arranged for the Queen Mother when Duchess of York, but the room in which Princess Margaret was born is not shown. *Duncan's Hall*, showing portraits of James IV and Mary, Queen of Scots, is of particular interest both as the oldest part of the castle, when it may have served as a guardroom, and also as the setting of Shakespeare's 'Macbeth'. The *Family Exhibition* includes the sword and watch of the Old Pretender, Claverhouse's bullet-proof jerkin and boots, and photographs of the Strathmore family.

The castle stands within a magnificent *Park* landscaped towards the end of the 18C. It includes the Italian Garden of two acres enclosed by high yew hedges, and a nature trail through Douglas firs and hardwood trees.

From Glamis there are alternative roads to Brechin; a southerly one through Forfar and Aberlemno, and a slightly longer (3m) northerly one through Kirriemuir and Finavon. The former passes the ancient priory of Restenneth and then the notable group of Pictish stones at Aberlemno; the latter will be chosen by lovers of the works of J.M. Barrie as also by those with the time to divert up the beautiful glens of Prosen and Clova.

Glamis to Brechin via Forfar and Aberlemno.

5m **Forfar** (13,000 inhab. *Inf.*) lies at the east end of the small loch on the shores of which was fought one of the last battles between the Picts and Scots before the combining of the two kingdoms in c 845. Today a lively place of some character with its often narrow and in part cobbled streets, Forfar was in ancient times the place where Malcolm Canmore is said to have first conferred surnames and titles on the Scottish nobility, and, in a more recent context, a wartime base for Polish troops. Both occasions are remembered; the latter by a plaque on the District Council building in the town centre, and the former by an octagonal turret, formerly the cross of c 1640, which, reached by steps out of Canmore Street, marks the site of Canmore's castle. Forfar *Museum and Art Gallery* (Tel: 0674-73232) is largely devoted to local history and activities, the exhibits including the burgh regalia, material on local archaeology and the flax industry, the 'Forfar bridle', used as a gag for witches who were mercilessly hounded here, and paintings largely of regional interest.

Restenneth Priory, 1½m east of Forfar off B9113, is supposed to have been founded in c 710 by the Pictish King Nechtan for St. Boniface, then refounded in c 1153 by Malcolm IV for Augustinians from Jedburgh. The tall tower, primitive both in its stonework and detail, is certainly pre-Norman (spire 15C), and what is particularly interesting is that the lower part is considerably older than the upper, this leading to the suggestion that this may in fact have been a west porch of Nechtan's ancient church. The rest of the church is of the 12C. *Dunnichen Hill*, 3m east of Forfar to the south of A932, was the site of the battle of Nectansmere (685), in which Egfrith of Northumbria was killed by the Pictish King Brude, this ending Anglian penetration into this part of Scotland.

B9134 is now followed out of Forfar to reach in *5m* the village of **Aberlemno**, famed for its *Pictish Stones, four of which are to be seen, one in the churchyard and three others beside the road in the village. The stone in the churchyard, dating from the 8C, bears on one side a Celtic cross, with entwined beasts, and on the other a vivid battle scene. The largest stone beside the road also shows a Celtic cross, this time flanked by two sorrowing angels holding books, while on the reverse there is a hunting scene above two typically Pictish symbols. More symbols decorate the remaining two simpler stones.—*2m Melgund Castle*, on the right down a side road and now a ruin, is said to have been built by Cardinal Beaton.

4m **Brechin** (7500 inhab. *Inf.*), perched on a steep slope above the South Esk, is most noted for its Cathedral and associated Round Tower. This squat little *Cathedral*, founded by David I in 1150 and now the parish church, is successor to an early Culdee abbey, but of David I's work nothing visible survives. As seen today the oldest parts of the building, the nave piers, date from the 13C, while the broad, projecting tower, with a low spire, though begun in the early 13C took some two centuries to complete. The choir was ruined at the Reformation, and in 1807 the transepts were demolished, but, later, more sensitive influences prevailed and in 1900–02 the choir was roofed and reglazed and the transepts at the same time rebuilt. For most visitors entering the cathedral the south west corner, beside an arc of the base of the Round Tower, will prove the most interesting, here being a number of ancient graveslabs (10–13C), some showing good strapwork, a carved cross of the same period, and the cathedral's silver and pewter.

The *Round Tower* (87ft) was built by Irish masons between 990 and 1012 and is the older of the only two Scottish mainland round towers of this kind, the other being at Abernethy (Rte 33D). In Ireland some 80 of these towers survive and, as in Ireland, the probability is that there was once an associated detached church, the predecessor until the 13C of the cathedral then started. On the west side there is a narrow doorway, 6ft above ground level, with typically Irish inward inclining jambs, the whole surrounded by a beaded moulding and surmounted by a Crucifixion, this last being rare in Pictland where the figure of Christ never appears on the crosses to be seen on so many sculpted stones. At the sides are two Culdee ecclesiastics.

In the small town the steep High Street was until the late 18C a main route for traffic crossing Brechin bridge, until then the only one over the South Esk. Here in High Street today a circle of stones set into the road marks the site of the mercat cross, demolished in 1767, while in various corners of the town neat plaques draw attention to the past. To the north, across the main through road, can be seen parts of the walls of

Brechin Round Tower. Built by Irish masons between 990 and 1012 and probably associated with the predecessor of the adjacent 13C cathedral

the chapel of the *Maison Dieu* hospice founded in 1267. The local *Museum* (Tel: 0674-73232) is in the public library in St. Ninian's Square in the east part of the town.

Glamis to Brechin via Kirriemuir.

Glamis is left by A928 for (*4m*) **Kirriemuir** (5000 inhab. *Inf.*), visited as the birthplace of J.M. Barrie (1860–1937) and as the 'Thrums' of his stories. *Barrie's Birthplace* (NTS. Tel: 0575-72646) is at 9 Brechin Road, and here today a museum recalls Barrie's achievements in the world of letters, at the same time indicating the various local places which feature in the novels. The outside washhouse, said to have served as his first theatre, now houses a Peter Pan display. Also of interest in the town are the quaint old Town Hall and a shield on the new Town Hall recording gratitude for the hospitality given to Polish army units in 1940–41, while, 1m west by B951, *Loch of Kinnordy Nature Reserve* (RSPB. Tel: 031-556-5624) is a marsh at which birds can be watched from hides.

GLENS PROSEN AND CLOVA. Two of Scotland's loveliest glens, Prosen and Clova, can conveniently be toured from Kirriemuir. **Glen Prosen**, the western and more modest of the two and penetrating the mountains for some 12 wooded miles, has, for much of its length, roads along both sides, that on the south being the more scenic and incidental. A good circuit can be made from Kirriemuir by heading north for Pearsie and then *Glenprosen* village which is where the two roads meet. From here *Runtaleave*, the head of the glen so far as the road is concerned, is 3m farther. The return can be made down the north side, below the hilltop Airlie Monument commemorating the 8th Earl (1856–1900), killed in the South African War, and passing a roadside memorial to Captain Scott and Doctor Wilson, the Antarctic explorers who here, at Wilson's home, planned their ill-fated expedition of 1910–11.—**Glen Clova** (B955) penetrates some 14m from its foot at *Dykehead*, soon offering a road choice either side of the broad valley as far as *Clova*, from where a small road, now close-hemmed by mountains, continues another scenic 3m to the Forestry Commission's *Glen Doll* picnic site, in fine surroundings beside the South Esk.—Glen Clova enjoys a historical association as the scene of the so-called Start, an abortive attempt by the young Charles II in 1650 to shake himself free of his fanatical Presbyterian supporters. After resting at Cortachy (a castle amid fine trees beside the road near Dykehead) he rode up the glen to Clova, where, however, his Highlander partisans failed to keep the promised rendezvous and Charles was forced to return more or less captive to the sermons and suffocating austerities of Presbyterian Perth.

The main axis of this Route continues (below) from Kirriemuir. But if the next objective is Edzell, then the choice should be the pleasant ridge-road which, starting from Dykehead and travelling by way of Fern and Kirkton of Menmuir, affords splendid views over the coastal levels. Rather over half-way along this road, 2m beyond Kirkton, a sign at a crossroads points north to the White and Brown Caterthuns, two notable examples of hill-forts which enjoy the bonus of being easily accessible from a parking area, itself worth a visit for the views both inland and towards the coast. The *White Caterthun* (976ft), only a few hundred yards away to the west and owing its name to its stonework, dates from about the 1C and preserves one of the most impressive stone and earthwork defensive complexes in Britain, comprising a rampart, perhaps once as much as 40ft thick, a ditch and outer earthworks. The

Brown Caterthun (943ft), generally probably of earlier date but spanning several structural periods, shows at least four and probably as many as six concentric defences, each provided with several entrances.

Assuming the main Route is followed, Kirriemuir is left by B957 for *(8m)* **Finavon** where A94 is joined. Here Finavon Dovecot, one of the largest in Scotland, is a twin-chambered sloping-roof type with some 2100 boxes, many of which are still in use, while nearby *Finavon Castle*, now a crumbling ruin but once a sturdy keep of the earls of Crawford, although built in the late 16C stands on foundations of c 1300; it collapsed in 1712 through undermining by a stream.—*7m* **Brechin**, see above.

From Brechin, A94 is the fast road to Stonehaven, but this Route makes a more interesting northerly loop, following B966 through Edzell and Fettercairn to rejoin A94 near Fordoun.—*3m* The village of *Inchbare* stands at a crossroads, a short way to the east being *Stracathro Church*, in the churchyard of which, on 10 July 1296, John Balliol renounced his crown in favour of England's Edward I, formally handing over the realm of Scotland to Edward's representative, the Bishop of Durham. Near here, too, in 1452, was fought the battle in which the Earl of Crawford, a partisan of the Douglases in their struggle against James II, was defeated by the king's supporters under Huntly.—*2m Edzell* is a neat modern village, best known for its castle.

*****Edzell Castle** (AM. Tel: 031-244-3101) is 1m west of the village, and as it is approached the earthworks can be seen of the earlier Norman stronghold. Adjoining this was the parish church, transferred in 1818 to

Edzell Castle. The Summer House at a corner of the early 17C Pleasance

its present site, and in its graveyard are a Celtic stone and the burial aisle of the Lindsays of Glenesk.

History. The original castle was the stronghold of the Stirlings of Glenesk. In the mid 14C the Stirlings were replaced by the Crawford Lindsays, who in the 16C, with an eye more to shelter and comfort than to defence, indulged themselves with the elegant new castle seen today. This comprises the towerhouse (early 16C), to which was added (1580) the mansion around the courtyard, followed in 1604 by the Pleasance, the achievement of Sir David Lindsay, Lord Edzell. In 1562 Mary, Queen of Scots, while making her northern progress, stayed here and held council. Later the castle was twice visited by James VI, and in the 18C it suffered from occupation by Hanoverian troops.

Entrance is by way of a breach in the courtyard east wall, the tower-house then being ahead left, joined by the shell of a range of buildings to the lower and much damaged Round or North Tower. The Great Hall is inside the tower-house on the first floor.

But Edzell's unique feature is its *Pleasance, or walled garden, created, as noted above, by Sir David Lindsay in 1604 and especially remarkable for its symbolic sculpture. It is contained within a square enclosure, with the arms of its creator and its date appearing over a doorway in the north east corner. The walls are decorated with bas-reliefs (copies of German originals after Dürer) of the Cardinal Virtues (west), the Liberal Arts (south), and the Planetary Deities (east), these last being executed with particular strength. The walls are also indented with large square holes (flower-filled in summer) which, seen from a distance, form, in combination with their surrounds, the Lindsay arms. The box hedge (1932) in the centre spells the family motto, 'Dum spiro spero'—'While I breathe I hope'. In the south corner once stood the Bath House, an unusual luxury by early 17C standards; it was pulled down at an unknown date, but the foundations were exposed in 1855 and show that the building was a comfortable and elegant affair with bath, dressing and sitting room, this last with a fireplace. The Summer House, at the east corner, is provided with a stone bench round the wall, a small stair-turret and a closet with twin privies.

GLEN ESK. Edzell stands at the mouth of wooded **Glen Esk** which curves some 14 northward and westward miles into the mountains, along its course offering both scenery and a touch of history; history because it was probably up this valley that Macbeth fled before crossing the mountains by the Fir Mounth to meet his end at Lumphanan, north beyond Deeside. There is prehistory, too, in the form of *Colmealie Stone Circle*, a rough, unpretentious, almost miniature affair found some 6m out of Edzell beside some farm buildings a few yards up a track from where the road touches the river. Not far beyond comes the *Glenesk Folk Museum* (Tel: 03567-236) where the exhibits tell the story of everyday life in the glen between 1800 and modern times. The road ends at *Invermark Castle*, the shell of the tall tower-house—typical with its high, barred entrance and windows—which once deterred raiders descending out of the mountains to pillage the rich glen and the open lowlands at its foot. Beyond Invermark, a track leads in about a mile to *Loch Lee*, set below high brown mountains and once home to a village community, as evidenced by a ruined church (on, it is said, an ancient Culdee site) and its forlorn graveyard.

From Edzell village B966 heads east for (*5m*) **Fettercairn**, a trim small place which welcomes the visitor through a turreted arch, built to commemorate a visit by Queen Victoria and Prince Albert in 1861. Of more interest, in the pleasing square, stands the shaft of a *Mercat Cross*, bearing marks indicating the length of the Scots ell and also an iron hasp to which the jougs were attached. In fact this was not properly Fettercairn's cross, but that of the township of Kincardine (see below). *Fasque* (Tel: 05614-201), rather over 1m north of Fettercairn on B974, is a mansion of 1809, acquired soon after that date by the father of the statesman W.E. Gladstone. The latter spent his honeymoon here but made his home at his wife's Hawarden Castle (see 'Blue Guide Wales'). Life in Victorian times is the theme here, while a deer park and deer farm provide outdoor interest.

B974, the lonely and scenic Cairn o' Mounth road, passes Fasque on the left and then, on the right before reaching Clattering Bridge, an earthwork known as *Green Castle*, believed to have been the stronghold of Finella, daughter of the lord of Angus reputed to have murdered Kenneth II while on a pilgrimage from Kincardine to the shrine of St. Palladius at Auchenblae (see Kincardine Castle, below). The lady's name survives as Strath Finella which runs north east from Clattering Bridge. Beyond the Cairn o' Mounth watershed at 1488ft, the road descends to reach Deeside at Banchory some 15m from Fettercairn.

Laurencekirk, 4m south east of Fettercairn by B9120, is the chief town of a fertile district known as The Howe of the Mearns. The small town, founded by Lord Gardenstone in 1779 as a centre for linen weaving, also became famed for its snuff boxes of exceptional design (by Charles Stiven) with a concealed hinge and pin.

Still travelling north east on B966 this Route in under *2m* passes (north) earthworks and foundations on a mound, these marking the site of *Kincardine Castle*, the sole vestige, apart from the shaft of its cross in Fettercairn, of the royal residence and associated township which once flourished here. Here, it is said, Kenneth II was murdered in 994 by a lord of Angus, and from here, too, in 1296, John Balliol wrote to Edward I offering to abdicate.—*4m* **Auchenblae**, where the ruined *Chapel of St. Palladius* (1243) recalls in its dedication an early Irish churchman said to have brought Christianity to the Mearns and to have been buried here by his disciple Ternan who erected a shrine over his master's tomb.—Rejoining A94 this Route soon reaches (*4m*) *Bridge of Mondynes*, just north west of which is *Glenbervie*, home of Burns's ancestors whose graves, including that of his great-grandfather, James Burnes (sic), will be found in the churchyard. Nearby there is a Burns memorial cairn.

7m **Stonehaven** (8500 inhab. *Inf.*) can almost be said to be two towns, with Old Stonehaven around the harbour and 19C New Stonehaven above. For the visitor the old town is the more picturesque and interesting, here being the late 16C *Tolbooth*, built to serve as a storehouse and later, in 1748–49, used as a prison for the local Episcopal clergy, who nevertheless managed, through a barred window, to baptise children held up to them. Today the building houses a small museum of local history and fishing (Tel: 0779-77778).

For *Dunnottar Castle*, immediately south of Stonehaven, see Rte 35.

The road known as the **Slug Road** (A957), linking Stonehaven with Crathes on Deeside, was completed in 1800. The *Auquhollie Stone*, interesting because of its clear Ogham inscription, stands north of the road a short way out of Stonehaven (turn right opposite the entrance to Rickarton House, then left; the stone is on the right just beyond the first farm).

The **Elsick Mounth Road** (B979), farther north east, also links Stonehaven with Deeside, near Peterculter. This is a much older road, said indeed to have been used by the Romans whose camp of *Raedykes*, one of their northernmost main marching camps, lies along the ridge between B979 and A957. The camp was probably never fully finished and may be the site of the battle of Mons Grampius (84) in which the northern tribes were defeated by Agricola (but Bennachie, see Rte 40, is the more favoured site).

Now following A92 this Route passes (*5m*) **Muchalls Castle** (Tel: 0569-30217) which, though comparatively small, is a complete and typical example of a 17C laird's house, still in private occupation today. Built in 1619–27, the house is noted for its moulded ceilings and a secret stairway. Along the coast between Muchalls and Aberdeen there is a chain of what were once busy fishing villages—Muchalls, Newtonhill, Portlethen and Findon, this last giving its name (Finnan) to smoked haddock—which today, though, are increasingly developing as extensions of Aberdeen.—*10m* central **Aberdeen**, see Rte 36.

30 Perth to Dundee (Direct)

A85.—This road traverses the level tract between the Sidlaw Hills and the Tay, here temporarily opening as a wide estuary before narrowing to pass between Dundee and the north east tip of the Fife peninsula. Known as the Carse of Gowrie, this tract has long been famed for its fertility, though less perhaps for its tourist interest and Rte 33D (only 6m longer) offers a more interesting alternative south of the Tay and through northern Fife.

SOME HOTELS. See **Perth** (Rte 26) and **Dundee** (Rte 34).

Total distance 22m.

Perth, see Rte 26, is left by either Perth or Queen's Bridge, and then Gowrie Street followed by Dundee Road. A85 runs below the steep slope of Kinnoull Hill, passing *Fairways Heavy Horse Centre*, while across the Tay stands ruined *Elcho Castle*, both places described under Rte 26.—*10m Megginch Castle Gardens* (Tel: 08212-222) include ancient yews, for which an age of 1000 years is claimed, a 16C rose garden, a 19C flower parterre and a dovecot. The castle (no adm.) is an enlargement of a 15C original. Immediately east of Megginch, *Errol Station Heritage Centre* (Tel: 05754-222) should attract railway enthusiasts; here, at a station of 1847, a booking office and waiting rooms have been restored to their 1920s appearance, while in the former porter's house an exhibition recalls the railways of Tayside. To the north of A85, along the minor parallel road running with the Braes of the Carse, there are two castles (both no adm.) of minor historical and some architectural interest. *Fingask*, with a tower of 1594 and additions of 1675, twice provided refuge for the Old Pretender, while *Kinnaird Castle*, 2m north east of Fingask, is a tall (restored) 15C tower.

Back on A85, between *4m Inchture* and *2m Longforgan*, will be seen the stately *Castle Huntly* (no adm.), the tower of which, much altered in the 17–18C and now incorporated into a college, was first raised in 1452 by Lord Gray of Fowlis, Master of the Household to James II. This same Lord Gray also built, in 1453, the *Church of St. Marnan* at Fowlis Easter, 2m north of Longforgan, where some curiosities will be found both within the church and in its churchyard. In fact Lord Gray's church was successor to a chapel of c 1150, built when these lands were given by David I to William Maule as a reward for military service; later, in 1377, the estate passed by marriage to the Grays who in 1242 dedicated the chapel to St. Marnan, an Iona contemporary of Columba. Today, a harsh note in an otherwise tranquil spot, jougs still hang by the west door, while in the churchyard an ancient cross and tomb invite speculation. In fact the former probably has nothing to do with the latter, if only because it stands at the tomb's foot rather than at its head. It has been suggested that the cross may mark, or have marked, an early church meeting-place, and that the graveslab, ornamented with a hunting horn, may cover a 16C forester. Inside the church are a bronze alms dish (German, 1487), embossed with a scene of the Garden of Eden; 15C oak doors which were once part of the rood screen; and, of particular interest, pre-Reformation paintings on oak, quaintly representing the Crucifixion, the Virgin, St. John the Baptist and St. Catherine, with an entombment below.

From Fowlis Easter Dundee can be reached by minor roads passing close to *Camperdown Park* (see Rte 34). Along A85 (*2m*) **Invergowrie**, now a suburb of Dundee, is said once to have been a favourite residence of Alexander I.—*4m* central **Dundee**, see Rte 34.

31 Edinburgh to Stirling via Dunfermline, Culross and Alloa

A90 across the Forth Bridge. A823 to Dunfermline. A994 and B9037 to Culross and Kincardine. A977 and A907 to Alloa and Stirling.—Of no particular scenic merit, this Route runs through the south west corner of Fife (see Rte 33).

SOME HOTELS. **Dunfermline**. *King Malcolm*, Queensferry Road, KY11 5DS. Tel: 0383-722611. **Airth**. *Airth Castle*, FK2 8JF. Tel: 0324-83411. **Alloa**. *Royal Oak*, Bedford Place, FK10 1LJ. Tel: 0259-722423.

Total distance 36m.—*13m* **Dunfermline**.—*7m* **Culross**.—*4m* **Kincardine**.—*5m* **Alloa**.—*7m* **Stirling**.

From central **Edinburgh** (see Rte 18) Queensferry Road (A90) in *10m* reaches and crosses the *Forth Road Bridge*, for which, as also for the adjacent railway bridge and the approach from Edinburgh, see Rte 9. Here, by the bridge's north end, Rte 32 continues north, while Rtes 33A and 33C head east across Fife. This Route takes A823 which cuts off north west for Rosyth and Dunfermline. *Rosyth* lies around the anchorage of St. Margaret's Hope, much of the land here having been acquired by the government in 1903 to house the naval base and dockyard, and it was between Rosyth and Dunfermline in 1651 that a battle was fought between Cromwell's troops and supporters of Charles II, the latter mostly Macdonalds. Decisively defeated, the clan suffered heavy losses and their chief, Hector Macdonald of Duart, was taken prisoner.

3m **Dunfermline** (52,000 inhab. *Inf.*), most royal of royal burghs, and since at least Malcolm Canmore's time (11C) intimately associated with the births, lives and burials of Scotland's royalty, is visited today for the abbey, monastery and palace ruins which reflect that past, as also, in a more modern context, as the birthplace of the munificent philanthropist Andrew Carnegie.

History. The name Dunfermline means Fort of the Crooked Linn, this probably referring to the primitive castle which Malcolm Canmore held here beside a bend in the burn running through Pittencrieff Glen, where what may well be the remains of this fort can still be seen as a mound called Malcolm's Tower. The Saxon princess Margaret, sister of Edgar Atheling and fleeing from the Normans, was shipwrecked in the Forth and brought to Dunfermline where Malcolm married her in 1067. Malcolm and Margaret then built their palace and, a little later, founded a priory. This palace was to remain a favourite with successor kings, and the priory, promoted to abbey by David I, superseded Iona as their place of burial. Edward I held court here during his second invasion of Scotland (1303). And Charles II stayed here in 1651 before his march to defeat at Worcester, and it was while here that he was forced to accept the Covenants.

The *Andrew Carnegie Birthplace Museum* (Tel: 0383-724302) is a weaver's cottage at the corner of Moodie Street and Priory Lane in the lower, south part of the town. The museum and the associated memorial hall tell the story of Carnegie's youth, of the fortune he made, and of his munificent benefactions.

Born here in poor circumstances, Andrew Carnegie (1835–1919) emigrated with his family to Pennsylvania, there rising to enormous wealth and power through his flair in the iron and steel industries. He became renowned as a philanthropist, his gifts amounting to millions of dollars in both America and Britain. Nor did he forget his native town, which has benefited much from the Carnegie Dunfermline Trust (1904), Pittencrieff Glen, baths, library, etc., as well as an annual festival of music and drama, being among the causes supported. Dunfermline is the headquarters of this local trust, of the Carnegie Hero Fund, and of the United Kingdom Trust.

The abbey and the monastery and palace ruins, forming a compact group a short way up the hill, can be approached along either side, by Monastery Street on the west or St. Margaret Street (with a car park) on the east.

The *Abbey Church* is in two parts; a Norman nave of 1150 and a spacious Gothic choir, built by William Burn in 1817–22 and serving as parish church.

The nave, standing in part on the foundations of the earlier church, is a substantial relic of the church begun by David I in 1128 when he raised Malcolm Canmore's and Margaret's priory to the rank of abbey. An elegant choir and transepts, added in 1250, were wrecked by Reformers in 1560 and finally swept away in 1817 to make way for Burn's choir-church. Malcolm and Margaret, who both died in 1093, were buried in a special chapel (now only foundations) outside the church. Their sons (Edgar, Alexander I and David I) and their descendants (Malcolm IV, Alexander III and Robert Bruce) all lie in the church.

Seen from the outside the *Nave is somewhat marred by the great size of the buttresses added in the 16C. The imposing west doorway is flanked by towers, the one on the north rebuilt with its spire in c 1590, the other surviving longer until rebuilt in 1887 after being damaged by lightning. The interior is of six bays, with tall round piers and round arches, the south west arch, however, built by James VI in Gothic style. The east piers are typically grooved with zigzags and spirals, and the elaborate zigzag Norman mouldings on the inner arch of the north porch contrast with the later groined roof. The aisles have original quadripartite vaults and blind arcading; the triforium and clerestory are plain. In the north aisle there is a memorial to George Durie, the last abbot (1560), and the glass of the large, 'historical' west window was designed by Noel Paton.

The Choir (parish church) carries a heavy square tower, the balustrade of which incongruously flaunts in large stone letters the words 'King Robert the Bruce'. Beneath the pulpit is the grave of Robert Bruce (1274–1329), marked by a memorial brass. During the excavations in 1818 Bruce's body was revealed wrapped in a shroud interwoven with threads of gold and encased in two lead coverings; it was placed in a new coffin and reburied. Outside the choir, at the east end of the church, are the foundations of the Shrine of St. Margaret, the burial place of herself and her husband. Nearby (north east) is the sarcophagus tomb (1875) of Robert Erskine (1685–1752), minister of the abbey and one of the leaders of the Seccession movement.

The *Monastery* domestic buildings were ranged south of and below the church, the chief remains today—its stones, as also those of the palace, were pillaged in 1610 for the building of Pittencrieff House (see below)—being those of the refectory, which must have been a fine hall indeed judging from its elegant window of seven lights, the upper parts filled with quatrefoils. An arch crosses the road to what is left of the *Palace*, at times also doubling as guest house for the abbey. Destroyed by fire in 1304, when Edward I left, the palace was rebuilt by James IV in 1500 and it was occupied by Mary, Queen of Scots, in 1561. But today a kitchen is about all that identifiably remains of this favourite royal residence and, indeed, nursery, for here were born (to Margaret) Maud, wife of Henry I of England, and her brothers, later kings Edgar, Alexander I and David I; David II (1324) and James I (1394); and the children of James VI/I, Elizabeth (1596), afterwards Queen of Bohemia, and, in 1600, Charles I.

Opposite the west door of the Abbey Church is an entrance to *Pittencrieff Glen*, once Malcolm Canmore's park, today a large ornamental estate with superb gardens, presented to the town by Andrew Carnegie in 1903. Here Canmore's memory lives on in the ruin of *Malcolm's Tower* beside the burn, while *Pittencrieff House* (Tel: 0383-722935 or 721814) houses a museum of local history and a distinguished costume collection. The house, built in 1610, in part with stones pillaged from the monastery and palace, has known many owners, the last individual being Andrew Carnegie who was laird for a brief year before in 1903 handing over the property to the town.

Dunfermline's *Public Library* (Tel: 0383-723661), just east of the abbey, owes its origin (1883) and much of its later prestige to Carnegie and the Dunfermline Trust. It houses the distinguished Murison Burns Collection of Burns material, this including books, pamphlets, prints and even commemorative pottery. Just north of here, in High Street by the 19C guildhall, stands the cross of (in part) 1626, while the site of its predecessor of 1396 is marked out on the ground. High Street, followed east, becomes East Port, off which Viewfield Terrace drops south to a car park conveniently placed beside *Dunfermline Museum* (Tel: 0383-721814). Here the local story is attractively told, some emphasis being placed on the damask linen industry, illustrated by examples of this craft together with a handloom of 1835, complete with Jacquard harness and pattern cards.

A994 and B9037 are now followed west for (7m) ***Culross** (pron. Cooross), but noting, beside the road just east of the town, the remains of *St. Mungo's Chapel* (NTS), built in 1503 by Glasgow's Bishop Blacader.

Culross is the traditional site of a 5 or 6C religious house, presided over by St. Serf or Servan. St. Mungo, or Kentigern, founder of Glasgow cathedral and patron saint of that city, is said to have been born here. The story goes that his mother, Thenew, of a pagan family, secretly married the Christian King Owen of Strathclyde. Disowned then by her father she was forced to flee from her home in Lothian, crossing the Forth alone in a small boat which was driven ashore at the spot now marked by this chapel. And here she gave birth.

During the 16–17C Culross was a busy community, thriving through its trade in coal and salt, its salt-pans being visited by James VI who made the town a royal burgh in 1588. The coal and salt trades were much expanded by the energetic and businesslike Sir George Bruce (died 1625).

Culross survives as perhaps the most perfect example of a small Scots town of the 16–18C. That this is so is in large part due to the care and imagination of the National Trust for Scotland which, over the last 50 years, has acquired and restored many buildings. The lower town, beside the Forth, is connected with the upper and the abbey by steep, narrow flagstone streets.

The *Palace* (AM. Tel: 031-244-3101) was built in 1597, and extended by a north wing in 1611, for Sir George Bruce, and, with its stepped gables and pantiled roofs set about an open court with terraced gardens

The Pineapple, Kincardine. An 18C Garden Folly

behind, is a charming example of the smaller type of Scottish town mansion. Many of the panelled rooms are, in typical Scottish style, painted all over with scenes from the scriptures etc. The *Town House* (NTS. Tel: 0383-880359), or tolbooth, dates from 1626 except for its tower which is of 1783. Handed over to the National Trust by the local council in 1975, the building now houses a Visitor Centre with an audio-visual presentation.

Behind the palace stands the Cross, supported by a modern shaft, and here too is the curious, corbelled-out turret known as the *Study of Bishop Leighton* (NTS. Tel: 0383-880359).

The *Abbey*, at the top of the town, was founded for Cistercians by Malcolm, Earl of Fife, in 1215. The church, dating in large part from c 1300 but rebuilt under James IV, preserves intact its choir and splendid central tower, these parts now serving as parish church. The nave, however, of which the south wall is probably original to 1215, is in ruins. In a chamber on the north side are the alabaster effigies of Sir George Bruce (died 1625) and his numerous family. Of the monastic buildings little survives, much of their stone having been used in the building of Abbey House (no adm.) just above; begun in 1608 and altered in 1670, the house was remodelled in 1952.

Continuing west, B9037 in *4m* reaches **Kincardine**, a small river port at the north end of a fine bridge of 1936. Connoisseurs of follies will cross the bridge to see the bizarre *Pineapple* (NTS. Picnic area; off B9124 to the north of Airth), built in 1761 by an unknown architect as a garden retreat. Sir John Dewar (1842–1922), inventor of the vacuum flask, was born in Kincardine, and *Tulliallan Castle* (1824), at the north end of the town, was occupied by the Polish General Sikorsky as his headquarters during the 1939–45 war. Beyond extends an important Forestry Commission tree nursery.

3m **Clackmannan**, reached by A977 and A907, stands just to the south of the latter road and rewards the short diversion with a stepped 17C *Cross*, the tower of the old *Tolbooth* (1592), which, with its courtroom, prison and jailor's dwelling once extended some 40ft to the east, and the mysterious *Stone (Clach) of Mannan*, all these grouped in the village square. The stone, then recumbent, was placed on its present shaft in 1833 and is sometimes said to be sacred to the pagan god, Mannan. *Clackmannan Tower* (no adm. but well seen from outside), on a hill to the west appropriately known as King's Seat, is a tall and ancient tower said to have been a residence of Malcolm IV. *Gartmorn Dam Country Park* (Tel: 0259-214319), a short way north of Clackmannan, offers a nature reserve, a reservoir with the oldest dam in Scotland and a visitor centre.

2m **Alloa** (26,000 inhab.) is essentially an industrial town, although *Alloa Tower*, in the lower east part of the town, provides a reminder of medieval times. Dating from the 15C the tower was built by the Erskine family (later earls of Mar) and was at times in turn the childhood home of James V, Mary, Queen of Scots, James VI and his sons Henry and Charles. Alloa stands at the south east end of the *Links of the Forth*, the tortuous stretch of the river between here and Stirling, so famed for its fertility that a saying runs 'A crook o' the Forth is worth an earldom o' the North'.—*2m* **Tullibody**, in which there is a small pre-Reformation church, of which John Knox recorded that the French troops sent to help Mary of Guise, 'expert enough in such feats, tuke down the roof to make ane brig over the Devon', and so escaped to Stirling. Robert Dick (1811–66), the geologist (see also Rte 61, Thurso), was born here.—*5m* **Stirling**, see Rte 23.

32   Edinburgh to Perth

A90 across the Forth Bridge. M90 to Exit 5. B9097, B920 and A911 around Loch Leven to Kinross. M90 to Perth.—Farmland, with hills.

SOME HOTELS. **Kinross**. *Granada Lodge*, Kincardine Road (by M90), KY13 7NQ. Tel: 0577-64646. *Green*, 2 The Muirs, KY13 7AS. Tel: 0577-63467. *Windlestrae*, The Muirs, KY13 7AS. Tel: 0577-63217.

Total distance 45m.—*10m* **Forth Bridge (north)**.—*10m* **M90 Exit 5**.—*6m* **Scotlandwell**.—*4m* **Kinross**.—*15m* **Perth**.

From central **Edinburgh** (see Rte 18) Queensferry Road (A90) in *10m* reaches and crosses the Forth Road Bridge, for which, as also for the adjacent railway bridge and the approach from Edinburgh, see Rte 9. Here, at the north end of the Forth Bridge, Rte 31 bears west while Rtes 33A and 33C lead off east.—M90 now crosses a western part of Fife (see Rte 33), to the west, between Exits 4 and 5, being *Blairadam Forest*, an estate bought by William Adam in 1731.

10m **M90 Exit 5** where the motorway is left for an anticlockwise circuit of Loch Leven. However, at Gairney Bank, immediately north up B996, visitors with an interest in Scottish Church history will find a roadside monument commemorating the foundation here in 1733 of the first Secession presbytery.

Loch Leven, celebrated as much for its pink trout as for the imprisonment and romantic escape of Mary, Queen of Scots, is 3½m long by 2m broad and a *National Nature Reserve*, the most important freshwater area in Britain for migratory and breeding wildfowl, notably pink-footed and greylag geese and many varieties of duck (Restricted access. Tel: 031-447-4784). There are two principal islands, on one of which, near Kinross, stands Loch Leven Castle (see below); on the other, *St. Serf's Island* at the south east, are the ruins of a priory, founded on the site of an earlier Culdee settlement. Andrew Wyntoun (died c 1420), one of the earliest of the Scots chroniclers, was prior here.

B9097 in under *2m* reaches *Vane Farm Nature Centre* (RSPB. Tel: 0577-62355), the first nature centre to be established in Britain. In a converted farm building, the Centre has arranged displays explaining the local geography, geology, wildlife, botany etc., while, additionally, there are a picnic area, a nature trail, and a hide from which between late September and April feeding wild geese and duck can be observed.—*2m* New Gullet Bridge whence B920 is followed north for (*2m*) *Scotlandwell* with, in the village, an ancient well from which Agricola's soldiers are said to have drunk in 84 and where also, it is claimed, Bruce was cured of leprosy by the local Red Friars who had established a hospice here in 1250 (he is nonetheless generally believed to have died of leprosy in 1329). By way of contrast, nearby Portmoak airfield is a gliding centre, good use being made of the thermals produced by Bishop Hill to the north.—*1m* Kinnesswood, for *Michael Bruce's Cottage* (Tel: 031-556-0307), birthplace of Michael Bruce (1746–67), known as the Gentle poet of Loch Leven and author of the 'Ode to the Cuckoo'; the cottage shows material illustrating 18 and 19C village life. Beyond, A911 curves west to pass the ruin of *Burleigh Castle*, an early 16C tower with a rather later courtyard wall, once a stronghold of the Balfours and several times visited by James VI.—*1m* Milnathort, where Rte 25C comes in from Stirling.

Kinross (3000 inhab. *Inf.*) is under *2m* south of Milnathort. The 17C *Tolbooth* was repaired and decorated in 1771 by Robert Adam, adjacent being *Kinross Museum* (Tel: 0738-32488) bearing a plaque recording the gratitude of the Polish Tank Training Centre, here between 1942–48.

But the main tourist objective here is *Loch Leven Castle* (AM. Tel: 031-244-3101), the island-prison of Mary, Queen of Scots. A compact square tower standing in a court surrounded by a curtain wall, the castle dates in part from the early 14C when, in 1335, it was unsuccessfully besieged by the English who attempted to drown the place by damming the river Leven and thus raising the loch level. The round tower, at an angle of the wall, is an early 16C addition, as are also probably the remains of a hall and kitchen.

Here Mary was brought on 16 June 1567 after her surrender at Carberry Hill, and here she remained for nearly 11 months in the custody of the local laird, Sir William Douglas. Her treatment was unsympathetic, she was much of the time in poor health and she suffered a miscarriage, thought to have been of twins. In Mary's time the surrounds of the castle were very different to what the visitor sees today; the island was even smaller and the loch nearly four times larger. The tower, at this time entered through a low round-headed door on the first floor, comprised two vaulted chambers below (a store and a kitchen) and three storeys above, the wooden floors of which have long disappeared. Here dwelt Douglas and his wife. Their prisoner was probably held in the round tower (described by Scott as 'rude and inconvenient'), and here, on 23 July 1567, threatened by Lord Lindsay, 'the rudest, most bigoted and fiercest of the confederated lords' who was 'so unmanly as to pinch with his iron glove the arm of the poor queen' (Scott), Mary signed a deed of abdication in favour of her son, and another appointing her half-brother, Moray, regent.

Many attempts to rescue the queen were made, but eventually through her personal charm she succeeded in touching the heart of George Douglas, youngest brother of Sir William. His undisguised devotion led to his expulsion from the island, but he left behind him a like-minded kinsman, William Douglas, a lad of 16 who, on the night of 2 May 1568, while everybody was at supper, got hold of the keys, placed the queen in a boat, and, having locked the gates behind him, threw the keys into the water. On reaching the shore, Mary was received by Lord Seton, George Douglas and Sir James Hamilton and escorted to Niddry Castle (see Rte 8). Thirteen days later she was defeated at Langside.

M90 is now rejoined for (*11m*) *Exit 9* for Rte 33D.—*4m* central **Perth**, see Rte 26.

33   Fife Peninsula

Fife, now one of the local government regions of Scotland, has since long ago been known as the Kingdom of Fife, perhaps because the region is close to Abernethy, an ancient Pictish capital, or perhaps simply because it has long been one of the richest and most self-contained parts of Scotland. One of its latest assertions of independence was its successful opposition to official plans to split Fife between Tayside and Lothian under the 1975 local government reorganisation. Properly Fife embraces also the district extending south west from Loch Leven as far as Kincardine and including Dunfermline. This area is described under Rte 31.

The Fife peninsula, bounded on the north by the Firth of Tay and on the south by the Firth of Forth, is some 30–35m long by 20m broad. Scenically the outstanding feature is the string of quaint and picturesque ancient little fishing ports lining the east part of the south coast (roughly Largo to Crail, known as the East Neuk); otherwise Fife is generally farming land, with some high moorland patches. Of many interesting and historical sites, special mention may be made of Falkland Palace, the round tower at Abernethy and the town of St. Andrews.

Fife is described in four sections: A. Edinburgh to St. Andrews round the coast. B. St. Andrews. C. Edinburgh to Dundee via Falkland and Cupar. D. The North (Perth to Dundee).

A. Edinburgh to St. Andrews round the Coast

A90 across the Forth Bridge. A921 from the north side of the Forth
Bridge to Kirkcaldy. A955 to Leven. A915 to Kirkton of Largo. A917 to
Crail and St. Andrews.

SOME HOTELS. **Aberdour**. *Woodside*, High Street, KY3 0SW. Tel:
0383-860328. **Burntisland**. *Inchview*, Kinghorn Road, KY3 9EB. Tel:
0592-872239. **Kirkcaldy**. *Anthony's*, 18 West Albert Road, KY1 1DL. Tel:
0592-265627. **Leven (Lundin Links)**. *Old Manor*, Leven Road, KY8 6AJ.
Tel: 0333-320368. **Anstruther**. *Craw's Nest*, Bankwell Road, KY10 3DS.
Tel: 0333-310691, **Crail**. *Balcomie Links*, KY10 3TN. Tel: 0333-50237.
Croma, Nethergate, KY10 3TU. Tel: 0333-50239.

Total distance 55m.—*10m* **Forth Bridge (north)**.—*4m* **Aberdour**.—*2m*
Burntisland.—*5m* **Kirkcaldy**.—*10m* **Largo**.—*5m* **Elie**.—*5m*
Anstruther.—*4m* **Crail**.—*10m* **St. Andrews**.

From central **Edinburgh** (see Rte 18) Queensferry Road (A90) in *10m*
reaches and crosses the *Forth Road Bridge*, for which, as also for the
adjacent railway bridge and the approach from Edinburgh, see Rte 9.
Here, at the north end of the Forth Bridge, Rte 31 bears west while Rte
32 continues north and Rte 33C aims north east. This Route drops into
the small town of **Inverkeithing**, granted a charter by William the Lion
in 1165 and the birthplace of Sir Samuel Greig (1735–88), the admiral
who created a Russian navy for Catherine the Great (plaque in High
Street). More about this admiral can be learnt at the *Inverkeithing
Museum* of local history (Tel: 0383-413344), at the west end of the town
and housed in what was once the 14C friary and hospice of the Grey
Friars. At the east end of the town stands the *Cross* (1399; with unicorn of
1688), near here also being the *Town House* of 1755; the attractive, turreted 17C *Church Hall* or *Fordell's Lodging*; and the *Church* (1826 but
with a medieval tower) in which there is a late 14C font.

2m A921 skirts the industrial area and new town of *Dalgety* which has
grown near where once stood the seat of the Earl of Moray, granted
lands along this coast by Bruce. *St. Bridget's Church*, dating from 1244
and now roofless, is by Dalgety Bay to the south east of the town. The
east part represents the old church, the structure to the west being a
later two-storey building with a laird's loft and a burial vault.

2m **Aberdour** is a small summer resort whose castle, ancient church
and dovecot form an exceptionally attractive medieval group. The
Castle (AM. Tel: 031-244-3101), standing on 14C foundations, has as its
core a 14C tower on to which other buildings were grafted during the 16
and 17C. Originally a stronghold of the Morays, the castle later passed
to the Douglas earls of Morton, and today preserves some murals. *St.
Fillan's Church* is part Norman and part 16C, the Norman parts being
the chancel, the chancel arch, the north wall of the nave and the
windows of both chancel and nave. There is a leper-squint in the west
wall, and the exterior south wall bears a tablet to Robert Blair (died
1666) who was at one time tutor to Charles I.

Aberdour is also a place from which to reach **Inchcolm Island**, with
the ruin of *St. Colm's Abbey* (AM. Tel: 031-244-3101. See also Rte 18,
Edinburgh, F.). First this was a priory, founded for Augustinians in 1123
by Alexander I in gratitude for the help given by the island's hermit
when he was shipwrecked here, and it is just possible that a primitive

cell on the north west may have been that of this hermit. Alexander's priory was raised to abbey in 1235, the remains of which include a small 13 or 15C church; an octagonal chapter house with a stone roof (c 1283); and a 14C cloister, with vaulted dormitory, refectory and guesthouse above. In Shakespeare's 'Macbeth', St. Colme's Inch is mentioned as the burial place of the defeated Sweno of Norway, and a hog-backed gravestone west of the church may date from this time.

2m **Burntisland** (6500 inhab. *Inf.*), with sands, and backed by Links in summer the scene of a programme of enterprising events, happily enough accepts the accolade of Playground of Fife. Staider visitors, and especially those with a feel for unusual church architecture, may well prefer to make for the interesting church, while romantics may pause outside Rossend Castle and ponder the fate of Pierre Chastelard.

Tradition is that the harbour was used by Agricola in 83 and that his troops also built a fortified camp on Dunearn Hill. Mary, Queen of Scots, visited here in 1563 (the occasion of the Chastelard affair), and James VI in 1601 when, at a General Assembly in the church, he suggested the need for a new translation of the Bible, this suggestion eventually leading to the Authorized Version of 1611. In 1651 the town is said to have surrendered to Cromwell, on the pragmatic condition that he repaired its harbour and streets.

The *Church is one of the most original and most remarkable post-Reformation churches in Scotland. As long ago as 1120 David I granted land for a church on this site, but the first was not built until 1234. The present building (1592) is octagonal in plan, with an external stair to a Sailors' Loft and a tower of 1749. Particularly noteworthy are the superb canopied central pew (1606) and the elaborately carved and painted Trades' Lofts (17 and 18C).

It was to *Rossend Castle* (no adm; restored as offices), then a 15C tower, that Mary, Queen of Scots, came in 1563, pursued by her over-romantic admirer, the French poet Pierre Chastelard. Found hiding under Mary's bed, he was pardoned, but soon again, and equally unsuccessfully, hid in her room. This time there could be no pardon and he was beheaded in St. Andrews the following day. Romantic to the end he went to the scaffold reading Ronsard's 'Hymne de la Mort' and as his last words declaimed 'Adieu, toi si belle et si cruelle, qui me tues et que je ne puis cesser d'aimer'. In the following century a house was grafted on to the original tower, and a painted ceiling (c 1610) from this, discovered by accident in 1957, is now in the Royal Museum of Scotland (Queen Street) in Edinburgh. *Burntisland Museum* (Tel: 0592-260732), at 102 High Street, offers a local history gallery and a walk-through reconstruction of a town fair of 1910, this latter based on a contemporary painting.

Approaching (*2m*) **Kinghorn** the coastal road is successor to the track along which Alexander III rode in 1286—as far, that is, as the spot where a roadside monument (of 1883) now records his death. The king was returning in the dark to the royal residence at nearby Pettycur when, it is said, his horse stumbled and he fell. Some such violent death had been predicted by an apparition at his wedding feast in Jedburgh Castle the previous year; and, the previous day, Thomas the Rhymer, challenged by the Earl of Dunbar to predict the morrow, had replied that it would be a day of calamity.

The fortified island of **Inchkeith** is 3m south east. In 1547, after the battle of Pinkie, the English planted a fort on the island, but from 1549 to 1567 it was garrisoned by the French.

3m **Kirkcaldy** (46,000 inhab. *Inf.*), chartered since 1363 and a royal burgh since 1644, is a busy place which successfully combines industry with the amenities of a coastal resort, and which also has a notable museum and art gallery. Once little more than one long street—and it still stretches along over 4m of waterfront—it was, and sometimes still is, known as the 'Lang toun of Fife'.

Michael Scot, the Wizard, was born near here (at Balwearie, 1½m south west) in c 1175. Adam Smith also was born here in 1723 and returned to write his 'Wealth of Nations', and Robert Adam, born in 1728, was another distinguished native. Thomas Carlyle was a teacher at the burgh school.

In the town centre stands the imposing *Town House* (by Carr and Howard, 1939–56) with, on top, Kirkcaldy's patron, St. Bryce, blessing the people. The Museum and Art Gallery will be found above the War Memorial Gardens near the station.

Museum and Art Gallery (Tel: 0592-260732). While the museum part offers much of interest—local archaeology, history, geology and natural history, as also material on Smith and Carlyle—it is the *Art Gallery that achieves distinction, with a small but brilliant collection in which many of the works are by Scottish artists. Names represented here include Andrew Geddes, S.J. Peploe, Henry Raeburn, W.Q. Orchardson, William McTaggart (a whole room, including his touching 'Helping Granny'), W.R. Sickert, L.S. Lowry and L.E. Boudin.

In front of the Museum and Art Gallery a plaque commemorates Sir Sandford Fleming (1827–1915), native of Kirkcaldy, chief engineer of the Canadian Pacific Railway and author of Standard Time, while, across from the War Memorial Gardens, Adam Smith is remembered by the *Adam Smith Centre*, with a theatre and other facilities.

In the lower town, skirting the Forth, the Esplanade is the scene in spring each year of the Links Market, with origins reaching back to 1304 and believed to be the largest street fair in Britain. To the east, in High Street, near the docks, *Sailor's Walk* is a group of 17C houses restored by the National Trust for Scotland. Among Kirkcaldy's several attractive parks, *Ravenscraig*, to the east beside the shore and with a nature trail, is perhaps the most worth a visit, if only to see the ruin of Ravenscraig Castle. Dating from 1460, the castle was begun by James II as a dower-house for his wife Mary of Gueldres, but the work stopped three years later when the lady died. James III handed the place over to William Sinclair, Earl of Orkney, and it was finally demolished by Monk in 1651.

Dysart, once a royal burgh in its own right but since 1930 integrated as an eastern suburb of Kirkcaldy, is an old port and still a place of character, with some quaint streets and houses with stepped gables, several of these restored by the National Trust for Scotland. The *John McDouall Stuart Museum* (Tel: 0592-260732), in Rectory Lane, should be of particular interest to Australians. Here, in the (NTS) restored 17C house in which the explorer was born in 1815, is shown material on his journeys between 1858–62 and, in particular, on his south to north crossing through Australia's central desert.

Beyond Dysart, West Wemyss, Coaltown of Wemyss and East Wemyss follow one another in quick succession, the name deriving from 'weems', or caves, of which there are several along this coast, although most are in poor condition and difficult of access. *Wemyss Castle* (no adm.), on a rocky height overlooking the sea just north of West Wemyss, dates from the 15–17C (restored) and is said to have been the place where Mary first met Darnley five months before their marriage, while ruined *Macduff's Castle*, to the east of East Wemyss, was in all probability a stronghold of the ancient earls of Fife.

5m (from Kirkcaldy) *Buckhaven*, now industrial, recalls its fishing past at the Buckhaven Museum (Tel: 0592-260732) above the library in College Street. *Methil*, just beyond, is also industrial, while sandy *Leven* caters for the beach visitor who may, at the Museum (Tel: 0592-260732) at the library, enjoy an exhibition of photographs and postcards recalling Victorian and Edwardian holiday Leven.—At (*4m* from Buckhaven) *Lundin Links* three large standing stones can be seen on the golf links.

1m **Largo** comprises Upper and Lower Largo, the former also known as *Kirkton of Largo*, with a parish church first consecrated in 1243 although the chancel is the only pre-Reformation survival. More interesting perhaps are a Pictish stone in the churchyard and a tablet on the churchyard wall recording that it was built in 1657 by one John Wood (possibly a descendant of Sir Andrew Wood, see below, buried here) 'after 55 years absence returning from his travels'. *Lower Largo* was the birthplace in 1676 of Alexander Selkirk, better known as Robinson Crusoe; he was the son of a cobbler and his statue, nicely traditional in pose and clothing, stands at the cottage. Another Largo seaman was Sir Andrew Wood (died 1515), captain of the famous Scottish warship 'Yellow Carvel' and victor of a naval engagement in the Forth in 1498 when he both defeated and captured the English admiral, Stephen Bull.

A915 now heads north for St. Andrews while this Route takes A917 to keep along the coast, though perhaps briefly diverting along B942 to *Colinsburgh*, a village founded in the 18C by Colin, Earl of Balcarres, a staunch Jacobite, as a home for his soldiers when it seemed clear that the Stuart cause was finally lost.—*5m* **Elie**, and its westerly continuation *Earlsferry*, are both summer resorts with good sands on which rockhounds may sometimes find garnets. Earlsferry owes its name to a tradition that it was from here that Macduff, fleeing from Macbeth, was ferried across the Forth, while Elie preserves the more modern story that Lady's Tower, to the east of the harbour, was the beach house from which a noted local beauty, Lady Janet Anstruther, was wont to bathe—but not before she had sent a servant through the streets ringing a bell to warn people to keep away.

For the next ten or so miles A917 runs with the East Neuk, the stretch of coast along which are strung Fife's several quaint little ports. Not that these are the only attractions here, for within the ports, and between them, will be found ruined castles, ancient and interesting churches, a notable fisheries museum and even a visitable lightship. Ruined *Ardross Castle* (14C) appears first, closely followed by *Newark Castle* on its headland, once the home of the Abercrombies but in c 1649 bought by General David Leslie, the Covenanter commander, who became Lord Newark. Then, in (*2m* from Elie) **St. Monance**, there is the ancient *Church of St. Monan*, built by David II in c 1362 in gratitude for his recovery at the saint's shrine from a wound. Today the church comprises transepts and choir, with a squat square tower surmounted by an octagonal steeple, while a groined roof and ogee-headed sedilia are features of the interior.

2m **Pittenweem**, the principal fishing base along this coast and with medieval and even earlier religious roots, was the place where Robertson and Wilson in 1736 robbed the customs collector, a crime which led to Wilson's being hanged in Edinburgh (Robertson escaped) and the subsequent riot and lynching of the guard commander, Captain Porteous (see Rte 18, Edinburgh, Grassmarket). Today a plaque on a house in Routine Row, near the parish church in the east part of the town, recalls the crime. This *Parish Church* preserves its tower of 1588, with a balustrade on top and the old prison, where doubtless Robertson and Wilson were held, at the foot, here also being the Cross of 1711. Immediately east, in the grounds of the Episcopal church, are the remains of a priory founded in 1114 and later (1318) associated with that on the Isle of May (see below); that this was a sizeable place with land extending some way farther is evident from the length of old wall which bounds the seaward end of Abbey Walk Road.

A yet older religious link is provided by *St. Fillan's Cave*, said to have been the retreat of the 9C hermit whose relic, cherished by Inchaffray Abbey, was so effectively used to bless Bruce's army before Bannockburn. Since long ago treated as a shrine, and later physically connected to the priory above, the cave was at one period used as a store for fishing gear until rededicated in 1935. At the east end of the harbour *The Gyles*, restored by the National Trust for Scotland, form a pleasing group of 16C houses.

Two very opposed themes—domestic architecture of the 16–17C and a steam railway—may prompt short diversions northward. *Kellie Castle* (NTS. Tel: 03338-271) is on B9171 3m north west of Pittenweem. Although its oldest part is traced to c 1360, this castle is essentially a good example of 16–17C domestic architecture, consisting of two 16C towers united by a 17C range with some notable plasterwork and panelling with painted landscapes. Kellie was built by the Oliphants, but sold in 1613 to Thomas Erskine, 1st Earl of Kellie, the man who killed Ruthven in the Perth Gowrie Conspiracy. Abandoned in 1830, the castle was restored from 1878 by Professor James Lorimer. The layout of the walled garden is late Victorian.—*Lochty Private Railway* (Tel: 0592-264587) is on B940, less than 2m north of Kellie Castle. Opened in 1967 as the first preserved steam passenger line in Scotland, the railway represents a section of the former East Fife Central Railway and today operates a short steam-hauled passenger service.

1m (from Pittenweem) **Anstruther** (3000 inhab. *Inf.*) is more grandly and more properly the 'United Burgh of Kilrenny, Cellardyke, Anstruther Easter and Anstruther Wester', which locally abbreviates to 'Anster'. Until the departure of the herring in the 1940s Anstruther was a main centre of Scotland's herring fishing, and it is thus appropriate that the town should now be the home of the *Scottish Fisheries Museum* (Tel: 0333-310628), housed mainly in a group of buildings known as St. Ayles, but also in two adjoining houses and at the harbour. In addition to the range of exhibits there is a lecture hall for special exhibitions and an aquarium with wall tanks and a floor pool.

During the 15C St. Ayles Chapel stood here, on the site of the north building, and a relic survives in the double-pointed arch window-head rebuilt into the present structure and overlooking the courtyard. The building known as Abbot's Lodging, on the east side of the courtyard, is of the early 16C and served as quarters for the Abbot of Balmerino when he visited Anstruther, presumably to check on the operation of the charter of 1318 which gave to his abbey the right to lease booths to the local fishermen.

The museum illustrates many aspects both of sea fishing and of the life in fisher communities, all imaginatively interpreted by means of model and actual boats, tableaux in authentic costume and several striking paintings. The West Room and West Gallery are devoted to the days of sail, a period evoked by beautifully made boats, fishing nets and gear, a diorama of fishing methods, nostalgic photographs, as also paintings by John McGhie, Sam Bough and ordinary fishermen. The Courtyard Gallery, by contrast, displays marine engines, while the Long Gallery (with a whaling exhibition in an adjacent corridor) shows a map of fishing communities and a tableau of ancillary trades such as gutting, packing and coopering. The Ship Loft, with a huge mural of a harbour scene, is devoted to steam; in the Courtyard are the wheelhouse from a modern trawler, as also various small boats and gear; and the Abbot's Lodging shows a typical fisher family room of c 1900, net loft above. In the Harbour there are actual veteran vessels, these including two restored fishing boats, 'White Wing' and 'The Reaper'.

The two adjoining houses serve as both storage area and galleries, among the themes being sea salmon fishing and 'This Modern Age'.

The *North Carr Lightship* (Tel: 0334-53722), now calm in Anstruther harbour but from 1933–75 stationed at the treacherous Carr Rocks off Fife Ness, is a maritime museum of a different kind in which the visitor can see at first hand the cramped conditions under which a lightship crew worked and lived.—*Cellardyke*, the eastern part of Anstruther and the old fishing centre, owes its curious name to the cellars and dykes, built respectively below and above the hill, to protect fishing gear; and the name Cardinal Steps Bathing Pool recalls that the pool occupies the site of the landing steps below a palace which Cardinal Beaton once owned here.

In May–September there are boat excursions to the **Isle of May**, c 6m to the south east in the mouth of the Firth of Forth (Tel: 0333-310103). The small battlemented Beacon is a relic of a lighthouse of 1636. Long before this, though, there was a Benedictine priory here, founded by David I in c 1153 but abandoned in c 1312 when its inmates moved to the doubtless greater comfort of Pittenweem. And strange things are said to have happened here. When, for instance, St. Adrian was murdered here by Norsemen in c 870, his stone coffin miraculously floated across to Anstruther where it is still identified in Anstruther Wester churchyard. And when once the Devil visited here, he became so enraged about something that he hurled a huge stone at the church at Crail, the stone landing against the churchyard wall where it can still be seen.

Just north east out of Anstruther the road passes *Kilrenny*, where the church, with a 15C tower, traces its origin to a foundation of c 865, before reaching (*4m*) **Crail**, a royal burgh since 1310 under a charter granted by Bruce. This is a picturesque small place, especially around the harbour area, with partly cobbled and tree-lined streets, restored crow-stepped and red-tiled 17–18C houses, a mercat cross topped by a unicorn and a *Tolbooth* (or Town House) dating in part from the 16C. And there are glimpses here of a remoter past, in three ancient stones to be found at the interesting *Collegiate Church of St. Mary*, in part reaching back to the 12 or 13C. Here the stone in the entrance lobby is 8C Pictish. There is another stone, near the door, showing an indentation said to be the result of generations of local bowmen sharpening their arrow tips, while, outside the churchyard gate, there is a third stone, the one which the Devil hurled at the church from the Isle of May. And in the churchyard a ghoulish touch is provided by a solid, square building of 1826 bearing the inscription 'Erected for securing the dead', a visible reminder of body-snatching days. The town's *Museum and Heritage Centre* (Tel: 0333-50869), in Marketgate, well illustrates most aspects of Crail's varied past, including even material on the wartime Royal Naval Air Station.

Fife Ness, beyond Crail, is the eastern promontory of the Fife peninsula. It was at *Balcomie* tower, to the north of the minor road out to the Ness, that Mary of Guise, just landed in Scotland as the bride of James V, was received and entertained in 1538, while opposite, running south from the road, a ridge and earthwork known as *Danes Dyke* is said to have been thrown up either by, or as a protection against, the Norsemen.

A917, heading north out of Crail, in *3m* passes *Cambo Country Park* (Tel:

0333-50810) with farm animals (including rare breeds), nature trails and a length of shore.—*7m* **St. Andrews**, see Rte 33B, immediately below.

B. St. Andrews

One of the historic towns of Scotland—secular, spiritual and academic—and hallowed in the world of golf, St. Andrews (11,500 inhab.), stretches along a broad generally east to west axis, with the sea on the north and South Street defining the south. At the east end are the harbour and the venerable ruined cathedral, at the west the Royal and Ancient Golf Club, while, between, three streets fan out westward from the vicinity of the cathedral. These are North Street, Market Street and South Street, this last being the main street. All three are flanked by gracious and dignified buildings and, with their narrow connecting streets, make up a legacy of thoughtful planning and good taste.

Tourist Information. South Street. Tel: 0334-72021.

SOME HOTELS. *Old Course and Country Club*, Old Station Road, KY16 9SP. Tel: 0334-74371. *Scores*, 76 The Scores, KY16 9BB. Tel: 0334-72451. *St. Andrews Golf*, 40 The Scores, KY16 9AS. Tel: 0334-72611. *Rufflets*, Strathkinness Low Road, KY16 9TX. Tel: 0334-72594.

History. That St. Regulus, or Rule, bearing the relics of St. Andrew, was shipwrecked here in the 4C is one of the many convenient legends of Scottish history. It seems more likely that these relics were brought here in the mid 8C, at about which time a Culdee settlement was founded, its chapel first being on a rock by the shore, this soon followed by a church on Kirk Hill, traces of a successor of which (St. Mary of the Rock) can still be seen. In due course this Culdee settlement became a priory and bishopric which, by the beginning of the 10C, had superseded Abernethy in the primacy of Scotland.

Much happened during the 12C, starting with the appointment as bishop in 1124 of Robert, prior of the Augustinian house at Scone, a move which soon led to an influx of Canons Regular, the founding of the cathedral in 1160, and, forty years later in 1200, the start of the construction of the castle as an episcopal residence. Promotion to archbishopric came in 1472, one of the first to hold this rank being William Schevez or Schivas (died 1497), counsellor of James IV.

The 15C saw the start of some 150 years darkened by religious burnings and murder. John Risby was one of the first to suffer, burnt here in 1407 for heresy, followed a few years later (1433) and for the same offence by the Bohemian Paul Crawar. Patrick Hamilton went to the stake in 1528, and the burning by the Catholic Cardinal Beaton of the Protestant George Wishart in 1546 was almost immediately avenged by the former's murder. Another victim (1558) was Walter Myln, the last Reformation martyr (Reformation martyrs are commemorated by the *Martyrs' Monument* on the green near the sea at the north west of the town a short distance east of the Royal and Ancient club house). But the 16C was also something of a royal century, starting in 1538 with the ceremonial welcome of Mary of Guise before her marriage to James V and followed in 1563 and 1564 by visits by her daughter Mary, Queen of Scots. And in 1583 the young James VI found shelter here after his experience at Huntingtower.

The **University** of St. Andrews, the oldest in Scotland, was founded in 1412 by Bishop Henry Wardlaw and confirmed the following year by a bill of Pope Benedict XIII. In 1450 the college of St. Salvator was founded and in 1512 that of St. Leonard, the two being merged in 1747, though St. Leonard's has now been revived as a postgraduate college. St. Mary's College, founded in 1538, houses the theological faculty.

Golf. The Royal and Ancient Golf Club, now the world's premier club and the ruling arbiter on the game, was founded in 1754, as the Society of St. Andrews Golfers, by 22 'noblemen and gentlemen being admirers of the ancient and healthful exercise of golf'. The autumn meeting, when the captain for the ensuing year plays himself into office, is the principal event of the year.

There are four (Links Trust) courses, all of 18 holes and all to the north west of the town. The *Old Course* (4m), always the favourite, starts from the Royal and Ancient Golf Club House. The others are the *New Course* (3¾m), the *Jubilee Course* (2¾m) and the *Eden Course* (3½m). All the above are the property of a Links Trust and, on payment of a green fee, are open without introduction or the need to belong to a club. However, advance reservation (at least eight weeks) is advisable (Links Management Committee, Golf Place, St. Andrews, Fife. Tel: 0334-75757) and for the Old Course there is also a ballot system (Tel: 0334-73393). *Balgove Links* provides a fifth course.

The description below starts from West Port, at the west end of South Street, continues through the town to the cathedral, then returns westward past the castle and through the university fronting North Street to end at the Royal and Ancient club house. The total distance on foot is about 1½m.

West Port, one of the few surviving Scottish city gates, was rebuilt in 1589, but the side arches are 19C additions as is the figure of David I. Beyond, in South Street and the turnings off it, there are many pleasing 18C houses, as also older buildings. On the south the first place of interest is *Blackfriars Chapel*, a fragment (1525) of the church of the Dominican friary founded in 1274 by Bishop Wischart but destroyed by a Reformation mob in 1559. The chapel now stands within the grounds of Madras College, a school founded in 1832 from a bequest of Andrew

Bell, a native of St. Andrews who made his fortune in India. Beyond, on the right, is the *Town Hall* (Tourist Information).

Holy Trinity Church, opposite the Town Hall, was founded in 1410 but has since been many times altered, the two most notable architectural events being an indifferent rebuilding of 1799 followed in 1906–09 by rescue by MacGregor Chalmers who in his redesign followed the old lines and retained as much as possible of the original work, including the fine tower which is pre-Reformation. It was in this church in 1547 that John Knox preached his first public sermon, but, despite this, and certainly unexpected in a Presbyterian church, the most striking feature of the interior (south transept) is the elaborate marble monument to the Catholic Archbishop Sharp, carved in Holland and erected by his son, with a fulsome inscription and a representation of the archbishop's particularly brutal murder (see Rte 33C, Magus Muir). To the south east is the Memorial Aisle, with two surviving choir stalls (c 1505) and the silver Book of Remembrance (in a shrine recess), made after the last war, while on the north side the Playfair Aisle commemorates Sir Nigel Playfair (1874–1934), actor and theatre manager, and members of the family. The east and west windows, and 11 others in the church (1910–50), are the work of Douglas Strachan.

The pulpit, lectern and font commemorate 'A.K.H.B.' (Dr Boyd), minister of this church in 1865–99; he was appointed Moderator of the General Assembly, and, as A.K.H.B., became known as the author of 'The Recreations of a Country Parson' and 'Graver Thoughts of a Country Parson'.

St. Mary's College, on the south side of South Street beyond the Town Hall, is readily identified by the coats-of-arms of past chancellors on the street façade. Founded in 1538 by Archbishop Beaton, the college has since 1579 been the theological faculty of the university. The older buildings form two sides of an attractive quadrangle in which a thorn tree planted by Mary, Queen of Scots, still flourishes.

Beyond Abbey Street, and again on the south, *St. Leonard's School*, a girls' residential school since 1877, occupies the site and some of the old buildings of St. Leonard's College which was founded in 1512, on the site of an older hospice, by Prior John Hepburn and Archbishop Alex Stewart; the latter was natural son of James IV, with whom he died at Flodden (1513). Until 1747, when the college was united with St. Salvator and the domestic buildings were sold, this college enjoyed great distinction. George Buchanan was principal in 1566–70, John Knox resided here, and it was here that so many of the youthful Reformers studied that the phrase to have 'drunk at St. Leonard's Well' became accepted as meaning having imbibed Protestant doctrine. The school's library is in *Queen Mary's House*, at the east end of South Street, a 16C house once belonging to a merchant, Hugh Scrimgeour, in which Mary, Queen of Scots, probably stayed (1563–64) and Charles II certainly did in 1650.

South Street ends almost opposite the cathedral entrance (see below), on the right here being *The Pends*, two fine 14C arches, once the chief entrance to the precinct of the priory which is surrounded by a daunting defensive wall (16C but on earlier foundations) 25ft high, c 1m in circumference and distinguished at intervals by towers, gunloops and carved heraldic panels. On the right, beyond The Pends, is the entrance to *St. Leonard's Chapel*, founded in 1512 as the chapel of St. Leonard's College. After a period as a parish church (1578–1671), the chapel stood neglected until 1910 when the university began a long programme of restoration successfully completed in 1952. Pends Road drops down to the harbour (the main pier of which was rebuilt in the 17C with stones from the cathedral and castle ruins).

Facing the cathedral entrance, a group of 16–17C houses known as *Dean's Court* stand on the site of the former Archdeacon's Lodging. Here the arms over the old gateway are those of George Douglas, the young man who engineered the escape of Mary, Queen of Scots, from Loch Leven.

For all that it is in ruins, the ***Cathedral** (AM. Tel: 031-244-3101), with its lofty, near perfect east end wall, still impresses both visually and as an example of 12C and later achievement. The Church of St. Rule, of earlier date than the cathedral, is also within this precinct.

History. Although founded in 1160 by Bishop Arnold, the cathedral was finished and consecrated only in 1318, in the presence of King Robert the Bruce. Later these walls saw both pomp and despair, the former exemplified by the marriage of James V

St. Andrews Cathedral. The 12C east front, with its original triple lancets but 15C main window

and Mary of Guise, the latter by the trial and condemnation for heresy of such as Patrick Hamilton, George Wishart and Walter Myln. John Knox can probably be blamed for the cathedral's loss of its images and 'popish' ornaments, but there is no evidence that the Reformation brought structural damage, and it was probably a combination of neglect and the elements that led to the ruinous state recorded as early as 1649, by which time the place was being freely pillaged for stones for the town's defences and the harbour, not to mention the citizens' houses which continued to benefit until as recently as about 1826.

When perfect the cathedral was 355ft long and about 160ft wide across the transepts, the largest in fact in Scotland. Today the only significant remains standing are parts of the east and west ends (from the visitor's point of view the two essentials here), entirely isolated from one another, and a part too of the south wall of the nave. The remainder of what must have been a truly beautiful edifice survives as no more than a ground plan defined by lines filled with granite chips.

The 12C *East Front* stands balanced and perfect, with flanking turrets, three narrow round-headed lancets at the bottom, and above (a 15C insertion), a large pointed window. The *West Wall* (1273–79; not the original front which was two bays farther west) has a deeply recessed central doorway, surmounted by a blind Early English arcade and flanked by a turret still propped by a flying buttress. From here runs the south wall of the nave of 11 bays, the west bays having late 13C windows, while those to the east are of a century earlier.

On the east side of the cloister is the triple entrance to the chapter house of c 1250, extended east by Bishop Lamberton in 1313–21. Between this and the south transept is a slype, once vaulted, while to the south is what was the warming room (now museum, see below) above which was the dormitory. The undercroft of the refectory, on the south side of the cloister, was reconstructed in c 1899.

Close to the south east angle of the cathedral is the **Church of St. Rule**, built in 1127–44 by Yorkshire masons for Bishop Robert (see town history). The nave has vanished, but the oddly narrow choir survives as does also the slender *Tower* (108ft. Fee for ascent of 158 steps). The same ticket admits to the *Museum*, in the former warming room in the cloister, showing Early Christian carved stones, medieval monuments, and various local relics.

Kirk Hill, between the precinct and the foot of the pier, is probably the site of the earliest Culdee settlement, here today being traces of the church of St. Mary of the Rock (c 1250). In the cliff below, a short way north west, is *St. Rule's Cave*, perhaps better known as Lady Buchan's Cave after an 18C lady who fitted it up as a summer house.

The **Castle** (AM. Tel: 031-244-3101), long the august palace of the bishops, the scene too—at any rate as seen through modern eyes—of much barbarity, survives as no more than a shattered ruin on a rock beside the sea some 300 yards north west of the cathedral.

History. Started by Bishop Rogers in 1200 as the bishop's palace, the castle was rebuilt after Bannockburn by Bishop Lamberton and has since several times been modified. Later, it was the prison of Gavin Douglas, Bishop of Dunkeld, and of many early Reformers, and in 1546 the scene of two barbarous deaths. The first, in March, was that of George Wishart, burnt at the stake in front of the castle by Cardinal Beaton who showed no mercy to Reformation leaders and watched the burning in comfort from the castle walls. But next, two months later, it was Beaton's own turn, when several friends of Wishart, headed by Norman Leslie, son of the Earl of Rothes, seized the castle, butchered Beaton and hung his corpse over the battlements. Joined by many Reformer adherents, including John Knox, they held out until the castle was taken by a French fleet in July 1547, when Knox and many of the garrison were sent to the galleys at Nantes. The castle passed into the possession of the town in the 17C.

A modern bridge crosses the moat to the entrance, flanked by guardrooms, beyond being the courtyard, with the castle well. In the so-called Sea Tower, at the north west angle, there is a strange bottle-shaped dungeon, some 25ft deep, in which several Reformers are said to have been held, and into which also the body of their persecutor Beaton was thrown and covered with salt—'to await', said Knox, 'what exsequies his brethren the bishops would prepare for him'. At the north east angle is the Kitchen Tower, while the strong tower at the south west angle is supposed to have contained Beaton's apartments.

North Castle Street, followed south, crosses North Street, near the intersection, at 12 North Street, being the **Preservation Trust Museum** (Tel: 0334-72152). Here, in a reconstructed 17C house, can be seen a 19C grocer's shop, a chemist of the same period, and, on the upper floor, a nostalgic collection of scrapbooks, postcards, photographs and much else to carry the visitor back to the St. Andrews of a century or so ago.

Many of the main university buildings line the north side of North Street, first coming *Younger Hall* (1929), beyond which is **St. Salvator's College**, founded on this site in 1450 by Bishop James Kennedy (grandson of Robert III and Chancellor of Scotland) and still a main focus of university life. However, of Kennedy's original building the only survivor is the church, now the university chapel, with a lofty tower. Inside are Bishop Kennedy's elaborately decorated tomb and, in the vestry, a mace of Kennedy's time (made in Paris in 1461) still borne on ceremonial occasions. The *Crawford Centre for the Arts* (Tel: 0334-74610), at 93 North Street and a part of the university, presents exhibitions of Scottish and other art as well as theatre and music.

Mellow and dignified though the streets are today, a tour of this area of St. Andrews ends on a sombre note. It was before the gate of St. Salvator's that Patrick Hamilton, the first martyr of the Scottish Reformation (see also Rte 57, Fearn), was burnt in 1528, his courageous death achieving the opposite of what his persecutors hoped, for, it was said, 'the reek of Patrick Hamilton infected all it blew on'. College Street, opposite St. Salvator's, links North Street to Market Street, a St. Andrew's cross on the ground marking the site of the old market cross, beside which the Bohemian Paul Crawer was burnt for heresy in 1433 and the compulsively romantic Pierre Chastelard met his end in 1563 (see Rte 33A, Burntisland).

The shore road westward from the castle is The Scores, this becoming Gillespie Terrace and ending opposite the Royal and Ancient club house. Here, close to one another, are the *Martyrs' Monument*, a museum, and a sea life centre. The museum is the *British Golf Museum* (Tel: 0334-73423) run by the Royal and Ancient Trust; the museum traces the development of the game from its beginnings down to the present day and also offers a programme of films. The *Sea Life Centre* (Tel: 0334-74786) shows a range of native British marine life, including seals, of which it is hoped to build up a breeding colony.

St. Andrews *Botanic Garden* (Tel: 0334-72021), in the south west of the town and entered from The Canongate, originated as a walled garden of 1889 near St. Mary's College and moved to this present site in 1960, since then winning international recognition for both display and range of plants.—*Craigtoun Country Park* (Tel: 0334-73666), 2m south west of St. Andrews, includes visitor and countryside centres as also a variety of other popular features.

C. Edinburgh to Dundee via Falkland and Cupar

A90 across the Forth Bridge. B981 and B921 to Glenrothes. A92 and A912 to Falkland. Minor roads followed by A92 to Cupar. A916, B939 and unclassified south around Cupar through Ceres to Dairsie. A91, A919 and A92 to Leuchars and Dundee. Road improvements, especially in western Fife, may bring some changes in numbering and distances.

SOME HOTELS. **Glenrothes**. *Albany*, North Street, KY7 5NA. Tel: 0592-752292. **Falkland**. *Hunting Lodge*, High Street, KY7 9BZ. Tel: 0337-57226. **Cupar**. *Eden House*, 2 Pitscottie Road. Tel: 0334-52510. *Fernie Castle* (5m west), Letham, KY7 7RU. Tel: 033781-381. See also **St. Andrews**, Rte 33B.

Total distance 60m.—*10m* **Forth Road Bridge (N)**.—*8m* **Lochgelly**.— *7m* **Glenrothes**.—*5m* **Falkland**.—*10m* **Cupar**.—*4m* **Ceres**.—*2m* **Pitscottie**.—*3m* **Dairsie**.—*4m* **Leuchars**.—*5m* **Newport-on-Tay**.—*2m* **Dundee**.

From central **Edinburgh** (see Rte 18) Queensferry Road (A90) in *10m* reaches and crosses the *Forth Road Bridge*, for which, as also for the adjacent railway bridge and the approach from Edinburgh, see Rte 9. Here, at the north end of the Forth Bridge, Rte 31 bears west while Rte 32 continues north and Rte 33A follows the coast eastward. For *Inverkeithing*, just below and east of the north end of the bridge complex, see Rte 33A.

This Route follows B981 and B921 north and north east past industrial *Cowdenbeath* and (*8m*) also industrial *Lochgelly*, both of these places once centres of a coal mining district. *Lochore Meadows Country Park*, 2m north of Lochgelly off B920, is the outcome of an internationally acclaimed reclamation project under which a drab and desolate mining wasteland has been transformed (Tel: 0592-860086).

B921 in *5m* reaches *Glenrothes Airfield* at a crossroads. Here enthusiasts for ancient early Christian stones will divert 1m south along B922 to see the *Dogton Stone*, off the road to the west near Dogton Farm where permission may be asked to park the car and advice sought on the path (200 yards) to follow to avoid damage to crops. Dating from the 10C and, though the top and arms are now missing, once a cross, it is still possible to make out a horse on the east face and a serpentine design on the south.

2m **Glenrothes** (34,000 inhab. *Inf.*), designed for the needs of the local collieries but, now that these are exhausted, devoted to light industry, is an interesting 'new town' development which has benefited from being individual rather than a satellite to some city. Some of the buildings (generally 1960 on) merit attention, as do also many examples of contemporary sculpture. Among the buildings are *St. Columba's Church* (1960), by Wheeler and Sproson, with a lofty, detached steel and glass tower and a mural by Alberto Morocco; *St. Paul's Church* with an altarpiece by Benno Schotz, who also devised the statue at the town centre; and the imposing *High School* (1966) with a patterned glass façade. As to the sculpture, Glenrothes boasts what must surely be an almost unique assemblage, largely because in 1968 the Development Corporation appointed an artist, David Harding, 'to contribute creatively to the external built environment of the town'.

Glenrothes offers all the many facilities to be expected of such a development, including *Balbirnie Park*, with a craft centre and a stone circle, the latter interesting both as such and for having been moved 100 yards when threatened by road construction. Near **Markinch**, now effectively an east suburb but claiming once to have been the Pictish capital of Fife, are the ruins of *Balgonie Castle* (Tel: 0592-750119), with a late 14 or early 15C tower and residential quarters added largely during the 17C when the castle was the home of Alexander, Lord Leven (died 1661), commander of the Scots at Marston Moor. Garrisoned by Rob Roy in 1719, Balgonie thereafter was largely unoccupied until recent years saw restoration work on the tower in 1971 followed by current work aiming at total restoration. The castle is home to Eddergoll Studios, active in a number of crafts, notably leatherwork and tapestry weaving.

Falkland, *5m* north by A92 and A912, could scarcely provide a greater contrast to Glenrothes, the latter uncompromisingly of today, Falkland a dignified little royal burgh of 1458, particularly rich in restored 17 to 19C small houses and its name synonymous with that of the elegant palace built and loved by James IV and V (history exhibition in the town hall). But humbler people lived here too, one such being Richard Cameron, the Covenanter leader (see Rte 11, Sanquhar), who was born here and became the village schoolmaster.

Falkland Palace (NTS. Tel: 0337-57397). Visits are by guided tour only, lasting 40 minutes. Visitor Centre, shop, etc.

History. An earlier castle here, mentioned in a charter of 1160, belonged to the Macduffs, the powerful earls of Fife, and in 1371 passed to Robert III's ambitious brother, the Duke of Albany, who in 1402 reputedly here starved to death his nephew David, Duke of Rothesay and heir to the throne. The dry, official announcement, however, was that that 'dissolute prince' had 'died by the visitation of providence and not otherwise' (be this as it may, Albany seemingly deemed it prudent to expiate by founding the Albany Aisle in Edinburgh's St. Giles Cathedral). In 1425 Albany's son and grandsons were all executed by James I and the castle became royal property.

The Palace, begun by James IV in about 1500, became a favourite seat of the Scottish court, and the phrase 'Falkland bred' implied courtly manners. It was James V though who completed and embellished Falkland (1525–42), and it was here that he died in 1542, broken-hearted after his defeat at Solway Moss. A few

Falkland Palace. The creation of James IV and V and long a favourite seat of the Scottish court

days before his death, he learnt of the birth of his daughter, Mary, and commented: 'God's will be done; it cam wi' a lass and it'll gang wi' a lass'—a reference to the fact that the Stuarts had obtained the throne by marriage to Bruce's daughter. Later, Mary and her son, James VI, both highly appreciated the fine hunting in this neighbourhood, and it was from Falkland that James rode to Perth and the drama of the Gowrie Conspiracy. Charles I in 1633 and Charles II in 1650 visited Falkland, but in 1654 it was occupied and part burned by Cromwell's troops; in 1715, after Sheriffmuir, Rob Roy occupied the palace and levied contributions from the town. In 1887 the Falkland estates were purchased by the 3rd Marquis of Bute, Hereditary Constable, Captain and Keeper, who restored the south wing, and in 1952 the National Trust for Scotland was appointed Deputy Keeper.

The south wing presents to the street an elegant ornamental façade with narrow mullioned and grated windows, and has an imposing gatehouse of c 1537, flanked by loop-holed round towers and containing the Keeper's Apartments.

The inner court was originally enclosed on three sides. Here the façade of the south wing is somewhat French in character, perhaps reflecting the taste and influence of James V's two French wives; it is divided by buttresses, faced with Renaissance columns and entablatures, the upper windows being flanked with medallion heads of kings, queens and dignitaries. The east wing has a similar but less elaborate façade, while on the north side of the court can be seen the foundations of the great hall begun by James IV.

In the restored interior of the south wing, a corridor with 17C Flemish tapestries, a 19C oak ceiling, and stained glass showing the escutcheons of Scottish monarchs and their consorts, leads to the Chapel Royal which retains its original walls and ceiling. The royal apartments were in the damaged east wing, in which the King's Bedchamber and the Queen's Room have been restored. Here, too, may be pointed out the door by which the youthful and adventurous James V was wont to sneak out in disguise, and a dungeon dubbed 'Rothesay's' by Scott in his 'Fair Maid of Perth'.

In the Garden, which contains the royal tennis court of 1539, are indicated the sites of the keep and curtain wall of the early castle of the Macduffs.

Minor roads lead east through Newton of Falkland and *Freuchie* to reach A92, Freuchie having once been the place to which Falkland courtiers who had in some way offended were banished. Hence the Fife expression of derision, 'Awa tae Freuchie and eat mice'.—*6m Pitlessie* provided the scene for the painter David Wilkie's first and possibly most famous work, 'Pitlessie Fair', now to be seen in Edinburgh's National Gallery. The artist was born in 1785 in the manse of Cults, just south east of Pitlessie.—*4m* **Cupar** (6000 inhab. *Inf.*) has a charter of 1381. The town claims, though, to have been a royal burgh some 200 years before this, and it does seem to be fact that Alexander III held an assembly here in 1276. Cam the earls of Fife had a stronghold here, too, on the north east hill (Castlehill). Although today a shopping and administrative centre, Cupar manages to retain something of the air of an old burgh, with quite dignified main streets, narrow wynds, several 18 and 19C houses, and, at the head of Crossgate, a *Cross* of 1683, scarcely improved by a Victorian unicorn. The *Old Parish Church*, on the south west hill, although effectively of 1785, nevertheless retains three bays and a tower of 1415, the spire being an addition of 1620; in the churchyard are buried the hands of Hackston of Rathillet (see Magus Muir, below) and also the heads of two other Covenanters dismembered in Edinburgh.—The *Scottish Deer Centre* (Tel: 033781-391), 3m west by A91, offers close contact with red deer.

A91 provides the direct road to St. Andrews, or, using A92, to Dundee.

However, there are several places of varied interest to the south and east of Cupar, so this Route makes a loop using A916, B939 and a minor road to regain A91 at Dairsie.

A916, followed south out of Cupar, in under 2m passes between the mansion of Hill of Tarvit (east) and Scotstarvit Tower (west). *Hill of Tarvit* (NTS. Tel: 0334-53127) architecturally provides a good example of the work of Robert Lorimer who in 1906 remodelled this mansion of 1696. Here too are to be seen antique furniture, Flemish tapestries, Chinese porcelain and bronzes, Dutch paintings and also paintings by Raeburn and Ramsay. The keys of *Scotstarvit Tower* are held at Hill of Tarvit. Dating from c 1579, this L-shaped building of five storeys was the home of Sir John Scot (1585–1670), a noted scholar, geographer and cartographer.

2m **Ceres** (on B939), little more than a village, is the home of the *Fife Folk Museum* (Tel: 033482-380), housed in 18 and 19C cottages and the 17C weighhouse near the medieval bridge, as also of the *Provost*, a strange 17C stone figure at the village crossroads, said to represent a former provost and to have been carved by a local man. This jovial fellow, long lost until found in the undergrowth of a nearby garden, was set up in his present position in 1939.—2m *Pitscottie* crossroads. Here, although this Route now takes a minor road heading due north, connoisseurs of 17C Covenanting murders will first continue 3½m along B939 to the crossroads immediately south of Strathkinnes. *Magus Muir* (sign 350 yards south of the crossroads) is where on the night of 3 May 1679 a party of Covenanters, headed by Balfour of Kinloch and Hackston of Rathillet, waylaid and butchered Archbishop Sharp (the Episcopalian Archbishop of St. Andrews) in the arms of his daughter, herself wounded in her vain efforts to protect her father. Later Hackston was caught and dismembered in Edinburgh, his hands being buried in Cupar old churchyard. Today a path (about ½m) leads to two monuments, one to five Covenanters executed in connection with the murder but in fact innocent, the other (100 yards away) marking the site of the murder.

From Pitscottie a minor road runs north through *Dura Den*, a narrow

Murder of Archbishop Sharp on Magus Muir. His gallant daughter Isabella was wounded as she threw herself between her father and the assassins

sandstone cleft noted for important discoveries of fossil fish, to (1m) *Kemback*, with, in the ruin of the earlier church, the effigy of the wife of Miles Graham, one of the murderers of James I in 1437. Reputedly she betrayed her husband, albeit under torture, and her ghost now haunts the neighbourhood. A short way beyond, the road crosses *Dairsie Bridge*, a bridge of three arches built in c 1522 by Archbishop Beaton across the Eden. The ruin above the river is *Dairsie Castle*, on the site of a predecessor in which David II may have spent a part of his youth, while the nearby *Kirk of Dairsie* was built in 1621 by Archbishop Spottiswood as part of his vain endeavour to bring Scotland into conformity with England. A91 is joined at *Dairsie*, rather under 2m north of Kemback, this road in 2m reaching *Guardbridge* from where A919 is followed north.

2m **Leuchars**, a village justly celebrated for its 12C **"*Church*, the east end of which is perhaps the most beautiful fragment of Norman work in Britain. Here the exterior of the apse is arcaded, with superb blind arches and pilasters showing axe marking, while, inside, the mouldings of the arches at the entrances to the choir and apse are of great richness.—The nearby RAF station was the base of a Norwegian squadron during the last war and a memorial stands by the entrance. *Earlshall Castle* (Tel: 033483-205), 1m east of Leuchars, dates from the 16C. Inside the castle the main features are the painted ceiling in the long gallery and a collection of Scottish weapons, while the grounds (nature trail etc.) are known for their topiary.

Tentsmuir Forest, to the north of Leuchars and occupying the north east corner of Fife between the Tay and Eden estuaries, spreads over an area of some 5m from north to south and 3m from east to west. Here will be found a Forestry Commission picnic area, and woodland and shore trails along which may be seen deer as well as many bird species, these perhaps including capercaillies, terns, eider and waders, while seals are common on the Eden sandbanks. There are also two nature reserves. *Tentsmuir Point* (open access), at the north east corner, comprises foreshore (Abertay Sands, a winter roost for wildfowl), an area of dunes and some patches of marsh. The other reserve is *Morton Lochs* (restricted access. Tel: 0334-54038) which are artificial lochs lying between B945 (at Kirktonbarns) and the forest. On the main migration path of wildfowl and waders, the lochs, then badly silted, were in 1976 deepened and given islands and promontories.—It is of interest that Tentsmuir has yielded some of the earliest evidence of man's presence in Scotland, c 8000 years ago.

5m **Newport-on-Tay** is a summer resort at the south end of the Tay Road Bridge, beside which there is a large car park with a splendid view across to Dundee; but with, also, a memorial to five men who lost their lives during the bridge's construction.

The *Tay Road Bridge* (toll) was built in 1963–66. Over a mile in length and with a height of 120ft above the water, the bridge has 42 spans, these including four wider ones of 250ft for navigation.

The *Tay Rail Bridge*, 2m west of the road bridge, was built in 1883–88 about 20 yards west of the site of its predecessor (1871–78), the central spans of which collapsed in a gale during the night of 28 December 1879 when a train was crossing, around 100 people losing their lives as the train plunged into the water. The graceful curve of the present bridge is 2m long, has 73 pairs of piers, and the rails are 92ft above the water.— Prior to the construction of the bridge, the train brought its passengers to Tayport, whence they crossed the river by ferry. One of the oldest in Scotland, this ferry is mentioned in records of as long ago as 1474.

2m **Dundee**, see Rte 34.

D. Northern Fife (Perth to Dundee via Newburgh)

A912 and A913 to Newburgh. Unclassified to Balmerino and Newport-on-Tay. A92 to Dundee.—This Route provides an alternative to Rte 30.

SOME HOTELS. As the distance of this Route is only 28m, see **Perth** (Rte 26) or **Dundee** (Rte 34). See also **Cupar** on Rte 33C.

Total distance 28m.—*4m* **M90, Exit 9**.—*4m* **Abernethy**.—*3m* **Newburgh**.—*10m* **Balmerino Abbey**.—*5m* **Newport-on-Tay**.—*2m* **Dundee**.

Perth (see Rte 26) is left by crossing the South Inch by Edinburgh Road, A912 then running through Bridge of Earn to cross M90 and reach (*6m*) *Aberargie* where A913 forks east.—*2m* **Abernethy**, now no more than a large village and not officially in Fife, was once a Pictish capital, an important Church (Culdee) centre in 862–87, and also, or so it is said, the place where in 1072 Malcolm Canmore did homage to William the Conqueror. Today, though, Abernethy's fame is through its *'Round Tower*, one of only three such in Scotland, the others being at Brechin and on the Orkney island of Egilsay. With a lower part ascribed to the 9C and the upper, presumably replacement, to the 11 or 12C, Abernethy's tower is 74ft high and tapers in circumference from 48 to 32ft. At the tower's foot there is a Pictish stone incised with ritual designs.

3m **Newburgh**, with, in High Street, the *Laing Museum* (Tel: 0334-53722), the theme of which is social aspects of Victorian Scotland.—This Route now follows the minor coastal road eastward, this soon passing *Lindores Abbey*, once one of the great religious communities of Fife but now scanty ruins; the arch of the main entrance and a part of the west tower are about the only features standing. The abbey was founded in 1191 for Tironensians by David, Earl of Huntingdon, on his return from a crusade. Later the unhappy Duke of Rothesay (see Rte 33C, Falkland) was buried here, and, later still, the abbey was still of sufficient importance to attract a visit by John Knox who records the burning of the monks' mass books.

The minor coastal road continues for *10m* to **Balmerino Abbey** (NTS. View only from outside during restoration), unusual if not unique for having been jointly founded in 1229 by both a king, Alexander II, and his mother Ermengarde, the latter buried here in 1234. As at Lindores the remains are scanty, if more compact, and it is not easy to picture this as a once flourishing Cistercian colony from Melrose; the abbey, in fact, which controlled the fishing at Anstruther where its abbot's house survives as a part of the Scottish Fisheries Museum. Balmerino was largely destroyed by the English in 1547, attempts to rebuild being cut off by the Reformation.

For the **Tay Bridges** and (*5m*) **Newport-on-Tay**, see Rte 33C which is joined at the latter.—*2m* **Dundee**, see Rte 34.

34 Dundee

Lying along the north shore of the Firth of Tay, here 2m wide and crossed by road and rail bridges (for both of which see Rte 33C), Dundee (175,000 inhab.) is a busy commercial and industrial city and port which, despite the demolition of much of the heart of the old town—a 19C insensitivity unusual in Scottish cities—nevertheless achieves an

DUNDEE

0 yards	1000
0 kilometres	1

A929 TEALING & FORFAR

TROTTICK

Golf Course

Caird Park

Mains Castle

FINTRY

KINGSWAY EAST

KINGSWAY EAST

OLD CRAIGIE

Cemetery

Baxter Park

ARBICATH ROAD

CRAIGIE

BROUGHTY FERRY ROAD

A92 CLAYPOTTS & ARBROATH

A930 BROUGHTY FERRY

EAST DOCK ROAD

Central Area
(See inset plan)

CAMPERDOWN DOCK

VICTORIA DOCK

HARBOUR

CITY SQUARE

way
on

Firth of Tay

Tay Road Bridge (Toll)

Tay

River

Car Park

N

NEWPORT-ON-TAY

ST ANDREWS

acceptable if unexciting blend of the modern style and of some solid, handsome older buildings.

Tourist Information. 4 City Square. Tel: 0382-27723.

SOME HOTELS. *Angus Thistle*, 101 Marketgait, DD1 1QU. Tel: 0382-26874. *Stakis Earl Grey*, Earl Grey Place, DD1 4DE. Tel: 0382-29271. *Queen's*, 160 Nethergate, DD1 4DU. Tel: 0382-22515.

History. Dundee seems to have been made a royal burgh by William the Lion in about 1190, thereafter quickly developing to become one of the chief towns of Scotland and one known also to Wallace who received some schooling here. Later it was the first town in Scotland wholeheartedly to accept the Reformed religion, George Wishart, burned at St. Andrews in 1546, being a leading figure. It was also a town which knew all too much of war—in 1547 the forces of England's Henry VIII held, plundered and burned the town for a week; in 1645 it was stormed by Montrose; and in 1651 it was taken and treated with the utmost severity by Cromwell's General Monk.

Graham of Claverhouse ('Bonnie Dundee' of ballad), born here in 1649, is perhaps the best known historical name associated with the city; he became hereditary constable of Dundee in 1683 but enjoyed the title of Viscount Dundee for less than a year before his death at Killiecrankie. The Old Pretender spent a night here in 1716, and the Jacobites held the town from September 1745 until after Culloden. William Lyon Mackenzie, the turbulent Canadian politician, was born in Dundee in 1795.

Dundee ships have explored the Arctic (in search of Franklin) and the Antarctic (Scott's 'Discovery' in 1901), and whaling was important during the latter half of the 18C.

In CITY SQUARE, which may be regarded as the modern city centre, stands *Caird Hall*, a distinguished building with a façade of columns, built in 1914–23 chiefly with a bequest from Sir James Caird (died 1916), a prominent Dundee industrialist. From City Square the description below tours in three directions: the Waterfront; to the north east towards Seagate and the old city centre; and to the west and north for several points of interest. Finally, three short sections describe some of Dundee's parks; the eastern suburb of Broughty Ferry and Claypotts Castle; and also Tealing Dovecot and Earth-House, some 5m north off A929.

WATERFRONT. Imediately south east and south of City Square, a complex of roads provides the approaches to (east) the Tay Road Bridge into Fife (see Rte 33C), and (west) the station and airport and A85 for Perth (Rte 30). In the latter direction the *University Botanic Garden* (Tel: 0382-66939), with a visitor centre, is off Riverside Drive. Within the above complex of roads, the waterfront area includes a leisure centre, a hotel and the Tay Bridge Monument. Farther north east, beyond the Tay Road Bridge, is Victoria Dock, today the home of two museum ships. **HMS Unicorn** (Tel: 0382-200900), a wooden frigate of 46 guns, was launched in Chatham in 1824 and now provides an insight into contemporary naval life, while the other ship is the **Royal Research Ship Discovery** (Tel: 0382-201175), Captain Scott's Antarctic ship built in Dundee in 1901 for the expedition of 1901–04.

EAST OF CITY SQUARE, within the angle of High Street and Commercial Street, *St. Paul's Episcopal Cathedral* (by George Gilbert Scott) occupies the site of the old castle (plaque), destroyed in c 1314. A plaque also marks the site of the birthplace of Admiral Duncan (1731), victor of Camperdown against the Dutch in 1797, and an adjoining house was where the Old Pretender stayed. No. 8 Castle Street, beside the cathedral, may interest philatelists as the place where stood the shop and printing works of James Chalmers, inventor in c 1834 of the adhesive postage stamp. Seagate leads north off Commercial Street, a plaque on the south side recalling the old town centre where stood the cross and tolbooth, while in Cowgate, the parallel street to the north of Seagate, are *St. Andrew's Church* (1774), a typical example of the work of Samuel Bell, and, just north east, the *Wishart Arch* (or East Port, or Cowgate Port), dating from 1591 and the only surviving city gate. The arch's name honours George Wishart, the Reformer burnt at St. Andrews in 1546, who, in 1544 from this gate's predecessor, at a time when Dundee was stricken by plague, preached in two directions, to the plague-stricken outside and to the still unaffected within.

WEST AND NORTH OF CITY SQUARE. Nethergate runs south west, soon passing on the north the so-called **City Churches**, a large cruciform pile comprising three churches under one roof, now surrounded on three sides by the Overgate Centre. The dominant feature here is the fine 15C tower of *Old Steeple* (or *St. Mary's Tower*), the only surviving part of the pre-Reformation church of St. Mary.

The story here is one of remarkably determined survival against the English and other disasters. It all started in c 1195 when David, Earl of Huntingdon, survived a storm at sea and, in obedience to a vow made during the storm, founded a chapel here. This was destroyed by the English in 1296 and again in 1385, but, such was the sanctity of this site, a church was rebuilt before 1480. The nave was battered down by an English fleet in 1547, and in 1651, when Monk assaulted Dundee, the garrison took to the Old Steeple and gallantly held out until burning straw was heaped against its base. Despite all this the building was gradually extended until by 1783 it embraced the four churches of St. Mary, St. Paul, St. Clement and St. John. Then in 1841 disaster struck again, this time as a fire which caused almost complete destruction. But, as always, the churches were rebuilt, although after this the congregation of St. Paul was accommodated elsewhere.

Beside Nethergate stands the *Cross*, a replica of the one that stood in Seagate but incorporating the original shaft. And in the pedestrian precinct a plaque with a biographical summary commemorates William Lyon Mackenzie (1795–1861), born in Dundee and in 1834 first mayor of Toronto, Canada.

Nethergate continues west, with, on its south side, *St. Andrew's RC Cathedral* containing a mosaic reredos of 1963 by Walter Pritchard, depicting Christ the King and Saints Peter and Clement. Opposite and beyond are the buildings of the **University** (1967).

The original University College was endowed by John Boyd Baxter and Miss Baxter of Balgavies, and opened in 1883 in some old houses on this site. It was incorporated with the University of St. Andrews in 1890–95 and again, after a brief separation, in 1897. In 1954 the college combined with others to form Queen's College, and independence from St. Andrews and individual university status were finally achieved in 1967.

To the north of the City Churches and the Overgate Centre is **The Howff**, for three centuries, until 1857, the city's chief burial ground, a sombre, eerie place yet a treasure-house for the connoisseur of quaint tombstones and the backward glimpses afforded by their inscriptions. And there are touches of history here too, for once this was the orchard of a Franciscan monastery, founded by Devorguilla Balliol in c 1270 and destroyed in 1548. Then in 1564 Mary, Queen of Scots, gave the ground to the town, and from then on it was used not only as a burying ground but also as a meeting-place (howff) of the Incorporated Trades, a practice which continued until the opening of a Trades Hall in 1778.

Near the north west corner of The Howff, on the corner of Barrack Street and Meadowside, is the **Barrack Street Museum** (Tel: 0382-23141), the primary theme of which is local natural history.

The city's **McManus Galleries** (Tel: 0382-23141), in Albert Square just north east of The Howff, are housed in the former Albert Institute, a substantial Victorian Gothic building of 1867, enlarged in 1887 and with, in front, a statue of Burns (by John Steell). Museum exhibits con-

centrate on regional collections of archaeological and general histori-
cal material, the latter including an instructive gallery on Trade and
Industry, while the Art Gallery shows works by Flemish, Dutch, French,
British and, in particular, Scottish artists with some emphasis on the
Victorian years. The recently restored Albert Hall provides a fine set-
ting for sculpture, paintings, silver and antique furnishing.

PARKS. Four Dundee parks may be mentioned. **Dudhope Park**, the
nearest to the city centre, less than 1m to the north west of City Square,
includes *Dudhope Castle* (no adm.), of some interest as being, at least in
its early form, the 14C successor of Dundee's original castle, the site of
which is now occupied by St. Paul's Cathedral. At one time a seat of the
Scrimgeours, whom Wallace had appointed hereditary constables of
Dundee, both the castle and its accompanying title passed through several hands until acquired by Claverhouse in 1683. In turn wool mill,
barracks and part of a college of technology, the structure has undergone constant alteration. Behind rises *Dundee Law* (571ft; view indicator), crowned by Dundee War Memorial.

On **Balgay Hill**, roughly 1m west of Dudhope Park, stands the *Mills
Observatory* (Tel: 0382-67138) with a ten-inch refracting telescope and
other instruments, as also a planetarium and displays on astronomy and
space exploration.—In **Caird Park** (north, beyond the ring road) is 16C
Mains Castle (or *Fintry Castle*), built in c 1550 by Sir David Graham and
now restored.

Camperdown Park (Tel: 0382-23141), 3m north west of central
Dundee off A923, is a large park offering a nature trail, a golf course,
riding, a *Wildlife Centre* and an adventure play-ground re-enacting the
Battle of Camperdown. *Camperdown House*, at the park's centre, is an
imposing mansion built by William Burn in 1824 for Robert Duncan, son
of Admiral Duncan, the victor of Camperdown.

BROUGHTY FERRY AND CLAYPOTTS CASTLE. **Broughty Ferry**, a
coastal suburb to the east of Dundee, is popular for the sandy beaches
between here and Monifieth a couple of miles north east. *Broughty
Castle* (Tel: 0382-76121), conspicuous by the sea, was first built in the
15C, occupied by the English in 1547 after their victory at Pinkie, and
stormed in 1550 by French auxiliaries in Scots service. Today the castle
houses a museum devoted largely to the ecology of the Tay and to the
maritime aspects of Dundee's past, with some emphasis on whaling.
Claypotts Castle (AM. Tel: 031-244-3101), just north of Broughty Ferry
at the intersection of A92 and B978, is one of Scotland's most complete
Z-plan tower-houses, with two round towers, stepped gables and intact
roof. Although the castle dates from 1569–88, the lands of Claypotts are
of far earlier identification, being mentioned in a document of 1365 in
connection with the abbey of Lindores (Rte 33D) which at that time was
the superior of Dundee's St. Mary's church. When the castle was built
the lands were owned by the Grahams of Claverhouse, but were forfeited to the Douglases in 1689 after Dundee's death at Killiecrankie.

TEALING DOVECOT AND EARTH-HOUSE. 5m north off A929. This is a
worthwhile diversion if only for the most unusual and attractive design
of the *Dovecot* which is built in the shape of a small house; dated 1595, it
bears on a gable the initials of Sir David Maxwell. The *Earth-house*,
well seen because it is now roofless, has an exceptionally long curving
passage. Immediately on the right inside, at ground level, there is a
cup-and-ring stone, much older of course than the earth-house and certainly once set up as a ritual stone elsewhere.

For Dundee to **Perth** (direct), see Rte 30; to **Perth** via Balmerino and Newburgh, see
Rte 33D; to **Edinburgh** via Cupar and Falkland, see Rte 33C; to **Montrose** and
Stonehaven, see Rte 35.

35   Dundee to Stonehaven via Montrose

A92.—Generally cultivated land, with coastal towns and coastal views, rocky in the northern part.

SOME HOTELS. **Carnoustie**. *Carlogie House*, Carlogie Road, DD7 6LD. Tel: 0241-53185. **Arbroath**. *Seaforth*, Dundee Road, DD11 1QF. Tel: 0241-72232. *Windmill*, Millgate Loan, DD11 1QG. Tel: 0241-72278. **Montrose**. *Park*, 61 John Street, DD10 8RJ. Tel: 0674-73415. *Carlton*, 139 High Street, DD10 8QN. Tel: 0674-77237.

Total distance 48m.—*10m* **Carnoustie**.—*6m* **Arbroath**.—*12m* **Montrose**.—*12m* **Inverbervie**.—*7m* **Dunnottar Castle**.—*1m* **Stonehaven**.

Dundee (see Rte 34) is left by A92, passing *Claypotts Castle* (see Rte 34) and in *6m* reaching the intersection with B962. Here *Ardestie Earth-house*, within the north west angle of the intersection, is roofless and thus offers a painless opportunity to study the layout of one of these curious and unexplained excavations; and this site is of added interest for its association with an Iron Age settlement, the foundations of the houses being clearly seen, as also the line of an internal drain and what seems to have been a shallow tank, possibly used for keeping shellfish fresh. Nearby *Carlungie Earth-house* is also roofless and shows a long, twisting passage off which branch three short secondary passages; it is reached by driving another mile east along A92 and then following a minor road north for half a mile.

Two country parks, both to the north, are within easy reach of the Ardestie intersection. *Monikie Country Park* (Tel: 082623-202) is 2m north off B961 and *Crombie Country Park* (Tel: 02416-360) a further 2m north east off the same road. Both parks offer wildlife, guided walks, ranger services, angling and children's picnic and play areas.

At (*4m*) *Muirdrum* A92 intersects B9128 (north) and A930 (south), a short way down the latter being **Carnoustie** (9000 inhab. *Inf.*), known for its sands and golf courses. About 2m north west of Muirdrum, on the left off B9128, once stood Panmure House, built in the later 17C and demolished in 1955; but the gates survive, not opened since the 4th Earl fled to France after the collapse of the '15.

6m **Arbroath** (24,000 inhab. *Inf.*), royal burgh of 1599 and popular holiday resort, is best known for its ruined and historic abbey and also for St. Vigean's Museum. But there are other places of interest too. For instance the *Art Gallery* (Tel: 0674-73232), in the Library, Hill Terrace, the place for paintings by local artists or by other Scottish artists who have painted this district. Or the *Signal Tower Museum* (Tel: 0674-73232), in Ladyloan west of the harbour, which is housed in what was once the shore base of the Bell Rock lighthouse and illustrates the history of Arbroath, with particular reference to fishing, flax and the Bell Rock (see below). And there is also the *Cliffs Nature Trail*, 3m in length and for the most part using reasonable paths (booklet from Tourist Information).

*Arbroath Abbey (AM. Tel: 031-244-3101), in the town centre, is an outstandingly beautiful ruin of red sandstone, essentially Early English in period though also with many traces of Norman.

History. The story behind the foundation of this abbey is interesting both in itself and as being perhaps typical of the kind of incident which could lead to a foundation. The murder at Canterbury of Thomas à Becket led to a rebellion by the English barons and Scotland's King, William the Lion, himself an English landowner, joined in. He was defeated and captured at Alnwick (1174) on the very day that Henry II suffered penance by being scourged by the Canterbury monks. So impressed was William by this coincidence that on his release and return to Scotland he founded Arbroath (1178) as a Cluniac priory dedicated to Becket. There were two fires during the construction, and the building was not finished until 1233, 19 years after its founder's death. The priory was promoted to abbey in 1285.

Undoubtedly the abbey's most historic moment was in 1320 when the Estates of Scotland met here and formally asserted Scotland's independence of the English Crown (Declaration of Arbroath), sending a letter to Pope John XXII acknowledging Robert Bruce as king. However it was not until 1324 that Rome addressed Bruce as king and not until 1328 that England's Edward III fell in line.

The abbey was sacked by Ochterlony of Kelly (Kelly Castle is 2m west of Arbroath) in c 1600, but its ultimate ruin was due to post-Reformation neglect and the town's habit of removing and then either selling or using the stones. Among famous abbots were Bernard de Linton, the probable author of the declaration of independence; the three Beatons (Cardinal David, and two Archbishops James, uncle and nephew of the cardinal); and Gavin Douglas, Bishop of Dunkeld.

Above the fine semicircular west doorway, with its deep Early English mouldings, is an arcade of six pointed arches, but of the rose-window only the lower arc remains. Much of the north west tower and part of the south west survives. The south wall and south transept remain, showing some pier bases, this south transept, with arcades and triforium intact, having a magnificent circular window, known as the 'Round O of Arbroath', once always kept lighted as a beacon for navigation. Next to this transept there is a vaulted structure with remarkable acoustics, probably formerly the sacristy, surrounded within by sedilia.

At the east end were once three rows of lancets, emphasising the length of the church, but of these only the lowest now survives.

The massive gatehouse tower flanks an arch, or pend, above which was the chamber in which the Declaration was signed. The *Abbot's House, to the south, shows a fine vaulted kitchen, while the hall above, still with some 13C tiles, has been restored and fitted up as a Museum showing documents, relics and sculpture, among this last being a headless effigy with the feet resting on a lion which is supposed, though really on no more evidence than this lion, to represent the abbey's founder, known to have been buried before the high altar.

St Vigean's Museum (AM. Tel: 031-244-3101), in a converted cottage in Arbroath's north west suburbs (sign off A92), shows an important collection of Pictish and Celtic Early Christian sculptured stones. The stones are admirably arranged and displayed, and the lively detail on many of them repays study.

Inchcape (Bell) Rock. This rock, covered by water at high tide, is 11m out to sea south east of Arbroath and is said to have taken the name of Bell Rock from a bell placed there by an abbot of Arbroath; later, tradition continues, the bell was removed by a pirate, Sir Ralph the Rover, hoping to trap ships but in fact himself being wrecked here ('Sir Ralph the Rover tore his hair, He curst himself in his despair'—as Southey put it in his ballad).

7m **Red Castle**, a stark red sandstone ruin overlooking Lunan Bay, can be well seen below A92 and is easily reached by a minor road. Although dating from the 15C the castle replaced an earlier stronghold built for William the Lion by Walter de Berkeley, probably as a defence against the Danish pirates who even in William the Lion's time constantly raided this coast. William may well have stayed here from time to time during the building of his priory at Arbroath, and later, in 1328, Bruce gave the castle to his son-in-law Hugh, 6th Earl of Ross. Eventually, in 1579, the place seems to have met an undignified end, being largely destroyed during a marital feud between Lady Invermeith, the then occupant, and her divorced husband, James Gray.

5m **Montrose** (12,000 inhab. *Inf.*) fills a broad tongue of land projecting southward between the sea and *Montrose Basin*, a tidal lagoon about 2m square through which the South Esk reaches the sea. An effort made to drain the basin in 1670 was foiled by a storm, and it survived to become today a nature reserve which is a rich habitat for migrating waders and wildfowl as also huge flocks of geese.

The town's connection with James Graham, the great Marquis of Montrose, is small; merely that he was born in 1612 at Old Montrose, on the south west side of the Basin.

History. Montrose has many times been touched by history; military, political and even educational. The castle here was taken by Edward I in 1296, and it was here that John Balliol personally made his submission after his formal abdication at Stracathro near Brechin. Then, in the following year, Wallace destroyed the castle, while in 1330, according to Froissart, it was from Montrose that Sir James Douglas sailed for the Holy Land, carrying with him the heart of Bruce. The year 1554 brought a more erudite note when John Erskine of Dun established here Scotland's first school for the teaching of Greek, the first teacher being a Frenchman, Pierre de Marsiliers, and his pupils including the Reformers George Wishart and Andrew Melville. Later, the '15 ended here with the secret embarkation on 4 February 1716 of the Old Pretender and the Earl of Mar.

Well planned, with a spacious wide High Street and several dignified if modest buildings, this is a town of quiet distinction. The *Old Church*, in High Street, with its pinnacled square tower carrying a graceful steeple of 1834 by Gillespie Graham, sets the tone, near it being the *Old Town Hall* of 1763, though with additions of 1813. Behind, in Panmure Place, is the *Museum and Art Gallery* (Tel: 0674-73232), with good displays illustrating local history, the Pictish stones, material on whaling, and the geology collections being of some note; also, in the garden beside Museum Street, can be seen a length of the stone balustrade of the old Montrose suspension bridge (1828–1928). To the east stands the *New Town Hall* (1963) interestingly constructed in the body of a 19C church, and, beyond, links extend to a sandy shore. Visitors with an interest in sculpture will probably wish to take in the *William Lamb Memorial Studio* (Tel: 0674-73232) at 24 Market Place, where a selection of the works of this Montrose sculptor and etcher (1893–1951) is shown in his studio.

Two places near Montrose also perhaps merit a visit. *House of Dun* (NTS. Tel: 067481-264), 4m west of Montrose on A935, was rebuilt in 1730 by William Adam from the earlier house in which John Erskine (see History) was born. The plasterwork is notable, and the house also shows mementoes of the Regency period, the wife of the then owner having been a natural daughter of William IV and the actress, Mrs Jordan. Very different, and of specialised appeal, is the *Sunnyside Museum* (Tel: 067483-361) in Sunnyside Royal Hospital at Hillside, 3m north of Montrose on A937. This hospital of 1781 was Scotland's first mental hospital and its museum tells its story and that of psychiatry in Scotland.

12m **Inverbervie** lies on the south bank of Bervie Water, while on the north side is Bervie Brow (450ft) and its promontory *Craig David*, the place where David II and his queen landed in May 1341 after nine years of exile in France during the ascendancy of the Balliols; his ship was driven ashore by a storm and the rock known as the King's Step is said to be the spot where he actually set foot in Scotland. The town was made a royal burgh the following year.

At (*2m*) *Roadside of Kinneff* a minor road leads 1m south east to **Kinneff Church** where (in association with Dunnottar Castle, see below) this Route touches one of the several adventures of the regalia of Scotland (see also Rte 18, Edinburgh, Edinburgh Castle). During the Cromwellian wars the Scottish regalia were brought to Dunnottar for safety, and when the castle was besieged in 1652, Ogilvy, the governor, determined to hold out until the regalia were secreted away. This was achieved through the ingenuity and courage of Mrs Grainger, wife of the minister of Kinneff, who obtained permission to enter the castle ostensibly to visit Ogilvy's wife. When she left, it was with the crown in her apron, while her serving woman carried the sword and sceptre in a bundle of flax. The story further insists that the English commander courteously helped Mrs Grainger into the saddle. Back at Kinneff Mrs Grainger handed the regalia to her husband who hid them beneath the pulpit where they rested in safety until the Restoration eight years later.

But the church as seen today dates largely from 1738 and only a part survives—with monuments to the Rev. Grainger and Ogilvy—of the original church which sheltered the 'Honours of Scotland'. Romantically though the story may read at a distance of over 300 years, it was scarcely so for some of those concerned, though all—Ogilvy and his lady, the minister and his—emerged with credit, refusing, even under torture, to reveal anything. Their rewards came with the Restoration when Ogilvy received a baronetcy and the Graingers a pension.—In about *3m* north from Roadside of Kinneff, along a cliff path from the coastal village of Crawton, *Fowlsheugh Nature Reserve* (RSPB) shelters a large seabird colony, best in April–July.

2m **"Dunnottar Castle** (Tel: 0569-62173), an isolated and extensive ruin, sprawls over a great crag, surrounded on three sides by sea and rocks and on the fourth by a deep cleft left when the crag split from the main cliff. Among the most theatrically sited in Scotland, the ruins are more akin to those of a fortified township than of just a castle.

History. During the Dark Ages this rock was the site both of a Pictish fort and of an Early Christian chapel, the former recalled by the 'Dun' in this place's name, the latter by the fact that the ravine down which the castle is approached is known as St. Ninian's Den. Records indicate that there was a castle here in the early 13C, and also that a church (of St. Ninian) was consecrated here in 1276. In 1297, when the English held the castle, Wallace stormed it, burning many of the garrison who had taken refuge in the church. However, despite this, Dunnottar remained in English hands.

The oldest surviving buildings today are the great square tower and chapel, said to have been built by Sir William Keith, great Marischal of Scotland, in c 1392. The gatehouse (c 1575) was the strongest in Scotland and, like the 'lodging' in the courtyard, was built by the 5th Earl Marischal. In 1645, the 7th Earl Marischal, a stubborn Covenanter, withstood a siege by Montrose, who in revenge wasted the country for miles around and burned the town of Stonehaven. As the Chronicler vividly puts it, the country was 'uterlie spoilzeit, plunderit and undone'. There followed the Cromwellian siege and the incident of the regalia as described above (Kinneff Church). In 1687 Dunnottar was the prison of 167 Covenanters, held under brutal circumstances in a dungeon (the 'Whigs' Vault') open to the sea. Finally, the staunchly Jacobite 10th Earl Marischal had to forfeit the estate in 1716, and thereafter the castle was gradually dismantled.

Signs identify the various buildings which make up these complex and sprawling ruins, and the local booklet explains their detail. The outstanding features are the once formidable *Gatehouse* (1575); the huge *Well*, 30ft across and 25ft deep; the *Drawing Room*, with its modern (1927) painted and carved ceiling; and the breathtaking view from the *Marischal's Suite*, perched high above the rocks. Also the exceptionally interesting great range of *Domestic Buildings*—immense kitchen, with sink, sluice and ovens; the bakery and its capacious oven; wine vault and brewery. Finally there is the grim *Whigs' Vault* (the name Whig was bestowed on 17C Scottish Presbyterians), the prison for over two summer months in 1684 of 122 men and 45 women. Many died, and in desperation 25 attempted an escape along the rock face. Only ten got away, some were killed and the others were cruelly punished. The *Covenanters' Stone*, in Dunnottar churchyard, commemorates those who died as prisoners or in attempting to escape.

1m **Stonehaven**, see Rte 29.

VI NORTH EAST

North East Scotland is made up of a wooded and undulating agricultural and pastoral centre, bordered by the sea to the north and east; by
Deeside, famed for its forest and mountain beauty and its royal associations to the south; and, to the west, by high bare moor and mountain.
Round the coasts, especially in the north east, there are stretches of
steep cliff and rock (notably *Bullers of Buchan*, south of Peterhead), but
for the most part the through-roads run inland and short diversions
must be made to see the coast's scenery and small ports.

That the fertile lowland districts were widely inhabited in prehistoric times is clear from the many stone circles, those in the south east
corner even being of a distinctive local style (Recumbent Stone). The
North East moves into history in the 9C with the union of Dalriada and
Pictland by Kenneth Macalpine, among the best known (thanks to
Shakespeare) of his shadowy early successors being Duncan and Macbeth. The former may have been murdered at *Forres* (though more
probably he was killed in battle), as were others before him, and Macbeth probably met his end at *Lumphanan*, near Deeside, where the
great motte on which stood his primitive stronghold can still be seen.
By the 13C power was largely in the hands of the Norman Comyns, earls
of Buchan, the first Comyn having married a daughter of a local chief. (It
was this Comyn who in 1219 founded *Deer Abbey*.) But Bruce's struggle
against the English was equally a struggle against the Comyns, and in
1307 he twice defeated them (at *Slioch*, near Huntly, and at *Barra Hill*,
near Inverurie), thereafter laying waste the land and installing his own
supporters in the former Comyn strongholds. To Sir Adam Gordon went
Strathbogie, later *Huntly Castle*, and there followed some 250 years
during which the Gordons (later, earls of Huntly) ruled the North East
like kings. Their sway ended with the bizarre events of 1562.

The 4th Earl was as powerful and arrogant as any of his forerunners, and his third
son, Sir John Gordon, a swashbuckling character who had let it be known that he
was a candidate for the hand of the queen, Mary. Mary marched north, intending

to combine a formal royal progress with curbing the Gordons. Her progress, however, became a running skirmish with Sir John, whose intention it was to abduct her. She wisely avoided the Gordon stronghold of Huntly and made for the royal castle at Inverness, where she interpreted the refusal of the governor, another Huntly son, to admit her as evidence of open rebellion. She gained admittance, however, and hanged the governor from the battlements. Back in Aberdeen, Mary outlawed both the Earl and Sir John. The former's redoubtable countess then came on the scene, urging her husband to fight because she had been advised by her witches that that evening he would lie unscratched in Aberdeen's tolbooth. The rival forces met at *Corrichie* (15m west of the city) and both the Earl and Sir John were captured. The former promptly died of heart failure, and his unwounded body was dumped in the tolbooth, thus at least satisfying the promise of the witches. Later the body was embalmed, brought to Edinburgh, and formally tried for treason. Sir John was executed, with Mary an unwilling spectator.

Thus ended the era of absolute Gordon power, for centuries the main feature of life throughout the North East, and although there was a half-hearted rebellion by Errol, Huntly and others against James VI in 1594 (this resulting in the destruction of Errol's *Slains Castle*, as also of much of the Gordon *Huntly Castle*), and although Montrose was active here, generally the North East remained loyal to the Crown. Little enthusiasm was shown for the Jacobite cause, although George Keith, the 10th Earl Marischal, was exiled for permitting the Old Pretender to land at Peterhead, and although the Earl of Mar raised the latter's standard at Braemar.

To a majority of visitors the North East will mean upper Deeside, which many will reach from the south, by crossing the Cairnwell Pass (Rte 28) to *Braemar*, from where the North West rather than the North East may well be the next objective. This can best be achieved by taking the old (Hanoverian) military road north from *Balmoral*, this becoming the *Lecht Road* where it crosses the high moor (2100ft) before descending to *Grantown-on-Spey*, whence roads radiate in all directions. Twenty miles north west of here, near Inverness, are two of the most important sites in this part of Scotland. These are the battlefield of *Culloden*, the last battle to be fought on British soil and one which not only ended all the hopes of the House of Stuart but also signalled the end of a centuries old Highland way of life; and, nearby, *Clava Cairns*, an outstanding group of prehistoric tombs and stones.

But not everybody will head north west and for those who travel down Deeside there are several places meriting a stop. These are described under Rtes 37A and 37B, the former being the main road and the latter the smaller B9119 a short way to the north. This latter road is less crowded, and passes some unusual sites, such as *Culsh Earth-house*, near Tarland; the great walled motte at *Lumphanan*, associated with Macbeth; and *Craigievar Castle*, perhaps Scotland's most perfect tower-house, virtually untouched since its building in the 17C.

The remainder of the North East is described under Rte 36 (Aberdeen); five Routes radiating from the city; and Rte 43, which travels the length of the north coast.

Aberdeen, the 'Granite City', with its striking yet dignified inner city buildings, granite and sandstone 14–15C cathedral, and its large harbour area around which anyone can wander more or less at will, deserves at least a day. The radiating Routes all end at places along the north coast and the one chosen will depend on individual taste and plans. Rtes 39 and 40, though, follow roughly parallel courses through the heart of the North East and most principal sites are close to them, e.g. the sculptured stones, stone circle and other sites between *Inverurie* and *Insch*; the great castles of *Kildrummy*, *Huntly* and *Balvenie*, each with its story of past bloodshed and all notable as ruins; and the whisky distilleries strung along the '*Whisky Trail*'.

Along the north coast there are many little-visited corners, but **Elgin** stands out as the principal centre. Within the town is the cathedral, one of the loveliest ruins in Scotland, while, as a change from ruins, *Pluscarden Abbey* to the south west shows how a flourishing modern religious community can be grafted on to what was left by the old. Near Elgin also are 12C *Birnie Church*, with its surrounding ancient standing stones certainly one of Scotland's oldest sites continously used for ritual, first pagan then Christian; *Spynie Palace*, fortified home of Elgin's bishops; and *Duffus Castle*, where a medieval stone keep balances uneasily on an older motte. To the west is *Forres*, associated with Macbeth and today visited for the famed *Sueno Stone* with its vivid battle scenes. A few miles before Inverness, *Culloden* and *Clava Cairns* lie just to the south.

36 Aberdeen

Granite, solid and confident, and with a population of some 170,000, Aberdeen's foundations are its distinguished university and its port at the mouth of the Dee, the latter, still active with fishing, in recent years also bringing a new prosperity as a service and supply base for companies exploiting North Sea oil and gas. Within and around the city there is much of historic and artistic interest—a good two days here would not be wasted—while for the visitor with other tastes there are the attractions of superb sands, a long esplanade, golf links and all the best in family entertainment.

> **Tourist Information**. St. Nicholas House, Broad Street. Tel: 0224-632727, or, for accommodation, 637353.
>
> **Railway and Bus Stations**. Guild Street.
>
> **Airport**. Dyce, 6m north west.
>
> SOME HOTELS. All the following have parking. **Main City**. *Caledonian Thistle*, Union Terrace, AB9 1HE. Tel: 0224-640233. *Royal*, 1 Bath Street, AB1 2HY. Tel: 0224-585152. *Copthorne*, 122 Huntly Street. Tel: 0224-630404. *Douglas*, Market Street. Tel: 0224-582255. **Old Aberdeen**. *Cairn Northern*, 1 Great Northern Road, AB9 2UL. Tel: 0224-483342. **Airport**. *Skean Dhu*, Argyll Road, AB2 0DU. Tel: 0224-725252.

History. Undoubtedly there were prehistoric settlements along this estuary of the Dee, and undoubtedly, too, Romans, Picts and Scots were here. Later, in 1136, David I allowed a tithe to be levied on all craft in and out of the Dee. But the earliest existing charter as a royal burgh is that of William the Lion of 1179. In 1306 Bruce sought and received refuge here. The year 1337 was another important date, for after the destruction of the castle and the burning of the town by Edward III Aberdeen was rebuilt on a more generous scale. During the 17C Montrose three times occupied the city, twice as a leader of the Covenanters and once as a royalist, then Commonwealth military occupation followed for some years after 1651. Although Jacobite declarations were made in 1715 and 1745, Aberdeen was never really in sympathy; the contrary, indeed, since it was from here that Cope embarked for Dunbar and his defeat at Prestonpans, and in the following year Cumberland stayed six weeks here prior to Culloden.—The *University* includes Marischal College in the city centre and King's College in Old Aberdeen. Although in 1641 Charles I chartered the two as a single university, they separated at the Restoration and their present union dates from 1860.

Aberdeen is both conveniently visited and conveniently described as three districts: the Main City, the Harbour and beyond, and Old Aberdeen.

The Main City

The central area is quite compact and most places of interest can comfortably be visited on foot. Union Street (begun in 1800, its name commemorating the union of the parliaments of Great Britain and Ireland) is the city's long and main east–west axis, the description below starting beyond the east end, at the Mercat Cross, and then travelling westward along Union Street and its northern parallels, Upper Kirkgate and Schoolhill.

In the middle of Castle Street—with parallel Justice Street less a street than an open rectangle off the east end of Union Street—stands the *Mercat Cross of 1686, perhaps the most notable such in Scotland with its unicorn and hexagonal base on which are panels with medallion heads of monarchs from James I to VII/II, together with heraldic coats-of-arms. This Mercat Cross was of course the focus of commercial activity, while the **Town House** (contact City Archivist. Tel: 0224-642121), forming the corner with Broad Street, provided the administration, today's striking building of 1860–80 incorporating the tower and spire of the tolbooth (1616 and 1704; entrance to Lodge Walk), long the prison and the place outside which public executions took place until as recently as 1867. Within the Town House is the *Charter Room*, showing the charter granted by William the Lion as also the burgh records, complete but for one volume, from 1398 to the present day. A (Tolbooth) Civic History Museum is planned for the early 1990s.

There is much of both historical and current interest to be found in the close surrounds of Castle Street, starting with the fact that this was indeed the approach to Aberdeen's castle, destroyed in 1337 by Edward III and now represented by a cluster of high-rise buildings immediately to the east behind the Salvation Army Citadel. A more modern, and transatlantic interest awaits in King Street (north), for here **St. Andrew's Cathedral** (Bishop Seabury Visitor Centre. Tel: 0224-314765 or 640290) is the Mother Church of the Episcopal Communion in America, with a memorial commemorating Samuel Seabury, first bishop in the United States, consecrated in Aberdeen in 1784. The interior here is most striking with its contrast between the white of the walls and pillars, the blue east window and the sharp bright colouring of the ceiling coats-of-arms, those above the north aisle being of all the American States, those above the south aisle of all those Aberdeenshire families who held loyal to the Jacobite cause.

Nearby (at 21 Castle Street) are *Peacock Printmakers* (Tel: 0224-639539), an association founded in 1974 to encourage printmaking (etchings, screenprints, lithographs, relief prints) in the north east of Scotland. For the visitor there is a viewing gallery, a museum and explanatory display, and the opportunity to buy members' work. The adjacent *Artspace Galleries* (Tel: 0224-639539) mount exhibitions by local, national and international artists.

From the east end of Castle Street, Justice Street and Beach Boulevard lead across Queen's Links to reach Beach Esplanade, over 2m in length from the Don in the north to the harbour entrance at the south. Here, in the area around the seaward end of Beach Boulevard, are such resort attractions as a beach ballroom, a leisure centre, a children's village and adventure playground, and an amusement centre and park. At its south end Beach Esplanade ends at *Footdee* (or, locally, Fittie), a planned fishing village built in 1809 to replace an older settlement.

In Marischal Street, leading south out of Castle Street, there can be dark echoes, for here the offices of the Bank of Scotland occupy the site of the town mansion of the Earl Marischal, from a window of which in 1562 Mary, Queen of Scots, was forced to watch the execution of Sir

John Gordon, her swashbuckling but little encouraged admirer who, openly expressing intentions of abduction and marriage, had harried her state progress into the North. At this same time the body of Sir John's father, the Earl of Huntly, who had rebelled, been defeated at Corrichie on Deeside, then died of heart failure, lay across the way in the tolbooth prior to being embalmed and taken to Edinburgh for a ghoulish trial for treason (see North East introduction, above).

The **Aberdeen Maritime Museum** (Tel: 0224-585788) will be found in Shiprow, leading south west roughly opposite the tolbooth and, until as late as the mid 18C, the city's only connection with its upper harbour. The museum is housed in Provost Ross's House (1593), once the home of a late 16C merchant and in the 18C that of Provost Ross, another merchant with substantial maritime interests. The museum is arranged on three levels, of which the ground floor is partly administrative with museum and NTS shops and partly allotted to temporary exhibitions and an introductory room. On the first floor the central feature is the Picture Gallery, the museum themes on one side being Fishing and Aberdeen Harbour and, on the other, Wrecks and Rescues, the North Boats (vessels to Orkney and Shetland), and the Duthie Room, the 1884 office of a shipowner. Above, on the second floor, the themes are Local Shipbuilding and Shipowning, the London Boats (the Aberdeen Steam Navigation Company operated from 1835 until the early 1960s), a Viewing Platform (hand-rivetting) and North Sea Oil and Gas.—The building, owned by the National Trust for Scotland, is leased to the city. In addition to a NTS shop there is an admirable video presentation on NTS Grampian properties.

From the west end of Castle Street there is a westward choice between Union Street, stretching away for a somewhat daunting straight mile, or a more broken northerly arc following Broad Street, Upper Kirkgate, Schoolhill and Union Terrace, this last rejoining Union Street well along its length. This northerly arc, by far the more interesting, is the course now followed.

The short length of Broad Street is dominated by two conspicuous and wildly contrasting buildings—on the west side the towering modern slab of **St. Nicholas House** (Municipal offices. *Tourist Information*) and, opposite, the pinnacled splendour of ****Marischal College**, since 1860, with King's College in Old Aberdeen, forming Aberdeen University but founded here three centuries earlier than this, in 1593, by George Keith, the cultured 5th Earl Marischal. Keith's early college occupied the buildings of the Greyfriars' monastery, defunct since the Reformation, these remaining in use until c 1844 by which date they had been replaced by the first buildings of the present quadrangle; today the monastery lives on as no more than a seven-light gable from its church, preserved and incorporated in the present Greyfriars Church, a rebuilding of 1903 at the college's south front. The college, flaunting that breathtaking pinnacled façade of 1906, is considered to be one of the world's most extravagant granite achievements, and the *Mitchell Hall*, with a window illustrating the history of the college, and the *Portrait Gallery* are open at reasonable times when not in use for functions. The *University of Aberdeen Anthropological Museum* or *Marischal Museum* (Tel: 0224-273131) illustrates the arts, crafts and customs of peoples worldwide from ancient to modern times, a section being devoted to Scotland's, and especially Grampian's, prehistoric inhabitants.

Opposite—almost hiding beside St. Nicholas House, dwarfed by it and providing yet another contrast in this corner of Aberdeen—is ***Provost Skene's House** (Tel: 0224-641086). Built in c 1545, and now

Aberdeen's oldest surviving example of a private house, this pleasant turreted place came to the Skene family in 1654 and is named after Sir George Skene, provost of Aberdeen (1676–85) and known to have carried out extensive repairs and restoration. Of more historic interest, and indicative of the status at the time of a house such as this, is that the Duke of Cumberland chose this as his residence for some six weeks before Culloden, the house at this period (1732–1832) being split into two. Acquired by the city in 1926, the house is now the perfect frame for several exquisitely period-furnished rooms (Georgian, Regency, Victorian), while other attractions include a video on the history of the property, and also (top floor) instructive material on local civic and domestic life and on the archaeology of Aberdeen and Grampian.

Upper Kirkgate, leading west, crosses shopping precincts, immediately beyond on the left, set back in green surrounds, being the **Church of St. Nicholas** (access also from Union Street). In origin a 12–15C structure, first mentioned in 1157, this is no ordinary church. Long the largest parish church in Scotland, it was divided into two at the Reformation, but, with what is known as the Transept—a kind of common vestibule between the West and East churches—in effect the building is in three parts. Some ancient effigies and memorials, interesting in their local context, and some curiosities reward the visitor. The *West Church*, a rebuilding of 1755, shows some good contemporary woodwork, but is better known for four large embroidered panels (Finding of Moses. Finding of Jephthah. Esther. Susanna and the Elders), attributed to Mary Jamesone, daughter of the painter George Jamesone (?1587–1644). The *East Church*, although a rebuilding of 1877, preserves its 15C crypt (St. Mary's chapel), a simple little stone-vaulted place, founded in 1420 and in part restored in 1898, which over the years has also served some surprising secular purposes. During the 17C, for instance, witches were imprisoned here, and iron rings to which these much-feared wretches may have been secured are shown; in the following century a plumber took over, using this crypt as his workshop; and in the early 19C the poor shuffled through here to receive their portion from a soup kitchen. But, bar possibly those iron rings, no secular physical reminders survive, though from the crypt's spiritual years there are fragments of 16C stalls and some 17C panels and seats.

The so-called *Transept*, above an older structure discovered below the floor and now covered, has a spire replacing one lost by fire in 1874 and also a carillon of 48 bells dating from 1932. Here, in Collison's Aisle (north), an effigy may be that of Alderman Davidson, killed at Harlaw in 1411 and leader of the Aberdonians in the battle (see Rte 40), while a tablet to the wife (died 1568) of Canon Heriot recalls the name of the first Protestant minister of Aberdeen. In Drum's Aisle (south) there are reminders of the lands of Drum (Rte 37A) in the forms of the 15C effigies of Forbes of Drum and his wife, and also of a rare medieval brass, an unfinished inscription to Sir A. de Irwyn, known to have died in 1457 and thus a close descendant of Bruce's standard bearer. Here, too, are an interesting Mortification List, spanning 1616 to 1792, and a tablet to Robert Gordon, founder of Gordon's College (see immediately below).

Schoolhill is now ascended to pass, on the right at the top of the rise and marked by an archway, *Gordon's College* founded in 1739 as Robert Gordon's College for the board and education of the sons of burgesses. The central block (1746) is by William Adam, and the statue by the arch is of General Gordon of Khartoum, no relation, though, to the college's founder. Roughly opposite, at 61 Schoolhill, is *James Dun's House* (Tel: 0224-646333), the 18C town house of a former master and rector of Aberdeen Grammar School, now restored as a museum mounting varied exhibitions and video presentations.

The city *Art Gallery (Tel: 0224-646333), on the corner of Schoolhill and Blackfriars Street, shows good permanent collections of 18–20C art, the emphasis however being on contemporary work. The ground floor is devoted largely to the decorative arts, the collection of silver, and in particular of Aberdeen work, being especially notable and the subject of a video, 'All that Glisters'. The fine art gallery, on the upper floor, includes the unique *Macdonald Collection of 92 portraits of British artists, nearly all painted by themselves, while names such as Raeburn, MacEvoy, Zoffany, Reynolds, Romney, Augustus John, Toulouse Lautrec and Orpen give a measure of the gallery's quality and scope. Additionally the gallery mounts a full programme of temporary exhibitions, music recitals, dance, poetry readings and lectures.—The austere Memorial Court opens out as a part of the ground floor.

Woolmanhill, running north west, recalls that this was once the site of the wool market.

Schoolhill now becomes Rosemount Viaduct, with, on the right, *His Majesty's Theatre* (1906) and, opposite, an open space with a defiant statue of Wallace and a seated one of Prince Albert. Here Union Terrace, with a statue of Burns, bears south beside gardens above the railway to join Union Street, with a statue of Edward VII on the corner of Union Bridge, not immediately recognised as a bridge now that the south side is built over.

From this point many visitors may well return east, passing the Union Street entrance to the Church of St. Nicholas, marked by an Ionic colonnade of 1820 built in emulation of London's Hyde Park Corner. There remain, however, places of interest westward along Union Street, at least as far as (c ½m) the point where the street ends, forking right as Alford (becoming Albyn) Place and left as Holburn Street. On the right, with classical columns, is the *Music Hall* of 1820, while just beyond in Huntly Street the spired RC *St. Mary's Cathedral* dates from 1860–80. Crown Street, opposite the Music Hall, leads by way of Crown Terrace (opposite the main *Post Office*) to *St. John's Church*, of interest to connoisseurs of fonts, the one here, early 16C and showing the Five Wounds of Christ, having originally been in the now ruined church at Kinkell (Rte 40). At the west end of Union Street can be seen the Tudor edifice of *Christ's College* (1851), academically linked with the university's Faculty of Divinity. *Satrosphere* (Tel: 0224-213232), at 19 Justice Mill Lane, just south of this west end of Union Street, is a hands-on science and technology exhibition.

WEST BEYOND UNION STREET. Albyn Place, with distinguished 19C granite mansions, becomes Queen's Road off which, in just under 1m from the west end of Albyn Place, leads Viewfield Road, with the *Gordon Highlanders' Regimental HQ and Museum* (Tel: 0224-318174). In *Hazlehead Park*, beyond, there is a memorial (Sue Jane Taylor) to the victims of the Piper Alpha oil rig tragedy of 1988.

SOUTH OF UNION STREET. From the west end of Union Street, Holburn Street in 1½m reaches the *Bridge of Dee*, on the road to Stonehaven. A structure of seven ribbed arches bearing inscriptions and coats-of-arms, this bridge was built by Bishop Dunbar in 1520–27, but widened in 1842 when its west face was replaced so as to preserve the medieval appearance. Nearby, off Riverside Drive, Ruthrieston Pack Horse Bridge is in origin of 1694. Central Aberdeen can pleasantly be regained by following Riverside Drive along the left bank of the Dee, this road passing *Duthie Park*, with gardens, exotic birds, an aquarium, winter gardens and, in summer, a boating pond and other amusements.

The Harbour and Beyond

Market Street, dropping south off Union Street opposite St. Nicholas Centre, and with on the right the older *Market Centre*, soon reaches the harbour at its north west corner. Nearby, in Shiprow, is the *Maritime Museum* (see above), a prior visit to which could greatly add to the interest of a tour of the harbour area.

History. It was in 1136 that the port received its first recorded formal recognition when David I allowed a shipping tithe to be levied. But despite impressive growth in both fishing and continental trade little was done over the long medieval centuries throughout which the harbour remained essentially an uncontrolled estuary of islands and shifting sands. Then in 1596 came the first awakening when, to raise money for improvement, James VI allowed Aberdeen to impose charges on ships using the harbour, the result being the construction in 1607 of a bulwark along the south shore of the estuary near the river mouth, the aim being to increase tidal scour and thus deepen the entrance.

But over another century and a half would elapse before it became accepted that the port could no longer cope with the accelerating trade resulting from the Act of Union and James Smeaton was called in to advise, his main recommendation being the construction of the North Pier (1780). Telford soon followed (1802) with several proposals, and, although these were not fully accepted, the mid 19C saw the extension of the North Pier, the construction of a southern breakwater, the development of Victoria Dock and the start of work on various quays. But the major undertaking of the 19C was the diversion (1869–73) of the Dee (which hitherto had run through what is now Albert Basin), this enabling sandbanks to be reclaimed and the harbour to begin to assume its present basic plan.

During the present century improvements have been constant and major, and since 1969, though the basic geography remains, the port has been virtually rebuilt to meet the needs of fishing, roll on/roll off, and oil-related activities.

Unlike many ports, Aberdeen allows virtually unrestricted motor and pedestrian access, but the Harbour Board do ask visitors to appreciate that this is a busy area, to drive slowly and generally to exercise caution.

Market Street reaches the harbour at its north west corner, near *Upper Dock* (the west extension of Victoria Dock), a corner which recalls the earliest quayhead which lay just to the rear of today's Trinity Quay, here running east. Here, too, in 1582, the first crane was erected, and from here, also, the narrow, cobbled Shiprow provided the only access to the trading area around the Mercat Cross. Trinity, Regent and Waterloo quays mark the north side of *Victoria Dock*, developed in the 19C after Telford's proposals, honoured in 1848 by the entry of the royal yacht carrying Queen Victoria and her family, and in the 1970s drastically modified by the removal of the dock gates. The *P. and O. Ferries*

Aberdeen in the 16th century

(Shetland) Terminal now operates on Jamieson's Quay on the south side of the Upper Dock.

Market Street continues south to pass on the left the modern **Fish Market**, Scotland's largest, opened in 1982 by the Queen, accompanied by Princess Anne. The bustling auction (Mon.–Fri.: best visited 07.00 to 08.00) is popular with early-rising visitors, who may care to reflect that they are witnessing an activity already well established as long ago as 1281 when an agent of Edward I came to Aberdeen charged with buying 100 barrels of sturgeons and 5000 salt fish. *Albert Basin*, beyond, with Commercial Quay along its north and Albert Quay along its south, in part representing the former channel of the Dee, was developed as a result of the river's diversion in 1869–73.

Market Street now reaches Victoria Bridge, crossing the modern course of the Dee. North Esplanade West, becoming Riverside Drive, passes *Duthie Park* before reaching *Bridge of Dee*, for both of which see above. Across the river, Sinclair Road, leading east, in about half a mile reaches a point offering a good view northwards across the harbour; beyond, Greyhope Road very roughly marks the line of the bulwark built in 1607. With views across to Footdee and the North Pier, Greyhope Road rounds a golf course and passes the foot of the southern breakwaters to reach the grassy headland of *Walker Park*, with *Girdleness Lighthouse*.

Old Aberdeen

Although incorporated with Aberdeen proper since 1891, Old Aberdeen, 1½m north of the main city, remains an aloof, academic and even venerable quarter offering a total contrast to the bustle of Union Street and its surrounds. By car, Old Aberdeen is best reached by way of King Street (from the east end of Union Street), then (left) a short distance up St. Machar Drive. On foot, the direct and pleasantest route is from Broad Street along Gallowgate, Mounthooly, King's Crescent, Spital and College Bounds.

Old Aberdeen comprises two distinct parts, separated by the busy St. Machar Drive, a useful and necessary road but one on which Old Aberdeen's two sections prefer to turn their backs. To the south is High Street, with King's College; to the north the cathedral with, beyond, the ancient Brig o' Balgownie. Some of the streets impose car restrictions.

SOUTH OF ST. MACHAR DRIVE. The north end of High Street is straddled by the *Town House* of 1788, used as such until the incorporation with Aberdeen proper in 1891 and now a library.

Beyond are the gracious buildings of **King's College** (16C and later), founded by Bishop Elphinstone in 1495 during the reign of James IV and thus a century older than Marischal College, the other component of Aberdeen's university. The *Round Tower*, through the passage in the south east corner of the quadrangle, is a defensive work of 1525, while *Cromwell's Tower*, east of the chapel, dating from 1658 and originally a hall of residence, was in part paid for by contributions by some of Cromwell's officers, one of these being General Monk. But most visitors will aim for the *Chapel*, built in 1500–05 with an elegant lantern tower, the crown of which was rebuilt after a storm in 1633 (Tel: 0224-480241). First Catholic, then Protestant, the chapel is now interdenominational. The antechapel, arranged as a war memorial, is separated from the chapel proper by the former rood screen. The main features of the main chapel are a double row of canopied stalls, some with misericords; the pulpit (1540; brought from the cathedral and much restored) bearing the heads of Scottish kings from James I to VII; and, offering a more modern touch, the seven windows by Douglas Strachan. Bishop Elphinstone, founder of college and chapel, lies below the floor (though his elaborate cenotaph of 1931 is outside on the lawn) and another floor slab commemorates Hector Boece (died 1536), the Scottish historian and the college's first principal; while, against the east wall, an altar has been converted to serve as the tomb of Peter Udny, a sub-principal who died in 1601.

The curious and incongruous oriental gateway (c 1830) on the other side of High Street and marking the way to halls of residence was once the gate to nearby Powis House and reminds of that family's associations with the Middle East.

NORTH OF ST. MACHAR DRIVE. Opposite High Street the road called Chanonry passes *Cruickshank Botanic Gardens* (Tel: 0224-272704. Ext. 5247), the university's gardens with extensive collections, shrubs, alpines, heather, succulents and rock and water gardens being among the features here.

*St. Machar's Cathedral (Tel: 0224-485988), part ruin but its nave intact, is a place of mellow antiquity, imposing yet simple, its granite touched by sandstone and the whole a monument to three bishops who, though spanning two centuries, seem to have shared a common sensitivity. In its name, the cathedral recalls a saint who may have been a follower of Columba and who, on a mission to convert the Picts, is said to have planted a chapel here during the 6C; the title of cathedral recalls a bishopric, reputedly founded at Mortlach (see Rte 39) by Malcolm II in 1010 and transferred to Aberdeen by David I in 1137.

Be the above as it may, the earliest stonework surviving is of the 14C, this—finely carved sandstone and the work of Bishop Kininmunde, 1356–62—comprising (east exterior) two of the external piers at the crossing, now partly buried in the modern gables, and a portion of the ruined transepts. The rest of the cathedral—except for the sandstone steeples added to the two west towers by Bishop Gavin Dunbar in c 1522—is largely granite, mainly of the 15C and the work of Bishop Leighton (Lichtoun) whose tomb recess is in the north transept which he founded in 1424. Bishop Dunbar's handsome canopied tomb is in the opposing transept.

Before entering the cathedral it may add interest to the view of the exterior to picture that it once had a central tower, completed in c 1512 but which collapsed in 1688, owing, it is said, to the removal of stones from the choir by Cromwell's soldiers building a fort over 30 years earlier on Aberdeen's Castle Hill.

The nave now serves as parish church. Here the principal feature is Bishop Dunbar's flat ceiling of panelled oak (c 1520; restored), with its 48 shields glittering with the blazonries of Pope Leo X, the Emperor Charles V, St. Margaret, the kings and princes of Christendom, and the bishops and nobles of Scotland. Also of interest, and all well explained by notices, are a small 15C wall effigy of Canon Dodds, near the east end of the south aisle; in the north west corner an effigy (reconstructed) of Bishop Leighton; the font, by Hew Lorimer in 1953, showing St. Machar baptising in the Don; the war memorial window by Douglas Strachan; and the Charter Room, showing documents, seals and other relics.

Beyond the cathedral, to the north west in Tillydrone Road, now stands the so-called *Wallace Tower* (no adm.), interesting as a Z-plan tower-house built in central Aberdeen's Nether Kirkgate in 1616 and rebuilt on this site in 1963.

*Brig o' Balgownie, or Auld Brig o' Don (no cars), spanning a deep pool of the Don and the oldest medieval bridge in Scotland, is roughly ¾m north of the cathedral. On foot the bridge can be reached through

Seaton Park, but motorists should drive north along King Street, soon bearing left along Don Street. In bare architectural terms this is a late 13 to early 14C (restored 1607) bridge in the form of a pointed arch 62ft wide. But there is more to this beguiling corner. Bruce, for instance, is involved, seemingly personally ordering the completion of work begun in the 1280s but held up by the wars of the time, while an early bishop, Cheyne, is credited with carrying out his king's wishes and completing the bridge by perhaps 1320. And this despite Thomas the Rhymer's gloomy prediction that the bridge would fall should it be crossed by an only son riding a mare's only foal. Centuries later Byron, in his 'Don Juan', named 'Balgounie Brig' as one of his Scottish nostalgia, adding in a note—and doubtless well aware that the dark pool below was the haunt of witches—'I still remember ... the awful proverb which made me pause to cross it, yet lean over with a childish delight, being an only son'.

For Aberdeen to **Stonehaven**, **Forfar** and **Perth**, see Rte 29; to **Banchory** and **Braemar**, see Rte 37A; to **Echt** and **Tarland**, see Rte 37B; to **Grantown-on-Spey**, **Nairn** and **Forres**, see Rte 38; to **Dufftown** and **Elgin**, see Rte 39; to **Huntly** and **Fochabers**, see Rte 40; to **Macduff** and **Banff**, see Rte 41; to **Peterhead** and **Fraserburgh**, see Rte 42.

37 Aberdeen to Braemar (Deeside)

Two roads are described below. The first, Rte 37A along the main A93, closely follows the Dee; the second, Rte 37B, choosing roads roughly parallel a few miles to the north, joins Rte 37A at the west end of Muir of Dinnet, some two thirds of the distance to Braemar. There is little difference in either mileage or in scenery—the best of the scenery starts to the west of Muir of Dinnet—and the choice is therefore likely to be made principally on grounds of what there is to be seen, though noting that the several linking roads allow a meandering flexibility between the alternatives. Stone circle and earth-house enthusiasts will choose Rte 37B.

Two points may be borne in mind. First, that Deeside is a popular touring area and that A93 can be a busy road in summer. Second, that, although Deeside offers a choice of moor and mountain walks, this can be treacherous terrain and local advice should always be sought before adventuring far.

A. Via Peterculter and Banchory

A93.—Pleasant, pastoral river valley scenery gradually becomes increasingly wooded and Highland, especially after Ballater as the Grampian mountains and their south east spur, The Mounth, close in. The main road runs with the north side of the Dee, but for much of the way good but less used roads, scenically little different, follow the south bank; there are several bridges.

SOME HOTELS. **Banchory**. *Banchory Lodge*, Dee Street, AB3 3HS. Tel: 03302-2625. **Aboyne**. *Birse Lodge*, Charlestown Road, AB3 5EL. Tel: 03398-86253. **Ballater**. *Craigendarroch*, Braemar Road, AB3 5XA. Tel: 03397-55858. *Darroch Learg*, Braemar Road, AB3 5UX. Tel: 03397-55443. *Monaltrie Lodge*, 5 Bridge Square, AB3 5QJ. Tel: 03397-55417. **Braemar**. *Braemar Lodge*, Glenshee Road, AB3 5YQ. Tel: 03397-41627. *Invercauld Arms*, AB3 5YR. Tel: 03397-41605.

Total distance 54m.—*8m* **Peterculter**.—*9m* **Banchory**.—*8m*
Kincardine O' Neil.—*4m* **Aboyne**.—*4m* **Dinnet**.—*6m* **Ballater**.—*7m*
Crathie (Balmoral).—*8m* **Braemar**.

Aberdeen (see Rte 36) is left by Union Street, Holburn Street and Great
Western Road.—*8m* **Peterculter** recalls through its name that until
early medieval times the lands here on both sides of the Dee made up
the district of Culter, pronounced, then as now, Kooter. Then in the late
12C William the Lion granted the south bank to the Knights Templar
who built a chapel to St. Mary. This south bank then became, and still is,
Maryculter, while the north, already with a chapel to St. Peter, became
Peterculter. The ruin of the Templars' chapel, later used by the Hospi-
tallers and then parish church until 1787, is in Templars' Park by the
river south bank (access west off B979 and B9077), while by contrast
there is also at Maryculter a family theme park (*Storybook Glen*. Tel:
0224-732941), a landscaped glen with many excitements for younger
children. *Blairs College* (by appointment. Tel: 0224-867626), about 1½m
east of the B979 river bridge by B9077, is for visitors with a Stuart
interest. A Roman Catholic foundation of 1827, the college owns important portraits of Mary, Queen of Scots (including one found at Douai
after the French revolution) as also portraits and memorabilia of other
Stuarts.

Leaving Peterculter A93 crosses the Leuchar Burn, from the bridge
over which can be seen a statue of Rob Roy. Quite why this far from
worthy character merits this honour is unclear; all that seems known is
that he once crossed this burn on his way back from Aberdeen, and that
this statue is the third in a long succession.

3m ***Drum Castle** (NTS. Tel: 03308-204) presents an astonishing but
balanced contrast between its massive, battlemented late 13C keep and
the gracious Jacobean mansion grafted on to it in 1619. The keep seems
to have been built in 1296 by Richard Cementarius, who somewhat
improbably combined the post of provost of Aberdeen (the city's first)
with that of royal mason. But soon afterwards, in 1324, Bruce conferred
the lands of Drum on his standard and armour bearer, William de Irwin,
whose descendants remained in possession until 1975 when the estate
passed to the National Trust for Scotland. Within the castle are family
portraits, antique furniture and suchlike, while the grounds of 400 acres
offer woodland walks, an arboretum and an adventure playground.

4m ****Crathes Castle** (NTS. Tel: 033044-525) is at the heart of a district
known as Leys, granted in 1323 by Bruce to Alexander Burnett (Bur-
nard) whom he appointed Royal Forester of the Forest of Drum, the then
huge forest here which Bruce designated a royal hunting reserve.
These early Burnetts lived not here at Crathes, but in a wooden dwelling on a loch island, now represented by a marsh 2m north west and to
the east of A980, and today's castle—a tower-house sprinkled with turrets, dormers and gables, its fairy quality enhanced by the many facets
glimpsed from different corners of the grounds—though begun in 1553
was not completed and occupied until 1594. Extensions were grafted on
during the 17 and 19C, much of this part now replaced by rebuilding
after a fire in 1966.

In the main hall hangs the ancient jewelled and ivory Horn of Leys,
said to have been presented by Bruce as a token of tenure. And at the
top of the castle the Long Gallery, with a rare 17C oak ceiling, affords
some original views over the grounds. In between—and the glory of
Crathes—are the Room of the Nine Nobles, the Room of the Green Lady
and the Room of the Muses, each with its crowded painted ceiling, the
work of unknown artists but men of imagination and skill for, working
awkwardly above their heads, they also had to adapt their work—a

weird mixture of pictures, designs and lengthy written messages—to the constricting run of the panels and beams.

Inside, like any other tower-house, Crathes may seem cramped. Outside, though, it is generous with space, its 600 acres offering no fewer than eight gardens, separated either by borders or by yew hedges of 1702; several nature trails, including one for the disabled; an adventure playground, as also a NTS Visitor Centre, picnic area and suchlike.

2m **Banchory** (5300 inhab. *Inf.*), its name meaning Fair Hollow and certainly pleasantly enough sited between the hills and the Dee, has a story reaching back to St. Ternan, who came here in the 5C to convert the Picts and, it is thought, established himself and his small monastery at the spot now occupied by the churchyard, in which survive traces of a medieval church. James Scott Skinner, fiddler and composer known as the Strathspey King, born in Banchory in 1843, is remembered by a memorial and by material in *Banchory Museum* (Tel: 0779-77778) in local government buildings towards the west end of High Street. Just south of the town the Dee is joined by the Feugh, crossed by the narrow *Bridge of Feugh* (1790), beside which there is a footbridge from which the visitor may be lucky enough to see salmon leaping up the ledges. For Banchory south to *Fettercairn* by B974 (Cairn o' Mounth) and to *Stonehaven* by A957 (Slug Road), see Rte 29.

A980, leading north out of Banchory, in just over 1m passes the west end of the marsh area where was once the loch on a crannog of which the early Burnetts of Crathes had their home. And here, too, many centuries earlier, St. Ternan may have found a reasonably safe refuge among the pagan Picts. Beyond, the road is joined by B977, 2m due north of the intersection, on the east slope of *Hill of Fare*, being the site of the battle (Corrichie) of 1562 at which the great Gordon Earl of Huntly was defeated by the adherents of Mary, Queen of Scots, under Moray, the Earl himself dying of a heart attack.

At (*8m*) **Kincardine O' Neil** the ruined *Church of St. Mary* was originally associated with a hospice erected here in 1231 by Allan Durward to serve the needs of indigent travellers using the bridge which his father Thomas had built to link with the track making for the Cairn o' Mounth pass (today B974). Although that once so important bridge has long disappeared, the church remains, together with what are probably traces of the hospice in the form of foundations of an east extension to the church. A mile or so beyond the village, a minor road branches north for Lumphanan (see Rte 37B), within the north west angle of the junction being the *Gallows Stone*, originally standing on a nearby hillside which from feudal times until as recently as 1747 was the site from which justice was dispensed.

4m **Aboyne** is a village set around a large green, first laid out in 1676 and the scene today of the annual (August) Aboyne Games, one of the main events of the Highland season. *Aboyne Castle* (no adm.), to the north of the village and dating from 1671–1869, replaced 13C Coull Castle the scattered remnants of which can be seen beside B9094 2m north (see Rte 37B).—The scenic **Glen Tanar** ascends south west from Aboyne to traverse the forest of the same name, its oak, shipped down the Dee until well into the 19C, once much in demand for shipbuilding. The pleasant sylvan road, starting from Bridge o' Ess on B976 south of the river, soon reaches a parking and picnic area opposite which a footbridge leads to the *Braeloine Interpretive Centre* (Tel: 0339-2072) for waymarked walks and material explaining the farming, forestry and wildlife of this estate. The Fir Mounth, a track climbing across the mountains to cross the watershed at 2364ft and reach Glen Esk in some 12m, may well be the route used by Macbeth when fleeing from Dunsinane to defeat and death at Lumphanan.

Continuing west, A93 reaches (*4m*) **Dinnet**, beyond the village running between Loch Kinord on the north and, on the south, *Muir of Dinnet*, the latter, together with a considerable area to the north of the road, forming a national nature reserve of heath, scrub and birch, broken by fen and open water and important for breeding and wintering wildfowl.—*2m* **Junction with A97**, where Rte 37B joins. For *Burn o' Vat, Loch Kinord, Loch Davan* (all within the area of the nature reserve) and the battle of 1335 fought below the hill of *Culblean*, see the end of Rte 37B.—Of (*3m*) **Tullich**, claiming once to have been a royal burgh, little now remains bar a ruined church of c 1400, built on the site of an early chapel founded in perhaps the 5C though the worn Pictish stones shown here are of about the 7C. The church is traditionally associated with the dance known as the Reel of Tulloch (Tullich), said first to have been danced here by a congregation as a means of keeping warm when their preacher was late in arriving. Just beyond the church, B972 branches away to bypass Ballater and cut through the steep and wooded Pass of Ballater. This Route stays with A93 which almost at once crosses the old railway track, now a pleasant walkway where once ran Queen Victoria's royal train.

1m **Ballater** (1180 inhab. *Inf.*) owes its existence to an old woman and a Jacobite. The former did no more than cure herself of scrofula by obeying a dream and bathing in water near the north foot of Pannanich Hill, 2m south east of Ballater. The Jacobite was Francis Farquharson of Monaltrie, captured at Culloden, sent to London, sentenced to be hanged and at the last minute reprieved, though his home, Monaltrie House to the north of today's town, was burnt down by government troops. Exiled for 20 years, he returned home and shrewdly exploited the old woman's lead, building Pannanich Lodge—today Pannanich Wells Inn, 2m east on B976—as a spa. So successful was this venture that in 1800 Francis Farquharson's nephew, William, decided to continue the exploitation by starting to lay out what would become Ballater, soon in the 19C, as it is today, a spacious small planned town and summer centre in lovely surrounds of woodland and mountain.

The car and the holiday coach have now taken the place of the railway, which, running from Aberdeen, ended here, Queen Victoria having made clear that she would not tolerate its coming any closer to Balmoral. She made good use of it, however, and over many years Ballater's station enjoyed a royal cachet. It was Queen Victoria, too, who in 1885 opened the present *Royal Bridge* across the Dee, the latest in a series of four, two predecessors being wrecked by floods in 1799 and 1829, while the third was a wooden affair of 1834.

GLEN MUICK, ascending for some 8m southward into woods and mountains, is both scenic and of royal Victorian interest. Just outside Ballater, by the junction with the south Deeside road, a typical turn-of-the-century scene is recalled by a cairn commemorating an occasion in 1899 when Queen Victoria, out for a drive, by chance met, and then reviewed, a battalion of the Gordon Highlanders, shortly before their embarkation for South Africa. Farther south, 2m up the west bank of the Muick, is the mansion of *Birkhall*, built in 1715, later bought by Prince Albert, and in 1856 rented by Florence Nightingale who from here, encouraged by Queen Victoria ('Such a head! I wish we had her at the War Office' was the queen's opinion), started the pestering which persuaded the army authorities to form the Army Medical Service, later to become the Royal Army Medical Corps.

The longer road (the Capel Mounth), running with the Muick's east bank, passes the cascade of *Linn of Muick* to end just short of Loch

Muick at *Spittal of Glenmuick*, with a mountain rescue post and a Scottish Wildlife Trust's visitor centre. Here, in this area, there are two more royal associations. *Allt-na-Giubhsaich*, a short mile away to the north west across the river, is a shooting lodge used by the queen and Prince Albert and known to them as The Hut (it has since been much enlarged). From here a track climbs to the, in part precipitous, eyrie of *Lochnagar* (3786ft), more than once ascended by the queen, although she did have the benefit of ponies. *Glas-allt-Shiel*, on the west shore of the loch towards its south end, was a less happy place, built by the queen as a retreat in 1868 and sometimes called her 'Widow's house'. From here another track climbs Lochnagar, while a second heads west for *Dubh Loch* at 2090ft.

From Spittal of Glenmuick the road continues as the *Capel Mounth* track, climbing to 2250ft before descending to Braedownie in Glen Clova (see Rte 29).

Leaving Ballater, A93 in *1m* is joined by B972 at *Bridge of Gairn* at the west end of the Pass of Ballater, here being the *McEwan Gallery* (Tel: 0338-55429) showing 18–20C watercolours and oils, many by Scottish artists and of Scottish landscapes.

Already forecast by Ballater's pass and surrounds of steep and wooded hills, the scenery now changes, becoming distinctly Highland as A93 accompanies the Dee's upper reaches. In some *4m* from Bridge of Gairn, soon after a picnic site, there is a Standing Stone to the right of the road, site of the spot where in the 9C St. Manire founded a chapel. Beyond, in *1m*, on the south bank of the river and reached by a private suspension bridge, stands *Abergeldie Castle* (c 1550; no adm.), home in turn of Queen Victoria's mother, of Eugenie, widow of Napoleon III, and of the future Edward VII and his princess, Alexandra.—*1m* **Crathie**, where the church, a neat little granite place of 1895 and housing many royal gifts, will for most people be associated with church attendances by the royal family when in residence at adjacent Balmoral. The church is successor to a simple predecessor of 1804 in which Queen Victoria worshipped for most of her reign, starting in 1848 when she first came to Deeside.

Balmoral Castle, a personal royal home as opposed to an official residence, is just across the river from Crathie. The grounds and an exhibition are open, except when the family are here (Tel: 03397-55306).—Once a 16C tower of the Gordons (enlarged c 1835) stood here, on an estate first leased and then in 1852 bought by Prince Albert. Today's large, white granite Scottish Baronial mansion—beyond a sweep of lawn and framed by trees—can architecturally be credited to William Smith, city architect of Aberdeen, acting very closely, though, with the prince. In 1855 the family moved in, whereupon the adjacent Gordon tower was demolished, to be recalled only by a stone marking its site. Of interest around the grounds and estate, generously planted by Prince Albert with conifers and other trees, are Queen Victoria's garden cottage; the gardens originally planned by Queen Mary; and seemingly countless statues, memorials and cairns each telling of some royal person or event.—*Lochnagar Distillery* (Tel: 03384-273), off B976 about a mile east of Balmoral, dates from 1845 and has been offering tours ever since an invitation was accepted by Queen Victoria and Prince Albert soon after the distillery opened.

Beyond Crathie, A93 loops with the Dee, then, straightening, passes, just under *2m* from Crathie, the *Cairn na Cuimhne*, a mound with a few trees beside the river below the road. A modest enough spot now, possibly only fleetingly glimpsed because traffic can be fast here, this was once the important rallying place of the Farquharsons; before each foray each man deposited a stone, removing it when and if he returned, the balance recording the clan's loss.—*3m Invercauld Bridge*, where the Dee is crossed, was built by Prince Albert when the old bridge of 1752, still to be seen and evocatively attractive a few yards downstream, became royal property and the south Deeside road through the estate was closed. *Invercauld House* (no adm.), soon seen to the north, a 15–16C core with additions and the seat of the Farquharsons, is the place from which in 1715 the Earl of Mar called out the clans in support of the Old Pretender.

3m **Braemar** (400 inhab. *Inf.*), a scattered village at 1100ft near where the Cluny joins the Dee, may be small but is nonetheless, and on several counts, one of the best known of Highland names—for history, for scenery and walks, for two castles, for the most prestigious of all Highland Gatherings, and even for its festival and theatre.

Braemar Castle (Tel: 03397-41219), a towered and turreted fortress-home beside A93, was built (though on ancient foundations) by the Earl of Mar in 1628; attacked and burnt by the Farquharsons in 1689; garrisoned by Hanoverian troops after the '15; and, after the '45, repaired and again garrisoned to protect the military road from Perth across Dee and Speyside to Fort George on Moray Firth. Later, it was acquired by the Farquharsons of Invercauld who converted the castle to residence. Among notable features are the round central tower, the iron gate, the barrel-vaulted ceilings, and the star-shaped curtain wall, loopholed for muskets, which represents the defensive work carried out after the '45.

Within the village there survives, but only just, the far older and very different *Kindrochit Castle*, today no more than an ancient fragment. The name means Head of the Bridge, and this once formidable stronghold commanded all the glens converging on this point. A castle here is thought to have been occupied by Malcolm Canmore in the 11C, but today's stones date from a 14C fortified hunting lodge of Robert II. Rebuilt in about 1390, Kindrochit was, and has remained, derelict since about 1600 by which time the powerful Braemar Castle was taking shape.

It was on a mound now covered by the *Invercauld Arms* that the Earl of Mar raised his standard in 1715, an event commemorated by a stone (1952) on the roadway opposite, as also by a plaque inside the hotel where, furthermore, latter-day Jacobites may still drink a toast in the Earl of Mar's bar. At an angle across the road is the *Invercauld Festival Theatre*, used for a range of Scottish entertainments over the July–September period; formerly a church, converted in 1949, the theatre shows some striking murals. Finally, a cottage, on the left a short way along Glenshee Road (A93), is the place where R.L. Stevenson spent the summer of 1881 writing 'Treasure Island'.

The **Braemar Royal Highland Gathering* (first Saturday in September), under royal patronage and frequently attended by royalty, is Scotland's most prestigious Gathering. The site, now, and since 1905, is the Princess Royal and Duke of Fife Memorial Park in the west area of the village, but previous sites have included Braemar Castle, Balmoral and Invercauld House as, doubtless, many others over the centuries since that day when, it is claimed, Malcolm Canmore summoned the clans to the Brae of Mar for contests which would enable him to select the bravest and best as his soldiers. (Seats may be reserved, after about 20 March, by application to the Bookings Secretary, B.R.H.S. Society Office, Braemar, Aberdeenshire. Remittance and stamped addressed envelope must accompany applications. Accommodation queries should be addressed to the Area Tourist Office, 45 Station Road, Banchory, AB3 3XX.)

TO LINN OF DEE (west, 6m). This minor road in under 2m arrives at a point commanding a view of the opening of Glen Quoich, ascending north west towards the piled heights of the Cairngorms, 2m farther on being Victoria Bridge leading across to Mar Lodge, completed in 1898 but successor to other lodges occupying sites nearby. Next comes the hamlet of *Inverey*, with a monument of 1934 recalling the birth here of John Lamont (1805–79), son of a local forester who, after attending the Scots Benedictine College at Ratisbon, turned secular, studied in Munich and later became, as Johannes von Lamont, astronomer royal of Bavaria. A glen track ascends Glen Ey to reach, in a long mile, the site known as the *Colonel's Bed*, a small gorge in which Colonel John Farquharson successfully hid while fleeing after Killiecrankie. The public road ends at **Linn of Dee** bridge, a scenic spot where the Dee forces itself through a narrow rock cleft.

Braemar, with nearby Inverey and Linn of Dee, are well known as starting places for walks and climbs. The choice extends from local walks of a mile or two, through mountain climbs (e.g. Lochnagar, 3786ft; Morrone, 2819ft), to ambitious undertakings such as down Glen Tilt to Blair Atholl, some 29m, or even into or across the Cairngorms. The favourite Cairngorm routes are either by Lairig Ghru, the pass below the west of Ben Macdhui, or by Glen Derry and Glen Avon. Private estates, the importance of not disturbing deer or birds, and the height and remoteness of some of the treks all impose certain restrictions and it is most important to seek local advice before setting off. The 'Braemar Official Guide' suggests and describes a number of walks.

For Braemar over the *Cairnwell Pass* to **Perth**, see Rte 28.

B.   Via Echt and Tarland

A944 out of Aberdeen, after 6m diverging on to B9119 as far as Ordie. A97 to junction with Rte 37A near west end of Muir of Dinnet. A93 to Braemar.—Pastoral and agricultural countryside gradually becoming more wooded and undulating. Highland scenery west of Muir of Dinnet. *Note*: A torch will be necessary for Culsh Earth-house.

SOME HOTELS. See Rte 37A.

Total distance 55m.—*13m* **Echt.**—*11m* **Intersection with A980** (for **Craigievar** and **Lumphanan**).—*6m* **Tarland.**—*2m* **Ordie.**—*4m* **Muir of Dinnet** (Rte 37A).—*19m* **Braemar**.

Aberdeen (see Rte 36) is left by Union Street, Albyn Place and Queen's Road, passing Hazlehead Park, A944 being exchanged in *6m* for B9119.— *4m Garlogie*, a village just to the south of which is *Cullerlie Stone Circle*, a ring of eight boulders within which are several small cairns, perhaps used for cremations. It has been suggested that this may have been the tomb of a chief, with the cairns representing dependants, perhaps ritually killed at the time of his burial.—*3m* **Echt**, just over 1m north west of which is the *Barmekin of Echt*, an isolated conical hill (900ft) crowned with five rings of Iron Age fortifications notable for their several entrances (reached by a farm road off B977 and then on foot).—*1m Sunhoney*, a farm behind which there is a circle of sizeable stones, pleasingly set in a ring of trees. This circle is of the Recumbent Stone type, the recumbent monolith here being exceptionally long (17ft).

A stop should surely be made at *(1m) Midmar* where, to the south of the road, can be seen an attractive turreted castle (1575; no adm.). More interesting, though, is the 17C church, less for itself, though the private door for the laird is unusual, than for the fact that there is a stone circle in the churchyard and that this site has therefore been used for ritual purposes, if with breaks, over a period of several millenia. The circle shows the usual local recumbent stone and flankers, and traces can also be seen of some structure that stood just inside of these three stones. For *Hill of Fare* (Battle of Corrichie), rising to the south of Midmar, see Rte 37A.

In *9m* B9119 is crossed by A980, with Craigievar Castle just to the north and Lumphanan and its Macbeth associations a short distance to the south.

The great thing about ****Craigievar Castle** (NTS. Tel: 03398-83635) is that for all practical purposes no one has changed it. This slim tower-house, arguably Scotland's purest and loveliest—smooth below as a concession to defence, but crowned with a seemingly haphazard collage of turrets, stepped gables, cupolas and precipitous roofs—stands today virtually as it did in 1626 when it was completed for William Forbes, Baltic merchant (he was known as 'Danzig Willie') and brother of the Bishop of Aberdeen. Lighting has never been installed here, so, it has to be said, a

Romantic Craigievar. Unchanged since completed for 'Danzig Willie' in 1626

tour of the interior can sometimes be disappointing. Yet this very lack of light, coupled with other features, can sharply bring home the discomforts with which this place's owners, not to mention their servants, had to contend, while, even on a dull day, the splendid decorated plaster ceilings, and especially that in the hall, can still provide their own illumination. The tour around the rooms reveals some surprising domestic aspects, portraits by Raeburn, and, to the architecturally aware, that the builders' external lightheartedness was not as haphazard as might appear. The grounds offer a picnic area and walks.

A980, followed south from the crossroads, almost at once enters territory associated, in tradition if not in fact, with the last hours of Macbeth. On the left, under a mile before reaching Lumphanan, a small ring of trees up on the slope is known as *Macbeth's Cairn*, reputedly the actual spot at which he met his end. Beyond, just south west of **Lumphanan**, the *Peel Ring* is a huge and particularly good example of an early medieval motte, complete with wall, earthworks and ditches. The stone wall is probably of the 12 or 13C, but before this there would have been a wooden palisade, behind which, it could well be, Macbeth in 1057 made his last stand against Malcolm Canmore, dying either here or perhaps while struggling up that hill to the north.

Continuing west from the crossroads, B9119 almost at once passes *Corse Castle* (1581; no adm.), a small but satisfactory ruin in the grounds of Corse House. The castle belonged to William of Craigievar's brother, Patrick, later Bishop of Aberdeen, who had a unique constructional problem because of a visit by the Devil who, being worsted in an argument, flew off in a rage, carrying with him the whole of the front of the castle.

4m ***Culsh Earth-house**, beside the road, is one of the best and most accessible of these unexplained tunnel excavations, the particular features here being exceptionally massive roof slabs and a passage which is not only wider and higher than others but also ends in a broadening rather than a true chamber.—*2m* **Tarland**, just south of which, on a rocky knoll beside B9094, is what is left of *Tomnaverie Stone Circle*, an example of the Recumbent Stone type. *Coull Castle*, on the left a little farther along B9094, was the ancient predecessor to Aboyne Castle. Once a great stronghold of five towers, built in imitation of Kildrummy and belonging to the Durwards, it is said to have been destroyed in the early 14C in one violent night of fire, so that, today, it survives as no more than fragments on a rise.

2m **Ordie** crossroads where B9119 is exchanged for A97 southwards, a road which runs below *Culblean Hill* (2m west. 1983ft), scene of a historic battle of 1335, during the wars with England's Edward III, which may be said to have confirmed Bannockburn, fought 20 years earlier. The two lochs, *Davan* to the north and *Kinord* to the south, squeezed within the angle of A97 and B9119, also played their part in events which started with the siege by the pro-English Earl of Atholl of Kildrummy Castle (see Rte 38), held by the wife of David II's adherent, Sir Andrew de Moray (for Atholl's wife, see Rte 38, Loch-in-Dorb). Moray, approaching from the south, installed himself in the Hall of Ruthven, a small castle on an island in Loch Davan, and, learning of this, Atholl marched south to challenge him, the result being the battle (commemorative stone beside A97) in which Atholl met both defeat and death. After the battle one of Atholl's adherents, Sir Robert Menzies, took refuge on a fortified crannog in Loch Kinord from where, wisely, he negotiated his return to the Scottish cause. Three hundred years later, in 1646, this crannog castle, held for Charles I, was surrendered to the Covenanter Leslie and then demolished, so effectively that it has disappeared.

A97 passes, on the right, *Burn o' the Vat*, a popular picnic area with a short path to a fissure in the Vat burn with a curious rounded cauldron and cascade behind which various people are supposed to have hidden, including 17C freebooters and a fugitive of the '45.

4m **Junction with A93**. For from this point to (*19m*) *Braemar*, see Rte 37A.

38   Aberdeen to Nairn and Forres via Grantown-on-Spey

A944 to Dunecht. Unclassified to Castle Fraser and Monymusk. B993 to Tillyfourie. A944 to Mossat. A97, B973 (on some maps A944) and A939 through Tomintoul and Grantown-on-Spey to Dava fork. A939 to Nairn or A940 to Forres.—After Alford, increasingly high and open moor, beyond Corgarff Castle following the fine 18C military Lecht Road rising to 2100ft with stome steep gradients. Beyond Grantown, moor followed by woods.

SOME HOTELS. **Alford**. *Haughton Arms*, AB3 8QA. Tel: 09755-62026. **Kildrummy**. *Kildrummy Castle*, AB3 8RA. Tel: 09755-71288. **Strathdon**. *Colquhonnie*, AB3 8UN. Tel: 09756-51210. **Tomintoul**. *Richmond Arms*, The Square, AB3 9ET. Tel: 08074-209. **Grantown-on-Spey**. *Garth*, The Square, PH26 3HN. Tel: 0479-2836. *Seafield Lodge* Woodside Avenue, PH26 3JN. Tel: 0479-2152.

Total distance 95m to Nairn or 92m to Forres.—*15m* **Castle Fraser**.—*11m* **Alford**.—*7m* **Mossat**.—*2m* **Kildrummy Castle**.—*15m* **Cogarff Castle**.—*10m* **Tomintoul**.—*12m* **Grantown-on-Spey**.—*8m* **Dava**.—*15m* **Nairn** or *12m* **Forres**.

Aberdeen (see Rte 36) is left by Union Street, Albyn Place and Queen's Road, passing Hazlehead Park.—*12m Dunecht*, from where a minor road heading north west in *3m* reaches ***Castle Fraser** (NTS. Tel: 03303-463). Here a Fraser father and son, working between 1575 and 1636 with the local master masons Bel and Leiper, achieved a castle and home which ranks as perhaps the most splendid of the Castles of Mar.

From Castle Fraser minor roads wander *3m* north west to the village of **Monymusk**, today apart and quiet but, if local tradition is accepted, resounding with martial activity one day in 1307 when Bruce and his army camped on Camp Field to the east of Monymusk House before moving out to defeat John Comyn at Barra Hill (see start of Rte 41). The house (no adm.) traces its roots to an early priory, first Culdee and then in the 13C Augustinian, which at the Reformation became a part of a castle (of the Forbes), this in turn developing into today's mansion; and the village church, too, dates well back, as a Norman survival of c 1170, restored in 1929. *Pitfichie Castle*, a tower 1m north along the west bank of the Don, well shows how a round tower attached to the corner of a keep gave defensive command along two sides, while the road up the other side of the Don in 4m reaches the more peaceful objective of the Forestry Commission's *Don View Visitor Centre* with exhibits about local forestry and walks.

From Monymusk B993 and A944, rejoined at Tillyfourie, in *8m* reach **Alford** (1100 inhab. *Inf.*), scene in 1645 of a battle won by Montrose against the Covenanters but visited today for its museum of transport and its narrow-gauge railway. The *Grampian Transport Museum* (Tel: 09755-62292) offers a bright, outstanding display (cars, motor cycles, vans etc) spanning from vintage to relatively modern, while the *Alford Valley Railway* (Tel: 09755-62326; museum at the station), the only 2ft narrow-gauge passenger line in Scotland, operates rides to nearby Haughton Country Park and thence to Murray Park. Alford also offers its *Alford-Donside Heritage Centre* (Tel: 09755-62221), a small museum of local history.—Three castles around Alford merit mention. *Balfluig Castle* (basically 1556), 1m south east, was a tower-house of the Forbes who now occupy 19C *Castle Forbes*, 3m north east. *Terpersie Castle* (4m north west), probably built in about 1561, has a poignant story, for it was here that the then owner, George Gordon, who had fought at Culloden, was captured and later executed, after having been inadvertently given away by his own children.

Just outside Alford A944 turns sharply right, at about the point where Montrose won his battle, to cross the Don and then closely follow the river for most of the way to (7m) *Mossat* where Rte 39 to Dufftown and Elgin breaks away north. This Route turns south and in *1m* reaches *Kildrummy*, beside whose church are the remains of a medieval predecessor, with a 14C tomb of Forbes of Brux and an Elphinstone vault of 1605. Beyond (*1m*) appears ruined **Kildrummy Castle* (AM. Tel: 031-244-3101), visually formidable and exciting, architecturally instructive, historically both important and the scene of treachery and intrigue.

History. First built in the early 13C on the orders of Alexander II, the castle later fell to England's Edward I who ordered alterations in 1296–1303. Soon after this the Scots gained the castle, Bruce sending his wife and children here for safety when he fled to Rathlin in 1306. But the Scots' tenure was as shortlived as its end was bloody. Besieged again by the English, Kildrummy fell, through, it is said, the treachery of its blacksmith who, having been promised as much gold as he could carry, fired the place, thus leaving the defenders no choice but to surrender. Bruce's wife and children escaped to Tain (Rte 57), but his brother Sir Nigel was executed; the garrison was all 'hangyt and drawyn'; and the promise made to the blacksmith was honoured by the pouring of molten gold down his throat. In 1335 the castle, since Bannockburn in Scots' hands and defended by Lady Moray, again came under siege, this time though being saved by Sir Andrew Moray's victory at Culblean (see end of Rte 37B). In 1404 Alexander Stewart, illegitimate son of the 'Wolf of Badenoch' (and later victor of Harlaw, see Rte 40), here kidnapped the widowed Countess of Mar (it was he who had had her husband killed), then forced her to marry him and bestow on him the title of Earl of Mar. Later, Kildrummy became the seat of the Erskines of Mar, and it was here that the final plans were laid for the '15. After this rebellion's failure the castle was forfeited and much dismantled.

Despite such a history the ruins survive as an extensive and solid example of two stages of late 13–early 14C defensive building. There is the original courtyard system of a broad ditch and curtain wall with several round towers and, larger than the others and with its own well, a main keep, at the time of its building regarded as the last stand for defence. Then there is the twin-towered gatehouse, almost certainly an addition by Edward I and indicative of how defence thinking was shifting from the idea of a central keep to one forward on the perimeter. Within the complex, the layout of the domestic buildings—hall, solar, kitchen—can be traced below the inner side of the north wall, while, projecting from the east wall, the chapel gable (mid 13C) with its three elegant lancets provides a softer though almost incongruous note in this setting of brute strength.

Adjacent, and associated with a hotel, are *Kildrummy Castle Gardens* (Tel: 09755-71264 or 71277), main features of which are alpines, shrubs and a water garden.

Meeting the Don, A97 turns west with the river to pass (rather over *3m* from Kildrummy Castle) *Glenkindie House*, in the grounds of which there is an earth-house, distinctive for having only a short passage but also a second chamber reached from the main chamber through a restricted hole (ask permission at the house's westernmost lodge, from where the earth-house is a short way away in a clump of trees on the left of the drive. Torch needed for inner chamber). This Route now remains with the river Don for some 12m as far as, approaching Corgarff Castle, the junction with A939.

1m Bridge of Buchat, close to which is *Glenbuchat Castle* (no adm. but well seen from outside), a late 16C Gordon tower, of interest for later belonging to the tough and colourful John Gordon, popularly known as 'Old Glenbucket of the '45'. A staunch Jacobite, he fought at Culloden at the age of 68, escaped to Norway and in 1750 died impoverished in France. An apposite inscription over the door reads 'No thing on arth remanis bot fame'. *Glenbuchat Church*, 1m up the glen, will attract anyone with a feel for 17–18C Highland churches, of which this is a particularly attractive example. In origin of the 15C, and still preserving some stonework of that period, the church underwent reconstruction in 1629 and again towards the close of the 18C, noteworthy features now being the belfry and, inside the church, the laird's loft of 1828 and the box pews with their tables and moveable partitions.

A97 now turns south and in about *2m* is exchanged for B973 (on some maps A944) which accompanies the river west and in rather over *1m* passes *Colquhonnie Castle*, beside a hotel, a small ruin begun by Forbes of Towie in the 16C but never finished, because, it is said, three successive lairds fell off the top and were killed. A short *1m* beyond, at **Bellabeg**, the road crosses the Water of Nochty, on the far side being the *Doune of Invernochty*, a large grassy motte marking the site of the early (12C or before) stronghold of the Earl of Mar before the construction of Kildrummy. The Lonach Highland Gathering—so called from the name of a nearby hill and well known for its March of the Clansmen from Inverernan, 2m south west—is held usually towards the end of August. Just beyond the Doune of Invernochty the road offers a glimpse, on the left and steeply below in the trees, of graceful *Poldullie Bridge*(leading to the village of *Strathdon*), a single arch built in 1715 by Jack Forbes of Inverernan, who, soon afterwards was executed for his part in the '15. *CandercraigGardens* (Tel: 09756-51226), about 1m farther, are Victorian walled gardens.

In another *5m* (from Bellabeg), and still running with the Don, the road joins A939, the latter representing the Hanoverian military road of 1752–54 from Perth via Braemar to Fort George on the Moray Firth. Nor is it long before the traveller is made uncompromisingly aware of this, for in *2m* appears **Corgarff Castle** (AM. Tel: 031-244-3101), the stark and ugly Hanoverian conversion into a fortified barracks of a mid 16C tower which, not much later in that same century, in 1571, was the scene of a particularly horrific example of clan history. It arose out of the feud between the Gordons and the Forbes, during which Corgarff, defended by the wife of the absent Alexander Forbes, was besieged by Adam Gordon of Auchindoun. The tower was set on fire and, rather than surrender, the gallant defender chose to perish in the flames together with her children and entire household. Later, and rebuilt, the tower sheltered Montrose in 1645 and in 1745 was used by the Jacobites. But it was in the following year that the Hanoverians began to give Corgarff its present barracks form, a conspicuous feature of which is the star-shaped loopholed wall of 1748. The castle remained in military occupation until 1830, in the later years playing a useful role in the suppression of smuggling, largely of whisky.

If Corgarff represents one aspect of the Hanoverian presence, the **Lecht Road**, which climbs steeply away northwards from 1330ft to 2100ft, represents a very different one, an achievement remarkable enough in the mid 18C and still admired and used today. From the shelter of a modern car the seemingly endless bleak moorland can be accepted and quickly traversed, but conditions were assuredly very different for the men of the five companies of the 33rd Regiment, credited, on a stone at *Well of the Lecht*, 2m north of the summit, with the building of the road from this point down into the valley of the Spey. Notorious for its snowfalls, the Lecht is today provided with skiers' tows (Lecht Ski Company, Corgarff AB3 8YP. Tel: 09754-240).

10m (from Corgarff) **Tomintoul** (*Inf.*), in the midst of barren moorland and laid out by the Duke of Gordon in 1779, is the highest village in the Highlands (1160ft) though, curiously, not in Scotland (see Rte 10, Wanlockhead and Leadhills). The *Museum* (Tel: 0309-73701) illustrates the local scene, touching aspects such as wildlife, geology, climate and local history with a reconstructed rural kitchen as an attractive feature.

A DISTILLERIES CIRCUIT. Two whisky distilleries (successors of the 200 or so illicit ones which flourished in this part of Scotland before the Distilleries Act of 1823), both along B9008, can be visited from Tomintoul in a scenically pleasant circuit of some 20 miles. Both distilleries offer a video, a tour, a free dram and a visitor centre and shop. The first, *Tamnavoulin* (Tel: 08073-427), the name meaning The Mill on the Hill, has its visitor centre in the restored old mill and there is also a riverside picnic area. Beyond, at *The Glenlivet* (Tel: 08073-427), the visitor centre is in the converted original maltings. The nearby castle (*Blairfindy*) dates from 1564 and was successor to *Drumin Castle*, a fragment amid farm buildings which may be glimpsed to the right at the start of the return leg of this circuit along B9136 (no adm., but explanatory notice beside the road). It was in Glenlivet in 1594 that James VI in person defeated the rebel earls Huntly and Errol.

From Tomintoul A939 descends off the moors into the broad and wooded valley of the Spey which it reaches at (*12m*) **Grantown-on-Spey** (1600 inhab. *Inf.*). Laid out in 1776 by Sir James Grant (enlightened, energetic and responsible for many roads, towns, village improvements and suchlike in and around Strathspey), and with a dignified length of wide, tree-lined main street, this is a spacious and sheltered place which, at the hub of several important touring roads, has become an established summer centre as also a base for winter sports.

This Route here crosses, but does not continue with the Spey. For places to the south west—such as *Castle Roy*, *Boat of Garten* (Strathspey Railway), *Loch Garten* (ospreys) and *Carrbridge*—see Rte 50. The scenically pleasant **Strathspey** extends some 20m north east to *Craigellachie* (on Rte 39), the main A95 running south and B9102 north of the river. The four places of specific interest—three distilleries and an agricultural museum—are described as from Craigellachie.

Castle Grant, on the north outskirts of Grantown and the chief seat of the Grants for five centuries, is structurally a successful combination of a 15C keep and 18C extensions carried out by Robert and John Adam.

8m **Dava**, a road fork at which a decision must be made between A939 to Nairn or A940 to Forres. Each road passes close to a site of interest— Ardclach Bell Tower off A939; Randolph's Leap off A940—but a linking road (B9007) through Relugas enables both to be visited. But first a short diversion of 2m south west from Dava may be made to the bleakly sited moorland loch of *Loch-in-Dorb*, a lost place now but one which with its island castle, still surviving as a ruin, was of considerable importance during the 13–15C. First, in the 13C, the Comyns built the castle; in 1303 Edward I took it and greatly strengthened the defences; in 1336 the anglophile Countess of Athol (for her husband, see Culblean, at the end of Rte 37B) held out against David II until the siege could be raised by

England's Edward III; and in 1372 the castle became a lair of the 'Wolf of Badenoch'. Finally, in 1456, Loch-in-Dorb's story ended with its dimantling by James II.

TO NAIRN (A939). *5m Ferness*, a village where B9007 is crossed, the northward stretch of which, beyond Relugas, passes close to Randolph's Leap (see below). —*1m Logie Bridge*, crossing the Findhorn, a river which drops off the high moor to cut a beautiful wooded and winding course through defiles and steep-sided hills. Just beyond, a minor road and lane in about 1m arrive at **Ardclach Bell Tower** (key at reasonable hours from cottage), a curious detached and fortified two-storeyed belfry of 1665, perched high above the Findhorn and combining the functions both of look-out and of summoning worshippers to the old church. Beside the approach lane stands a monument to Donald Mitchell (born 1782), Scotland's first missionary to India. From here some of the best of the Findhorn can be enjoyed by continuing along the minor road for about 3m to *Dulsie Bridge* where the river forces through a narrow cut below the valley coming in from the west.—*9m* (from Logie Bridge), **Nairn** see Rte 43.

TO FORRES (A940). In *7m* B9007 joins from the south west, providing a link across to Ardclach Bell Tower and the approach to (in 1m) *Randolph's Leap*, where amid beautiful woodland the Findhorn tumbles through a small gorge, in one spot with rocks only 10ft apart. A plaque tells the somewhat involved story behind the name, while a stone marks the astonishingly high level of the flood of 1829.—*5m* **Forres**, see Rte 43.

39   Aberdeen to Elgin via Dufftown

A944 to Dunecht. Unclassified to Castle Fraser and Monymusk. B993 to Tillyfourie. A944 to Mossat. A97, B9002 and A941 to Elgin.—Generally pastoral, but moor and upland between Alford and Dufftown, especially across the desolate Moor of Cabrach approaching the latter. Between Dufftown and Rothes, several distilleries.

SOME HOTELS. **Mossat (Kildrummy)**. *Kildrummy Castle*, AB3 8RA. Tel: 09755-71288. **Craigellachie (Charlestown of Aberlour)**. *Aberlour*, High Street, AB3 9QB. Tel: 0340-871287. **Rothes**. *Rothes Glen*, IV33 7AH. Tel: 03403-254.

Total distance 67m.—*33m* **Mossat**.—*18m* **Dufftown**.—*4m* **Craigellachie**.—*12m* **Elgin**.

For Aberdeen to (*33m*) *Mossat*, see Rte 38.—*3m Auchindoir (St. Mary's) Church*, within the angle of A97 and B9002, though now a ruin, has features making a visit worthwhile. In origin a parish church of the 13C, the shell still shelters a 16C sacrament house, considered to be one of the best in Scotland, a Transitional door with a semicircular arch and dog-tooth moulding, and, in the north wall, a still graceful lancet. *Craig Castle* (Summer only and by appointment. Tel: 04648-202), just north and overlooking a wooded glen, has as its oldest feature a keep of 1528 or earlier, while the armorial decorative work and the gateway of 1720 are also notable.

B9002 in *4m* joins with A941 which heads across the *Moor of Cabrach*, a desolate tract below mountains of around 2000ft, to descend to bridge Glen Fiddich. Ahead—stark, forbidding yet inviting on its high moorland skyline—appears **Auchindoun Castle** (AM. Tel: 031-244-3101), reached by a track off A941 about 1½m short of Dufftown. The prehistoric earthworks scattered around tell that this lonely upland site was a defended one centuries before Auchindoun's central tower was built, probably in the 15C by James III's mason and favourite Robert Cochrane, later to become the stronghold of that Adam Gordon who in 1571 achieved notoriety through the burning of Corgarff and its household. A curiosity here is the absence of the normal tailored cornerstones, all removed to become parts of Balvenie Castle in Dufftown.

11m **Dufftown** (1700 inhab. *Inf.*) might be described as a place of four origins, all visibly surviving—Mortlach church with pre-Norman and earlier roots; Balvenie Castle representing the medieval centuries; the town itself, the creation in 1817 of James Duff, 4th Earl of Fife; and the district's whisky distilleries which since the late 19C have made their ever popular contribution.

The focus of this rather quaint small town is its pleasing central *Clock Tower* housing the local *Museum* (Tel: 0309-73701) telling Dufftown's story from Mortlach to whisky. *Mortlach Church*, $\frac{1}{2}$m south, is basically 12C and something of this medieval building survives in the walls, while the lancets in the choir are 13C and the north aisle jumps into the 19C. But fact begins to mix with tradition as this church's earlier origins are sought. Ancient stones suggest an early Christian foundation, it is said by St. Moluag in 566, while tradition also tells that in 1010, in celebration of a victory over the Norsemen, Malcolm II lengthened the church by a measure of three spears, at the same time founding a bishopric, which, however, David I in 1137 transferred to Aberdeen where it is now represented by St. Machar's cathedral.

Balvenie Castle (AM. Tel: 031-244-3101), on the north outskirts of Dufftown, survives as the substantial ruin of what was originally the 13C moated, courtyard stronghold of the Comyns. Some of the masonry undoubtedly belongs to this period, and on the south west and north west sides the ditch can still be seen, but there was major rebuilding during the 15 and 16C, the 4th Earl of Atholl (1542–79) being responsible for the tower-house which changed the castle's character from fortress to a nobleman's mansion. Balvenie was visited by Edward I in 1304, by Mary, Queen of Scots, in 1562, and in 1746 by Cumberland when the castle was occupied by his troops. See also Auchindoun Castle above.

To the north of the castle, *Glenfiddich Distillery* (Tel: 0340-20373), though dating from 1887, is briskly modern, with a visitor theatre, video presentation in six languages and the latest in whisky technology. This is the only distillery in the Highlands in which malt whisky is actually bottled on the premises, this enabling the visitor to follow the whole process, 'from the barley to the bottle', with a free dram to close the tour.

4m **Craigellachie** more or less marks the east end of Strathspey, the river crossed by a modern bridge (1973) just below Telford's graceful, iron single-span predecessor of 1815.

A DISTILLERIES CIRCUIT. From Craigellachie a westerly round of some 17m takes in three distilleries (tours, visitor centres, free drams, shops) and an agricultural museum. A95 is followed south west through Charlestown of Aberlour to reach in some 6m *Glenfarclas Distillery* (Tel: 08072-245), founded in 1836. Just beyond, at Marypark, B9102 is taken north for Knockando where there are two more distilleries, namely *Cardhu* (Tel: 03406-204) and *Tamdhu* (Tel: 03406-221). Farther east, at Archiestown, is *Ladycroft Agricultural Museum* (Tel: 03406-274). Thence B9102 in 4m joins A941 just north of Craigellachie bridge.

3m **Rothes**, with, at the south, the surviving wall of its castle, and, to the west, *Glen Grant Distillery* (Tel: 03403-413).—*9m* **Elgin**, see Rte 43.

40 Aberdeen to Fochabers via Huntly

A96 to Inverurie. B9001 and unclassified roads to Harlaw, Daviot
(Loanhead Stone Circle), Pitcaple Castle, Chapel of Garioch and the
Maiden Stone. B9002 and A97 to Huntly. A96 to Fochabers.—Pastoral
and agricultural countryside, becoming higher and more wooded after
Oyne.

SOME HOTELS. **Inverurie**. *Strathburn*, Burghmuir Drive, AB5 9GY.
Tel: 0467-24422. *Gordon Arms*, Market Place, AB5 9SA. Tel: 0467-20314.
Pitcaple. *Pittodrie House*, AB5 9HS. Tel: 04676-444. **Huntly**. *Castle*,
AB5 4SH. Tel: 0466-2696. *Gordon Arms*, AB5 5AF. Tel: 0466-2288. **Keith**.
Fife Arms, Regent Street, AB5 3DZ. Tel: 0542-462351.

Total distance 61m.—*16m* **Inverurie**.—*15m* **Insch**.—*6m* **Leith
Hall**.—*7m* **Huntly**.—*10m* **Keith**.—*7m* **Fochabers**.

From the roundabout beyond the east end of Castle Street, **Aberdeen**
(see Rte 36) is left by way of West North Street, Causewayend and Great
Northern Road. In the suburb of *Bucksburn*, *4m* out of the city centre,
A947 breaks away north for Dyce airport and Rte 41.—*8m* **Kintore**
which, though small and quickly passed, nevertheless merits a few
minutes pause, and not only because, surprisingly, this place has been a
royal burgh since 1506 and, indeed, claims to have been first chartered
by Kenneth II as reward for help in fighting the Picts. The *Town House*
of 1737 is quaint with its external curving stairs, while the *Church*
shows a pre-Reformation sacrament house, with a panel with angels
displaying a monstrance, and, in the yard, a Pictish stone combining
Christian and pagan symbols.

4m **Inverurie** (7000 inhab. *Inf.*), said to have been made a royal burgh
by David I, though this status more probably dates from a charter given
by Mary, Queen of Scots, is the largest centre within a district rich in
prehistory and Pictish stones. Thus the *Museum* (Tel: 0779-77778) here,
in the Public Library in the Square, though small, is of particular
interest for its local material.

*The Bass, on the south east of the town beside B993, and the stones in
the adjacent churchyard, together remind of medieval and earlier
times. The Pictish stones, one bearing a lively figure of a pony and
another a clear 'spectacle' symbol, provide, as do all such, a tantalising
glimpse into Dark Ages ritual. But The Bass requires no explanation;
only imagination. Strictly military in purpose, this great mound, today
green and bare, was thrown up in 1160 by David, Lord of Garioch and
brother of Malcolm IV, to serve as the base, steep and surrounded by a
formidable palisade of sharpened stakes, on which to place his wooden
tower crowned with its defensive platform. From this would have
grown the more sophisticated stone castle visited by Mary, Queen of
Scots, in 1562. Just beyond The Bass a small road leads due south for 1m
to ruined early 16C *Kinkell Church*, of interest because the parson here,
Alexander Galloway, was well known as an artistic designer of sacrament houses and the one here bears his initials and the date 1524.
Another curiosity is a tombstone of Gilbert de Greenlaw, killed at
Harlaw (see below), economically re-used in 1592, possibly by a Forbes.

The *Brandsbutt Stone*, off A96 on the north west outskirts of Inverurie, stands as another reminder of this district's Pictish past, this one
not only with typical symbols but also bearing an Ogham inscription.

There are several sites of interest either side of the next 6m of A96.
This Route therefore now chooses a meandering course along generally
minor roads before first crossing, and then briefly rejoining A96 just
before its fork with B9002 which is then followed.

Near the Brandsbutt Stone, B9001 forks north, in *1m* reaching a road to the left leading to *Harlaw House* in the grounds of which a monument of 1911 marks the site of the Battle of Harlaw of 1411 and may also remind the visitor of some characters met elsewhere.

The Countess of Ross, niece of Donald, Lord of the Isles, renounced her title and entered a convent, Donald at once claiming the earldom, marching southward against James I, burning Dingwall and Inverness and threatening Aberdeen. Opposing him here was the self-made Earl of Mar, that same Alexander Stewart, illegitimate son of the 'Wolf of Badenoch', who, at Kildrummy, had forced the Countess of Mar, whom he had widowed, to marry him and give him the title. Mar won the battle, and Donald was forced both to renounce his claim and declare allegiance to the Crown. But the cost was heavy, among the killed being Alderman Davidson of Aberdeen and Sir Alexander de Irwyn of Drum, both of whom, the former by an effigy and the latter by a brass, are remembered in Aberdeen's St. Nicholas church.

In *3m* farther along B9001 a side road, through Daviot, in *1m* reaches *Loanhead Stone Circle*, one of the leading examples of the Recumbent Stone type. A ring of rough erect stones surrounds a scatter of small stones, all that is left of what was once a large burial cairn, while pottery discovered here indicates that, perhaps 1000 years later, this place was inhabited, rather than used just for ritual and burial. There are other stone and earthworks adjacent. From here minor roads wander generally south west to *3m Pitcaple Castle* on A96, a 15–16C castle with two round towers and 19C additions, still in use as a family home. Beneath a tree in front of the house both Mary, Queen of Scots, and Charles II are said to have danced, the former in 1562, Charles in 1650. But the latter year witnessed also a less happy occasion when Montrose arrived as a prisoner, preceded by a crier announcing him as James Graham, traitor.

A96 is crossed opposite Pitcaple, a small road being followed to (*1m*) *Chapel of Garioch*. The ruined tower (1530) of *Balquhain*, beside the road 1m east of here, was a seat of the Jacobite Leslies. In 1746 Cumberland ordered that it be burnt, but, so the story goes, a tenant of the Leslies bribed the soldiers to use damp straw. Beside the road, *1m* north west of Chapel of Garioch, stands the magnificent *Maiden Stone* (9C), ranking among the most beautiful of Scotland's Early Christian monuments and taking its name from the comb and mirror carved at the foot. Of red granite and standing 10ft high, the stone bears a Celtic cross and Pictish symbols, including, on one side, a man between marine monsters, and, on the other, beasts, an 'elephant' and the mirror and comb.

The wooded ridge of *Bennachie* (1773ft), by some authorities held to be the site of Mons Graupius, rises immediately to the south west, with, on Mither Tap (1698ft), the east summit, the remains of a hill-fort. Around Bennachie the Forestry Commission have laid out some of their finest forest walks, one car park being just west of the Maiden Stone and another at Puttingstone to the south of Oyne.

This Route now briefly touches A96 before bearing left along B9002, beside which stands the pile of *Harthill Castle* (no adm.), probably begun by Patrick Leith of Barnis and completed by his son John in 1601. Less than a century later the last laird, hopelessly in debt, burnt the castle, rather than have it seized, and fled to London.—*2m* (from the Maiden Stone) *Oyne*, followed by (*3m*) **Insch**, 2m north of which (at Myreton, off the Largie road) there is another fine stone, the *Picardy Stone* (7 or 8C) showing a variety of symbols, including double disc, serpent and mirror. Excavation in 1856 revealed that the stone stood above a grave.

Just beyond Insch, the hill of *Dunnideer* rises emphatically above the railway to the north of B9002. Iron Age people built the first fort here, this, judging by the quantity of vitrified stone still tumbled around the hilltop, destroyed by fire perhaps 2000 years ago. A thousand or more years later, in the early 13C, some of the Iron Age fort's stones were used in the building here of one of the earliest stone castles in Scotland, the simple tower, today no more than a battered fragment, of a Balliol nobleman.

6m **Leith Hall** (NTS. Tel: 04643-216), approached by way of a splendid avenue, offers a change from castles, for although the core here is a turreted tower-house of 1649, essentially Leith is now a large but unpretentious and attractive country mansion around a central courtyard. James Leith, the first to build here, seems to have come from a family which once lived in Leith, near Edinburgh, but moved to Aberdeen to become by the 14C prosperous shipowners, and in large part the exhibits in the house reflect the long tradition of military service later given by the Leiths and associated Hays. Prominent among these was Andrew Hay who achieved the distinction of being pardoned after Culloden, the document being among those shown here. Gardens, trails with a bird observation hide, Soay sheep, Highland cattle, a picnic area and even carved Pictish stones are among the attractions around the grounds.

In *2m* B9002 meets A97 below the high ground of *Clashindarroch Forest*, rising, 2m south west of this road junction, to *Tap o' Noth* (1851ft) crowned by a vitrified Iron Age fort. Much of this forest grows at between 1000 and 1500 ft and access roads, some only for walkers, climb the valleys which break these eastern slopes and meet Strath Bogie which is now followed north as A97.

5m **Huntly** (4000 inhab. *Inf.*), within the confluence of the rivers Deveron and Bogie, tends to be overshadowed, historically and touristwise though not physically, by its famed ruined Gordon castle. Yet

Huntly Castle, showing the 5th Earl's elegant oriel windows of 1602

this small town, though essentially a Gordon creation, has an identity of its own and, indeed, on the evidence of the two standing stones in the attractive Square, infinitely earlier origins than its castle. But in medieval times the town of course grew with the castle, being chartered in 1545 and then in the later 18 and 19C laid out and extended to settle to the plan it shows today. Material illustrating something of the town's development can be seen in the *Library Museum* in the Square (Tel: 0779-77778), while—an indication of the town's architectural merit—a leaflet obtainable from Tourist Information guides around an Architectural Trail.

The *Castle (AM. Tel: 031-244-3101), until 1544 known as Strathbogie Castle, is reached by Castle Street, running north from the Square to pass below an arch formed by buildings of Gordon Schools (founded in 1839 by the Duchess of Gordon), beyond being the fine approach avenue. Essentially what survives here are the Norman motte and bailey, the later tower-house palace, and the foundations of a court.

History. In both strategic and tactical terms the castle's site is an obvious choice, the former because it commands the roads from Strathdon and Aberdeen to Moray, the latter because of the defensive advantage provided by the two rivers.

Early history is of course that of the motte, 12–13C stronghold of the Scottish-Norman Duncan, Earl of Fife, and the place also in which in 1307, during his campaign against the Comyns, Bruce rested after an illness before moving out to defeat the Comyns at Barra Hill. Just before Bannockburn, though, the then lord turned against Bruce, as a result losing his lands to the latter's loyal supporter, Sir Adam Gordon of Huntly (Gordon) in the Borders. In 1449 the Gordons were made earls of Huntly, but only three years later, during the civil disputes of 1452, their wooden castle was destroyed by the Douglas Earl of Moray. Replacement of the wooden structure by stone had probably already started before Moray's attack, which of course accelerated the process.

For the next century the Gordon earls of Huntly held autocratic sway over this part of Scotland, and it was here in 1496 that James IV, a frequent visitor, attended the marriage between Perkin Warbeck and Lady Catherine Gordon. Then in 1552 the colourful and energetic 4th Earl pulled down most of the 15C structure and built much of the basic palace fabric as seen today. But it was he, too, who, by rebelling against Mary, Queen of Scots, and being defeated at Corrichie, closed the era of Gordon power.

The 5th Earl also rebelled (against James VI) in 1594, his defeat in Glen Livet leading to the subsequent destruction of much of the castle. However, three years later he made his peace with the king, became 1st Marquis of Huntly and set about restoring his home. A man of refined taste, it is to his restoration that belong the building's most beautiful architectural features. The 2nd Marquis lost his head after supporting Charles I, first suffering the cruelty of being imprisoned in his own castle. After this, and with the move later of the family to what is now Gordon Castle at Fochabers, Huntly inevitably fell into disrepair.

The building is greatly complicated by the centuries of destruction, rebuilding and alteration. The main part, though, is the 4th and 5th earls' 16–17C Palace, using the older vaults as its foundations. Features are the elegant row of oriel windows (1602) with the stonework names of the 1st Marquis (5th Earl) and his wife; the elaborate heraldic ornamentation (which should be imagined as emblazoned in colour), particularly the *vertical panel above the main doorway, probably the finest heraldic doorway in Britain; and the fireplaces, again with heraldic and other ornamentation.

Below the palace is the 15C vaulted Dungeon, rather more roomy than in some castles but not much less grim. It is reached by a gloomy narrow passage, with outer and inner doors, the latter killing any lingering hopes of escape by opening into the dungeon several feet above its floor level. Along the basement passage walls can be seen graffiti, possibly the work of bored guards.

Outside the palace, on the north, the visitor stands within the outline of the Court, the remains on the west and east sides being respectively

16 and 17C but those on the north the foundations of what must have been a massive 15C tower. Within the court are the remains of a stable, possibly originally a chapel.

The Motte is self-evident; and across the grass on the east side of the castle runs the ancient cobbled entrance causeway.

10m **Keith** (4600 inhab. *Inf.*) claims roots reaching back to before 700, when those living here beside the Isla were converted to Christianity by St. Maelrubha, and certainly existed as a community by the 12C when William the Lion chartered this place to Kinloss Abbey. Today Keith really represents an amalgam of three places. Old Keith, beside the river, dates from medieval times, a nice survival here (off Regent Street) being the *Auld Brig*, built in 1609 by Thomas Murray and Janet Lindsay whose names are cut into the south face; New Keith, above and to the east of the river, was laid out by the 2nd Earl of Seafield in 1750; and Fife Keith, on the opposite bank of the Isla, was founded by the Earl of Fife in 1817.

In addition to the Auld Brig, a church, an ancient tower and a distillery all merit a visit. *St. Thomas's Church*, in Chapel Street in the south part of New Keith, was built in 1830 with a façade copied from that of Santa Maria de Angelis in Rome. Inside are an 'Incredulity of St. Thomas', painted by François Dubois and presented by Charles X of France; a statue of St. John Ogilvie, Scotland's first post-Reformation saint, born near Keith in 1580, hanged in Glasgow in 1615 and canonised in 1976; and modern stained-glass windows, by Father Ninian Sloane of Pluscarden Abbey. *Milton Tower*, in Station Road, survives as Keith's oldest building; part of a larger castle, built in 1480, this was long the seat of the Ogilvie family. *Strathisla Distillery*, in Seafield Avenue to the south of the station, was established in 1786 and is thus one of the oldest in Scotland (Tel: 05422-7471).—*Newmill*, just north of Keith, was the birthplace in c 1800 of James Gordon Bennett, founder of the 'New York Herald'.

7m **Fochabers**, see Rte 43.

41   Aberdeen to Macduff and Banff

A947 to Oldmeldrum. A920 to Pitmedden. B999 and B9170 to Methlick. B9005 to Fyvie. A947 to Macduff (Banff).—Generally pastoral and wooded.

SOME HOTELS. **Oldmeldrum**. *Meldrum House*, AB5 OAE. Tel: 06512-2294. **Fyvie**. *Vale*, AB5 8JP. Tel: 06516-376. **Turriff**. *Union*, Main Street. Tel: 0888-63704.

Total distance 54m.—*16m* **Oldmeldrum**.—*18m* (via Pitmedden and Haddo) **Fyvie**.—*8m* **Turriff**.—*12m* **Macduff** and **Banff**.

From the roundabout beyond the east end of Castle Street, **Aberdeen** (see Rte 36) is left by West North Street, Causewayend and Great Northern Road.—*4m Bucksburn*, whence Rte 40 follows A96.—*1m* **Dyce**, a name best known as Aberdeen's airport.—*11m* **Oldmeldrum**, 1m south of which, just east of B9170, rises *Barra Hill* (634ft) where in 1307, on Christmas Eve, Bruce decisively defeated John Comyn who may have camped within the hill's Iron Age fort.

From Oldmeldrum A947 provides the direct road to Fyvie. This Route, however, takes an eastward loop, starting along A920, to include a clutch of outstanding National Trust and other sites.

5m ***Pitmedden Garden and Museum** (NTS. Tel: 06513-2352). The *Garden* here is no ordinary garden, but the Great Garden laid out in 1675 by Sir Alexander Seton and recreated with all its elaborate floral designs by the National Trust. There are four formal parterres, three being taken from designs recorded as having been used in the gardens of Edinburgh's Holyrood House in 1647, while the fourth is a heraldic design based on Sir Alexander Seton's coat-of-arms (he was the first Baronet Pitmedden). Pitmedden also offers a *Museum of Farming Life*, with some both interesting and curious farming and domestic material, a visitor centre, an exhibition on formal gardens, picnic area, woodland and farmland walks (rare breeds of livestock) and an adventure play-ground.

Udny Castle (no adm. but well seen from the road) is a dramatic battlemented and turreted tower of the 15–17C, while the old church-yard in *Udny Green*, immediately south of the castle, contains a burial enclosure of the Setons of Pitmedden and also a mort-house for the prevention of body-snatching.

*Tolquhoun Castle (AM. Tel: 031-244-3101) is just north west (*1m*) of Pitmedden off B999. The castle's situation beyond an unusually large, gently sloping forecourt, with an old yew tree pleasance along its west side, and the structurally and functionally abrupt contrast between a fortified exterior and a mainly residential inner court, combine to give Tolquhoun a distinction and interest all its own.

History. Unlike so many castles, Tolquhoun suffered little if at all from hostile attack. In the 14C it belonged to the Prestons, but in 1420, through the marriage of a Preston daughter, it passed to Sir John Forbes, the probable builder of the Auld Tower, sometimes still called Preston's Tower, the oldest part of the castle seen today. In 1584 the laird was the cultured William Forbes, who not only much enlarged Tolquhoun but took steps to ensure that posterity would know this; a precise inscription at the gatehouse reads 'Al this wark, excep the auld tour, was begun be William Forbes 15 Aprile, 1584, and endit be him, 20 October, 1589'. His master mason was Thomas Leiper, who was also responsible for his employer's elaborate tomb in the churchyard at Tarves (see below). For financial reasons, the estate had to be sold by the laird in 1716, though the castle remained occupied until the mid 19C.

The visitor's first impression is of a defensive stronghold, and even at the arched forecourt entrance there are gunloops, tactically constructed so that the central opening gives forward while the others are angled. Many such will also be seen in the castle itself. Two corner towers, one round and one square, provide the usual protection along all four of the castle's walls, while the main gatehouse, where the above inscription will be found, continues the defensive theme with its flanking drum towers, barred windows, two guard rooms and gunloops.

Beyond the gatehouse, in the inner court, there are still gunloops and heavily barred windows, while to the left is John Forbes's ruined Auld Tower, with a vaulted cellar. The well, too, is probably a survival from the older period. But the emphasis here is residential and domestic, the main rooms being along the south and west sides, with a wide stairway leading to the upper floor with the hall and laird's room, a practical feature of the latter being the private stair from the kitchen.

1m Tarves, where can be seen the elaborate tomb (by Thomas Leiper) of William Forbes and his wife, a Gothic structure with Renaissance detail and statuettes of the occupants.

1m ***Haddo House**, at the heart of a splendid and much varied park, is approached from the south. The complex comprises the house, gardens and grounds, 177 acres of the last forming a Country Park controlled by Grampian Regional Council. (*House*. NTS. Tel: 06515-440. *Country Park*. Tel: 06515-489).

Long the seat of the Gordon earls and marquises of Aberdeen, Haddo House was planned in 1731, for the 2nd Earl, by William Adam (father of Robert), to replace the old House of Kellie (burnt by Covenanters in 1644) which for centuries had been the home of the Gordons of Methlick. The house is a masterpiece of symmetry, particularly pleasing being the high central section with its matching curving flights of stairs up to the first floor balcony, this being the normal entrance until 1880 when the 1st Marquis (7th Earl) inserted the present ground level door. Inside the house the elegant yet unpretentious rooms opening off the long curving passageway contain a notable collection of portraits, of which the most treasured is that by Lawrence of the 4th Earl, prime minister from 1852–55 and the man largely responsible for rescuing a neglected estate and making it what it is today. Here too are portraits of some of his friends and colleagues, such as William Pitt, Castlereagh, Wellington and Peel. The Chapel (1880), with stained glass by Burne-Jones, was the last work of the architect G.E. Street.—Features of the *Country Park* are a tree trail (booklet), bird hide, picnic area and interpretive centre.

The **Haddo House Choral and Operatic Society**, founded in 1945 by June, Marchioness of Aberdeen, and with its own theatre beside the house, has made its name as one of Scotland's leading musical bodies. Productions include opera and concerts in which internationally known artists often appear, and also performances of classic drama. For information contact the Choral Secretary, Tel: 06515-666.

From *Methlick*, *2m* north west of Haddo, B9005 heads north west, in a good *2m* arriving at the hamlet of Stonehouse, from where a farm track and path in c $\frac{3}{4}$m reach *Gight Castle*, above the steep wooded bank of the Ythan. This is the sad and decaying ruin of the once formidable tower-house of the lawless Gordons of Gight, perhaps worth a visit as such and certainly worth one by anyone in search of Byronic associations. For this was the home of Lady Catherine Gordon, 13th laird in a succession reaching back to 1479 and mother of the poet Byron (1788), who was forced to sell Gight in 1787, in order to pay the gambling debts of her dissolute husband, 'Mad Jack' Byron. Thomas the Rhymer predicted 'when the herons leave the tree, the lairds of Gight shall landless be', and, sure enough, in 1787 the herons did exchange Gight for Haddo.

6m **Fyvie Castle** (NTS. Tel: 06516-266), spanning from the 13C to Scottish Baronial and one of the stateliest castellated mansions in Scotland, is a place of five towers and of five families.

History. In the early 13C there was a keep here in the royal forest, but in 1338 the lands were granted to Sir James Lindsay, Earl of Crawford. This family, though, does not count among the five because the estate soon passed by marriage to Sir Henry Preston, builder of the south east and oldest surviving tower (*Preston Tower*). Later, and again by marriage, Fyvie went to the Meldrums who put up the *Meldrum Tower* (south west). However by 1596 the Meldrums, by then bankrupt, sold out to Sir Alexander Seton, and it was he who was responsible for the great central *Seton Tower*, with its twin drums, as also for the upper works and north west wing. In 1733 Fyvie was again sold, this time to the 2nd Earl of Aberdeen, the builder at the same time of Haddo House and remembered here by the *Gordon Tower* (north east). A third sale, in 1889, brought the estate to Alexander Forbes-Leith, an American industrialist and descendant of the Leith-Hays of Leith Hall (see Rte 40), who in 1890 raised the *Leith Tower* (north west) and, as Lord Leith, gave Fyvie its turn-of-the-century opulence. The above, of course, is a simplification; inevitably there was constructional overlapping, and it seems also virtually certain that the Preston Tower incorporates something of the earlier keep.

Acquired by the National Trust for Scotland in 1984, Fyvie was opened to the public in 1986.

Architecturally the two outstanding earlier features inside the castle are the great *wheel stairway, built by Sir Alexander Seton, bearing his crest and ascending through five floors; and, in the 17C morning room, the contemporary plaster ceiling and panelling. Otherwise the ambience here is the recreation of the lifestyle and taste of an immensely wealthy Edwardian, among the highlights being the many portraits, notably by Raeburn as also by Lely, Kneller, Romney, Opie and Hoppner; the 17C Brussels tapestries; the collection of armour in the entrance hall; and the billiard room which Lord Leith created out of the 18C kitchen.

From *Fyvie*, where the church merits a glance because of the Celtic stones built into its gable, this Route heads north on A947.—*4m Towie (Tolly) Barclay Castle* (by appointment. Tel: 08884-347), a square and turreted 16C red tower with modern (1970s) upper floors which was once the home of the Barclays, the family to which belonged Prince Michael de Tolly, marshal in the Russian army during the Napoleonic wars.—*4m* **Turriff** claims early roots as the capital of a 6C Pictish prince. From more recent times the town enjoys the modest distinction of having been the scene of the first skirmish of the Civil War. In what has become known as the 'Trot of Turriff' (1639) a party of Royalist Gordons routed the Covenanters under the Master of Forbes. *Delgatie Castle* (written application), 1½m north east, a satisfying tower-house well seen from the minor road which passes it, dates from the 11–13C but has additions mainly of about 1570. Features of the interior are pictures and arms, painted ceilings of about 1590, and a portrait of Mary, Queen of Scots, hanging in the room which she used for three days in 1562. *Craigston Castle* (written application), on B9105 4m north east of Turriff, has been a seat of the Urquharts since the castle's building in 1604–07. Architecturally a main feature is a four-storey arch linking the two central towers.

8m Eden Castle, 1m west of A947 down a side road, is today a mere tower remnant. Built in the 16C for the Meldrums, and later passing to the Leslies, the castle's downfall is ascribed to the curse of a mother who asked the laird to control her wayward son, which he effectively did by drowning the boy in the river.—*4m* **Macduff** and **Banff**, for both of which see Rte 43.

42   Aberdeen to Peterhead and Fraserburgh

A92, A975 and A952 to Peterhead. A952 and B9033 to Fraserburgh.— Scenically generally dull roads across open and sometimes bleak farming land, but plenty of rewarding coastal dunes and cliffs.

SOME HOTELS. **Ellon**. *Mercury*, South Road, AB4 9NP. Tel: 0358-20666. **Newburgh**. *Udny Arms*, Main Street, AB4 0BL. Tel: 03586-89444. **Peterhead**. *Waterside Inn*, 1 Fraserburgh Road, AB4 7BN. Tel: 0779-71121. *Palace*, Prince Street, AB4 6PL. Tel: 0779-74821. **St. Combs**. *Tufted Duck*, AB4 5YS. Tel: 03465-2481. **Fraserburgh**. *Royal*, Broad Street. Tel: 0346-28524.

Total distance 46m.—*12m* **Newburgh**.—*10m* **Cruden Bay**.—*6m* **Peterhead**.—*18m* **Fraserburgh**.

Aberdeen (see Rte 36) is left from Castle Street by King Street, the road soon crossing the Don into (*2m*) *Bridge of Don*.—*5m Balmedie Beach*, below sand dunes, offers a picnic area and other facilities. The junction with A975 is reached in another *3m*, this road being followed for *2m* **Newburgh**, once an important port on the Ythan estuary.

Beyond the river bridge A975 runs with the north west boundary of the **Sands of Forvie Nature Reserve** (Tel: 035887-330), an area of 1774 acres stretching with the shore for some 4m from the estuary of the Ythan to the village of Collieston. One of the largest and most untouched dunes systems in Britain, and embracing foreshore, dunes and estuary spit, with also some heath, rough pasture and even cliff, the reserve is not only of considerable botanical interest but is also known for flocks of wintering wildfowl as also for breeding eider and terns. But this tract was not always so desolate, and indeed was probably not swamped by the dunes until possibly the late 17C. The foundations of a Bronze Age village were excavated here in 1951, and the small, sad ruin of *Forvie Church* (close to the shore; 1m by path from east side of A975 bridge) is evidence of a medieval village, thought to have been swamped in a great gale of 1688 or, if a more colourful explanation is preferred, because of the curse pronounced by the three daughters of the local laird, smarting at being cheated of an inheritance.

Collieston, a village with its roots in fishing and smuggling, is 1½m south of *Old Slains Castle*, given by Bruce to Sir Gilbert Hay (whose successors later became earls of Erroll) but now no more than a fragment, the result of being blown up by James VI in 1594 when the 9th Earl, together with the Earl of Huntly, unsuccessfully rebelled.

Ellon (4m north west of Newburgh by main road, or 5m west of Collieston by minor road. 6500 inhab. *Inf.*), though today in large part a commuter town for Aberdeen, is a place of ancient origin, claiming in fact to have been a Pictish settlement before 400 BC. Later, Bruce's enemies, the (Comyn) earls of Buchan, ruled here, dispensing Norman justice from a site now marked by a monument beside the car park in Market Street. Today the river is crossed by a modern bridge, beside its picturesque predecessor of 1793, itself successor to what was long an important ford protected by Ellon's castle, a fragment of which can be glimpsed on the terrace above the north bank.—Another neglected medieval tower, that of *Esslemont*, stands 2m west beside A920.

10m (from Newburgh) **Cruden Bay** which, in modern terms, is the landfall of a North Sea oil pipeline and the start of the pipe section which continues south to Grangemouth. *New Slains Castle*, an extensive ruin overlooking the bay, recalls an earlier importance, for this was the great castle built in c 1597 by the 9th Earl of Erroll when, having been pardoned by James VI for his rebellion, he returned from exile and chose this site rather than that of the destroyed old castle near Collieston. Much restored in 1837, the castle fell into decay after loosing its roof in 1925. Bram Stoker, author of 'Dracula', was a regular visitor to this district over the turn of the century and Slains is said to have inspired his setting of the vampire count's lair.—The *Bullers of Buchan*, rather over *1m* north of Cruden Bay and reached from A975, is a breathtaking natural feature where a cliff-edge path balances along the rim of a sheer 200ft-deep rock chasm, probably once an immense cave of which the roof has collapsed. Although particularly awesome in rough weather when the waves pound in through the natural archway—or boil, or bull; the name is a corruption from Norman French—this corner of the coast is in fact at any time worth a visit for its savage cliffs and rocks alive with seabirds.

5m **Peterhead** (17,000 inhab. *Inf.*), solidly build in pink granite from local quarries, is, after Aberdeen, the largest town in Scotland's North East.

History. Peterhead was founded in 1593 by George Keith, 5th Earl Marischal, and for over a century the town's growth depended on this family; until, in fact, 1716 when the 10th (and last) Earl and his brother, James Keith, were exiled for having permitted the secret landing here of the Old Pretender. In the early 19C Peterhead was a busy whaling port, this being followed by the boom in herring fishing.

The town is best known for its immense harbour-bay, rounded by A952 approaching from the south. The north arm uses the island-promontory of Keith Inch, while the southern is a long breakwater constructed between 1886 and 1912 by convicts from the prison near its base. In the town, in front of the *Town House* of 1788, stands a statue of James Keith, of interest as much for its subject as for its provenance. In exile, James Keith became a close adviser of Frederick the Great of Prussia as also a field marshal in his army, in which capacity he was killed in battle in 1758; then in 1868 William I of Prussia presented this statue, which had long stood in Berlin, to Peterhead. The *Arbuthnot Museum* (Tel: 0779-77778), in St. Peter Street, tells the local story, with emphasis on whaling and fishing.

DIVERSION TO DEER ABBEY AND ADEN COUNTRY PARK. **Deer Abbey** (AM. Tel: 031-244-3121) is 10m west of Peterhead by A950. Although there is not a great deal left to be seen, these ruins are pleasantly sited and have some features of modest interest.

History. A Celtic monastery was founded by St. Drostan in the 7C at Old Deer, a village just south east of today's Deer Abbey. Of this Celtic monastery there is now no structural trace, although it has been suggested that the parish church stands on its site. There is, though, a priceless scholastic trace—the famed 'Book of Deer', now in the University Library at Cambridge. This, perhaps the most precious literary relic of the Celtic Church, is a 9C Latin manuscript of parts of the New Testament, annotated in Gaelic in the 11 or 12C by the monks of Deer, these Gaelic marginal notes being the earliest example known of written Scottish Gaelic.

Deer Abbey as seen today was founded—presumably with some link, however tenuous, to its Celtic predecessor—by William Comyn, Earl of Buchan, for Cistercian monks from Kinloss. It survived the overthrow of the Comyns by Bruce and thrived until the late 16C, after which it was abandoned and plundered as a source of building material. The site was bought in 1809 by the Ferguson family, their Admiral Ferguson in 1854 destroying virtually all that was left of the church in order to build a mausoleum on its site. This was removed in 1930, but two gravestones remain and the mausoleum's portico now forms the site's entrance.

The chief remains are to the south, though these were partly 'restored' in 1809. The buildings here, beyond the cloisters, were the kitchen and parlour, above which would have been the refectory and dormitory. Beyond is the abbot's house, between which and the infirmary to its north can be traced the main drain, carrying away from the reredorter at the north west angle of the abbot's house and then turning towards the river. Architectural fragments are preserved, these including two sedilia arches, a curious piscina with a basin on either side, and a part of an altar with a cavity for relics.

Aden Country Park (Tel: 0771-22857), just east off A950, is centred on the now restored Home Farm of the parent estate, the farm now housing the *North East of Scotland Agricultural Heritage Centre*, portraying local farming, both past and present. Other features of the park include woodland, riverside and lakeside walks, a tree nursery and picnic areas.

Leaving Peterhead A952 crosses the river Ugie, in *2m* reaching, in the village of the same name, late 16C *Inverugie Castle*, the birthplace in 1696 of that Marshal James Keith whose statue stands in Peterhead. Abandoned when the Keith brothers were exiled in 1716, their castle is now a sorry ruin, well reflecting Thomas the Rhymer's prediction, 'Inverugie by the sea, Lordless shall thy landis be'. *Ravenscraig Castle*, a short way upstream, dates from the 15C and belonged to the Cheyne family before passing to the Keiths.—*2m St. Fergus*, with a North Sea gas terminal.

4m Crimond, just before which a minor road north east is worth exploring for a mile or so to the remains of ancient *St. Mary's Chapel* (perhaps founded in the 10C but structurally more likely 13C) from where there is a view across the often desolate but nevertheless interesting expanse of *Loch of Strathbeg*; interesting because, though now fresh water and a bird sanctuary (RSPB visitor centre; access road signed in Crimond village), this was until as recently as 1720 a bay of the sea, and, it would seem, a lively enough place with a castle, a port and even the royal burgh of Rattray. In 1720, though, a storm blocked the channel with sand, and, today, Rattray and its castle, a few yards beyond the chapel, survive as no more than a farm name and, immediately east, traces of earthworks.

In well under *2m* beyond Crimond A952 meets the junction with B9033. *Mormond Hill* (768ft), rising 4m to the west, bears on its slopes a white horse and a white stag, both formed by exposing the quartzite. The horse is attributed to a Fraser who wished to commemorate his charger, killed on a battlefield; the stag, attributed to the laird of nearby Cortes, was cut in 1870.—From this road junction A952 provides the fast approach to Fraserburgh, as also the opportunity to visit (about halfway, and 1m west along B9032) *Memsie Cairn*, a Bronze Age heap, impressive for its size but without a visible entry.

This Route now starts a short eastward loop along B9033 into a countryside of flat fields, dunes and long, open beaches, in *3m* reaching the former fishing but now mixed and residential shore village of *St. Combs*. West of the village, desolate on the flats beside the road, rears the stark fragment of *Inverallochy Castle*, surviving from the 13C as a reminder of the once powerful Norman Comyns. Beyond, *Inverallochy* and *Cairnbulg*, quaint with their rows of low granite 19C cottages, are astonishing twin one-time fishing villages, intimate either side of a now canalised stream yet, as will readily be seen, intensely individual.— *Cairnbulg Castle* (no adm.), seen to the south of B9033, is built around a core which, like Inverallochy, was Comyn but which—and in later centuries much changed—has since 1375, though with a break, been Fraser.

5m (from St. Combs) **Fraserburgh** (12,500 inhab. *Inf.*), a somewhat austere place but important with its port, fishing and industry, was founded in 1546 by Sir Alexander Fraser, laird of Philorth (Cairnbulg Castle). Two buildings of modest historical and architectural interest merit note. One, on Kinnaird's Head, is what is left of *Kinnaird Castle*, built in 1574 by the grandson of the town's founder, later much altered, and its top floor removed in 1787 to make place for a lighthouse, claiming to be the first in Scotland. The other, below, is the strange so-called *Wine Tower*, its purpose never satisfactorily explained but probably a 16C watch tower.—For Fraserburgh westward to *Inverness*, see Rte 43.

43   Fraserburgh to Inverness

B9031 to Macduff. B9139 to Portsoy. A98 to Fochabers. A96 to Elgin, Forres and Nairn but with north or south loops between Elgin and Forres. B9090, B9091 and B9006 to Cawdor, Culloden and Inverness.— In the east, an undulating road, a little back from high, grassy cliffs and linking some picturesque fishing townships and villages, on and close to pleasant bays and beaches. West of Banff, a busier road, flatter and farther inland, but with many side roads to the coast. Views across Moray Firth up the northern coast and towards the Highlands.

SOME HOTELS. **Macduff**. *Highland Haven*, Shore Street, AB4 1UB. Tel: 0261-32408. **Banff**. *Banff Springs*, Golden Knowes Road, AB4 2JE. Tel: 02612-2881. *County*, 32 High Street, AB4 1AE. Tel: 02612-5353. **Cullen**. *Seafield Arms*, 19 Seafield Street, AB5 2SG. Tel: 0542-40791.

Buckie. *Cluny*, 2 High Street, AB5 1AL. Tel: 0542-32922. **Fochabers**. *Grant Arms*, 42 High Street, IV32 7DX. Tel: 0343-820202. *Gordon Arms*, 89 High Street, IV32 7DH. Tel: 0343-820508. **Elgin**. *Mansion House*, The Haugh, IV30 1AW. Tel: 0343-548811. *Park House*, South Street, IV30 1JB. Tel: 0343-547695. **Forres**. *Ramnee*, Victoria Road, IV36 0BN. Tel: 0309-72410. **Nairn**. *Golf View*, Seabank Road, IV12 4HD. Tel: 0667-52301. *Clifton*, Viewfield Street, IV12 4HW. Tel: 0667-53119.

Total distance 90m.—*20m* **Macduff**.—*12m* **Cullen**.—*10m* **Fochabers**.— *8m* **Elgin**.—*12m* (direct by A96) **Forres**.—*11m* **Nairn**.—*12m* **Clava Cairns** and **Culloden**.—*5m* **Inverness**.

From **Fraserburgh** (see Rte 42) the main road westward is A98, looping far inland and with little of interest. This Route chooses the coastal B9031 which, with some steep hills, is slow but scenic and a lot more interesting.

4m **Rosehearty**, founded in 1684 by Lord Forbes of Pitsligo and long a thriving port, is now essentially a dormitory for Fraserburgh. The Forbes' stronghold was *Pitsligo Castle*, ½m south, now a ruin but originally built in 1424 by the Frasers, later passing to the Forbes who considerably extended the castle in about 1570 (heritage centre under consideration). Another castle ruin, seen across the fields to the east, is that of *Pittulie Castle*, also built by the Frasers and dating from the late 16C. Beside the road, a short way south of Pitsligo Castle, are the old (1633) and new (1890) *Churches of Pitsligo*, the former a ruin with a Forbes family vault, the latter with a Forbes loft and some fine locally-carved Jacobean panels transferred here from the earlier church. The name Lord Pitsligo's Cave, on the shore 1½m south west of Rosehearty, recalls the staunchly Jacobite 4th and last Lord Pitsligo (Alexander Forbes), who, having fought in both the '15 and '45, spent the remainder of his life (some 46 years, until his death in 1792 at the age of 84) as a hunted fugitive.

4m **New Aberdour**, a foundation of 1798, from where a road drops down to *Aberdour Bay*, associated with St. Drostan, said to have landed here in about 575 at the spot marked by St. Drostan's Well, today with a stone canopy of 1884 serving as a memorial to Andrew Findlater, editor of Chamber's Encyclopedia. One of Drostan's first acts was to found a church, the predecessor of the part-Norman church the ruin of which is beside the road down to the bay; Drostan then moved inland to convert the locals and found the monastery of Old Deer (see Rte 42). The Jane Whyte memorial, also at Aberdour Bay, honours a local woman who in 1884 'brought ashore a lifeline from the raging sea and saved 15 men from a wreck'.—From New Aberdour, B9031 continues west past the dizzily-sited below-the-cliffs villages of *Pennan* and *Crovie* (steep and narrow approach) to reach (*6m*) *Gardenstown*, a terraced, cliffside village started in 1720 by Alexander Garden. St. John's Chapel, seen to the west of the village, is said to have been built in 1004 in gratitude for the defeat of a Norse raid.

6m **Macduff** (4000 inhab. *Inf.* at Banff), until 1783 a fishing village called Doune, was created by the 2nd Earl of Fife who gave the new Doune his family name. The fishing harbour is the key to the town, over which a fine view can be enjoyed from the high *War Memorial Tower* on the Hill of Doune behind. *Tarlair*, just east, was a spa during the 19C, but the medicinal well no longer flows and has been replaced by a more modern and more popular facility in the form of an open-air swimming pool, superbly sited within the rocky bay.—For Macduff to *Aberdeen*, see Rte 41.

Across the Deveron, and climbing in steeply linked terraces above the south west shore of its bay, **Banff** (3500 inhab. *Inf.*) is a place of some style and character, reflecting, though, more of its 18–19C antecedence than that it was granted a charter by Malcolm IV in 1163 and further privileges by Bruce and Robert II. Of this ancient past there survives in fact only a fragment of the *Old Castle*—no more than a few walls and a ditch—once a royal residence and the birthplace in 1618 of the ill-starred Archbishop Sharp (the new castle, built on the same site by William Adam for Lord Deskford in 1750, is now a municipal building). A similar contrast is provided by *St. Mary's Church*, with a pre-Reformation aisle remnant surviving in the old cemetery opposite the post office while its imposing successor (1790; steeple 1849) is one of a distinguished clutch of generally 19C buildings in the south part of the town. *Banff Museum* (Tel: 0779-77778), in High Street, fills in on local history, while, to the south of the town beside the golf links, *Duff House* (AM. Tel: 031-244-3101), designed by William Adam in about 1740 for the 1st Earl of Fife, is a notable example of Georgian Baroque. The house is is to become the home (from about 1993) of the Scottish Collection of Country House Art.

From Banff, B9139 heads west, in a little over 5m passing just south of ruined *Boyne Castle* (c 1580) in the wooded glen of the Burn of the Boyne, successor to an earlier castle on the coast and long a seat of the Ogilvies until forfeited after the family's support of the Young Pretender.—2m **Portsoy**, much of which is a conservation area, is known for its several restored 17 and 18C buildings as also for its ser-pentine marble, with its subtle green and reddish colouring once par-ticularly popular in France where it was even incorporated into the palace of Versailles. The stone is still to be found in a vein to the west, and it is worth going down to the picturesque small 17C harbour, beside which *Portsoy Marble* (Tel: 0261-42404) offers viewing and a shop. From Portsoy the village of *Fordyce* is only 3m south west, a quaint spot clustered around a tower-house of 1592 and with a curious small church with a belfry of 1661.

A98 runs to the south of Sandend Bay, *Sandend* itself providing the approach to ruined Findlater Castle standing sheer above the shore (park at Barnyards of Findlater, 1m west of Sandend; rough path; dan-gerous ruins). Built by the Ogilvies in 1455, Findlater later had a Gordon governor who in 1562 arrogantly refused even to reply when Mary, Queen of Scots, requested entry.

5m **Cullen** (1500 inhab. *Inf.*) is divided into an upper and a lower town by the long viaduct of the railway, closed since 1967 but surviving today as a monument as much to 19C engineering as to the power exercised by a laird of the time, the railway company having been forced to built this viaduct in 1886 when the Countess of Seafield refused to allow the line to cross the grounds of Cullen House, 1½m south. Today sections of the track serve as a pleasant coastal path, while *Cullen House* (built by the Ogilvies in about 1600 when they abandoned Findlater Castle but since much extended) has been converted into flats.

Beside the house's gates was the site of Old Cullen, established in about 1300 but in 1822–30 replaced (by the Earl of Seafield) by what is now the well planned upper town, still centred on its *Cross* (1696, but with an older plaque of the Madonna) which the citizens brought with them. The *Auld Kirk* (signed; about 1m), though, survived unmolested. Essentially of the 14C, though incorporating 12C work, the church well merits a visit for the fine sacrament house in the north wall; for the imposing Seafield Loft of 1602; and for the huge Baroque tomb, with his armoured effigy beneath the canopy, of Alexander Ogilvy, who died in 1554, the year after he had made the church collegiate. This same Alexander Ogilvy can be met again in ruined *Deskford Church*, 4m

south, where the finely carved sacrament house of 1551 bears a somewhat self-satisfied inscription recording that it was provided by him
and his wife.

Descending to the lower town, A98 touches Cullen Bay, with its three
distinctive red sandstone rocks known as the 'Three Kings of Cullen', to
reach in *5m* **Buckie** (7500 inhab.), on A942, an important fishing port
and, appropriately, home of the *Buckie Maritime Museum* (Tel: 0309-
73701). Beyond, the road fringes *Speymouth Forest* (picnic area, walks)
before reaching (*5m*) **Fochabers**, a regularly planned small town placed
here in 1776 when transferred from its site close to *Gordon Castle* (no
adm.) which, with old Fochabers' mercat cross by its entrance gates, is
passed just beyond the town. Long belonging to the Gordons, and
architecturally rarely left alone, the castle passed in 1836, on the death
of the last Duke of Gordon, to the Duke of Richmond and Gordon. All
manner of bygones, including a collection of horse-drawn vehicles, are
shown at the town's *Folk Museum*, interestingly housed in a converted
church, while *Baxters Visitor Centre* (Tel: 0343-820393), just west of
Fochabers on A96, tells the story of this well-known fine food firm started in 1868 when George Baxter, one of the many gardeners at Gordon
Castle, opened a modest local shop. Today, a Victorian kitchen and an
exact replica of George Baxter's original shop recall the past while a
video presentation and factory tour confront the visitor with today's
contrasts.—For Fochabers to *Huntly* and *Aberdeen*, see Rte 40.

The river Spey is now crossed, offering roads descending either side.
B9104, descending the east bank, in 4m reaches *Spey Bay*, where the
Tugnet Ice House Museum (Tel: 0309-73701), set up in an ice house
building of 1860, tells much about the Spey, with some emphasis on
salmon and wildlife. The other bank is served by B9015 for *Garmouth*
and *Kingston*, the former the place where Charles II landed in June
1650 after signing the Covenants. Kingston, at the estuary mouth, was
so named in 1786 by two Yorkshiremen from Kingston-upon-Hull who
came to buy timber from the Duke of Gordon and then stayed to establish a shipbuilding village; their yard closed in 1815, but wooden ships
continued to be built here until 1890. The return to A96 may be made
through the village of *Urquhart*, with a rough Stone Circle beside the
road and once the site of a Benedictine priory founded by David I and in
1454 absorbed by Pluscarden (see below).

8m **Elgin** (18,000 inhab. *Inf.*), though most visited for its historic and
still beautiful ruined cathedral, is a place with a past and a personality
of its own even if much of what is to be seen along its pleasing long and
broad High Street tends to be a replacement or token of that past.

History. Of ancient if shadowy origin, and first mentioned in 1190, Elgin was long a
royal residence, and the occupation of its castle by Edward I in 1296 marked the
northern limit of the English penetration. The 14 and 15C at least twice saw major
destruction, in 1390 when a part of the town was burnt by the 'Wolf of Badenoch'
(see also cathedral history) and in 1452 when the experience was repeated during
the struggle between Huntly and Douglas. Attention in later centuries focused
more on the cathedral, but the town as such was back in the news in 1746 when the
Young Pretender spent 11 days here before Culloden.

The axis of the town is the High Street, long, broadening and aligned
from west to east to end by the cathedral. *Lady Hill*, beside the west end
and now with a lofty column commemorating the last Duke of Gordon
(died 1836; see Gordon Castle above), was the site of the ancient castle,
today only fragmentary traces but remembered also by its chapel of St.
Mary from which this hill takes its name.

High Street still preserves a few of the old arcaded houses which
once gave it elegant character, while a hotel off the south side occupies

Thunderton House, the site (rather than the castle) of the royal residence, later the mansion of successive aristocratic families, and in 1746
the headquarters chosen by the Young Pretender. In the middle of the
street stands *St. Giles Church* (a replacement of 1828), with on its west
side a fountain marking the site of the tolbooth, and, at its east end, the
Muckle Cross, originally erected in c 1650, destroyed in 1792 and rebuilt
in 1888. The *Little Cross* (17C; restored), at the east end of High Street,
marks the old boundary between the town and cathedral lands, while
opposite is *Elgin Museum* (Tel: 0343-543675), founded in 1842 by the
Elgin Society and noted especially for its collection of fossils. To the
south of Little Cross and entered from Abbey Street are the remains of a
Franciscan friary, founded, though on another site, by Bishop John
Innes in 1479 and now incorporated into a convent with the charming
Greyfriars Chapel, well restored in 1896 by the 3rd Marquis of Bute.

Also worth a visit is *Old Mills* (Tel: 0343-540698), in Oldmills Road in
the west part of the town, a restored 17C meal mill with roots in a royal
charter of 1230 granting rights to the monks of Pluscarden.

••Elgin Cathedral (AM. Tel: 031-244-3101) was described by Bishop
Barr in the 14C as 'the ornament of the district, the glory of the kingdom,
and the admiration of foreigners'. Today, though long in ruins, Elgin's
cathedral still merits similar praise.

History. The see of Moray was in existence before 1124, but for the following
century the bishops' seat moved around between Birnie, Spynie and Kinneddar
(for all of which, see below), settling only when this cathedral was founded in 1224.
From then on, though, Elgin's story was to be punctuated by disasters. In 1270,
probably before it was even completed, the structure was badly damaged by fire,
and a century later, in 1390, the 'Wolf of Badenoch', having quarrelled with the
bishop and been excommunicated, descended upon the town and cathedral with
his 'wyld, wykked Helendmen'. The cathedral was then rebuilt with a central
tower which, however, fell in 1506, was raised again in 1558, and collapsed once
and for all in 1711. In 1555 the place was desecrated by what came to be called the
'Bloody Vespers', a murderous brawl between the Dunbar and Innes families, to be
followed, only 12 years later in 1567, by (on the orders of the Privy Council) the
removal of the lead from the roof in order to raise funds for paying the troops. In
1640 the beautiful rood screen, recorded as richly adorned and painted with bibli-
cal subjects, was torn down, and ten years later Cromwell's soldiery smashed the
tracery of the west windows. The cathedral then gradually declined into ruin,
despite the devoted attention early in the 19C of a poor shoemaker called John
Shanks, whom the government appointed official Keeper in 1825.

The ruins now visited are those of a cathedral the length of which was c
260ft and the breadth across the transepts c 120ft. Two imposing west
towers (before 1390) flank a handsome portal, deeply recessed with
mouldings, now, like so much of the cathedral's carving, much defaced.
The window above surmounts an interior arcade of four bays. Of the
Nave of six bays with double aisles about all that remains are the
stumps of some of the piers. The *Transepts* are known as the Dunbar
Aisle (north) and the Innes Aisle (south), the façade of the latter including the oldest work in the cathedral, dating from 1224 and a part which
escaped, or at any rate survived, the attack by the 'Wolf of Badenoch'; it
is pierced by a doorway with toothed moulding surmounted by a pointed oval, the round arch appearing in the upper range of windows above
the pointed.

The *Choir*, flanked by side chapels, has a graceful clerestory of
double and triple lancets of c 1270, while the raised chancel is lighted
from the east by two rows of five lancets, each framed in rectangular
mouldings, the whole surmounted by the perfect Omega window. The
south choir aisle, which has managed to keep its 15C vault, was once a
burial place of the Gordons. The tomb at the east end is that of Bishop

Winchester (died 1460); in the centre is the tomb of the Gordon 1st Earl of Huntly (died 1470); and farther west there is an armed effigy of Hay and Lochloy (died 1422).

On the north side of the central space will be found a cross-slab (9–10C), carved on one side with a cross on the arms of which are the symbols of four priests; on the other side are figures of a knight carrying his hawk, a 'spectacle' symbol, a broken mace and a half-moon.

Between the north aisle of the choir and the octagonal chapter house is the small so-called *Lavatory* with a piscina which in the 18C played its part in a remarkable story. In 1748, one Gilzean Anderson, the half-crazed widow of a soldier, returned to her native Elgin and made her home in this corner of the cathedral, using this piscina as a cradle for her baby. The boy survived, enlisted in the Hon. East India Company, rose to Lieutenant General and amassed a fortune, a part of which he bequeathed to Elgin.

The interesting octagonal *Chapter House*, though originally of the 13C, is better preserved than most of the cathedral, partly because it was well rebuilt after the 'Wolf of Badenoch's' raid and partly also because it was used as a courthouse until 1731. The elegant central pier and the groined roof are the features here.

Just north west of the cathedral stand remains of the *Bishop's House*, dating from 1557 and bearing bishops' arms. Of the four gateways in the cathedral precinct wall, the only survivor is the east gate, by the river and known as *Pann's Port*.

For Elgin to *Dufftown* and *Aberdeen*, see Rte 39.

Leaving Elgin, A96 continues to provide the axis of this Route. However, as far as Forres (12m), this main road is of little interest, so northerly (c 23m) and southerly (c 16m) loops are suggested as alternatives. Of the two the northerly loop is by far the more incidental and varied, though, to the south, little Birnie Church has deep prehistoric and Culdee roots while, in sharp contrast, thriving Benedictine Pluscarden Abbey is of both monastic and architectural importance. A generous network of roads should allow a course to be plotted to embrace sites of individual choice.

Northerly Loop (Lossiemouth, Burghead, Kinloss)

A941, leading north out of Elgin, in rather over 1m passes (east) a turn to the hamlet of *Spynie*, in the churchyard of which is buried Ramsay MacDonald (died 1937; see below), just north being **Spynie Palace** (no adm. but well seen from outside), the great ruined castellar palace of the bishops of Moray, serving as seat of the see until the consecration of Elgin in 1244 and thereafter as bishop's palace until 1686. Even in ruin the most splendid bishop's palace in Scotland, Spynie uncompromisingly illustrates that medieval bishops were—and indeed had to be—as feudal and military as their lay contemporaries. The early castle (14C) was a curtain-walled court, complete with angle towers and protected on the south and east by a moat, to which early in the 15C Bishop John Innes added his arms over the main entrance. But Spynie's most prominent feature is the massive David's Tower (c 1470–80), built by Bishop David Stewart as defence against the Gordons, whose chief, the Earl of Huntly, he had rashly excommunicated. A century later, in 1562 and with the Gordons no quieter, Mary, Queen of Scots, stopped here during her combined royal progress and running campaign against that family.—A contrast is provided by *Kinneddar*, now little more than a churchyard beside B9135, 2m north, but also, before Elgin, a seat and castle of the see of Moray.

Lossiemouth (7000 inhab.) is one with *Branderburgh*, the former representing the older town, founded as a port for Elgin after the Lossie silted up, the latter a 19C creation by the local laird, Colonel Brander, to meet the needs of the booming herring fishing industry. The sea is still the theme here (Fisheries Museum), balanced now though by the air as represented by the adjacent RAF airfield. James Ramsay MacDonald, the first Labour prime minister, was born in 1866 at 1 Gregory Place (south east Lossiemouth), where the house, with a plaque, can be seen, though only from the outside.

B9040 fringes the north of the airfield and in 4 or so miles meets a turn south into the village of **Duffus**, for an ancient church and a spectacular castle. *St. Peter's Kirk*, a humble, lost little place just east of the present village, has roots and some stonework of at least 1226, the base of a 14C tower, the remains of a 16C porch, and, in the churchyard, the shaft of the 14C parish cross, this last reminding that this church stood at the heart of its village until planned 'new' Duffus arose in the early 19C. About *Duffus Castle*, though, 1½m south east, there is certainly nothing humble. Although of no particular historical significance—the castle was a seat of the De Moravias, or Murrays, and in 1151 David I stayed here when founding Kinloss Abbey—this place is a theatrical complex rising out of the flat fields; a great circular ditch protects a large motte on which balance a battered tower and bailey wall, both of about 1300, the former split open, sliding, and dramatically illustrating the hazards of building massive stone keeps on earthen mottes never designed to support such. *Gordonstoun School* (no adm), 1m north east of Duffus village, educated the Duke of Edinburgh and the Prince of Wales.

Burghead, 4m west of Duffus, is a small fishing town laid out in the early 19C along a stubby headland that had already known successive Iron Age and Norse forts. Today the attraction here is the intriguing *Burghead Well*. Within the Iron Age defences, cut into the rock and fed by a spring, this is in fact something of an archaeological mystery in terms both of date and purpose. Doubtless Iron Age defenders, and probably others before them, drank from this spring, the site later perhaps being converted to use as an early Christian baptistry, some evidence for this being the steps down into the water and, in the corners, a basin and a pedestal.

From Burghead B9089 in 7m reaches *Kinloss*, with, just south of the west part of the town, *Kinloss Abbey*, today a sorry, minor ruin, but once an important Cistercian foundation (1151) of David I who, lost in the forest, chose this site, then a clearing, after being guided to it by a white dove. After the Reformation the buildings served as a quarry, but there survive a round-headed archway, the vaulted east end of the church, and a part of the abbot's house. *Findhorn*, a fishing village and small resort 2m north at the narrow entrance to Findhorn Bay, is the third village of this name; its two predecessors, to the north west, were both swept away, the first in 1694 by storm-driven sand and the second by a flood in 1701.—*Forres* (see below) is reached in 3m.

Southerly Loop (Birnie and Pluscarden)

Birnie Church, 2½m south of Elgin on a minor road between A941 and B9010, secluded and modest though it is now, nevertheless represents a religious site, first pagan and then Christian, in use, if perhaps with breaks, from millenia ago until today. Several standing stones—one by the Minister's Gate, others incorporated in the churchyard wall—define a site of prehistoric ritual, followed in c 500 by a Celtic church dedicated to St. Brendan and followed again in 1140 by the present small Norman building, seat of the bishopric of Moray before Kinned-dar, Spynie and Elgin and believed now to be Scotland's oldest parish church in unbroken use for worship. Architecturally an odd feature is that there is no east window, lighting coming through round-headed Norman windows; spiritually, the saying goes that to be thrice prayed for in Birnie Kirk will 'either mend ye or end ye'.

Pluscarden Abbey (Tel: 034389-257), 5m south west of Birnie by minor roads, is a religious house on a far grander scale, ancient in origin but today occupied and being restored by Benedictine monks.

History. The abbey was founded in 1230 by Alexander II for the little known order of the Valliscaulians whose parent home in France was the priory of Val des Choux, the valley of the cabbages. Although damaged by Edward I in 1303, the abbey's worst experience came in 1390 when, as a dependency of the see of Moray, it was attacked and burnt by the 'Wolf of Badenoch', enraged at his excommunication by the bishop. In 1454 Pluscarden absorbed the priory of Urquhart and became Benedictine, remaining such until suppression in 1560. There followed centuries of post-Reformation decay, with the abbey's buildings frequently serving as a quarry, until Pluscarden was bought by the Marquis of Bute. His son gave it to the Benedictines of Prinknash in England who since 1948 have followed a steady programme of restoration.

The main block of the abbey is made up of the east wing of the monastery, with the chancel, transepts and central tower of the church. Of the nave only foundations survive, but a part of the cloister has been restored. Inside the church, features of particular note are traces of murals (c 1500) showing St. John writing the Book of Revelations on Patmos; in the north transept, windows by Sadie McLellan (1960) portraying symbols showing the role of Mary in Christ's life; in the chancel (restored 1980) a 16C sacrament house from Flanders; and the Lady Chapel (opened on request), almost entirely of original masonry from the abbey's founding in 1230 but, by contrast, with modern windows made in the abbey workshops. The abbey's precinct wall, surrounding three sides, is, after that of St. Andrews, the longest in Scotland.

From Pluscarden, *Forres* (see immediately below) is reached in 8m by minor roads followed by B9010, passing close to *Blervie Castle*, a 16C tower, successor perhaps of the wooden castle in which Malcolm I may have been murdered in 954.

12m (from Elgin by A96) **Forres** (8500 inhab. *Inf.*) is a pleasant small town, its name inseparable from Shakespeare's 'Macbeth' but otherwise far removed from its usually violent royal connection going back to the 10C and the shadowy kings of Scotia.

History. King Donald I was killed at Forres in c 900, and his son, Malcolm I, is said to have lived here, perhaps being murdered at Blervie Castle, 4m south east, in 954. Malcolm's son, Duff, was in turn slain by the governor of Forres in 967. In the early 11C Duncan I held his court here, and it was on their way to attend it that Macbeth and Banquo met on the 'blasted heath' (see below) the 'weird sisters', just three of the witches for which Forres was notorious. Whether Macbeth's subsequent murder of Duncan took place here, or at Cawdor, or, as placed by Shakespeare, at Inverness, or if indeed he was murdered at all, will probably never be agreed. Forres continued to be a royal residence, but after the foundation of the powerful bishopric at Elgin in 1224 the castle's, and with it the town's, importance declined.

The castle has long disappeared, its site above the west end of High Street now marked by a memorial to a doctor hero of the Crimea, but something of the town's past can be experienced in the *Falconer Museum* (Tel: 0309-73701) in Tolbooth Street and named after Dr Hugh Falconer (1808–65), palaeontologist and botanist. Another aspect of the past is offered by *Dallas Dhu Distillery* (AM. Tel: 031-244-3101, or 0309-72938), 1m south, with a visitor centre, video presentation and picnic area.

But it is *Sueno's Stone* that provides the most exciting link with the local past, suggesting as it so vividly does that a great battle was fought here, though by whom against whom remains guesswork; that Sweyne of Denmark defeated Malcolm II in 1008 is one suggestion, but that this was the scene of a Norse defeat is also advanced. Whatever its story, here is a slim shaft, 23ft high, dated to the 9–11C, and bearing martial carving of mounted and foot soldiers, of headless bodies and bodiless heads (a number of skeletons were found here in 1813) and, particularly interestingly, of what may be a broch.

Forres lies beside some attractive and also unusual scenery provided by the river Findhorn, ascending south through its cuts towards Randolph's Leap and Ardclach Bell Tower (see Rte 38) and, close to Forres, entering the almost enclosed pocket of Findhorn Bay. This bay is flanked on the west by Culbin Forest, now covering a large area of dune formed largely by a storm of 1694. A panoramic impression of much of the district can be enjoyed from *Nelson's Tower*, erected in 1806 by admirers of the admiral on a hill at the south east of Forres.

For Forres to *Grantown-on-Spey* and *Aberdeen*, see Rte 38.

4m **Brodie Castle** (NTS. Tel: 03094-371), just north of A96, represents an unbroken family association since these lands were granted to the Brodies in 1160 by Malcolm IV. The early castle was burnt in 1645 during the Civil War, thereafter being largely rebuilt and extended in both the 17 and 19C. The interior shows an outstanding collection of paintings—embracing 17C Dutch, 18C and early 19C English watercolours and French Impressionists—notable late 17C plasterwork, French furniture and porcelain of varied provenance. A woodland walk, wildlife hide, adventure playground, and a picnic area are all to be enjoyed in the park.—*Darnaway Estate Visitor Centre* (Tel: 0309-72213), 1½m south of A96 roughly opposite Brodie Castle, offers an estate exhibition, woodland walks, picnic area and suchlike.

Hardmuir, or, more popularly, *Macbeth's Hillock*, to the north of A96 about a mile after leaving Brodie Castle and now disappointingly cultivated and wooded, is supposed to be the 'blasted heath' on which Macbeth consulted the witches.—*4m* **Auldearn**, where 17C *Boath Dovecot* (NTS) now stands on the motte which once supported the 12C royal castle of Eren. But, however peaceful the dovecot, the emphasis here is on battle, for here on 9 May 1645 Montrose raised his standard as a prelude to one of his most brilliant victories in which—and NTS provide an excellent plan and explanation—with 1500 foot and 200 horse he routed a force of Covenanters under General Urry.

3m **Nairn** (7500 inhab. *Inf.*), today essentially a family resort with long beaches backed by links, was long regarded as marking the boundary between the Lowlands and the Highlands, James VI remarking that the inhabitants of one end did not understand the language of the other. However it is now many years since Gaelic was spoken here, though the *Fishertown Museum*, in King Street, captures something of the past, with particular emphasis on herring fishing (Tel: 0667-52064).—For Nairn to *Grantown-on-Spey* and *Aberdeen*, see Rte 38.

At Nairn this Route quits A96 to take a more southerly line along B9090 for Cawdor Castle, the prehistoric site of the Clava Cairns and the battlefield of Culloden. An alternative northerly loop visiting Fort George is described immediately below.

TO INVERNESS VIA FORT GEORGE. B9092 and unclassified roads in 8m reach **Fort George** (AM. Tel: 031-244-3101), built in 1748, guarding the narrow neck of Moray Firth and ranking as one of the most outstanding examples in Britain of Hanoverian military architecture; an irregular polygon with six bastions, the fort accommodated some 2000 men and today houses the *Museum of the Queen's Own Highlanders* (Seaforth and Cameron. Lovat Scouts. Tel: 0463-224380). From Fort George, B9006 and B9039, passing Inverness Airport, in some 6m meet A96 close to *Castle Stuart* (Tel: 0463-790745), ancient seat of the earls of Moray. From here Inverness is reached in 5m by A96, off which in 1m a minor road leads south to Culloden.

Continuing the main Route, B9090 out of Nairn in *5m* reaches **Cawdor Castle** (Tel: 06677-615), the 14C seat of the Thanes of Cawdor, the title promised to Macbeth by the witches on the 'blasted heath' (see Hardmuir above). But this was in 1040, the castle of which date stood about a mile to the north east, whereas what is seen today is a sturdy central tower of 1372 (fortified 1454) surrounded and softened by now mellow 16C buildings (remodelled in the 17C). Inside, there is much of interest, whether 17C Flemish and English tapestries; several portraits by artists such as Cotes, Romney, Lawrence and Reynolds; or curiosities ranging from the iron gate of Loch-in-Dorb Castle, through muskets captured from the French in 1797 when Lord Cawdor repulsed their farcical invasion of Wales (Fishguard), to some homely 18 and 19C domestic and kitchen equipment. Outside, gardens and several nature trails (booklet) ensure that the best of the beautifully wooded grounds is enjoyed.

Beyond Cawdor, and just after crossing the Nairn, B9090 is exchanged for B9091, close to the road junction and *2m* from Cawdor being the entrance to *Kilravock Castle* (Tel: 06678-258), an estate dating back to the 13C and since 1460, when the keep was built as successor to an earlier structure, the seat of the Roses of Kilravock. In 1553 the 10th Baron added what is now the main part of the castle, and it was he who nine years later here entertained Mary, Queen of Scots. Two centuries later, on the eve of Culloden, the 17th Baron, though not a Jacobite, dined the Young Pretender.—*1m* Croy where B9091 merges to become B9006.

4m B9006 reaches a triangle of minor roads (enclosing the Cumberland Stone) just short of Culloden battlefield site (see below). *Clava Cairns (NTS and AM), with Camster's cairns on Rte 59 one of the two most exciting and archaeologically important cairn groups on Scotland's mainland, will be found less than a mile to the south across the river Nairn. Probably overlapping the Stone and Bronze ages (say 2000–1500 BC), here are three large burial mounds, each surrounded by standing stones, and also, at the north west of the site, a small stone circle on its own. Two of the cairns, those at the south west and north east, are passage-grave type, i.e. the burial chambers are approached by long narrow passages through the cairns. The central cairn is ring-type, and, though with no entrance, is unique in having unexplained stone pavements radiating from it. Many of the standing and other stones bear the mysterious ritual cup indentations and other markings, these best seen in some profusion on a kerb stone on the north side of the north east cairn. Within the small stone circle—modest compared to its neighbour cairns and possibly therefore representing a more modest burial—a depression suggests a grave, and one of the stones bears many cup markings.

*Culloden Battlefield (NTS. Site always open. Visitor Centre, Tel: 0463-790607) lies either side of today's B9006 (there was no road here at the time of the battle), extending for about 1½m westward from the

Cumberland Stone road triangle. Fought on 16 April 1746 between the Young Pretender and the Duke of Cumberland, Culloden, the last land battle of any significance to be fought in Britain, not only ended for ever any serious hopes that the Stuarts might regain the throne but also signalled the beginning of the end for a Highland way of life that had endured for centuries.

The Young Pretender's army, covering Inverness, consisted of some 5000 Highlanders, ill-armed, ill-fed and exhausted by an abortive attempt to surprise the enemy the night before. Against them the Duke of Cumberland advanced from Nairn at the head of 9000 men. The action began at 1 pm with an artillery duel, opened by the Jacobites but in which the Hanoverians quickly gained the upper hand, slaughtering the lines of Highlanders. The latter's only chance lay in the famed élan of a Highland charge, but for various reasons—the Young Pretender seems to have been willing to leave the initiative to Cumberland—the order came too late and, despite a fearless impetuosity which almost miraculously swept through the devastating grape-shot and even broke the Hanoverian first line, the attack faltered and the few survivors broke in retreat which quickly became a general Jacobite rout. Of the Hanoverian troops only 76 were killed, but 1200 Highlanders fell.

The carnage was enormously increased by Cumberland's brutal order to spare none of the wounded. For several days after the battle search parties massacred wounded clansmen who had dragged themselves into the neighbouring woods and farms, while Cumberland's cavalry even killed off spectators who had come out from Inverness. And when, after the capitulation of the town, the provost of Inverness ventured a protest against the inhumanity of the soldiery, it was only to be kicked down the stairs.

Now owned by the National Trust for Scotland and with its heart restored to something like its original topography, this site is something of a shrine, combining much of historical and military interest with more than a touch of Highland poignancy still insistent after two and a half centuries.

The natural boulder known as the *Cumberland Stone* is not, as sometimes supposed, the spot from which the Duke directed the battle—he was in fact well forward—though it is reasonable to accept that he was here beforehand, perhaps using this position as one from which to make his tactical plan. From here B9006 within 500 yards reaches the Hanoverian lines, near here being the NTS *Visitor Centre* which admirably explains the battle and its significance by means of a historical display and a video programme, backed up, for those in search of more detail, by a guide book and battle map folder. Here, too, a survivor of the battle, is *Old Leonach Cottage*, now given period furnishing.

The next 500 yards represent the heart of the site; initially the gap between the two armies but soon the field of battle. Most features of interest are to the south of B9006, paths from the Visitor Centre passing the *Well of the Dead*, a spring at which wounded Highlanders were killed while trying to drink; the scattered stones of the *Graves of the Clans*; the *Memorial Cairn* (1881) overlooking the scene of the fiercest of the fighting; and, to the west, the *Irish Stone* (1963) honouring the Irish who fought in the Jacobite cause.

From Culloden B9006 in *5m* reaches **Inverness**, see Rte 51.

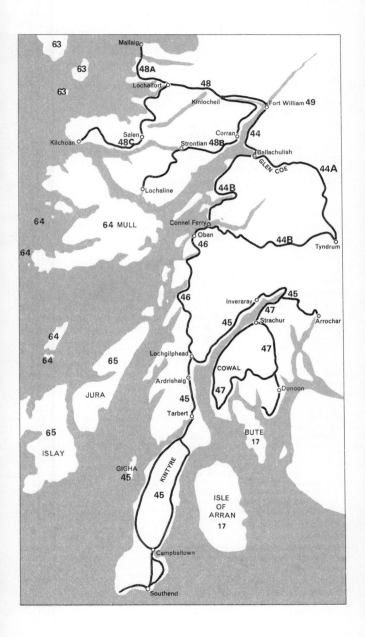

With minor variations the part of Scotland covered by Rtes 44 to 48 corresponds to the former county of Argyll (less its islands) which, under the local government reorganisation of 1975, became absorbed into the Region of Strathclyde. The name has nevertheless been retained here, because for centuries this has been Argyll (the Coast of the Gaels), a name which, whatever new artifical boundaries may be imposed, will surely live on in popular and local usage.

Geographically, as covered by the following five Routes, Argyll comprises, from north to south, the scenic chunk of land (virtually an island) lying between A830 (Fort William to Lochailort) in the north and the Sound of Mull in the south (the splendid districts of Ardgour, Kingairloch, Sunart, Morvern, Moidart and Ardnamurchan); and a true mainland defined by Glen Coe in the north, by the sea on the west, by A82 and Loch Lomond on the east, and southward tapering away into the long thin finger of Kintyre and the many-pronged peninsula of Cowal.

With scenery ranging from Highland and fretted coastal grandeur to forest and rich farming land; with a concentration of prehistoric sites unequalled elsewhere in Scotland, except perhaps in Orkney; historically the ancient cradle of Scotland, associated also with Columban Christianity; and having along its coast the embarkation ports for most of the Inner and Outer Hebrides, Argyll has long been a magnet for tourists.

The grandest scenery is in the north. Here, behind the lovely coasts of Moidart and Ardnamurchan, are the mountains of *Moidart*, *Sunart* and *Ardgour*, while across Loch Linnhe rises *Ben Nevis* (not actually in Argyll) with to its south the peaks that enclose *Glen Coe*. From here a wilderness of high mountain runs away south, across lonely Glen Etive towards the mass of *Ben Cruachan*, rising 3695ft above Loch Awe and with a power station built deep within its southern flank. The mountain mass ends with the heights of *Argyll Forest Park* filling the north east corner of Cowal, but even if, west and south from here, the mountain grandeur eases, Argyll still continues as a scenic country of hills, moor, woods and, above all, seascapes.

The historic interest of Argyll—and, however remote in time, the physical reminders are plentiful—is to be found mainly in the south, though two places of outstanding importance, Glen Coe and Glenfinnan, are in the north.

The extraordinary valley of burial cairns and ritual stones to the north of *Lochgilphead* evidences a sizeable and active population here in prehistoric times. In the early centuries of the Dark Ages Gaelic-speaking Celts (Scots), immigrants from Ireland, began to appear, people who by the end of the 5C had driven out or assimilated the native inhabitants and founded the small Kingdom of Dalriada, with its water and bog surrounded capital on the hill of *Dunadd*. With them these people are said to have brought from Ireland the sacred Stone of Destiny. By the mid 6C Christian missionaries were coming across, amongst them St Columba who by tradition landed at *Keil* at the foot of Kintyre, later moving on to establish himself on Iona. In 574 he is thought to have come to Dunadd and there officiated at the first Christian 'coronation', that of his kinsman Aidan. The Norse era followed, with raids and the establishment of coastal settlements which gradually became independent territories over which the Dalriadic kings lost power. (Kintyre remained under Norse influence until the 13C). Meanwhile the capital of Dalriada is said to have moved (with the Stone of Destiny) to *Dunstaffnage*, north of Oban, and it could have been from here (c 850) that Kenneth Macalpine, partly by arms and partly by diplomacy, joined his kingdom to that of the central Picts and moved his court and the Stone of Destiny away from Argyll to Scone.

In Argyll there followed centuries during which the clans grew, spread and fought one another. During the early 12C a native ruler of Morvern, Somerled, a descendant of a branch of the Dalriadic royal house and married to the daughter of a Norse chief, rose to great power and through his three sons founded the various branches of Clan Macdonald. (It would be a Macdonald, John of Islay, who in 1386 would formally assume the title of Lord of the Isles, a lordship which claimed sway over plenty of mainland as well.) Later in the 12C Cailein Mor (Great Colin) of Loch Awe started the Campbell line, their chiefs later becoming earls, marquises and dukes of Argyll. These clans and others fought for power and land throughout Argyll, sometimes recognising, sometimes defying the Scottish kings. At the opening of the 14C Bruce was in Kintyre, occupying *Tarbert Castle*, but it was not until 1495 that royal authority was really asserted when James IV at *Mingary Castle* received the submission of the Macdonald Lord of the Isles. In the 17C Argyll had its share of the violence of the Civil War, and thereafter it was three times to achieve historical note. In 1685, after the Marquis of Argyll had tried to support Monmouth's rebellion, the Marquis of Atholl was ordered to punish the rebels, a task which the men of Atholl, eager to avenge Argyll's destruction of Atholl in 1653, discharged with brutal efficiency; secondly in 1692, with the infamous massacre of Glen Coe; and finally in 1745 when the Young Pretender raised his standard at Glenfinnan.

With its long, separated peninsulas Argyll is a scattered area for touring, but the route suggested below takes in most of what is best, both of history and scenery. The approach may be made either through Cowal or from Loch Lomond to *Inveraray*, long the headquarters of the Campbells (Argylls). South from here the unusual *Auchindrain Museum* is passed on the way to *Lochgilphead*, whence if time allows Kintyre may be toured. Otherwise the Oban road is taken, along or close to which are several important sites. These are the *Achnabreck Farm* cup and ring-marked rocks just outside Lochgilphead; *Castle Sween*, possibly the oldest stone castle in Scotland; *Dunadd*, Dalriada's first capital, where carvings possibly associated with early kingship ritual still survive; the concentration of prehistoric burial cairns and ritual stones between Dunadd and Kilmartin; and **Oban** itself, the principal town of Argyll and port for many excursions, notably to Mull and Iona. Just north is *Dunstaffnage Castle*, perhaps the site of Dalriada's second capital, then at *Connel* a diversion may be made c 14 miles east, to visit the four-hundred megawatt power station deep within the mountain of *Cruachan*. North from Connel the road leads to Loch Leven, down to which descends *Glen Coe*, as notorious for its massacre as it is renowned for its scenery.

A short way north of Loch Leven the *Corran* car ferry crosses Loch Linnhe to the western peninsula. Here there is a choice of roads: to *Lochaline* (car ferry to Mull); or west along Loch Sunart into *Ardnamurchan*, with *Mingary Castle* and, beyond, the lighthouse that stands on the most westerly point of mainland Britain; or, either north or through the centre, to the Fort William to Mallaig road, with *Glenfinnan* (monument and National Trust Visitor Centre) and other sites associated with the launching of the '45.

44 Tyndrum to Fort William

There is a choice of two beautiful Highland roads—A. Via Glen Coe (46m) or B. Via Connel (68m)—the two joining at South Ballachulish, on Loch Leven 13m short of Fort William. Both historically and scenically the Glen Coe road is the better known, though in fact the Connel alternative provides more varied and better loch scenery, passes more places of interest and allows a short diversion to Dunstaffnage Castle and Oban, both described under Rte 46. Separated by a wild mountain mass pierced by several long sea lochs, the two roads offer no connecting links.

A.   Via Glen Coe

A82.—High, bare moor and mountain, followed by a descent through sombre and steep-sided Glen Coe and finishing at sea level with views across the long narrow arm of Loch Linnhe to the mountains of Ardgour.

SOME HOTELS. **Glen Coe** (east, at head of the glen). *King's House.* Tel: 08556-259. **Glencoe**. *Glencoe, PA39 4HW.* Tel: 08552-245. **Ballachulish**. *Ballachulish, PA39 4JY.* Tel: 08552-606. **Onich**. *Lodge on the Loch*, Creag Dhu, PH33 6RY. Tel: 08553-238. *Allt-Nan-Ros*, PH33 6RY. Tel: 08553-210.

Total distance 46m.—*17m* **Glen Coe** (*White Corries—King's House*).—*10m* **NTS Glen Coe Visitor Centre**.—*6m* **South Ballachulish**.—*4m* **Corran Ferry**.—*9m* **Fort William**.

The **Railway** does not run through Glen Coe but leaves the road in 9m at Loch Tulla to traverse the desolate *Moor of Rannoch*—a national nature reserve known for its variety of mire flora and fauna—and reach lonely *Rannoch Station* (see Rte 27). Just north of the station the watershed is crossed close to little *Loch Chlaidheimh*, the name meaning 'sword' and deriving, it is said, from a meeting between two chiefs who had agreed to parley unarmed. Both in fact wore swords, so, having failed to outwit one another, they hurled their weapons into the water. Just beyond *Corrour*, beside Loch Siolaig, the line reaches its highest point (1354ft) before descending along the east shore of *Loch Treig*, so furrowed by burns that the track requires some 150 bridges. For Hydro-Electric use of Loch Treig, and the road from the north end of the loch to Fort William, see Rte 50.

For **Tyndrum**, and the approach from Glasgow, see Rte 20. A82 leads into increasingly lonely country, soon crossing the watershed at 1045ft and in *6m* reaching the hamlet of *Bridge of Orchy*, below (east) Beinn Dorain (3524ft), the 'stormy mountain' of the poems of Duncan Ban MacIntyre, the 'Burns of the Highlands', born beside nearby Loch Tulla (see also Rte 44B). From here A8005 winds a brief 3m north west before petering out as a hill track which, constructed for military purposes in 1751, represents the old road and traverses the empty tract of Black Mount before rejoining A82 in some 8m near White Corries chairlift and King's House Hotel. Beyond Bridge of Orchy, in *3m*, A82 touches the north east corner of Loch Tulla, a spot from which a path leading north east in 1m reaches the ruin of *Achallader Castle*, a stronghold originally of the Fletchers but later of the Glenlyon Campbells, said here to have put the finishing touches to the plot for the Glencoe massacre.

In *8m* a small crossroads is reached, the south arm of which (the old military road mentioned above) is the approach to *White Corries* ski centre, with tows and a chairlift, the latter riding to 2100ft and affording sweeping views (Tel: 08556-226). The road opposite is for *King's House Hotel*, an inn once important as a military stage but now a grandly sited modernised hotel. Just beyond (1m), a small road descends south west down remote and scenic *Glen Etive, in 11m (from A82) reaching Loch Etive (see also Rte 44B, Taynuilt).

King's House Hotel marks the upper entry to *Glen Coe, Scotland's most famous and most infamous glen, a great cleft of wild mountain grandeur down which, and surprisingly gently, the road descends for some 12m to sea level. With a name inescapably associated with the massacre of 1692, Glen Coe is equalled only by Culloden in its echoes of clan lament, but whereas Culloden stands for gallant sacrifice in honest battle, here the story is one of treachery and the murder of the harmless and defenceless. But however much the glen's savage and often dark slopes may be cited as reflecting that shameful February night, the prosaic fact is that in the main the massacre took place some ten miles below, where the glen is almost soft and green. Nevertheless the association is unavoidable, and since this valley surely witnessed both the approach of the Campbells and also the desperate flight of some of the Macdonald survivors, a summary of the story seems appropriate here.

The Highlanders had not willingly accepted William and Mary in place of James VII/II, and the London government fixed 31 December 1691 as the final date for submission. Macdonald of Glen Coe had delayed until the last moment, and when at length he went to Fort William he found no magistrate there competent to receive his oath and was forced to go to Inveraray, far to the south on Loch Fyne. When the papers arrived in Edinburgh, a few days late, they were suppressed by the Under Secretary of State, Sir John Dalrymple, Master of Stair, who was eager to use this opportunity of making an example and issued instructions which included the words 'To plunder their lands, or drive off their cattle, would be only to render them desperate; they must all be slaughtered, and the manner of execution must be sure, secret and effectual'. The task fell to Campbell of Glenlyon, who was instructed 'to fall upon the rebels and put all to the sword under seventy', and in particular to ensure that 'the old fox and his cubs do on no account escape your hands'.

Such were the orders received by Campbell of Glenlyon on 12 February 1692, by which date he and his 128 soldiers (feigning that they were on their way to Fort William where, however, their accommodation was not yet prepared) had already lived for two weeks on friendly terms with their Macdonald hosts. The massacre began at four the following morning, and of the 200 Macdonalds some 40 were slain, scant attention being paid to the age limit and the victims including the very aged, the bedridden and children. Others died from exposure, and even more would have perished had not storm and snow prevented Glenlyon's soldiers from blocking the passes as ordered.

Three years later, as the result of an official inquiry, the Scottish parliament voted that the killing had been murder. But King William's guilt was slurred over, and he, in his turn, sheltered the Master of Stair, who suffered only dismissal, while Glenlyon and his soldiers, by now serving in Flanders, escaped untouched.

If Glen Coe's infamy is perhaps largely for the historically sensitive, its scenery is for all, much of this (though not the site of the massacre) now in the care of the National Trust for Scotland who own some 14,000 acres stretching from upper Glen Etive across the Coe to include the great rock wall of Aonach Eagach. Outstanding walking and climbing country rich in Highland flora and fauna, its detail, together with the story of the massacre, is explained at the Trust's Visitor Centre (see below).

Descending the glen from King's House the road in under *3m* curves west below (north) the *Devil's Staircase*, a section of an old drover and military road, now in disrepair, which climbs and crosses the hills (1754ft) to reach Kinlochleven. Beyond, to the north as the road drops into the pass proper, hangs *Aonach Eagach*, while opposite rise the *Three Sisters*, with, towards their west end and high on the face of Aonach Dubh, a cleft known as *Ossian's Cave*, traditionally if improbably the birthplace of the bard. *Loch Achtriochtan*, haunt of watersprites, is skirted to reach (*7m*) the *NTS Visitor Centre* (Tel: 08552-307). Just beyond, the road rounds *Signal Rock* (across the river; footbridge), once a look-out and rallying place of the Macdonalds, to enter the lower glen which, with (*3m*) *Glencoe* village on sea Loch Leven, was the main scene of the massacre. In the village the *Glencoe and North Lorne Folk Museum* (Tel: Ballachulish Tourist Information, 08552-296), housed in restored crofts, shows bygones, Macdonald and Jacobite relics, and agricultural and local slate industry material.

From Glencoe village the round of Loch Leven can be made, which, though scenic, is slow and adds some 15m.

1m **Ballachulish** (1000 inhab. *Inf.*) was long known for its slate quarries which flourished between 1693 to 1955. On the island of St. Munda in the loch there are Macdonald graves.—*2m* **South Ballachulish**, where Rte 44B joins from the south, combined Rte 44 here crossing the bridge spanning the narrow neck of Loch Leven.

From here northward the drive is more relaxed, for the most part along a straight fast road beside the narrow inner arm of Loch Linnhe with views across to the alternating valleys and high ground of Ardgour (see Rte 48B).—*4m* **Corran** *Ferry* (Crossing 5 minutes. Daily, frequent. Tel: 08555-243) provides a car ferry service to Ardgour and a good road link across Morvern to Lochaline and the ferry to Mull.—*9m* **Fort William**, see Rte 49.

B.   Via Connel

A85 to Connel. A828 to South Ballachulish. A82 to Fort William.—
Highland and loch scenery, particularly fine at the Pass of Brander
where the road skirts Loch Awe below Ben Cruachan (3695ft). From
Connel northwards, sea lochs and islands.

SOME HOTELS. **Taynuilt**. *Polfearn*, PA35 1JQ. Tel: 08662-251.
Ardanaiseig. *Ardanaiseig*, PH35 1HE. Tel: 08663-333. **Connel**. *Falls of Lora*, PA37 1PB. Tel: 063171-483. **Port Appin**. *Airds*, PA38 4DF. Tel: 063173-236. **Keil** (**Duror**). *Stewart*, Glen Duror, PA38 4BW. Tel: 063174-268.

Total distance 68m.—*12m* **Dalmally**.—*6m* **Cruachan Power Station**.—
5m **Taynuilt**.—*6m* **Connel**.—*15m* **Port Appin (Lismore)**.—*11m* **South Ballachulish**.—*13m* **Fort William**.

For **Tyndrum**, and the approach from Glasgow, see Rte 20. A85 runs with green Glen Lochy below (south) the heights of Ben Lui (3708ft) to merge with Glen Orchy coming in from the north east and in *12m* reach **Dalmally**. From here a short diversion south west along the old Invera-ray road in 1m reaches *Monument Hill*, providing a splendid view towards Kilchurn Castle and across the islanded waters of northern Loch Awe. The monument is to Duncan Ban MacIntyre (1724–1812), the 'Burns of the Highlands', but more interesting perhaps, and certainly more intriguing, is the flat stone beside it, seemingly of unknown origin and bearing a neat incised cross.

Just beyond Dalmally A85 touches the north east arm of **Loch Awe**, a huge long and narrow loch slicing some 23m south west, the southern and main part of which is described under Rte 46. However, Macnaughtons and Macarthurs may choose to divert 3m south along A819 for a glimpse of two islands, *Innis Fraoch* with a ruined castle of the former and *Innishail* with the remains of a 13C church and a Macarthur burial ground. *Inistrynish*, beside A819 just south east of Innishail and now no longer an island but a stubby promontory, has a name (Isle of sculptors) inviting speculation, one suggestion being that this was once perhaps the site of a colony of tomb carvers.

Ruined *Kilchurn Castle* (No adm., but well seen from outside), occupying a spit jutting into Loch Awe's north east arm, is an oblong structure with a square keep, the latter built in 1440 by Sir Colin Campbell of Glenorchy, ancestor of the Breadalbane family. The remainder represents addition of 1693 by Ian, Earl of Breadalbane, whose arms, together with those of his wife, are over the gateway. Until 1740 the castle was occupied by the family, but in 1746 it was garrisoned by

Hanoverian troops and in 1879 the top of one of the towers fell in a gale. From Lochawe village, a short way beyond, there are summer cruises on the Edwardian steamer, 'Lady Rowena' (Tel: 08382-440).

A85 now hugs the north east and north west arms of Loch Awe to reach (6m from Dalmally) *Cruachan Power Station (Tel: 08662-673), a reversible pumped-storage development which uses energy from thermal stations at times when the load is low (night and weekends) to pump water from Loch Awe to a reservoir filling a high corrie on Ben Cruachan. The water stored here is then used to generate electricity to meet daytime peak loads, two inclined shafts supplying water to reversible pump/turbines in a power station deep within the mountain and the water then being carried down to Loch Awe by a single tailrace.

Opened by the Queen in 1965, Cruachan represents Scotland's first large pumped-storage installation. For the visitor the attractions are a picnic area beside the loch; a Visitor Centre with displays and literature explaining the scheme; and a drive along the tunnel (about ½m) to the power station in the heart of the mountain. This last—whether for technical interest, or simply as an experience, or even for botanical reasons for a special leaflet is provided describing the plants growing here in totally artificial conditions—is very popular and, since the number of visitors that can be accepted is limited, the Electricity Board advise early arrival.

Immediately beyond the power station, and still beside the water, A85 enters the **Pass of Brander**, scenically quickly narrowing as the loch becomes the river Awe, historically the scene of a battle (1308) between Bruce and Clan MacDougall of Lorne.

5m **Taynuilt**, now a pleasant village resort, was once Scotland's main iron-smelting centre, using charcoal from the oak and beech forests which in the 18 and 19C still covered this district. This period is well recalled by restored *Bonawe Iron Furnace* (AM. Tel: 031-244-3121) which was opened in 1753 and operated until 1874. The furnace prided itself on the cannon and shot it provided for the navy, and the Nelson monument near the church was erected by the ironworkers in 1805 immediately after Trafalgar, even before, it is said, the admiral's remains had reached England. Here the river Awe flows into *Loch Etive*, curving here to run west to meet salt water at Connel or to pierce some 12m north east to the lonely reaches of Glen Etive which in turn ascends to the heights above Glen Coe. From the pier there is a good view up the loch on which there are cruises between Easter and mid October (Tel: 08662-430).

GARDENS DIVERSIONS. *Barguillan Garden* (Tel: 08662-333), 3m south west of Taynuilt on the Glen Lonan road, a secluded garden with a loch, is a sanctuary for woodland and water birds.—A longer diversion (B845, 20m return) may be made southward up Glen Nant (forest trail) to reach *Kilchrenan*, 3m east of which are *Ardanaiseig Gardens* (Tel: 08663-333), dating, with the house, from 1834 and affording spectacular views across northern Loch Awe (see also Some Hotels above).

3m *Achnacloich Woodland Garden* (Tel: 063171-221), on a promontory into Loch Etive, provides incidental walks and views westward towards Mull and eastward to the mass of Ben Cruachan.—3m **Connel**, which, though only a village, marks a water and road junction of some importance. Here a narrow channel links Loch Etive with the wide, islanded intersection of Loch Linnhe, the Firth of Lorne and, coming in from the west, the Sound of Mull, the resultant tides and currents forming, below Connel's bridge, the churning water known as the *Falls of Lora*. And here, too, Rte 46 joins from the south, Dunstaffnage Castle and Oban being respectively only 3 and 5m away.

This Route now bears north on A828 to cross the bridge, just beyond which a minor road branches east for (4m) ruined *Ardchattan Priory*, named after St. Cathan, a companion of St. Columba. A Valliscaulian house founded by the MacDougalls in 1231, this was later the site of a parliament convened by Bruce in 1308, notable for probably being the last at which Gaelic was officially spoken. *Ardchattan Gardens* (of the adjacent house) are open to visitors (Tel: 0631-75274).

Along the west side of **Benderloch**, a straggling village a short *3m* north of Connel, rises a small, rough ridge bearing traces of walls and vitrified fortification.—*2m* **Barcaldine Sea Life Centre** (Tel: 063172-386), beautifully situated beside a wooded and rocky shore and perhaps the largest and most modern presentation in Britain of native marine life—ranging from octopus through herring and catfish to seals—is particularly popular for these last which may include rescued orphan pups which are trained for survival on release to the wild.

A828 rounds (*5m*) the head of Loch Creran, beyond running with **Strath of Appin**, a name perhaps most associated (at any rate by readers of Stevenson's 'Kidnapped' and 'Catriona') with the 'Appin Murder' of 1752 when Colin Campbell of Glenure was shot by an unknown hand. Someone had to pay, so James Stewart ('James of the Glens') was accused, tried at Inveraray by a Campbell judge and a Campbell jury, and hanged near Ballachulish, presumably by a Campbell hangman (see also Keil, below).

At (*5m*) **Appin** a minor road bears west for *Dalnashean Garden* (Tel: 063173-221) and *Port Appin* from where a ferry (no cars) crosses to the island of **Lismore** (Crossing 10 minutes. Roughly every 2 hours, but less frequent on Sunday. Also by arrangement. Tel: 063173-217, which number will also provide information on boats for viewing seals. Car ferry from Oban. Caledonian MacBrayne, Tel: 0475-33755). The island is perhaps more of ecclesiastical and scholastic than popular interest, having been the seat of the bishopric of Argyll (1200–1507), the bishops enjoying the title of 'Episcopi Lismorenses', and being also known for the 'Book of the Dean of Lismore', a manuscript collection of English and Gaelic poems, compiled in the 15C and of value to scholars for the light it throws on the works of Ossian. In more popular terms Lismore, the Great Garden, is some 10m long by 1m broad and served for most of its length by a road (B8045). Pleasant walking country, the island offers two ruined castles and a broch. *Coeffin Castle*, on the west coast in the north half of the island, dates from the 13C and was probably built by the MacDougalls of Lorne; *Tirefour Broch* is 1m south east by the other coast; and *Achanduin Castle* (13C), by the west coast in the island's south, was that of the bishops.

1m Portnacroish, from where *Castle Stalker*, the restored 16C tower house built by the Stewarts of Appin, is well seen on its islet (By arrangement. Tel: 08832-2768 or 063173-234). A short way farther north, at Appin Home Farm, *Appin Wildlife Museum* (Tel: 063173-308) is the interesting private collection of a retired forest ranger. The road now hugs Loch Linnhe to reach in *5m* the hamlet of *Keil*, burial place of James Stewart, falsely hanged for the 'Appin Murder', and then in another *5m* **South Ballachulish** where Rte 44A is joined. For South Ballachulish to (*13m*) **Fort William**, see Rte 44A.

45 Arrochar to Lochgilphead and Kintyre Peninsula

A83 (with B8024) to Campbeltown, following the west coast of Kintyre. B842, B8001 and A83 from Campbeltown to Tarbert along the east Kintyre coast.—Initially splendid Highland scenery across Argyll Forest Park and as far as Loch Fyne. Beyond, an always scenic mixture of cultivated land, wood, hills and moorland, most of the way beside wide sea lochs or open water with views across to Cowal and the islands of (east) Arran and (west) Gigha, the latter distantly backed by Islay and Jura.

SOME HOTELS. **Arrochar**. *Arrochar*, G83 7AU. Tel: 03012-484. **Inveraray**. *Great Inn*, PA32 8XB. Tel: 0499-2466. *Loch Fyne*, PA32 8XT. Tel: 0499-2148. **Lochgilphead**. *Stag*, Argyll Street, PA31 8NE. Tel: 0546-2496. **Tarbert**. *Columba*, PA29 6UF. Tel: 0880-820808. *Stonefield Castle*, PA29 6YJ. Tel: 0880-820836. **Isle of Gigha**. *Gigha*, PA41 7AD. Tel: 05835-254. **Bellochantuy**. *Putechan Lodge*, PA28 6QE. Tel: 05832-323. **Campbeltown**. *Seafield*, Kilkerran Road, PA28 6JL. Tel: 0586-54385. **Carradale**. *Carradale*, PA28 6RY. Tel: 05833-223.

Total distance 157m.—*7m* **'Rest-and-be-thankful'**.—*14m* **Inveraray**.—*30m* **Lochgilphead**.—*4m* **Junction with B8024**.—*30m* **Tarbert**.—*5m* **Kennacraig**.—*13m* **Tayinloan (Gigha)**.—*18m* **Campbeltown**.—*9m* **Saddell Abbey**.—*17m* **Claonaig**.—*10m* **Tarbert**.

Arrochar (also on Rte 20)—at the head of Loch Long, a bare 2m from ever popular Loch Lomond and sheltered below the piled heights of Argyll Forest Park (see Rte 47)—is a lively holiday and touring centre. A83, rounding the curve of the loch, soon starts to climb **Glen Croe**, with, reached in *3m* from Arrochar, *Ardgartan Forest Office*, starting point for some rugged and long forest walks. Ascending below Ben Arthur (north. 2891ft)—also known as the Cobbler from the Gaelic meaning forked peak—the modern road in *4m* smoothly breasts the pass at *'Rest-and-be-thankful'*, a watershed at 860ft earning its name from a stone so inscribed and recalling the repair of the road by the army in the 18C. In fact the stone is beside the adjacent old, or military road, and it was up this far steeper and more hazardous ascent that— 'doubling and doubling with laborious walk'—the poet Wordsworth and his sister coaxed their horses in 1803.

From 'Rest-and-be-thankful' the road drops through the open moorland of Glen Kinglas to reach in *4m* the junction with A815 marking the start of Rte 47 into the peninsula of Cowal. Just beyond, *Strone Gardens* (Tel: 04996-284) include a pinetum boasting the tallest tree in Britain, the 'Grand Fir', c 188ft.

After rounding the head of Loch Fyne A83 changes direction south west, heading deep into Campbell country with (*10m*) its 'capital' of **Inveraray** (1000 inhab. *Inf.*), a pleasant planned 18C town, approached over elegant contemporary bridges crossing the Aray and Shira and best known for its prestigious castle.

The town originally clustered around its first castle, its fortunes being those of the castle and its masters, the Campbells—earls, marquises, and finally dukes of Argyll. When on his succession in 1743 the 3rd Duke decided to build a new castle, he at the same time planned to move the whole village and thus much improve the surrounds of his new home. A notable example of 18C town planning, and to a large extent the work of William Adam, today's Inveraray dates therefore in concept from 1743, though the plans were not finalised until the 1750s and it took close on another 100 years to complete town and castle as seen today.

Within the town there are three points of interest, the most popular being *Inveraray Jail* (Tel: 0499-2381) by the shore, closed in 1889 and now opened as a tourist attraction with courtroom (1820), cells, wax figures and a crime and punishment exhibition. Also in the town is the 16C *Cross*, while a large gateway beside the Great Inn (John Adam, 1750) admits to an avenue which passes the Episcopalian Church, known for its *Bell Tower* (Tel: 0499-2433), containing some of Scotland's finest bells, several named after saints and so inscribed. There are exhibitions on vestments and campanology.

*Inveraray Castle (Tel: 0499-2203) is a Gothic-revival fairy-tale towered and turreted palace, as rewarding externally as it is within.

History (family and castle). Great Colin (Cailean Mor), founder of the fortunes of the powerful but politically not always astute Campbell family, was Sir Colin Campbell of Lochow (Loch Awe). He died in 1296, and all the later chiefs have taken the name MacCailean Mor. His son married the sister of Bruce and his descendants became earls in 1457 and dukes (of Argyll) in 1701. Archibald, 8th Earl (beheaded 1661), leader of the Covenanters, became marquis in 1641. His son, who unwisely supported Monmouth's rebellion, was likewise beheaded (1685). The 8th Duke (died 1900) was a distinguished author and Liberal statesman, and the 9th Duke (died 1914) married Princess Louise, daughter of Queen Victoria.

The castle, replacing one of the 15C of which some ruins survive, was begun for the 3rd Duke in c 1746 by Roger Morris, assisted by William Adam and possibly using a sketch by Vanbrugh. The splendid decorated interior was completed by Robert Mylne in 1772–82 for the 5th Duke. The top storey and the conical caps to the towers represent rebuilding after a fire in 1877. The castle was again swept by fire in 1975, the roof and the upper floor being destroyed, but restoration began immediately and was completed by 1978.

The castle is known for its magnificently decorated rooms and many treasures; the French-style decorative painting, with grisailles by Guinand and flowers and other work by Girard, can hardly be surpassed. The treasures include 18C Beauvais tapestry; oriental and European porcelain, including Japanese Imari ware (early 18C), Chinese blue and white, Meissen and Derby; fine displays of arms in decorative patterns; and 18C furniture. The distinguished collection of portraits includes works by, amongst many others, Kneller, Raeburn, Hoppner, Gainsborough, Batoni, Ramsay, Cotes, Winterhalter and Gavin Hamilton.

Adjacent to the Castle is the *Combined Operations Museum*, recalling that Inveraray was the Second World War's first British Combined

Old Castle of Inveraray. Dating from the 15C but now a ruin, this predecessor of today's splendid 18C castle was long the home of the Campbell chiefs

Operations training base; a base through which passed over a quarter of a million troops of many nations.

A walk through the castle grounds leads north for 1m to a 17C dovecot (*Carlunan*) and, over 1m beyond, the little *Falls of Aray*. A longer walk ascends the Shira to *Rob Roy's House*, a ruin where the outlaw is said to have lived for some time. From here *Ben Bhuidhe* (3156ft) may be ascended by following the ridge.

In less than *2m* A83 passes the *Argyll Wildlife Park* (Tel: 0499-2264) where in a setting of woodland, pond and burn the visitor can meet over 100 species of wildfowl, owls, and all manner of Scottish mammals.—*4m* **Auchindrain Museum of Farming Life** (Tel: 04995-235) illustrates life on a typical joint-tenure or strip-system farm, common in the Highlands until the late 18C. Such places were more multiple-tenancy villages than farms, paying a communal rent, in the case of Auchindrain to the Duke of Argyll. The museum includes a visitor centre, as also 18 and 19C crofts and farm buildings, complete with livestock and furnished with contemporary farm and domestic equipment.—*2m Furnace*, so called from a now long abandoned 18C iron smelting furnace, historically interesting for having profited from charcoal resulting from Hanoverian government deforestation aimed at removing a ready shelter for Highlander rebels. Today the granite quarries are the important feature here.—*3m Crarae Glen Gardens* (Tel: 0546-86633), dating from about 1912, are essentially within a glen sheltering many varieties of rare trees and shrubs.—*2m Minard Castle* (By appointment, Tel: 0546-86272), by the loch shore, though with later extensions is 16C in origin.—*4m Lochgair* is a village pleasantly fringing an inlet of the same name.—*6m Kilmory Castle Gardens* (Tel: 0546-2127) date from the late 18C and at one time supplied plants for London's Kew Gardens. Later neglected, the gardens are now being restored to include woodland walks, a nature trail, borders and rock, rose and water gardens.

7m **Lochgilphead** (2500 inhab. *Inf.*), an unpretentious local and holiday lochside centre, has a wide main street originally designed to serve as a market and a church containing a window by Burne-Jones. For *Achnabreck Farm*, 1m north, with rocks bearing notable cup and ring markings, as also for Lochgilphead to Oban, see Rte 46.—*2m* **Ardrishaig** is at the start of the *Crinan Canal* which permits small boats to pass from Loch Fyne across the isthmus to the west coast at Crinan. Surveyed by Watt and constructed to Rennie's plans between 1793–1801, the canal, now used mainly by pleasure craft, is interrupted by 15 locks over a distance of nine miles.

In *2m* the junction is reached with B8024. From this point the main A83 reaches Tarbert in 9m, but, though pleasant enough with views across to Cowal, there is nothing of specific interest along this stretch (other than Stonefield Castle Gardens, for which see below under Tarbert). This Route therefore chooses the westerly loop provided by B8024 (30m to Tarbert) around the peninsula of KNAPDALE, a much slower road, but more interesting and affording views towards Jura and Islay. For anybody with a feel for very early Christianity, St. Columba's Cave will be incentive enough to opt for this road.

5m Achahoish, from where a small road (for Ellary) rounds the head of Loch Caolisport and in 3m reaches **St. Columba's Cave**, archaeologically proven (in the 19C) to have been occupied as long ago as the Middle Stone Age (c 8000 BC), traditionally associated with St. Columba's arrival in Scotland (6C) and certainly used for Christian ceremony at about that time. There is not, of course, a lot to be seen, and some imagination and sensitivity help here, but there is a rock-shelf with an altar, and, above, carved crosses, while a large basin, perhaps a Stone

Age mortar, may have been used as a font. That this place was occupied until at least medieval times is indicated by traces of houses and the ruin of a (? 13C) chapel in front of the cave. Alongside there is a second, smaller cave in which, should the light be just right, it is possible to make out a faint cross on the rear wall.

Running with the shore of Loch Caolisport B8024 in *10m* (from Achahoish) reaches the *Kilberry Stones* (AM; signed, west of B8024), a group of medieval gravestones collected over the last century from various parts of the Kilberry estate. There is also a large boulder reputedly once used for trials of strength.—*3m Carse*, where, on the right just beyond the river bridge, are three standing stones.—Beyond, B8024 completes its loop by turning north to run beside West Loch Tarbert and in *11m* rejoin A83 just north of Tarbert.

1m **Tarbert** (1500 inhab. *Inf.*) is a sheltered small town at the head of the short East Loch Tarbert which is picturesquely overlooked by a ruined castle, built by Bruce in 1325, later rebuilt and known to have been a residence of Robert II and James IV. A more modern castle, *Stonefield Castle* (2m north on A83. Tel: 0880-820836), now a hotel, is a Scottish Baronial pile built by W.H. Playfair in 1837. The grounds comprise some 50 acres of scrub and woodland with some rare trees from South Africa and New Zealand as also venerable rhododendrons originating as seed collected in Sikkim in about 1850. Mainly a fishing and yachting centre, Tarbert marks the north tip of the long, narrow peninsula of KINTYRE, reached by crossing the 'tarbert', the little isthmus, 1m long, which separates East from the far longer and more important West Loch Tarbert. Today, in a car, the isthmus is barely noticed, a matter of two minutes. But it is perhaps worth recalling that this is a historic mile and that others had a more strenuous crossing. That wily Viking, King Magnus Barfud, for instance, who in 1198 negotiated a treaty giving him all the land he could sail around and then, taking the tiller of a galley and hoisting a sail, had himself hauled across so that he could claim Kintyre; or Bruce who dragged his ships across on his way to attack Castle Sween; and indeed, though with more peaceful intent, local fishermen who regularly portaged right up until the opening of the Crinan Canal in 1801.

5m **Kennacraig**, for the car ferry to Islay (see Rte 65), and the junction also with B8001 along which this Route later returns northward completing the circuit of Kintyre. Affording fine views across West Loch Tarbert and of Knapdale beyond, A83 in *7m* kinks south of *Dunskeig* (reached by minor road from Clachan), a combined dun and hill-fort nearly 500ft high and commanding the loch entrance, to descend to (*1m*) **Ronachan Bay**, on some maps Dunskeig Bay and also sometimes called *Seal Bay*. This last name is well deserved for the rocks offshore are favourites with seals—some of them Atlantic grey seals, Britain's largest wild animal; and, should the seals pall, then there is still the pleasure of fossicking for the dazzling white quartz lying among the profusion of sea pinks. A few yards farther south, and *Corriechrevie Cairn*, one of the largest in Kintyre, overlooks the road, while *1m* farther (not visible from the road, but reached by a short track) will be found the *Ballochroy Stones*, comprising three standing stones, a burial cist and, adjacent to the east, a boulder showing cup markings.

4m **Tayinloan**, for the car ferry to the island of **Gigha** (Crossing 20 minutes. Roughly four crossings daily each way. Caledonian Mac-Brayne. Tel: 088073-253 or 0475-33755).

History. Standing stones and cairns prove prehistoric occupancy, but in more recent times, by at least the 15C, the owners were the McNeills, related to those in Knapdale. Aggressive action by the Macleans in 1530 decimated the Gigha McNeills and the island was sold to Macdonalds in 1554, who in turn sold it to Sir

John Campbell of Calder. Hector McNeill of Taynish repurchased the island in 1590 and it remained in the family until 1865. The cemetery bears frequent witness to the Gigha McNeills, probably the oldest branch of this clan.

Pronounced, roughly, 'gear'—the name derives from the Norse for God's Island—Gigha covers some six square miles and supports a permanent population of about 150. The principal visitor objective is *Achamore Gardens* (Tel: 05835-253), 50 acres of shrub and woodland created by Sir James Horlick between 1944 and 1973.

Running for the most part close to the shore, A83 in *6m* reaches Glenbarr Abbey, with a *Clan Macalister Centre* (Tel: 05832-247), beyond skirting (*3m*) *Bellochantuy Bay*, with a hotel, before bearing south east to reach (*9m*) **Campbeltown** on Kintyre's east coast (6600 inhab. *Inf.*). Market and shopping centre for a wide district, and tucked comfortably around the head of its bay, the town has a particularly inviting waterfront.

History. Whether or not, as is sometimes claimed, this place was antecedent to Dunadd (see Rte 46) can safely be left to the visitor's individual judgement. What is certain is that until the mid 17C the town was Kinlochkerran, a name recalling the Irish St. Kieran, contemporary of Columba and Aidan, both so closely associated with Dunadd. The 17C, though, saw the end of the long strife between the Campbells of Inveraray and the Macdonalds of Kintyre, the latter being defeated (finally at Dunaverty, see below) and their lands given to Archibald Campbell, 7th Earl of Argyll, who quickly substituted his own family name for that of the saint. *Castlehill Church*, above the town, was the rallying place in 1684 for the 9th Earl's rebellion in support of Monmouth. In 1774 Flora Macdonald, emigrating with her family to Carolina, set sail from Campbeltown.

Campbeltown Museum (Tel: 0586-52366), in the Library in Hall Street, ranges farther than its name implies and shows geological, archaeological and general cultural material relative to the whole of Kintyre. But perhaps the town's main focus of interest is the 15C *Campbeltown Cross* (facing the harbour), with highly elaborate ornamentation and an inscription to Edward McEachern and his son Andrew. Originally in Main Street, near the town hall, the cross was removed during the last war and later erected on its present site. Also worth a visit is *Davaar Island*, off the entrance to the bay; in fact an island only at high tide, and at other times linked by a shingle bank known as the Dhorlin. In summer there is a ferry service, the objective being a cave in which there is a painting of the Crucifixion, the work (1887) of Archibald Mackinnon, inspired by a dream. In 1934 the picture was retouched by the artist, then aged 80.

TO SOUTHEND AND MULL OF KINTYRE (south and west c 20m). There is a choice of two roads to Southend on the south coast; the inland road (B842, 10m), or a more scenic, but hilly and winding coastal road (14m). The latter, known as the Learside (leewardside) road and affording views of Ailsa Craig, passes, first, the village suburb of Kilkerran, a reminder of Campbeltown's earlier name, and then the Dhorlin shingle spit across to Davaar.

Southend is a holiday village, immediately south of which is the promontory of *Dunaverty*, once an arrogant stronghold of the Macdonald Lords of the Isles but in 1647 the scene of the bloody close of the Kintyre Macdonald story. Catholic, and supporters of Montrose (who had sided with Charles I), the Macdonalds, some 300 in number, were hunted the length of the peninsula by the Covenanter general, Leslie, and here turned to make their last stand. But, deserted by their Irish allies who sailed away, without water, and led to believe that their lives would be spared, they surrendered. They should have known better, because only two years earlier, at Philiphaugh in the Lowlands, Leslie had shot over a hundred of his prisoners. And here he did the same thing, sparing only one lad.—The island of *Sanda*, 2½m south east, is said to have hidden Bruce in 1306 and is also traditionally associated with St. Ninian after whom a ruined chapel is named (boat in summer from Southend or Campbeltown. Tel: Campbeltown Tourist Information, 0586-52056).

Keil, just west of Southend, claims to be where St. Columba first landed in Scotland, the evidence being footprints in a flat rock at the top of a hillock just beyond a ruined medieval chapel said to be successor of one he founded here.

Beyond Keil Point a minor road across *Mull of Kintyre*, the name given to the peninsula's south west tip, in 6m drops very steeply to Mull lighthouse, built in 1788 and later remodelled by Robert Stevenson. From here Ireland is only 12m distant, the view extending along its north coast, off which lies the island of Rathlin, refuge of Bruce and the strongest claimant to have been the home of the spider from which he drew encouragement.

B842, taken north out of Campbeltown and with increasingly closer views of Arran, in *9m* reaches **Saddell Abbey**, today scanty ruins but once a rich Cistercian house founded in c 1164 by the redoubtable Somerled, said to be buried here. Although his grave is not identified there is an outstanding collection of carved graveslabs showing hounds, stags, galleys, warriors and their weapons and much else. To the north the central mountain is *Beinn an Tuirc* (1490ft), the highest peak in Kintyre. The name means Mountain of the Boar, and traditionally it was here that Diarmuid, a remote ancestor of the Campbells, slew a fierce boar, the origin of the boar's head which appears on the Campbell arms.

17m **Claonaig**, for a car ferry to Lochranza on Arran (see Rte 17). At *Skipness*, 2m north east, the large ruined 13C castle has a part contemporary curtain wall with later 13 and 16C extensions, the latter incorporating windows of the original chapel. Adjacent is the ruined (? 14C) church of St. Brendan with early Gothic doorways and windows.—From Claonaig B8001 and A83 reach **Tarbert** in *10m*.

46   Lochgilphead to Oban and Connel

A816 to Oban. A85 to Connel.—Undulating, open and pastoral with seaward and island views. Approaching Oban, some woodland and moor.

SOME HOTELS. **Crinan**. *Crinan*, PA31 8SR. Tel: 054683-261. **Kilmelford**. *Cuilfail*. Tel: 08522-274. **Kilmelford (Arduaine)**. *Loch Melfort*, PA34 4XG. Tel: 08522-233. **Kilninver**. *Knipoch*, PA34 4QT. Tel: 08526-251. **Island of Seil**. *Willowburn*, Clachan Seil, PA34 4TJ. Tel: 08523-276. *Easdale Inn*, Easdale, PA34 4RF. Tel: 08523-256. **Oban**. *Columba*, North Pier, PA34 5QD. Tel: 0631-62183. *Manor House*, Gallanach Road, PA34 4LS. Tel: 0631-62087. *Caledonian*, Station Square, PA34 5RT. Tel: 0631-63133.

Total distance 37m.—*2m* **Cairnbaan (Dunadd)**.—*3m* **Kilmartin**.—*2m* **Carnasserie Castle**.—*18m* **Kilninver**.—*7m* **Oban**.—*5m* **Connel**.

For **Lochgilphead**, see Rte 45. A816 runs beside the Crinan Canal to reach in *1m* **Achnabreck Farm**, where permission can be asked to walk ½m to find one of the largest known and clearest complexes of cup-and-ring markings. The markings are incised across two flat rock faces, the first in a clearing in the wood beyond the top left corner of the field, the other just beyond.

1m Cairnbaan is a hamlet from which B841 and the Crinan Canal bear west along the northern flank of Knapdale Forest, for forest walks and a choice of scenic drives either side of Loch Sween.

KNAPDALE FOREST AND LOCH SWEEN. In 3m west of Cairnbaan, B841 crosses B8025 at the village of *Bellanoch*. *Crinan* is just over a mile farther west, while B8025 northward crosses the bleak flats of Moine Mhor to reach Kilmartin and its prehistoric sites (see below). B8025, followed south, in 1m reaches a fork offering a choice between the west or east sides of Loch Sween, both roads being dead ends after respectively 10 and 12 miles.

Loch Sween, West. It was northward along this road that the cattle herds were driven after being brought across from Islay and Jura to the road's terminal jetty at Keillmore. About a mile short of the jetty a c 13C chapel, now re-roofed, houses medieval graveslabs and a carved Celtic cross, perhaps of the 10C.

Loch Sween East. In 9m the road reaches *Castle Sween, its keep dating from the 11 or 12C and probably the oldest stone one on Scotland's mainland. The MacSweens, of Norse origin (Sueno), were here first, but they lost their title in 1262 to the Earl of Menteith. In an effort to regain their lands they sided with the English around 1300–10, as a result losing everything in Scotland and being forced to find their future in Ireland. In c 1308 Alexander Macdonald installed himself here, only to be besieged and defeated by Bruce who achieved surprise by hauling his ships across the isthmus at Tarbert. Later, in about 1325, Bruce made the McNeills constables of Sween, a position they held for over 200 years until a McNeill heiress married a Macmillan, the latter then acquiring the Knapdale lands and the title of constable. Finally, in 1647, the castle was destroyed by the royalists. Despite the castle's age and story a surprising amount survives, primarily, of course, the ancient keep (unusual in being greater in area than in height), but also some 13C extensions, the kitchen with oven and storage recesses, and, in the round tower, what appears to be a large drain or rubbish shaft.

Kilmory Knap Chapel, 3m beyond and dating from the 13C, has been roofed with glass and shelters a collection of Celtic and later sculptured stones, the collection including 15C Macmillan's Cross showing a hunting scene on one side and a crucifixion on the other.

Just beyond Cairnbaan A816 crosses the little river Add, ahead now rising the bare and rocky hill of ***Dunadd**, on several counts—as the ancient Dalriadic capital; as a dramatic example of a fort of its period (c 500–850); for its association, real or guessed, with Aidan, Columba and original Christian and royal ritual—one of the most evocative sites in Scotland. And the setting is in tune, too; a rough hump of a hill set on the bleak Moine Mhor, drained now but otherwise little changed and still carrying the standing stones of an even more ancient people. As the hill is climbed traces of walls and buildings can be made out, but it is at the top that Dunadd has left its tantalising message—a carved boar, for instance, a footprint, a deep basin and even some Ogham writing—all surely playing their part in ancient royal ceremony, perhaps even the first Christian coronation in Britain, when, in 574, Columba officiated at that of Aidan. And tradition goes farther, suggesting that the throne used for this, and possibly earlier ceremonies, was the Stone of Destiny, later moved to Dunstaffnage, then Scone, and finally by Edward I to Westminster.

Dunadd stands on the southern edge of an astonishing concentration of ****Prehistoric Sites**; standing stones, burial cairns, cists, a stone circle, and several cup-and-ring clusters cut not only into cist slabs and standing stones but also covering seemingly random flat rocks. Most of the sites—all with admirable and detailed explanation boards—lie just below the west side of A816 between Dunadd and (*3m*) *Kilmartin*, sprinkled along a modest valley which over the later Stone and Bronze ages—millenia before Aidan and Columba performed their ceremonies on Dunadd's platform—must have been of deep and persistent ritual significance.

Most of the sites (all normally with open access) are well signed. First, 1½m north of Dunadd, will be seen on the west a fine group of six standing stones, some of them cupmarked; then, almost at once, there is a small, signed parking area off the right of the road. This is for visitors to *Dunchraigaig Cairn* in a small clump of trees across the road. Bronze Age, and once 100ft in diameter, evidence has been excavated here of both cremated and other burials. In an enclosure in the adjoining field on the north are the *Baluachraig Rocks*, flat faces profusely carved with cup, ring and other markings. After driving a short way farther north along A816, a left turn is made on to B8025, followed shortly by a right turn along a minor road crossing the Kilmartin burn, this turn rounding a field with another good cluster of standing stones. *Ri-Cruin Cairn* will be found a few yards farther on the left. The next road to the right soon reaches the attractive small *Templewood Stone Circle*, in fact two circles. The northern, found during excavations of 1974–80, is the earlier (before 3000 BC) but was soon superseded by the southern circle, today still showing something of a central cist, surrounded by stones at the base of one of which (north) there is an unusual spiral marking. *Nether Largie Cairn South*, across the road from Templewood, is interesting because it is possible to get into the shored-up chamber which has partitions. The cairn is believed to have been used for cremations by Stone Age people, then for uncremated burials by their Bronze Age successors.

A track now heads north for Nether Largie Mid and North cairns, both of the Bronze Age. The former is little more than a pile of stones and an exposed cist, but *Nether Largie North*, part reconstructed, has been given a glass roof. On the end slab of the cist can be seen axe and other markings, while the capstone alongside bears axe heads and numerous cups.—The last cairn is *Glebe Cairn* (reached from the north end of Kilmartin), associated with two rings of small standing stones, all, however, now covered.

In *Kilmartin* the church gateway forms a pleasing and original style of war memorial, while in the churchyard will be found two collections of medieval graveslabs, some the work of Loch Awe sculptors. The church itself houses early Christian crosses, accompanied by photographic and other explanatory material. A ruined 16C tower in the north of the village was once that of the rectors, but **Carnasserie Castle**, *2m* north beside A816, is far more rewarding. It was built in the 16C by John Carswell, the first Protestant Bishop of the Isles, a scholar whose translation of Knox's liturgy into Gaelic (1567) was perhaps the first book ever published in that language, and has a number of features of modest architectural interest. Above the entrance, for instance, there are frames for inscribed panels, only one of which, however, survives; there are the string-courses running round the exterior; and traces of the courtyard survive, with, above the gateway, the initials (1681) of Sir Douglas Campbell and his wife, the then owners.

LOCH AWE. Opposite the castle B840 bears north east for (3m) **Loch Awe**, a huge loch cutting for a narrow 23m towards scenery of increasing grandeur and eventually discharging through the river Awe below the lofty mass of Cruachan (see Rte 44B, which describes the north end of the loch). Macarthurs, Macnaughtons, Macdonalds and, above all, Campbells were the principal clans along these shores, and the Campbell slogan 'It's a far cry to Loch Ow' was a defiant boast of the inaccessibility of their fastness. Today, though, roads run with both banks, that along the east being the better and rather more interesting. Along this latter, ruined *Fincharn Castle* (reached in 2m beyond the hamlet of Ford where the road splits), once a Macdonald stronghold, stands on a rock ledge beside the water. Beyond, the six miles of Eredine Forest must be crossed before the next point of interest, namely *Innis Sherrich Chapel*, dedicated in the 13C to St. Findoc and standing on an islet, perhaps once a crannog and reached still, and only at low water, by stepping stones. Just north, and on another islet, ruined *Ardchonnel Castle* (15C) was a lair of the Campbells. Continuing north east, the road reaches Rte 44B in some 16m close to Dalmally.

Along the west shore the road in 1m skirts Torran Farm, amid the buildings of which there is a large standing stone. From here on the drive is through the forests of Inverliever and Inverinan with many walks, picnic sites and view points (information at *Dalavich*, reached in another 8m). From Dalavich one road continues through Inverinan Forest and beside the loch to reach (in 8m) Kilchrenan (see Rte 44B). Another road, highly scenic but in places narrow and steep, heads roughly north west from just north of Dalavich to fringe lovely *Loch Avich* and in 11m return to this Rte 46 at Kilmelford.

In *4m* (from Carnasserie Castle) A816 drops to the head of *Loch Craignish*, on the right on the descent being a large standing stone beside the remains of burial cairns.—*8m Kilmelford*, with the small road (see above, Loch Awe) to Loch Avich and Dalavich.—*6m Kilninver*, where B844 diverts to the islands of Seil, Easdale and Luing, all popular day excursions from Oban.

SEIL, EASDALE AND LUING. **Seil** is reached in 4m by way of the delightful, humpbacked *Clachan Bridge*, built in 1791 and popularly known as the Atlantic Bridge. From Easdale, on the west coast, a ferry (No cars; crossing 5 minutes, daily, more or less as required. Tel: 08523-338) plies to the small island of **Easdale** on which there is a Folk Museum (Tel: 08523-370, evenings), illustrating, with some emphasis on slate, the island's social and industrial story of the 18 and 19C.—**Luing**, to the south and the largest of the islands, is linked by car ferry from Seil across Cuan Sound (Crossing 5 minutes; daily, frequent. Tel: 08523-252). Slate was long the principal industry here, and Luing slate was used to roof Iona cathedral, but farming is now the main activity. From Luing there are summer boat excursions to Mull (Lochbuie); Lunga; Jura and Scarba, with, between them, the whirlpool of Corrievreckan; and the Garvellach Islands, with beehive cells and other early monastic traces (L. MacLachlan, Jubilee Cottage, Isle of Luing. Tel: 08524-282).

4m **Cleigh**, where a minor road to the right leading direct to Connel enables Oban to be avoided. This minor road soon briefly fringes *Loch Nell*, touching the loch at a point where a crannog islet can be seen and passing, 300 yards farther on the left by a house, the so-called Serpent Mound, an earthwork some 300ft long and thought to be a relic of pagan worship. Beyond, some 2m east of Oban, this road passes *Barranrioch Rare Breeds Farm Park* (Tel: 063177-223), with rare domestic breeds, as also deer and, for the children, close contact with a variety of small animals.

Just beyond Cleigh a road (to Kilbride) bears west off A816 and in 1m reaches *Lerag's Cross* of 1526; after long lying in three pieces beside the ruined church, it was repaired and erected on its present mound.

3m **Oban** (7000 inhab. *Inf.*), well situated on the shore and slopes of its bay which is protected by the island of Kerrera, combines much of the dignity of the 19C with the needs of modern tourism for which it is a dedicated, if in summer somewhat overtaxed centre. Ferries and cruises are what really count here, an industry born of the development of steam during the 19C and the consequent surge in tourism leading to today's emphasis on sea, road and combined excursions.

Ship services, cruises, excursions. Excursion possibilities from Oban can be bewildering in number, method and choice. Timetables and services are subject to annual alterations, but some of the main possibilities are outlined below.

Caledonian MacBrayne operate car and passenger ferries to Mull (Craignure), Barra (Castlebay) and South Uist (Lochboisdale); also to Mull (Tobermory), Coll, Tiree, Colonsay, Islay and Lismore. Popular day excursions, combining ship and coach, visit Mull, Iona and Staffa; while, with a little planning, motorists can tour Mull, visit Iona, ferry across the Sound of Mull to Morvern (Lochaline), drive to Mallaig and thence continue by ferries to Skye and the Outer Hebrides. For all the above contact Caledonian MacBrayne Ltd, Ferry Terminal, Railway Pier. Tel: 0631-62285 or 0475-33755.

Other local excursions include Duart Castle, Torosay Castle and Grasspoint, all on Mull; Loch Etive; Kerrera; and coach tours to, for instance, Cruachan power station and the islands of Seil, Easdale and Luing. For all these contact Tourist Information or local travel firms.

On the hill above the town two curious, uncompleted buildings attract attention; the circular *McCaig's Tower* is a folly built in 1897 by a local banker anxious to combine easing unemployment with perpetuating his own name, while the other building, to the south and intended as a hydropathic establishment, was abandoned when funds ran out.

Oban's main street is George Street, flanking the harbour in which seals sometimes compete with ferries for the visitor's attention. Railway Quay forms the south arm, North Pier the other, on the latter being *A World in Miniature* (Tel: 0631-66300), showing about 50 displays of miniature furniture, dioramas, room settings and suchlike, all the work of over 250 of the finest miniaturists in Britain. Some 300 yards to the north, at the north end of George Street, the *Highland Discovery Centre* (Tel: 0631-62444) provides a visitor centre and video presentations on changing themes relating to the Highlands and Islands.

In the south part of the town, on Lochavullin Industrial Estate, *Oban (Caithness) Glassworks* (Tel: 0631-63386) enables the varied crafts of glass-making to be watched.

To the north, Corran Esplanade skirts the bay to reach the Catholic *St. Columba Cathedral* (1922, Sir Giles Scott) and the movingly sculpted War Memorial, beside which is the *Dog Stone* to which Fingal used to secure his dog Bran. Farther on, on a bluff, stand the ruins of *Dunollie Castle*, once a 12 or 13C stronghold but now reduced to a keep and fragments.

Dunollie has long belonged to the MacDougalls, Lords of Lorne, and their descendant preserves the Brooch of Lorne (see Rte 20) in nearby Dunollie House (no adm). Originally kept at Gylen on Kerrera (see below), the brooch was taken at the burning of Gylen Castle in 1645 and for nearly 200 years hidden in the Campbell house of Braglenbeg in Glen Euchar, 8m south east of Oban. It was returned to the MacDougalls in 1826.

Kerrera, the island protecting Oban's harbour, is reached by frequent

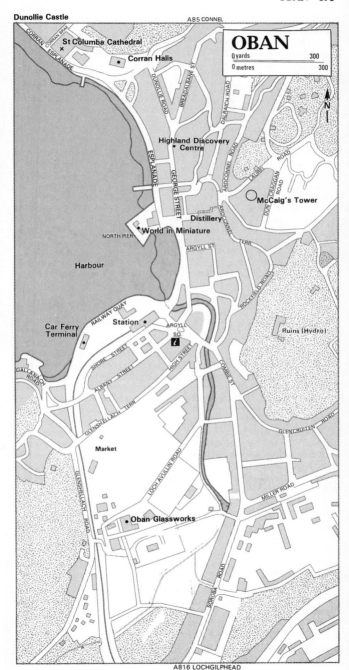

Dunollie Castle

A85 CONNEL

St Columba Cathedral

Corran Halls

OBAN

0 yards _____ 300
0 metres _____ 300

CORRAN BRAE

CORRAN ESPLANADE

DUNOLLIE ROAD

BREADALBANE ST

DALRIACH ROAD

Highland Discovery
• Centre

ARDCONNEL ROAD

LAUREL

DUN CHRAGGAN
ROAD

ROAD

N

ESPLANADE

GEORGE STREET

McCaig's Tower

Distillery

•World in Miniature

ARDCONNEL

TERR

NORTH PIER

ARGYLL ST

Harbour

ROCKFIELD ROAD

RAILWAY QUAY

Station •

ARGYLL
SQ.

Ruins (Hydro)

Car Ferry
Terminal

GALLANACH
ROAD

SHORE STREET

HIGH STREET

COMBIE ST

ALBANY STREET

GLENSHELLACH TERR

GLENCRUITEN ROAD

Market

LOCH AVULLIN ROAD

MILLER ROAD

GLENSHELLACH ROAD

•Oban Glassworks

SOROBA

ROAD

A816 LOCHGILPHEAD

ferry (no cars) from Gallanach, 2m south of Oban. Alexander II died on Kerrera in 1249 during an expedition against the Norsemen in the Hebrides, and 14 years later Horseshoe Bay was used by Hakon's fleet on its way south to defeat at Largs. *Gylen Castle*, a MacDougall stronghold at the south end of the island, was destroyed by Cromwell's troops in 1645. The obelisk at the north end honours David Hutcheson, founder of the west coast steamer services.

Leaving Oban A85 in *2m* reaches *Dunbeg*, close to **Dunstaffnage Castle** (AM. Tel: 031-244-3121), guardian of the entrance to Loch Etive and also, it is said, of the Stone of Destiny, brought here from Dunadd. Thus Dunstaffnage would have been the site of the court of Kenneth Macalpine, first king of the combined Scots and Picts, at any rate until he moved, together with the stone, to Scone. Later the castle passed to the MacDougall lords of Lorne, and, later still, in 1746 when garrisoned by Hanoverian troops, Flora Macdonald was held here for some days.

Seeming almost to spring from the rock platform, the castle—an irregular four-sided ruin with three round towers—dates mainly from the 13C (400 or so years later than when the Stone of Destiny may have been here) and has a contrasting 17C tower-house above its entrance. Features are the walls, in places 66ft high and 10ft thick; the large well with its neat surround with four small turrets; and the ruined chapel which, with 13C lancets, is the burial place of the Campbells of Dunstaffnage, hereditary captains of the castle.

3m **Connel**, see Rte 44B.

47 Cowal

Cowal is the name given to the peninsula bounded on the west by Loch Fyne and on the east by the Firth of Clyde and Loch Long. Pierced from the south by several long, narrow sea lochs, the peninsula hangs like a claw above the island of Bute which, separated by the beautiful waters of the two Kyles of Bute, falls away to the south. Cowal enjoys varied scenery, ranging from the great peaks and forests of *Argyll Forest Park* in the north east to pastoral, forest and sea loch landscapes towards the south. The main town is *Dunoon*, a leading Clyde resort and the scene at the end of August of the Cowal Highland Gathering. It is only this south east corner that can be said to be really populated, though in summer the peninsula's small roads sometimes carry a good deal of touring traffic.

By road Cowal can be reached from A83 near Strone Gardens in the north (Rte 45), the approach chosen by this Route, which then makes an anticlockwise circuit. Other approaches are the ferries across the Clyde from Gourock to Dunoon or the ferry from Bute to Colintraive.

> From near Strone Gardens, A815 to Strachur. A886 and B8000 to Kames. A8003, A886, B836, A815 and A885 across to Dunoon. A885 and A815 back to Strachur.
>
> SOME HOTELS. **Strachur**. *The Creggan's Inn*, PA27 8BX. Tel: 036986-279. **Kilfinan**. *Kilfinan*, PA21 2AP. Tel: 070082-201. **Dunoon**. *Enmore*, Marine Parade, PA23 8HH. Tel: 0369-2230. *Ardfillayne*, West Bay, PA23 7QJ. Tel: 0369-2267. *Abbeyhill*, Dhailling Road, PA23 8EA. Tel: 0369-2204. **Ardentinny**. *Ardentinny*, PA23 8TR. Tel: 036981-209.
>
> Total distance 75m.—*9m* **Strathur**.—*15m* **Otter Ferry**.—*4m* **Kilfinan**.—*6m* **Millhouse**.—*13m* **Auchenbreck**.—*12m* **Dunoon**.—*4m* **Ardbeg**.—*12m* **Strachur**.

Argyll Forest Park, spread across most of north east Cowal, was the first

Forestry Commission Forest Park to be created in Britain (1935) and has since then grown from bare hillsides or infant plantations into one of Scotland's finest expanses of Highland forest. The park, not all of which is afforested, stretches from Strone Point, between Holy Loch and Loch Long, up the shores of Loch Eck and north east across Loch Goil to beyond Glen Croe. Official roads (as opposed to Forestry Commission no-cars roads) serving the park are, towards the south, A880 rounding Strone Point to run up Loch Long to Ardentinny, whence an unclassified road cuts north west across Larach Pass (533ft) to descend to meet A815 which traces the length of Loch Eck (for A815, see the latter part of this Route); in the north, A83 from Arrochar up to 'Rest-and-be-thankful' (see Rte 45); and, in between and with B828 providing a link from 'Rest-and-be-thankful', B839. This last breaks away south east near the start of this Route and follows Hell's Glen (719ft)—green, with steep sides and moorland, but scarcely meriting its name—before dropping sharply to *Lochgoilhead* to continue as an unclassified road to pass forest walks and reach (13m from Strone Gardens on Rte 45) *Carrick Castle*, a gaunt keep beside lower Loch Goil, dating mainly from the 15C though it is said to occupy the site of a Norse fort and to stand on 12C foundations. An Argyll stronghold, the castle was burned in 1685 by the men of Atholl.

The park provides a network of forest roads (for walkers only) as also many and varied forest walks. Information from Forest Offices at *Kilmun* on A880 beside Holy Loch (see below) and *Ardgartan* (see beginning of Rte 45).

Leaving A83 near *Strone Gardens* (see Rte 45) A815 in 2m meets the junction with B839 (see above), a curiosity opposite the junction being white stones in the shape of a heart which mark the traditional wedding place of the Argyll tinkers. Just beyond, on the south side of A815, is the stone cist of *Ardno Cairn*. Continuing beside Loch Fyne, opposite Inveraray over 1m wide, the road in 7m reaches the junction with A886 which is now followed, A815 representing the return journey. For *Strachur*, a short way along A815, see at the end of this Route. In another 3m this Route moves on to B8000 to stay with the coast, while A886 provides a cut across to the head of Loch Riddon, useful for those not wishing to make the complete circuit.

In *4m* B8000 touches *Lachlan Bay*, on the right being the humble ruin of a Celtic chapel, standing within a typical large circular stone cashel or enclosure, while across the little river, and in stark contrast, rises ruined *Castle Lachlan*, guardian of this remote bay. A tower of the MacLachlans, in part 12C but mainly early 16C, the castle was razed after Culloden.

8m Otter Ferry, where a stop is worthwhile just south of the junction with the road leading east across to Glendaruel. From here, against the skyline to the south east, can be seen the Iron Age hill-fort of *Barr Iola* with its tumbled walls, while connoisseurs of chambered cairns will divert 1m east along the Glendaruel road for *Carn Bàn*, the covering of which was removed during the 18C to reveal the stones of the main chamber, still well seen.—*4m Kilfinan*, where the church of 1754 may stand on a Celtic site and certainly does stand within an ancient burial ground, some of the early medieval stones from which have been collected together in the 17C Lamont vault against the exterior north wall of the church.

From (*6m*) *Millhouse*, where this Route angles sharply east with B8000, an extended circuit can be made southward, rounding Tighnabruaich Forest to reach Ardlamont Point (Coast of the Lamonts, the clan of southern Cowal) and return beside the western of the Kyles of Bute pass-

ing Carry Point, a Forestry Commission picnic site with views of Bute
and Arran.—*1m Kames* is a small resort beautifully sited opposite Bute,
while *Tighnabruaich*, *1m* farther north, is a similarly sited but larger
resort and sailing centre. Beyond Tighnabruaich, and now on A8003, this
Route passes (*2m*) *Caladh Castle Forest Trail* (1½m with some steep sections) and, travelling high above the water and with frequent parking
places, in *8m* meets A886 at the head of Loch Riddon, accompanying this
road south for *1m* to the road junction at *Auchenbreck*. (Here A886 in 4m
arrives at *Colintraive*, on the east Kyle of Bute and with a car ferry across
to the island. Crossing 5 minutes. Daily, frequent. Tel: 0475-33755. A
grassy mound in the field near the ferry marks an ancient burial cairn.)

From Auchenbreck B836 loops around the head of Loch Striven, at this
point, in front of the farm at *Balliemore*, being two standing stones. Loch
Tarsan, soon passed on the north, is a power reservoir with dams in Glen
Lean and Glen Tarsan.—*7m Clachaig*, with ruined mills at which gunpowder was made throughout the second half of the 19C.—In *2m* B836
joins A815, within the angle being a mound, possibly artificial, on the top
of which is a burial place of the Campbells of Ballochyle.

This Route now heads south for Dunoon. For Holy Loch and A815
northward up Glen Eck, see below after the description of Dunoon.

1m Sandbank, where there is a choice of roads, either the direct A885
or the coastal A815. The latter kinks within *Lazaretto Point*, so called
from the quarantine station which operated from here during the Napoleonic wars, a stone wall and turret still marking the limits of the station,
and then passes *Hunter's Quay*, for the Western Ferries car ferry to Gourock (Daily, frequent. Tel: 041-332-9766). The slightly more direct inland
road runs close to *Adam's Grave*, massive burial cairn slabs just west of
the road on the slope between Ardnadam Farm and the houses of
Sandbank.

2m **Dunoon** (10,000 inhab. *Inf.*) is a lively Clyde resort ranking as the
'capital' of Cowal. The famous Cowal Highland Gathering takes over on
the last Friday and Saturday in August (Secretary, Cowal Highland
Gathering, 2 Hanover Street, Dunoon PA23 7AV. Tel: 0369-3206).—
Caledonian MacBrayne car ferry to Gourock (Crossing 20 minutes;
daily, frequent. Tel: 0475-33755).

History. The town's early history is that of the old castle, traces of which can still be
seen. Built in the 13C, on the site of an earlier stronghold, the castle was taken in 1296
by Edward I, given by Bruce to the High Stewards, surrendered to Edward Balliol,
then retaken by Robert Stewart who in 1371 became King Robert II. Thus the castle
became a royal possession. In 1471 the Earl of Argyll and his heirs were made hereditary keepers by James III, the picturesque condition being that they should pay a
red rose, should such be demanded. When the present Queen visited Dunoon in
1958, the Duke of Argyll's representative, the Captain of Dunstaffnage, duly presented her with a red rose.

But in the 17C events associated with the castle were anything but picturesque. In
1646 the Marquis of Argyll, briefly master of Scotland, took the opportunity to
destroy the castle of his Lamont enemies at Toward, 6m to the south, thereafter
bringing some 200 prisoners to Dunoon where they were massacred and thrown
into mass graves. Forty years later, in 1685, the castle's story closed when the men of
Atholl burnt and razed it. Dunoon then relapsed into an unimportant village until in
the late 18C tourism began to grow.

The modern 'castle' (Castle House) was built in 1822 by James Ewing,
Provost of Glasgow, as a 'marine villa', and is now used for municipal
purposes. The remains of the real castle are on *Castle Hill*, above the
pier, at its foot being a statue (1896) of Burns's Highland Mary, born on
the site of the farm of Auchnamore behind the town. To the west of Castle
Hill is the old *Moot Hill*, where once justice was administered. There
had, though, been little justice for the Lamonts in 1646, and when last

century the road round Castle Hill was being built some of the mass graves were unearthed; the victims of the massacre are now remembered by a stone Celtic cross erected in 1906 by the Clan Lamont Society.

To the south of Dunoon A815 skirts the coast to pass ruined Knockamillie Castle and then, beyond Toward Point, *Toward Castle*, the 15C tower-house of the Lamonts, destroyed by Argyll in 1646. Beyond, a road continues north beside Loch Scriven to reach *Inverchaolain* (12m from Dunoon) with many ancient Lamont graves.—Off Dunoon lie the *Gantock Rocks*, marked by a beacon built by Robert Stevenson.

This Route now returns north to reach (*4m* from Dunoon) *Ardbeg* at the head of **Holy Loch**, traditionally owing its name to the wreck here of a shipload of earth from the Holy Land destined for the foundations of Glasgow cathedral. *Kilmun*, 1m south on A880, is worth a visit for both church and forestry reasons. The church (1841) is by Thomas Burns, but of the collegiate church founded here in 1441 by Sir Duncan Campbell only the tower survives. In the vault lies the 8th Earl and 1st Marquis of Argyll, beheaded in 1661; and in the churchyard lies Elizabeth Blackwell (1821–1910), the first woman to get her name into the British Medical Register. At Kilmun, too, a Forestry Office (with an arboretum) provides information on the many forest walks throughout Argyll Forest Park. The road which continues around Strone Point to reach *Ardentinny* and beyond has already been mentioned under Argyll Forest Park at the beginning of this Route.

Heading north from Ardbeg, A815 almost at once passes **Younger Botanic Garden** (Tel: 0369-6261), an outstation of Edinburgh's Royal Botanic Garden and known for its collection of flowering trees and shrubs, its extensive plantings of many species of conifers, and, above all perhaps, for the spectacular Californian giant redwoods, planted between 1865–70 and providing the entrance avenue. *Glen Massan* (c 5m; dead-end road) ascends north west through scenic country to end on a desolate tract of high moor.

A815 now runs with the east shore of **Loch Eck**, a scenic gash of water, 6m long and only a few hundred yards wide, lined on the east by Loch Eck Forest and on the west by the heights of Benmore, lifting to well over 2000ft. At (*4m* from Ardbeg) *Coylet Inn*, high on the hillside opposite can be seen a deep cleft, long a refuge during times of clan strife and the place where, at the beginning of this century, papers were found relating to the Argyll rising of 1685.—*6m Glenbranter*, just north of the loch's end, was an estate once owned by Sir Harry Lauder, here still standing the memorial he set up to his son, killed during the 1914–18 war, as also a cross to his wife who died in 1927.—*2m Strachur*, approaching which the outline of an unusual rectangular motte can be made out in the angle between A815 and the track to a saw mill. In the village the church of 1787 is of interest on three counts; the circular enclosure suggests an early Celtic origin, the church walls incorporate carved stones which came from a chapel nearby, and a little watchman's hut provides a ghoulish reminder of the days of body-snatching.

Just beyond Strachur A815 merges with A886, to complete this circuit of Cowal.

48   Fort William to Mallaig (Also the districts of Ardgour, Kingairloch, Sunart, Morvern, Moidart and Ardnamurchan)

One of several claimants to the title of 'Road to the Isles', A830 runs west from Fort William, bearing north at the coast to reach Mallaig. To the south of this road extends a broken, roughly rectangular peninsula—some 25m broad and stretching 30m southward to the Sound of Mull—embracing the districts of Ardgour and Kingairloch in the east, bordering Loch Linnhe; Sunart in the centre; Moidart and Ardnamurchan in the west; and Morvern to the south. Broken almost into several islands by the long waters of lochs Shiel and Sunart, the whole area is splendidly scenic, country of Highland impact in the north, easing southward into varied mountain and moor, yet still impressive, particularly around the lochs and near the rocky coast with basalt cliffs and views towards the islands.

Rte 48A below describes Fort William to Mallaig; Rte 48B, Kinlocheil to Lochaline through Ardgour, Kingairloch and Morvern; Rte 48C, Lochailort to Kilchoan through Moidart and Ardnamurchan.

A.   Fort William to Mallaig

A830.—Highland grandeur, combining mountains, inland lochs, sea lochs and islands.

SOME HOTELS. **Glenfinnan**. *Glenfinnan House*, PH37 4LT. Tel: 039783-235. *Stage House Inn*, PA37 4LT. Tel: 039783-246. **Lochailort**. *Lochailort Inn*, PH38 4LZ. Tel: 06877-208. **Arisaig**. *Arisaig House*, Beasdale, PH39 4NR. Tel: 06875-622. *Arisaig*, PH39 4NH. Tel: 06875-210. **Mallaig**. *Marine*, 10 Station Road, PH41 4PY. Tel: 0687-2217. *West Highland*, PH41 4QZ. Tel: 0687-2210.

Total distance 41m.—*11m* **Kinlocheil**.—*5m* **Glenfinnan**.—*9m* **Lochailort**.—*9m* **Arisaig**.—*7m* **Mallaig**.

The **West Highland Railway** accompanies the road. After a long absence, steam trains now run on certain days during the summer. Leaflet from any principal British Rail Scotland station. Supplement to normal fare. Tel: 0397-703791.

For **Fort William**, see Rte 49; to *Inverlochy Castle* and (*2m*) the *Caledonian Canal*, see Rtes 50 and 51. The canal is crossed immediately below Neptune's Staircase, a tight sequence of eight locks, built between 1805–22 and raising the canal by 64ft. There are more locks a short distance below, where the canal enters Loch Linnhe at Corpach, and, just beyond, along the road, stands an obelisk honouring John Cameron of Fassfern who fell at Quatre Bras in 1815, the major skirmish which preceded Waterloo. Continuing west, A830 soon fringes *Loch Eil*—a lovely sheet of water, 8m long, ¾m broad and forming a westward extension of Loch Linnhe—to reach (*6m*) *Fassfern* where the Young Pretender spent a night, four days after raising his standard at Glenfinnan.—*3m Kinlocheil*, just beyond which Rte 48B breaks away.

5m **Glenfinnan Monument and Visitor Centre** (NTS. Tel: 039783-250), at the head of Loch Shiel, mark where, on 19 August 1745, the

Young Pretender raised his standard, the signal for a venture which, despite victory at Prestonpans and an advance as far south as Derby, would end in April 1746 with disastrous defeat at Culloden. Some authorities have, however, long questioned whether the monument in fact marks the precise spot at which the standard was raised, suggesting that this may instead have been a knoll about a quarter of a mile away on the west bank of the river Finnan. Here a rock, exposed by a heath fire, bears the date 1745 and a Latin engraving thought to be Victorian. In 1990, on the occasion of the annual Gathering, NTS unveiled a plaque saying that this rock is in fact the correct site.

On 22 June 1745, unknown to his father (the Old Pretender), and optimistically assuming French help, Prince Charles Edward sailed from France with only seven companions. He reached Loch nan Uamh, some 12m west of here, on 25 July, but initially failed to raise any Highland enthusiasm and was in fact criticised for arriving without French backing. However, having gained Macdonald support, and having also shamed the influential Donald Cameron of Lochiel into joining him, he ostentatiously sent his ship away on 4 August and fixed a rendezvous for 19 August at Glenfinnan. Meanwhile, while the clans were rallied, he waited at Kinlochmoidart (see Rte 48C).

The prince spent the night of 18 August with Macdonald of Glenaladale, halfway down Loch Shiel, and the next morning was rowed to the rendezvous. After a slow start men and promises began to pour in, and in the afternoon the standard was raised, the Old Pretender being formally proclaimed King James VIII and the prince his regent.

The *Glenfinnan Monument*, bearing a statue of a Highlander (by John Greenshields), was erected in 1815 by Macdonald of Glenaladale, descendant of that Macdonald whose support had meant so much in getting the venture started, while the NTS *Visitor Centre* vividly tells the subsequent story, large maps showing the progress of the campaign and tracing also the prince's confusing wanderings after Culloden. The Glenfinnan Gathering and Games are held here annually on the Saturday in August nearest to the anniversary.

Loch Shiel reaches over 20m south east to Acharacle (see Rte 48C), here at Glenfinnan, and for over half its length, a scenic sheet of water with rocky wooded sides below mountains approaching 3000ft in height.

Moving into increasingly grand scenery, road and railway split respectively north and south of Loch Eilt and in 9m from Glenfinnan reach *Lochailort*, where Rte 48C heads south beside the loch of the same name. Next comes islanded *Loch nan Uamh*, beside which a cairn recalls that this otherwise quiet scoop out of the Sound of Arisaig saw both the start and finish of the '45, both the hopeful arrival and the defeated, dispirited departure of its leader. On the latter occasion he had an escort of two French frigates ('Mars' and 'Bellona') which, far too late, had brought money and arms for his cause (see also Rte 51, Loch Arkaig). A small English naval force, one of whose captains was later Earl Howe, engaged the French, but was too weak to hold them.

9m **Arisaig**, sheltered at the head of Loch nan Cealt, itself protected by a barrier of rocks and islets, is a small resort and yachting centre, best known perhaps, together with Mallaig, for Hebridean day cruises, some coordinated with West Highland Railway steam services. The choice varies from year to year but will probably include such islands as Eigg, Muck, Rhum, Canna, Mull, Soay and Skye, as also Loch Hourn, Loch Duich, Loch Coruisk and Loch Nevis.

Approaching (5m) *Morar* the road crosses a narrow isthmus with the sea on one side and, on the other, Loch Morar, remarkable for its great depth of over 1000ft. It was on the largest of the group of islands near the loch's west end that Lord Lovat was captured two months after

Culloden; an intriguer, he had been playing both sides, but was now taken to London and beheaded.

2m **Mallaig** (1000 inhab. *Inf.*), at the end of the road and the end of the railway, is, with Arisaig, important for its ferry and passenger services to Skye and other islands, as also for boat excursions into some of Scotland's most splendid sea loch scenery. Caledonian MacBrayne (Tel: 0475-33755) operate the ferry to Armadale on Skye (see Rte 62); also services (no cars) to Rhum, Eigg, Muck and Canna (see Rte 63).

B.   Kinlocheil to Lochaline

A861 to Strontian. A884 to Lochaline.—Mountain and sea loch, with distant views across to the heights above Glen Coe.

SOME HOTELS. **Ardgour (Corran)**. *Ardgour*, PH33 7AA. Tel: 08555-225. **Strontian**. *Kilcamb Lodge*, PH36 4HY. Tel: 0967-2257. *Ben View*, PH36 4HY. Tel: 0967-2333.

Total distance 53m.—*11m* **Camusnagaul.**—*10m* **Ardgour.**—*5m* **Inversanda.**—*8m* **Strontian.**—*19m* **Lochaline**.

From just west of **Kinlocheil** on Rte 48A, A861 skirts the southern length of Loch Eil to round the north east point of Ardgour at *(11m)* *Camusnagaul* with a passenger ferry to Fort William (Crossing 10 minutes. No cars; daily except Sunday, roughly every 2 hours. Tel: 03977-483). Now heading south beside Loch Linnhe, A861 in *10m* reaches **Ardgour (Corran)** on the west shore of the Corran Narrows (car ferry. 5 minutes; daily, frequent. Tel: 08555-243).—*5m Inversanda*, where there is a choice between continuing down the coast to turn inland at Loch a' Choire, or taking the main road west up Glen Tarbert which, below Garbh Bheinn (north, 2903ft) and Creach Bheinn (south, 2798ft), two of the higher Ardgour peaks, in *8m* reaches the pleasant small centre of **Strontian** (pron. Stronteen). Here *Ariundle Nature Reserve*, to the north, is known for its Atlantic mosses, liverworts and lichens, while, to the north again, are the long disused lead mines (care needed), opened in 1722 and in 1790 the source of the discovery of Strontianite of which Strontium 90 is an isotope. The mines provided much of the lead used in the bullets fired during the Napoleonic wars, and were at one time worked by French prisoners.

From Strontian this Route turns south on A884, while A861 continues west beside Loch Sunart to reach (8m) *Salen* on Rte 48C.

A884 for a short distance fringes the south shore of Loch Sunart before bearing south between the districts of Morvern (west) and Kingairloch (east) to reach in *15m* the hamlet of *Claggan*, just beyond which, at the head of Loch Aline, is ruined *Kinlochaline Castle*, the 15C square turreted tower of the chiefs of Clan MacInnes. From here a track down the east side of the loch leads to a promontory into the Sound of Mull to which still clings the ruined sentinel keep and broken wall of *Ardtornish Castle*, built in c 1340 and until the end of the 15C a principal stronghold of the Lords of the Isles.—*4m* **Lochaline**, known industrially for its silica quarries used in the manufacture of high grade optical glass, and by tourists for the car ferry to Fishnish on Mull (see Rte 64. Crossing 15 minutes. Daily, roughly hourly, but with some gaps. Caledonian MacBrayne, Tel: 0475-33755).

The road west along the north shore of the Sound of Mull (dead-end after 10m) passes *Fiunary*, once a home of the Macleods and the name incorporated in his title by Lord Macleod, founder of the Iona Community (1938). Beyond, in 2m by the shore, are the ruins of *Caisteal nan Con*, another link in the chain of strongholds between Dunollie (Oban) and Mingary on Ardnamurchan.

C.   Lochailort to Kilchoan

A861 to Salen. B8007 to Kilchoan.—At first between the islanded Sound of Arisaig and the heights of Moidart (nearly 3000ft). After a flat patch at Acharacle, a scenic run beside Loch Sunart and into the empty country of Ardnamurchan.

SOME HOTELS. **Acharacle**. *Dalilea House*, PH36 2JX. Tel: 096785-253. **Glenborrodale**. *Glenborrodale Castle*, Ardnamurchan, PH36 4JP. Tel: 09724-266.

Total distance 34m.—*10m* **Kinlochmoidart**.—*6m* **Acharacle**.—*2m* **Salen**.—*6m* **Glenborrodale**.—*10m* **Kilchoan**.

Leaving **Lochailort**, on Rte 48A, A861 for nearly 10m runs through the rocky coastal scenery of Moidart, below Ross Bheinn (2895ft) and with panoramic views along the shore and across to Eigg and Muck.—*10m Kinlochmoidart*, where Old Kinlochmoidart House, now a ruin, was destroyed by Government troops in 1746 because this was where the Young Pretender stayed while the clans were rallied to Glenfinnan. Dalelia, 2m south of here on Loch Shiel, was where the prince embarked to be rowed up the loch to overnight with his staunch ally Macdonald of Glenaladale.—*5m Blain*, from where a small road leads north for (2m) *Castle Tioram*, lone on an islet in Loch Moidart but accessible at low tide. This was the 13–14C keep of John of Moidart, but has also a later tower of c 1600. The ancient seat of the Macdonalds of Clan Ranald, the castle was burnt by its chief in 1715 to prevent its falling into Campbell hands when he joined Mar's uprising.

The scenery now surprisingly changes as (*1m*) **Acharacle** is reached, a small centre lying in a patch of oddly open flat country at the south foot of narrow and snaking Loch Shiel (see also Rte 48A).

2m **Salen** on Loch Sunart. From here A861 in 8m meets Rte 48B at Strontian, but this Route branches west to follow B8007 along the scenic northern shore of the loch where seals may often be seen, especially from a point just west of (*6m*) *Glenborrodale*. Beyond, the road takes a large inland loop to round Beinn nan Losgann (1026ft) and in *10m* reach **Kilchoan**, adjacent to which is ruined *Mingary Castle*, a 13C stronghold of the McIans, a branch of the Macdonald Lords of the Isles. Standing on a rock promontory and once the formidable guardian of the entrances both to Loch Sunart and to the Sound of Mull, Mingary long served the Lords of the Isles but eventually was witness, too, to their downfall, for here in 1495 James IV received their submission as also that of other island chiefs. Later, in 1625, the castle was taken by the Campbells; in 1644—an eventful year—it was seized on behalf of Montrose, besieged by Argyll, and then relieved; and in 1745 it suffered the indignity of being garrisoned by Hanoverian troops who even built a barrack within the walls.

Ardnamurchan Point, 5m north west of Kilchoan and with a lighthouse of 1846, is the most westerly mainland point in Britain.

From Kilchoan–Mingary there is a ferry (no cars) to Tobermory on Mull (Crossing 35 minutes. Daily except Sunday. Caledonian Mac-Brayne, Tel: 0475-33755).

VIII   THE NORTH

The North, as covered by this section, includes all the mainland northward from the roads linking Mallaig to Fort William (see Rte 48 in the previous section), and Fort William by way of the Spey valley and the Cairngorms to Inverness (Rte 50). It divides naturally into three zones—the Northern Highlands, that vast empty spread of mountains, lochs, glens, and burns that to many people represents the true Scotland; Inverness and the well-populated and fertile strip to its north; and the Far North, a land of rolling barren moor and bleak peat bog.

The above three zones are outlined in turn below. One feature, however, is common to all, namely brochs, those cunningly constructed defensive towers erected by people of perhaps the 1 and 2C. Traces of some 500 of these have been recorded throughout Scotland's North, including the islands, and the practised eye will soon readily pick out the distinctive stone-mounds that tell where a broch once rose. Some, though, still stand, and the mainland's two best preserved may be seen in *Glen Beg*, not far from Kyle of Lochalsh on the west coast (Rte 52).

Throughout any tour of the North it is also often worth reflecting that the peaceful valleys and lower moors, today so empty of anything but sheep, were until the 19C the home of large crofting communities, those Highlanders who for centuries until Culloden had marched out of their mountains to fight for whatever cause their chief was supporting. These people disappeared during the Clearances, leaving virtually no trace of their long presence, though at *Croick Church* in Strath Carron (Rte 57) their names and messages scratched on the glass are a moving reminder of their forced departure.

THE NORTHERN HIGHLANDS (Rtes 49–55; also much of Rtes 56 and 58) divide into six mountain districts: Ben Nevis, the Cairngorms, the Monadhliath Mountains, Glen Affric, Wester Ross and Inverpolly.

Ben Nevis, above Fort William (Rte 49), is known more for being Britain's highest mountain (4406ft) than for its scenic merit. Being without a cone or peak, from the roads which run near it the mountain appears simply as a towering, rounded mass and hides the buttresses and corries that are a feature of the north side. Ben Nevis is a walker's and climber's mountain rather than a motorist's. For the latter, though, there is *Glen Nevis*, the wild valley which curves southward round the mountain's foot.

The **Cairngorms** (Rte 50), a mountain mass with six peaks over 4000ft, lie between the Spey valley and upper Deeside, the approach by car being from the former, from *Aviemore*. The magnificent Ski Road (the only road into these mountains) climbs for some 10 miles through *Glen More Forest Park* to end at car parks at 2000ft whence chairlifts take the visitor to within 500ft of the summit of *Cairngorm* (4084ft).—Near Aviemore there are several places worth a visit. These include the Highland Wildlife Park at *Kincraig*; the Landmark Visitor Centre at *Carrbridge*, vividly covering 10,000 years of Highland history; near *Loch Garten* a nature reserve with nesting ospreys; and between Aviemore and *Boat of Garten* the steam line of the Strathspey Railway Association.

The **Monadhliath Mountains** (roadless, but fringed by Rtes 50 and 51) mass between the Spey valley and Loch Ness and the Great Glen, the geological split which cuts clean across northern Scotland. West of Loch Ness is **Glen Affric** (Rte 53), with its woods, lochs and mountain background one of Scotland's loveliest. A single road ascends the glen to end at *Loch Affric* at its head.

From the Great Glen a scenic road (Rte 52) crosses the mountains to *Kyle of Lochalsh* on the west coast, which may also of course be reached by a choice of more northerly roads. North of Kyle of Lochalsh, behind and along the coast, **Wester Ross** (Rte 55) offers exciting mountain and coastal touring country which includes the famous *Torridon* and *Beinn Eighe* range where the pink sandstone is capped with quartzite. Wester Ross can be entered from the south, from Loch Carron, near which a diversion can be made to cross the Pass of *Bealach-nam-Bo* (2054ft), one of the highest roads in Scotland; from the centre, at Achnasheen, passing *Beinn Eighe* and *Loch Maree*; or from the north at the spectacular Corrieshalloch Gorge. A road skirts much of the length of the coast along which are the well-known sub-tropical *Inverewe Gardens* and also *Gairloch*, a popular holiday centre.

The most northerly mountain district of the Northern Highlands is that made up of **Inverpolly Nature Reserve** and adjoining *Glencanisp* (Rte 56), together a confusion of high, isolated peaks, moor and lost lochs, as remote and wild as anywhere in Scotland. By car the best of Inverpolly can be seen from the narrow, winding road which rounds the reserve's southern and western sides to reach the village of *Lochinver*.

INVERNESS AND THE COASTAL STRIP (end of Rte 51. Rte 57). **Inverness** is a crowded town, useful to the visitor if of only limited tourist interest. About 5 miles east are *Culloden* (site of the battle) and *Clava Cairns* (prehistoric site), both places well worth a visit (Rte 43).

North from Inverness there is a well populated fertile coastal strip, largely made up of two peninsulas, *Black Isle* and *Tain*, separated from one another by Cromarty Firth. *Loch Fleet*, north of Dornoch, marks the end of this strip for beyond here the high ground closes in. From the south end at Beauly and from the north at Bonar Bridge fan out all the principal roads across to the western and northern coasts.

This strip has little in common with the Highlands that back it, nor is it of particular scenic attraction. Nevertheless it is not without places of interest. Among such are, from south to north, the ruins of 13C *Beauly Priory* and, on Black Isle, those of 14C *Fortrose Cathedral*, with, beyond, the quaint small town of *Cromarty*; above Evanton, the deep cleft of *Black Rock Ravine*; *Tain*, with its ancient church and chapel, and with a foot in history as the place whence in 1307 Bruce's wife and daughter were seized from sanctuary; and finally *Dornoch*, a quiet holiday centre with fine sands, a famous golf course and a cathedral dating from the 13C.

THE FAR NORTH (Rtes 59–61; also the northern parts of Rtes 56 and 58). The Far North includes the former counties, now districts, of *Sutherland* (north west) and *Caithness* (north east), the principal towns being *Dornoch* in the south (see above) and, in the north, *Wick* and *Thurso*, the latter with the car ferry for Orkney. For many the lure of the Far North will be simply that it is Britain's barren and sparsely populated tip, with at one end *John O'Groats*, Pentland and Orkney views, and day excursions to the islands, and, at the other, promisingly named *Cape Wrath*. Yet there is more to the Far North than this. This was the home of some of Scotland's earliest inhabitants; a land in later centuries long under Norse occupation (Sutherland was the 'South Land' for the Norsemen of Caithness); and a place which during the last 150 years has seen events as contrasting as the evictions of the Clearances and the construction of the nuclear power station at Dounreay.

Scenically Caithness and Sutherland are very different. Caithness, away from its east shore stacks and cliffs, is one third black peat bog and generally flat with fertile coastal strips. Sutherland, by contrast, apart from some wooded and cultivated valleys running in from the coasts, is a land of high, barren moor and bog, broken by numerous lochs and fringed to the west by commanding peaks. As to the coasts, the main road up the east is pleasant enough though not outstanding, while that along the north may prove disappointing because for much of its way it stays inland, giving only occasional views of the sea. Nevertheless the visitor who explores almost any of the many little roads down to the shore will find surprisingly rewarding lost corners with fine beaches and strange cliffs and rocks. Undoubtedly the most scenic road in the Far North is in the north west corner from *Kylesku* to *Durness* (Rte 56). This winds through a forbidding mountain wilderness of rock-strewn glens, glacial boulders and dark lochs, here and there touching a wild and broken coast with many islands. The village of *Scourie*, half-way, provides a break and, as along the other coasts, there are side roads to unexpected corners. One such is to *Tarbet*, with a close view across to the bird sanctuary island of *Handa*.

The Far North is rich in prehistoric monuments, many easily accessible yet in surroundings where the road, usually small, is the only modern touch. In the east for example, off A9 between Latheron and Wick, the *Grey Cairns of Camster*, with their horned-chamber complex, stand alone out on the peat bog, while not far away in equally unspoilt settings are the 200 or so little stones of the unexplained *Hill o'many Stanes* and the unusual megalith oval of *Achavanich*. Across in the west, beside *Loch Eriboll* (Rte 61), can be found an earth-house about as intact and as hidden as when it was built in perhaps the 1C; this is just one of the many prehistoric remains in the district around *Durness*. Brochs abound in the Far North more than anywhere else on the mainland, but mostly only as mounds of stones. The best preserved is *Dornadilla* (south of Loch Hope, Rte 58), a small broch, part of the surviving wall of which may still be about its original height. Other recognisable brochs are the two north and south of *Brora* on the east coast.

The Norsemen have left little visible evidence of their years of settlement. Instead this period lives on in place names: 'Lybster' meaning farmstead; 'by', village; 'Wick', bay. Nor is there a great deal from medieval and later times. The principal such sites are *Dornoch*, with its cathedral and part of its bishop's palace; a number of castle ruins either side of *Wick*; and some ancient churches between John O'Groats and Dounreay (*Canisbay*; *Dunnet*, with a perhaps 14C saddleback tower; the 12 or 13C St Peter's Church in *Thurso*; and the ruined 12C *Chapel of St Mary*, on the coast 5 miles west). In contrast, just beyond this last, there sprawls the *Dounreay* nuclear power station.

But the Far North does have its modern ruins, and everywhere the traveller will find abandoned buildings, roofless and crumbling. These do not, as might be thought, date from the Clearances (of that period virtually nothing remains), but are evidence of more recent depopulation throughout this remote region which has little to offer its youth.

49   Fort William and Environs

Tourist Information. Cameron Square. Tel: 0397-703781.

SOME HOTELS. *Mercury*, Achintore Road, PH33 6RW. Tel: 0397-703117. *Alexandra*, The Parade, PH33 6AZ. Tel: 0397-702241. *Clan Macduff Motorlodge*, Achintore Road, PH33 6RW. Tel: 0397-702341. *Croit Anna*, Achintore Road, PH33 6RR. Tel: 0397-702268.

Ferry to *Camusnagaul* on Ardgour (Crossing 10 minutes. No cars. Daily, except Sunday, roughly every 2 hours. Tel: 03977-483.—For other loch cruising possibilities, ask Tourist Information). —**West Highland Railway**. To Mallaig for Skye. Steam trains on certain days in summer. Tel: 0397-703791 (see also Rte 48A).

History. Ignoring nearby Inverlochy Castle (see Rte 51), with a story reaching back to at least the 13C and even, though less probably, to the 8C, Fort William's relatively short history began in 1655 when General Monk built an earthwork fort here. This was replaced by stone during the reign of William III—the settlement being briefly known as Maryburgh in honour of his queen—the new fort achieving the distinction of successfully holding out against the Jacobites during both the '15 and the '45. During the later 19C the fort was pulled down to make way for the

FORT WILLIAM
AND ENVIRONS

0 yards   1000

0 kilometres   1

railway which, ironically, was to bring tourism, growth and prosperity to a place originally conceived, to quote Dr Johnson, with the purpose of subduing 'savage clans and raving barbarians'.

For Fort William to **Tyndrum**, see Rte 44; to **Mallaig** and the district to the south, see Rte 48; to **Inverness** via the Spey Valley and the Cairngorms, see Rte 50; to **Inverness** via the Great Glen and Loch Ness, see Rte 51.

Fort William (11,000 inhab.), amid splendid mountain and water scenery, and at the foot of Ben Nevis (Britain's highest mountain), is a rail, waterway and, above all, a road hub, a magnet for tourists yet on the whole spacious enough to absorb them.

Of the fort nothing survives, and the visitor in search of the local story should, instead, make for Cameron Square, with a visitor centre, Tourist Information and the *West Highland Museum* (Tel: 0397-702169) in which local history, natural history, folk material and the '45 are the principal themes.

From the tourist point of view Fort William is almost synonymous with Ben Nevis, well explained by means of an exhibition, video and model at the *Ben Nevis Centre*, with also a Scottish Craft Exhibition, in High Street (Tel: 0397-704406).

*Ben Nevis (4406ft) is in fact little seen from the town, and what small part is visible appears as no more than a high, rounded hump. Although Britain's highest mountain, it lacks a definite peak and thus its height and great mass are not readily appreciated. The mountain's main features are the deep Glen Nevis (see below) on the south; the impressive buttresses and gullies on the north, best seen approaching Fort William from Spean Bridge; and the grand corrie on the north east at the head of which a narrow ridge connects the summit with the spur of Cairn More Dearg (4012ft).

The mountain is easily enough climbed by a choice of approaches, but there can be hazards and Tourist Information advice should be sought before setting out. On the summit are the ruins of an observatory, built in 1823 to study sunspots but closed in 1904, and the views, of course, can be immense, except to the north east where the Cairngorms shorten the horizon. To the south, Loch Linnhe, the Glen Coe mountains, Ben More on Mull, Ben Cruachan and the Paps of Jura can be visible, and even, if exceptionally, the coast of Ireland. To the south east stand Ben Lawers and Schiehallion; to the north east a glimpse can be caught of Loch Laggan on the approach to the Spey valley. The line of the Great Glen and its lochs can be traced, while, far to the west, are the ragged peaks of the Cuillins (Skye), the hills of Rhum and the Sgurr of Eigg.

*Glen Nevis, comfortably ascended by car, hooks for a wild and rugged 6m below the western and southern flanks of the mountain. *Glen Nevis House* (no adm.), reached in 1½m, was the headquarters during the '45 of Donald Cameron of Lochiel while he unsuccessfully tried to take Fort William. Beyond, by the farm of *Achriabhach*, the road crosses the river, here tumbling as rapids down a small ravine, and soon ends at a car park in a highly scenic setting beside a waterslide.—A walk of 1m, in places rough, leads through a gorge to a waterfall, beyond this continuing east over a pass (1320ft) to (another 10m) *Loch Treig* and *Correur Station*, close to the highest point (1354ft) of the Glasgow to Fort William railway.

50   Fort William to Inverness via Spey Valley and the Cairngorms

A82 to Spean Bridge. A86 to Kingussie. B9152 to Aviemore. A95 and B9153 to Carrbridge. A9 (with diversion along B9154 at Loch Moy) to Inverness.—As far as Loch Laggan, often bleak moor below mountains rising to over 3000ft. Later, as far as Aviemore, down the broad and in part wooded Spey valley, with the Monadhliath Mountains to the north and west, and the Grampians, including the Cairngorms, to the east. Beyond, mixed moor, wood and pastoral land.

SOME HOTELS. **Spean Bridge**. *Spean Bridge*, PH34 4ES. Tel: 039781-250. **Laggan**. *Gaskmore House*, PH20 1BS. Tel: 05284-250. **Newtonmore**. *Alvey House*, Golf Course Road, PH20 1AT. Tel: 05403-260. *Ard-Na-Coille*, Kingussie Road, PH20 1AY. Tel: 05403-214.

Aviemore. *Four Seasons*, Aviemore Centre, PH22 1PF. Tel: 0479-810681. *Highlands*, Aviemore Centre, PH22 1PJ. Tel: 0479-810771. *Stakis Coylumbridge*, PH22 1QN. Tel: 0479-810661. **Boat of Garten**. *The Boat*, PH24 3BH. Tel: 047983-258. **Carrbridge**. *Struan House*, PH23 3AS. Tel: 047984-242.

Total distance 82m.—*9m* **Spean Bridge**.—*26m* **Laggan**.—*7m* **Newtonmore**.—*3m* **Kingussie**.—*6m* **Kincraig**.—*6m* **Aviemore**.—*6m* **Carrbridge**.—*19m* **Inverness**.

For **Fort William**, see Rte 49. For Fort William to *Spean Bridge* by B8004 along the Caledonian Canal, see Rte 51.

Leaving Fort William A82 crosses the Nevis and immediately enters **Inverlochy** with the long pier of the aluminium company, the factory of which, with its pipes running down the mountain, is to the east of the road. The waters of Loch Treig (east of Ben Nevis), raised 40ft and combined by means of a tunnel-pipe with those of lochs Moy and Laggan, are led by another tunnel beneath Ben Nevis to the aluminium works. For ancient *Inverlochy Castle* (not to be confused with the nearby 19C hotel of the same name), signed down A830, see Rte 51.—*Nevis Range* ski complex (Tel: 0397-705825) is passed before *9m* **Spean Bridge**, where this Route switches to A86 while Rte 51 follows A82 from the nearby *Commando Memorial*. Those Commandos would surely have savoured the scene near Spean Bridge over two centuries earlier, on 16 August 1745, when a mere dozen of MacDonald of Keppoch's Highlanders, armed with little more formidable than bagpipes and blood-curdling cries, routed two companies of government troops on their way from Fort Augustus to reinforce the garrison at Fort William. The troops fled back to Loch Lochy where, meeting more Highlanders, they wisely surrendered (to become, two days later, enforced spectators at Glenfinnan), while Spean Bridge achieved its modest mention in history as the site of the opening skirmish of the '45.

3m **Roybridge**, immediately south of which the hamlet of *Keppoch* was in 1688 the scene of Scotland's last real clan battle, sparked, as so often, by the fact that the MacDonalds of Keppoch held these lands by clan tradition, whereas the Mackintoshes had a 'sheepskin grant'. To settle the matter, and enjoying government support, the Mackintoshes attacked, only however to be defeated. This, of course, the government could not accept, and troops were soon sent to finish off the MacDonalds.—From Roybridge a road ascends for 9m up **Glen Roy**, on either side of which are the geologically famous *Parallel Roads*, mountainside terraces left by the slowly sinking waters of the ice-dammed lake that once filled this valley. The 'roads' are clearly seen because they date from the comparatively recent geological time known as the Loch Lomond Advance, a very late Ice Age build-up of some 10–11,000 years ago. The area is a national nature reserve (2887 acres) and a booklet (normally obtainable from Tourist Information) explains the geology in some detail.

6m **Loch Moy** (sometimes called Loch Laggan Reservoir), with a dam 180ft high and 700ft long and occasionally unattractively empty, is linked by tunnel to Loch Treig, 2m south, whence water flows through another tunnel under Ben Nevis to the aluminium works at Inverlochy.—Beyond, the road skirts Loch Laggan proper to reach (*11m*) *Kinloch Laggan*, between which and (*6m*) *Laggan* the Mashie is joined by the Spey (north), in the angle between the two rising *Dun-na-Lamb*, a hill-fort 600ft above the valley.

From Laggan a diversion can be made westward to enjoy a few miles of the infant Spey and experience, too, some touches of the Jacobite and Hanoverian stories. For this road (a century later much used by drovers), though built in 1735 by General Wade for the easier control of the Highlanders, in fact in 1745 achieved the opposite, proving a boon for the Young Pretender who advanced south east from Bridge of Oich through Corrieyarrick Pass and, on reaching Garvamore (7m from Laggan), seized Cluny Macpherson and persuaded him and his 400 men to join his cause. The motor road ends beyond the Spey, but Wade's continues as a track through Corrieyarrick (2507ft) to descend through Glen Tarff to Fort Augustus at the south end of Loch Ness.

2m Cluny Castle was the home of Cluny Macpherson (see just above), who, unable of course to return home after Culloden, instead—and despite a large reward offered for his capture—managed to hide for nine years in a cave in the cliffs of *Craig Dhubh* which hang above the road about *3m* farther on. Macpherson graves, including those of clan chiefs, will be found in the small burial ground below the castle, while more about this clan can be learnt at *(2m)* **Newtonmore** (1000 inhab.) where there is a *Clan Macpherson Museum* (Tel: 05403-332). The clan rally and Newtonmore Highland Games are held on the first Saturday in August.—For Newtonmore to *Pitlochry* and *Perth*, see Rte 27.

3m **Kingussie** (1000 inhab. *Inf.*) is 'capital' of the historic and sizeable district of Badenoch, bounded by the Monadhliath, Grampian and Atholl mountains and anciently the territory of the Comyns until their defeat by Bruce. Bruce then gave part to Randolph, Earl of Moray, retaining the remainder for the Crown, this part later being granted to Alexander, son of Robert II and notorious as the 'Wolf of Badenoch'. But of the medieval stronghold of the Comyns and the 'Wolf' all that survives, just south across the Spey, is an exceptionally large motte, support now for the ruined shell of *Ruthven Barracks*, as stark and ugly visually as is their story. Built in 1718 to control the Highlanders, and in 1734 enlarged by Wade—two years before the poet James Macpherson of Ossianic renown was born in the adjacent village—the barracks were in 1745 at first held successfully against the Jacobites (by Sergeant Molloy and only 14 men) but later fell to the Young Pretender. And it was to this grim Hanoverian outpost that the pathetic remnants of the prince's army rallied after Culloden, only to have such hopes as they may have still held abruptly extinguished by the curt message that every man should seek his safety in the best way he could. So they blew up the barracks and scattered.

More pleasantly, Kingussie is the home of the admirable *Highland Folk Museum* (Tel: 0540-661307). Founded in 1935 on Iona by Miss I.F. Grant, an authority on Gaelic and clan history, the museum here is now in two parts, open air and indoors. The former shows a 'blackhouse' from Lewis, a click mill and a salmon smokehouse, while indoors there is a farming section, a kitchen scene, and a gallery showing Highland furniture and domestic bygones.

Between Kingussie and Aviemore, a distance of 14m, there is a choice of three close and parallel roads, A9 and B9152 keeping north of the Spey while B970 serves the other bank. A9 will be for those in a hurry; a combination of the other two, conveniently linked by a bridge halfway at Kincraig, will provide the easiest approach to several points of interest; B970 will be chosen by those set on exploring the Badenoch mountains' glens of *Tromie* and *Feshie*.

Leaving Kingussie, B9152 passes the war memorial, interestingly set on a prehistoric tumulus, and then a monument to James Macpherson (see above), builder of the mansion of Balavil (2m from Kingussie) on the site of ancient Raits Castle, once a Comyn stronghold and the scene of a massacre by the Mackintoshes. The story goes that Comyn had invited his Mackintosh enemies to a feast in pretended reconciliation, but had arranged that each Comyn would kill a Mackintosh as soon as the boar's head—long a customary signal for violent death—was brought on. However the Mackintoshes were forewarned and slew the Comyns instead.

6m **Kincraig** is known for its *Highland Wildlife Park* (Royal Zoological Society of Scotland. Tel: 05404-270), with both drive-through and walk-through sections. The former shows deer, bison and Highland cattle; the latter, wolves, bears, wildcats, eagles and well over 50 other species, while a picnic area and children's farm are among other attractions. *Insh Church*, sitting on a morraine knoll above Loch Insh immediately south of Kincraig, claims that its site was once sacred to the Druids and that it has been continuously used for Christian worship since the coming of Celtic missionaries in the 6 or 7C; a claim supported inside the church by an ancient Celtic bell and a hollow stone said to have been used as a font by St Adamnan.—*3m Alvie*, to the south of which there are three monuments, the most conspicuous being that atop Tor Alvie, a 90ft-high column erected in 1840 to the last Duke of Gordon (died 1836) and bearing inscriptions in Gaelic, Latin and English. Nearby, and more modest, a cairn of 1815 put up by the Marquis of Huntly honours the Highland soldiers who fell at Waterloo, while the third monument, an obelisk nearer the river to the south, remembers Bonnie Jean, Duchess of Gordon (died 1812), who reputedly recruited for the Gordon Highlanders by giving a kiss to those who joined. Another who lived near Alvie, and who is buried here, was Sir George Henschel (1850–1934), the conductor and composer.

In *2m* beyond Alvie, and just short of Aviemore, B970 (the start of the 'Ski Road' into Glen More Forest Park and the Cairngorms, see below) crosses the Spey into *Inverdruie*, with three attractions all associated with the **Rothiemurchus Estate** (Tel: 0479-810858). The first to be reached, on the left just after B970 crosses the Spey, is the *Fish Farm and Fishing Centre* with myriad fish which can be viewed and fed and the rearing of which is explained. A short way beyond are the adjacent *Estate Visitor Centre* and the *Cairngorm Whisky Centre*. The former provides an introduction to this large Highland estate—owned in turn by Comyns, Gordons, Shaws, Mackintoshes and, since 1580, Grants—and also advises on the many possibilities open to visitors, these including ranger-accompanied forest and wildlife walks, a farm tour, a land-rover estate tour, fishing and clay pigeon shooting. The whisky centre includes a video, a small museum and a tasting room.—The Rothiemurchus Estate includes *Loch-on-Eilean* (2m south of Inverdruie), an exceptionally lovely loch, surrounded by pines below a mountain backdrop and with an island castle, started in the 15C by Lachlan of Mackintosh but later enlarged and passing, as part of the estate, to the Gordons and then the Grants. Until the loch was dammed during the 18C the castle could be reached by causeway, an approach which in 1688 tempted an attack by adherents of James VII/II who, however, reckoned without the spirit of the laird's wife who in her husband's absence put up a successful resistance. A nature trail makes the circuit of the loch and a visitor centre (Tel: 0479-810647), in a converted croft, tells the story of the local ecology, with particular reference to the pine forest.

1m (by B9152 from junction with B970) **Aviemore** (1500 resident inhab. *Inf.* on B9152 at south approach to the town. Tel: 0479-810363) has come a long way since it was a settlement beside Wade's military road, later, with the coming of the railway in the 19C, becoming an unassuming though stylish small resort.

All this changed during the 1960s with the arrival of the *Aviemore Centre* (Tel: 0479-810624), Europe's first purpose-built leisure, sports and conference centre with, among today's features, hotels, restaurants, ice rink, swimming pool, theatre, cinema and dry ski slope. Although the Centre inevitably dominates Aviemore, there are other things here, including even a reminder of the prehistoric past in the shape of a few stones of a small ring-cairn, signed (east) off the main road towards the north of the town; while more recent nostalgia is catered for by the steam trains of the *Strathspey Railway* (Tel: 047983-692; for restaurant trains, 047983-258). Plying between Aviemore (Speyside station) and Boat of Garten, the headquarters of the Strathspey Railway Association (museum), the trains keep alive five miles of a line opened in 1863 and officially closed in 1965. *Craigellachie Nature Reserve* (Nature Trail), immediately west of Aviemore beside A9, provides a mixture of birchwood and moor rising to 1700ft, while geological features include the Craigellachie Rock, historically the rallying place of Clan Grant whose war cry was 'Stand fast, Craigellachie!'. This clan occupied the lands between this Craigellachie and that 37m away at the foot of Strathspey; there are twin Grant mausoleums at Duthil on the road from Carrbridge to Grantown-on-Spey.

Aviemore, together with its Centre, offers a range of year-round special and inclusive holiday arrangements, including winter sports and many other recreations. There are also concessions by British Rail. Write: Aviemore and Spey Valley Tourist Centre, Main Road, Aviemore, PH22 1PP. Tel: 0479-810363.

*Glen More Forest Park and the Cairngorms

Glen More Forest Park lies close to the south east of Aviemore, while beyond lifts the mass of Cairngorm, with the Cairngorms National Nature Reserve. The area is reached by the fine scenic 'Ski Road' (buses) which starts at Coylumbridge, 2m south east of Aviemore, and, after crossing the Forest Park, in another 8m reaches the chairlifts at the foot of Cairngorm.

Climbs and Walks. The whole district abounds in possibilities for climbs and walks, ranging from simple, well-marked local nature trails to strenuous undertakings to summits or across the mountains to Braemar (28–30m). Many of the walks trace old drover roads, and many tackle high, wild country which should only be attempted in good weather by those with experience and specialist clothing and equipment. Although in general the walks are public rights of way, and there are no restrictions within the Forest Park, elsewhere there can at certain times of the year be restrictions for reasons of bird protection and deer culling. Advice on the Cairngorms generally, and particularly on climbs and walks, can be obtained from Aviemore Tourist Information, the Forestry Commission Information Centre at Glenmore, or the Rothiemurchus Visitor Centre at Inverdruie.

Glen More Forest Park, covering the north west slopes of Cairngorm, was first known as Queen's Forest, to commemorate the Silver Jubilee of King George V and Queen Mary in 1935, and was given its present name in 1948. With 4000 acres of forest ringed by mountains, the heart of the park is *Loch Morlich* (camping, caravanning, swimming, boating) at the east end of which are the admirable *Forestry Commission Information Centre* (Tel: 047986-271) and *Reindeer House*, the latter the headquarters of the Reindeer Company which, weather permitting, arranges viewing walks with the herdsman (Daily, assembly 11.00. Reindeer are usually seen within half an hour, but good walkers may join a longer tour. Tel: 047986-228). The local herd of Swedish reindeer was introduced in 1952, but the animals seen today are Scottish-born descendants. And here, too, a boulder commemorates the Norwegians who trained in this area during the last war.

Leaving Loch Morlich, the road climbs past the *Coire na Ciste* car park at 1800ft (snack bar and facilities, winter only), with two chairlifts serving several ski tows, to reach the *Coire Cas* car park at 2100ft, offering, weather permitting, all year access to the summit (Tel: 047986-261). The westerly view, even from the car park, is superb, and as often as not reindeer graze the area. A first chairlift reaches the *Shieling* halfway station (2500ft. Snack bar and facilities), from where a second (White Lady) lifts to the summit station at 3600ft, with the Ptarmigan snack bar, the highest eating place in Britain. From here a path reaches the summit (4084ft) of *Cairngorm*.

The **'Cairngorms**, a concentration of splendid mountains lying between Aviemore on the Spey and Braemar on Deeside, represent the highest mountain mass in Britain, with six peaks of over 4000ft. Of granite, the massif is famous for the now rare transparent crystals of brownish quartz, often quite large, known as 'cairngorms'. The *Cairngorms National Nature Reserve* covers some 100 square miles of the southern part of the region. Established between 1954–66, and the largest nature reserve in Britain, it is partly owned by Scottish Natural Heritage but is mainly private estates (Rothiemurchus, Glenfeshie, Glen Avon and Mar Lodge). The reserve has a sub-arctic summit plateau with distinctive arctic-alpine plant and animal communities, and amongst the wildlife that may be seen are mountain hare, wild cat, deer, ptarmigan and eagles.

Aviemore is left by A95, in *4m* reaching the junction with B9153 (for Carrbridge). Here an eastward diversion may be made to (2m) **Boat of Garten**, so called from the ferry that operated here until the bridge was built in 1898 and today the home of the *Strathspey Railway Association* (see above). *Loch Garten* (2m south east) is a nature reserve established in 1959 to safeguard the first pair of ospreys to breed in Scotland for some 50 years. There is an RSPB information point and observation hut (Tel: 0479-83694) providing fixed binoculars, an intimate view of the nest by means of a video relay from a camera near the tree, and a programme of nature reserve walks. The diversion may be continued for another 4m along B970 to Nethy Bridge, just beyond which, and standing on a motte, is *Castle Roy*, or Red Castle, a ruined curtain-wall stronghold of the Comyns, dating from the 12C and one of the oldest castle ruins in Scotland.

2m (by B9153) **Carrbridge**, most visited for the imaginative *Landmark Visitor Centre* (Tel: 047984-614). Here, though the principal attraction is a dramatic multi-screen presentation and exhibition, there is also much else and especially for children. Other features include indoor and outdoor forestry exhibitions; a steam-powered saw mill; a lofty observation tower commanding a fine view of the Cairngorms; a woodland maze; a pine forest nature centre, with nature and tree-top trails; and an adventure playground. Nor should Carrbridge be left without a glance at its picturesque arch of a bridge of 1717, built after two men had been drowned at the ford. Specially designed to be above flood level, the bridge was nonetheless badly damaged by water in 1829, in the same storm which produced that spectacular flood recorded at Randolph's Leap on the nearby river Findhorn. And those with an association with the name Grant may wish to divert the short distance east to Duthil where they will find the family's twin mausoleums.

This Route now joins the trunk A9, crossing the Findhorn at (*8m*) *Tomatin*, where the distillery may be visited (Tel: 08082-234), and in another *2m* branching to the right along B9154 for *Loch Moy*, the heart of Mackintosh territory for over 600 years. The chiefs' island castle was replaced in c 1700 by a mansion north of the loch, this being burnt in 1800 and replaced by two successor mansions, the second, today's Moy Hall (no adm.), dating from 1955. Near here, in February 1746, took place what was to be known as the 'Rout of Moy', an affair remarkably similar to that at Spean Bridge the previous year. Scorning the ambivalence of her husband (the Mackintosh), the lady of Moy (Scott's 'gallant amazon') sheltered the Young Pretender and, on learning that Lord Loudoun, governor of Inverness, was advancing with 1500 men, despatched the Moy blacksmith and six or so men into the night to reconnoitre. Hearing the enemy approach, the blacksmith's band scattered, skirling clan rallies on their bagpipes and yelling Lochiel, Keppoch and their own war cries. Convinced that they had blundered into the main Jacobite army, Loudoun's men turned tail while later, back at Moy, the prince informed the Mackintosh that he must regard himself as his wife's prisoner.

4m Daviot, where B851 leads north east for Culloden (Rte 43) while this Route rejoins A9 for (*5m*) **Inverness**, see Rte 51.

51 Fort William to Inverness via the Great Glen and Loch Ness

A82 and A830 out of Fort William to Banavie. B8004 beside the Caledonian Canal to rejoin A82 short of Spean Bridge. A82 (alternative B862 and B852 south of Loch Ness) to Inverness.—Scenically pleasant, though, for the Highlands, unspectacular, most of the distance being beside the string of lochs (Lochy, Oich, Ness) which fill the Great Glen, the geological split across northern Scotland. The lochs have green and often wooded hilly shores, with, frequently, mountain background. A82 carries a lot of traffic in summer.

SOME HOTELS. **Invergarry**. *Glengarry Castle*, PH35 4HW. Tel: 08093-254. **Fort Augustus**. *Lovat Arms*, PH32 2BE. Tel: 0320-6206. *The Brae*, PH32 4DG. Tel: 0320-6289. **Invermoriston**. *Glenmoriston Arms*, IV3 6YA. Tel: 0320-51206. **Drumnadrochit**. *Drumnadrochit*, IV3 6TU. Tel: 04562-218. *Polmaily House*, IV3 6XT. Tel: 04562-343. **Foyers**. *Foyers*, IV1 2XT. Tel: 04563-216. **Inverness**. *Craigmonie*, Annfield Road, IV2 3HX. Tel: 0463-231649. *Kingsmills*, Culcabock Road, IV2 3LP. Tel: 0463-237166. *Palace*, Ness Walk, IV3 5NE. Tel: 0463-223243. *Caledonian*, Church Street, IV1 1DX. Tel: 0463-235181.

Total distance 61m.—*7m* **Gairlochy**.—*16m* **Invergarry**.—*6m* **Fort Augustus**.—Either: *6m* **Invermoriston**.—*12m* **Drumnadrochit**.—*14m* **Inverness**. Or: *14m* **Foyers**.—*10m* **Dores**.—*8m* **Inverness**.

The **Caledonian Canal**, following the Great Glen, links Loch Linnhe in the south with Moray Firth in the north, but only about 22m of its 60m length is true canal, the remainder taking advantage of the succession of lochs. The route was surveyed by James Watt in 1773, construction was begun by Telford in 1803, and the canal was opened in 1822; it turned out, however, to be too shallow and was not finally completed until 1847. For many years it was much used, particularly by sailing boats anxious to avoid the long and often hazardous voyage around Scotland's northern coast. Today, owing to the small capacity of the 29 locks as also the greater seaworthiness of modern ships, the canal is much less active, though it remains popular with pleasure and other small craft.

For **Fort William**, see Rte 49. For Fort William by A82 to *Spean Bridge*, see Rte 50.

This Route leaves Fort William by A82 but in just over *1m* bears briefly west on A830 (Rte 48) rounding ruined *Inverlochy Castle*, dating probably from the late 13C, though a curious legend insists that this was the site of a Pictish city, the king of which is said to have signed a treaty with Charlemagne in 790. More certainly, this was a Comyn stronghold and, later, the scene of three battles, in 1429, 1431 and, more importantly, in 1645 when the Covenanters under Argyll were defeated by Montrose.— *1m. Banavie*, where the Caledonian Canal is crossed immediately below the tight sequence of the eight locks known as Neptune's Staircase, raising the canal 64ft and representing one of Telford's biggest problems. From Banavie B8004 takes this Route along the canal's west bank, in 3m crossing the mouth of *Glen Loy*, down which the Young Pretender marched from Glenfinnan, and in another 2m reaching *Gairlochy*.

Here a diversion can be made north beside Loch Lochy and then west for a look at **Loch Arkaig**, which, its north shore with a road, cuts westward through the mountains of Lochaber for some 13m. *Achnacarry House* (no adm. except to *Clan Cameron Museum*, Tel: 0397-772473), on the isthmus between Loch Lochy and Loch Arkaig and the seat of Cameron of Lochiel, recalls Donald Cameron of Lochiel who, after initial doubts about the Young Pretender's venture, eventually gave his support after being taunted with wishing to stay at home and learn about his prince's fate from the newspapers. He must surely have later rued his decision for he was wounded at Culloden and soon afterwards died in France, while Cumberland destroyed his castle here, now a ruin beside its early 19C successor. *Murlaggan*, at the road's end, was the scene of one of the last Jacobite rallies in 1746, an occasion on which, it is said, treasure belatedly given by the French was cast into the loch to prevent its falling into government hands.

At Gairlochy B8004 carries this Route back across the canal, here about to lose itself in Loch Lochy, and in 2m reaches the junction with A82, within the intersection being the *Commando Memorial* (Scott Sutherland, 1952), standing watch above the rough Lochaber land over which the commandos trained during the last war and remembering those among them who lost their lives. From here, too, there is an excellent view of Ben Nevis. For *Spean Bridge*, 1m farther, see Rte 50.

Fringing the east shore of Loch Lochy A82 in *11m* reaches *Laggan*, on the neck between lochs Lochy and Oich and the scene of at least two skirmishes, for the second of which—and it was bloodless—see Rte 50, Spean Bridge. But there was nothing bloodless about the defeat here in July 1544 of Clan Fraser by Clan Macdonald in an affray known as the Battle of the Shirts because both sides discarded their plaids, so hot was the weather. Beyond, beside the road on the west shore of Loch Oich, the *Well of the Heads* (1812)—seven men's heads above a spring—is a bizarre monument to a grim story. In the 17C Keppoch, head of a branch of the MacDonells, sent his two sons to be educated in France but himself died while they were away, leaving the management of his affairs to his seven brothers who, greedy to share these lands, murdered the lads on their return. But the family bard—an improbable but efficient avenger—had the murderers put to death and presented their heads to the chief of the clan at Glengarry, having first washed them in this well where an inscription in Gaelic, English, French and Latin records this 'ample and summary vengeance'.

3m **Invergarry**, where the ruins of *Invergarry Castle* cling on in the grounds of Glengarry Castle Hotel. Successor to earlier castles, this was long the seat of the chiefs of the MacDonells of Glengarry and it would have been here that the Keppoch bard would have made his presentation of the seven murderers' heads. A century or so later, in 1746, there was vengeance on another scale when Cumberland razed this staunchly Jacobite home.—For A87 westward to *Kyle of Lochalsh*, see Rte 52.

If Invergarry Castle, halfway up Loch Oich, recalls the '45's merciless end, *Bridge of Oich*, only 2m farther north, recalls the high hopes of its beginning, for here—and with strong government forces only just up the road at Fort Augustus—the Young Pretender wheeled southward, to march through the Pass of Corrieyarrick and onward deep into England.

4m **Fort Augustus** (1000 inhab. *Inf.*), at the head of famed Loch Ness, and offering a choice of onward roads, comes as an obvious halfway halt along this Route.

History. That this place was inhabited in very early times is proved by Cherry Island, a loch crannog just offshore to the north of the town, as also by the town's ancient name of Kilcumein, meaning Church of Cumein, a successor of St. Columba. After the '15, Hanoverian government barracks were built here, on the site now occupied by the Lovat Arms Hotel behind which a fragment of barrack still survives. In 1724 Wade made the village his headquarters (for his roads in this district, see below), in 1729 starting the construction of a new fort in a tactically better situation beside the loch. This he named Fort Augustus, after William Augustus, Duke of Cumberland, then only a boy but later to earn such notoriety in these parts. Captured by the Jacobites during the '45, the fort was soon retaken by government troops after Culloden, and it was here that Cumberland was presented with the head of Roderick Mackenzie, a young Edinburgh lawyer who had gallantly encouraged his captors in their belief that he was the fugitive Young Pretender (see also Rte 52, Glen Moriston). The remains of the by then redundant fort were sold in 1867 to Lord Lovat, who in 1876 presented them to the Benedictine Order for the founding of an abbey and school.

Fort Augustus stands at the crossing of four of *General Wade's Military Roads.* One of these has been followed by this Route from Fort William. Another, now a footway, leads across to Glen Moriston. A third, now also only a track but the one used by the Young Pretender at the start of his southward march, ascends Glen Tarff to cross Corrieyarrick Pass and reach the Spey. And the fourth, described below, makes for Inverness by way of the south east shore of Loch Ness.

Fort Augustus Abbey (Tel: 0320-6234), a boys' school since 1878, is, theologically, successor to two older abbeys; that of St. Adrian and Denys, founded in Hanover in 1645, and that of St. James of the Scots, founded at Regensburg in Bavaria in about 1100 and later an important post-Reformation centre for Scottish Catholics. Architecturally, of course, the abbey represents Wade's fort, the greater part of the ground floor of which has been incorporated into the abbey buildings which range in date from the 19C East Cloister, Chapter House and St. Andrew's Chapel to the nave of 1956 and the porch of 1968. Of particular interest inside are a model of the fort, a curious pagan Roman stone with carvings of the Mother Goddesses, and some finely worked vestments.

For walkers there is *Inchnacardoch Forest*, with a trail (4m) starting from the Forest Office (Auchterawe, just south west of Fort Augustus. Booklet obtainable here or from Tourist Information) and combining forest with the bank of the river Oich.

Loch Ness is 24m long, an average of 1m broad, and in places 900ft deep. It has never been known to freeze. Fed by eight rivers and countless streams, the loch's only outlet is by the river Ness into the Moray Firth.

These are the natural facts, to most visitors probably of scant interest compared to the loch's fame as the home of its monster, affectionately known as Nessie. Real or imagined, Nessie is of ancient lineage, recorded by that respected 7C biographer St. Adamnan as having been not only seen but also effectively dealt with by St. Columba. On his way to convert Brude, king of the Picts, Columba ordered a servant to swim across the river Ness and bring back a boat. However, no sooner was the servant in the water than the monster attacked, and the man's life was only saved by the monster's retreat when confronted by Columba's sign of the Cross and shouted invocation. Over the years, and increasingly since the construction of A82 in the 1930s, there have been several sightings and even photographs, and the monster has been the object of serious scientific investigation using the most modern devices, but so far all has been without conclusive result. Meanwhile even the most sceptical find it hard not to scan the loch's surface.—Cruises from Fort Augustus and Inverness.

From Fort Augustus there is a choice of roads (both 32m) either side of Loch Ness to Inverness. A82, on the north, is the faster and generally more interesting. B862 and B852, to the south and following the general line of Wade's military road, offer a quieter and rather more scenic alternative.

To Inverness North of Loch Ness

Leaving Fort Augustus, Cherry Island crannog is seen just offshore.— *6m* **Invermoriston** where the northern arm of Rte 52 bears away west up Glen Moriston.—*7m* **Balbeg**, beyond which the *Cobb Memorial* cairn, beside the road and loch and bearing in Gaelic the words 'Honour to the brave and to the humble', commemorates John Cobb who lost his life on the loch in 1952 while attempting to break the world waterspeed record.—*3m* **Castle Urquhart** (AM. Tel: 031-244-3121), at its most impressive when viewed from the road above, is a large but battered ruin, less interesting as such than for its theatrical situation. Successor to an Iron Age fort which once stood on this bluff, and once one of the largest castles in Scotland, Urquhart was occupied and strengthened by Edward I, later passing through several hands until 1509 when James IV gifted it to John Grant of Freuchie. It was he who built most of the structure seen today, his descendants remaining in possession until the present century even though the castle was blown up in 1692 for fear it might fall into Jacobite hands.

While pausing to view the castle visitors may also note that more monster sightings have been reported from this point than from anywhere else along either side of the loch.

The road kinks around Urquhart Bay for (*2m*) **Drumnadrochit**, home of the *Loch Ness Monster Centre* (Tel: 04562-573) with an informative, objective exhibition as also features such as a kilt shop, a glass blower and a House of Heraldry. From Drumnadrochit A831 runs westward up wooded Glen Urquhart for Corrimony cairn, Glen Affric, Glen Cannich and Strathfarrar, for all of which see Rte 53—*14m* **Inverness**, see below.

To Inverness South of Loch Ness

Affording view points, B862 climbs to 1162ft before in *11m* arriving at the junction with B852. Beyond, along B862, Loch Mhor, 5m long, was formed by joining lochs Garth and Farraline when the river Foyers was dammed for hydro-industrial purposes. From the road junction B852 drops sharply to (*3m*) **Foyers**, beside the loch, on the descent passing the *Falls of Foyers*, once spectacular enough to earn praise from Burns but much tamed by industrial projects, first aluminium smelting (until 1968) and then pumped storage.

2m Inverfarigaig, near which are picnic areas and a small Forestry Commission visitor centre (Tel: 04563-249) near the start of a forest trail (1½m and in places steep; booklet) up to a mountain view point overlooking the meeting of two river gorges. But there is a reminder, too, that all was not always peaceful here; Inverfarigaig Fort. Best seen and reached from the road heading north east out of the village, this Iron Age stronghold stands atop a rock above the mouth of the river Farigaig and still shows remains of a thick wall, traces of vitrification and a subsidence that may indicate the position of a well.

Between Inverfarigaig and (*8m*) *Dores*, where B862 rejoins from the high ground, the road—here pretty precisely representing Wade's—fringes Loch Ness, across the water from Castle Urquhart and with some inviting picnic spots. Beyond Dores the loch edges away from the road as it tapers to become the closely parallel river Ness and Caledonian Canal, the road in *5m* (beyond Sconiport) reaching a minor road (east) leading in about 1m to the *Knocknagael* or *Boar Stone*, a rough Pictish block of the 7 or 8C bearing the outline of a wild boar and also a mirror symbol.—*3m* **Inverness**, see immediately below.

Inverness (39,500 inhab. *Inf.* 23 Church Street. Tel: 0463-234353) is a sizeable and busy centre, popularly dubbed 'Capital of the Highlands'. And, administratively, this it certainly is for the town is the headquarters of Highland Region, Scotland's largest local government authority, as also of the important Highlands and Islands Enterprise, not to mention lesser bodies. But the tourist anticipating a Highland ambience may well be disappointed for, visually at any rate, the Highlands are at best a distant promise. A road, rail and even air hub (airport at Dalcross, 8m north east), the emphasis here tends to be on administration, commerce and industry. Yet this should not deter the visitor, for Inverness is a town with ancient roots and one which can reward with some odd corners.

History. According to St. Adamnan, St. Columba visited the Pictish king Brude in about 565 at a castle 'near the Ness'. This may have been Craig Phadrig (see below), site of an Iron and Dark Ages fort. Equally it may have been the early predecessor of Macbeth's 11C stronghold (where Shakespeare placed the murder of Duncan), the site of which is Auld Castle Hill to the east of the present Castle Hill. Macbeth's castle was razed by Duncan's avenger, Malcolm Canmore, and it was either he (in 1057) or David I (c 1140) who founded a new castle on the existing site, the latter also granting the town a charter as a royal burgh.

In the War of Independence, Inverness was three times occupied by the English, and when Bruce retook it in 1307 he followed his usual policy of destroying the castle. In later reigns town and castle alike suffered from the savagery of the Highlanders and were the scene of many assemblies called by Scotland's kings in their attempts to control the clans. In 1562 Mary, Queen of Scots, attempting a northern progress, was refused admission to the castle by Alexander Gordon, son of the arrogant rebel Earl of Huntly, but later the castle surrendered, Mary moved in and Gordon and several others were hanged from the walls. In the following century Cromwell appreciated the town's strategic importance, in 1652–57 building a strong fort, known as 'The Sconce', on the right bank of the Ness beside its mouth, using for the purpose stones from the abbey of Kinloss and the cathedral at Fortrose. This, however, was pulled down at the Restoration.

Inverness Castle was occupied by the Jacobites in 1715, and again in 1745 by the Young Pretender who blew it up, leaving little remaining. The site was finally cleared in 1834 to make way for the present buildings.

Caledonian Canal and Loch Ness cruises. There is a choice of cruises, these including a *Loch Ness Monster Tour* (bus and boat, tour leaving from Railway Station rear car park. Tel: 0463-233999) which visits Urquhart Castle and the Loch Ness Monster Exhibition at Drumnacrochit. Others are *Scot II* (Tel: 0463-233140, from Muirtown Locks on the Caledonian Canal), a boat built in 1932 as a canal tug; and *Jacobite Cruises* (Tel: 0463-233999) from Tomnahurich Bridge on the canal.

Inverness is split by the Ness, the main part occupying the right bank. Here, beside High Street, the heart of the town is the *Town House* of 1880, in front of which stands the restored Cross on a base enclosing the Clach-na-Cuddain (Stone of the tubs), a rough block on which women carrying water from the river rested their tubs; a homely, domestic scene not easy to picture alongside today's traffic. The stone is of misty origin and the source of many local tales, one being that it was used as a coronation stone, another that the prosperity of Inverness depends upon its staying where it is. In the Town House are a beam from Cromwell's fort, and some good paintings and heraldic stained glass, while in the Council Chamber are the framed signatures of members of Lloyd George's cabinet which met here in 1921, the first British cabinet meeting held outside London.

Behind the Town House are the castle and the museum. The *Castle*, a dominating 19C structure on the site of that of Malcolm Canmore or

B9161 Cromwell's Fort — B865

RIVER NESS

Friars Bridge

GEORGE STREET

ABBAN ST.

A862 Craig Phadrig

WELLS STREET

MUIRTOWN ST.

KENNETH STREET

FAIRFIELD ROAD

PLANEFIELD ROAD

MONTAGUE ROW

GLENURQUHART ROAD

A82 Tomnahurich Hill

CELT

QUEENS STREET

KING STREET

GREIG STREET

DUNCRAIG STREET

TOMNAHURICH

ARDROSS PLACE

ARDROSS STREET

St. Andrew's Cath.

Eden Court Th.

SIDE ST.

DOUGLAS ROW

CHAPEL STREET

FRIARS LA.

FRIARS STREET

ROSE ST.

STROTHERS LA.

• Dunbar's Hosp.

High Church

SCHOOL LA.

ACADEMY STREET

Station

(Motorail)

Footbridge

BANK STREET

HUNTLY STREET

Abertarff Ho.

FRASER STREET

CHURCH STREET

QUEENSGATE

UNION STREET

BARON TAYLOR'S ST.

Eastgate Centre

BANK ST.

HIGH STREET

ARDCONNEL TER.

Steeple

BRIDGE ST.

Town House

CHARLES ST.

Monster Video

YOUNG ST.

NESS BANK

BRIDGE

Mus

Castle

CASTLE ST.

HILL STREET

CROWN STREET

ALEXANDER PL.

HUNTLY STREET

NESS BANK

CASTLE ROAD

CASTLE VIEW P.

ARGYLE ST.

ARGYLE TER.

CULDUTHEL ROAD

OLD EDINBURGH ROAD

NESS WALK

RIVER NESS

BISHOP'S ROAD

HAUGH ROAD

MAYFIELD ROAD

B853

INVERNESS

0 yards — 400

0 metres — 400

N

A828 A9

A862 Craig Phadrig

A82 Tomnahurich Hill

Pringle Woollen Mill — B862

David I, is now the home of law courts and local government offices, though a link with the past survives in the courtyard in the form of the well (rediscovered and restored in 1909) while a Jacobite touch is provided on the terrace by a statue of Flora Macdonald. *Inverness Museum and Art Gallery* (Tel: 0463-237114) illustrates the Highland as much as the Inverness story, themes covered including archaeology and social and natural history and of particular note being the collection of Highland silver.

The principal shopping area is represented by the network of streets generally to the north and north east of the Town House, the focus increasingly being the *Eastgate Centre* near the railway station.

High Street extends west as Bridge Street, on the corner of the latter and Church Street being the lofty *Steeple* of 1791, once the jail. Church Street (with *Tourist Information*) leads to most places of interest in this sector of the town. *Abertarff House* (Tel: 0463-232034), on the left beyond Fraser Street, dates from 1592 and incorporates a rare example of an old stair-tower; long the town residence of the Lovats, the house was restored by the National Trust for Scotland in 1963 and is now the Trust's Highland office. Beyond, and again to the left, stands the *High*

Church, a rebuilding of 1772 but still preserving its 14C tower and with also, in the yard, a curious 17C colonnaded enclosure. Just to the north, in Friars Street, leading off Friars Lane beside the High Church, is *Friars Burying Ground,* on the site of a Dominican priory founded in 1233 and surviving as no more than a broken pillar. And, in Church Street to the east of the High Church, there is *Dunbar's Hospital* (1688; restored), originally an almshouse, now with its row of dormer windows a mellow example of 17C domestic building.

Students of Cromwellian architecture must continue a good half mile northwards—by way of Chapel Street, Shore Street and Cromwell Road—to reach the site of *Cromwell's Fort,* destroyed at the Restoration except for a clock tower.

Also on this east side of the river, in Dores Street about 1m south of Ness Bridge, is the *Clan Tartan Centre* (James Pringle Woollen Mill. Tel: 0463-223311) with an archive computer, a restaurant and a shop.

The Ness is crossed by Ness Bridge, immediately across which, at 4–9 Huntly Street, the *Loch Ness Monster Video Show* (Tel: 0463-222781) covers, amongst other material, the search for the monster. Other points of interest on this western side of the river are all to the south, first coming *St. Andrew's Cathedral* (1868); a handsome, roseate edifice with an octagonal chapter house and elaborate interior, it serves the see of Moray, Ross and Caithness. The adjacent *Eden Court Theatre,* completed in 1976 and incorporating a 19C house build by Bishop Eden, is a theatre, conference centre and gallery for exhibitions by contemporary artists. *Tomnahurich* (Hill of the Fairies), a 220ft-high hill $\frac{1}{2}$m south west of the cathedral, has been beautifully laid out as a cemetery which serves also as a notable local view point, while *Ness Islands* ($\frac{1}{2}$m south of the cathedral), linked to one another and the river's banks by footbridges, and even with a miniature railway, form an original public park.

Finally, anyone with a feel for the remote past will make for *Craig Phadrig* (2m west of Inverness, off A9), a 550ft hill bearing a fort, archaeologically dated to about 500 BC but thought also—though 1000 years later—to have been Brude's fastness and the place visited by St. Columba, set on converting the pagan king and citing, it is surely reasonable to surmise, his recent successful brush with the monster of the Ness.

For Inverness east along the coast to **Fraserburgh**, see Rte 43; to **Aviemore** and **Fort William** (via Spey valley), see Rte 50; for the Glens of **Strathfarrar**, **Cannich** and **Affric**, see Rte 53; to **Kyle of Lochalsh**, see Rte 54; to **Ullapool** and **Durness**, see Rte 56; to **Bonar Bridge**, see Rte 57.

52 Invergarry or Invermoriston to Kyle of Lochalsh

A87 from Invergarry, or A887 from Invermoriston joining A87 just short of Loch Cluanie. A87 to Kyle of Lochalsh.—Highland scenery, the approach from Invergarry being the finer. Scenic diversion to Glenelg brochs.

SOME HOTELS. **Shiel Bridge**. *Kintail Lodge*, IV40 8HL. Tel: 059981-275. **Glenelg**. *Glenelg Inn*, IV40 8JY. Tel: 059982-273. **Dornie**. *Loch Duich*, IV40 8DY. Tel: 059985-213. **Balmacara**. *Balmacara*, IV40 8DH. Tel: 059986-283. **Kyle of Lochalsh**. *Lochalsh*, Ferry Road, IV40 8AF. Tel: 0599-4202.

Total distance 46m from Invergarry or 49m from Invermoriston.—*12m*

Junction A87/A887.—
14m Pass of Stachel (Glen Shiel).—5m Shiel Bridge.—8m Eilean
Donan Castle (Dornie).—7m Kyle of Lochalsh.

FROM INVERGARRY. Leaving **Invergarry** (see Rte 51), A87 quickly
climbs into superb Highland scenery, riding above lochs Garry and
Loyne as long views open out westward across lonely, wild country
towards Loch Quoich and Loch Hourn. A tempting minor road (steep
and narrow along its final 3m), breaking away from A87 3m out of Invergarry, traces most of the length of the vista, fringing lochs Garry and
Quoich (the latter with a large rock-filled dam) and in 20m ending at
Kinlochhourn at Loch Hourn's narrow head, still some 12m short of the
loch's broader mouth into the Sound of Sleat (for cruises into Loch
Hourn, see Rte 48, Arisaig and Mallaig). The return to A87 must be made
by the same road, but this matters little for the reversed views are
wholly different.—In *12m* from Invergarry the junction with A887 is
reached.

FROM INVERMORISTON. From **Invermoriston** on Rte 51, A887 ascends
the wooded valley of Glen Moriston beside its tumbling river. It was in
this glen, towards its west end and short of the junction with A87, that
the heroic Roderick Mackenzie, hiding here after Culloden and in
appearance not dissimilar to the Young Pretender, was set upon by
soldiers and, though mortally wounded, had the presence of mind to cry
out 'Ah, villains! You have slain your prince'. The ruse in large measure
succeeded, for Mackenzie's head, having first been shown to Cumberland at Fort Augustus, was sent to London where so many people
swore that it was that of the prince that, if only for a while, the urgency
of the hunt was much relaxed. Near where this happened, some *14m*
from Invermoriston, the road bridges the small river Doe, some 2½m up
which there is a cave called *Corriedoe* in which the Young Pretender
hid from 24 to 28 August 1746, three weeks after Mackenzie's death in
the glen below. In another *1m* A887 meets A87.

After skirting the north shore of Loch Cluanie, A87 starts the descent of
Glen Shiel through the *Pass of Stachel*, a scenic defile overhung by
peaked and jagged mountains rising to well over 3000ft and gashed by
gloomy corries. It was here (about *14m* from the A87–A887 junction) that
a skirmish was fought in 1719 during one of the lesser known attempts
to put the Old Pretender on the throne.

The Earl of Seaforth, since the '15 a fugitive in France and Spain, in 1719 sailed from
Spain with ten ships and 6000 soldiers. However, storms at sea took their toll and
only two frigates with some 300 men reached the island of Lewis, where Seaforth
raised a few hundred Highlanders (mainly Macraes and Mackenzies) and then
crossed to Eilean Donan and Kintail, taking up position across the Pass of Stachel.
Attacked by government troops under General Wightman, the Highlanders and
Spaniards more than held their own. But when Seaforth was wounded the impetus
of the rebellion died, the Spaniards surrendered and the Highlanders dispersed.

Just beyond, the road and the river Shiel together descend below the
towering mass (north) of the *Five Sisters*, scenically one of the most
dramatic features of the NTS wild and mountainous Kintail Estate, to
reach in *5m* **Shiel Bridge**, at the head of Loch Duich and offering a
diversion as scenically splendid as it is archaeologically interesting.

DIVERSION TO GLENELG BROCHS (west, 12m. Dead-end unless the car
ferry to Kylerhea on Skye is used). Once a military highway, today's
unclassified road hairpins spectacularly from sea level up to the *Pass of
Mam Ratagan* (1116ft), with a car park and orientation table—an easy

enough ascent for a modern car, but one which Johnson and Boswell found daunting as they coaxed their weary horses upwards beside a precipitous edge, Johnson at one point calling out for help as his mount staggered under its rider's ungainly weight. The wide view embraces much of Glen Shiel, defined in part by the great barren wall of the Five Sisters, while, beyond, other vistas open up as—more decorously on this side—the road descends along the flank of Glen More with the mountains of Skye ahead.

At its foot the road forks, the north prong in 2m reaching the car ferry to Skye (Summer only. Frequent weekday service. Crossing 4 minutes. Tel: 059982-224), while the south west prong at once passes the drab, rectilinear ruin of *Bernera Barracks*, built in c 1722 and until the end of the century this road's military objective.

Less than a mile south from the village of Glenelg a small wooded road turns inland along Glen Beg to reach the two best preserved brochs on Scotland's mainland. These—appearing suddenly as the road leaves the trees—are *Dun Telve* on the right, and, a short way farther on the left, *Dun Troddan*. With walls over 13ft thick at the base and rising respectively to 33 and 25ft, the two combine well to show the main features of broch construction, with massive circular bases, entrance passages, guard cells, parts of the stairway and the typical internal gall-eries. Leaving these brochs the road continues only for another mile, beyond becoming a track heading for woods and heights and in half a mile arriving at *Dun Grugaig*, a fort of a type which preceded the brochs. Now little more than base wall and tumbled stones, this fort is larger in circumference than the brochs below and semicircular in design with the open side defended by a precipitous drop into a narrow, hidden glen. Along the approach track can be seen traces of another ancient stone and earthwork ring-enclosure.

The coastal road runs for another 9m to *Arnisdale* on the north shore of Loch Hourn.

Beyond Shiel Bridge, and still in grand mountain scenery, A87 rounds the head of Loch Duich, just to the east being the National Trust for Scotland's *Kintail and Morvich Countryside Centre* (Tel: 059981-219), where the Trust's Kintail Estate is described and advice is given on the many climbs and walks, notably—and most strenuously—to the *Falls of Glomach*, some 5 mountain miles to the north east.

Running with the north shore of Loch Duich, A87 in *8m* reaches **Eilean Donan Castle** (Tel: 059985-202), rooted firmly to its islet at the end of a short causeway, guardian of the confluence of three lochs, and picturesque favourite of Scotland's poster designers. Successor to an Iron Age fort, the castle was built in 1220 by Alexander II to deter Viking penetration, later passing to the Mackenzie earls of Seaforth and in 1719 (see Glen Shiel above) achieving the surely unique distinc-tion of first being garrisoned by Spanish soldiers and then being blown apart by a Hanoverian warship. After 200 years as a ruin, Eilean Donan was rebuilt and now shows Jacobite, Mackenzie and Macrae relics.

Beyond (*2m*), Rte 54 (A890) comes in from the north, while, in another *2m* and now beside Loch Alsh, A87 passes *Lochalsh Woodland Garden* (NTS. Tel: 059986-207), with, in the Coach House, a natural history display.

3m **Kyle of Lochalsh** (700 inhab. *Inf.*), separated from Skye by the narrow Kyle Akin, is the terminus of the railway from Inverness and of this principal road approach to Skye. For *Skye* and the car ferry to the island, see Rte 62. A toll bridge is planned to open in 1994–95.

53   The Glens South West of Inverness (Strathfarrar, Cannich and Affric)

To the south west of Inverness three lovely glens pierce deep into the mountains. These are Glen Strathfarrar, Glen Cannich and Glen Affric, this last being the best known, scenically the most dramatic, and also enjoying the best road with plenty of places to park. Hydro-electric schemes are present in the forms of dams and power stations, but much care has been taken not to mar the magnificent Highland scenery, which indeed many would judge improved by the enlargement of modest lochs into sizeable reservoirs. The glens, all with dead-end roads (but note that Strathfarrar is a power company private road, normally open only to walkers), can be approached from Beauly (on Rte 54, 10m west of Inverness) or from Drumnadrochit (Rte 51) on Loch Ness. The text below assumes the former.

The base road is A831, the village of Struy marking the foot of Glen Strathfarrar, while Cannich is the gateway for the other two.

SOME HOTELS. **Struy**. *Cnoc*, IV4 7JU. Tel: 046376-264. **Cannich**. *Cozac Lodge*, Glen Cannich, IV4 7LX. Tel: 04565-263. *Glen Affric*, IV4 7LW. Tel: 04565-214.

Total distance (Beauly to Cannich) 17m.—*10m* Struy, for *Glen Strathfarrar* (14m to head).—*7m* **Cannich**, for *Glen Cannich* (9m to head) or *Glen Affric* (9m to head).

From **Beauly** (see Rte 54) A831 ascends the small but picturesque gorge of the river Beaulieu, blocked by dams at *Kilmorack* and (5m) *Aigas* at both of which the sluices are opened daily to allow fish to make their way upstream (admission to Aigas, with a viewing chamber. Tel: 0463-782412).—*5m* **Struy**, a hamlet at the confluence of the Farrar and the Beauly, the latter here looping south west and now called the river Glass.

GLEN STRATHFARRAR. The road up the glen belongs to the power company and is normally open only to walkers. Much of the way wandering through fine woods and past lochs, the road in 4m ends at the large sheet of *Loch Monar*, stretching for 8 narrow miles below mountains, many of which rise to well over 3000ft.—*Culligran Deer Farm* (essential to telephone in advance, 046376-285) can arrange landrover tours to see the red deer.

A831, now ascending Strath Glass, in *4m* passes the curious *Well of St. Ignatius*, heavily carved and incorporating a shrine of 1880, and in another *3m* reaches **Cannich**, a scattered hamlet at which Strath Glass, Glen Cannich, Glen Affric and Glen Urquhart all meet. Here a short diversion should be made 3m east down Glen Urquhart to *Corrimony Cairn*, a large prehistoric burial cairn, surrounded by a circle of 11 standing stones and with its entrance passage still roofed. When excavated in 1952, evidence was found of a crouched burial.

GLEN CANNICH, thickly wooded with bare mountains looming above, fringes small lochs and, widening in its upper reach, in 9m ends at *Loch Mullardoch* with an impressive dam and a tunnel through which water is fed to Loch Beneveian in Glen Affric. Walkers can explore the narrow length of the loch (9m) below mountains lifting to 3775ft on the north and 3880ft on the south.

*GLEN AFFRIC effectively means *Loch Beneveian*, for the road (9m long, and generous with parking sites from some of which there are forest walks) hugs this wooded, island-studded water for 6m, threading a constant contrast between the dark and light greens of pine and birch and, beyond the dam, riding well above the water and enjoying splendid mountain vistas. Near the start, at *Fasnakyle Switching Station*, display boards explain the hydro-electric scheme; and, at the road's end (770ft), a plaque reminds that Affric was once Clan Chisholm land. Glen Affric shelters one of the largest surviving remnants of the ancient Caledonian pine forest, in 1990 fenced by the Forestry Commission (for protection from deer) as part of a regeneration project.

54   Inverness to Kyle of Lochalsh via Achnasheen

A862 to Muir of Ord. A832 to Achnasheen. A890 and A87 to Kyle of Lochalsh.—After leaving the fertile coastal strip at Muir of Ord the road rises gradually across open moorland hills, passing a succession of lochs. Mountains define the west view and the landscape becomes increasingly wild and Highland beyond Achnasheen.

SOME HOTELS. **Beauly**. *Priory*, The Square, IV4 7BX. Tel: 0463-782309. **Muir of Ord**. *Ord Arms*, IV6 7XR. Tel: 0463-870286. **Strathconon** (11m west of Marybank). *East Lodge*, IV6 7QQ. Tel: 09977-222. **Strathpeffer**. *Holly Lodge*, Golf Course Road, IV14 9AR. Tel: 0997-21254. **Garve**. *Inchbae Lodge*, Inchbae, IV23 2PH. Tel: 09975-269. **Achnasheen**. *Ledgowan Lodge*, Ledgowan, IV22 2EJ. Tel: 044588-252.—For **Balmacara** and **Kyle of Lochalsh**, see Rte 52.

Total distance 76m.—*10m* **Beauly**.—*2m* **Muir of Ord**.—*4m* **Marybank**.—*8m* **Garve**.—*17m* **Achnasheen**.—*25m* **Stromeferry**.—*10m* **Kyle of Lochalsh**.

Railway. The railway (British Rail's 'Great Scenic Railway') for the most part follows a similar course to the road. In the east, though, the line continues north beyond Muir of Ord to Dingwall before bearing west. It then climbs a steep and scenic gradient to *Raven Rock* before rejoining the road at Loch Garve. Thereafter rail and road run together as far as Stromeferry, where the railway continues close to the shore to reach Kyle, while the main road cuts across the peninsula. The time from Inverness to Kyle of Lochalsh averages a little over three hours.

Leaving **Inverness** (see Rte 51) A862 crosses the Caledonian Canal (which here joins the sea through a series of six locks) at *Clachnaharry*, meaning Watchman's Stone—the place where the citizens maintained a watch for raiding Highlanders—and then for a while fringes the south shore of Beauly Firth before bridging the Beauly river at the point where A831 carries Rte 53 south west to the glens of Strathfarrar, Cannich and Affric.

10m **Beauly** (1100 inhab.) derives its name from the French 'beau lieu', this in turn associated with the now ruined priory, once the 'Monasterium de bello loco'. A pleasant enough small place—though hardly meriting the claim implicit in its name—Beauly is closely associated with the Lovat family, chiefs of Clan Fraser, whose Beaufort Castle (2m south; no adm.) is the 19C successor of their castle destroyed by Cumberland in 1746 (for the fate of the then Lord Lovat, see Rte 48, Loch Morar). In the town square a striking monument commemorates the raising by the 16th Lord Lovat of the Lovat Scouts for service in the South African war, a stirring inscription recording that Lord Lovat 'desired to show that the martial spirit of their forefathers still animates the Highlands today', while, nearby, more modestly at the priory entrance, stands the shaft of the old mercat cross.

Beauly Priory (AM. Tel: 031-244-3101) was founded in c 1230 by Sir John Bisset of the Aird for French Valliscaulian monks. Today the most noteworthy features are the three rare and beautiful 13C triangular windows, with trefoils, in the south wall; the window-arcading in the chancel; and the 13C west doorway of the south transept. The north transept (restored 1901) is the burial place of the Mackenzies of Kintail, with a monument to their Sir Kenneth (died 1391), opposite which is the restored tomb of Prior Mackenzie (died 1479). The priory façade, with its three lancets, was built after 1530 by Abbot Reid, later Bishop of Orkney.

2m **Muir of Ord** marks an important crossroads, this Route here branching north west along A832, while A862 continues north to join Rte 57 at Dingwall. Guided tours may be made of *Ord Distillery* (Tel: 0463-870421), established in 1838.—*4m Marybank*, whence a small road runs west for 22m up lonely Strathconon, while, a short distance beyond Marybank, signs off A832 direct to the *Neil Gunn Memorial*; he was a much respected local writer and the drive up to the memorial rewards with some fine views.

Strathpeffer (1300 inhab. *Inf.*), on A834 3m north of Marybank, comes as something of a surprise. In the 18C sulphur springs were discovered here, the town soon becoming a popular spa, and although those elegant days are now long gone the town's wide street, gardens and many hotels still recall its gracious past. At or close to The Square are *Tourist Information* (with a visitor centre; Tel: 0997-21415); a water-tasting pavilion; the *Pump Room*, with a summer exhibition of turn-of-the-century photographs; and a *Doll Museum* (Tel: 0997-21549). For visitors in search of crafts there are specialist shops at the restored Victorian station at the east entrance to the town, while for those with a feel for clan conflict and legend there is the *Eagle Stone*, reached by a path (sign; 100 yards) a short way up the road opposite the large Ben Wyvis Hotel. An eagle is the crest of Clan Munro and the stone commemorates a successful affray of 1411 by the Munros against the Macdonalds, while legend is provided by the Seer of Brahan who foretold that ships would tether to the stone should it fall three times; it is said that it has already fallen twice.

Castle Leod (no adm.), immediately north east of the town, dates from c 1616.—East above the town rises the ridge called *Druim Chat* (Cat's Back), on top of which stands the vitrified fort of *Knockfarrel*, reached by a track by the burn bridge on A834 ½m north east of the town.—The mass of *Ben Wyvis* (3429ft) lifts some 10m to the north of Strathpeffer; there are proposals for a rack railway to the summit.

Beyond *Contin* (*4m* from Marybank) A832 runs through *Torrachilty Forest* and reaches (*2m*) *Rogie Falls* where, in a wooded and rocky setting, a foot suspension bridge leads the visitor over rapids.—*2m* **Garve**, from where Rte 56 bears north along A835 for Ullapool, while this Route continues with A832 above *Loch Luichart*, the first reservoir in the Highlands to be used for the generation of electricity. In 1955 the railway track here was raised 20ft and a new station built; traces of the old line can still sometimes be traced. From the west end of the loch (*Grudie Bridge*, 6m from Garve), a track ascends for 4½m to Loch Fannich, 9m long and in wild and remote surroundings.

Now in lonely open moorland, A832 heads westward past small lochs and along Strath Bran to reach in *11m* the bleakly sited and scattered hamlet of **Achnasheen** with a station, the railhead for such places in

Wester Ross (see Rte 55) as Loch Maree, Gairloch and Inverewe Gardens. Here this Route exchanges A832 for A890, the former road now representing one of the approaches to the heart of Wester Ross.

Both westward and southward Achnasheen is the gateway to much of Scotland's grandest Highland scenery, and as this Route now aims south west towards Loch Carron it is into increasingly wild and broken country, the watershed (634ft) soon being crossed between lochs Gowan and Scaven.

In *18m* the head of **Loch Carron** is reached, a sea loch in two parts, the inner loch (6m long) being separated by a narrow neck from the open outer loch. Just before reaching the loch's head, the road splits, this Route and the railway fringing the south shore. (For the north shore, see Rte 55. It should be noted that despite the name Stromeferry there is in fact no ferry across Loch Carron's neck.)—*7m* **Stromeferry**, where the main road carries this Route south to join A87 and approach Kyle of Lochalsh along the shore of Loch Alsh. The railway, though, continues along the south shore of the now open part of Loch Carron, this section of the track having been built in 1897, before which the line ended at Stromeferry. Much of the new track had to be blasted out of the rock and the line represents what was at the time a major engineering achievement.

Dropping south from Stromeferry, A890 in *5m* joins A87, from which point to (*5m*) **Kyle of Lochalsh** see Rte 52.

55 Wester Ross (Loch Carron to Corrieshalloch)

This Route is concerned with a splendid scenic triangle the apex of which is Garve (Rtes 54 and 56); its base line is the great sweep of broken coast that curves northward from Kyle of Lochalsh to Ullapool. As well as this magnificent coast, the area includes the famous NTS Torridon mountain estate, equally famed Loch Maree, and the well-known subtropical Inverewe gardens.

Wester Ross can be approached along any of three principal roads. From the south the entry is from Loch Carron. The central approach comes in from Achnasheen direct to Loch Maree. In the north, close to Corrieshalloch Gorge, A832 forks off A835 to fringe the coast southwards. The road from Garve to Corrieshalloch is described under Rte 56, and that from Garve through Achnasheen to Loch Carron under Rte 54. The description below travels the road from Loch Carron, northward past Torridon, Loch Maree and Gairloch (the only place in the whole area of any size), to Corrieshalloch.

A896 from Lochcarron to Kinlochewe, A832 to Gairloch and Corrieshalloch.

SOME HOTELS. **Lochcarron**. *Lochcarron* IV54 8YS. Tel: 05202-226. **Shieldaig**. *Tigh-an-Eilean*, IV54 8XN. Tel: 05205-251. **Torridon**. *Loch Torridon*, IV22 2EY. Tel: 044587-242. **Kinlochewe**. *Kinlochewe*, IV22 2PA. Tel: 044584-253. **Gairloch**. *Creag-Mor*, IV21 2AH. Tel: 0445-2068. *Gairloch*, IV21 2BL. Tel: 0445-2001. **Poolewe**. *Pool House*, IV22 2LE. Tel: 044586-272. **Aultbea**. *Aultbea*, IV22 2HX. Tel: 044582-201. **Dundonnell**. *Dundonnell*, IV23 2QR. Tel: 085483-204.

Total distance 89m.—*4m* **Kishorn (Ardarroch)**.—*9m* **Shieldaig**.—*6m* **Torridon**.—*9m* **Kinlochewe**.—*19m* **Gairloch**.—*5m* **Poolewe (Inverewe)**.—*37m* **Corrieshalloch**.

For *Loch Carron* and its south shore, see Rte 54. On the north shore the straggling village of **Lochcarron** is also known as Jeanstown. *Strome Castle*, 3m south west and on the loch's narrow neck across from Stromeferry, is a small and muddled ruin (NTS) the destruction of which was reputedly caused by the stupidity of the castle women. Long a stronghold of the Macdonalds, the castle was always a thorn in the flesh of the neighbouring Mackenzies. In 1602 Kenneth Mackenzie of Kintail laid siege to this irritant and succeeded in taking the castle and then blowing it up because Strome's women, after drawing water at the well, carelessly emptied it all into the gunpowder vat instead of the water vat and thus rendered the defenders helpless.

Leaving Lochcarron A896 climbs across a peninsula to reach (*4m*) **Kishorn (Ardarroch)** at the head of the loch of the same name and offering—though only to the confident motorist with a sound car—the opportunity to divert westward into the scenic and interesting Applecross Forest peninsula.

APPLECROSS DIVERSION (c 35m from Kishorn to Shieldaig). Access here in the south is by the difficult but spectacular pass of *Bealach-nam-Bo* (2054ft), narrow, steep and with many hairpins, though the descent to the village of *Applecross* on the west coast is by comparison gentle. In Gaelic the village is known as A Chromraich (Sanctuary), a reminder of a monastery founded here in 673 by St. Maelrubha (died 721), a monk from Bangor in Ireland. The monastery, which soon made this remote place second only to Iona as a Christian centre, was destroyed by the Norsemen, a fate probably also suffered by its founder, though not here but at Skaill (see Rte 60, Strath Naver). Local tradition is that the saint's body came back to Applecross for burial; but see also Loch Maree below.

Southward from the village the road passes largely depopulated hamlets before reaching (4m) *Toscaig*. Northward it rounds the bay beside which is *Applecross Chapel*, the now forlorn and abandoned relic of St. Maelrubha's venture, a remote and evocative corner with an ancient burial ground which may or may not be its founder's resting place. A venerable stone at the entrance commemorates Abbot Macoggie, who left here in 801 to become bishop of Bangor, while inside the chapel there are fragments of a Celtic cross, found beneath the turf here and probably set up in the 8C. Beyond, the road follows the coast, first of the Inner Sound with views across to Raasay, and then of Loch Torridon, to rejoin A896 in some 20m at Shieldaig.

9m (direct from Kishorn) **Shieldaig**, off which an island of the same name is an NTS nature reserve almost entirely covered in Scots pine. Here the road turns abruptly eastwards close to the south shore of Upper Loch Torridon to reach (*6m*) the **Torridon Countryside Centre** (NTS. Tel: 044587-221), a visit to which—with its displays, video presentation, deer museum, and advice on walks and climbs—is essential for any understanding of the magnificent *Torridon Estate* which looms high above. Formerly owned by the earls of Lovelace, the estate of 16,000 acres came to the National Trust for Scotland in 1967. Bounded on the north east by the summit ridge of Beinn Eighe (3309ft, and combining seven individual summits linked by narrow ridges nearly 5m long), and including peaks such as *Liathach* (3456ft) and *Beinn Alligin* (3232ft), the estate, together with the Beinn Eighe National Nature Reserve (see below) immediately to the north, ranks as one of Scotland's most scenically splendid and naturally interesting mountain masses, a tract as certain to excite the casual layman visitor as it will the naturalist or geologist. For the former the wildlife includes deer, mountain goat, wild cat and eagles; for the latter there are those red sandstone peaks, some 750 million years old, their tops conspicuous with white quartzite, some 150 million years younger.

Much the same might be written about **Beinn Eighe National Nature Reserve** (11,757 acres), across Beinn Eighe on Torridon's north, acquired primarily for the preservation and study of the sizeable remnant of Caledonian pine forest and distinguished for being the first national nature reserve to be declared in Britain. *Aultroy Visitor Centre* (Tel: 044584-258), on A832 1m north west of Kinlochewe, shows an excellent illuminated physical model of the district, and leaflets are available for two nature trails, both starting from a car park 2m farther up the road.

Running below Liathach and Beinn Eighe, A896 in 9m arrives at **Kinlochewe** where A832 comes in from Achnasheen and the east to carry this Route north west past the Aultroy Visitor Centre and along much of the 12 mile length of *Loch Maree. Varying in width and with its surprising variety of scenery, this is one of Scotland's loveliest and best known lochs. The name is thought to derive from St. Maree or Maelrubha, the monk who founded the monastery at Applecross and who, tradition claims, was for a while a hermit on the Isle of Maree in the loch's wider part where, dismissing the claims of Applecross, the locals insist that he was buried. The first stretch of the south shore with its Caledonian pine forest is a part of the Beinn Eighe reserve, while farther on, beyond the islands and where the road leaves the loch (*12m* from Kinlochewe), comes a Forestry Commission picnic area, starting point for forest walks; one of these (short) affords views of Victoria Falls, visited by Queen Victoria when she stayed at the Loch Maree Hotel, while another, the Tollie Path, provides 5m of rough hill walking across to Poolewe. Across the loch the grandest feature is the towering mass of *Slioch* (3260ft), so steep that its corries can be traced from foot to summit.

Leaving the loch A832 cuts across to the sea and (*7m*) **Gairloch** (*Inf.*), a sizeable village and very popular holiday centre straggling around the broad bay of the same name. The local *Heritage Museum* (Tel: 044583-243) provides admirable displays illustrating the long story of these western Highlands.

Beyond Gairloch the road to (*5m*) **Poolewe** passes a view point affording breathtaking vistas seaward across to northern Skye with the mountains of Harris far beyond, and inland up the length of Loch Maree. Poolewe, at the head of Loch Ewe and owing its name to the curious pool formed where the river enters the sea, is best known for *Inverewe Gardens* (NTS. Tel: 044586-200 or, for visitor centre, 229). Created by Osgood Mackenzie in 1862, and the property of Scotland's National Trust since 1952, these famous sub-tropical gardens sprawl over a steep promontory jutting into Loch Ewe with its mountain backdrop. Although in the same latitude as icy Labrador and Siberia, the Gulf Stream here makes possible a luxuriance and variety at all times of the year. Among the huge variety of plants are examples from South America and South Africa, Himalayan lilies, and giant forget-me-nots from the South Pacific.

The road beyond Poolewe was once known as 'Destitution Road', a reminder that it was built during the famine of 1851. Although lacking the scenic grandeur of the country around and to the south of Loch Maree, the road nevertheless affords open sea loch views and mountain vistas, the dominating feature being *An Teallach* (the Forge) lifting to 3484ft above the southern shore of Little Loch Broom. *6m Aultbea.—*

17m Dundonnell, 14m beyond which A832 joins A835 and Rte 56 at *Corrieshalloch* (Falls of Measach).

56   Inverness to Durness via Ullapool, Lochinver and Scourie

A862 to Muir of Ord. A832 to Garve. A835 through Ullapool to Drumrunie. Unclassified roads through Inverpolly National Nature Reserve to Lochinver. A837 and A894 to Laxford Bridge. A838 to Durness.—Beyond Garve, and increasingly so north of Ullapool, highly scenic, with the wild grandeur of Inverpolly followed by dark rock-strewn glens and lochs and a rugged, fretted coast between Kylesku and Durness.

SOME HOTELS. **Ullapool.** *Mercury*, North Road, IV26 2UD. Tel: 0854-2314. *Royal*, Garve Road, IV26 2SY. Tel: 0854-2181. **Lochinver.** *Inver Lodge*, IV27 4LU. Tel: 05714-496. *Park House*, IV27 4JY. Tel: 05714-259. **Kylesku.** *Kylesku*, IV27 4HW. Tel: 0971-2231. **Scourie**, *Scourie*, IV27 4SX. Tel: 0971-2396. *Eddrachilles*, Badcall Bay, IV27 4TH. Tel: 0971-2080. **Kinlochbervie.** *Kinlochbervie*, IV27 4RP. Tel: 097182-275.

Total distance 132m.—*24m* **Garve.**—*20m* **Corrieshalloch Gorge.**—*12m* **Ullapool.**—*9m* **Drumrunie.**—*20m* **Lochinver.**—*15m* **Kylesku (Unapool).**—*8m* **Scourie.**—*6m* **Laxford Bridge.**—*4m* **Rhiconich.**—*14m* **Durness.**

For Inverness to (*24m*) **Garve**, see Rte 54.—In a bleak moorland of bare, rounded mountains A835 fringes the south shore of *Loch Glascarnoch*, formed by the damming of the Glascarnoch river and linked by tunnels with Loch Vaitch to the north and the power station on Loch Luichart to the south. The water divide (915ft) is crossed between the north end of the loch and the small Loch Droma, to the south of the road just beyond.

20m (from Garve) *****Corrieshalloch Gorge** (NTS.) is a spectacular mile-long 200ft-deep schist-eroded ravine into which the *Measach Falls* plunge 120ft. A suspension bridge just below the falls was built by John Fowler, engineer of the Forth railway bridge, and there is a good observation platform a short way farther downstream. Rte 55 joins here from Gairloch. Just beyond (*2m*), *Lael Forest Garden* (FC; walks, leaflets), showing some 150 different trees and shrubs from many parts of the world, borders the east side of the road.

Running now with the east shore of Loch Broom A835 in *10m* enters **Ullapool** (800 inhab. *Inf.*), a sprawling whitewashed township established in 1788 by the British Fisheries Society, still active with fishing but increasingly important as a lively tourist centre and as the port for the car ferry (see Rte 66) to Stornoway on the island of Lewis. *Ullapool Museum* (Tel: 0854-2356) covers many aspects of Wester Ross, including the Clearances, geology, crofting and wildlife, while in summer there is a choice of boat excursions, islands, seals and birds being the principal attractions (Mackenzie Marine. Tel: 0854-2008. Murdo Mackenzie. Tel: 854-2200). The *Summer Islands*, a scattered and sparsely inhabited group some 12m to the north west, today largely concerned with fish farming, are perhaps the most popular objective, with time ashore on Tanera Mor, where in summer there is a post office which issues special stamps, or on Carn nan Sgeir, a bird island on the southern edge of the group. *Isle Martin* (RSPB; no landing), just round Rhue point immediately north west of Ullapool, is also popular.

Leaving Ullapool A835 soon touches the coast, with a view across to Isle Martin, and then in *9m* reaches *Drumrunie*, little more than a road junction offering a choice between A835, a scenic direct road north-ward, or the minor road westward for Inverpolly National Nature Reserve.

DIRECT ROAD NORTHWARD. A835 in some 3m reaches scenically sited *Knockan Cliff Information Centre* (Tel: 085484-254) providing information on the Inverpolly reserve and starting point for geological and nature trails. A short way farther north (3m), at Elphin and in a fine Highland setting, comes the *Highland and Rare Breeds Farm* (Tel: 085486-204) with all manner of animals, a farm walk, pets' corner and theme shop. Beyond, A835 meets A837 at Ledmore on Rte 58.

*Inverpolly National Nature Reserve** (Knockan Cliff Information Centre, see small print above), with Inverpolly Forest, is a remote and wild confusion of moor, woodland, burns, lochs and lofty, isolated mountain peaks, the reserve in the north merging with *Clencanisp Forest* to form one splendid scenic whole. The principal peaks in the reserve, rising as a half circle around the south end of lonely Loch Sionascaig, are *Cul Mor* (2787ft), *Cul Beag* (2523ft) and the craggy pinnacle of *Stac Polly* (2009ft), while Glencanisp is dominated by *Canisp* (2779ft) and the distinctive sugarloaf of *Suilven* (2399ft).

The unclassified road now followed—narrow, twisting and slow most of the way to Lochinver—first runs below mountains towering high to the right (Cul Beag and Stac Polly) while below on the other side stretch the dark and winding lengths of lochs Lurgainn and Baddagyle. After *8m* this Inverpolly circuit bears right.

The road ahead rounds Loch Osgaig to reach *Achiltibuie*, with two attractions: the Hydroponicum (Tel: 085482-202), described as a space-age garden in which plants grow without soil, and a Smokehouse (Tel: 085482-353) with a viewing gallery. For boat excursions, apply at the Post Office, Tel: 085482-200.

The Inverpolly circuit crosses the small river Polly and meanders north-ward, often through rowans providing a colourful photographic fore-ground for shots towards the wall of eastern peaks hanging above the reserve's inner fastness of moor, bog and loch.

12m **Lochinver** (300 inhab. *Inf.*), a largish village, the only place of any size between Ullapool and Scourie and famed for its scenic coast, is a popular objective which can be overcrowded in summer.

Motorists with time may continue by following the northerly loop (some 19m) offered by B869, narrow, twisting, sometimes steep, but generous with its ever varying views along the islanded coast and out into the waters of the Minch or across the breadth of Eddrachillis Bay. This Route, however, now chooses A837 which soon runs with the shore of *Loch Assynt*, in *10m* from Lochinver reaching the junction with A894, the end-point of the Strath Oykel arm of Rte 58 which describes nearby ruined Ardvreck Castle and Calda House.—*5m* **Kylesku (Unapool)**, where, amid broken and sombre scenery, a fine bridge of 1984 now speeds the motorist across the rocky, islanded confluence of three lochs, Cairnbawn seaward to the west, Glendhu and Glencoul probing east and south east into the mountains. As in so many places, a boat best provides the isolation and the views, excursions here including the three lochs, seal islands, a heronry and, at the head of Loch Glencoul, *Eas Coul Aulin*, claiming to be Britain's highest waterfall (Tel: 0971-2239).—*8m* **Scourie** (250 inhab.) is a sizeable village and useful stop along several miles of for the most part empty road.

In *3m* A894 makes a neat loop around the north west of *Loch a' Bhagh Ghainmhich*, which is a lot of name for what is little more than a lochan. Here a very minor road, splitting into a diamond and returning to this same spot, affords ever varying island-studded seaward views as it meanders for some 6m through a weird landscape in which there is as much freshwater loch as solid soil and rock. Narrow, twisting, blind and in places abruptly steep, this minor road serves two places from which boat excursions can be made. One, on the west, is *Tarbet*, for the seabird reserve of Handa Island (Tel: 0971-2156 or 2140). The other, to the north east, is *Fanagmore*, for cruises into Loch Laxford, with its islands, seals and birds (Tel: 0971-2409).

3m **Laxford Bridge**, a name deriving from the Norse for salmon. Here the Loch Shin arm of Rte 58 ends, while this Route continues north along A838 into a strange and forbidding mountain wilderness of dark, rockstrewn glens, perched glacial boulders and black sombre lochs.— *4m Rhiconich* marks the head of grand *Loch Inchard*, flanked on its north east side by a tempting road which rides high above the water to reach the small port of *Kinlochbervie*, a hamlet developed after 1947 for white fish and lobster fishing.

Leaving the sea, now, and aiming north east through a remote and tumbled landscape, A838 in *5m* reaches a surprise in the form of a well beside the road. Dated 1883, it charmingly expresses the gratitude of the surveyor of this road, one Peter Lawson, for the kindness extended to him by the local people—a gentle touch above the rock-strewn wasteland beyond which, to the south east, Strath Dionard emerges from the mountains. Descending, the road in *4m* touches the sandy *Kyle of Durness*, in another *3m* reaching *Keoldale* for the ferry to Cape Wrath, for which, as also for (*2m*) **Durness**, see Rte 61.

57   Inverness to Bonar Bridge

A9 to Tore (for Black Isle). A835 to Dingwall. A862 and A9 to Tain (for Tain peninsula). A9 to Bonar Bridge, but the construction of a new road (A9) across Dornoch Firth from roughly Tain to Clashmore (Rte 59) may affect this road numbering.—This Route explores a fertile coastal-estuaried strip with unexciting seaward views but, inland, hills rising to moor and mountain, notably Ben Wyvis (3433ft). The Route includes the peninsulas of Black Isle and Tain, the two separated by Cromarty Firth.

SOME HOTELS. **Fortrose**. *Royal*, Union Street, IV10 8TD. Tel: 0381-20236. **Cromarty**. *Royal*, Marine Terrace, IV11 8YN. Tel: 03817-217. **Dingwall**. *National*, High Street, IV15 9HA. Tel: 0349-62166. *Royal*, High Street, IV15 9HL. Tel: 0349-62130. **Tain**. *Royal*, IV19 1AB. Tel: 0862-2013. **Bonar Bridge**. *Bridge*, Dornoch Road, IV24 3EB. Tel: 08632-685.

Total distance (excluding Black Isle and eastern Tain peninsula) 50m.—*7m* **Tore**.—*5m* **Dingwall**.—*6m* **Evanton**.—*16m* **Tain**.—*15m* **Ardgay**.—*1m* **Bonar Bridge**.

From **Inverness** (see Rte 51) A9, using the interesting low Kessock Bridge of 1980 (*Inf.* a short way beyond the north end of the bridge), quickly crosses the narrows linking Beauly Firth to the west and the larger Moray Firth to the east and in *7m* reaches **Tore**, unimportant in itself but at the junction of five main roads and the place from which to start a round of Black Isle.—Motorists wishing neither to tour Black Isle nor to visit Dingwall may continue north along A9 which crosses inner Cromarty Firth to a junction with A862 3m north east of Dingwall.

Black Isle

Black Isle is not in fact an island, but a thick tapering promontory, some

16m long from Tore to Cromarty and up to 8m broad, jutting out north east between Moray Firth on the south and Cromarty Firth on the north. The origin of the name is uncertain, but one suggestion is that it is a translation from the Gaelic Eilean Dubh, itself perhaps a corruption of Eilean Dubhthaich (St. Duthus Isle; St. Duthus, died 1065, Bishop of Ross). A simpler, though almost equally unsatisfactory theory is that, because of the mild climate, the area remains clear when the surrounding landscape is white with snow. A rather lost, quiet district of farm and woodland, there are a number of places of interest, some good beaches, and coastal flats with a variety of seabirds.

The description below makes an anticlockwise circuit of some 33m, but first a diversion to *Redcastle* (2m south west of Tore) may be considered, where the parish church of c 1450, ½m west of the hamlet, was formerly the church of the parish of Killearnan, this name deriving from St. Ierman, a nephew of St. Columba. The ruined castle above the hamlet, originally built in 1178 by William the Lion, was later owned by James Stewart, Marquis of Ormond, son of James III.

A832 leads east from Tore to *Munlochy*, just south of which is Drumderfit Hill, scene in 1400 of a Macdonald disaster when the defenders of Inverness first smuggled strong drink into the clan camp and then slaughtered the fuddled Highlanders. Fringing the head of Munlochy Bay, a seabird reserve, the road soon reaches *Avoch*, north west of which is the Rosehaugh estate, during the 17C the property of Sir George Mackenzie, Lord Advocate of Scotland and notorious as the 'bloody advocate' because of his persecution of the Covenanters. Another, and more reputable Mackenzie, Sir Alexander (1735–1821), explorer of Canada and discoverer of the river which received his name, also lived near Avoch, though his home, Avoch House, later burnt down.

Fortrose, though with a population of under 1000, is, with Cromarty, one of the two principal towns of Black Isle. The main feature here is the *Cathedral*, the small, ruined red sandstone fragment of a church founded by David I for the see of Ross, completed in 1485 by Abbot Fraser, a monk from Melrose, and two centuries later pillaged by Cromwell to provide stone for his fort at Inverness. Against the north wall is the canopied tomb of Euphemia, Countess of Ross and builder of this aisle in about 1395, while the west end is a burial place of the Mackenzies of Seaforth; some of the tablets here are worth reading. Beside the cathedral stands the pleasing, detached 13C Chapter House. A road runs across the golf links to *Chanonry Point* with a lighthouse and a view across the Moray Firth narrows to Fort George. Traditionally it was here on Chanonry Point that Coinneach Odhar, the Seer of Brahan, met his painful end. Required by the Countess of Seaforth to describe what her absent husband was doing, he rashly replied that he was in the arms of a French woman, whereupon the outraged countess promptly ordered him burnt to death in a barrel of tar. A stone here records the event.

Adjacent **Rosemarkie** claims to have been the forerunner of Fortrose as a bishopric, this perhaps the successor of a monastic church and school traditionally founded here in the 6C by St. Moluag and rededicated in 716 by St. Boniface. *Groam House Museum* (Tel: 0381-20961) is a Pictish centre in which the star exhibit is a fine decorated cross-slab, thought to date from the 8C and now known as the Soul of Rosemarkie. Also here are fragments of other decorated crosses, photographs and reproductions of several Ross and Cromarty stones, and video films both about Picts and about the Seer of Brahan.

The walk along the cliffs north east from Rosemarkie will be familiar to geologists through the writings of Hugh Miller. A832, however, runs inland.

With some attractive narrow streets and old cottages, **Cromarty** is a quiet township at Black Isle's tip which marks the south side of the narrow entrance to Cromarty Firth. *Hugh Miller's Cottage* (NTS. Tel: 03817-245), a thatched cottage of 1711 which was the birthplace of the noted geologist (1802-52), is now a museum showing geological specimens and material relating to Miller's work as geologist, writer and stonemason. Also of interest are the *Court House* of 1782, now a museum of local history (Tel: 03817-243); the *Cross* (14C; repaired 1744); and the *East Church* with three mid 18C lofts (one for the laird, one for the schoolmaster and his pupils, and the third an investment to raise income from pew rents). And there is also the roofless *Gaelic Chapel*, on a hill above the town, built for the Highlanders who flocked to the cloth mills in the latter half of the 18C; a statue of Hugh Miller (H. Ritchie, 1859) adjoins the chapel and in the churchyard there are tombstones carved by him.

An undemanding road returns westward, providing views across to industrialised Invergordon and farther afield to the wide spread of the mountains. *Udale Bay*, with Nigg Bay across on the north side of the firth, together form a nature reserve, important for its migratory wildfowl as also for the large number of wader species. Farther west (5m), on the shore below B9163, stands the small 15C ruin of *Craig Castle*, an Urquhart stronghold and once also a seat of the bishops of Ross. Beyond, A9 crosses inner Cromarty Firth some 3m north east of Dingwall.

From Tore A835 in *5m* reaches the town of **Dingwall** (5000 inhab.), a busy centre at the head of Cromarty Firth. The birthplace of Macbeth, the town was colonised by the Norsemen and it is to them that it owes its name ('Thing Volle' meaning Council Place). In 1226 Dingwall was made a royal burgh by Alexander II, but of the old *Castle* only a few stones remain, at the foot of Castle Street, and the principal place of interest today is the *Town House* of 1730, today a good museum of local history (Tel: 0349-62116), this including material on the distinguished military career of Sir Herbert MacDonald (1853-1903) who rose from the ranks and fought at Omdurman; he is also commemorated by a monument on nearby Mitchell Hill. In front of the Town House stands Dingwall's weathered and resited Mercat Cross. Also of interest, if only as an entertaining curiosity, is an *Obelisk* on a mound in a car park a short way behind the Town House. It bears a worn inscription stating that it was 'Erected by George, 1st Earl of Cromartie, who d. 1714 and is buried 3ft 6in southward hereof'—a curious arrangement apparently chosen by the earl to thwart his wife's declared intention of dancing on his grave. In fact the present obelisk is a small replica (1916) of the original which tapered to 50ft, and, whatever the countess's opinion of her husband, it seems that he was popular enough with other ladies for tradition insists that the mound was raised by the women of Dingwall as a sign of respect for their lamented laird.

Running north east beside Cromarty Firth, the road (A862, becoming A9) passes below (*4m*) *Foulis Castle* (no adm.), seat of the chief of Clan Munro. A condition of the clan's tenure was that a snowball should be presented to the king whenever he visited, a feat apparently possible because the north-facing corries of Ben Wyvis are rarely completely free of snow.—*2m* **Evanton** village is at the foot of *Black Rock Ravine*, a remarkable cleft—2m long, less than 12ft wide and in places a sheer 200ft deep—through which surges the river Glass. The '*Indian Temple*' crowning Knock Fyrish (1483ft) to the north above Evanton was put up by General Sir Hector Munro (1726-1805) of nearby Novar House as a

means of easing local unemployment while at the same time achieving a
touch of self-glorification, for the structure is said to represent the gateway to an Indian town taken by him in 1781.

Beyond Evanton (2m) A836, avoiding Invergordon and Tain, provides
a short cut across high ground, with long views up and down the coast
(view indicator on Struie Hill above the descent to Dornoch Firth). This
Route, however, keeps with A9, bypassing the industrial complex of
Invergordon and in *14m* reaching **Tain** (2000 inhab. *Inf.*), a sturdy small
town in which what first strikes the visitor is the attractive 16C (rebuilt
1707) *Tolbooth* with its conical spire and small angle turrets. But while
appreciating this, a thought should surely be spared for those simple
crofters of the 19C to whom Tain was a notorious centre of the ruthless
administration of the Clearances. To them there could have been nothing attractive about the 'sharp-pointed house' from which emanated
orders for their dispossession and in which, if they resisted, they were
likely to find themselves imprisoned.

But Tain's story reaches way back beyond the Clearances. To Norse
days, for the town's name is a corruption of the Norse 'Thing', meaning
Council; to its patron St. Duthus, born here in c 1000 and later a distinguished Bishop of Ross; to Malcolm Canmore who granted a charter; to
medieval days as a sanctuary, once sought, though in vain, by the wife of
Bruce; and to 1587 when a second charter was conferred by James VI.
Something of the above is recalled in the town's museum; in St. Duthus
Church; and in ruined St. Duthus Chapel. From the main street, a narrow
road (signed) drops down north to pass the museum and church, and
then the station, to reach, close by the shore, the chapel.

St Duthus Chapel, a ruin in a cemetery, was built around the 11 or 12C
and traditionally both stands on the site of the cottage in which Duthus
was born and also houses his bones which are known to have been
brought to Tain in 1253 from Armagh in Ireland where he died in 1065.
Neither tradition is solidly based, and it may well be that the relics were
buried in the ancient church which once stood on the site of today's. The
chapel was built as a prayer cell with accommodation for a resident
hermit charged with guarding the saint's shrine. It stood also within the
sanctuary of the Girth of Tain, which, however, was violated on at least
two occasions. The first was in 1307 when the Earl of Ross seized Bruce's
wife and daughter who had fled here from Kildrummy (see Rte 38); the
second was in 1427 when a freebooter, McNeill of Creich, chased an
enemy into the chapel, then burning it and all who were inside, though
it has been suggested that the offender was in reality a Mackay,
masquerading under the name of his McNeill grandmother.

St. Duthus Church, built in c 1360, stands on the site of its early medieval predecessor, traces of which can still be seen in the chapter house.
The new church soon became something of a competitor to the chapel
on account of the saint's bones—they disappeared in 1560—and was
long a place of pilgrimage, among its penitents being James IV who
came here each year between 1493 and 1513 in expiation for his part in
the death of his father (see Sauchieburn, at the end of Rte 23). Especially
noteworthy are the beautiful east window, with five stained glass sections, and other windows depicting two historical events, namely Malcolm Canmore and Margaret conferring their charter, and the Scottish
parliament of 1560 adopting Knox's Confession of Faith.—Adjacent
Tain Museum (Tel: 0862-2140) houses a Clan Ross Centre.

EAST OF TAIN. A short way south of Tain B9165 heads east off A9 for *Hill
of Fearn*, birthplace and boyhood home of Peter Fraser (1884–1950),
Prime Minister of New Zealand from 1940–49, and, just beyond, **Fearn**

Abbey. A Premonstratensian abbey founded in 1221 by Farquhar, 1st Earl of Ross, at Edderton (see below) was removed to Fearn in 1238 because of the greater fertility of the soil here. The young Patrick Hamilton, the first martyr of the Scottish Reformation (burnt at St. Andrews in 1528), was titular abbot, and at his death Fearn was annexed to the see of Ross. Later, the abbey church was converted to parish church, but was the scene of a tragedy in 1742 when the roof fell in, killing 44 people. Today the again largely restored church embodies the nave and choir of the old abbey church.

Beyond, on the coast, *Shandwick* has to the south of its bay a red sandstone cliff below which fossils may be found, while above the village, and protected by glass, stands a fine carved stone. Another fine stone, in Edinburgh's Queen Street Royal Museum of Scotland, was found at Hilton of Cadboll, just to the north. Tradition is that these Shandwick and Hilton stones mark the graves of Norse princes lost in a shipwreck on a local reef.

B9165 out of Fearn leads north east towards Tarbat Ness, along which is the village resort of **Portmahomack**, with a small harbour (improved by Telford) and a quaint Victorian iron fountain recording the introduction of 'gravitation water' in 1887. Nearby ruined *Ballone Castle* of the 15–16C was typical Z-plan with diagonally opposed towers; built for the Earl of Ross and later passing to the Mackenzies, the castle was abandoned in the early 19C. *Tarbat Ness*, with one of the highest lighthouses in Britain, guards the south entrance towards Dornoch Firth.

A new road (A9; early 1990s), crossing Dornoch Firth, provides a direct link to Clashmore and Dornoch (both Rte 59), but this Route heads west to Bonar Bridge.—Curving north west out of Tain the road in *6m* reaches *Edderton*, the original site chosen in 1221 by the Earl of Ross for his abbey, moved a few years later to Fearn. Of this—it was here for only a brief 17 years—nothing of course survives, but, to the north of the village, there is a reminder of even earlier days in the form of a tall stone bearing Pictish symbols and traditionally commemorating a battle with the Norsemen.

9m Ardgay is at the head of Dornoch Firth and at the foot of **Strathcarron**, the latter a strath to be explored to its road's end at Croick (10m) by anybody sensitive to the poignancies of the Clearances. Once this land was the crofting home of the Rosses, but in 1845 the landowner decided that they must make way for more profitable sheep. Quiet roads trace both banks of the brown and boulder-strewn Carron as it drops seawards through lightly wooded and gentle country, but in 1854 the scene at *Gruinards*, on the right bank, was anything but gentle when 70 Ross women stood resolute until, with 20 of their number injured, they were swamped by a small army of eviction agents. Higher up the strath, Clencalvie too was Ross, and its evicted families, having nowhere else to go, camped beside *Croick Church*, a modest white-pebbled small place built, somewhat surprisingly, to a plan by Telford. Here they scratched their record on the glass of the window, leaving messages still to be read today. 'Glencalvie people was in the churchyard here, May 24 1845'; 'This house is needy refuge'; 'Glencalvie people, the wicked generation'—did they perhaps see their plight as some form of punishment? Nor is this all here, for outside the west edge of the churchyard are the collapsed but unmistakeable remains of a broch, a reminder of a refuge of other peoples perhaps 2000 years earlier.

1m **Bonar Bridge** (500 inhab. *Inf.*), on the north side of the head of Dornoch Firth, lies beyond a bridge spanning the channel linking the head of the firth with the loch known as the Kyle of Sutherland; built by

Telford in 1812 and rebuilt after a flood of 1892, the bridge has since been widened. It was near *Carbisdale Castle* (Youth Hostel) at the north of the Kyle that Montrose made his final stand in 1650, being routed and then surrendered to his enemies by MacLeod of Assynt (see Rte 58).—For Bonar Bridge to the *North West*, see Rte 58; to *John O'Groats*, see Rte 59.

58 Bonar Bridge to the North West

Three roads, all wandering across remote and open moor, fan north west away from Bonar Bridge. To the west coast the choice is between Strath Oykel (A837 to Loch Assynt) or Loch Shin (A838 to Laxford Bridge). Scenically, at least by Highland standards, the Strath Oykel road is not outstanding, but its northern part affords good views of the mountains and this road has the advantage that it heads directly for Ullapool and Lochinver and the wild country of Inverpolly and Glencanisp that lies between. The Loch Shin Road is pleasant and varied, though not until the end of the loch's rather dreary 16m length.

The road to the north coast (A836 to Altnaharra, then unclassified to Hope on Rte 61) would be hard to equal for sheer space and remoteness and has also the merit of offering, at Altnaharra, a choice of two other approaches to the north coast.

For all three roads the start is common as far as (4m, by A836) Invershin where the Strath Oykel road bears west. The other two split 8m farther north beyond Lairg.

> **Key distances**. Bonar Bridge via Strath Oykel to *Loch Assynt* (junction with A894), 37m.—Bonar Bridge via Loch Shin to *Laxford Bridge*, 45m.—Bonar Bridge via Altnaharra to *Hope*, 49m.
>
> SOME HOTELS (see also Rtes 57, 56 and 61). **Inchnadamph**. *Inchnadamph*, IV27 4HL. Tel: 05712-202.—**Lairg**. *Sutherland Arms*, IV27 4AT. Tel: 0549-2291. **Altnaharra**. *Altnaharra*, IV27 4UE. Tel: 054981-222.

Via Strath Oykel to Loch Assynt

At *Invershin* A837 bears west, almost immediately crossing the river Shin (waterfall 1m north by B864) and in a further 6m merging with A839 from Lairg. In another 3m A837 reaches a spot called Tuiteam-Tarbhach, site in c 1397 of a bloody affray between the MacLeods of Assynt and Lewis and the Mackays of Sutherland; it was a decisive Mackay victory, only one MacLeod returning to Lewis and he later dying of his wounds.

Beyond Oykel Bridge wooded landscape gives way to moor as gradually the western mountains rise into view, first among them being *Canisp* (2779ft) and to the right *Breabag* (2670ft) and *Ben More Assynt* (3273ft). Beyond Loch Craggie (4m after Oykel Bridge) appear the grand isolated peaks of Inverpolly and Glencanisp Forest; from south to north *Cul Beag* (2523ft) with *Stac Polly* (2009ft) behind, and then *Cul More* (2786ft), followed by *Suilven* (2399ft).

A837 is joined by A835 (for the Highland and Rare Breeds Farm and Knockan Cliff Information Centre, both a short way south west by A835, see Rte 56), beyond the junction heading due north and in about 4m passing (east) *Inchnadamph Nature Reserve* (3200 acres), an area mainly of specialist geological interest, lying as it does at the west foot of an area of disturbed limestone of Cambrian age and being ringed by the Glencoul, Ben More and Moine thrusts. In the south part of the reserve there are caves and fissures in which prehistoric human and animal bones have been found, while botanists may note that willow scrub found in the peat hollows is of a type common in Scandinavia but rare in Scotland.

As Loch Assynt is approached a memorial on a hillock near the south east corner of the loch commemorates two late-19C geologists (Peach and Horne) who did much to interpret the geology of this part of the Highlands. Beyond, on its promontory, appears the stark fragment of *Ardvreck Castle*, a stronghold (c 1490) of the MacLeods and the grim place in which Montrose was held after his defeat at Carbisdale near Bonar Bridge, while just to the south stand the remains of *Calda House*, a Mackenzie mansion built in the 17C but later abandoned after destruction by a fire.—Here Rte 56 is joined.

Via Loch Shin to Laxford Bridge

From *Invershin* A836 continues north for *Lairg* (600 inhab. *Inf.*), 2m beyond which A838 angles away north west beside the not very interesting shore of *Loch Shin*—a narrow hydro-electric reservoir some 17m long—and soon the mountains begin to bar the westward view; *Ben More Assynt* (west, 3273ft), *Ben Leod* (ahead, 2597ft) and *Ben Hee* (north, 2864ft).

Beyond the end of Loch Shin the scenery markedly improves. The hills close in and the road threads a series of lochs and woods between mountains of increasing height, until finally squeezing between the abrupt, quartzite-capped pinnacle of *Ben Stack* (2356ft) and its companion loch to accompany the lovely Laxford river below the great scree face of *Arkle* (2580ft) to the north. Rte 56 is joined at *Laxford Bridge*.

Via Altnaharra and Strath More to Hope

For Invershin to *Lairg*, see above. The road steadily rises across desolate moor to cross the watershed (828ft) at *The Crask*, 1m north of Crask Inn, and reach the remote hamlet of **Altnaharra** at the west end of Loch Naver. Here there is a choice of three roads to the north coast. To the east, B873 skirts part-wooded Loch Naver, beyond joining Rte 60 at Syre; in the centre, A836 continues north across moorland (730ft) before descending to the west shore of *Loch Loyal*, with its extension Loch Craggie forming a lovely sweep of water below (west) the huge granite mass of *Ben Loyal* (2504ft) with its four splintered peaks.

But this Route turns west along a narrow, unclassified road which after 6m of lonely moor and dark bog meets the watershed at *Loch Meadie* before finding the mountains and dropping into steep-sided green Strath More. Here, in a grand and lovely setting beside the river with *Ben Hope* (3040ft) towering above, there survives a tantalising echo from this valley's Iron Age past; the unusually small broch of *Dornadilla* (or Dun Dornaig or Dornaieil), once a home and refuge, today still remarkably well preserved and with the higher part of its wall probably still representing the original height. Just beyond, at *Alltnacailleach*, there is a good waterfall, and, beyond again, the road runs above peaceful Loch Hope to join Rte 61 at *Hope*.

59 Bonar Bridge to John o'Groats

A9 (but number may change as far as about Clashmore).—Generally a narrow coastal strip between the mountains and the sea. At first the coast is flat, but to the north of Loch Fleet it becomes undulating and in places steep, with cliffs. Beyond Dunbeath the mountains ease down to moorland, and from Wick northwards the scene is flat and bleak, though in places with impressive cliffs.

SOME HOTELS. **Dornoch**. *Dornoch Castle*, Castle Street, IV25 3SD. Tel: 0862-810216. *Royal Golf*, Grange Road, IV25 3LG. Tel: 0862-810283. **Golspie**. *Golf Links*, Church Street, KW10 6TT. Tel: 04083-3408. **Brora**. *Links*, Golf Road, KW9 6QS. Tel: 0408-21225. *Royal Marine*, Golf Road, KW9 6GS. Tel: 0408-21252. **Helmsdale**. *Navidale House*, KW8 6JS. Tel: 04312-258. **Wick**. *Mercury*, Riverside, KW1 4NL. Tel: 0955-3344.

Total distance 90m.—*14m* **Dornoch**.—*10m* **Golspie**.—*5m* **Brora**.—*10m* **Helmsdale**.—*19m* **Latheron**.—*5m* **Clyth**.—*10m* **Wick**.—*17m* **John o'Groats**.

From **Bonar Bridge** (see Rte 57) the wooded road skirts the north side of Dornoch Firth, passing or running close to a variety of minor sites. On the promontory into the firth, 3m out of Bonar Bridge, a search—in summer the undergrowth can be dense—should reveal the remains of a vitrified fort called *Dun Creich*, within it being an unidentified medieval ruin, while at (2m) *Spinningdale*, and more easily seen, a ruin below the road is that of a mill. In a further 2m, opposite *Ospidale House*, a stone column beside the road is said to commemorate the death in battle of a Norse chieftain called Ospis. Next comes *Skibo Castle* (no adm.), built in 1898 by Andrew Carnegie on the site of an old castle to which Montrose was brought after his capture at Loch Assynt and imprisonment in Ardvreck. Near *Clashmore* a new A9 comes in from the south and, just beyond, A949 is followed south east for Dornoch, to the south of this road and approaching the town being a lone standing stone.

14m (from Bonar Bridge) **Dornoch** (1000 inhab. *Inf.*) is a dignified, almost sleepy town, clustered solid around a spacious centre dominated by the squat cathedral, admirably in keeping in local stone. With its miles of sands, golf courses and other amenities this is a popular yet still quiet family resort.

History. Middens discovered at Earl's Cross on the links prove that there were people living here perhaps 3000 years ago. Dornoch's first recorded building, however, was the church of St. Barr which must have stood here in about 600. Later there was a Norse settlement, then in 1224 Gilbert de Moravia (Murray), Bishop of Caithness, started building the present cathedral and Dornoch became the seat of the bishops, who built their castle alongside. In 1570 Dornoch was the victim of a clan feud between the local Murrays and the Mackays of Strathnaver, the town being pillaged and both cathedral and bishop's castle burned. In 1722 the last witch in Scotland was burnt here; the unfortunate was Janet Horne, condemned for transforming her daughter into a pony, riding her to a witches' coven, and there having her shod by the Devil. In 1942 the Norsemen returned, this time as the Norwegian Brigade which was based here for training and whose stay is recorded by a plaque in the cathedral.

Dornoch Cathedral was begun in 1224 as described above, but after the fire of 1570 all that was left intact was the tower with its spire, the rest being roofless. The choir and transepts were restored in 1616 and the nave in 1634, but major restoration had to wait until that sponsored by the Duchess of Sutherland between 1835–37 and carried out by William Burn—a drastic undertaking which included what was virtually a rebuilding of the nave. A happier restoration was that of 1924, as part of the 700th anniversary commemoration, when the plaster was stripped away to reveal once again the beautiful 13C stonework of the crossing, the choir and the east sides of the transepts. No fewer than 16 earls of Sutherland are said to lie here. At the west end are a statue of the 1st Duke (by Chantrey) who died in 1833 and is even more ostentatiously commemorated by a giant figure high above his Dunrobin Castle (see below), and the mutilated effigy of Sir Richard de Moravia, brother of the cathedral's founder and killed in battle against the Norsemen at nearby Embo (see below).

The town *Cross*, still showing its ancient shaft, is against the north side of the cathedral wall, but all that survives of the once formidable *Castle of the Bishops* is its sturdy tower, now a part of Dornoch Castle Hotel. Also in the Square, in the old jail, is the *Dornoch Craft Centre* (Tel: 0862-810555) showing crafts and offering a glimpse of 19C prison life.

The northward journey can be continued either by returning direct to A9 or, more interestingly, by taking the minor shore road through Embo and Skelbo. Just outside Dornoch the *Earl's Cross* (see above) stands on the links between the road and the shore, site of prehistoric discoveries but itself probably marking the boundary in the 13C between the lands of the earls of Sutherland and those of the bishop; once it bore on either side their respective arms. At *Embo*, by the entrance to a caravan site, are preserved the scanty, tumbled remains of two prehistoric burial chambers (c 2000 BC), while the caravan site is itself of interest as successor to a Clearances village into which evicted crofters were herded and invited to farm the unpromising, sandy surrounds. Beyond, *Skelbo Castle*, now a small ruin on a grassy mound overlooking Loch Fleet, dates from the 14C but is successor to an older, wooden affair owned by that Richard de Moravia, killed at Embo, whose effigy lies in Dornoch's cathedral. And hither in 1290 came Edward I's commissioners, eager to greet the child Maid of Norway as Queen of Scotland and bride of their king's son, but soon to be shattered by the news of her death at sea.

Immediately beyond Skelbo A9 is rejoined and the head of Loch Fleet crossed by a long causeway raised by Telford in 1815 to carry the new road superseding the ferry that had plied for centuries.—*10m* (from Dornoch) **Golspie**, a long, straggling village closely associated with the Sutherlands, their splendidly carved loft of 1739 being the main feature of St. Andrew's Church, while high above the village on Ben Vraggie (1293ft; sometimes shown as Beinn a' Bhragaidh) presides the colossal figure of the 1st Duke, a man as much abused for his Clearances evictions as he was praised for the improvements he sponsored. At Golspie, too, bearing hard round the church along an insignificant road, a high inland loop can be made (c 22m) to Brora), first across the shoulder of Ben Horn (1706ft) and up on to a desolate windswept plateau, then by contrast curving northwards and eastwards to drop the length of a glorious open valley, its foot filled by *Loch Brora*, wooded, tranquil and with green meadows creeping into its waters. This is a district rich in cairns, burial chambers, brochs, settlement remains and field systems, the discovery of which should tempt the dawdler armed with a detailed map.

Dunrobin Castle (Tel: 04083-3177), from the 13C the seat of the earls, later the dukes of Sutherland, stands on a natural terrace by the sea, once marking the end of the series of ferries which crossed the succession of firths to the south. Said to have occupied the site of a broch, the original castle was a square keep with angle-turrets, built by Robert, 2nd Earl of Sutherland, in c 1275 (hence the castle's name). Over the years this was extended by a tower and hall wing which eventually enclosed a courtyard, until in the 19C Sir Charles Barry carried out the large extension which resulted in today's Scottish Baronial complex. In 1915, when in use as a naval hospital, the castle was damaged by fire, this leading to further reconstruction by Sir Robert Lorimer. Visitors today can still see the massive ancient keep and some of the 19C rooms, while in the grounds there is a Victorian museum showing Pictish stones and much of local interest.

Two quite good broch remains can be found beside A9 either side of (5m) **Brora**, a small town known for the spinning of Shetland wool. The broch to the south is immediately east of the road just before it crosses the railway; the other (Cinn Trolla), 3m north and close to the railway, is better, with an internal diameter of over 30ft, traces of domed chambers, and outworks about an entrance passage. When excavated in 1880 two headless skeletons were found here. Not far beyond, on the west a short way before the Glen Loth road, a stone in a layby records the death near here in about 1700 of the last wolf in Sutherland.—*10m* **Helmsdale** (1000 inhab. *Inf.*) is a grey-built township, largely beside Strath Ullie well below A9. On the south side of the road bridge spanning the valley, a layby was the site of a castle the ruins of which were removed in 1970. Built in 1488 by the 7th Countess of Sutherland, the castle was the scene in 1567 of the murder of the 11th Earl and his wife at the instigation of George Sinclair, Earl of Caithness. More about this, as also about many aspects of the Highlands past—Picts, Vikings, witches, the Clearances, the Kildonan gold rush—can be learnt at *Timespan* (Tel: 04312-327), a visitor centre using vivid life-size sets and video programmes; down below in the valley, Timespan also offers a riverside herb garden with rare and medicinal plants.

Now winding round ravines, A9 climbs to a plateau (750ft) which ends towards the sea in the bold and rocky *Ord of Caithness* (the south limit of the Caithness coast), a place of ill omen for Sinclairs who prefer not to cross the Ord on a Monday ever since a large party of the clan marched across on that day on their way to Flodden, whence none returned. Beside the sea, at (*10m*) *Berriedale*, are the scanty remains of a castle, once a fortress of the earls of Caithness, while, just west of A9, Langwell Gardens (Tel: 05935-237) were laid out in 1916 within a surround of much earlier walls.—*5m* **Dunbeath** takes its name (Fort of the Birches) from a broch, traces of which still survive at the confluence of the Dunbeath Water and the Houstry Burn, and ancient records mention a siege of as long ago as the year 680. The Dunbeath *Preservation Trust* exhibition recalls the local past (Tel: 05933-233). From the village a minor road ascends some 6m west to *Braemore*, a hamlet near which the royal Duke of Kent (1902–42) lost his life in an air accident.

1m Llaidhay Caithness Croft Museum (Tel: 05932-208) is an 18–19C croft complex, with house and byre together under one roof and an adjacent barn which is a good example of cruck roof construction, a method essential here due to the local shortage of timber.—*3m* **Latheron**, with a *Clan Gunn Heritage Centre and Museum* in the 18C old parish church, as also, within the north east angle of A9 and A895, standing stones and a strange hilltop belfry, sited here so that the summoning bell could be heard throughout the scattered valleys of the parish.

From Latheron a worthwhile diversion—of prehistoric interest; a triangle of some 12m back to A9 at Lybster—may be made north along A895 to *Achavanich*, approaching which Loch Rangag, with broch remains on a low spit, lies below the road; though little more than a tumble of stones, the site is of interest for the traces of a ditch and embankment defence across the neck. The *Achavanich Standing Stones*, some 40 surviving out of a probable original 60, are just down the unclassified road which hairpins south east. The oval shape, open to the south east, is one of only two known sites of this design, and speculation is added by a once large burial cist just outside the oval's mouth. The unclassified road meets A9 at *Lybster*, where there is an inscribed Celtic cross near the north wall of the churchyard.

5m (direct from Latheron) *West Clyth*, where prehistoric interest again suggests a diversion, this time 6m north to the *Grey Cairns of Camster*, a complex of burial cairns in a remote and desolate peat moorland landscape that can have changed little since Stone and Bronze Age peoples brought stones here and erected these massive monuments. Today well restored and given skylights to help the visitor supple enough to crawl inside, they include a round and a long cairn, the former, with complete original passage, being one of the best examples of its kind on Scotland's mainland. The long cairn—200ft by 65ft and known as the horned type—has separate chambers as well as its entrance passage. Human and animal remains, pottery and stone artefacts have all been found here.

The *Hill o' Many Stanes*, on a hillock just off A9 *3m* beyond West Clyth, is a perhaps even more remarkable prehistoric site where no explanation is offered for over 200 small stones painstakingly arranged in 22 rows to form a kind of fan.

In *8m*, approaching Wick, the shattered *Castle of Old Wick* survives from the 12–14C as little more than a clifftop fragment. Originally a Cheyne stronghold, it later passed to the Sutherlands; but the castle's weakness was its lack of a good well, this leading to its surrender after a siege in 1569 and its abandonment a century or so later. There are fine cliffs around here, to the south of the castle being the Brig o' Trams, a stack connected to the shore by a natural arch.

2m **Wick** (8000 inhab. *Inf.*)—the name deriving from the Norse 'Vik' meaning Bay—is a busy northern centre with an airport and a harbour at the mouth of the river.

History. Wick was mentioned in the sagas as early as 1140 and later became a royal burgh, at which time, though, the place was no more than a scatter of houses and a church on the north bank of the river. In 1808 the British Fisheries Society commissioned Telford to lay out a model village on the south side, this being called, then as now, Pulteneytown. The inner harbour was completed by 1810, the outer by 1831, and there were major improvements as soon as 1868. But the harbour, for various reasons never very successful, declined in importance with the disappearance of the herring and the arrival of the railway; today it is largely used by whitefish boats.

The old town, north of the river, with the narrow, winding High Street and the wider Bridge Street, is the main shopping district. Here the parish church (1830), at the west end of High Street, is adjoined by the older *Sinclair Aisle*, the burial place of the earls of Caithness. Two main places of interest, however, will be found south of the river, one being the *Wick Heritage Centre* (Tel: 0955-3385) in Bank Row. With some emphasis on the fishing industry, and recalling also local past domestic and farming life, features include the interiors of a lighthouse, a kippering shed and 19C homes and workshops. The other, on Harrowhill, is *Caithness Glass* (Tel: 0955-2286) where the crafting of glass can be watched and the result purchased.

Noss Head, with a lighthouse, is 3m north of Wick beyond the airport, and from a car park short of the lighthouse a path leads to two adjacent clifftop ruined castles, *Sinclair* and *Girnigoe*, the latter of the 15C and the former early 17C. Both were residences of the earls of Caithness, Girnigoe being where the 4th Earl, suspecting that his son (the Master of Caithness) was plotting against him, imprisoned him from 1570–76 and then murdered him. In 1672 the 6th Earl sold his estates to Campbell of Glenorchy, but the sale was disputed by another Sinclair, Sinclair of Keiss (7m north). Campbell thereupon invaded and laid siege to Girnigoe, this being the expedition to which the ballad 'The Campbells are coming' is believed to refer. Both castles were deserted in 1679, soon collapsing into ruin. *Ackergill Tower*, 2m west of the twin castles, dates from the 14–15C, but was enlarged in 1852.

The stretch of coast between Wick and John o' Groats seems to have been among the earliest inhabited parts of Scotland, and, although nothing can now be seen, excavation during the 19C and more recently has shown that Middle Stone Age people lived here, holding on to their primitive way of life even after more advanced New Stone Age and even Iron Age cultures were flourishing in the more fertile hinterland.

In *5m* from Wick, A9 touches a loch beside which a minor road north west in 4m reaches Lyth, with the *Lyth Arts Centre* (Tel: 095584-270), home during summer of a programme of contemporary art exhibitions.—*2m Keiss*, with remains on the cliff of its medieval castle, has a small harbour just to the north of which are traces of two brochs.— At the (*2m*) *John Nicolson Museum*, at Auckengill (Tel: 0955-3761. Ext. 242), named after a respected local antiquarian, the theme is local archaeology with some emphasis on brochs and the Iron Age. A short way beyond, just south of Ness Head, stands ruined 15C *Bucholy Castle*—*8m* **John o'Groats**, see Rte 61.

60 Helmsdale to the North Coast

A897 up Strath of Kildonan to Kinbrace. Then choice between A897 via Strath Halladale to Melvich, or B871 via Strath Naver to Bettyhill.— Moor, peat bog and wooded strath, with some mountain backdrop.

HOTEL. **Forsinard** (south send of Strath Halladale). *Forsinard*, KW13 6YT. Tel: 06417-221.

Total distance to Melvich 37m; to Bettyhill 44m.—*16m* **Kinbrace**. Then either *21m* **Melvich**; or *15m* **Syre**.—*13m* **Bettyhill**.

From **Helmsdale** (see Rte 59) the road, accompanied by the railway, gradually ascends *Strath of Kildonan*, also known as *Strath Ullie*, a wide valley of slowly rising, mostly open and bald moor, with at its upper end distant mountain views. This parish of Kildonan (see also Timespan at Helmsdale) suffered severely during the Clearances, losing four-fifths of its people (some 2000) between 1801–31, but there was a temporary surge in population when Suisgill and other burns became the scene of gold panning in 1868–69. Cairns and broch remains invite discovery with the help of a large-scale map, and gold panning can still provide entertainment, if with little likelihood of profit.

In some *12m* the *Suisgill Burn* is crossed, a large broch remain being visible just west of the road a short way beyond.—*4m* **Kinbrace**, a desolate and scattered hamlet at which a choice is offered between A897 along Strath Halladale or B871 up the Helmsdale river and then along Strath Naver. Scenically there is little to choose between the two roads, but that via Strath Naver is wilder, rather more interesting and provides, at Syre, a road west to Altnaharra and Rte 58.

STRATH HALLADALE, green and well cultivated, once defined the boundary between Mackay and Sutherland territory.—*7m Forsinard* (hotel)—*14m Melvich* is on Rte 61.

STRATH NAVER. From Kinbrace to (*15m*) **Syre** in Strath Naver B871 makes its way across wide, open moor affording long vistas, especially south to the mountains which rise beyond the large, bleak lochs that feed the Helmsdale river. Syre, and Skail 2m north, two sparse communities strung along some four miles, are associated with St. Maelrubha, thought to have been murdered here by the Norsemen in c 722, while a more recent association is recorded by a stone beside the road at the north end of Skail, this recalling the days of Napoleonic danger and the first gathering of the 93rd Sutherland Highlanders on the formation of the regiment in 1800.

Strath Naver has not always presented the tranquil face it does today. At the time when the Sutherland Highlanders gathered, the fertile 10m from the loch to Skailburn was strung with crofter hamlets, the people being Mackays despite their living on Sutherland land. Nineteen years later all the inhabitants had been evicted and their homes burned; many died, and an eye-witness of 1819 has described how on one unforgettable night he counted the flames of 250 crofts, including his own. For the *Strath Naver Museum* at Bettyhill-Farr, see Rte 61.

From Syre B873 bears south east along Loch Naver for Altnaharra on Rte 58. B871 continues north from Syre to reach in *10m* the junction with A836 and (a further *3m*) **Bettyhill**, see Rte 61.

61   John o' Groats to Durness

A836 to Tongue. A838 to Durness.—For much of this Route the road keeps inland, giving only occasional views of the sea. Rather bleak landscape between John o' Groats and Thurso, along which stretch can be seen, though sadly decreasingly, distinctive local stone slab fences, the only evidence today of an industry which once supplied flagstones for the pavements of cities as far apart as Paris and Melbourne. West of Thurso the scenery gradually changes until west of Melvich the road is winding across mostly bare moor while the coast becomes bolder. The visitor who explores almost any of the many little roads down to the shore will find surprisingly rewarding lost corners, with some fine beaches and strange cliffs and rocks.

SOME HOTELS. **John o' Groats**. *John o' Groats House*, KW1 4YR. Tel: 095581-203. **Thurso**. *Pentland*, Princes Street, KW14 7AA. Tel: 0847-63202. *Royal*, Traill Street, KW14 8EH. Tel: 0847-63191. **Bridge of Forss**. *Forss House*, KW14 7XY. Tel: 084786-201. **Melvich**. *Melvich*, KW14 7YJ. Tel: 06413-206. **Tongue**. *Ben Loyal*, Main Street, IV27 4XE. Tel: 084755-216. *Tongue*, IV27 4XD. Tel: 084755-206. **Durness**. *Parkhill*, IV27 4PN. Tel: 097181-209.

Total distance 87m.—*11m* **Dunnet**.—*8m* **Thurso**.—*9m* **Dounreay**.—*21m* **Bettyhill**.—*12m* **Kyle of Tongue**.—*8m* **Hope (Loch Eriboll)**.—*18m* **Durness**.

John o' Groats (*Inf.*), though not, as often supposed, the northernmost point of Britain's mainland (this is Dunnet Head) is nevertheless the accepted opposite to Cornwall's Land's End, 876m away.

The curious name goes back to one John de Groot, a Dutchman who inexplicably settled in this remote corner during the reign of James IV, a mound with a flagstaff close to the hotel being said to mark the site of his house. In order to avoid family precedence disputes between his eight descendants, the house was octagonal in shape, had eight doors and was centred on an octagonal table; thus each man entered by his own door and could maintain that he was sitting at the head of the table. A more prosaic story is that John worked a ferry across to South Ronaldsay and built a shelter for his waiting customers, with eight recesses to protect them from the wind whatever its direction.

Scattered around an uninviting landscape the village affords seaward views across Pentland Firth and its islands to Orkney (8m away). Since 1989 in part under the same ownership as Land's End, there are now plans for the development of a complementary northern tourism complex. In summer there is a popular passenger ferry to Burwick on Orkney's South Ronaldsay (roughly four times daily; Orkney coach tour. Tel: 095581-353).—For John o' Groats south to *Bonar Bridge*, see Rte 59.

Pentland Firth, a name more meaningful in its older version, Pictland Firth, is notorious for its swirling tides and treacherous currents; when the tide is rising the main current sets from west to east, changing direction on the ebb, but the coastal currents run in opposition, forming the dangerous 'roosts' or races. Set in the firth are the island of *Stroma* and, farther east, the group of the *Pentland Skerries*.—From John o' Groats a road runs east (2m) to **Duncansby Head** (210ft), the spectacular north east promontory of Scotland. To the north and north west, between Duncansby and Stroma, are the *Boars of Duncansby*, a reef the name of which reflects the force of the sea here, while to the south the three *Stacks of Duncansby* rise as obelisks out of the sea.

2m Canisbay, where the church has something from several centuries, though not from as far back as 1222, the year in which a church here is first mentioned. The present church is probably 15C in origin, two aisles being added in the 17C and a new tower in the 18C. *Gills Bay*, a short way north west of Canisbay, is under consideration as the terminal for a car ferry to Burwick on Orkney's South Ronaldsay. Beyond, in *4m*, the *Castle of Mey* (no adm., though the gardens are open in aid of charity on certain days in July and August), built between 1566–72 and once a seat of the earls of Caithness, was acquired in 1952 by the Queen Mother.— *5m Dunnet* is a scattered village well known for its sands and with an unusual church showing a saddleback tower which may be 14C in origin. In Dunnet pavilion there are displays, including aquaria, illustrating local natural history and geology. *Dunnet Head* (4m north; road), the most northerly point of mainland Britain, is an appropriately bold and lofty (400ft) sandstone promontory. The view seaward to Orkney and in both directions along the coast is splendid, and if, as scholars judge probable, this is the Cape Oras of the Greek historian Diodorus Siculus (c 50 BC), then Dunnet Head can claim to be the first place in Scotland to be mentioned by a writer.—*3m* **Castletown** was where in 1824 the Caithness flagstone industry was founded. The village was built to house the workers, and both village and port flourished until skilfully laid and polished flags were defeated by drab, poured concrete.

5m **Thurso** (9000 inhab. *Inf.*), of Norse origin—the name 'Thors-a' meaning Thor's river—straddles the river of the same name, in the north part being the long, narrow harbour and a pleasant promenade overlooking Thurso Bay.

History. Modest though Thurso is today, this was in medieval times the principal port for the trade between Scotland and Scandinavia and in the 14C of such importance that its weights and measures were adopted throughout Scotland. Later the town became busy with the flagstone industry, while today the ferry service from Scrabster to Orkney and the nuclear power station at nearby Dounreay combine to boost local activity.

From the east the town is entered across Thurso Bridge, ahead being a church (William Burn, 1853), opposite which is a statue, perhaps by Chantrey, of Sir John Sinclair (1754–1835), financier, agricultural writer and economist; he and his daughter Catherine, the latter known as a writer of fiction, lived at Thurso Castle (no adm.) to the north east of the town. Traill Street, bearing right beyond the bridge, soon passes Manson's Lane, on the corner being the picturesque small *Meadow Well* from which the townspeople drew their water until well into the 19C and the market too where local fishwives sold their fresh fish.

Farther into the town, at the Town Hall (1872) in High Street, will be found the *Heritage Museum* (Tel: 0847-62459), serving as a folk museum and as home for a notable collection of stones and fossils, including the bequest of Robert Dick (1811–66), a local baker who made a name as both botanist and geologist. *St. Peter's Church*, close to the harbour, dates from the 12 or 13C and may have been built by Bishop Gilbert de Moravia, better known for Dornoch's cathedral; rebuilt during the 17C, the church was not used after 1832 and soon became a ruin. The oldest part is the choir, with a semicircular apse within a square end, while the large south gable window with five lights is also noteworthy. *Harald's Tower*, to the north east of the town, built in the early 19C by Sir John Sinclair (see above) as a Sinclair burial place, stands above the grave of Harald, Earl of Caithness, slain in a battle near here in 1196.

On the west outskirts of Thurso A836 passes (left) *Pennyland Farm* (a name recalling Norse days when land was rated for tax as mark, ounce or penny), birthplace of Sir William Smith (1854–1914), founder of the Boys' Brigade, while just beyond a fork branches to Scrabster Pier whence the car ferry plies to Stromness in Orkney (see Rte 67).

5m Bridge of Forss, just beyond which a minor road south (for Shebster) passes below the hilltop *Cnoc Freiceadain Cairns*, two longmound, horned burial chambers, curiously set at right angles to one another; the cairns apart, the short climb is rewarded by a splendid view. By the shore, about 1m north of the above turn off A836, the small ruined *St. Mary's Chapel* (*Crosskirk*) dates probably from the 12C and is notable for its very low doors.

4m **Dounreay** nuclear power development establishment, with its dome and great spread of buildings, appears as something of a modern shock in a district which seems essentially more attuned to the past than to a technological present (Tours and exhibition. Tel: 0847-62121, Ext. 656). *Reay, 2m* beyond, the place from which Lord Reay, chief of Clan Mackay, takes his title, has a church of 1739, typical of the local style of that period with a small belfry tower and external stair.—Just short of (*6m*) *Melvich* A897 brings in Rte 60 from Strath Halladale.

13m **Bettyhill** (*Inf.*) is named after Elizabeth, 1st Duchess of Sutherland. At the east end of the village the former church of Farr (1774), with a contemporary pulpit and a Celtic cross, has been converted into a *Strath Naver Museum* (Tel: 06412-342), a private museum run by volunteer enthusiasts which tells the story of the Strath Naver Clearances (see also Rte 60) and illustrates also the local way of life at and around that period. One section is devoted to Clan Mackay. *Invernaver National Nature Reserve*, across the Naver estuary, contains the finest collection of northern plant communities (of mixed mountain and coastal types) in the north of Scotland, breeding birds also here including the greenshank, ring ouzel and twite or mountain linnet.

Passing the junction with B871 (see Rte 60, via Strath Naver) A836 in *12m* overlooks the **Kyle of Tongue**, a broad, shallow inlet, the tapering head of which lies below the serrated peaks of Ben Loyal and the long east shoulder of Ben Hope. The township of *Tongue*, on this east side, is dominated by ruined Castle Varrich, a 14C Mackay stronghold said to be successor to a Norse fort. Since 1972 crossed by a causeway, the Kyle is part blocked at its foot by the Rabbit Islands, to which it is possible to walk at low water, while along the Kyle's west side a small road soon loses itself in a quiet corner of sandy beaches, cliffs, curious rocks and islands.

Across the causeway the main road rises to a wilderness of mixed moor and bog known as *A'Mhoine* to reach (*8m*) *Hope* where Rte 58 joins from Altnaharra. Beyond, **Loch Eriboll** fills the scene below, a long, beautiful and very deep inlet which in 1939–45 sheltered assembling Allied convoys and, the war won, saw the surrender of German submarines, thus confirming a prophecy of the Seer of Brahan that a war would end at

Eriboll. Here, too, seven centuries earlier, assembled Hakon's Viking galleys, only to sail fearfully away convinced—and rightly so because they were soon defeated at Largs—that an eclipse of the sun was harbinger of disaster. From an even remoter age hut circles can be found here, though not easily amid the bracken. One group lies between two small lochs just north of where the road turns south, a broch remnant also surviving just to the east of the huts; another group awaits discovery to the right of the road about 1m south of Eriboll estate. And on the loch's west side—by a burn bridge just north of the turn to Port Nancon jetty; identified by two modest cairns beside the east verge of the road—there is, hidden in the undergrowth, an intact and wholly unspoilt *Earthhouse* complete with curved stair and long passage finishing at a round chamber (torch necessary; may be flooded).

17m (from Hope) *Smoo Cave* is an immense triple-chambered cliff cavern, the outer chamber—some 200ft deep and 120ft high with gaping holes in the roof—being easily accessible from the beach. Access to the second cavern, with a waterfall, is difficult; to the third impossible without special equipment and arrangements.

1m **Durness** (*Inf.*), the Scottish mainland's most north west village, is a popular stop along the coastal round, the ending point of Rte 56, and the place at which to arrange a visit to Cape Wrath (see below). It is also interesting to go a mile or so west to *Balnakeil* where a former military camp has since 1964 been a craft village (summer only) with several individual workshops. Balnakeil Bay is a glorious curve of white sand beside which is the now roofless *Durness Old Church*, built in 1619 but on the site of an older church mentioned in Vatican records as having contributed to the third crusade. Here are two memorials. One, prominent in the burial ground, is to Rob Donn (1740–78; born Mackay), a famed local bard; a horizontal slab between the memorial and the church may mark his grave. The other memorial, inside the church (south wall with a skull and crossbones), is to Donald MacMurchov, a notorious highwayman who arranged to be buried here in return for his financial help to the then Lord Reay who wished, but could not afford, to rebuild the church. The large 18C farmhouse opposite the church stands on the site of a summer residence of the bishops of Caithness.

*Cape Wrath—the name has nothing to do with the often wild sea, but comes from the Norse 'hvarf' meaning 'point of turning'—is the 523ft high north west extremity of Britain's mainland, a headland of precipitous gneiss cliffs veined with pink pegmatite. The immense view extends east along the coast and across to Orkney (Hoy, 60m), and west to the Butt of Lewis (45m) and even Harris beyond (80m). Far out to sea may be seen Stack Skerry and Skule Skerry (37 and 42m north east) and the island of Rona (40m north west). The fort-like lighthouse was built in 1828.

Cape Wrath is reached by the Kyle of Durness ferry (no cars) at Keoldale, 1½m south of Durness (May–Sept: First sailing about 09.30 daily. Tel: 097181-376). The ferry connects with a minibus service. Bird enthusiasts can leave the bus on the way and walk about a mile to *Clo-Mor Cliffs*, the highest in Britain. The road to the cape crosses a bleak moor called *The Parph*, once notorious for wolves.

IX THE HEBRIDES

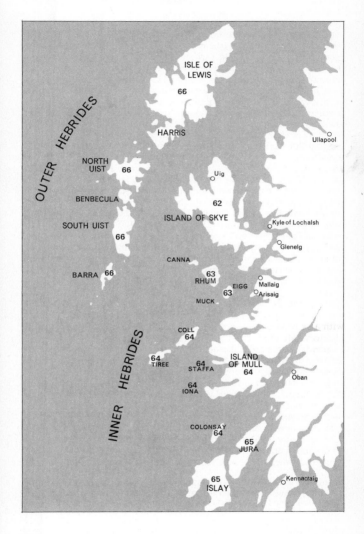

The Hebrides comprise between 40 and 50 islands and innumerable barren islets and reefs. They divide themselves into the Outer and the Inner Hebrides. The latter, which include the large island of Skye, lie, as their name suggests, fairly close to the mainland and stretch some 150 miles from the north of Skye opposite Gairloch to the south of Islay opposite Kintyre. (Smaller islands, close inshore, are not included here but are described under the appropriate mainland Routes.) The Outer Hebrides straggle 130 miles from the Butt of Lewis in the north to Barra

Head in the south. They are separated from the mainland or the Inner Hebrides by the North Minch (40 miles between Lewis and the mainland); the Little Minch (25 miles between Harris or North Uist and Skye); and the Sea of the Hebrides (60 miles from Barra to the mainland).

The **Inner Hebrides** are described below as four Routes: Skye, and then the three groups of islands as served, from north to south, by the ports of Mallaig, Oban and Tarbert (Kennacraig). The **Outer Hebrides** are described as one Route, because it is possible, given careful planning and timing, to motor the length of the group.

Information on communications to and within the islands is given with each island or group of islands. The warning must, though, be sounded that services are seasonal (some are, in whole or in part, summer only) and may be changed at short notice; visitors are therefore strongly advised to arm themselves with the current edition of 'Getting around the Highlands and Islands', providing up-to-date information on sea, road, rail and air services. The principal operator for sea services is Caledonian MacBrayne Ltd, The Pier, Gourock, PA19 1QP. Tel: 0475-33755. Contact should be made with this headquarters office if plans involve more than one crossing or if information is required on the various cruises and special discounts offered. For air services the operators are British Airways. Tel: 0345-222111; and Loganair, Glasgow Airport, Paisley, Renfrewshire. Tel: 041-889-3181. The main islands are reasonably well served by car ferries. Services can, however, be crowded in summer (advance booking is recommended) and careful planning of both ferries and accommodation, which on some islands is limited, is advisable. This is particularly the case if it is wished to travel the length of the Outer Hebrides where the services from Harris to North Uist and from South Uist to Barra may not be daily. Roads throughout the islands are good, if narrow and often winding.—For Hebridean luxury cruises ('Hebridean Princess') of a week or more, Hebridean Island Cruises Ltd., Acorn Park, Keighly Road, Skipton, North Yorkshire, BD23 2UE. Tel: 0756-701338.

Scenically the Hebrides offer a variety ranging from the barrenness of Barra to the jagged mountains of Harris and Skye, while at every turn there seems to be a different kind of coastline. In addition the visitor can enjoy remote places with a way of life noticeably different from that on the mainland, where there is little in the way of 'development', and where the Gaelic culture and language still flourish. It is, however, worth remembering that one aspect of this is that Sunday is strictly observed, few facilities then being available. Prehistoric and early Christian sites will be found on many of the islands, the great ritual site of *Callanish* on Lewis being outstanding among the former while *Iona* is of course a cradle of Scottish Christianity.

History. In the 6C St. Columba and other missionaries came to the Hebrides, preaching to and converting the early tribes. The Norsemen started to arrive in the 8C, first as raiders then as settlers. They called the islands 'Sudreyjar', or 'Southern Islands', a form which has been preserved in the title of the Bishop of Sodor and Man, though the bishops' jurisdiction over the Hebrides ended in the 14C. During the early 12C Somerled, a native chief of Morvern who had married a daughter of one of the Norse kings, rose to power, controlling many of the inner islands. But Norse domination continued elsewhere, not ending until 1266, three years after the Battle of Largs, when Magnus, Earl of Orkney, abandoned all claim. The formal title, 'Lord of the Isles', was first adopted by a descendant of Somerled, John Macdonald of Islay (died 1386). The power of the Lords of the Isles was finally annexed to the Crown by James IV. In 1748, with the abolition of heritable jurisdictions, the title vanished. In the early 19C the Hebrides suffered severely under the Clearances, these leading to mass emigration and a decline in population which still continues, today's population being only about one third of that of a hundred years ago. Unemployment is high, though the situation is easing through job creation projects and multi-million-pound investment by Highlands and Islands Enterprise.

62 Skye

Skye is both the largest (c 600 sq.m) of the Hebrides, and also the most scenic, in parts wild and lonely, its Cuillin Mountains (c 3000ft) the barest, most precipitous and most impressively awesome in Britain. The coasts, constantly broken by sea lochs, present striking and often strange cliff scenery, and throughout the island there are reminders of its prehistoric and medieval peoples. The island's weak point is its climate, and it is not for nothing that it is known as the Misty Isle.

This is a famed and popular holiday objective. Yet by and large the crowds head for the focal points such as Portree and Dunvegan, and even in summer it is possible to find remote and uncrowded corners.

Tourist Organisation. Isle of Skye Tourist Board, Portree. Tel: 0478-2137.

Communications. There are three *Car Ferry* services from the mainland:

1. From Kyle of Lochalsh to Kyleakin, this link also serving the train from Inverness. Crossing 5 minutes. All year, daily, frequent (Caledonian MacBrayne. Tel: 0475-33755). But note that a toll bridge is planned for 1994–95.

2. From Glenelg to Kylerhea. Crossing 5 minutes. Mid May–mid Sept: Mon.–Sat., frequent (M. A. Mackenzie, Glenelg. Tel: 059982-224).

3. From Mallaig to Armadale, this link also serving the train from Fort William. Crossing 30 minutes. Summer: Mon.–Sat., up to five services daily. Winter: Restricted service; no cars (Caledonian MacBrayne. Tel: 0475-33755).

Internal Bus Services, with seasonal timetables and no Sunday services, are infrequent. In summer there is a choice of day excursions from Portree. Information from Highland Omnibuses Ltd, Portree. Tel: 0463-233371.

SOME HOTELS. **Kyleakin**. *Dunringell*, IV41 8PR. Tel: 0599-4180. *King's Arms*, IV41 8PH. Tel: 0599-4109. **Broadford**. *Broadford*. Tel: 04712-204. **Ardvasar**. *Ardvasar*, Sleat, IV45 8RS. Tel: 04714-223. **Isle of Raasay**. *Isle of Raasay*, IV40 8PB. Tel: 047862-222. **Sligachan**. *Sligachan*, IV47 8SW. Tel: 047852-204. **Dunvegan**, *Atholl House*, IV55 8WA. Tel: 047022-219. *Harlosh*, IV55 8ZG. Tel: 047022-367. **Portree**. *Rosedale*, Beaumont Crescent, IV51 9DB. Tel: 0478-3131. **Kensaleyre**. *Kesaleyre House*, IV51 9XE. Tel: 047032-210. **Duntulm**. *Duntulm Castle*, IV51 9UF. Tel: 047052-213. **Flodigarry**. *Flodigary* IV51 9HZ. Tel: 047052-203.

History. With early Christian missionaries, Norse occupation and the Lords of the Isles and their long struggle against the Crown, Skye's history is that of the Hebrides generally. Thereafter local history is largely one of clan disputes between the Macdonalds (of Trotternish, Sleat, etc.), the Mackinnons (of the east coast), the MacLeods of Lewis (Vaternish and Dunvegan) and the MacLeods of Harris (Duirinish and Minginish).

In 1745 loyalties were divided, but what will always be remembered is that it was from Benbecula to Kilbride Bay just north of Uig that the Skye girl, Flora Macdonald, brought the Young Pretender (disguised as Betty Burke) 'over the sea to Skye'. He remained just under a week, walking first to Portree where—at Mac-Nab's Inn, now the Royal Hotel—he said goodbye to Flora. There followed two nights on Raasay, a return to Skye, and a long walk to Elgol where the Mackinnons gave him a banquet in a cave and a boat to Mallaig on the mainland.

In 1881–85, after a succession of bad harvests and poor fishing seasons, Skye experienced serious crofter riots, the main centres being Loch Sligachan in the east and the Duirinish peninsula in the north west.

*The Cuillin Mountains

The Cuillin Mountains, across the southern part of Skye and with peaks of well over 3000ft, are a tumbled, irregular mass of rough gabbro on basalt, a firm rock affording some of the best climbing in Britain. But these are also Britain's wildest and most difficult mountains and there are few peaks which can be reached without experienced rock climbing or at least a good deal of rough scrambling. Furthermore these mountains can also, and with little warning, disappear within cloud and mist, while for mineralogical reasons the compass is not necessarily reliable. Walking and climbing are therefore only for the experienced and properly equipped, or for others under expert guidance. *Glen Brittle*, with a road (from near Carbost) all the way to the coast, runs close below the mountains' west flank.

Kyleakin to Broadford

A850. 8m.—**Kyleakin** is a straggling, functional village beside the straits (⅓m wide) of the same name, this deriving from Norway's Hakon who sailed through here in 1263 on his way to defeat by Alexander III at Largs. *Castle Moil*, a ruin overlooking the straits, once known as Dun Akin and built as a defence against marauding Norsemen, was by the 12–15C a Mackinnon keep. The story goes that one enterprising chatelaine, known as 'Saucy Mary', stretched a chain across the strait and levied a stiff toll from passing shipping.

In 4m Skye's small airport is passed, Glen Arroch from here carrying an unclassified road south east to the ferry at Kylerhea. In another 2m A851 angles away for Ardvasar and the Armadale ferry. **Broadford** (*Inf.*), at the junction with A881 for Elgol, is a straggling village beside the bay of the same name and below the red granite mass of *Ben-na-Cailleach* (2403ft).

Armadale to Broadford

A851. 17m.—*Armadale* is simply the ferry terminal, the associated village being **Ardvasar**, just north east of which is *Armadale Castle*, built for Lord Macdonald in 1815–19 by Gillespie Graham near the site of a former house which in 1690 was bombarded from the sea by government forces and burned. Here now is the *Clan Donald Centre* (Tel: 04714-227), with a museum (Museum of the Isles), audio-visual presentation, gardens and an arboretum.

A851 provides the obvious road northwards, but a minor road making a circuit (c 12m) to the north west and rejoining A851 near Knock Castle is well worth considering as an alternative. Small, twisting and slow through lonely country, this road reaches and for 4m runs with the opposite coast with views across to Elgol and Rhum. Ruined *Dunscaith Castle*, guarding an arm of a coastal bay and seeming to spring from the natural rock, was a 15–16C stronghold of the Macdonalds. But legend is easy to accept here too; that the Irish hero Cuchulainn once came here to learn the art of war from the Amazon Queen of Skye who boasted 100 warriors. Beyond, at *Ord*, this diversion leaves the coast and in 4m meets A851.

Knock Castle is a creeper-clad remnant on the rocky arm of a bay of the Sound of Sleat. Belonging to the Macdonalds of Sleat, it too, like Moil and Dunscaith, has its heroine, a lady dubbed Mary of the Castle after her gallant and successful defeat in the 15C of a siege by the

MacLeods. Beyond, *Isleornsa*y, with bathing and fishing, takes its name from an island close inshore on which are a lighthouse and the ruin of a chapel. Skirting the small sea loch Loch na Dal, the road heads inland for *Broadford*.

Broadford to Elgol

A881. 14m.—A very scenic run (the most scenic in Skye) towards the southern foot of the Cuillins.

Rounding the foot of Ben-na-Cailleach (2403ft) the road in a little over 2m passes on the right a ruined church (*Cill Chriosd*), traditionally on a site where in the 7C St. Maelrubha had a cell. About 2m farther, on the left within a road fork, *Clach na Annait* is a standing stone the name of which, as also of an adjacent well, is associated with that of a shadowy pagan goddess. Skye marble quarries are now on both sides of the road which loops Loch Slapin to reach the hamlet of *Kilmarie*, a mile or so to the east of which, on the shore, is *Dun Ringill*, all that is left of a Mackinnon fort, possibly 9C in origin. Soon after Kilmarie, too, is the start of a path to (3m) *Camasunary* on Loch Scavaig.

From Camasunary a path continues another 3m to Loch Coruisk; this path involves a difficult and even dangerous section known as the Bad Step and is only for the experienced. Beyond Camasunary another path makes for (8m) Sligachan; about halfway, Harta Corrie slices away west, near the corrie's mouth being the so-called Bloody Stone, site of the last clan battle (1601) between the Macdonalds and the MacLeods.

Elgol is a haphazard village scattered around its steep cliff from which there are views across to Rhum and several other islands. It was here that—no longer Betty Burke but disguised as a manservant called Lewie Caw—the Young Pretender was received by the Mackinnons, given a banquet in what is now called *Prince Charles's Cave* (south of the village) and then sent on his way to the mainland.

Sligachan Bridge, Isle of Skye, between Kyleakin and Portree

Loch Scavaig and *_Loch Coruisk_ are together in perhaps the wildest setting in Skye. The former is a broad sea loch, its head overshadowed by bare and fretted peaks. Loch Coruisk (or Coire Uisg, Cauldron of Water), beyond across a narrow neck, lies within the very foot of the dark, towering Cuillins and is considerd by many to be Scotland's most dramatic loch (Boat from Elgol, sailings according to demand from 10.30. R. Mackinnon, Tel: 04716-213. J. Mackinnon, Tel: 04716-235). Sailings may also be possible to the island of _Soay_, 4m west off the mouth of Loch Scavaig; the bulk of the island's inhabitants moved to Mull in 1953.

Broadford to Sligachan and Dunvegan (Duirinish and Vaternish)

A850 to Sligachan. A863 to Dunvegan. 35m.—With the large island of Scalpay rising to 1298ft close offshore, the road turns beside Loch Ainort to pass _Luib Folk Museum_ (Tel: 047022-296), illustrating local living conditions in the early years of the present century. Beyond, at the loch's head, there is a choice between the main road across the peninsula between lochs Ainort and Sligachan or, rather more interestingly, the small road which rounds it. The two roads meet just before _Sconser_, from where a car ferry serves the island of _Raasay_ (Mon.—Sat., about four crossings daily. 15 minutes crossing. Caledonian Mac-Brayne. Tel: 0475-33755).

Raasay is some 15m long but uneven in width, with a road serving the length of the island as far as ruined _Brochel Castle_, long a home of the MacLeods of Raasay, and then (as the result of one man's work over ten years with pick and shovel because the local council was unwilling to finance a road) on to _Arnish_. The road builder, Calum MacLeod (died 1988), who also tended the lighthouse on Rona, is honoured by a cairn (1990) and his road now has a tarmac surface. A staunch Jacobite, the local MacLeod of 1745 joined the Young Pretender with 100 men, and the following year it was Raasay MacLeods who sheltered him for two nights. Soon afterwards, government troops landed and laid waste the estate.—Both Raasay, and the smaller island of _Rona_ to the north, may be visited in summer by excursions from Portree.

Sligachan, at the head of its loch, is at the junction of the roads to Dunvegan and (10m) Portree, as also of Glen Sligachan up which a path leads in 8m to Camasunary (see Broadford to Elgol above). A863, crossing an isthmus, in large part beside the small river Drynoch, in 6m reaches _Drynoch_ at the head of Loch Harport, a deep, narrow sea loch some 6m long, and from near here the small Glen Brittle road (see also The Cuillins above) drops southward below the west flank of the mountains to reach an unexciting shore in 8m.

Now heading north west above Loch Harport A863 in 4½m passes the prominent hill fort of _Dun Taimh_ before descending to loop around a bay and reach _Struan_, a point at which to pause, for both the best preserved broch on Skye and an earth-house are nearby. The former (Dun Beag) is on a hill to the right of the road opposite a turning to Ullinish. The latter may be found, though not easily, by taking the Ullinish road for ¼m to a gate on the right; the nearside of the hillock should then be followed round north east for about 400 yards, the earth-house being below the rock outcrop. Beyond Struan, and beyond the head of little Loch Caroy, the road breasts a short rise, at the top (left, opposite a road signed to Upper Feorlig) being the collapsed remains of two chambered cairns.

Dunvegan, the village at the head of the large sea loch of the same name, is best known for its castle. From here, too, there are boat excursions to see the seal colonies on the loch's islets (Tel: 047022-206).

Dunvegan Castle (Tel: 047022-206) has, since at least 1200, been the seat of the chiefs of Clan MacLeod. The present castle—a massive pile showing almost every building style from the 15 to the 19C—was formerly accessible only from the sea by a small gateway with a portcullis opening on to the rocks but is now entered by way of a bridge across a ravine which once served as a dry moat.

Inside the castle one focus of popular interest is the Fairy Flag, which is shown in the Drawing Room, originally the great hall of the 14C keep. This mysterious silken banner of Middle Eastern origin and dated to somewhere between the 4 and 7C is said to possess the magical property of being able to save the clan from danger. But only on three occasions, two of which though—one being at Trumpan, see below—have already been expended. Legends surround the flag, the most romantic of which is that it came to the MacLeods through the love of a chief for a fairy; forced to part at Fairy Bridge (see below), the fairy presented the chief with the silken coverlet she had drawn over their child. More prosaically, and perhaps more probably in view of the silk's Middle Eastern origin, other tales link the flag with the crusades.

Among much else of interest are, in the Dining Room, the ancient Dunvegan Cup, an Irish drinking vessel of the 10C bearing silver ornamentation of 1493, pictures by Ramsay and Raeburn, and an early charter granted by James IV; just outside the Drawing Room, the Dungeon with its grim oubliette; and many interesting pictures, mementoes of the '45 and letters from distinguished visitors such as Sir Walter Scott and Dr Johnson, a portrait of whom (by Zoffany, after Reynolds) hangs in the Fairy Tower.

Duirinish, a moorland hammerhead immediately west of Dunvegan, is essentially MacLeod, with two prominent hills called MacLeod's Tables and, off Idrigill Point at the peninsula's south tip, three basaltic stacks known as MacLeod's Maidens, a name traditionally honouring a MacLeod chieftain's wife and daughters drowned here in a shipwreck.

B884 traverses the northern area of the irregular peninsula, soon passing the remains of a broch on the left of the road opposite the turn to Uginish. Beyond (4m from Dunvegan) is the *Colbost Folk Museum* (Tel: 047022-296), an authentic crofter blackhouse of the 19C. From Colbost a minor road north in 3m reaches Boreraig, long the site of a piping school established by the famous piping family of MacCrimmon of Duirinish, hereditary pipers (c 1500–c 1800) to the MacLeod chiefs. Here, today, the *Piping Heritage Centre* (Tel: 047081-284) tells much about bagpipes, the MacCrimmons and other piping families. B884 breasts a rise, approaching the crest of which a memorial stands as a reminder that Duirinish was one of the main centres of the crofter riots of 1881–85, and then descends to the Glendale *Skye Watermill* to end after another 2m at *Milovaig*.

The northward finger of **Vaternish** is soon reached by taking the Portree road (A850) out of Dunvegan, this in 3m reaching *Fairy Bridge* (see Dunvegan Castle). From here B886 in 4m kinks into *Stein*, scene of an 18C attempt by MacLeod of MacLeod to establish a fishing industry, defeated by the high cost of salt. Beyond, another 4m of unclassified road ends at *Trumpan*, of interest on three counts, most notoriously perhaps for the bloody business of 1579 between the Macdonalds and the MacLeods. While the latter were at worship a party of Macdonalds landed and burned down the church, all the MacLeods who were inside perishing. However, on returning to their boats, the Macdonalds found the rest of the MacLeods waiting for them, and since the MacLeods had brought the Fairy Flag the fate of the Macdonalds was sealed and all were killed.

More tangible links with the past are provided here by the Trial Stone and the grave of Lady Grange. The former long provided a simple form of justice; accused persons were blindfolded and if they then succeeded in inserting a finger in the hole they were judged innocent. The unfortunate Lady Grange (died 1745), though, was given no option. The wife of a Jacobite Edinburgh judge, she threatened to reveal a plot (1734) on which she had stumbled, whereupon her husband promptly packed her off to remote St. Kilda and left her there until 1742.

From Fairy Bridge A850 crosses 19m of mainly dull moorland to reach Portree. For *Skeabost* and *Tote*, reached in 13m, see below.

Portree and Trotternish

Portree (1500 inhab. *Inf.*) owes its name (in Gaelic Port-an Righ), meaning Port of the King, to a state visit by James V. The only town on Skye, and the island capital, this is a picturesque and incidental small place, though with little of formal interest beyond perhaps the room at the *Royal Hotel* in which the Young Pretender took his leave of Flora Macdonald, courteously if optimistically remarking 'For all that has happened I hope, Madam, we shall meet in St. James's yet'.

In summer, Portree offers a choice of coach, boat and combined excursions.

Trotternish is a long oval peninsula reaching some 23m northward from Portree. It provides some good mountain and coastal scenery; the little port of Uig for car ferries to Harris and North Uist; a croft museum; Flora Macdonald's grave; and several other sites of varied interest. The road described starts and finishes at Portree, making a clockwise circuit of some 55m.

Four miles out of Portree the road forks, the westerly prong (for Dunvegan) soon bridging the river Snizort at *Skeabost*. Here, on an island just below the bridge (stepping stones), scanty remains are of a chapel traditionally associated with St. Columba, while a search around the tumbled burial ground should reveal three crusaders' slabs. Nearby to the north, on the road up to the hamlet of *Tote*, stands Clach Ard, the Stone on the Hill, bearing a variety of Pictish symbols.

A856 heads north above the east shore of Loch Snizort Beag, home once of prehistoric peoples, for the sizeable hump of a burial cairn survives near Kensaleyre at the head of the loch's nearer arm while, about 1m farther, there are twin small standing stones between the road and the water. Beyond, off to the left, the name *Kingsburgh* recalls the Young Pretender who, having landed farther north, found refuge in the predecessor of the present house. And it was here, too, that Johnson and Boswell met Flora Macdonald. Next, the little river Hinnisdal is crossed, beyond, on the shore, standing the shattered ruin of *Caisteal Huisdean*, stronghold of a 17C pirate, Hugh Gillespie; his end came when he unwisely plotted against his Macdonald lord, the latter then sealing him up in a dungeon at Duntulm (see below) with a piece of salt beef and an empty water jug.

Uig, a neat village at the head of the sheltered bay of the same name, is important as the pier for the car ferries to Tarbert on Harris and Lochmaddy on North Uist (see Rte 66). The north side of the bay is marked by the imposing height of Ru Idrigil, just north of which, by the shore, Skudaborg was an Iron Age fort. From Uig, too, a small road, passing the foot of the The Quiraing (see below), provides a cut across to the east coast.

Along the 2m between Uig and the hamlet of *Linicro* the road again skirts land with Young Pretender associations. He and Flora Macdonald came ashore near Prince Charles's Point (just north of Kilbride Point), Flora then leading her companion to nearby Monkstadt House, home of Sir Alexander Macdonald. Finding, however, that government officers had already quartered themselves there, the pair made their way south to Kingsburgh and Portree.

The road now runs inland along the flank of the hills with lower ground to the left in part representing *Loch Challuim Chille* (St. Columba's Loch), long drained and reclaimed but once the site of a small Celtic monastery, identifiable today only as a raised area with fragments of a cashel wall, a chapel and a causeway towards the shore.

Next, at Kilmuir, comes the *Skye Museum of Island Life* (Tel: 047052-279), housed in a group of cottages and of particular interest for its collection of old documents and photographs, while just up a side road, in the local burial ground, are the grave and monument of Flora Macdonald (died 1790). Adjacent lies a well preserved crusader slab.

Bearing north east and then east to round the peninsula's tip the road now runs with a cliff-edged, rock-strewn shore with basaltic columns and the gaunt ruin of *Duntulm Castle*, dating from the 17C but on the site of earlier Macdonald strongholds and the place, too, where the pirate Hugh Gillespie met his cruel end. Beyond, at *Flodigarry*, the house beside the hotel was the first married home of Flora Macdonald; she married Allan Macdonald of Kingsburgh in 1750 and her seven children were all born here. *The Quiraing* (1781ft; best approached from the small road across to Uig) now rises on the west above Staffin Bay; here a dramatic complex of towers and pinnacles surrounds a grassy amphitheatre known as the Prison and long used for hiding cattle.

Farther south, after rounding Staffin Bay, the road touches *Loch Mealt* where the distinctive remains of a broch can be seen on a small promontory from the north shore. The loch empties as a little stream, falling 300ft into the sea over a sheer cliff, and from here there is a good view of *Kilt Rock*, so called from the coloured strata and the way in which the basalt column resembles the folds of a kilt (the cliff edge is brittle and dangerous). Beyond, the river Lealt is crossed at a point where the stream cascades by waterfall stages into a ravine, and soon the black obelisk of the *Old Man of Storr* comes into sight at the foot of *The Storr* (2360ft), a cliff fretted with pinnacles and crags and notorious for its treacherously loose rocks. Storr Forest Walk, however, though steep, provides a path towards the Old Man and also views across to Raasay.

Lochs Leathan and *Fada*, below the road, serve as a hydro-electric reservoir, and a cave on the shore east of Loch Fada (accessible only by boat) was the point where the Young Pretender landed from Raasay; he slept in a byre about 2m farther south and walked thence to Elgol. A good hill-fort (*Dun Torvaig*) is passed on the left just before the descent to Portree.

63 Inner Hebrides reached from Mallaig (Eigg, Muck, Rhum and Canna)

Tourist Organisation. Fort William and Lochaber Tourist Board, Fort William. Tel: 0397-3781.

Access. No car ferries. For passengers:—1. Caledonian MacBrayne operate a year-round circuit service about four times weekly, though less frequently to Muck which is served by local boat from Eigg. The round trip requires about 7 hours. Tel: 0475-33755.—2. Arisaig Marine

(Arisaig, 5m south of Mallaig) also operate summer only cruises and scheduled services. Tel: 06875-224.

Accommodation, where available at all, is modest and limited. For addresses contact Fort William and Lochaber Tourist Board, as above.—**Transport**. Bicycles can be hired.

Eigg (5m by 2½m) is topographically notable for the *Sgurr of Eigg* (1292ft), a strangely shaped hill in the south of the island, a mass of black glassy pitchstone which has assumed columnar forms. The *Singing Sands*, beside the bay of Camas Sgiotaig at the north west, are another, if minor, natural feature, the sand here 'singing' when displaced by walking feet, or even when scoured by the wind, while in *Kildonnan* churchyard a Celtic slab survives as evidence of early Christianity.

Muck, 2m long, at most 1m broad, and with a population of about 25, lies 3m south west of Eigg. The smallest and most southerly of the group, the island is probably best known for its unenviable name, deriving perhaps, and equally unenviably, from a Gaelic form meaning pig, which animal the island was once judged to resemble.

Rhum, 8m by 8m and roughly diamond in shape, rises steeply to a fine volcanic mountain cluster culminating in *Askival* (2659ft), this name and others recalling the period of Norse occupation. Inhabited since perhaps 6500 BC, the population in the later 18C grew to over 400, but in 1827–28, the time of the Clearances, the entire population, at least partly by compulsion, emigrated to America. The island then became the home of sheep, and later (1845) Red deer were re-imported by the sporting Earl of Salisbury. From 1888 to 1957 Rhum was a private estate of the Bulloughs, of Lancashire, who in 1901 built *Kinloch Castle*, now run as a hotel and hostel by Scottish Natural Heritage, the predecessor of which, the Nature Conservancy Council, acquired the island in 1957. Today Rhum is a National Nature Reserve and Biosphere Reserve, outstandingly important on several counts—geologically, botanically, ornithologically, for the study of Red deer and for research in woodland re-creation and management.

There are two nature trails for day visitors (at Kinloch) and permission to camp or use bothy accommodation may be obtained from the Reserve Office at The Whitehouse, Rhum, PH43 4RR. Tel: 0687-2026.

In contrast to Rhum, **Canna** (NTS. Tel: 0687-2477), 5m by 1½m, is lowish and fertile, its highest point being under 700ft. The harbour is at the east end, just to the north being *Compass Hill* (458ft), so named because the rich iron deposits in the basalt cliffs are said to distort ships' compass readings. The island offers minor antiquities—the ruin of a tower on a stack between the harbour and Compass Hill is traditionally where a jealous Lord of the Isles confined his beautiful wife; a mutilated sculptured cross represents early Christianity and, nearby, a standing stone recalls even earlier islanders.—The adjacent small island of *Sanday* is reached by a bridge.

64   Inner Hebrides reached from Oban (Mull, Iona, Staffa, Coll, Tiree, Colonsay and Oronsay)

The **Tourist Organisation** covering the above islands is the Oban, Mull and District Tourist Board, Argyll Square, Oban, Argyll. Tel: 0631-63122.

For **Communications** (see also Rte 46, Oban) and **Accommodation** see under individual islands.

Island of Mull

Access. Caledonian MacBrayne operate car ferry services from Oban to Craignure and Tobermory, and from Lochaline (see Rte 48) to Fishnish. Also a passenger service from Mingary/Kilchoan (see Rte 48) to Tobermory. For detail apply Caledonian MacBrayne, Tel: 0475-33755. Additionally, in summer, several private operators run excursions to such places as Grass Point, Duart Castle and Torosay Castle (for details apply Tourist Information or local travel firms).

Internal Bus Services. The two principal routes are Tobermory—Salen—Craignure; and Craignure—Pennyghael—Bunessan—Fionnphort (for Iona). For details on both these services, Bowman's Coaches, Craignure. Tel: 06802-313.

Short routes also operate (not Sun.) between Tobermory and Calgary; and Salen, Gruline and Ulva. Tel: 0688-2220 and 06803-321.

SOME HOTELS. **Craignure**. *Isle of Mull*, PA65 6BB. Tel: 06802-351. **Salen**. *Salen*, PA72 6JE. Tel: 0680-300324. *Glenforsa*, Aros, PA72 6JW. Tel: 0680-300377. **Tobermory**. *Tobermory*, 53 Main Street, PA75 6NT. Tel: 0688-2091. *Harbour House*, 59 Main Street, PA75 6NT. Tel: 0688-2209. **Dervaig**, *Druimnacruish*, PA75 6QW. Tel: 06884-274. *Druimard*, PA75 6QW. Tel: 06884-345. **Tiroran**. *Tiroran House*, PA69 6ES. Tel: 06815-232. **Fionnphort**. *Achaban House*, PA66 6BL. Tel: 06817-205.

Mull is an island for coasts; for seaward vistas which are splendid in virtually every direction. Along the north east the shore as such is relatively uneventful, lining the narrow Sound of Mull beyond which rise the heights of Morvern, but elsewhere the coast is so fretted that, while its total length adds up to some 300 miles, only three miles separate Salen on the Sound from the Atlantic bay of Loch Na Keal. To the south of Loch Na Keal the larger Loch Scridain bites in from the west, its southern arm, with some good cliff scenery, extending far westward as the Ross of Mull. Beyond waits Iona.

Inland the island scenery is pleasant and varied, that in the southern part, with the mountain pile of Ben More (3171ft) being the finest.

The description below—starting at Craignure which is where most visitors will arrive—heads first for Tobermory and then completes an anticlockwise circuit of the main island, with, on the way, a diversion along the length of the Ross of Mull to Fionnphort.

Total distance (excluding Ross of Mull) 84m.—*5m* **Fishnish**.—*6m* **Salen**.—*9m* **Tobermory**.—*6m* **Dervaig**.—*5m* **Calgary**.—*12m* **Ulva Ferry**.—*7m* **Gruline**.—*17m* **Junction with A849** (for **Fionnphort**).—*11m* **Strathcoil**.—*6m* **Craignure**.

Craignure is best known for two castles, Duart and Torosay, as also perhaps for the *Mull and West Highland Railway*, a 10.25 gauge miniature line linking Craignure with Torosay (Tel: 06802-494).

Torosay Castle (Tel: 06802-421), 1½m south of Craignure, is a 19C Scottish Baronial creation by David Bryce, surrounded by terraced gardens laid out by Robert Lorimer and notable for a statue walk with 19 life-sized figures by the 18C Venetian Antonio Bonazza. The house, largely furnished in Edwardian taste, shows family portraits by such artists as Sargent and De Lazlo, and wildlife works by Landseer, Thorburn and Peter Scott.

Duart Castle (Tel: 06802-309), dramatically guarding Duart Point and well seen from the Oban ferries, dates from about 1250 and, with one break, has always been the home of the chiefs of Clan Maclean. Burnt by Argyll in 1691, Duart was confiscated half a century later after Culloden, but repurchased and restored in 1912 by the then chief, Sir Fitzroy

Maclean. In the keep can be seen the cell in which the officers of Tobermory's Spanish galleon were held after their ship had been blown up by
Donald Maclean.

5m Fishnish for the car ferry across to Lochaline (see Rte 48).—*4m*
Pennygown, where the ruined chapel is worth a visit for a late Celtic
cross-shaft, bearing a Madonna and, curiously, a ship and a griffon.—*2m*
Salen, the village at the north end of the narrow neck across to Loch Na
Keal and the Atlantic, is traditionally the place where St. Columba
landed on his way to Iona after Aidan of Dalriada had granted him that
island. *Aros Castle, 1m* north on a shore promontory, is a 13C ruin,
thought once to have been a stronghold of the MacDougalls of Lorne,
but *(7m) Aros Park* (Forestry Commission) is, by contrast, a quiet small
country park with a cliff walk, rhododendrons and a picnic and play
area.

1m **Tobermory** (800 inhab. *Inf.*) clusters cosily and picturesquely
around the shore and slopes of its wooded bay, sheltered by the island
of Calve. The bay provides one of the safest anchorages along Scotland's west coast and, with its attractive small town, is very popular
with yachting visitors.

History. The town was founded as a fishing port in 1788, but though it at first
prospered it was unable to survive the competition when the railway reached
Oban and the population quickly dropped from 1500 in 1843 to settle at around its
present modest figure. It was in the 16C, though, in 1588, that Tobermory Bay
earned its niche in history. In that year the 'Florida', a galleon of the Spanish
Armada, was driven in for shelter. Although the Spaniards were courteously welcomed and provided with victuals, it soon became clear that they were planning to
slip away without paying. Donald Maclean was then sent aboard to claim what
was due, only however to be locked up by the Spaniards. Resourcefully he got free,
reached the magazine and blew up and sank the ship, thus starting a treasure hunt
which continues today, even though, beyond some cannon and a few coins, nothing of great value has so far been salvaged.

There is a small museum, the *Mull and Iona Folk Museum* (Tel: 0688-
2182), interestingly housed in a former Baptist church, and the *Well of
St. Mary*, from which Tobermory derives its name, is beside a ruined
chapel just west of the town. Favourite walks are to Aros Park, mentioned above; and north round the point of Rubha-nan-Gall with a
lighthouse to *Bloody Bay*, scene in 1439 of a sea battle between John,
4th Lord of the Isles, and his rebel son Angus. *Ardmore Forest Walk*, just
behind and to the north of Bloody Bay, is also popular, a cliff path
rounding Mull's northernmost tip and providing splendid sea and
island views (motor access by unclassified road via Glengorm Castle).

Tobermory is left by B8073, the start of a generally narrow, twisting
and slow road, first across the north of the island and then beside the
west coast. After climbing, the road drops briefly to the sea at *(6m)*
Dervaig, with, near the old cemetery, a group of standing stones. The
village is the home of the *Mull Little Theatre*, Britain's smallest professional theatre (summer repertory. Tel: 06884-267), and also of the *The
Old Byre* (Tel: 06884-229) with exhibits on life on Mull and the island's
natural history. *Croaig*, 3m north west at the entrance to Loch Cuan,
was once a busy port to which drovers brought their cattle from the
outer islands before driving the herds across Mull to Grass Point,
whence they were shipped, or sometimes swam, to Kerrera and the
mainland.

The west coast is reached at *(5m) Calgary* (the modest hamlet ancestor of the great Canadian city), just beyond being *Treshnish Woodland
Garden* (Tel: 06884-249). Here the road curves southward and inland,
reaching the sea again in *5m* at *Burg*, with traces of an Iron Age fort just

seaward of the road. Just beyond (*1m*), in the burial ground of *Kilninian*, there is a very fine medieval slab, commemorating a chieftain complete with kilt and broadsword, while at *Ballygown*, less than *3m* farther, the quite substantial remains of a broch can be seen by the shore.

Since leaving Burg the road has been fringing Loch Tuath, off the mouth of which lie the **Treshnish Isles**, a string of basaltic rocks rising in terraces. The most southerly island is, from its shape, called the *Dutchman's Cap*, while at the north end of the string rise the cliff islets of *Cairn a' Burgh Mor* and *Beg* with a ruined fortress, besieged in James IV's campaign against the Lord of the Isles and later, in 1690 and 1715, held by Macleans in the Jacobite cause.—Closer in, and forming the loch's south shore, are the larger islands of *Gometra* and *Ulva*, the latter the birthplace of General Lachlan Macquarie (1761–1824), governor of New South Wales and an innovative penal reformer whose enlightened attitude made him so unpopular with the free settlers that he was recalled.

3m Ulva Ferry, whence occasional boat excursions (Tel: 06885-239; 06884-242; 0688-2165) may include Staffa, the Treshnish Isles, Lunga (sea-birds), Gometra, Ulva and Iona; some trips pass the Fossil Tree, a 50ft-high petrified tree, perhaps 50 million years old, within the basalt of the cliffs of the Ardmeanach peninsula.—Now bearing east beside Loch Na Keal, B8073 in *7m* reaches *Gruline*—at the head of the loch and marking the south end of Mull's narrow isthmus—the road (now B8035) curving south west along Loch Na Keal's south shore below the mass of *Ben More* (3171ft), a mountain thrown up in the same volcanic upheaval that formed Staffa.

Ardmeanach, the fine volcanic peninsula extending Ben More and forming the north shore of Loch Scridain, is separated from the mountain by Glen Seilisdeir which carries B8035 across the peninsula's base. *Inch Kenneth* (private), an island off Ardmeanach's north shore at the mouth of Loch Na Keal, is named after a follower of St. Columba; very fertile, and once serving as granary for Iona, the island was also anciently a stopping place on the way to Iona and, because of the storms which frequently delayed onward travel, it may well have been the enforced burial place of some kings and chiefs. *Gribun Rocks*, near where the road starts to angle across, are an impressive range of overhanging cliffs, while *Mackinnon's Cave*, about 2m down the coast and accessible only at low tide, provides a story. Never fully explored, and believed by some to tunnel clear across the peninsula, the cave takes its name from a piper who undertook to lead a party through the cave but was killed by a witch who had settled here; but she spared the piper's dog which was later seen roaming the peninsula's southern shore.

The road reaches Loch Scridain at (*13m* from Gruline) *Kilfinichan Bay*, whence a small road (to Tiroran), soon becoming a rough track (5m), leads to *Burg*, a National Trust for Scotland remote clifftop property.—In *4m* the junction with A849 is reached at the head of Loch Scridain.

TO FIONNPHORT (A849, west. 18m). For most of the way beside the south shore of Loch Scridain, this road travels the length of the Ross of Mull, in 3m reaching *Pennyghael* whence a road crosses the Ross to Carsaig, 4m south west of which along the shore, and accessible only at low water, are the *Carsaig Arches*. Here columnar basalt cliffs (750ft) have been eroded by the sea into astonishing caves and arches. Nuns' Pass, passed on the way, is said to have sheltered nuns driven out of Iona at the time of the Reformation.

Just beyond Pennyghael, at *Pennycross*, a memorial honours the Beatons, physicians for 300 years to the Macleans of Duart; and farther on, in the parish of Ardtun, approaching Bunessan, another memorial stands to the poet Mary Macdonald (1789–1872).

Fionnphort, at the road's end, is a straggling hamlet, notable principally for its huge car park for users of the ferry to Iona, a mile across the sound. In summer there are excursions to Staffa (Tel: 06817-373 or 338).

From the head of Loch Scridain, Glen More carries A849 eastwards, in *11m* reaching *Strathcoil* where there is a memorial to the Gaelic poet Dugald Macphail (1818–87).

From Strathcoil a small road diverges south west for Loch Buie (8m; dead-end), for some of the way closely following the shore of *Loch Spelve*, fanning out from its narrow entrance seen across the water. The grand basalt heights of Ben Creach (2290ft) and Ben Buie (2354ft) rise above the road as it fringes Loch Uisg to reach the village of *Loch Buie* at the head of its own loch. Here, to the north, is a stone circle and, to the south, the ruined keep of Castle Moy, 15C tower-house of Maclean of Loch Buie. A path continues to Carsaig.

4m Lochdon is at the irregular head of the shallow, meandering sea indent of the same name. The south point of the loch's entrance is *Grass Point*, ferry pier predecessor of Craignure. The small road to the point, branching off A849 just south of Lochdon, represents one of the most ancient ways on Mull, having been first an early pilgrim path and later a drovers' road in the days when Grass Point was the jetty from which the cattle were shipped to the mainland.—Passing close to Duart and Torosay castles, for both of which see at the start of this circuit, A849 in *2m* returns to *Craignure*.

*Island of Iona (NTS. Tel: 041-552-8391).

> **Access**. No cars. The two principal approaches are by excursion from Oban (see Rte 46) or by ferry from Fionnphort on Mull (Crossing 5 minutes. Mon–Sat., roughly hourly. Restricted service Sun. and in winter. Caledonian MacBrayne. Tel: 0475-33755).
>
> HOTELS. *Argyll*, PA76 6SJ. Tel: 06817-334. *St. Columba*, PA76 6SL. Tel: 06817-304.

Iona (3m long by 1½m wide) is, after Whithorn, the cradle of Scottish Christianity and rich also in later venerable associations. Austere, bare and often windswept, the island is owned by the National Trust for Scotland, except for the abbey and other sacred buildings and historic sites which are cared for by the Iona Cathedral Trust.

The main sites are all within a short walking distance of the pier and can normally comfortably be seen within the time allowed by excursions. Some of the island can also be toured by horse carriage.

In summer there are boat excursions to Staffa (Tel: 06817-373 or 338).

History. Iona, originally known simply as 'Ia' or 'Hy', was called 'Iova Insula' by Adamnan in his 'Life of Columba', a form transcribed by a careless copyist into Iona. Later it was named 'Icolmkill', 'Island of Columba of the Church'.

Excavation at Dun Bhuirg, on the west coast, has revealed that people lived here during the Iron Age, but it was in 563 that St. Columba left Ireland (where he was born in 521) and, with 12 companions, came to Iona, the nearest land from which he could no longer see his native shores. Here he founded a monastery of which nothing now remains, and hence he set out on those journeys which resulted in the conversion of the northern Picts and the spread of Christianity far and wide over Scotland, and even over Orkney, Shetland and Iceland. As religious head, he confirmed Aidan as King of Dalriada, thus formally establishing the early royal line. Columba died in Iona in 597, shortly after St. Augustine had arrived in Kent to convert the English. He was buried on Iona, but 200 years later, after a Norse raid in which 68 monks were murdered at Martyrs' Bay, his remains were taken back to Ireland (Kells) and all subsequent trace of them has disappeared. (But according to some authorities the bones were brought back to Iona and housed beside the cathedral in what is called St. Columba's Shrine). Iona, thus hallowed, early became a pilgrim objective, and it was the burial-place of the Scottish kings until super-seded by Dunfermline in the 11C. Throughout the Middle Ages the great West Highland chiefs were also brought here for burial.

The Norsemen pillaged the island over and over again during 9 and 10C. In 807 they burned and destroyed the monastery and all belonging to it. In 1203 Reginald, son of Somerled, founded a new monastery for Benedictines, and, a few years later, an Augustinian nunnery. Reginald's monastery, though covering much of its Celtic predecessor, does not coincide with it. The Benedictines' church served as the cathedral of the see of Argyll from 1507 until the Dissolution after 1570, and in 1617 it was annexed to the Protestant Bishopric of the Isles. In 1609 the church was the scene of the Statutes of Icolmkill, by which the Hebrides chieftains swore loyalty to the Stuart kings. In 1899 the 8th Duke of Argyll presented the cathedral to the Church of Scotland (Iona Cathedral Trust), restoration beginning soon thereafter. In 1938 the Iona Community was founded by Dr George Macleod and has since undertaken much restoration work in and around the cathedral. In 1979 the island was purchased from the Duke of Argyll by Sir Hugh Fraser, through whose generosity it came in December of that year to the National Trust for Scotland.

Among famous visitors to Iona have been Sir Walter Scott, who found it 'desolate and miserable'; Keats came in 1818 and Wordsworth in 1835, here writing three sonnets. Dr Johnson, another visitor, wrote: 'That man is little to be envied whose patriotism would not gain force upon the plain of Marathon, or whose piety would not grow warmer among the ruins of Iona'.

The main path is followed from the ferry, soon reaching the *Nunnery Church* (c 1200, with late 13C additions). It comprises a nave, with an aisle, adjoining which is the Lady Chapel still with some of its vaulting. To the south of the church are the remains of the cloister court, chapter house and refectory. The neighbouring *Church of St. Ronan* (14C) serves as a stones museum. Here can be seen, among other nuns' and priests' tombs, the tomb of the last prioress (died 1543), whose effigy in hood and cloak occupies one half of the slab, the remainder being broken away.—The 15C *Maclean's Cross*, passed farther along the path, is 11ft high and carved with great force and excellence of design. On the left there is a church built by Telford.

In *St. Oran's Cemetery*, or *Reilig Odhrain*, the oldest Christian burial-place in Scotland, 48 Scottish, 8 Norwegian, 4 Irish and 2 French kings are said to rest. The last king buried here was Duncan (1040), murdered by Macbeth, but, sadly, only one of the existing slabs (a plain red stone with a Celtic cross) may be of one of these kings. The many other carved slabs (15C and later) are mainly those of island chieftains, and they were only arranged in their present ridges in 1868. The ashes of Marjory Kennedy-Fraser (1857–1930), collector and transcriber of Gaelic songs, were also buried here. Here too lies Dr John Beaton of Mull (died 1657), physician to James VI and last of his famous medical family (memorial at Pennycross on Mull).—*St. Oran's Chapel*, probably on the site of a Celtic cemetery, is a small chamber of Norman style, now restored, said to have been built by Queen Margaret (1080). It is entered by a low, deeply recessed doorway, with chevron mouldings. Inside is the trefoiled canopy of the tomb of Lachlan Mackinnon (died 1489), and here too lie the first two Lords of the Isles (1386 and 1420).

The **Cathedral** (Tel: 06817-404) is the principal building on the island. In front is preserved a section of the *Street of the Dead*, a roadway of red marble, perhaps of the 13C. Opposite the west façade stands *St. Martin's Cross* (10C), 14ft high and boldly carved with Runic ornaments and figures; while to the left is the graceful 10C *St. John's Cross*, restored from fragments in 1926 but twice blown down since. Near the well a broken shaft is all the remains of *St. Mathew's Cross*. The restored cell or chapel at the north west angle of the nave is *St. Columba's Shrine* (see History), while *Tor Abb*, a mound just west of the cathedral, has the remains of a cell which may have been that of the saint.

Dating mainly from the early 16C, the cathedral has undergone many later additions and restorations, including those of the present day. Cruciform in plan, its chief external feature is the low square Tower (70ft) above the crossing, with four windows, filled with tracery of elegant design, different in each case. Inside the church the arches supporting the tower and the carved capitals of the columns in the choir should be noticed. In the Chancel are tombs of Abbot Mackinnon (died 1500) on the north, and Abbot Mackenzie (died 1489) on the south. Also on the south side are three sedilia in the Gothic style of the 14C. The elaborate Sacristy doorway (north) dates from 1500. The south transept contains a monument (1912) to the 8th Duke of Argyll (died 1900), who presented the cathedral to the Church of Scotland. From the north transept with Norman arches, the *Cloister* is entered. It incorporates two medieval pillars and has in its centre a group 'The Descent of the Spirit', by Jacques Lipchitz (1960).

Restored monastic buildings include the *Chapter House* (1955), still retaining its Norman doorway and the double arch supporting its vault; the *Refectory* (1949, no adm.); and the *Undercroft* on the west side. To the north are the *Reredorter* (1944) and the *Caretaker's House* (1950), preserving a gable of the old Abbot's House. Two buildings resting on Celtic pre-Benedictine foundations are the small *Michael Chapel* (rebuilt 1960) and the former *Infirmary*, now serving as a museum showing a stone known as Columba's Pillow, perhaps the saint's gravestone; the gravestone (from St. Oran's) of Angus Og (died 1326, an early lord of the Isles); the broken Mackinnon's Cross of 1489; and several other fine stones of chieftains and priors.

The above paragraphs cover the physical sacred aspects of Iona, but there are a number of other places of interest. *Dun-I* (332ft), for instance, towards the north end, not only recalls pre-Columban inhabitants but also provides an all-round survey of the island. On the east shore *Martyrs' Bay* is where 68 monks were killed by Norsemen in 806, while the *White Strand of the Monks* at the north east was the scene of the murder of the abbot and 15 monks as late as 986. On the south shore *St. Columba's Bay*, or, more evocatively, the *Port of the Coracle*, is traditionally the place where the saint landed. Other names are self-explanatory—Otters' Point, Spouting Cave, Meadow of the Lapwings; while yet others—Port of the False Man, Nest of the Red Haired Lad, Field of the Old Woman—simply stimulate speculation.

*Island of Staffa (NTS. Tel: 041-552-8391).

Access. Staffa may be seen by taking one of the excursions from Oban (Rte 46; no landing) or by boat as follows: *From Iona or Fionnphort (Mull).* Gordon Grant, Achavaich, Iona. Tel: 06817-338. Or David Kirkpatrick, Seaview, Iona. Tel: 06817-373. *From Ulva Ferry (Mull).* Iain Morrison, Penmore Mill, Dervaig, Mull. Tel: 06884-242. Or Brian Burgess, Castlecroft, Tobermory, Mull. Tel: 0688-2165.

Staffa (Norse 'Staphi-ey' meaning Island of the Pillars) was virtually unknown to the outer world before a visit paid to it in 1772 by Sir Joseph Banks, the explorer, who, on his way to Iceland, had been driven into the Sound of Mull where he learnt of this extraordinary place from a Mr Leach, an Irish visitor who had landed there a few days earlier.—Later visitors have included Queen Victoria and Prince Albert, the artist J.M.W. Turner, the poets and writers Keats, Wordsworth, Tennyson and Scott, and, most memorable of all, the composer Mendelssohn who here found the inspiration for 'Die Fingalshölle' or 'Hebridean Overture'.—Geologically what is now the north west coast of Scotland was once the scene of violent volcanic action, the subterranean disturbance finding a vent along a line from Skye to Ireland, the effects of which can be traced through Staffa, Mull (Ardmeanach), Islay and, in Ireland, Rathlin and the Giant's Causeway, all basically composed of the liquid basalt ejected to the surface.

Famous for its great caves and astonishing basaltic formations, Staffa is little more than 1½m in circumference, with a perpendicular face (140ft) towards the south and west and a more gradual slope on the north east. *Fingal's Cave* is the most spectacular of the caverns. It is 227ft long and the height from the water at mean tide is 66ft, the depth of the sea within being about the same. The sides at the opening are vertical and the whole of the sides, ground, and roof are composed of black pentagonal or hexagonal pillars divided transversely by joints at nearly uniform distances of 2ft.

Islands of Coll and Tiree

Communications. Both islands are reached by car ferry from Oban. Crossing times: Oban to Coll, 3 hours. Coll to Tiree, 1½ hours. Oban direct to Tiree, 3½ hours. 3 to 4 services weekly (Caledonian MacBrayne, Tel: 0475-33755). Also Air service from Glasgow to Tiree, continuing to Barra. (Loganair. Tel: 041-889-3181).

On Tiree a Post Office bus serves most places (Tel: 08792-301). Bicycles can be hired.

SOME HOTELS. **Coll**. *Isle of Coll*, Arinagour, PA78 6SZ. Tel: 08793-334. *Tig-Na-Mara*, Arinagaour, PA78 6SY. Tel: 08793-354. **Tiree**. *Kirkapol*, Gott Bay, PA77 6TN. Tel: 08792-729.

Coll is a flat crofting island, 12m long by 3m broad and with about 150 inhabitants, the majority of whom live in the village of *Arinagour*. Traces of brochs can be found, especially near the island's several lochs, and there are standing stones at Totronald in the south west part of the island. Near here, too, *Breacachadh Castle* (occasionally open. Tel: 08793-444) is a restored early 15C tower-house, perhaps built by Angus Og, to whom Bruce granted Coll, but later belonging to the Macleans.

Tiree, though low-lying and liable to be windswept—its Gaelic name means the Land lower than the waves—has a record of surprisingly sunny weather, statistics showing the longest sunshine hours in Scotland. Measuring 12m by 3m with some 800 inhabitants, the island offers the visitor sandy beaches and a golf course. There are also scattered dun and broch remains, the best being *Dun Mor Vaul* in the north east of the island, of particular interest for having started as a timber structure as long ago as the 6C BC before later becoming a stone broch.—*Skerryvore Lighthouse*, 10m south west out to sea, was built in 1843 but has not been manned since 1954. It can be seen from *Hynish*, at the south west of the island, where there is a small Skerryvore Museum (Tel: 08792-691).

Islands of Colonsay and Oronsay

Communications. Car ferry from Oban 3 times a week. Crossing 2¼ hours. This ferry continues to Port Askaig (Islay) 1¼ hours, and thence to Kennacraig, 2 hours. Colonsay can thus also be reached from the south from Kennacraig. Caledonian MacBrayne. Tel: 0475-33755.—The islands may also be reached by excursion boats in summer from Port Askaig on Islay.—*Oronsay* is reached by causeway at low water.

A Post Office bus serves most places (Tel: 09512-323). Bicycles can be hired.

HOTEL. *Isle of Colonsay*, PA61 7YP. Tel: 09512-316.

History. Colonsay was owned by the Macfies (or Macphies) at least from the 15 to 17C. They were dispossessed by the Macdonalds soon after 1615 and in turn the Campbells ousted the Macdonalds. By a land exchange agreement the McNeills acquired the two islands in 1700 and held them until 1904 when debt compelled sale.

The two islands (combined population some 200) owe their names to St. Columba and his companion St. Oran. But man had made his home here millenia before Christian times and excavations (on Oronsay) have revealed evidence of a Middle Stone Age settlement. Later archaeological traces include Iron Age duns and crannogs and, recalling the Norse years, a ship-burial site. But the emphasis remains early Christian with, on Oronsay, the ruins of a *Priory*, in all probability founded by St. Columba. It survives today as the remains of a 14C Augustinian house, together with crosses and graveslabs.

Together measuring some 9m from north to south, but barely 2m broad, the islands additionally offer a scenic mix of rocky hills and coastline with sandy beaches, rich bird life, seals, a golf course and *Kiloran Gardens* (Tel: 09512-312) with woodland, rhododendrons and rare shrubs.

65   Inner Hebrides reached from Tarbert/ Kennacraig (Islay and Jura)

Tourist Organisation. Mid Argyll, Kintyre and Islay Tourist Board, Campbeltown, Argyll. Tel: 0586-52056.

Access. *Islay* is reached by car ferry from Kennacraig on West Loch Tarbert to Port Ellen or Port Askaig. Crossing 2¼ hours. 3 to 4 services daily, but normally only one on Sunday. See also service from Oban via Colonsay (Rte 64). Caledonian MacBrayne. Tel: 0475-33755.—*Jura* is reached by car ferry from Port Askaig on Islay to Feolin. Crossing 10 minutes. Frequent, but less so on Sunday (Western Ferries. Tel: 049684-681).

Scheduled air service from Glasgow to Islay. (Loganair. Tel: 041-889-3181).

Internal bus services. On *Islay* services link the main centres of Portnahaven–Bridgend–Port Askaig–Bowmore–Port Ellen–Ardbeg. Operators are the Post Office, Port Ellen. Tel: 0496-2131; and B. Mundell Ltd, Tarbert. Tel: 049684-273. Services are infrequent, not Sunday, and to an extent geared to school requirements.

On *Jura* there is a service between the ferry at Feolin and Craighouse, with occasional onward connection to Ardlussa (Inverlussa). Infrequent and geared to school requirements. (Tel: 049682-221).

SOME HOTELS. **Port Ellen**. *Machrie*. Tel: 0496-2310. **Bowmore**. *Lochside*, 19 Shore Street. Tel: 049681-244. *Harbour Inn*, Tel: 049681-330. **Port Askaig**. *Port Askaig*, PA46 7RD. Tel: 049684-245.

On **Jura (Craighouse)**. *Jura*, PA60 7UX. Tel: 049682-243.

Island of Islay

Islay is the most southerly of the Hebrides; part arable and part moorland peat, the island measures some 25m from north to south and 20m across and has about 4000 resident inhabitants, the chief centres being Bowmore, Port Ellen and Port Charlotte, with farming, fishing and whisky distilling the principal occupations. With varied and in places rugged scenery, beaches, golf, fishing and some prehistoric and early Christian sites—and renowned too as an ornithological objective—the island attracts discerning summer visitors, yet is large and fragmented enough never to appear crowded. Topographically Islay is almost split into two by the sea lochs Gruinart and Indaal, the western hammerhead being known as the Rhinns.

Port Ellen to Kildalton Cross and Ardtalla (north east along the coast. 10m). Named after the wife of William Campbell, who started to rebuild here in about 1821, *Port Ellen* (1000 inhab.) is a neat little harbour backed by a genteel crescent of 19C stone cottages. Immediately to the east a lane bears north for Kilbride, within the farther angle being a tall standing stone and traces of a chapel. The former, easily seen, according to one story marks the grave of a Norse princess named Yula, her name perhaps the origin of this island's. The chapel—two fields away and not easily recognised because it survives as no more than a hollow in the turf marked out by a few rough stones—is dedicated to St. Lasar, an obscure 6C Irish nun, and is curious for two upright stones with holes through them, perhaps reminders of some ancient custom (like the Trial Stone at Trumpan on Skye), perhaps merely serving some prosaic constructional need.

Passing distilleries (Laphroaig, 1½m east of Port Ellen, may be toured by arrangement. Tel: 0496-2418), A846 soon reaches *Lagavulin*, its small bay guarded by ruined Dunavaig Castle, a tower dating from the 14C and probably built by John of Islay who in 1386 formally assumed the title of Lord of the Isles. Beyond, at *Ardbeg*, the road becomes minor as it fringes *Loch-an-t-Sailein*, the Loch of the Seals, though without binoculars few seals will be seen as they tend to favour the outer rocks.

**Kildalton Cross, the star among Islay's several Celtic and later crosses and by many held to be the most beautiful in Scotland, is 7m from Port Ellen. Dating from c 800 and probably the work of a sculptor from Iona, the green to grey local stone bears a wealth of well preserved and intricate patterns and scenes. Nor should the churchyard of the ruined chapel be ignored, for, though its stones cannot compare with the cross, they are nevertheless of interesting enough variety and span from medieval times to the 18C.

Beyond, the road continues a further 3m to *Ardtalla*, from where a path in another 3m reaches *McArthur's Head*, opposite Jura and marking the entrance to the Sound of Islay.

Port Ellen to Mull of Oa (west, across the peninsula of The Oa. 7m, but most of the last mile on foot). In 1m from Port Ellen a road bearing north for Kintra should be followed by anyone with a feel for ancient stones, for in 1½m, just before Kintra, *Druim an Stuin* stands on the left beside the road. It is not much of a stone, little more than a large boulder, but it is said to mark the grave of Godred Crovan, a Norse chieftain who drove Fingal out of the Isle of Man and made himself ruler of the western islands until his death here on Islay in 1095.

The peninsula, known for its caves and cliffs and once notorious for smuggling and illicit whisky distilling, rounds off as the *Mull of Oa*. Here a monument, erected by the American Red Cross, commemorates those who lost their lives in 1918 when the American troopships 'Tuscania' and 'Otranto' were lost, the former torpedoed off The Oa, the latter driven ashore on the west coast of the Rhinns.

Port Ellen to Bowmore and Port Askaig (north and north east. 21m). There is a choice of roads, A846 or the parallel B8016, both across dull peat-stacked lowland behind the great sandy crescent of Laggan Bay. A846 runs arrow-straight (its course was originally intended to be a railway), passing the airport and then kinking slightly to reach *Bowmore* (1000 inhab. *Inf.*), a neat, planned 19C township best known for its curious round church of Kilarrow (1767); the design was intended to thwart the Devil by denying him any corners in which to lurk. For a visit to Bowmore Distillery, Tel: 046681-441.

At *Bridgend*, 2m beyond Bowmore, the road for the Rhinns bears away west, while A846 continues north for (a further 7m) *Port Askaig* for the ferry crossing to Jura. Along this road, just beyond Ballygrant (5m from Bridgend), *Loch Finlaggan* lies a short mile to the north west. Finlaggan, with castle remains on an island, was from the 12–16C a home of the chiefs of Clan Donald.

The **Rhinns of Islay**, a hammerhead of land almost severed from the bulk of the island by the long bites of lochs Gruinart from the north and Indaal from the south, is in many ways—prehistoric, early Christian and as regards bloody clan strife—the most interesting part of Islay. For touring purposes the Rhinns conveniently divides into two distinct parts; a northern area reached by B8017, 2m west of Bridgend, and a southern district served by a road circuit starting at Port Charlotte.

A standing stone marks the start of B8017 which in 3½m reaches a road junction to the south west of the head of Loch Gruinart. Here a stone, the *Clach Mhic-illean*, stands where a Maclean chief was killed and recalls a vicious clan battle of 1598. The cause was the grant by James VI of land in Islay to Sir Lachlan Maclean of Duart on Mull. This, of course, the local Macdonalds would not accept, so 400 Macleans invaded here, only to lose their chief and suffer a defeat so crushing that only a handful returned to Mull. From this stone an uninviting road heads north, in 2½m reaching the ruined church of *Kilnave*, with a Celtic cross (c 8C) bearing weathered carving. Today a sad ruin across a bleak field, in 1598 this church held hope of sanctuary for a group of defeated and wounded Macleans, a hope, though, that was not realised because the Macdonalds fired the thatch and the Macleans all died beneath its blaze.

B8017, now heading west from the stone, reaches *Loch Gorm*, on a crannog islet near the south east of which are traces of the Macdonald castle which was the objective of the Maclean invasion. *Kilchoman Church*, beyond the south west of Loch Gorm, is more interesting, and especially for its fine Celtic cross, showing a clear Crucifixion and bearing small angels on its arms. Legend, if without evidence, suggests that this cross was erected by John of Islay in memory of his dead Scottish princess, the daughter of Robert II. And here, too, are several tombs showing quaint pygmy-like figures, thought to represent medieval (15–16C) churchmen, though local tradition insists that one stone (the one on which the effigy occupies the most space) was later used to mark the grave here of the luckless Maclean chief.

From Kilchoman it is necessary to return to Loch Indaal and Port Charlotte, a distance of 8m, before embarking on the Rhinns southern circuit.

At *Port Charlotte*, known for Islay cheese, are a Museum of Islay Life (Tel: 049685-358) and also the Islay Field Centre (Tel: 049685-288), for information on the island's natural history. The twin village-ports of *Portnahaven* and *Port Wemyss* (some 7m south) form a picturesque, haphazard corner with cottages reaching tentatively up turf slopes towards the 19C church which, serving both villages, nevertheless offers a separate door for each. A cluster of islands, once shelter for a jostle of fishing boats, marks the broken end of the Rhinns.

The return is made by the minor road which climbs away up on to the Rhinns' desolate, almost treeless central heights. Yet prehistoric people deliberately chose this place, leaving as evidence the great ring of weathered and battered stones known as *Cultoon Stone Circle* (3½m north of Portnahaven and about 100 yards west of the road). Most are prone, and the suggestion has been made that they never were raised, that the project, whatever its arcane purpose, may have been abandoned before completion. Today forlorn sheep are about all that move in a place once thronged first by this circle's builders and then by those who practised its rites.

Nor is *Kilchiaran Chapel* (2m farther, below the hills) without atmosphere, and it is easy enough to accept here that St. Columba did indeed beach his coracle in the sheltered bay, at once building a chapel on the nearest level ground above. Today a ruined medieval successor—dedicated to St. Kieran—shelters an aumbrey, a stoup and a slab bearing one of those pygmy figures found at nearby Kilchoman, while, outside, a fragment of a Christian cross stands close to a cup-marked stone suggesting that this spot was regarded as sacred perhaps 2000 years before the arrival of Columba.

Curving south east the road in 3m returns to Port Charlotte.

Island of Jura

Although so close geographically to Islay, Jura (28m from north to south by 8m broad) is scenically abruptly and dramatically different, splendidly Highland and with ever-changing seascapes. Halfway along its length the erratic gash of Loch Tarbert all but cuts the island into two; to the south lift the prominent *Paps of Jura*—An Oir, the Mountain of Gold, reaching 2576ft, Shiantiadh, the Holy Mountain, reaching 2477ft, and A Chaolais, the Mountain of the Strait, not far below at 2407ft. Red deer, too, are of the essence of Jura, for the island's name derives from the Norse for deer and today the herds still add up to some 5000 animals, most of them in the largely trackless fastnesses of the interior though not infrequently they approach the sparsely populated east coast.

The occasional standing stone proves man's very early presence here, but, at any rate numerically, he now seems in retreat for the 1500 or so inhabitants of the early 19C are now down to around 200, the cattle grazing of the past now superseded by estates given over to rod and gun.

The island's only road runs for 24m, curving within the coast between the ferry at Feolin and Jura's only village, Craighouse, from where—and for much of the way staying scenically high above the water—it follows the east coast past the head of Loch Tarbert to Ardlussa. The drive is essentially one of scenery, seascapes and, with any luck, deer. For the rest, a lone megalith is well seen to the right of the road 3m from the ferry. *Jura House* (Tel: 049682-213), reached in another 1½m, offers woodland walks and an organic garden; *Craighouse*, reached in another 3m, is a straggling shoreside village with a pleasant hotel and a distillery; and there are more standing stones near the settlement of *Tarbert*, the point at which Jura is less than a mile wide.

At *Ardlussa* the road ends, deteriorating into a track unsuitable for ordinary cars. This in another 7m reaches *Barnhill*, the house in which George Orwell wrote '1984', while, 3m beyond, Jura's northern tip looks across to the island of Scarba beyond the Strait of Corrievreckan, notorious for its whirlpools and tidal races.

66 Outer Hebrides

From north to south, and spanning 130 miles, the principal islands of the Outer Hebrides (the Long Island) are Lewis, Harris, North Uist, Benbecula, South Uist and Barra. Lewis and Harris are geographically one island; and North Uist, Benbecula and South Uist, linked by a causeway and a bridge, are effectively one. By using the car ferries between Harris and North Uist and between South Uist and Barra it is possible to tour the length of the group. But these ferries, with seasonal timetables, may not run daily, so some planning is necessary.

Each island has its own character. For the most part, though (with Harris the notable exception), the scenery tends to be open and bleak, and in this, coupled with their remote situation, lies much of the lure of these islands. Long sandy shores are fretted by countless sea lochs within which are scattered islands and islets. Likewise the often desolate moors are so sprinkled with hundreds of lochs that in many districts there is more water than land. Trees are few, and the scanty soil poor and often difficult to drain, so that farming is limited; lobster and other fishing, the manufacture of tweed and the harvesting of seaweed for the extraction of alginates are some main local activities of a people to whom Gaelic is the everyday language. In the south the population is largely Catholic.

Inhabited by man since earliest times, the islands are rich in prehistoric material.

Tourist Organisation. Western Isles Tourist Board, South Beach Street, Stornoway, Isle of Lewis, PA87 2XY. Tel: 0851-3088.

Access. Caledonian MacBrayne operate car ferries as below:

1. To Lewis (Stornoway) from Ullapool.

2. To Harris (Tarbert) from Uig on Skye.

3. To North Uist (Lochmaddy) from Uig on Skye.

4. To South Uist (Lochboisdale) from Oban.

5. To Barra (Castlebay) from Oban and Mallaig.

6. Between Harris and North Uist.

7. Between South Uist and Barra.

Timetables are seasonal. Advance reservation is strongly advised. Intending passengers planning a tour involving two or more islands should coordinate with Caledonian MacBrayne, Ferry Terminal, Gourock. PA19 1QP. Tel: 0475-33755.

Air Services, Lewis, Benbecula and Barra are served by scheduled air services. Apply British Airways (Tel: 0345-222111) for Lewis and Benbecula: Loganair (Tel: 041-889-3181) for Benbecula and Barra.

Internal Bus Services. See under individual islands.

Accommodation of virtually all middle grades is available. It is prudent, especially in summer, to book. For some hotels, see under individual islands.

Harris Tweed (or 'Clo Mor', big cloth) was originally woven by the islanders only for their own use, but later became much in demand particularly by sporting gentry who visited the islands. In 1909 the Harris Tweed Association was formed to protect the industry against imitators. Genuine Harris Tweed is a tweed made from pure Scottish wool, spun, dyed and finished in the Outer Hebrides and hand woven by the islanders in their own homes. Until the 1930s vegetable dyeing was still normal, the women producing the dyes from lichen, roots, heather, soot and vegetables; today modern dying processes offer a much wider range of colours. There is now a choice of over 5000 designs, of three weights, while a new 'gossamer' weave aims to meet modern demand for lighter and more delicate woollens. (Harris Tweed Association, 6 Garden Road, Stornoway, Isle of Lewis. Or: Ballantyne House, 84 Academy Street, Inverness, IV1 1LU).

Island of Lewis

Bus Services cover virtually the entire island but are operated by several different companies. Routes and information from Tourist Information, Stornoway.

SOME HOTELS. **Stornoway**. *Caberfeidh*, Manor Park, PA87 2EU. Tel: 0851-2604. *Crown*, Castle Street, PA87 2BD. Tel: 0851-3181. **Callanish**. *Creag Bhan*, PA86 9DY. Tel: 085172-341. **Uig**. *Scaliscro Lodge*, PA 86 9EL. Tel: 085175-325. *Baile-na-Cille*, Timsgarry, PA86 9JD. Tel: 085175-242.

The most northern of the Hebrides and, after Skye, the largest—at its longest and widest some 35m by 30m—Lewis is scenically an interior of moorland and countless small lochs behind coasts which are wildly broken in the south but smooth out as the island tapers towards its northern Butt. The focus is the town of Stornoway, halfway along the east coast, and it is here that the description below starts, before moving out into each of the island's four parishes.

Stornoway (5500 inhab. *Inf.*) is the island's port and capital, and also the headquarters of the local government Western Isles Area. Founded by James VI, something of the local story is illustrated in the *Stornoway Museum* in the Town Hall (Tel: 0851-3773), while *An Lanntair* (Tel: 0851-3307), on the upper floor, mounts an active programme of art (local artists) and other exhibitions. Two famous explorers have niches in the town's history. Alexander Mackenzie (1755–1820), famed in the annals of Canada, was born here and is remembered by a tablet on *Martin's Memorial Church* in Francis Street (the church stands on the site of his birthplace); and in *St. Peter's Church*, in the same street, can be seen David Livingstone's prayer book and a red granite font, brought from the Flannan Islands and one of the oldest in Scotland.

On the west side of the harbour stands *Lews Castle* (1856–63, and now a technical college), presented to the town by Lord Leverhulme (1851–1925) who in 1918 acquired Lewis and Harris and unsuccessfully tried to modernise the methods of farming and fishing. Beyond, it was near *Arnish Lighthouse*, marking the south entrance to Stornoway's bay, that the Young Pretender spent a night (memorial cairn). However his attempt to buy a boat was frustrated by two Lewis ministers. Across the harbour is the rock of *Holm* where on New Year's Day 1919 the troopship 'Iolaire' sank, over 200 soldiers and sailors being drowned.

The **Parish of Point** occupies the small peninsula which, with the airport at its west end, hooks east and north east out of Stornoway. Its only place of interest is the roofless 14C *Ui Chapel*, to be found at the peninsula's base, just north of the east end of the causeway. Said to have been founded by a MacLeod chief, it shelters an effigy which may be that of Roderick MacLeod (15C) as also a slab commemorating his daughter Margaret who died in 1503 and was the mother of the last abbot of Iona.

The large **Parishes of Barvas and Uig** cover most of Lewis to the north west and south west of Stornoway and include the length of the island's northern coast. These two parishes are toured below as a single anticlockwise circuit using A857 from Stornoway to Barvas (thence suggesting a diversion to the Butt of Lewis) and then A858 past Carloway and Callanish and back to Stornoway. The circuit, less diversions, is of some 45 miles.

Crossing desolate peat moor A857 in some 12m reaches the scattered village of *Barvas*. Here the main tour turns south west, but many visitors will elect first to divert to the Butt of Lewis (32m return to Barvas).

DIVERSION TO BUTT OF LEWIS. The road soon reaches two good prehistoric sites, followed by one from the Iron Age. First, at *Ballantrushal*, there is the huge Thrushal Stone (20ft), the tallest monolith in Scotland. Then, half a mile farther north along A857 (east, sign), comes *Steinacleit*, a collapsed burial cairn within a stone circle, an unusual feature here being an irregular outer stone surround. Finally, about 3m north of Steinacleit, the remains of a broch (*Dun Borve*) stand out against the western skyline.

Approaching Port of Ness the empty moor gives way to a surprisingly green and populated district with several sizeable villages. A minor road north (for Europie) almost at once passes Lionel Old School where the *Ness Historical Society* (Tel: 085181-576) shows artefacts, photographs and documents recalling local life of the past. The Society also offers, at Port of Ness, a restored 19C grain mill. Farther north, up this minor road, in the scattered village of *Europie*, the Church of St. Moluag dates from the 12C but is on the site of a 6C foundation by St. Moluag, a companion of St. Columba. Dedicated during the Norse period to St. Olaf, the church was restored and rededicated to St. Moluag in the early years of our century. The *Butt of Lewis*, with an attractive lighthouse, projects as a confusion of cliffs and rock pinnacles alive with seabirds. *Port of Ness* here is a small harbour from which the Nessmen sail in August and September to collect the 'guga', or young gannets, a favourite local delicacy, from Sula Sgeir, an islet 30m out to the north.

Heading south west from Barvas A858 in 3m reaches a sign (north) for *Arnol Blackhouse* (AM. Tel: 031-244-3101), a traditional crofter dwelling now preserved as a museum. Just beyond, at Bragar, there is a curiosity in the form of a whalebone arch, with, hanging from it, the harpoon which killed the whale in 1919, while, not far beyond the village, beside the road and a loch, can be seen a distinct broch mound. Beyond, again, at Shawbost, *Shawbost School Museum* (Tel: 085171-213), in a redundant church and illustrating the old way of life on Lewis, is an admirable local school achievement; and about 1m west of Shawbost (sign; $\frac{1}{3}$m walk) the same school has restored a Norse Watermill.

The road now enters the parish of Uig to reach (some 4m from Shawbost) *Dun Carloway*, the best preserved broch in the Hebrides, still about 30ft high on one side, and occupying a commanding position with a grand seaward view. At *Stonefield*, reached in 4m, an ancient standing stone is now set in a small modern housing estate; a modest prelude to the nearby **Standing Stones of Callanish*, an astonishing forest of megaliths planted on the moorland—at first sight apparently haphazard but in fact to a design—and, associated with the stones, traces of at least one chambered cairn. The central, flattened ring is of 13 stones surrounding a single stone (16ft and the highest at Callanish) and the small chambered cairn, this probably a later insertion. From the ring radiate rows of stones—five each to the east, west and south and a great avenue of 19 to the north—while just outside the ring stand two seemingly random stones, a tall one to the south west and a short one (re-erected in 1885) to the south east. Nor does Callanish stand alone, for nearby there are three other stone circles and several by comparison minor sites. Two of the stone circles, both visible to the south east and one with the remains of a cairn, are readily accessible just south of the main road; the third is a short way down B8011, glimpsed up the slope to the right.

DIVERSIONS TO GREAT BERNERA AND UIG SANDS. B8011 angling south at Garynahine just beyond Callanish provides the approach to Great Bernera and Uig Sands, both roads threading some of the loneliest country and best scenery on Lewis. *Great Bernera*, although geographically an island, is reached by a short bridge above the west end of which presides a fine group of three standing stones. Beyond, small roads meander about the island providing ever-varying loch and coastal views.—The road for *Uig Sands* (*Ardroil*) rounds the massif which fills the south west of Lewis. It was here, at Uig Sands in 1831, that the famous Uig Chessmen (now in the British Museum, London) were found; made of walrus ivory, the set may have been hidden by nuns from the Benedictine house known to have flourished at Mealista, at the road's end 6m farther down the coast. Today, in summer, the Uig

Historical Society opens an exhibition on the local crofting villages and families.—Nearly 20m out to the west are the *Flannan Islands*, or the Seven Hunters, with traces of hermits' cells and the scene of a mysterious tragedy in 1900 when three light-keepers disappeared without trace.

From Callanish, A858 travels across the well-named **Parish of Lochs** to reach Stornoway in 14m. However, if Harris is the objective, a minor road out of Achmore cuts across to A859 which is followed towards the increasingly impressive mountains of the Island of Harris, the border of which is at *Ardvourlie* on Loch Seaforth. After being forced to flee Scalpay (see below) the Young Pretender rowed up Loch Seaforth to land at Ardvourlie, thence walking to Arnish near Stornoway. *Seaforth Island* lies half in Lewis and half in Harris.

Island of Harris

> **Bus Services** run north to Stornoway and south to make a round of South Harris (Harris Garage Co, Tarbert. Tel: 0859–2441).
>
> SOME HOTELS. **Tarbert**. *Harris*, PA85 3DL. Tel: 0859-2154. **Scarista**. *Scarista House*, PA85 3HX. Tel: 085985-238.

Harris is split into North and South by the narrow isthmus (⅓m across) on which is the island's village capital and ferry port of **Tarbert** (*Inf.*). North Harris is mountainous with peaks of well over 2000ft. South Harris, in the east, is a wilderness of rock and small lochs, but in the west green downland drops to sweeps of yellow beaches.

Either side of the isthmus are West Loch Tarbert and East Loch Tarbert, the latter protected by the island of **Scalpay** (Car ferry from Kyles Scalpay. Caledonian MacBrayne. Tel: 0475-33755), with a population of around 500, largely engaged in fishing. During his wanderings the Young Pretender crossed to Scalpay where he was hidden by a farmer, Donald Cameron, while friends tried without success to buy a boat.—The *Shiant Islands*, 12m east of Scalpay, have sheer cliffs, the home of myriad seabirds (for boat hire from Tarbert or Scalpay, Tel: 085984-225).

North Harris. One road runs north to Stornoway. Another heads west between the mountains and West Loch Tarbert, a drive through lovely coastal scenery with many burns cascading down from above. Along this road, at *Bunaveneader*, can be seen the slip and other remains of a whaling station built by the Norwegians in c 1912, later operated by Lord Leverhulme, but abandoned in 1930. Beyond *Amhuinnsuidh Castle* (no adm.), built by the Earl of Dunmore in 1868, the road ends at *Husinish* (14m from Tarbert) opposite the island of *Scarp*, now uninhabited but with a modest niche in postal history. In 1934 the island was chosen for an experiment by which mail was to be delivered by a rocket designed by a German called Zucker. A special stamp was issued, but the rocket exploded on impact, damaging most of the mail, and the project was abandoned.

The peninsula of **South Harris** is circled by road, the distance from Tarbert back to Tarbert being some 40m. The east shore road is narrow, twisting and slow but runs through rugged, broken coastal scenery. The western loop is faster, but scenically very different, with downland and beaches.—An anticlockwise circuit (from and back to Tarbert) is described, Tarbert being left southward by A859 which in 5m (at the point where the return east coast road joins) curves west to reach the coast just short of *Horgabost*. From just south of this village, from where the road touches a sandy beach, the Standing Stone called Clach MhicLeoid can be seen on Aird of Nisabost to the north. Beyond, the road passes *Borve Lodge*, once home of Lord Leverhulme, and then *Scarista Post Office* about ½m south of which, in a field between the road and the sea, is another Standing Stone (Borvemore), this one close to several fallen stones, suggesting that there was probably a circle here. The road now curves southward to pass *Northton*, separated by a beach and dune isthmus from a peninsula (track and path) the central feature of which is the hill of Chaipaval (1092ft) affording splendid views which may even include St. Kilda (c 45m). At the south west corner of the peninsula there is a ruined chapel of obscure origins. *Leverburgh*, formerly Obbe, is the place chosen by Lord Leverhulme in 1923 for the establishment of a sizeable fishing port; although successful, the project was abandoned on Leverhulme's death two years later and most of the installations were demolished.

Out to sea to the south west, beyond the now uninhabited islands of Ensay and Killegray, are the islands of (north) Pabay and (south) Berneray. *Pabay*, uninhabited since 1858 when it was 'cleared', is now farmed from *Berneray* (200 inhab.) where a standing stone and other remains prove human occupation from millenia ago. Berneray can be reached by passenger ferry from Leverburgh, the service continuing to Newton Ferry on North Uist (Tel: 08767-230 or 250). The island can also be reached from the south by a small car ferry from Newton Ferry (Tel: as above).

Rodel St. Clement's Church (c 1500; restored 1787 and 1873) is known for the curious carvings on the exterior of its sturdy tower, these including strangely tilted figures wearing kilt and plaid. Long a MacLeod burial place, the most notable surviving tomb, with an armoured effigy, is that of Alastair Crotach; although the tomb is dated 1528, its occupant died many years later, in 1546.

Northward from Rodel, the small road threads a strange wilderness of rocks and countless small lochs above a broken coast to join A859 and regain Tarbert.

Island of North Uist

Bus Services cover most of the island and run also to Benbecula airport (Post Office, Lochmaddy. Tel: 08763-330).

SOME HOTELS. **Lochmaddy**. *Lochmaddy*. Tel: 08763-331. **Locheport**. *Langass Lodge*. Tel: 08764-285.

Vaguely circular in shape, though the geometry is distorted by several promontories, North Uist is scenically an island of high moorland and lochs on the east, while the west is by comparison green and fertile with long beaches. The chief centre is **Lochmaddy** (*Inf.*) on the east coast, apparently taking its name (Loch of the Dog) from the three doglike basalt islets at the harbour entrance. The loch, though only 5m long and with an entrance 1m wide, has a shoreline so tortuous that its length has been calculated to reach 360m.

A road (some 30m) circles the main island, this being described anticlockwise below. Heading north west this road rounds the hill of *Blashaval* to the west, on the lower north west slope of which there are three standing stones known as Na Fir Bhreige, or the False Men. One tradition is that these mark the graves of three spies who were buried here alive; another, more domestic, that the stones represent three men from Skye, turned to stone by a witch as retribution for having deserted their wives. Beyond, B893 leads north to (3m) Newton Ferry with a small car ferry to the island of Berneray and a passenger ferry to Leverburgh on South Harris (Tel: 08767-230 or 250). Continuing along A865 the hamlets of Grenitote and Solas are passed, beyond, beside the road, as it curves to travel south east, standing *Kilphedar Cross*, of obscure age and origin but transferred here from a nearby burial ground in 1830. From the road rise here the seaward view can include St. Kilda.

St. Kilda (the name in fact deriving from the Norn 'skilda' = shield), 45m west, comprises four islands and several islets, the largest, *Hirta*, being 3m long with stupendous cliffs over 1000ft in height. The entire population of 35 were evacuated at their own request in 1930, and the islands are now under the care of the National Trust for Scotland (Tel: 041-552-8391). Each year NTS working parties of volunteers are gradually restoring the village community. The other islands are *Soay* (home of the sheep of that breed), *Boreray* and *Dun*, all being alive with seabirds, these including the world's largest colony of gannets, the largest and oldest colonies in Britain of fulmars, and a large population of puffins.

Farther south, the nature reserve of *Balranald* (warden at Houghharry in summer), known for its variety of breeding birds, lies south west of the road which from here heads south east to reach (6m from Balranald) *Clachan* at a road junction. Here the left fork (A867) returns in 8m to Lochmaddy, but in 2m reaches the round chambered cairn of *Langash Barp*, to the south of the road on the slope of Ben Langash. Though partially collapsed, entry is still possible into a polygonal chamber, while around the exterior base are what appear to be small cists. A track rounds the south of the hill, a short way beyond its end being a prehistoric stone oval known as *Pobull Fhinn*, Finn's People.—*Locheport* (hotel), on B894, is 4m east of the Clachan junction.

To the west, some 10m from this road fork, are the *Monach Islands*, uninhabited and a national nature reserve which is a wintering ground for barnacle and white-footed geese. According to old records the Sound of Monach was until the 16C fordable at low water.

Leaving the island circuit, A865 now head south, in 3m reaching Carinish where there is a curious ruin known as *Teamphull na Trionaid* (Trinity Temple), twin church buildings founded on an earlier Celtic site in about 1200 by Beatrix, a daughter of Somerled, and later rebuilt by the wife of John Macdonald of Islay, first Lord of the Isles (she was daughter of Robert II; see also Kilchoman Church on Islay, Rte 65). It is said, too, that this was once an ancient seat of learning, attended by, amongst others, Duns Scotus. More certain is that Carinish was in 1601 the scene of a battle between the MacLeods of Harris and the local Macdonalds.

About a mile beyond Carinish the road breasts a rise, here cutting straight through the clear remains of a stone circle, while to the north east can be seen the distinct outline of a long cairn. Beyond, *North Ford* causeway, taking the road across to the island of Benbecula, was opened in 1960.

Island of Benbecula

Bus Services. For the service to Lochmaddy on North Uist, Tel: 08763-330. For services to western North Uist (Tigharry, Hosta, Scolpaig), Tel: 08765-247. For service to Lochboisdale on South Uist, Tel: 08705-237.

SOME HOTELS. **Liniclate**. *Dark Island*, PA88 5PG. Tel: 0870-2414. *Inchyra*, PA88 5PY. Tel: 0870-2176. **Creagorry**. *Creagorry*, PA88 5PG. Tel: 0870-2024.

Ignoring its many seaward promontories, especially to the east, Benbecula is a rough square, measuring some 5m by 5m and thus the smallest of the main islands of the Outer Hebridean chain. Scenically the island is to a large extent a flat broken area of sea and inland lochs, though on the west side there is a fertile district protected by sand dunes beyond which is beach. The principal village is Balivanich in the north west, alongside being the airport.

The direct road (A865) crosses the island in a little more than 5m, but it is a lot more interesting to make the westward loop provided by B892.

This road skirts the airport, ½m south east of which, on a promontory into Loch Dun Mhurchaidh, can be seen *Dun Buidhe*, an Iron Age survival with considerable stone remains and seemingly once a place of some strength. The road turns sharply west to round the airport, just to the south being a small ruin known as *Teampull Challuim Chille*, of unknown origin, but, if only from its name, almost certainly once a chapel. Beyond *Balivanich* the road drops southward, in 1m passing the ruined chapel *Nunton*; dating from the 14C the chapel was once that of a nunnery, wrecked at the Reformation and the nuns massacred. *Borve Castle*, on the left 2½m farther south, though now only a remnant, was a Clan Ranald stronghold until burnt by clansmen who opposed their Jacobite chief and supported George II. Opposite, a short way south of the road, there are traces of a chapel which probably belonged to the castle. Beyond, at *Liniclate*, a museum (Tel: 0870-2211) in the school shows material about the islands and also runs a wide-ranging pro-gramme of exhibitions.

A865 is soon rejoined, about 1½m northwards up this road being *Loch Olavat*, with islets showing evidence of three duns.

It was from the remote district of *Rossinish* in the broken north east of Benbecula that the Young Pretender and Flora Macdonald sailed 'over the sea to Skye'.

Benbecula is linked to South Uist by a bridge across *South Ford*.

Island of South Uist

> **Bus Services**. A service runs the length of the island between Benbecula airport in the north to Ludag in the south (Hebridean Coaches. Tel: 08705-237.
>
> SOME HOTELS. **Lochboisdale**. *Lochboisdale*, PA81 5TH. Tel: 08784-332. **Daliburgh**. *Borrodale*, PA81 5SS. Tel: 08784-444.

This is a long, thin island (20m by 7m) made up of a west coast of beaches, an interior of peat bog and lochs, and an east side of sea lochs and mountains, the highest being *Ben Mhor* (2033ft) and *Hecla* (1988ft).

Historically South Uist is associated with the Young Pretender's meeting with Flora Macdonald. The prince landed (from Scalpay) on 14 May 1746 in *Corodale Bay* on the east coast below Ben Mhor, thereafter hiding in a forester's hut. From a nearby cave (Prince's Cave) he watched government ships patrolling The Minch, but, though his stay may have been hazardous, it was not without its compensa-tions, for he apparently received many gifts of whisky and brandy and even won an all-night drinking marathon. He was looked after by Neil MacEachain Macdonald and through him met Flora Macdonald, aged 23 and on a visit from Skye to her brother at Milton, her birthplace. MacEachain proposed that she should return to Skye, taking the prince, disguised as a servant girl, with her. At first she refused, on the grounds that this could implicate her friends, but as soon as she met the prince her objections crumbled.

Corodale Bay and Prince's Cave are far from any road, but the island's north–south road passes Milton.

The description below travels the length of South Uist from north to south, soon crossing the large *Loch Bee* by causeway, just beyond the end of which, in Loch Duin Mhoir on the west of the road, there is an islet with clear traces of a dun and its causeway approach. To the east, 1½m farther, stands the 125ft-high granite statue of *Our Lady of the Isles* (Hew Lorimer, 1957). Within less than a mile the road is fringing *Loch Druidibeg*, spattered with islands and stretching over 2m east; a national nature reserve, the loch is the most important breeding ground in Britain of the greylag goose. Another road borders the north shore of the loch to reach the head of Loch Skipport, while in the south west of the loch, on an islet off the south shore (½m from the road), rectangular

Dun Roauill provides archaeological interest for its unusual shape and as perhaps the best dun on South Uist. Roughly opposite, to the west of A865 and standing in the middle of Loch an Eilean, *Caisteal Bheagram* is the ruin of a small 15 or 16C tower, and at *Howmore*, just to the south, the church offers a rare curiosity in the form of a central communion pew.

Continuing south, A865 passes (2½m from Howmore) below a lone megalith on the slope of Beinn a Charra, beyond, in another mile, reaching the turn (west) for *Ormaclete Castle*, a ruin standing within a farm. Built between 1701–08 for the chief of Clan Ranald, the castle had a short life and an undistinguished end when, in 1715, it was gutted by fire caused by over-enthusiastic celebration of what was prematurely reported to be a Jacobite victory at Sheriffmuir. *Flora Macdonald's Birthplace*, the home too of the brother she was visiting at the time of her meeting with the Young Pretender—today simply a memorial cairn within a low-walled ruin—can be seen up a track to the west of A865 halfway between the turns off to Kildonan and Milton. And opposite the latter turn an eastward track in 1m reaches a chambered cairn, part surrounded by standing stones.

At *Daliburgh* A865 bears east for (2m) **Lochboisdale** (*Inf.*), the island's port and capital. Off the southward road (now B888), in 1m, a road signed *Kilpheder* leads west through this hamlet, beyond, along a track and in the machar-covered dunes, being the remains of an Iron Age wheel-house, or aisled round-house, showing a circular outer wall, radiating dividers and a central hearth.

B888 breasts a rise on which stands a church (1963) containing attractive and unusual Stations of the Cross, the work of a Barra priest, Calum McNeil, beyond, on the south coast, being *Ludag*, a pleasant corner with seaward views of Eriskay, Barra and other small islands. (Vehicle boat to Eriskay. All year: Mon.–Sat., four return trips daily. Tel: 0851-3773 or 08786-261.—Passenger ferry to Eoligarry on Barra. Crossing 40 minutes. Tel: 08784-216).

It was on *Eriskay*, on Prince's Strand on the west shore, that the Young Pretender first set foot on Scottish soil on 23 July 1745. In 1941 the 'Politician' foundered here, carrying 20,000 cases of whisky, a wreck which became the subject of Compton Mackenzie's 'Whisky Galore'.—On *Stack Island*, to the south, the ruined castle was a lair of a notorious local Macneil pirate and wreck plunderer.

Island of Barra

Bus Service. Circuit of the island, including the airport and Eoligarry (Post Office, Castlebay. Tel: 08714-286).

SOME HOTELS. **Castlebay**. *Castlebay*, PA80 5XD. Tel: 08714-223. **Tangusdale**. *Isle of Barra*, PA80 5XW. Tel: 08714-383.

Barren, yet with an attraction all its own, Barra owes its name to St. Findbarr, or Barr, said to have converted the island during the 6C. **Castlebay** (*Inf.*), on the south, is the port and principal centre, on an island in its bay being *Kisimul Castle* (Tel: 08714-336).

History. The history of Barra is essentially that of Kisimul which, started in c 1060, is, in part at least, among the oldest stone castles in Scotland. The main tower dates from c 1120. The castle and the island were owned from 1314 by the Macneils (some put it earlier to 1030), acquired because a member of the clan fought for Bruce at Bannockburn. The castle was virtually destroyed by fire at the end of the 18C, and in 1838 Barra, together with the castle, was sold to John Gordon of Cluny. A century later, in 1937, Kisimul was bought back by the late Robert Lister Macneil (45th clan chief), an American architect. Restoration was completed by 1970 and the castle remains in (American) Macneil ownership.

A road (14m) circles the island, travelling north west out of Castlebay, soon passing the road serving the Vatersay causeway, and then, in under a mile, looking down on *Loch Tangusdale*, also known as Loch St. Clair, in which the small ruin of Castle Sinclair (or MacLeod's Tower) clings to an islet. The Isle of Barra Hotel is next passed, soon after which, west of the road opposite the turning to Borve, are two standing stones which, though modest, traditionally mark the grave of a raiding Norse warrior, defeated in single combat by a local champion. Just beyond, the road through *Craigston*—with a local cottage museum (Tel: 08714-336)—leads towards *Dun Bharpa*, a large collapsed chambered cairn part surrounded by standing stones (from the end of the surfaced road the continuing track may be followed for a few hundred yards, after which the cairn is reached by an easy though often wet climb north east).

Along the main road, a mile after the Craigston turn, a small cemetery is reached, a point at which it is worth crossing the dunes to the shore where many seals can normally be seen. Above the cemetery rises *Dun Cueir*, most easily climbed in about 10 minutes from the north and well worth the effort, not only for its commanding position but also because this is a much better preserved dun than many and one which still shows its thick wall and side passages.

At *North Bay* the island circuit should be broken for a diversion of some 4m into Barra's northern tip, the road soon rounding *Traigh Mhor*, the tidal sandy bay which at low water serves as the island's airfield (Cockle Strand). *Eoligarry*, beyond, is a scattered hamlet at the south end of which is the interesting *Cille-Bharra*, a group of three ruined chapels, perhaps of the 12C. One of these has now been roofed and shelters some weathered, carved graveslabs, probably of the 15–17C though local legend insists that they are Celtic, having been brought from Iona by a local chieftain requiring ballast for his galley; and, indeed, one stone does bear a faint picture of a galley. Compton Mackenzie, the author, is buried here—in sight of Eriskay, the setting for his 'Whisky Galore'—while across the road from the chapels *St. Barr's Well* is the spot where, after coming ashore, the saint struck the ground with his stave and out gushed water. From Eoligarry there is a passenger ferry to Ludag on South Uist (Crossing 40 minutes. Tel: 08784-216).

At North Bay, on an islet in the loch within the east angle of the two roads, stands a figure of St. Barr with his raised stave, the work (1975) of a local artist, Margaret Somerville. In another 4m, at *Brevig*, there are standing stones, beyond, high up on the south shoulder of Heavel (1255ft), standing the *Lady Star of the Sea*, a marble Madonna erected in 1954 by the Welcome Home Fund for Seamen.

A string of small islands runs away to the south, *Vatersay* being the nearest (just over 1m), inhabited, and since 1990 linked to Barra by causeway. The Annie James Monument, on the shore of West Bay, recalls the site of an emigrant shipwreck.— Boats can sometimes be hired to other islands, notably *Mingulay* whose towering cliffs are famous for nesting seabirds. Here Macphee's Hill is named after a rent collector who, on arriving on the island, found all the tenants dead from the plague; his terrified companions promptly rowed away, leaving Macphee marooned for a year. On *Pabbay* there are Pictish and Celtic Christian stones.

X ORKNEY AND SHETLAND

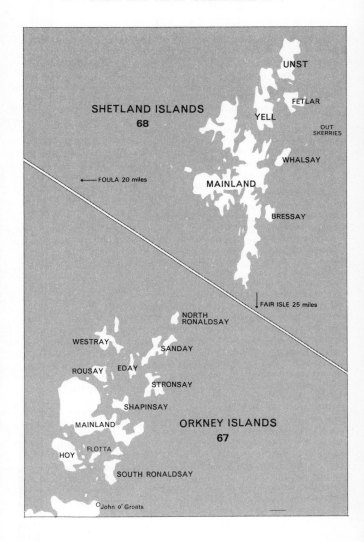

UNST

FETLAR

SHETLAND ISLANDS
68

YELL

OUT
SKERRIES

WHALSAY

←— FOULA 20 miles

MAINLAND

BRESSAY

↓ FAIR ISLE 25 miles

NORTH
RONALDSAY

WESTRAY

SANDAY

ROUSAY   EDAY

STRONSAY

SHAPINSAY

MAINLAND   ORKNEY ISLANDS
67

FLOTTA
HOY

SOUTH RONALDSAY

○John o' Groats

Although often spoken of as one, the two island groups of Orkney and Shetland are (if Shetland's Fair Isle is discounted) in fact separated by some 60 miles of often wild sea. Both groups are virtually treeless, they largely share a common history, both confusingly call their principal islands Mainland, and they have a common concern with oil. In other respects, though—and certainly from the tourist point of view—Orkney and Shetland are in total contrast; Orkney low-lying, scenically unexciting but offering by far the richest concentration of prehistoric monuments in Britain, Shetland a place of lonely peat upland, countless lochs and ever-present coastal scenery ranging from dark, peaceful inlets to precipitous cliffs alive with seabirds.

Common History. Both Orkney and Shetland were the home during the Stone Age of people of unknown origin; both were colonised by the Picts at about the time of the birth of Christ; both received early Christian missionaries (the frequently found place-name 'Papa' or 'Papil' was the Norse term for the Celtic priests); and both, after perhaps two centuries of Norse raiding and settlement, were annexed in 875 by Harold Haarfagr, who, set on unifying Norway, could no longer tolerate the raids on his coast by Orkney and Shetland-based vikings, or pirates. Thereafter, until 1468, the islands were governed by their own Norse earls of Orkney, the more stirring though not necessarily historically accurate aspects of whose story are told in the sagas, notably the Orkneyinga Saga recording the period from about 900 to 1200.

Some of these earls have left their mark. Thorfinn the Mighty was a virtually independent ruler from 1020–64, his territory including also the Hebrides, a large part of Scotland and a realm in Ireland. He is most associated with Brough of Birsay in Orkney where he had his hall and founded Christ Church. He defeated Duncan of Scotland and later may well have backed Macbeth over Duncan's murder. In the early 12C Thorfinn's grandson Magnus was one of two jointly ruling earls. A gentle man for his times he was murdered in 1116 by his co-earl Hakon. Paul of Orphir ruled next, in turn being supplanted by Magnus's nephew, the remarkable Rognvald, a cultured man and a poet, some of whose verses are in the Orkneyinga Saga. He founded St. Magnus Cathedral in Kirkwall in 1137, Magnus by then having been canonised (probably more on political than religious grounds), and also went on a crusade which took him as far as the Jordan. Later he also was canonised.

Scottish influence, however, gradually took over and from 1230, though still formally bound to Norway, the earls were all Scots. In 1468 Christian I of Norway and Denmark betrothed his daughter, Margaret, to James III of Scotland, and, being unable or unwilling to hand over the agreed dowry, instead pledged the islands, which even today theoretically remain in pawn despite their having been unilaterally annexed by Scotland in 1472. Later the islands were administered on behalf of the Crown by stewards, two of these, Earl Robert and his son Earl Patrick, being notorious tyrants. The latter was removed and executed in 1615, from which time Orkney and Shetland became administratively integral with Scotland.

Oil has been the modern event. Yet whatever changes it may have brought to the island way of life, these will be little apparent to the tourist visitor. Orkney's prehistoric sites are unaffected, both as such and in their settings, as is also, except for the one small area of Sullom Voe, Shetland's remote and lonely scenery.

Meanwhile, despite the 500 years since the pledging, Norse is still the source of most place names, the origin of the cadence in the local English speech, an occasional surviving influence in long-house-type building, and even the parent of some legal oddities and local festivals.

Inter-group Communications. _Sea._ Car ferry between Stromness (Orkney) and Lerwick (Shetland). Crossing 8 hours. Infrequent and seasonal. P and O Ferries, PO Box 5, Jamieson's Quay, Aberdeen, AB9 8DL. Tel: 0224-572615.—_Air._ Services between Kirkwall (Orkney) and Lerwick (Shetland) are operated by British Airways. Tel: 0345-222111. There is also an infrequent and seasonal service between Kirkwall (Orkney) and Fair Isle (Shetland) operated by Loganair, Glasgow Airport, Paisley. Tel: 041-889-3181.

67   Orkney

Its closest island some 6m from mainland Scotland across the Pentland Firth, the Orkney group numbers about 70 islands and islets of which 18 are inhabited, with a total population of some 19,000. The largest and most important, with the capital Kirkwall, is called *Mainland*, about 20m long, erratic in shape, and linked in the south by causeways to the islands of Burray and South Ronaldsay. The other islands divide themselves into the North and South groups. With the exception of Hoy (south), all the islands are low-lying or gently rolling agricultural land with few trees. There are scarcely any villages, in their place being dispersed houses and squat farms, the inhabitants largely concerned with the raising of cattle and sheep.

To the visitor Orkney is primarily important for its prehistoric monuments, of which the group has by far the richest concentration in Britain. There are sites of importance and interest on most islands, but those on Mainland are the most accessible and best known. Virtually all are to the west or north of Kirkwall, the best concentration being close to A965 around the south end of Loch of Stenness. Here, within a radius of less than 2m, are the great cairn of *Maes Howe*, the *Stenness Stones*, the *Ring of Brodgar* and *Unstan Cairn*. Other sites are scattered. The Stone Age village of *Skara Brae* is along the west coast, as is also, farther north, the *Brough of Birsay* archaeological complex, while the best broch, *Gurness*, is on Aiker Ness to the north east across from the island of Rousay.

In summer there is a choice of Mainland tours, these of course including the principal sites, and there is also a choice of island cruises, island day visits and suchlike. There are also scheduled bus services (not Sun.) throughout Mainland, but their use for touring the many scattered sites is not really practicable. A hired bicycle is one solution, but a car (own or rented) obviously gives the most flexibility. With a car it would be possible to cover most of Mainland's sites in one day, although this might be rushing places which deserve longer. Two or three days, though, should be ample, these also allowing time for the town of Kirkwall as well as for a run to Scapa Flow, famous as a naval base in the last two wars, and across the Churchill Barrier into South Ronaldsay.

Tourist Organisation. Orkney Tourist Board, 6 Broad Street, Kirkwall, Orkney KW15 1NX. Tel: 0856-2856.

Access. *Sea*. 1. The principal approach is by car ferry from Scrabster (Thurso) to Stromness. Crossing 2 hours. Basically Mon.–Sat., once or twice daily in each direction, but with Sunday and extra weekday crossings in summer. Advance booking advised. P and O Ferries, PO Box 5, Jamieson's Quay, Aberdeen, AB9 8DL. Tel: 0224-572615. 2. P and O Ferries also operate a car ferry (infrequent, seasonal; 8 hours) between Aberdeen and Stromness. 3. Passenger service John o' Groats to Burwick on South Ronaldsay. Summer only, roughly four times daily; 45 minutes; Orkney coach tour. Thomas and Bews, Ferry Office, John o' Groats, Caithness. Tel: 095581-353. 4. A car ferry between Gills Bay (west of John o' Groats) to Burwick on South Ronaldsay is under consideration for the early 1990s.

Air services between mainland Scotland and Orkney (Kirkwall) are operated by British Airways (Tel: 0345-222111) and by Loganair (Glasgow Airport, Paisley. Tel: 041-889-3181).

Inter-island Communications. See under North and South Islands.

SOME HOTELS (Mainland). **Kirkwall**. *Kirkwall*, Harbour Street, KW15 1LF. Tel: 0856-2232. *Lynnfield*, Holm Road, KW15 1RX. Tel: 0856-2505. **Stromness**. *Ferry Inn*, John Street, KW16 3AD. Tel: 0856-850280. *Stromness*, Victoria Street, KW16 3AA. Tel: 0856-850298. **Dounby**.

Smithfield, KW17 2HT. Tel: 085677-215. **Loch Harray**. *Merkister*, KW17 2LF. Tel: 085677-366.—Advance booking recommended. For accommodation on other islands, book through Tourist Information, Kirkwall.

Kirkwall

Kirkwall (6700 inhab. *Inf.* 5 Broad Street. Tel: 0856-2856), the island's capital and with a busy harbour, is dominated by its solid Cathedral of St. Magnus, beside which are the ruins of the Bishop's Palace and Earl's Palace, and also the Tankerness House Museum. This compact area is the tourist heart of Kirkwall and is reached from the waterfront (Harbour Street) by, in succession, Bridge, Albert and Broad streets.

History. Thanks to its harbour and the foundation of the cathedral in the 12C Kirkwall early became a place of local importance. In 1486 the town was made a royal burgh by James III, and, later, James V lodged in the Bishop's Palace and held meetings in Parliament Close.

The name Castle Street (off Broad Street) recalls the old castle. Built in the 14C it was so strong that its builder, Earl Henry Sinclair, was suspected of receiving help from the Devil. It was held by Balfour, governor of Orkney, in 1567 against the fugitive Earl of Bothwell, and was demolished in 1614 after the rebellion instigated by Earl Patrick (see Earl's Palace, below).

In 1650 Montrose mustered 2000 Orkneymen in Kirkwall, but half of them soon lost their lives by shipwreck.

Kirkwall derives its Norse name (Church Place) from a church dedicated in 1035 to St. Olaf, patron saint of Norway; a re-erected remnant (an arched doorway) of this church's 16C successor can be seen in St. Olaf's Wynd off Bridge Street.

The **'Cathedral of St. Magnus** is a sturdy cruciform structure of grey flagstone and patterned red and yellow sandstone, with a central tower and spire. The style is a severe and massive Norman.

History. Rognvald III, Magnus's nephew, founded the cathedral in 1137, the skeleton of the murdered St. Magnus being brought here from Thorfinn's Christ Church on Brough of Birsay. Two skeletons, one of them with a pierced skull, found hidden in chests within pillars (see below), are believed to be those of Magnus and Rognvald, thus making the cathedral unique in Britain for sheltering the remains of both founder and patron saint. The archbishops of York tried to claim suzerainty in the 12C, but the see was suffragan to Nidaros (Trondhjem, in Norway) until Orkney was annexed by Scotland in 1472, when it came under St. Andrews. The building of Rognvald's church apparently went on until well into the 13C, the transepts, with the three west bays of the choir and two east bays of the nave, with interlacing wall-arcades, being the oldest part of the church; the pointed arches supporting the tower are later. By about 1250 the three east bays of the choir were added, and the tower probably also dates from about this time. The steeple replaces a 17C one destroyed by fire in 1671. The church was finally completed in the 14–15C by the west extension of the nave.

At the Reformation the cathedral was saved by the townsmen, and it continued to have a succession of seven Protestant bishops. Cromwell's soldiers used the steeple as a prison and as a fortress, also turning the nave partly into a barrack and partly into a stable. After this the building fell into neglect, although the choir was used as the parish church. Major restoration took place in 1912–20.

The cathedral is unusual in that it is owned not by any religious assembly but, by royal charter (James III, 1486), by the citizens of Kirkwall.

Lining the Interior of the cathedral is a notable series of tombstones, largely of the 17C and many bearing informative identifications.

The description below starts beneath the fine west window, unveiled by the Queen in 1987 (handboards provide a detailed description of the window's symbolism), and then continues clockwise along the nave north aisle in which perhaps the most interesting feature is a hanging mort-brod of c 1690 with emblems of mortality, interesting both for itself and as the sole surviving example of this old type of Orkney

KIRKWALL CATHEDRAL

memorial. Nearby, above, can be seen a fragment of medieval vault painting. In the north transept stands the original Kirkwall Mercat Cross of 1621, removed from Kirk Green in 1954 and replaced by a replica. On the left, on entering the choir north aisle, is the memorial to the 833 men lost when HMS 'Royal Oak' was torpedoed in Scapa Flow in 1939, while, beyond and also in this aisle, is the cathedral's oldest tombstone, showing a cross and a sword and dated to the 13C. The choir is now rounded to reach the choir south aisle in which is the tomb of Lord Adam Steward (died 1575), natural son of James V.

In the raised Choir the massive piers of the central bay contain the remains of St. Magnus (south) and St. Rognvald (north) and, while here, it is interesting to compare the Norman work to the west and the later work of the east bays. The fine east window is ascribed to Bishop Stewart (c 1511) but may well be earlier, while, below, the site of the high altar is St. Rognvald's Chapel (Stanley Cursiter, 1966) with figures, by Reynold Eunson, of the saint, Bishop William the Old (died 1153) and Kol, the Norse master-mason builder of the cathedral.

High up, between the south wall of the choir and the south transept chapel, is the gloomy entrance to Marwick's Hole, known to have been used as a prison at least until the 18C. Beyond, an arched recess (probably 14C) in the south wall of the nave south aisle is a tomb of the Orkney family of Paplay.

The **Bishop's Palace** (AM. Tel: 031-244-3101), is almost entirely a 16C reconstruction on top of the original 12–13C building, of which only some ground floor masonry now remains. It was here, in the lower hall, that in 1263 King Hakon died after his disastrous defeat at Largs in the Clyde. The south extension was added by Earl Patrick Stewart, whose grandiose plan to join this palace to his own was ended by his downfall and execution. The tower, round outside but square within, bears a small statue, probably St. Olaf but possibly representing Bishop Reid (died 1558), who rebuilt the upper floors.

Across the road stands the more interesting and attractive ruin of the *Earl's Palace (AM. Tel: 031-244-3101), built by forced labour for the infamous Earl Patrick between 1600–07. Architecturally this is a gem of the period when castellation was beginning to be used more for ornamentation than defence. The palace is L-shaped, with particularly pleasing angle-turrets, each with its small room, while the enormous kitchens and storerooms and the great hall seem fitting setting for the magnificence and luxury enjoyed here by the earl and his friends. His initials (P.E.O., for Patrick, Earl of Orkney) stand by the hall's fireplace.

Earl Patrick behaved as a prince, never going out without an escort of 50 musket-
eers. Such was his behaviour in Orkney (farming out the revenues; imposing
forced labour; tampering with the weights and measures) that he spent much of his
time from 1609 onwards either imprisoned or on trial. In 1613, learning that his
castles had been seized, he sent his natural son, Robert, to Orkney to recapture
them. Robert, after some initial success, was defeated and executed. Soon after,
Earl Patrick too was executed for having instigated his son's revolt. Although
Steward of Orkney and Shetland, and though living in such magnificence, this
man was found 'so ignorant that he could scarce rehearse the Lord's Prayer' and
was granted a week's stay of execution so that he could 'better inform himself'.

Tankerness House Museum (Tel: 0856-3191) houses an admirable presentation of 4000 or more years of Orkney life. The building itself is a
beautifully restored example of a 16–18C Orkney merchant laird's
home with courtyard and garden; earlier the north and south wings
were the home of cathedral clergy. The museum has two out-stations,
the farm and folk museums Kirbuster and Corrigall (see under Northern
Mainland below).

Northern Mainland

A965 (alternative A964) to Stromness. A967, B9056 and A967 to Brough
of Birsay. A966 to Broch of Gurness. B9057 to Dounby. A986 and A965
to Kirkwall.—This circuit visits all the principal prehistoric sites on
Mainland.

Total distance 54m.—*10m* Maes Howe.—*5m* **Stromness**.—*7m* **Skara
Brae**.—*6m* **Brough of Birsay**.—*8m* **Gurness Broch**.—*5m* **Dounby**.—
13m **Kirkwall**.

There is a choice between Kirkwall and Stromness; the northerly
approach (A965, followed by this Route) passes several principal sites of
interest, while the southerly choice (A964) offers views across Scapa
Flow.

TO STROMNESS BY A964 (16m). Kirkwall is left through the suburb of St.
Ola in which at *Orkney Chairs* (Rosegarth House on A964. Tel: 0856-
3521) visitors may watch an unusual and local craft; chairs may be
bought here or will be delivered worldwide. Beyond, in some 8m from
Kirkwall, the road passes close to *Orphir Church* where a small apse is
all that survives of an 11 or 12C circular church, thought to have been
modelled on the Church of the Holy Sepulchre. It was probably built by
a crusader or pilgrim as the result of a vow made in the Holy Land,
possibly Earl Hakon who made a pilgrimage to Jerusalem as penance
for his murder of Magnus. Intact until 1757, the church was then
demolished to provide material for a new church, itself later
demolished. The fragment of foundation adjacent may be that of a 12C
Norse hall.—Beyond, A964 passes *Houton* (car ferry to Hoy), then heads
north for 5m to join A965 for Stromness.

Leaving Kirkwall, A965 crosses a causeway, just beyond (north) being
Grain Earth-house, the name being that of a local estate and having
nothing to do with the earth-house's possible purpose.—*4m Rennibister
Earth-house*, a particularly good example, was discovered in 1926 when
a farm vehicle broke through the roof; below there were several human
skulls and bones.

To the south along here there are two chambered cairns. One, on
Wideford Hill, shows a central chamber and three cells, two ring walls
and a smaller than usual entrance passage. The other, *Curween*, to the
south of (*3m*) Finstown and more easily accessible, is a communal burial
cairn of c 1800 BC. Merged into the empty slope of a hill and not much

visited, this cairn permits more feel of its ancient past than do some. Human and animal remains were found here, including those of 24 dogs, suggesting that this cairn may have been associated with some hunting ritual.

3m **Maes Howe* (AM. Tel: 031-244-3101)—the first of an astonishing trio of adjacent huge prehistoric monuments—is accepted as the finest chambered tomb in Europe. The roof has been rebuilt, the chamber is artificially lit, and because of the cairn's immense size entry is easy compared to most. The name, Great Mound, is certainly well justified, for this earth and stone hump is 115ft in diameter, 24ft high and over 300ft in circumference with a ditch averaging 45ft in width. Burrowing through the mound, a low, narrow passage, 36ft long, ends at the large inner chamber, off which open burial cells, each roofed and floored by massive single stones. The whole structure is an example of extraordinary strength and skill in the art of dry-stone building, some of the stones used being immense (one weighs over three tons).

Such a place must surely have been built for a line of powerful chiefs, but—and this is the added interest of Maes Howe—their rest was disturbed perhaps 2500 years later by Norsemen, the evidence being 24 runic inscriptions made in about 1150, in their way as fascinating as the mound itself. Many of these were carved by crusaders (probably Rognvald's expedition, known to have wintered in Orkney), one telling that the tomb's treasure was removed in the course of three nights, and another, intriguingly, that it is hidden somewhere to the north west. Yet another provides a very human touch with its record that two of a band, sheltering from a snowstorm, lost their wits and were thus a great hindrance to their companions. There are also 14 personal names, an animated dragon, a walrus or seal, and a knot of serpents.—*Tormiston Mill*, by the car park, is a good example of a large 19C watermill; it now houses a restaurant and a craft shop.

Half a mile to the west the *Standing Stones of Stenness* were perhaps contemporary with Maes Howe, perhaps even at some stage ritually associated with it. Only four stones still stand—thin local flags, one of them 17ft high—but there is evidence of others, including the rock-fill which held them upright. A ditch, cut through the rock but now silted, surrounds the site, and nearby towers the 18ft-high solitary Watch Stone.—Just a mile to the north west, beside B9055, the great *Ring of Brodgar* sits on a bleak moorland isthmus between lochs Stenness and Harray. Of a probable original 60 stones, 27 are still upright within a ditch surround, hacked out of the rock and with two entrance ways.

All around this area are scattered burial mounds, lone stones and other ancient traces, combining to stir speculation as to what compulsions drove prehistoric man and why he chose this corner.

In rather over *2m* beyond Maes Howe, *Unstan Cairn*, though a lot more modest, is nevertheless archaeologically important as one of the comparatively few cairns having both stalls and a cell, the former perhaps even being on two levels. Unstan is also important because its excavation in 1844 produced the largest collection of Stone Age pottery found on any Scottish site, this now being in Edinburgh's Royal Museum of Scotland (Queen Street), as also two seated human skeletons below some runic inscriptions.

3m **Stromness** (1800 inhab. *Inf.*; heritage trail leaflet), in marine terms now little more than the dock of the car ferry from Scrabster, as also for local boats serving the south islands, has in the past enjoyed several periods of prosperity. It was long a principal port on the northern sailing routes; for over 200 years, from 1670 to 1891, it was a base for Hudson Bay Company ships; it shared briefly with Kirkwall the North American rice trade; and from 1780 to the beginning of this century Stromness supplied stores and men for the Davis Strait whalers. All this meant that every trader sought to be on the waterfront, the outcome being today's mile-long, straggling narrow main street.

This main street—in sequence John Street, Victoria Street, Graham Place, Dundas Street, Alfred Street, South End and Ness Road—passes various points of interest, first coming the ferry terminal and then, a short way farther on the left, a fountain commemorating Alexander Graham who in 1743 so staunchly opposed the tax demands made by Kirkwall that Stromness was granted independent status. Adjacent, the *Pier Arts Centre* (Tel: 0856-850209), in an 18C house and warehouse, combines a permanent exhibition of 20C British art with a programme of temporary exhibitions and also a Children's Room encouraging children to produce and show their own work. Victoria Street runs into Graham Place, recalling Alexander Graham (see above; died 1783) whose house was on the east side. Beyond, in Alfred Street, *Stromness Museum* (Tel: 0856-850025) was founded in 1837 by the Orkney Natural History Society and has occupied this building since 1858. The museum is known for its natural history collections as also for material on the Hudson Bay Company, whaling, fishing, shipping, local history and the scuppered German fleet. *Login's Well*, across the road, long supplied visiting ships with water, and the cannon, beyond, is believed to have been that of an American privateer captured in 1813; installed on its present site, it long signalled the sighting of Hudson's Bay Company vessels.

Leaving Stromness northward, A967, followed in *4m* by B9056, in a further *3m* reaches **Skara Brae* (AM. Tel: 031-244-3101), in many ways Orkney's most exciting, and certainly one of the oldest sites. Lying beside the sandy crescent of the Bay of Skaill, this Stone Age settlement

Skara Brae. A furnished home of perhaps 3000 BC

of perhaps 3000 BC comes as a welcome change from burial cairns and ritual, enabling the visitor to see something of the everyday domestic life, rather than the death, of prehistoric man. That the village has survived, though, seems to have been because of a natural disaster; because this place was buried in sand and there remained for perhaps 4000 years until revealed by a storm in 1850. This is no scattered settlement, but a small, huddled place in which vague passages link individual 'houses' or rooms, each touchingly personal with its hearth, fish larder-pools, stone beds and other primitive furniture, all fashioned from local flagstone. There is evidence that doors of some kind protected what would have been by modern standards minute entrances, and the huts may be pictured as being roofed, perhaps with skins, perhaps with some local thatch.

Much has been found here—in the way of tools, beads, pottery, and stone and whalebone artefacts—all this suggesting several periods of occupation, all based, though, on the economy of the sea.

Heading north, B9056 in *4m* passes to the east of *Marwick Head*, with a clifftop memorial to Lord Kitchener, the 1914–18 war leader who was lost in these waters in 1916 when HMS 'Hampshire', in which he was travelling to Russia, was mined. Beyond, in some *2m*, is the ruined *Earl's Palace*, a 16C rebuilding on a site where the earls of Orkney had their palace prior to the rise of Kirkwall in the 12C.

Much more interesting, though, is the early Christian and Norse complex on *Brough of Birsay* (AM. Tel: 031-244-3101), the nearby tidal island reached by foot causeway at low water. The ruins are on the landward slope and, if it is not possible to cross, a distant impression can still be achieved. Brough of Birsay is most associated with Earl Thorfinn (died 1064) and this rather confusing site includes the ruins of his Christ Church, built over the foundations of an earlier Celtic church, with, to the south, the Celtic graveyard partly underlying the Norse. Christ Church was later promoted to cathedral, and to its north are the remains of its bishop's palace, with a cloister. Lower, by the shore, sprawl the quite extensive ruins of Earl Thorfinn's hall, much complicated by the foundations of an earlier hall and what is left of later ecclesiastical buildings. Finally, spreading up the hill, are the outlines of a number of Norse long-houses. The official booklet includes a detailed tour of this complex site.

From Mill of Boardhouse, just south east of Earl's Palace, a minor road leads south east to reach in rather over 2m *Kirbuster Farm and Folk Museum* (Tel: 0856-3191) with the last surviving Orkney 'firehoose', a room with a cosy peat central hearth. From here another minor road running north beside Loch of Hundland in 2m rejoins A966.

From Earl's Palace, A966, now heading generally east, in *7m* passes below *Burgar Hill*, crowned with electricity-generating windmills alongside an RSPB bird sanctuary. A visitor centre covers both themes, and the superb view includes (north) Rousay's Scabra Head with its fine natural arch.—In another *1m* the road reaches the junction with B9057 near which is the approach (north) to *Gurness Broch* (AM. Tel: 031-244-3101) on the shore of stubby, windswept Aiker Ness across from the island of Rousay. This site shows not only the best preserved broch in Orkney, but also, around and even within the broch, an interesting if highly confused and confusing sequence of other ruins. The broch was probably the primary structure, but over the centuries down to Norse times it became shelter for various domestic buildings, including, inside the tower, partitioned chambers and, outside, cells around a central hearth and also Norse long-houses. The broch tower has two special features. One is the unusual ground-level wall passage; the other is the well, with small rock steps down to a stone cistern of clear water. The local pamphlet can be recommended for any detailed understanding of this complex site.

B9057 is now followed south west, in rather over *3m* being a sign to the *Click Mill*, a tiny turf-roofed building which is the last surviving example in Orkney of one of these old horizontal watermills. Built in 1800, the mill is of a type much older in origin.—*2m Dounby*, whence A986 leads south east into the district of Harray to pass *Corrigall Farm and Folk Museum* (Tel: 0856-3191), a restored Orkney farmhouse of the mid 19C.—*4m* (from Dounby) *Orkney Farm Park* (Tel: 0856-76243), offering ten acres of landscaped walks along which are over 40 different rare breeds of domestic animals, most playing their part in a survival breeding programme.—In another *1m* this circuit is completed at the junction with A965, from which point Kirkwall is *8m* east, the road passing the cairns and earth-houses mentioned on the outward leg.

South Mainland and South Ronaldsay

A960 and B9052 to Churchill Barrier. A961 across Burray and through South Ronaldsay to Burwick.

Total distance 21m.—*3m* **Airport**.—*6m* **Churchill Barrier (north)**.—*4m* **Island of South Ronaldsay**.—*8m* **Burwick**.

3m Kirkwall Airport.—*3m Junction with B9052*. At points along the road from Kirkwall the tall *Convenanters Memorial* can be seen on cliffs to the north east. Dating from 1888 the memorial honours some 200 Covenanters who, made prisoners after Bothwell Bridge and being transported to America, were shipwrecked here in 1697.

DIVERSION INTO DEERNESS. A960 continues east to round a sandy bay and enter the peninsula of Deerness. The island of *Copinsay*, seen away to the south east, is an RSPB bird sanctuary. In about another mile the junction of B9051 and B9050 is reached, the former leading to the *Covenanters Memorial* (2m drive, followed by 1m walk). B9050 in 2m reaches the hamlet of Skaill, from where a minor road north in 1m reaches the car park for the short walk to *The Gloup*, a spectacular collapsed cliff-cave (unfenced and dangerous). From here a narrow and dangerous cliff path approaches (¾m) the Brough of Deerness where the remains of a chapel recall that here was once a Celtic monastery, much visited by pilgrims until the 17C.

In *3m* B9052 reaches the north end of the *Churchill Barrier*, a series of four causeways linking Mainland to South Ronaldsay across the small islands of Lamb Holm, Glims Holm and Burray and thus sealing off this end of Scapa Flow.

Scapa Flow is the large protected sea area, enclosed by Mainland on the north, then, clockwise, Burray, South Ronaldsay, Flotta and Hoy. Famous as a major fleet base in 1914–18 and 1939–45, Scapa Flow has again become a centre of marine activity with the development of *Flotta* as an oil pipeline landfall and tanker terminal, second only to Sullom Voe in Shetland. In neither war were the defences anything like as impregnable as hoped and in 1917 and 1939 respectively HMS 'Vanguard' and HMS 'Royal Oak' were torpedoed, both with grievous loss of life, the second of these disasters leading to the building of the Barrier. On Germany's surrender in 1918, the greater part of her fleet (70 ships, including 10 great battleships) was ordered to Scapa Flow, and here a few months later they were almost all either beached or scuttled by their crews. Seven remain, lasting but dangerous magnets for diving enthusiasts.

Crossing the system the wrecks seen on either side are those of the old boom-ships used to secure the entrance to Scapa Flow before the construction of the Barrier. But if these wrecks, however interesting, are ugly, a softer note is early provided by the *Italian Chapel* on Lamb Holm. Inside two drab wartime Nissen huts, this is a beautiful chapel ingeniously and imaginatively built out of scrap metal in 1943 by Italian war prisoners working on the road across the Barrier. The chapel was rededicated in 1960 when restored by the original designer, Domenico Chiocchetti.

The Barrier ends in *4m* on reaching the island of **South Ronaldsay**, close to the village of *St. Margaret's Hope* on the bay into which in 1290 sailed the ship on which the Maid of Norway had died. A more modern context is provided here by the *Orkney Wireless Museum* (Tel: 085683-462), illustrating Scapa Flow's wartime communications and showing also vintage wireless sets, while other aspects of bygone local life are recalled at the *Old Smithy* (Tel: 085683-366), a restored smithy with its forge and examples of locally-made agricultural machinery and tools.—*8m Burwick* is in summer linked to John o' Groats by passenger ferry (see Access above). Additionally, a car ferry link with Gills Bay, a short way west of John o' Groats, is under consideration for the early 1990s.—The *Tomb of the Eagles*, a stalled burial chamber 1m east of Burwick by B9041, is so called because, inexplicably, the claws of many sea eagles were found here (small museum. Tel: 085683-339).

South Islands

Access. The South Islands are Hoy, Graemsay and Flotta.
Car ferries (small, seasonal, infrequent; booking advised) serve all three islands, Hoy and Flotta daily, but Graemsay only once weekly. The operator is Orkney Island Shipping, 4 Ayre Road, Kirkwall, KW15 1QX. Tel: 0856-2044. Departures are from Houton (Orphir) to Longhope and Lyness on Hoy; also, for Graemsay, from Stromness. Additionally, there is a passenger ferry linking Stromness with Graemsay (three times weekly) and Moness on Hoy (daily). Operator: S. Mowat, Barkland, Cairston Road, Stromness. Tel: 0856-850624.

Hoy is the largest and principal island of the southern group and the only one likely to be of interest to the tourist. Measuring some 12m by 6m, the island has no bus service, but car hire can be arranged. The main centre is *Longhope* in the south, the other car ferry pier being at *Lyness*, 3m to the north and once the headquarters for the Scapa Flow naval base (Interpretation Centre). The entrance to Longhope Bay, separating Longhope from Lyness, is guarded on either side by Martello towers, built in 1813–15 as protection against marauding American privateers.

Hoy is Orkney's only hilly island, with *Ward Hill* in the north rising to over 1500ft. There is also outstanding cliff scenery, notably at the north west with the *Old Man of Hoy* (450ft; path from Rackwick), a sandstone stack on a basalt base, and *St. John's Cliff* (1140ft), the highest sheer cliff in Britain, this coast well seen from the Scrabster ferry. Archaeologically the island's principal site is the *Dwarfie Stone*, near the Rackwick road 2m from the pier at Moness. Dating from perhaps 3000 BC and unique as the only example in Britain of a rock tomb, this is a sandstone block out of which a passage and two chambers have been hollowed.—**Flotta** is largely given over to oil installations. Green and pastoral **Graemsay** boasts two fine 19C lighthouses.

North Islands

Orkney's northern islands form a low-lying archipelago some 25m broad and stretching away 30 or more miles north and north east from Mainland. Popular with bird-watchers, they are also rich in prehistoric, Norse and medieval sites, and arrangements for visiting the islands are continually improving. Nevertheless some planning is required, not only to coordinate travel and accommodation but also for visiting archaeological sites, not all of which are regularly open. There are few bus services, but bicycles can be hired on many islands. Intending visitors should first consult the Orkney Tourist Board in Kirkwall which provides excellently mapped and very detailed descriptive leaflets for each island.

> **Access by sea.** Orkney Islands Shipping (4 Ayre Road, Kirkwall, KW15 1QX. Tel: 0856-2044) operates roughly as below, but note that the ferries are small (8–12 cars) and services both seasonal and in some cases varying monthly; advance booking strongly advised. Variety of special cruises.
> *Shapinsay*. Car ferry from Kirkwall. Crossing 45 minutes. About four services daily.—Ask about special Balfour Castle Package Cruise which includes the seal island of Helliar Holm.
> *Rousay, Egilsay, Wyre*. Car ferry from Tingwall (14m north of Kirkwall). About four services daily, but Sunday in summer only. Crossing (to Rousay) 20 minutes.
> *Eday, Stronsay, Sanday, Papa Westray, Westray*. Passenger ferry. Monthly timetable variation but the general pattern offers Round the Islands on four days a week, leaving Kirkwall early morning and returning late afternoon.
> *North Ronaldsay*. Passenger ferry from Kirkwall. One return service weekly.

> **Access by air.** Loganair (Tel: 0856-3457) operate scheduled flights from Kirkwall to Sanday, Stronsay, Westray, Eday, North Ronaldsay and Papa Westray. Charters and round trips can be arranged.

Shapinsay (4m by 3m), largely concerned with farming, is the most intensely cultivated of all the Orkney islands. The ferry docks in Elwick Bay, of historic interest as the place chosen by Hakon in 1263 for the assembly of his 100 or more galleys before setting sail for Largs. On the island there are some sites of modest interest, the principal being *Balfour Castle* (Tel: 085671-282), a Scottish Baronial pile built in 1848 by David Balfour, member of a family of Fife origin, one of whom, Gilbert, Master of the Household to Mary, Queen of Scots, was given lands in Orkney in 1560. More modest is *Dishan Tower*, to the west of Balfour village, said once to have served as a dovecot. From prehistory there are various survivals, notably the standing stone of *Mor Stein* (3m east of Balfour by B9059 and a minor road north) and the remains of a chambered cairn known as *Castle Bloody* and standing on Shapinsay's only moorland to the south east of Mor Stein. Seals can be watched from many points around the coast, and visitors with an interest in literature may note that Quholm in the north east of the island was the home of the parents of the American writer Washington Irving.

Rousay (6m by 5m) is the best island for prehistory, the principal sites being within 5m of the pier and along the island's south shore road. Nearest, and all within 2m, are three burial cairns, the first being *Taversoe Tuick*, with two storeys each with its own entrance passage. Next comes *Blackhammer*, where the chamber shows seven divisions; in 1936 two skeletons were found here together with some pottery and flint artefacts. The last cairn is *Knowe of Yarso*, a stalled cairn with four compartments. Excavation here in 1934 revealed a large and baffling collection of bones—of 29 humans, 36 deer, several sheep and a dog—as also pottery, flint and bone artefacts.

But the best site, *Midhowe*, is 3m farther, with, adjacent to one another, a chambered cairn and a broch. The cairn is an exceptionally large one of the stalled type, in which the chamber is 76ft long and 7ft wide with 24 burial stalls arranged 12 on each side. The remains of 25 individuals were found here, together with pottery of the Unstan type. The adjacent broch, 30ft in diameter, is still in part 14ft high.—On the nearby island of *Eynhallow* (Norse for Holy Island) the ruined church probably belonged to a Benedictine monastery of c 1100.

On **Wyre** (3m by less than 1m) stands the ruin of the 12C stronghold of Kolbein Hruga, a Norse robber baron. With a keep and later outworks, this ruin is popularly known as *Cubbie Roo's Castle*. The nearby church was probably built by Hruga's son, Bishop Bjarni, in c 1190; it was partly rebuilt in the late 19C.

Egilsay (3m by 1m) is known for its 12C *Church of St. Magnus*, notable architecturally for its lofty round tower (Irish in design, but one of only three such in Scotland) and historically for standing on or close to the site where Magnus was murdered in 1116. Although now roofless, the church was in use until well into the 19C. A monument of 1938, just south of the church, is said to mark the actual site of the murder.

Stronsay, erratic in shape but roughly 6m from north to south, is flat and fertile with, at Whitehall in the north, a fish processing factory. On Lamb Head, at the south east tip of the island, there is a small broch, near a stone construction running into the sea which may represent a Pictish or Norse pier.

Sanday, 12m long and shaped like a grotesque fish, is archaeologically best known for *Quoyness Cairn* on the small south shore promontory of Els Ness. It shows a central chamber with six cells.

Eday (8m long) is separated from the small *Calf of Eday* by the narrow Calf Sound, the most scenic passage of the steamer route. A chambered cairn on the Calf is archaeologically of particular interest for being built above an earlier stone structure, perhaps a tomb or perhaps a minute home.

Westray, for the most part narrow, measures some 10m from north to south. The island's northern pier is at Pierowall, $\frac{1}{2}$m to the west being the quite extensive ruins of *Noltland Castle* (16C), built by Gilbert Balfour, Master of the Household to Mary, Queen of Scots, but in 1650 burnt by Covenanters. Features here are the hall, the vaulted kitchen and the tiers of gunloops in the wall, reminding that even on a remote island such as this attack could always be expected. There are also two medieval churches on Westray, *St. Mary's* (ruined; 13C south wall, remainder 17C) at Pierowall being historically interesting as successor to the church in which Rognvald heard Mass on his first arrival in Orkney in 1136. The other, and slightly older, church is *Crosskirk* (12C), on the shore near Tuquoy 3m south of Pierowall. Finally, Jacobite days are recalled by the name *Gentlemen's Cave*, to the north west on the south side of Noup Head, a refuge for several survivors of Culloden (difficult and dangerous access).

Papa Westray, 4m long and off the north east of Westray, is deeply associated with early Christianity. Not only does the island owe its name to the several hermits who once sought seclusion here, but ruined *St. Tredwell's Chapel*, beside the loch of the same name and built above a broch, is dedicated to that probably legendary saint, also known as Triduana, once believed to have had the power to cure diseases of the eyes (see also Rte 18F, Restalrig). Of unknown age, this chapel is also said to be on the spot at which Christianity first took root in Orkney.

But man was here millenia before the Christian hermits, as evidenced by *Knap of Howar* on the island's west coast. Dated to between 2400–

2800 BC these remains of two well-built side-by-side stone houses rank as the oldest still standing dwellings in north west Europe. And prehistoric man even reached the tiny *Holm of Papa*, leaving his mark with two chambered cairns, one a large one with a triple central chamber and several wall cells.

North Ronaldsay, forming a rough crescent 4m long, is Orkney's most northern island. Very low lying, it is surrounded by a dyke outside which the small native sheep live largely on the local rich red seaweed. The remains of a broch, *Broch of Burrian*, the hub of an extensive Iron Age settlement, guard the island's southern tip.

68 Shetland

The Shetland group, its principal island over 60 miles north of Orkney and on about the same latitude as the southern point of Greenland, comprises nearly 100 islands, of which only 12 are inhabited, and several of these precariously. The principal island, with the capital at *Lerwick* and the main airport 26 miles south at *Sumburgh*, is called *Mainland*; it is some 50 miles long and so indented that it varies in width from 20 miles to a few yards. The chief other islands are *Unst*, *Yell* and *Fetlar* to the north east; *Whalsay*, *Out Skerries* and *Bressay*, off Mainland's east coast; *Papa Stour* off the west shore; and, far to the south and west respectively, *Fair Isle* and *Foula*.

The name Shetland derives from the Norse 'Hjaltland' meaning 'High land', and for the most part the scenery is upland peat bog and grass or heath moor with countless small lochs, rising at *Ronas Hill* on Mainland to nearly 1500ft. The coast—and no place in Shetland is more than 3 miles from the sea—provides continual contrast, being in places pierced by long, tranquil, winding inlets or voes, and in places awesome cliffs battered by fierce seas into arches, fissures and stacks. Trees are rare, cultivation patchy, and almost everywhere there are sheep, including the distinctive Shetland black and brown, said to be identical with the wild sheep of Siberia. The small, hardy, native Shetland ponies will also be seen. Until the early 1970s the people were mainly fishermen, crofters or those serving local needs, but with the development of the oil installations some change has come, especially to Mainland. But the visitor in search of remoteness and scenery need have no fears since significant oil industrialisation is confined to the comparatively small Sullom Voe area of Mainland.

Two archaeological sites (*Jarlshof* and *Mousa*, the latter accessible only by boat in about May to Sept) are amongst the most important in Britain. These apart, it is the constantly changing coast that will most attract the visitor. Special arrangements are necessary for visits to the distant islands, but car ferries serve Unst, Yell, Fetlar, Whalsay and Bressay. In summer there are coach tours, but normal bus services, timed mainly to run from outlying districts into Lerwick in the morning, returning in the evening, are of little use to the touring visitor. A car gives most flexibility and is essential if time is a consideration. Even with a car at least three days should be allowed if the full opportunities of the coast are to be explored and sites such as Jarlshof and Mousa given the attention they deserve. Car transport to Shetland is expensive and the cost should be weighed against that of hiring; self-drive hire is efficiently organised and cars can be picked up either at the airport or in Lerwick, but there is heavy demand in summer and booking is essential.

Shetland knitwear, with its traditional designs, is world famous. The fine wool is not shorn but plucked or 'roo'ed' from the sheep's neck. Due though to mainland spinning the local knitwear is to a decreasing extent made purely of this soft wool. Shops in Lerwick and elsewhere offer a wide choice of knitwear at surprisingly low prices. In summer there are exhibitions in Lerwick at Isleburgh Community Centre and in the Town Hall (knitting, carding, spinning).

Birds. Many visitors are attracted to Shetland by the wealth of bird life, the birds dividing roughly into seabirds, northern birds, and migrants. The seabirds include gulls, auks, puffins, storm petrels, shags, guillemots, razorbills, fulmars (who first arrived about 100 years ago), and gannets (first seen in the early years of this century). These birds will be found in their thousands on the cliffs throughout Shetland, but special mention may be made of the nature reserves of Hermaness and Noss. Northern birds, some rare, include the red-necked phalarope, the whimbrel, skuas, and red-throated divers (known in Shetland as rain geese). The migrants are too varied to name. They are most numerous on the east side of the group, and Fair Isle, with its observatory, is internationally famous as a migration station.

Tourist Organisation. Shetland Tourist Organisation, Market Cross, Lerwick, ZE1 0LU. Tel: 0595-3434.

Access. By *Sea*, services are operated by P and O Ferries, PO Box 5, Jamieson's Quay, Aberdeen, AB9 8DL. Tel: 0224-572615. The principal and direct link is the overnight (14 hours) car ferry from Aberdeen, normally operating five times weekly. Another service (infrequent, seasonal) is from Aberdeen to Lerwick via Stromness on Orkney (Crossing Aberdeen–Stromness 8 hours; Stromness–Lerwick 8 hours).

Air services between mainland Scotland, Orkney and Shetland (Sumburgh) are operated by British Airways (Tel: 0345-222111); to Lerwick (Tingwall) by Loganair (Glasgow Airport, Paisley. Tel: 041-889-3181).

Inter-Island Communications. For ferries see under individual islands. Loganair operate scheduled air services from Tingwall to Fetlar, Unst, Whalsay and Fair Isle (Tel: 059584-246).

SOME HOTELS. **Lerwick**. *Grand*, Commercial Street. Tel: 0595-2826. *Kveldsro House*, Greenfield Place, ZE1 0AN. Tel: 0595-2195. *Shetland*, Holmsgarth Road, ZE1 0PW. Tel: 0595-5515. **Sumburgh**. *Sumburgh*, ZE3 9JN. Tel: 0950-60201. **Whiteness**. *Westings*, Wormadale, ZE2 9LJ. Tel: 059584-242. **Walls**. *Burrastow House*, ZE2 9PB. Tel: 059577-307. **Brae**. *Busta House*, ZE2 9QN. Tel: 080622-506. **Hillswick**. *St. Magnus Bay*, ZE2 9RW. Tel: 080623-372.

On **Yell**. *North Isles*, Sellafirth, ZE2 9DG. Tel: 095784-293. On **Unst**. *Baltasound*. Tel: 095781-334.

Lerwick and Scalloway

Lerwick and Scalloway are Shetland's two principal centres.

Lerwick (7000 inhab. *Inf.*), Britain's most northern town, has a lively harbour and waterfront, home to ships and sailors of many nations, especially Scandinavian and Russian. The town's business and prosperity have much increased as the result of the development of Sullom Voe (20m north) as an oil terminal.

History. The Iron Age and earlier people who lived here are represented by Clickhimin broch; the town's Norse origin by its name, meaning Clay Creek. Bressay Sound was long known as a refuge for seafarers and was an assembly place for Hakon's 200 galleys bound for Largs. But it was the use of the Sound by Dutch fishermen early in the 17C that led to the growth of Lerwick. In 1640 the Dutch fishing fleet's armed escort was attacked here and sunk by French warships. In 1653 a great boost was given to the town's future when 94 ships of Cromwell's fleet arrived, landing troops to build what is now Fort Charlotte, possibly the town's first permanent building. But the Dutch returned in 1673, burning part of the town.

Lerwick's Fire Festival, *Up Helly Aa*, a pagan survival welcoming the return of the sun, is held on the last Tuesday in January. A long procession with flaming torches is headed by a Viking chieftain and a replica of a galley. To end the festival the torches are thrown on to the galley to make a bonfire.

Another touch of the Norse tradition is provided by the *'Dim Riv'*, a replica of a Viking longship which takes visitors around the harbour (details from Tourist Information).

Lerwick's main street is Commercial Street, an attractively flagstoned, irregular and sometimes narrow road running roughly parallel with the waterfront. *Fort Charlotte*, near this street's north west end, was built in 1653, burned by the Dutch in 1673, repaired and given a new interior in 1781 when a large barrack block was added, and ranks today as the only intact Cromwellian military structure surviving in Scotland. The ramparts provide splendid views.

Above Commercial Street rises the district of Hillhead, where the *Town Hall* (Tel: 0595-3535) has some fine stained glass windows illustrating Shetland's story. Opposite, in a modern building, is the admirable *Shetland Museum* (Tel: 0595-5057) showing ship models and navigation instruments; prehistoric and early Christian material, the latter including the delightful Monks' Stone showing a procession of priests, sculptured stones from St. Ninian's Isle and replicas of the treasure found there; Shetland knitting; wireless telegraphy equipment; and articles salvaged from a Dutch East Indiaman wrecked on Out Skerries in 1711.

But *°Clickhimin Broch*, on the town's south west outskirts, the massive legacy left by Lerwick's prehistoric and Iron Age ancestors, will for many visitors be the town's most memorable site. Forming an island at the end of a causeway into a small loch, the broch—65ft in diameter and with walls 18ft thick and 15ft high—stands on a great stone platform with a gateway and an enclosure. The broch, though, is no more than the

A reconstructed view of Clickhimin Broch (Crown Copyright: reproduced by permission of Historic Buildings and Monuments, Scottish Development Department)

visible survival of one period in the life of a complex site, perhaps occupied from the 6C BC to the 5 or 7C AD and in turn primitive settlement, dun, broch and wheelhouse.

The island of *Bressay* (300 inhab.) is visited from Lerwick (Car ferry. Frequent. Tel: 0595-2024). For many the objective of the visit will be the small island of *Noss* 200 yards off Bressay's east shore, a bird sanctuary whose lofty headland of Noup of Noss (592ft) has a cliff-face alive with seabirds, including a colony of gannets (Visitors are ferried across by inflatable dinghy, but before leaving for Bressay should confirm with Tourist Information that the weather and sea conditions permit the crossing).

Scalloway (1000 inhab.), on the west coast 5m from Lerwick and until about 200 years ago the village capital of Shetland, is now mainly concerned with fish processing, one of the factories (L. Williamson. Tel: 059588-237) welcoming visitors. But Scalloway's most prominent feature is the stark ruin of *Earl Patrick's Castle*; built with local forced labour in 1600, in a medieval style already oldfashioned, the castle was abandoned on its owner's execution only 15 years later. In the harbour area a plaque recording a visit here in 1942 by Prince (later King) Olaf recalls that during the last war Scalloway was a base for Norwegian patriots carrying out clandestine operations, and that the expression to 'take the Shetland bus' meant to escape from Norway to Shetland. *Scalloway Museum* (Tel: 059588-256), in Main Street, tells the local story from prehistoric to 'Shetland bus' times.

Bridges connect Scalloway southwards with the islands of *Trondra* and *Burra* (west and east), their length (6m) served by a scenic if desolate road of moorland and waterscapes. The hamlet of Papil, at the south of West Burra, was an early Christian centre and the place where the Monks' Stone (see Shetland Museum above) was found as also the Papil Stone now in the Royal Museum of Scotland.

South Mainland (Lerwick to Sumburgh Airport and Jarlshof)

A970 (south), with diversion loop along B9122.—South Mainland is a long narrow finger of mixed moor and downland. The road follows the east side, generally running well above the shore and affording good coastal views.

Total distance 27m.—*13m* **Leebitton (Mousa)**.—*5m* **St. Ninian's Isle**.—*5m* **Croft House Museum**.—*3m* **Sumburgh Airport**.—*1m* **Jarlshof**.

Passing *Clickhimin Broch* the road in *3m* reaches *Hollanders' Knowe*, once a Dutch trading point but now marking the junction with B9073 for Scalloway.—*10m* **Leebitton**, below the road, is the pier for visits to the island and broch of ****Mousa**, reached in about 15 minutes (Tom Jamieson. Tel: 09505-367 to arrange mutually convenient timing. Summer only). This is by far the most complete of Scotland's more than 500 brochs and also, standing as it does on the shore of an empty island, one of the country's most exciting sites and one, too, with a colourful past. Here, it is said, the local Picts successfully sought refuge from Roman slave hunters; and here, many centuries later, in 1150 if the sagas are to be believed, a Norse nobleman hid with the famous beauty with whom he was eloping. Since then, and even allowing for some careful restoration, structurally and scenically not a great deal can have changed and Mousa still stands over 50ft in diameter, 45ft high and with walls tapering from 12ft to 7ft in thickness. And within the walls there are still galleries and stairways, by one of which a walkway around the tower's top can be reached.

In *3m* after rejoining the main road a worthwhile diversion can be made along the westerly loop provided by B9122, this in *2m* reaching the hamlet of *Bigton*. Here a small road drops to the sandy shore where the car may be parked and the isthmus crossed to **St. Ninian's Isle**, its bare and breezy downland, today occupied only by ponies and sheep, once the home of an early Christian monastic settlement. All that stands here now, easily reached and overlooking the isthmus, are the lower courses of a 12C chapel. But excavation in 1958 revealed the remains of a pre-Norse church, and, under a stone slab, a magnificent hoard of 8C Celtic silver, perhaps buried by the monks when faced with the threat of Viking raids. This silver is now in Edinburgh, but good replicas can be seen in the Shetland Museum in Lerwick. About ½m south of the chapel there is a Holy Well, seeping out from the peat as a small crystal clear spring.

In another *4m* B9122 rejoins A970 at *Boddam*, just south of which (*1m*) is the *Croft House Museum* (Tel: 0595-5057), convincingly preserving a picture of croft life as it was in the mid 19C. Here are the cottage, barn, byre and stable, all attached to one another and provided with the authentic household utensils of the day, while down the hill, beside a burn, a horizontal watermill, of original Norse design, still turns.

As the road drops to (*3m*) **Sumburgh Airport** there can be a distant view ahead of Fair Isle, while to the west rears *Fitful Head*, so named from the Norse 'hvitfugla' meaning white birds.

**Jarlshof (AM. Tel: 031-244-3101) is less than *1m* farther, near the hotel beside the south end of the main runway. This fanciful Norse name (an invention by Sir Walter Scott for his book 'The Pirate') is in fact highly misleading because this archaeological complex, accepted as being one of the most important in Britain, dates from at least the Bronze Age and displays the remains of five distinct periods of occupation piled around and on top of one another over perhaps 3000 or more years. The small Museum is well worth a visit, if only for its plan of the site as also for a series of pictures imaginatively illustrating how Jarlshof may have looked at various stages of its occupation.

The ruins, sprawling across a low promontory by the sea's edge, are inevitably confusing, but plaques well identify the various periods. From the Bronze Age there are huts, as well as evidence both of farming (with one of Britain's earliest cattle stalls) and of a metal worker's shop. The Iron Age is represented by two earth-houses, a broch with an outer defence wall (perhaps 1C) and also by rather later (3–8C) wheel-houses. These last, probably family homes, take the form of a number of individual recesses spoked around a central hearth and, with so much still clearly identifiable, are perhaps the most satisfying remains at Jarlshof. Norse settlement here of one kind or another probably spanned some 500 years (9–14C) but the builders of those centuries have left only a confusion of long-house remains. Next come the foundations of a medieval farmstead (14–16C), and then, most recent and most prominent, the walls of the 16C house of earls Robert and Patrick Stewart.

Nearby *Grutness Pier* is used by the boats for Fair Isle, while *Sumburgh Head*, notorious for its tidal races, has a lighthouse (1821, and only in 1975 converted from paraffin to electricity).

Across the bay, at the tip of its west arm (½m walk), the substantial ruin of *Ness of Burgi* was an Iron Age fort of what is known as the 'blockhouse' type, believed to have been the immediate predecessor of the brochs.

North Mainland (Lerwick to Esha Ness or Sandvoe)

A970 (north), followed by B9078 to Esha Ness.—Moor, inland lochs and seascapes.

Total distance 36m.—*5m* **Veensgarth.**—*5m* **Loch Girlsta.**—*6m*
Voe.—*5m* **Brae** (for **Sullom Voe**).—*6m* **A970 split,** followed by *9m*
Esha Ness or *9m* **Sandvoe.**

3m Bridge of Fitch where a branch of A970 leads off south west for
Scalloway.—*2m* **Veensgarth** is a scattered and characterless valley
community around a crossroads and Tingwall airfield. From here A971
(see West Mainland, below) heads north west for West Burrafirth and
Sandness, while B9074 drops south beside Loch of Tingwall to reach
Scalloway. A diversion of 2m as far as the south end of the loch should
be made by anyone attracted by Shetland's Norse period because this
Tingwall valley is historic as the meeting place of the island's parliament and law court, the Althing. The actual site is believed to have
been *Law Ting Holm*, a small promontory, in Norse days an island,
jutting into the north west corner of the loch. Beyond, B9074 skirts the
loch below (west) Gallows Hill—scene not only of hangings but also in
the early 18C of the burning of a mother and daughter, both accused of
witchcraft—to reach the foot of the loch where a standing stone
reminds that prehistoric man too regarded this valley as important.

More recent times, largely 19C, are recalled by the Shetland bygones
shown in the *Tingwall Agricultural Museum* at Veensgarth (Tel:
059584-344), a fascinating clutter covering crofting, fishing and domestic life, all housed in an 18C granary and stables. And something more of
this past and local atmosphere can be enjoyed by attending one of the
folklore evenings held here on certain days in summer (Bookings and
transport arrangements through Tourist Information).

In *5m* A970 runs beside *Loch Girlsta*, tracing its name to that of a
Norse maiden, Geirhilda, said to have died tragically and to be buried
on an island.

DIVERSION INTO LUNNA NESS (B9075, B9071 and unclassified; north
east, 14m to Lunna). B9075 branches east just beyond Loch Girlsta to
wind across remote and empty countryside with fine views to reach
(9m) *Laxo*, pier for the car ferry to Whalsay. (Laxo can also be reached
more quickly if less interestingly by continuing north along A970 for a
further 6m beyond Loch Girlsta and then turning east for 2m along
B9071). From Laxo B9071, becoming an unclassified road, continues for
5m to *Lunna*, halfway along Lunna Ness. Here the small church (1753)
has a leper squint, while, in a more modern context, Lunna House was
during the last war the headquarters of the Norwegian resistance.
Lunna is also the place where a North Sea oil pipeline crosses this
peninsula, making its landfall at Grut Wick (1½m north east), thence
running south west down the promontory to Cul Ness from where it
continues below the water to reach Sullom Voe.

From Loch Girlsta A970 heads due north for *(6m)* **Voe**, near which a
number of roads meet. B9071 leads east for (2m) Laxo and the car ferry to
Whalsay; A968 continues north for (9m) Toft and the car ferry to Yell,
and thence to Unst and Fetlar; B9071 wanders south west to meet the
West Mainland road (see below) at Bixter.

Beyond Voe A970 skirts *Olna Firth*, once busy as the last whaling
station in Shetland.—*5m* **Brae**, where the motorist curious about the
Sullom Voe oil terminal should take B9076 which, passing Scatsta airfield, in under 5m skirts the terminal complex, thence continuing for
another 4m to reach the Yell car ferry pier at Toft.

Sullom Voe Oil Terminal. During the last war Sullom Voe was an active, operational flying-boat base; today oil has taken over, as huge tankers are fed by the

North Sea pipelines. The terminal, with its tanker jetties, occupies the peninsula of *Calbeck Ness*, now joined to the mainland by reclaimed land, formerly part loch and part tidal pool.

In *1m*, at *Mavis Grind*, A970 crosses a short narrow isthmus where the Atlantic and the North Sea—the latter represented by the head of Sullom Voe, the former by a small sea loch—wash within a few yards of one another. Here the road enters the district of Northmavine, probably the most scenic in Mainland, in rather over *5m* reaching a road fork where A970 splits. A useful and very scenic link between this road's westward and northward arms is provided by an unclassified road running from the head of Ura Firth on the westward arm to skirt beautiful Ronas Voe and join the northward arm at this voe's head. Along this road a touch of history is provided by a monument known as the *Hollanders' Grave*, visible on the hill immediately west of Skeo Head Pier, 1m north of Ura Firth. This marks the grave of Dutch seamen killed in 1674 when their Indiaman, the 'Wapen van Rotterdam', sheltered in Ronas Voe where it was found and taken by the frigate 'Newcastle', though not without a fight.

TO ESHA NESS. A970 loops the head of Ura Firth, passing the small road described immediately above, and in *4m* ends at the village of *Hillswick*. Just before the village the westward road becomes B9078, this soon affording good if sometimes distant seaward views of strangely shaped scattered stacks. This road ends in *5m* at *'Esha Ness* (lighthouse) where, but with caution, the precipitous cliff edge can be approached with its view northward to the *Grind of the Navir* (Gateway of the Giants), a mile's length of awesome eroded cliffs, stacks and clefts facing the unbroken assault of the Atlantic and alive with screaming seabirds.

TO SANDVOE. Heading north from the road split, this northward arm of A970 in under *3m* passes close to the head of Ronas Voe (for the small road along the voe, see above), the high ground to the north west here rising to *Ronas Hill* (1475ft), Shetland's highest point. In *3m*, after skirting Colla Firth, the road reaches the oval *Loch of Housetter* with, clearly seen a few yards west of the road, two standing stones and, a short way north, a chambered cairn where, amid the rubble, the entrance passage can still be traced. Beyond, the road ends at (*3m*) the hamlet of *Isbister* or, beside its small voe, that of *Sandvoe*, while Mainland tapers away northward as a promontory ending as the narrow Point of Fethaland, continued, a mile or so away, by a scatter of skerries and stacks.

West Mainland (Lerwick to Sandness)

A970 to Veensgarth. A971 to Sandness.—Beside voes, followed by moorland broken by many small lochs.

Total distance 25m.—*5m* **Veensgarth**.—*10m* **Bixter**.—*2m* **Stanydale Temple**.—*3m* **Bridge of Walls**.—*5m* **Sandness**.

For Lerwick to (*5m*) **Veensgarth**, see North Mainland above. In *2m* A971 crosses *Wormadale Hill*, above the head of Whiteness Voe and affording grand views, before dropping to round the south end of *Strom Loch*, with, on an islet, fragments of Strom Castle, medieval in date, though almost certainly on the site of an Iron Age dun. The castle's story is shadowy, but it was perhaps an early residence of the Sinclair lords before the building of their castle at Scalloway. *Hjaltasteyn*, beside A971, shows and sells handcrafted jewellery using Shetland gemstones (Tel: 059584-351). Beyond, in rather over *3m*, the road kinks round the head of Weisdale Voe, a short way to the north here being *Kergord* with the largest stand of trees in Shetland. Weisdale was the birthplace in 1786 of the remarkable John Clunie Ross who settled in the Cocos Islands, becoming 'King' and having his sovereignty recognised by Queen Victoria.

5m **Bixter**, from where a road meanders northward for 10m to meet A970 at Voe. From just beyond Bixter, too, B9071 runs south to reach (4m, to the east) *Sand*, with fragments of a chapel traditionally, though apparently without evidence, built by the crew of a Spanish Armada galleon wrecked here.

In *2m* beyond Bixter an unclassified road leads south to reach in another 1½m the (probably wet) moorland path to (½m) the intriguing Stone Age site known as *Stanydale Temple*. Hut remains beside the path, and scattered generally around, tell that this uninviting and remote moor was once home to a sizeable Stone Age community, centred presumably on the heel-shaped 'temple'; called such because similar ancient buildings in the Mediterranean, and especially in Malta, are so classified, though it seems equally if not more likely that this place served some domestic communal purpose. Walls, some 12ft thick, enclose an oval chamber with stalls, and floor holes can be seen into which roof support poles would have been fitted. And a further puzzle is provided by the fact that wood traces found here have been analysed as spruce, a tree believed not to have existed in Scotland before the 16C, this prompting the suggestion that the prehistoric builders used driftwood washed across from America.

Along A971, in another *1m*, an unclassified road leads north for (4m) *West Burrafirth* for sailings to the island of Papa Stour.—*2m Bridge of Walls* where A971 splits, the left fork soon reaching *Walls*, for sailings to Foula. The right fork for some *5m* traverses a district of continual small lochs before curving through **Sandness**, a name embracing a group of crofting communities. Papa Stour lies a mile or so offshore, and Foula, over 20m away, may also be seen.

Islands of Yell, Fetlar and Unst

The islands of Yell, Fetlar and Unst are linked by car ferries. Toft (Mainland) to Ulsta (Yell), 20 minutes crossing. Gutcher (Yell) to Belmont (Unst), 10 minutes crossing, or one hour if routed through Fetlar. Gutcher (Yell) to Oddsta (Fetlar), 20 minutes crossing. The service through Yell to Unst runs daily, roughly hourly; Fetlar service roughly 4 services daily, but fewer on Sunday. Advance booking is advised. Tel: 095782-259 or 268.—Air services to Unst and Fetlar from Tingwall (Loganair).

Yell (17m by 6m; 1200 inhab.) is in large part made up of rolling peat moor. Between Ulsta (ferry) and Mid Yell there is a choice between a westerly or an easterly road. The former is rather faster; the latter more interesting and more scenic, passing crofts and hamlets and with views across to Out Skerries and Fetlar. Along this latter road, at Burravoe (4m from Ulsta), *Old Haa* (Tel: 095782-339), a large white crowstepped building dating from 1637 and the oldest building on the island, is a local museum and arts and crafts centre.

A drive northward from Gutcher is worth considering. In 4m, where the road curves and dips west at Brough, the oval Kirk Loch comes into view to the north, beside its west shore being the roofless *Kirk of Ness* (grass path a little farther down the road), a medieval church dedicated to St. Olaf but abandoned in 1750. Beyond, to the north between the church and the shore and half lost in sand and grass, there is an extensive and challenging wilderness of stone fragments, of (to the layman) unintelligible pattern but thought to represent perhaps thousands of years of prehistoric and later occupation. The cliffs here are magnificent, but their rims are brittle and dangerous. This drive should be continued for another 2m to Gloup where the *Fishermen's Memorial* (sign; short walk), on the hillside overlooking Gloup Voe, really tells its own story. During the 19C this voe was the home of a substantial fishing community, devastated on 20 July 1881 when in a great storm ten boats and 58 men were lost.

Fetlar (5m by 3m), the name being Norn for Fat Land, is Shetland's most fertile island. That prehistoric man took advantage of this is clear from the several cairns, brochs and other remains, while some ruined chapels represent medieval if not earlier Christianity. But it is as a nature reserve, and especially as a bird sanctuary—most popularly for the snowy owl—that Fetlar is best known. Visiting ornithologists are asked to contact the RSPB warden (Tel: 095783-246).

Unst (12m by 5m), a mix of bleak rolling downland and peat moor and Britain's northernmost inhabited island, is known for its ponies, cliff scenery and fine knitted work, though sadly this last is disappearing. The main road (A968) runs virtually the length of the island from the ferry pier at Belmont to the two scattered centres of Baltasound and Haroldswick, but within 2½m from the ferry both eastward and westward diversions should be made.

The first (east) rounds Uyea Sound, soon passes a standing stone and in 3m reaches *Muness Castle*, a desolate ruin in a not much less desolate landscape but interesting for having been built for Lawrence Bruce in 1598 by the same man who designed Scalloway's castle. This Lawrence Bruce was related to, and is reputed to have been almost as evil as, the notorious Earl Patrick, and this castle seems to have lasted not much longer than Scalloway, being burnt down, possibly by French privateers. Nevertheless, apart from the top storey—which was pulled down to provide material for the enclosure wall—the shell is more or less complete, among features being, below the windows, the shot-holes decorated with rings and trefoils; the decorated turrets; and, in the kitchen, the oven and sink, the latter still with its drain.—*Haaf Gruney*, an uninhabited island 2m south of Muness, is a national nature reserve where storm petrels breed amid the remains of a long-disused chromite mine.

The westward diversion (signed to Westing) in ½m reaches a yet smaller road leading down towards the sea and almost immediately passing a large, rough standing stone. Beyond, the road deteriorates into a track, at the end by the shore being the ruined 12C church of *Lund*, in use until 1785. Here will be found the graves of two merchants from Bremen (died 1573 and 1585), today just two names but in their time surely respected representatives of the Hanseatic trade; see also Whalsay, below. The Westing road continues north west, in 1m breasting a rise with, on the left, the grass-covered mound of a broch, notable for the extent of its surrounding earthworks. And in another mile, as the road dips to cross a burn by a stone bridge opposite a ruined house, will be found a restored, horizontal click mill of original Norse design.

A968 crosses a featureless landscape to reach first *Baltasound*, with the island's airfield to the south, and then the equally scattered community of *Haroldswick*, named after Harald Haarfagr (see Orkney and Shetland, Common History) who in 875 based himself first on Fetlar and then here before annexing the islands. Here is Britain's most northern post office, and visitors may have their mail franked to this effect.

Three roads fan northward out of Haroldswick. B9087 (north east) in a short mile reaches *Norwick*, Britain's most northern village and the home of the Unst Heritage Centre (Tel: 095781-528) at which the Unst History Group illustrates all manner of local activities ranging from the story of Shetland wool and knitting to a croft living room with its open hearth; the collection of old photographs is of particular interest. Beyond, in about 1m, an unclassified road reaches Britain's most northern house. The second road (unclassified) climbs due north to Saxa Vord (936ft), named, it is said, after a Norse giant but today crowned by Ministry of Defence installations and boasting that here, in 1962, was registered the British wind speed record of 177 mph, at which point the anemometer blew away. From here there is a superb view across the deep and beautiful inlet of *Burra Firth*, with, beyond its mouth, *Muckle Flugga* and its lighthouse. The west side of Burra Firth, between the firth and the open sea, forms *Hermaness National Nature Reserve*, one of Scotland's most important seabird sanctuaries, with skuas breeding on the moorland, and colonies of gannets, puffins, guillemots, kittiwakes and others on the 600ft-high cliffs. The base of the reserve is quickly (2m) reached by B9086 out of Haroldswick, the promontory then stretching over 2m north from the road's end.

Other Islands

Whalsay (5m by 2m; 1000 inhab.), 3m off Mainland's east coast, is reached by Loganair from Tingwall or by car ferry from Laxo (Crossing 30 minutes. Several times daily. Tel: 095782-268). The island prospers through fishing and fish processing, that this has long been the case evidenced by the so-called *Bremen Böd*, near Symbister pier, a 17C Hanseatic store and trading booth, the only complete surviving example in Scotland; today the building serves as a local interpretive centre for visitors. Nor need interest be confined to this pier area, for in the north east, beyond the hamlet of Isbister, there are the *Standing Stones of Yoxie*, a small complex dated to c 2000 BC, while nearby is the so-called *Bunzie House*, also of the Stone Age and, it has been suggested, perhaps serving as a kind of vestry for the priests.

Out Skerries form an island-group some 5m to the north east of Whalsay. Only the two main islands (adjacent and joined by a bridge) are inhabited, the 100 or fewer people living by fishing and fish processing in a modern, mechanised factory opened in 1970. The islands are reached by twice-weekly car ferry from Lerwick, the crossing requiring three hours. Tel: 0595-2024.

Papa Stour, volcanic in origin and with a coast that is all bays, stacks, natural arches and caves, of which it has some of the finest in Britain, measures some 3m by 2m and supports a population of some 40 people. As its name suggests—it means Great Island of the Priests—Papa Stour was associated with the early Christian hermits and missionaries. Later, until the 18C, the islet of *Brei Holm* off the east coast was used as a leper colony. Just off Mainland's west coast opposite Sandness, Papa Stour is reached by boat from West Burrafirth. Crossing 30 minutes. Tel: 059586-335.

Foula (Bird Island), 20m west of Papa Stour and measuring only 2m square, is a wild, remote island with cliffs 1200ft high, home to countless seabirds including the largest skua colony in Britain. Once 300 people lived here—many of them Norse descendants for the Norn language survived here until about 1800—but their number is now down to about forty. The island is reached by boat from Walls (Once or twice weekly. Tel: 03933-3232, but also consult Tourist Information, Lerwick, because the island can be isolated for lengthy periods by bad weather and visitors must rely on their own supplies).

Fair Isle (3m by 1m; population 80), lying halfway between Shetland and Orkney and since 1954 owned by the National Trust for Scotland, has a name long associated with intricate knitwear patterns, an art which some trace back to Spaniards wrecked here during the Armada of 1588. Today the local Cooperative sells island products worldwide. Otherwise—and increasingly since the establishment in 1948 of the Bird Observatory Trust—it is birds that rule here, the island being an internationally recognised ornithological habitat and an important migratory staging station.—By sea Fair Isle is reached by boat from Grutness. Twice weekly in summer. Once weekly in winter. Crossing three hours. Tel: 03512-222. For accommodation at the Bird Observatory, apply The Warden. Tel: 03512-258. Day visits can be made by Loganair from Tingwall.

INDEX

Topographical names are in **bold** print; names of persons in *italics*; other entries, including subsidiary indexes, in Roman print. Where there are two or more page references the more important are in appropriate cases printed **bold**.

Key Map to Atlas Pages

Motorway	
Trunk Roads	
Other Main Roads	
Secondary Roads	
Railways	

Castles, Mansions, Palaces and Towers   *

Abbeys, Chapels and Churches   ▪

Prehistoric, Iron Age and Roman sites   ◇

Other places of interest   ★

0   10   20 miles
0   10   20   30   40 kms

15

SHETLAND

FOULA

FAIR ISLE

14

ORKNEY

○Wick

OUTER
HEBRIDES
10

11

12

13

○ Inverness

Aberdeen ○

○ Fort
William

INNER
HEBRIDES
6

7

8

Dundee ○ **9**

Perth ○

○ St Andrews

Stirling ○

☐
GLASGOW

☐
EDINBURGH

Berwick
-upon
Tweed

2

○ Ayr

3

4

5

Dumfries ○

Stranraer ○

○ Carlisle

2500	
2000	
1600	Explanation of contours
1000	
600	
200	
100	Heights in metres
0	

○ Bell Rock

9

5

FE
SS

○ Dunbar
BARNS NESS

enton ○ Cockburnspath Fast
HILLS ○ Dunglass ★ ST ABBS HEAD
Abbey ○ Coldingham
St Bathans Eyemouth
anshaws ○ Edins Hall Burnmouth
Broch Chirnside Lamberton
Duns ○ Edrom Foulden ○ Berwick
upon Tweed
Ladykirk
★ Norham
ordon Coldstream
★ Hume
Mellerstain ○ Wark
Smailholm Carham
★ Floors ○ Kelso
○ Eckford ○ Yetholm
○ Morebattle
★ Cessford
○ Oxnam
○ Jedburgh Woden
Law
★ Carter Bar

THE BORDER

FOREST PARK

ENGLAND

Newcastle
Tyne

KINNAIRDS
HEAD

Troup
Head   Pitsligo   Fraserburgh
Portsoy   Banff Macduff   Inverallochy
Cullen   Aberdour   St Combs
Fordyce   Memsie   Loch of Strathbeg
Deskford   New   A952   Rattray
Pitsligo   Deer
Newmill   Delgatie   St Fergus
Keith   Turriff   Inverugie   Peterhead

A920   Huntly   Strath Bogie   Fyvie   Haddo   Bullers of Buchan
Tap o'   Leith   Tolquhon Tarves   Cruden Bay
Noth   Hall   Dunnideer   Old   Ellon   Slains
Rhynie   Loanhead   Meldrum   Pitmedden   Forvie
Insch   Oyne   Pitcaple   Sands
Auchindoir   Maiden   Newburgh
Mossat   Terpersie   Stone   Inverurie
Kildrummy   BENNACHIE   Kinkell
Glenkindie   Alford   Pitfichie   Kinmuck
Balfluig   Kintore
Craigievar   Monymusk
Corse   Midmar   B9119   Aberdeen
Lumphanan   Hill of   Echt   9
Culblean   Fare   A93   Peterculter
r of Dinnet   Kincardine   Crathes   Findon
Aboyne   o' Neil   Banchory
Glen Tanar   Muchalls
Forest

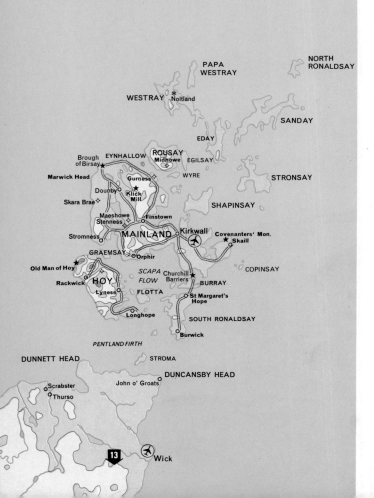

14

NORTH
RONALDSAY

PAPA
WESTRAY

WESTRAY ✳ Noltland

SANDAY

EDAY

EYNHALLOW

Brough
of Birsay ★

ROUSAY
◇ Midhowe

EGILSAY

STRONSAY

Marwick Head

Gurness ★

WYRE

Dounby ◇

Klick
Mill ★

SHAPINSAY

Skara Brae ◇

Maeshowe
Stenness ◇

Finstown

Stromness

MAINLAND

Kirkwall ★

Covenanters' Mon.
Skaill ★

GRAEMSAY

Orphir ◇

COPINSAY

Old Man of Hoy ★

SCAPA
FLOW

Churchill ★
Barriers

Rackwick

HOY

Lyness ◇

BURRAY

FLOTTA

St Margaret's ★
Hope

Longhope

SOUTH RONALDSAY

Burwick ★

PENTLAND FIRTH

STROMA

DUNNETT HEAD

DUNCANSBY HEAD

Scrabster ◇

John o' Groats

Thurso ◇

13 ★ Wick